Java 23 for Absolute Beginners

Learn the Fundamentals of Java Programming

Third Edition

Iuliana Cosmina

Apress®

Java 23 for Absolute Beginners: Learn the Fundamentals of Java Programming

Iuliana Cosmina
Edinburgh, UK

ISBN-13 (pbk): 979-8-8688-1040-4
ISBN-13 (electronic): 979-8-8688-1041-1
https://doi.org/10.1007/979-8-8688-1041-1

Managing Director, Apress Media LLC: Welmoed Spahr
Acquisitions Editor: Melissa Duffy
Desk Editor: Laura Berendson
Editorial Project Manager: Gryffin Winkler
Copyeditor: William McManus

Cover designed by eStudioCalamar

Cover Photo by Brigitte Tohm on Unsplash (unsplash.com)

Distributed to the book trade worldwide by Springer Science+Business Media New York, 1 New York Plaza, Suite 4600, New York, NY 10004-1562, USA. Phone 1-800-SPRINGER, fax (201) 348-4505, e-mail orders-ny@ springer-sbm.com, or visit www.springeronline.com. Apress Media, LLC is a California LLC and the sole member (owner) is Springer Science + Business Media Finance Inc (SSBM Finance Inc). SSBM Finance Inc is a **Delaware** corporation.

For information on translations, please e-mail booktranslations@springernature.com; for reprint, paperback, or audio rights, please e-mail bookpermissions@springernature.com.

Apress titles may be purchased in bulk for academic, corporate, or promotional use. eBook versions and licenses are also available for most titles. For more information, reference our Print and eBook Bulk Sales web page at https://www.apress.com/bulk-sales.

Any source code or other supplementary material referenced by the author in this book is available to readers on GitHub. For more detailed information, please visit https://www.apress.com/gp/services/source-code.

If disposing of this product, please recycle the paper

To all my teachers and mentors. I will be forever grateful.

Table of Contents

About the Author

Iuliana Cosmina is currently a lead software engineer for Cloudsoft, Edinburgh. She has been writing Java code since 2002. She has contributed to various types of applications, such as experimental search engines, ERPs, track and trace, and banking. During her career, she has been a teacher, a team leader, a software architect, a DevOps professional, and a software manager.

Iuliana is a Spring-certified professional, as defined by Pivotal, the makers of Spring Framework, Boot, and other tools. She considers Spring the best Java framework to work with. When she is not programming, she spends her time reading, blogging, learning to play piano, travelling, hiking, or biking.

- You can find some of her personal work on her GitHub account at `https://github.com/iuliana`.

- You can find her complete career path on her LinkedIn account at `https://linkedin.com/in/iulianacosmina`.

- You can contact her at `Iuliana.Cosmina@gmail.com`.

About the Technical Reviewer

Manuel Jordan is an autodidactic developer and researcher who enjoys learning new technologies for his own experiments about creating new integrations among them. Manuel won the 2010 Springy Award—Community Champion and Spring Champion 2013. In his little free time, he reads the Bible and composes music on his bass and guitar. Manuel considers constant education and training to be very valuable for any developer, along with refactoring and testing. Manuel offers Java and Spring services to companies. You can reach him primarily through his twitter account: `@dr_pompeii`

Acknowledgments

Writing books for beginners is tricky, because as an experienced developer, it might be challenging to find the right examples and explain them in such a way that even a nontechnical person would easily understand them. For this reason, I am profoundly grateful to the great people at Apress who have been by my side on the journey of writing this book. They provided valuable support and advice to keep this book at beginner level and approachable. A special thank you to the technical reviewer of this book, Manuel Jordan; his recommendations and corrections were crucial for the final form of the book.

Apress has published many of the books that I have read and used to improve myself professionally. It is a great honor to publish the third edition of this book with Apress, and it gives me enormous satisfaction to be able to contribute to the "making" of a new generation of Java developers.

I am grateful to all developers that have identified bugs in the text and the code and helped me make this edition of the book better than the previous ones.

Finally, I want to thank the Bogza-Vlad family: Monica, Tinel, Cristina, and Stefan. You are all close to my heart, and I miss you often.

CHAPTER 1

An Introduction to Java and Its History

Java has been consistently ranked among the top ten most popular programming languages in the world, and even after 28 years, it continues to be one of the most influential languages. Sun Microsystems officially released Java 1.0 in 1996, and it was able to overcome well-established languages like C/C++ to become one of the most commonly used programming languages. Over the years the number of Java's competitors grew to include C#, Groovy, Clojure, Scala, and Kotlin, among others, all of which have at some point been predicted to be the one that would bury Java, but clearly that has not happened (otherwise, you wouldn't be reading this book). This chapter is a short history lesson about the language you are about to learn; if you are not interested in the historical perspective, feel free to skip to Chapter 2.

How It All Started

In 1990, Sun Microsystems was an American company that was leading the revolution in the computer industry. When computers around the world started to be connected to the World Wide Web, the company decided to gather its best engineers to design and develop a product that would allow Sun to become an important player in the new emerging Internet world. Among those engineers was James Arthur Gosling, a Canadian computer scientist that is recognized today as the *father* of the Java programming language. Development of Sun's product would take five years of design and programming and one renaming (from Oak to Java because of copyright issues), but finally, on January 23, 1996[1], Java 1.0 was released for Linux, Solaris, Mac, and Windows.

---

[1] https://javaalmanac.io

© Iuliana Cosmina 2024
I. Cosmina, *Java 23 for Absolute Beginners*, https://doi.org/10.1007/979-8-8688-1041-1_1

The general tendency when reading a technical book is to skip the introductory chapter altogether. However, I encourage you to read this chapter. Personally, I was never much interested in the history of Java until I wrote the first edition of this book. I knew that James Gosling was considered the creator of Java and that Oracle bought Sun Microsystems in 2010, and that was pretty much it. I never cared much about how the language evolved, where the inspiration came from, or how one version was different from another. I just wanted to write code and get paid to do it. I started learning Java at version 1.5, and I took a lot of features for granted. Subsequently, I was assigned to a project running on Java 1.4, and I was quite confused, because I did not know why parts of the code I wrote were not compiling. Although the IT industry is moving very fast, there will always be that one client that has a legacy application, and knowing the peculiarities of each Java version is an advantage, because you know the issues when performing a migration.

When I started doing research for this book, I was mesmerized. The history of Java is interesting because it is a tale of incredible growth, success of a technology, and how a clash of egos in management almost killed the company that created it. Currently Java is the most commonly used technology in software development, and it is simply paradoxical that the company that gave birth to it no longer exists. Oracle, however, is still thriving and still investing in Java, so the future is looking pretty good for aspiring Java programmers.

This chapter describes each version of Java released so far, tracking succinctly the evolution of the language and the Java Virtual Machine (JVM).

Who This Book Is For

As the title *Java 23 for Absolute Beginners* indicates, this book is intended for absolute beginners. You don't even have to know what a programming language is; you just need to be familiar enough with your operating system to install the tools you need for Java development.

Most Java books for beginners start with the typical *Hello World!* example depicted in Listing 1-1.

Listing 1-1. The Most Common Java Beginner Code Sample

```java
public class HelloWorld {
    public static void main(String[] args) {
        System.out.println("Hello World!");
    }
}
```

This code, when executed, prints *Hello World!* in the console. However, because you are reading this book, I assume that you want to develop real applications in Java, and possibly want to have a realistic chance when applying for a position as a Java developer. If this is what you want and is who you are—a beginner with the wits and the desire to make full use of this language's power—then this book is for you. Based on that assumption, I will give you enough credit to start this book with a more complex example than *Hello World!*.

Java is a language with a syntax that is readable and based on the English language. So, if you are a logical thinker and have a working knowledge of the English language, it should be obvious to you what the code in Listing 1-2 does without even executing it.

Listing 1-2. The Java Beginner Code Sample a Smart Beginner Deserves

```java
package com.apress.ch.one.hw;

import java.util.List;

public class Example01 {
    public static void main(String[] args) {
        var items = List.of("1", "a", "2", "a", "3", "a");

        items.forEach(item -> {
            if (item.equals("a")) {
                System.out.println("A");
            } else {
                System.out.println("Not A");
            }
        });
    }
}
```

In this code example, a list of text values is declared; then the list is traversed, and when a text is equal to "a", the letter "A" is printed in the console; otherwise, "Not A" is printed.

If you are an absolute beginner to programming, this book is for you, especially because the sources attached to this book make use of algorithms and design patterns commonly used in programming. This book introduces you to the Java programming language, the core libraries, and tools any Java developer needs, and covers both imperative and declarative programming examples. So, if your plan is to get into programming and learn a high-level programming language, read the book, run the examples, write your own code, and you should have a good head start.

If you already know Java, you can use this book too, because it covers syntax and under-the-hood details for Java versions up to 23, and you will surely find some helpful tidbits that you did not know.

How This Book Is Structured

The chapter you are currently reading is an introductory one that covers a small part of Java history, showing you how the language has evolved and providing a glimpse into its future. Also, the mechanics of executing a Java application are covered, so that you are prepared for **Chapter 2**, which consists of instructions to set up your development environment and introduces you to a first simple application.

Starting with **Chapter 3**, fundamental parts of the language will be covered: packages, modules, classes, interfaces, annotations, objects, operators, data types, records, statements, streams, lambda expressions, and so on.

Starting with **Chapter 8**, interactions with external data sources are covered: reading and writing files, serializing/deserializing objects, testing and creating a user interface, writing a simple web application, interacting with it using the Java HTTP client, and packing it into a container image.

Chapter 12 is dedicated fully to the publish-subscribe framework introduced in Java 9 and reactive programming.

Chapter 13 will cover the Garbage Collector.

Most of the sources used in the listings in this book, and some that did not make it (to keep the book to a reasonable size), are part of a project named `java-23-for-absolute-beginners`. This project is organized in subprojects, also called *modules* (thus it is a *multimodule* project), that are linked to each other and have to be managed by something called **Apache Maven**. The sources that are not part of the Maven project are designed to be built separately.

Maven is something we developers call a *build tool*, and it provides the capability to build projects containing a lot of source code. To *build* a project means transforming the code written into something that can be executed. I choose to use multimodule projects for the books I write because they are easier to build and because common elements can be grouped, keeping the configuration of the project simple and nonrepetitive. Also, by having all the sources organized in one multimodule project, you get the feedback if the sources are not working as soon as possible, enabling you to notify the author to update them. I know that having a build tool introduces a certain level of complexity, but it gives you the opportunity to get comfortable with a development environment very similar to what you will work in as an Java developer. However, you don't need to worry about how to use build tools immediately, because **Chapter 2** starts by explaining how to run Java code directly, without needing a build tool.

Conventions

This book uses several formatting conventions that should make it easier to read. To that end, the following conventions are used within the book:

- Code or concept names in sentences appear as follows: `java.util.List`

- Code listings appear as follows:

```
public static void main(String[] args) {
    System.out.println("Hello World!");
}
```

- Logs in console outputs appear as follows:

```
01:24:07.809 [main] INFO c.a.Application - Starting Application
01:24:07.814 [main] DEBUG c.a.p.c.Application - Running in
debug mode
```

- {xx} is a placeholder, where the xx value is a pseudo-value giving a hint about the real value that should be used in the command or statement. For example, {YourVariableName}.

- Notice boxes labeled **IMPORTANT**, **WARNING**, **TIP**, **NOTE**, and **CAUTION** appear throughout the book. The name of the label conveys the importance and scope of the labeled statement.

- **Bold** font is used for chapter cross-references and important terms. It is also used to put emphasis on terms within the code. Underlining terms in code will be used for the same purpose.

- *Italic* font is used for somewhat important terms, humorous metaphors and expressions.

As for my style of writing, I like to write my books in the same way I have technical conversations with colleagues and friends, sprinkling jokes, giving production examples and making analogies to non-programming situations, because programming is nothing but just another way to model the real world.

When Java Was Owned by Sun Microsystems

The first stable version of Java was released in 1996. A very small team named **Green Team** worked on a prototype language named Oak (named by James Gosling after the oak tree in front of his house). The language was introduced to the world with a working demo—an interactive handheld home entertainment controller called the Star7. The "star" of the animated touch-screen user interface was a cartoon character named **Duke**, created by one of the team's graphic artists, Joe Palrang. Over the years, Duke (see Figure 1-1) has become the official Java technology mascot, and every JavaOne conference (organized by Oracle once a year) has its own Duke mascot personality.

Figure 1-1. *Duke, the Java official mascot (image source:* `https://www.oracle.com`)

The Green Team released Java to the world as open source via the Internet, because that was the fastest way to create widespread adoption. You can imagine that they jumped for joy every time somebody downloaded it, because that meant people were interested in it. The main advantage of making software open source is that contributions and feedback are provided by a large number of people from all over the world. For Java, the release as open source was a great decision, as it shaped the language that a lot of developers are using today. Even after 28 years, Java is still among the top-three most-used programming languages.

The Green Team was working for an American company named *Sun Microsystems*, founded in 1982. It guided the computer revolution by selling computers, computer parts, and software. One of their greatest achievements is the Java programming language. In Figure 1-2, you can see the company logo[2] that was used since Java's birth year until it was acquired by Oracle in 2010.

---

[2] `https://goodlogo.com/extended.info/sun-microsystems-logo-2385`

Figure 1-2. *The Sun Microsystems logo (image source:* `https://en.wikipedia.org/wiki/Sun_Microsystems`)

It is quite difficult to find information about the first version of Java, but dedicated developers that witnessed its *birth*, when the World Wide Web was way smaller and full of static pages, did create blogs and shared their experience with the world. It was quite easy for Java to shine with its applets that displayed dynamic content that interacted with the user. The development team got bigger and Java became much more than a web programming language. In trying to make applets run in any browser, the team found a solution to a common problem: **portability**.

Developers nowadays face a lot of headaches when developing software that should run on any operating system. And with the mobile revolution, things got really tricky. Figure 1-3 shows an abstract drawing of what is believed to be the first Java logo.

Figure 1-3. *The first Java logo, 1996–2003 (image source:* `https://www.oracle.com`*)*

Java 1.0 was released at the first edition of the JavaOne conference, which had over 6000 attendees. The language was really similar to C++ and was designed for handheld devices and set-top boxes. It evolved into the first version of Java, which provided developers the following advantages that C++ did not:

- **Security**: In Java, there is no danger of reading bogus data when accidentally going over the size of an array.

- **Automatic memory management**: A Java developer does not have to check if there is enough memory to allocate for an object and then deallocate it explicitly; the operations are automatically handled by the garbage collector. This also means that pointers are not necessary.

- **Simplicity**: Java has no pointers, unions, templates, or structures. Mostly anything in Java can be declared as a class. Also, confusion when using multiple inheritance is avoided by modifying the inheritance model and not allowing multiple class inheritance.

- **Support for multithreaded execution**: Java was designed from the start to support development of multithreaded software.

- **Portability**: One of the most known Java mottos is **Write once, run anywhere**. This is made possible by the Java Virtual Machine.

All these features made Java appealing for developers, and by 1997, when Java 1.1 was released, there were already approximately 400,000 Java developers in the world. The JavaOne conference had 10,000 attendees that year. The path to greatness was set. Before going further in our analysis of each Java version, let's clarify a few things.

How Is Java Portable?

I mentioned a few times that Java is portable and that Java programs can run on any operating system. It is time to explain how this is possible. Let's start with the simple drawing shown in Figure 1-4.

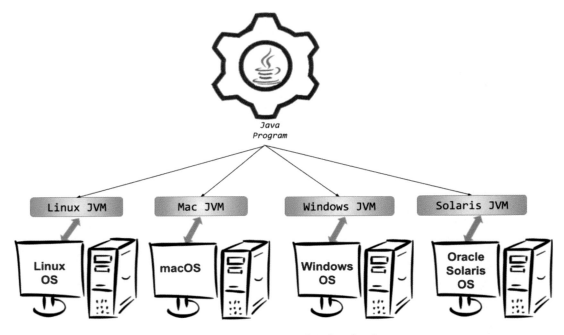

Figure 1-4. *Running a Java program on multiple platforms*

Java is what we call a **high-level programming language** that allows a developer to write programs that are independent of a particular type of computer. High-level languages are easier to read, write, and maintain. However, their code must be translated by a compiler or interpreted into machine language (unreadable by humans because is it made up of numbers) to be executed, because that is the only language that computers understand.

In Figure 1-4, notice that on top of the operating systems, a **JVM** is needed to execute a Java program. JVM stands for **Java Virtual Machine**, which is an abstract computing machine that enables a computer to run a Java program. It is a platform-independent execution environment that converts Java code into machine language and executes it.

So, what is the difference between Java and other high-level languages? Well, other high-level languages compile source code directly into machine code that is designed to run on a specific microprocessor architecture or operating system, such as Windows or Unix. By contrast, JVM mimics a Java processor, making it possible for a Java program to be interpreted as a sequence of actions or operating system calls on any processor regardless of the operating system. Sure, the compiling step makes Java slower than a pure compiled language like C++, but the advantage of portability makes it worth it. Also, Java is not the only member of the JVM languages family. Groovy, Scala, Kotlin, and Clojure are all very popular programming languages that run on the JVM.

Having mentioned the Java compiler, let's get back to Java 1.1, which was widely used even as new versions were released. It came with an improved **Abstract Window Toolkit** (**AWT**) graphical application programming interface (API, a collection of components used for building applets), inner classes, database connectivity classes (JDBC model), classes for remote calls (RMI), a special compiler for Microsoft platforms named the **JIT** (**J**ust **I**n **T**ime) compiler, support for internationalization, and support for Unicode. What also made Java 1.1 so widely embraced is that shortly after Java was released, Microsoft licensed it and started creating applications using it. The feedback helped further development of Java, and thus Java 1.1 was supported on all browsers of the time, which is why it was so widely deployed.

Information   A lot of terms used in this introductory chapter might seem foreign to you now, but as you read the book, these terms will start to make more sense as you are introduced to more information and they are used in context.

So, what exactly happens to developer-written Java code until the actual execution? The process is depicted in Figure 1-5.

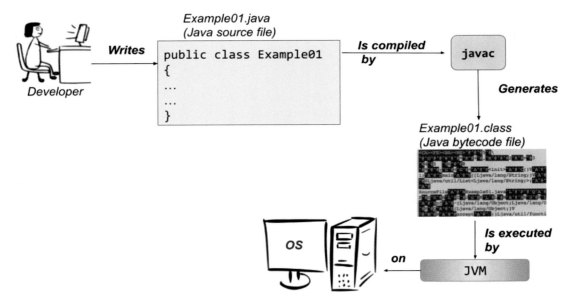

Figure 1-5. *From Java code to machine code*

Java code is compiled and transformed to bytecode that is then interpreted and executed by the JVM on the underlying operating system. This is what Java is: a compiled and interpreted general-purpose programming language with numerous features that make it well suited for the Web. Now that we've covered how Java code is executed, let's go back to some more history.

Sun Microsystem's Java Versions

The first stable Java version released by Sun Microsystems could be downloaded from the website as an archive named **JDK**, and its version at the time was 1.0.2. JDK is an acronym for **J**ava **D**evelopment **K**it. This is the software development environment used for developing Java applications and applets. It includes the **J**ava **R**untime **E**nvironment (**JRE**), an interpreter (loader), a compiler, an archiver, a documentation generator, and other tools needed for Java development. We will get into more details about the JDK in Chapter 2 in the section about installing it on your computer.

Starting with version 1.2, released in 1998, Java versions were given codenames.[3] The Java version 1.2 unofficial codename was *Playground*. It was a massive release, and this was the moment when people started talking about the *Java 2 Platform*. Starting with this version, the releases up to J2SE 5.0 were renamed, and *J2SE* replaced Java because the Java platform was now composed of three parts:

- **J2SE** (Java 2 Platform, Standard Edition), which later became JSE, a computing platform for the development and deployment of portable code for desktop and server environments.

- **J2EE** (Java 2 Platform, Enterprise Edition), which later became JEE, a set of specifications extending Java SE with specifications for enterprise features such as distributed computing and web services.

- **J2ME** (Java 2 Platform, Micro Edition), which later became JME, a computing platform for development and deployment of portable code for embedded and mobile devices.

With this release, the JIT compiler became part of Sun Microsystem's JVM (which basically means turning code into executable code became a faster operation and the generated executable code was optimized), the Swing graphical API was introduced as a fancy alternative to the AWT (new components to create fancy desktop applications were introduced), and the Java Collections Framework (for working with sets of data) was introduced.

J2SE 1.3 was released in 2000 with the codename *Kestrel* (maybe as a reference to the newly introduced Java sound classes). This release also contained Java Extensible Markup Language (XML) APIs.

J2SE 1.4 was released in 2002 with the codename *Merlin*. This is the first year that the Java Community Process members were involved in deciding which features the release should contain, and thus the release was quite consistent. This is the first release of the Java platform developed under the Java Community Process as JSR 59[4]. The following features are among those worth mentioning:

---

[3] https://www.java.com/releases/

[4] http://www.jcp.org/en/jsr/detail?id=59

- **Support for Internet Protocol version 6 (IPv6)**: This feature enables applications that run over a network to be written to work using networking protocol IPv6.

- **Nonblocking I/O**: I/O is an acronym for *input-output,* which refers to reading and writing data—a very slow operation. Making I/O nonblocking means to optimize these operations to increase speed of the running application.

- **Logging API**: Operations that get executed need to be reported to a file or a resource, which can be read in case of failure to determine the cause and find a solution. This process is called *logging* components to support this operation were introduced in this version for the firt time.

- **Image processing API**: Components developers can use this API to manipulate images with Java code.

Java's coffee cup logo made its entrance in 2003 (between releases 1.4 and 5.0) at the JavaOne conference. You can see it in Figure 1-6.

Figure 1-6. Java official logo 2003–2006 (image source: `https://oracle.com`)

Note   There are a few theories online about how the name *Java* was chosen. One theory is that it is a variation of the initials from the names of the Green Team members, James Gosling, Arthur Van Hoff, and Andy Bechtolsheim, and that the logo is inspired by their love of coffee.

J2SE 5.0 was released in 2004 with the codename *Tiger*. Initially it followed the typical versioning and was named J2SE 1.5, but because this was a major release with a significant number of new features that proved a serious improvement of maturity, stability, scalability, and security of the J2SE, the version was labeled 5.0 and presented like that to the public, even if internally 1.5 was still used. For this version and the next two, it was considered that 1.x = x.0. Let's list those features because most of them are covered in the book:

- **Generics** provide support for compile-time (static) type safety for collections and eliminates the need for most type conversions, which means the type used in a certain context is decided while the application is running. (**Chapter 4** has a full section about this topic).

- **Annotations**, also known as *metadata*, are used to tag classes and methods to allow metadata-aware utilities to process them (which means a component is labeled as something another component recognizes and does specific operations with it).

- **Autoboxing/unboxing** refers to the automatic conversion between primitive types and matching object types (wrappers). This feature is covered in **Chapter 5**.

- **Enumerations** define static final ordered sets of values using the enum keyword; also covered in **Chapter 4**.

- **Varargs** provide a shorthand for methods that support an arbitrary number of parameters of one type. The last parameter of a method is declared using a type name followed by three dots (e.g., `String...`), which implies that any number of arguments of that type can be provided and are placed into an array; covered in **Chapter 3**.

- An **enhanced for each loop** is used to iterate over collections and arrays too; covered in **Chapter 7**.

- **Static imports**, which provide a way to include existing static methods and constants into code; also covered in **Chapter 4**.

- Improvements for **RMI** (not covered in the book), Swing (**Chapter 10**), and introduction of the `Scanner` class (**Chapter 11**).

J2SE 5.0 was the first version available for Apple Mac OS X 10.4, and the default version installed on Apple Mac OS X 10.5. However, it was a pretty buggy release, and hotfixes for minor and not-so-minor bugs were released continuously until 2015.

In 2006, *JDK 6* (codename *Mustang*) was released with a little delay. Yes, yet another rename, using JDK again, because the two other products were not as successful. And yes, yet again a serious number of features were implemented in quite a short period of time. A lot of updates were required afterward to fix the existing issues. This was the last major Java release released by Sun Microsystems, as Oracle acquired this company in January 2010. The most important features in this release are listed next.

- **Dramatic performance improvements for the core platform**:
  Applications run faster and need less memory or CPU to execute.

- **Improved web service support**: Optimized the components that are
  required for development of web applications, like the `HttpServer`
  (used in **Chapter 10**).

- **JDBC 4.0**: Optimized the components that are required for
  development of applications using relational databases, covered in
  Chapter 11.

- **Many GUI improvements**: These included integration of `SwingWorker`
  in the API, table sorting and filtering, and true Swing double-buffering
  (eliminating the gray-area effect). Overall, components used to create
  interfaces for desktop applications were improved.

Shortly after (*in Java terms*), in December 2008, *JavaFX* 1.0 SDK was released. JavaFX is suitable for creating graphical user interfaces (GUIs) for any platform. The initial version was a scripting language. Until 2008, in Java there were two ways to create a user interface:

- Using AWT components, which are rendered and controlled by
  a native peer component specific to the underlying operating
  system; that is why AWT components are also called *heavyweight*
  components.

- Using Swing components, which are called *lightweight* because
  they do not require allocation of native resources in the operating
  system's windowing toolkit. The Swing API is a complementary
  extension of AWT.

For the first versions, it was never really clear if JavaFX would actually have a future and if it would grow up to replace Swing. Management turmoil inside Sun at the time did not help in defining a clear path for this project, either.

Oracle Takes Over

Although Sun Microsystems won a lawsuit against Microsoft, in which Microsoft agreed to pay Sun Microsystems $20 million for not implementing the Java 1.1 standard completely, in 2008, after some poor acquisition missteps and misdirected focus on Sparc instead of x86 architecture, the company was in such poor shape that negotiations for a merger with IBM and Hewlett-Packard began (but eventually failed). In 2009, Oracle and Sun announced that they agreed on a deal: Oracle would acquire Sun for $9.50 per share in cash, which amounted to a $5.6 billion offer. The impact was massive. A lot of engineers quit, including James Gosling, *the father of Java*, which made a lot of developers question the future of the Java platform.

Java 7

Note   Starting with this version, developers started using the term *Java* as an umbrella term for all Java related components: the language, the compiler, and the JVM. Thus, the titles of section starting now will follow the pattern: *Java {version}*.

It took five years for the Oracle developers to take over from the Green Team, but finally Oracle released JDK 7, codename *Dolphin*, in 2011. This first Java version released by Oracle was the result of an extensive collaboration between Oracle engineers and members of the worldwide Java communities, such as the OpenJDK Community and the Java Community Process (JCP). It contained a lot of changes, but a lot fewer than developers expected. Considering the long period between the releases, the expectations were pretty high. Project *Lambda*, which was supposed to allow usage of lambda expressions in Java (this leads to considerable syntax simplification in certain cases), and *Jigsaw* (making JVM and the Java application modular; there is a section in **Chapter 3** about them) were dropped. Both were released in future versions. The following are the most notable features of JDK 7:

- JVM support for dynamic languages with the new `invokedynamic` bytecode. Basically, Java code can use code implemented in non-Java languages (e.g., Python, Ruby, Perl, JavaScript, Groovy, etc.).

- Compressed 64-bit pointers (internal optimization of the JVM, so less memory is consumed).

- Small language changes grouped under project *Coin*:

  - Strings in `switch` statements, covered in **Chapter 7**

  - Automatic resource management in `try-with-resources` statements, covered in **Chapter 5**

  - Improved type inference for generics—the diamond `<>` operator, covered in **Chapter 4**

  - Binary integer literals: integer numbers can be represented directly as binary numbers, using the form 0b (or 0B) followed by one or more binary digits (0 or 1), covered in **Chapter 5**

- Multiple exception handling improvements, covered in **Chapter 5**.

- Concurrency improvements.

- New I/O library (new classes added to read/write data to/from files, covered in **Chapter 11**).

- Introduction of the `Timsort` algorithm to sort collections and arrays of objects instead of merge sort because it has better performance. Better performance usually means reducing consumed resources (memory and/or CPU) or reducing the time needed for execution.

Continuing development on a project with almost none of the original development team involved must have been a very tough job. That was made obvious by the 161 updates that followed, most of which were needed to fix security issues and vulnerabilities.

JavaFX 2.0 was released with Java 7. This confirmed that the JavaFX project had a future with Oracle. As a major change, JavaFX stopped being a scripting language and became a Java API. This meant that knowledge of the Java language syntax would be enough to start building GUIs with it. JavaFX started gaining ground over Swing because of its hardware-accelerated graphical engine called *Prism* that did a better job at rendering.

Note   Starting with Java 7, OpenJDK[5] was born, an open source reference implementation of the Java SE Platform Edition. This was an effort from the Java developers' community to provide a version of the JDK that was not under an Oracle license, because they assumed that Oracle would introduce stricter licensing for the JDK in order to profit from it. However Oracle ended up supporting the OpenJDK community, because the best ideas come from people passionate about Java.

Java 8

JDK 8, codename *Spider*, was released in 2014, and included features that were initially intended to be part of JDK 7. Better late than never, right? Three years in the making, JDK 8 contained the following key features:

- Language syntax changes:

  - Language-level support for lambda expressions (functional programming features)

  - Support for default methods in interfaces, covered in **Chapter 4**

  - New date and time API, covered in **Chapter 5**

  - New way to do parallel processing by using streams, covered in **Chapter 8**

- Improved integration with JavaScript (the Nashorn project). JavaScript is a web scripting language that is quite loved in the development community, so providing support for it in Java probably won Oracle a few new supporters.

- Improvements of the garbage collection process.

Starting with Java 8, Oracle dropped codenames to avoid any trademark-law hassles; instead, Oracle adopted a semantic versioning that easily distinguishes major, minor,

---

[5] https://openjdk.org

and security-update releases[6]. The version number matches the following pattern: `$MAJOR.$MINOR.$SECURITY`.

When executing `java -version` in a terminal (if you have Java 8 installed), you see a log similar to the one in Listing 1-3.

Listing 1-3. Java 8 Log for Execution of `java -version`

```
$ java -version
java version "1.8.0_381"
Java(TM) SE Runtime Environment (build 1.8.0_381-b09)
Java HotSpot(TM) 64-Bit Server VM (build 25.381-b09, mixed mode)
```

In this log, the version numbers have the following meaning:

- The 1 represents the major version number, incremented for a major release that contains significant new features as specified in a new edition of the Java SE Platform Specification.

- The 8 represents the minor version number, incremented for a minor update release that may contain compatible bug fixes, revisions to standard APIs, and other small features.

- The 0 represents the security level that is incremented for a security-update release that contains critical fixes, including those necessary to improve security. $SECURITY is not reset to zero when $MINOR is incremented, which lets the users know that this version is a more secure one.

- 162 is the build number.

- b12 represents additional build information.

This versioning style is quite common for Java applications; thus, this versioning style was adopted to align with the general industry practices.

---

[6] https://openjdk.org/jeps/223

Warning   Java SE 8u203 versions and more recent are provided under the new Java SE OTN License[7], so if you intend to use any of these versions in production, read the license carefully to understand what Oracle allows you to do with it and what it will cost you.

Java 9

JDK 9 was released in September 2017. The long-awaited *Jigsaw* project finally arrived. The Java platform was at last modular.

Important   Java modules were a big change for the Java world. It was not a change in syntax, nor was it just some new feature. It was a change in the design of the platform. Some experienced developers I know who have used Java since its first years had difficulties adapting. It was supposed to fix some serious problems that Java had been living with for years (covered in **Chapter 3**). You are lucky, because as a beginner, you start from scratch, so you do not need to change the way you develop your applications. Until Java 9, Java modular applications were developed using frameworks such as OSGi[8], which are a pain to use because they require additional configurations and special packaging. Jigsaw made configuring modules easier and made it a part of the Java application, not an additional configuration file interpreted by a build tool such as Maven.

The following are the most important features of JDK 9, aside from the introduction of Java modules:

- The Java Shell tool, an interactive command-line interface for evaluation declarations, statements, and expressions written in Java, covered in **Chapter 2**

- Quite a few security updates

---

[7]https://www.oracle.com/downloads/licenses/javase-license1.html
[8]https://www.osgi.org

- Support for `private` methods in interfaces, covered in **Chapter 4**

- Improved `try-with-resources`, enabling final variables to be used as resources, covered in **Chapter 5**

- Removal of _ (underscore) from the set of legal identifiers, covered in **Chapter 4**

- Enhancements for the Garbage-First (G1) garbage collector, which becomes the default garbage collector, as covered in **Chapter 13**.

- Internally, use of a new more compact `String` representation, covered in **Chapter 5**

- Concurrency updates (related to parallel execution, mentioned in **Chapter 5**)

- Factory methods for collections, covered in **Chapter 5**

- Updates of the image processing API optimization of components used to write code that processes images

Java 10

JDK 10 (a.k.a. Java 18.3) was released on March 20, 2018. Java 10 used a new versioning convention set up by Oracle: the version numbers follow a $YEAR.$MONTH format[9]. This release versioning style was supposed to make it easier for developers and end users to figure out the age of a release, so that they could judge whether to upgrade it to a newer release with the latest security fixes and additional features.

When JDK 10 is installed, running `java -version` in a terminal shows a log that is similar to the one in Listing 1-4.

Listing 1-4. Java 10 Log for Execution of `java -version`

```
$ java -version
java version "10" 2018-03-20
JavaTM SE Runtime Environment 18.3 build 10+46
Java HotSpotTM 64-Bit Server VM 18.3 build 10+46, mixed mode
```

---

[9] https://openjdk.org/jeps/322

The following are the most important features of Java 10:[10]

- A local-variable type inference to enhance the language to extend type inference to local variables (this was the most expected feature, and is covered in **Chapter 4**).

- More optimizations for garbage collection, covered in **Chapter 13**.

- Application Class-Data Sharing to reduce the footprint by sharing common class metadata across processes (this is an advanced feature and won't be covered in this book).

- More concurrency updates (related to parallel execution, mentioned in **Chapter 5**).

- Heap allocation on alternative memory devices. The memory needed by JVM to run a Java program—called *heap memory*—can be allocated on an alternative memory device, so the heap can also be split between volatile and nonvolatile RAM. (**Chapter 5** provides more details about memory used by Java applications.)

In June 2018, Oracle and other participants in the Java ecosystem announced a change to the release cadence model for Java SE: rather than having a major release planned for every two to three years (which would often become three to four years), followed by a long list of hotfixes, a new six-month feature-release-train model would be used.

Note   For releases after Java SE 8, Oracle designates one release every two years as a **Long-Term-Support** (**LTS**) release. Oracle customers using LTS releases for development will receive Oracle Premier Support and periodic update releases. Non-LTS releases are a cumulative set of implementation enhancements of the most recent LTS release, and support for them is limited until the following LTS release.

Caution   Java 9 and 10 are not LTS releases and therefore are not recommended for production use.

---

[10] https://www.oracle.com/java/technologies/javase/10-relnote-issues.html

Java 11

JDK 11[11] (a.k.a. Java 18.9), released on September 25, 2018, contains the following features:

- Removal of JEE advanced components used to build enterprise Java applications and Corba (very old technology for remote invocation, allowing your application to communicate with applications installed on a different computer) modules.

- Local-variable syntax for lambda parameters allow the var keyword to be used when declaring the formal parameters of implicitly typed lambda expressions.

- Epsilon, a low-overhead garbage collector (a no-GC, so basically you can run an application without a GC), providing more optimizations to the garbage collection, covered in **Chapter 13**.

- Introduction of the new HTTP client API.

- More concurrency updates (related to parallel execution, mentioned in **Chapter 5**).

- The Nashorn JavaScript script engine and APIs are marked as deprecated with the intent to remove them in a future release. ECMAScript language constructs evolve pretty rapidly, so Nashorn was getting difficult to maintain.

Aside from these changes, it was also speculated that a new versioning change should be introduced because the $YEAR.$MONTH format did not go so well with developers. (Why so many versioning naming changes, right? Is this really so important? Apparently, it is.) The proposed versioning change is similar to the one introduced in Java 9.

When JDK 11 is installed, running java -version in a terminal shows a log that is similar to the one in Listing 1-5.

---

[11] https://openjdk.org/projects/jdk/11

Listing 1-5. Java 11 Log for Execution of `java -version`

```
$ java -version
java version "11.0.20" 2023-07-18 LTS
Java(TM) SE Runtime Environment 18.9 (build 11.0.20+9-LTS-256)
Java HotSpot(TM) 64-Bit Server VM 18.9 (build 11.0.20+9-LTS-256, mixed mode)
```

As shown in Listing 1-5, JDK 11 was a **Long-Term Support (LTS) release** with several years of support.

Concomitant with the release of JDK 11, Oracle announced that they would start charging for Java SE 8 licenses, so small businesses that were trying to reduce their software costs started looking for alternatives. There are two free options: AdoptJDK and OpenJDK. AdoptOpenJDK[12] provides prebuilt OpenJDK binaries from a fully open source set of build scripts and infrastructure, for multiple platforms.

OpenJDK has the same code as Oracle JDK, depending on what provider you're using. Another advantage of OpenJDK is that, whereas Oracle JDK cannot be modified to suit the needs of a business application, OpenJDK can be modified because it is licensed under the GNU General Public License, which is quite permissive.

Also, if money is not an issue, Amazon Corretto, Azul Zulu, and GraalVM are all alternate JDKs optimized in one way or another.

Java 12

JDK 12[13], released on March 29, 2019, contains the following important features:

- A new experimental garbage collector (GC) algorithm named Shenandoah that reduces GC pause times.

- Modified syntax for the `switch` statement, allowing it to be used as an expression as well. Also, it removes the need for `break` statements, covered in **Chapter 7**.

- JVM Constants API, to model nominal descriptions of key class-file and runtime artifacts. This API can be helpful for tools that manipulate classes and methods.

---

[12] https://adoptopenjdk.net
[13] https://openjdk.org/projects/jdk/12

- Minor improvements to the G1 garbage collector, covered in **Chapter 13**.

- Class Data Sharing (CDS) archives to improve the JDK build process.

- Approximately 100 microbenchmarks[14] were added to the JDK source.

JDK 12 is part of Oracle's six-month release cadence introduced with JDK 9 in September 2017. JDK 12 is a feature release with a short support lifespan.

Java 13

JDK 13[15], released on September 17, 2019, contains a few important features, hundreds of smaller enhancements, and thousands of bug fixes. The most important features of this version are

- Improvement of the CDS archive support added in JDK 12

- Z Garbage Collector enhancements, covered in **Chapter 13**

- A new implementation of the Legacy Socket API

- More improvements for the `switch` expressions, covered in **Chapter 7**

- Support for text blocks (first preview), covered in **Chapter 5**

JDK 13 is a feature release with a short support lifespan as well.

Java 14

JDK 14[16], released on March 17, 2020, contains a big list of important features, enhancements, and bug fixes. The most important features of this version are

- Pattern matching for the `instanceof` operator, covered in **Chapter 6**.

- JFR Event Streaming API for collecting profiling and diagnostic data about a Java application and the JVM as they're running.

---

[14] https://openjdk.org/projects/code-tools/jmh
[15] https://openjdk.org/projects/jdk/13
[16] https://openjdk.org/projects/jdk/14

- More enhancements of the G1 garbage collector, covered in **Chapter 13**.

- The CMS (Concurrent Mark Sweep) garbage collector was removed.

- Support for the Z Garbage Collector for macOS, covered in **Chapter 13**.

- Records were introduced to provide a compact syntax for declaring classes that are transparent holders for shallowly immutable data, covered in **Chapter 4**.

- Foreign Memory Access API provides support for Java programs to safely and efficiently access foreign memory outside the Java heap.

- Improvements of the `NullPointerException` class to provide more precise details to easily identify the variable being `null`.

- The `jpackage` tool was introduced to provides support for native packaging formats to give end users a natural installation experience.

Although this release contains a lot of new features, most of them are available only in preview mode or are considered being in the `incubation` phase, making this release unstable and not a candidate for long-term support.

Java 15

JDK 15[17], released on September 15, 2020, contains considerable improvements to projects added in previous versions. The most notable features of this version are

- Removal of the Nashorn JavaScript Engine.

- Addition of sealed and hidden classes (Preview), covered in **Chapter 4**.

- **Text blocks** add support for multi-line string literal that avoids the need for most escape sequences, automatically formats the string in a predictable way, and gives the developer control over the format when desired, covered in **Chapter 5**.

---

[17] `https://openjdk.org/projects/jdk/15`

- The Edwards-Curve Digital Signature Algorithm (EdDSA) is now supported for cryptographic signatures.

- More enhancements for the Legacy DatagramSocket API.

- Biased Locking was disabled and deprecated, leading to performance increase for multithreaded applications.

- Records, second preview, covered in **Chapter 4**.

JDK 15 is just a short-term release that was supported with Oracle Premier Support for six months until JDK 16 arrived in March 2021.

Java 16

JDK 16[18], released on March 16, 2021, is the reference implementation of the version of standard Java set to follow JDK 15, which means that everything unstable in JDK 15 is expected to be more stable in JDK 16. Aside from that, the most notable features of this version are

- Introduction of a Vector API, to express vector computations that compile to optimal vector hardware instructions on supported CPU architectures, to achieve superior performance to equivalent scalar computations

- Strong encapsulation of JDK internals by default (covered in **Chapter 3**)

- Introduction of Foreign Linker API to provide statically typed, pure-Java access to native code

- Introduction of an Elastic Metaspace, which promotes return of unused HotSpot class-metadata (i.e., metaspace) memory to the operating system more promptly

- Added support for C++ 14 language features

- Final records release (covered in **Chapter 4**)

---

[18] https://openjdk.org/projects/jdk/16

JDK 16 is just a short-term release that was supported with Oracle Premier Support for six months until JDK 17 arrived in September 2021.

Java 17

JDK 17[19], the next **Long-Term Support** (LTS) release, will be supported by Oracle for eight years. It was released on September 14, 2021, as per Oracle's six-month release cadence for Java SE versions.

The list of features for JDK 17 are focused on the JVM internals to improve performance and deprecate/discard old APIs:

- Performance and implementation improvements for the Vector API introduced in JDK 16

- Refinements for sealed classes and interfaces, covered in **Chapter 4**

- Introduction of pattern matching for `switch` expressions, covered in **Chapter 7**

- macOS-specific improvements

- Enhancements for pseudo-random number generators (PRNGs), including introduction of new interfaces and implementations for PRNGs, which include jumpable PRNGs and a new class of splitable PRNG algorithms (LXM), covered in **Chapter 4**

- Enhancements on encapsulating JDK internals

- Foreign Function & Memory API, which merges two previously incubating APIs, the Foreign-Memory Access API and the Foreign Linker API, to allow developers to call up native libraries and process native data without the risks of JNI

When JDK 17 is installed, running `java -version` in a terminal shows a log that is similar to the one in Listing 1-6.

---

[19] `https://openjdk.org/projects/jdk/17/`

Listing 1-6. Java 17 Log for Execution of `java -version`

```
$ java -version
java version "17.0.9" 2023-10-17 LTS
Java(TM) SE Runtime Environment (build 17.0.9+11-LTS-201)
Java HotSpot(TM) 64-Bit Server VM (build 17.0.9+11-LTS-201, mixed mode,
sharing)
```

Java 18

JDK 18,[20] released on March 22, 2022, is another short-term release that focuses on updates of preview and incubator features:

- Vector API additions (third incubator)

- **Simple Web Server**, a command-line tool to start a minimal web server that serves static files only, covered in **Chapter 10**

- Introduction of the `@snippet` tag in JavaDocs to simplify inclusion of code in documentation, covered in **Chapter 9**

- Pattern Matching for `switch` expressions, second preview, covered in **Chapter 7**

- Deprecation of the finalization mechanism, in preparation for removal, covered in **Chapter 13**

Java 19

JDK 19,[21] released on September 20, 2022, is another short-term release that focuses on updates of preview and incubator features:

- Vector API additions (fourth incubator)

- Record Patterns, first preview, covered in **Chapter 6**

- Virtual Threads, first preview, covered in **Chapter 5**

---

[20] https://openjdk.org/projects/jdk/18
[21] https://openjdk.org/projects/jdk/19

- Pattern Matching for `switch` expressions, third preview, covered in **Chapter 7**

- Structured Concurrency (first incubator), covered in **Chapter 5**

Java 20

JDK 20,[22] released on March 21, 2023, is another short-term release that focuses on updates of preview and incubator features:

- Vector API additions (fifth incubator)

- Record Patterns, second preview, covered in **Chapter 7**

- Virtual Threads, second preview, covered in **Chapter 5**

- Pattern Matching for `switch` expressions, fourth preview, covered in **Chapter 7**

- Structured Concurrency (second incubator), covered in **Chapter 5**

- Scoped Values (first incubator)

Java 21

JDK 21,[23] the next **Long-Term Support** (LTS) release, will be supported by Oracle for eight years. It was released on September 19, 2023, as per Oracle's six-month release cadence for Java SE versions.

Over the years, the way Java features were proposed, implemented, and tracked was via JDK Enhancement Proposals (**JEPs**). JEPs represent individual proposals, but they can be categorized based on their scope and grouped in Java *projects*. These projects are named rather randomly. The following list depicts the most important projects that group most of the features introduced in this book:

- **Amber** is focused on Java language features and new syntax.

- **Babylon** is focused on extending the reach of Java to foreign programming models, such as SQL and machine learning.

---

[22] https://openjdk.org/projects/jdk/20
[23] https://openjdk.org/projects/jdk/21

- **Panama** is focused on improving and enriching the connections between the Java Virtual Machine and well-defined but *foreign* (non-Java) APIs, including many interfaces commonly used by C programmers.

- **Leyden** is focused on improvement of the startup time, time to peak performance, and footprint of Java programs.

- **Loom** is focused on exploring and incubating Java VM features and APIs built on top of them for the implementation of lightweight user-mode threads (fibers).

- **Valhalla** is focused on under-the-hood improvements of the Java object model to use memory less efficiently.

- **ZGC** is focused on the development and improvement of a scalable low-latency garbage collector capable of handling heaps ranging from 8MB to 16TB in size, with submillisecond max pause times.

- **VisualVM** continues the development of the VisualVM tool for monitoring Java applications.

The list of features for JDK 21 is longer because it is an LTS version and contains quite a few features that have reached maturity and improve the JDK a lot. The following list identifies the most important mature and preview features of JDK 21; for the full list, check the official page.

- **Virtual Threads** implementation is now ready for use, covered in **Chapter 5**.

- So is the **Generational ZGC**, covered in **Chapter 13**.

- Record Patterns are final too, covered in **Chapter 4**.

- Pattern Matching for `switch` expressions, final implementation, covered in **Chapter 4**.

- **Sequenced Collections**. Since the beginning, Java's collections framework has lacked a collection type that represents a sequence of elements with a defined encounter order. It also has lacked a uniform set of operations that apply across such collections. This now has been resolved by the introduction of the `SequencedCollection<E>` and `SequencedSet<E>` interfaces.

- **Generational ZGC**. Initially ZGC was nongenerational. With this release, the Generational ZGC maintains separate generations for young objects (recently allocated objects) and old objects (long-lived objects). Both generations are collected independently, focusing on quickly collecting younger objects. This allows ZGC to collect young objects—which tend to die young—more frequently.

- **Unnamed Patterns and Variables** (preview), or the return of the _ (underscore). The underscore was supported up to JDK 8, removed in Java 9, and it will finally be reintroduced in a version after JDK 21, for purposes similar to the ones in GoLang (The Go programming language), covered in **Chapter 4**.

- **Unnamed Classes and Instance Main Methods** (Preview). An alternative to JShell, this feature introduces an evolved version of the Java language, so that students can write their first programs without needing to understand language features designed for large programs. This means the ability to run Java code directly without the need to compile it. This is more practical for bits of Java code that span multiple lines, which are not that suitable for JShell, covered in **Chapter 3**.

- **Structured Concurrency**, first preview, covered in **Chapter 5**.

Java 22

JDK 22,[24] released on March 21, 2024, is another short-term release that focuses on updates of previews and incubator features introduced in previous releases:

- Unnamed Variables & Patterns, covered in **Chapter 4**.

- Foreign Function & Memory API.

- Statements before super (...), first preview, covered in **Chapter 4**.

- **Class-File API**, first preview. Under the hood, this is a very important change that will allow a project to use dependencies compiled with older versions of Java, as long as they use the same Class-File API.

---

[24] https://openjdk.org/projects/jdk/22

- **Launch Multi-File Source-Code Programs**, first preview. The Java application launcher is enhanced to be able to run a program supplied as multiple files of Java source code. For tiny applications, this makes it possible to skip using a build tool, covered in **Chapter 2**.

- **Stream Gatherers**, first preview. Enhancements of the Stream API to support custom intermediate operations, covered in **Chapter 8**.

- **Implicitly Declared Classes and Instance Main Methods**, second preview. This feature is an enhancement designed to allow students to write streamlined declarations for single-class programs and then seamlessly expand their programs to use more advanced features as their skills grow, covered in **Chapter 2**. It is the extension of "Unnamed Classes and Instance Main Methods" form Java 21.

- **Structured Concurrency**, second preview, covered in **Chapter 5**

Java 23

JDK 23,[25] released on September 17, 2024, is another short-term release that focuses on updates of preview and incubator features introduced in previous releases. This book aims to introduce you to the most interesting features up to this release, even if they are still in preview.

The most interesting features in this release are

- Primitive Types in Patterns, `instanceof`, and `switch`, first preview, covered in **Chapter 6**.

- **Markdown Documentation Comments**, covered in **Chapter 9**.

- **Stream Gatherers**, second preview, covered in **Chapter 8**.

- **ZGC: Generational Mode by Default**, covered in **Chapter 13**.

- **Module Import Declarations**, first preview, covered in **Appendix A** in the "Advanced Module Configurations" section.

---

[25] `https://openjdk.org/projects/jdk/23`

- **Implicitly Declared Classes and Instance Main Methods**, third preview, covered in **Chapter 2**.

- **Class-File API**, second preview. Again, under the hood, this is a very important change that will allow a project to use dependencies compiled with older version of Java, as long as they use the same class-file API.

- **Structured Concurrency**, third preview, covered in **Chapter 5**.

- **Flexible Constructor Bodies**, second preview of the feature allowing statements before `super(..)` invocations, covered in **Chapter 4**.

And this is where the details end. If you want more information on the first 25 years of the Java programming language, you can easily find it on the Internet[26].

Prerequisites

Before ending this chapter, it is only fair to tell you that to learn Java, you need to have an Internet connection and know a few things:

- Your way around an operating system, such as Windows, Linux, or macOS.

- How to refine your search criteria, because information related to your operating systems is not covered in the book; if you have issues, you must fix them yourself.

If you already know Java, and you bought this book out of curiosity, knowing about a build tool like Maven or Gradle is helpful, because the source code is organized in a multimodule project that can be fully built with one simple command. As previously mentioned, I've chosen to use a build tool because in this day and age, learning Java without one makes no sense; any company you apply to most definitely uses one.

Aside from the prerequisites that I listed, you also need install a JDK and a Java Editor, as covered in **Chapter 2**. You do not need to know math, algorithms, or design patterns. Actually, you might end up knowing a few after you read this book.

This being said, let's dig in.

---

[26] `https://www.freejavaguide.com/history.html`

Summary

Java has dominated the industry for more than 25 years. It wasn't always at the top of the most-used development technologies, but it has never left the top five. Even with server-side JavaScript smart frameworks, like Node.js, React, or TypeScript, the heavy lifting is still left to Java. Emerging programming languages like Scala and Kotlin run on the JVM, so maybe the Java programming language will suffer a serious metamorphosis in order to compete, but it will still be here.

The modularization capability introduced in version 9 opens the gates for Java applications to be installed on smaller devices, because to run a Java application, we no longer need the whole runtime—only its core plus the modules the application was built with.

Furthermore, there are a lot of applications written in Java, especially in the financial domain, so Java will still be here because of legacy reasons and because migrating these titan applications to another technology is an impossible task. Most of these applications might be stuck on JDK 8 because of their complexity and because they have a lot of dependencies that would require upgrading too.

There are also many frameworks written in Java, like Spring, Micronaut, Helidon Quarkus. By adopting the most recent version of Java, the teams developing them make sure that there is an incentive to keep the JDK alive and evolving.

Java will probably survive and be on top for many years to come. The fact that it is a very mature technology with a huge community built around it will help to ensure that it endures. Being very easy to learn and developer-friendly makes it remain the first choice for most companies. So, you might conclude at this point that learning Java and buying this book is a good investment.

This chapter has a lot of references. They are interesting to read, but they are not mandatory to understand the contents of this book. The same goes for the references cited in the rest of the chapters.

CHAPTER 2

Preparing Your Development Environment

To start learning Java, your computer needs to be set up as a Java development machine. Thus, here are the requirements:

- **Java** support on your computer is *kinda' mandatory* ☺.

- An integrated development environment, also known as IDE, which is basically an application in which you write your code. An IDE assists you when writing code, compiling it, and executing it.

  - The recommended IDE for this book is IntelliJ IDEA. You can go to the official website (`https://www.jetbrains.com/idea/`) to get the free community edition, which is sufficient for the purposes of this book.

  - Or you can choose the most popular free IDE for Java development: Eclipse (`https://www.eclipse.org/`).

  - Or you can try Apache NetBeans, which in the past was the default choice for most beginners because it was bundled with the JDK until version 8. It was taken out of the JDK in Java 9 and can now be downloaded from here: `https://netbeans.apache.org`.

- **Apache Maven** is a build tool used to organize projects, easily handle dependencies, and make your work easier in big multimodule projects. (It is mandatory because the projects in this book are organized and built with a Maven setup.)

© Iuliana Cosmina 2024
I. Cosmina, *Java 23 for Absolute Beginners*, https://doi.org/10.1007/979-8-8688-1041-1_2

- **Git** is a versioning system that you can use to get the source code for the book, and you can experiment with it and create your own version. It is optional because GitHub, which is where the sources for this chapter are hosted, supports downloading them directly as an archive.

Note   Any respectable software company uses a versioning system these days, so being comfortable with Git is a serious advantage when applying for a software developer position.

To write and execute Java programs/applications, you only need the Java **D**evelopment **K**it installed. *Nothing stops you writing Java code in Notepad, if that is what you want.* All other tools that I've listed here are needed only to make your job easier and to familiarize you with a real development job.

Important   You probably need administrative rights if you install these applications for all users. For more recent versions of Windows, you might even need administrative rights so you can install the necessary tools. This book provides instructions on how to install everything—assuming your user has the necessary rights. If you need more information, the Internet is here to help.

If the requirements seem like a lot to set up, do not get discouraged; this chapter contains instructions on how to install each tool and verify that it is working properly. Let's start by making sure your computer supports Java.

Installing Java

Here you are with your computer, and you can't wait to start writing Java applications. But first you need to get yourself a JDK and install it. For this, you need an Internet connection. Open your browser and go to `https://www.oracle.com/java/technologies/java-se-glance.html`.

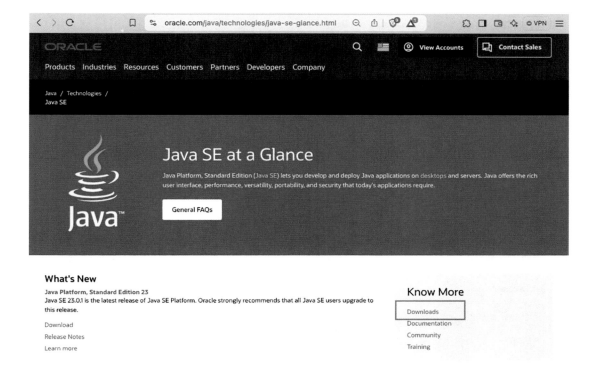

Figure 2-1. *Navigating the Oracle site to find the desired JDK*

On the Oracle site, you will find the latest stable Java version. Click the **Downloads** URL. You should be redirected to a download page similar to the one in Figure 2-2.

Java 23, Java 21, and earlier versions available now

JDK 23 is the latest release of the Java SE Platform.

Learn about Java SE Subscription

JDK 21 is the latest *Long-Term Support (LTS)* release of the Java SE Platform.

Earlier JDK versions are available below.

JDK 23   JDK 21   GraalVM for JDK 23   GraalVM for JDK 21

JDK Development Kit 23.0.1 downloads

JDK 23 binaries are free to use in production and free to redistribute, at no cost, under the Oracle No-Fee Terms and Conditions (NFTC).

JDK 23 will receive updates under these terms, until March 2025, when it will be superseded by JDK 24.

Linux   macOS   Windows

Product/file description	File size	Download
ARM64 Compressed Archive	228.92 MB	https://download.oracle.com/java/23/latest/jdk-23_linux-aarch64_bin.tar.gz (sha256)
ARM64 RPM Package	228.54 MB	https://download.oracle.com/java/23/latest/jdk-23_linux-aarch64_bin.rpm (sha256) (OL 8 GPG Key)
x64 Compressed Archive	231.64 MB	https://download.oracle.com/java/23/latest/jdk-23_linux-x64_bin.tar.gz (sha256)
x64 Debian Package	199.69 MB	https://download.oracle.com/java/23/latest/jdk-23_linux-x64_bin.deb (sha256)
x64 RPM Package	231.21 MB	https://download.oracle.com/java/23/latest/jdk-23_linux-x64_bin.rpm (sha256) (OL 8 GPG Key)

Figure 2-2. *The Oracle page where you can download the desired JDK*

JDK 23 is available for a few operating systems. You should download the JDK matching your OS. For writing this book and writing the source code, I am using a macOS computer, which means I will download the JDK with the `*.dmg` extension.

You need to accept the license agreement if you want to use Java for development. You can read it if you are curious, but basically it tells you that you are allowed to use Java as long as you do not modify its original components and do not make any profit from it. It also tells you that you are responsible for how you use it, so if you use it to write or execute nefarious applications you are solely responsible legally and so on.

If you want to get your hands on an early version of the JDK that was not officially released yet, this is the page where you have to go: `https://openjdk.org/projects/jdk`. At the time of writing this chapter, on that page, under *Releases*, version 24 is listed as *in development*, and an early access (unstable) JDK 24 is available for download.

Important   This book will cover Java syntax and details for versions up to and including Java 23. There are common details that remain the same from one version to another. Those won't be reviewed and changed, as the only thing that is different is the version number. It is recommended to download version 23 of the JDK to have full compatibility of the sources ensured.

After you have downloaded the JDK, the next step is to install it. The default configuration works well, so just double-click **Next** until you reach the final page, and then click **Finish**. This will work for Windows and macOS. The JDK is installed in a specific location.

In Windows, the default Java installation path is `C:\Program Files\Java\jdk-23`, but you can choose to install it in a different path, something simpler and without spaces like `C:\tools\jdk-23,` for example.

In macOS, the default path is `/Library/Java/JavaVirtualMachines/jdk-23.jdk/Contents/Home`.

On Linux systems, depending on the distribution, the location where the JDK is installed varies. My preferred way is to get the `*.tar.gz` from the Oracle site that contains the full content of the JDK, unpack it, and copy it to a specific location. Also, my preferred location on Linux is `/home/iuliana.cosmina/tools/jdk-23.jdk`.

Tip   Using a PPA (repository; also known as a Package Manager) installer on Linux will put the JDK files where they are supposed to go on Linux automatically and update them automatically when a new version is released using the Linux (Global) updater utility. But, if you are using Linux proficiently, you've probably figured out you can skip this section by now.

Another way to make things easy on a Linux or Unix system is to use SDKMAN. This is my favorite way to install Java in recent years, as SDKMAN can manage multiple Java versions and can automatically switch between depending on the project being worked on based on a configuration file named `.sdkmanrc`. Get it from here: `https://sdkman.io`.

After installing Java, if you go to the location specific to your operating system, you can inspect the contents of the JDK. As an example, in Figure 2-3, on the left are the contents of JDK 23, and on the right are the contents of JDK 8.

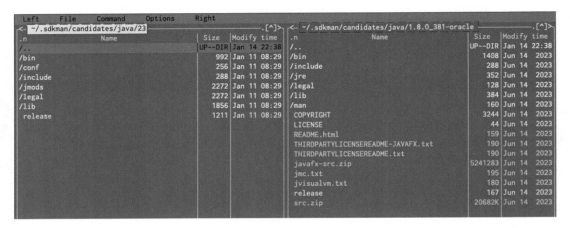

Figure 2-3. *JDK version 8 and version 23 contents comparison*

I chose to make this comparison because, starting with Java 9, the content of the JDK is organized differently. Until Java 8, the JDK contained a directory called jre that contained a Java Runtime Environment (JRE) used by the JDK. For people interested only in running Java applications, the JRE could be downloaded separately.

The lib directory contains Java libraries and support files needed by development tools.

Starting with Java 9, the JRE is no longer isolated in its own directory. Starting with version 11, Java has become fully modular. This means a customized "JRE" distribution can be created with the modules specifically needed to run an application. This means there are no JREs to download on the Oracle site starting with Java 11.

The most important thing you need to know about the JDK is that the bin directory contains executables and command-line launchers that are necessary to compile, execute, and audit Java code. The other directories are the jmods directory, which contains the compiled module definitions, and the include directory, which contains the C-language header files that support native code programming with the Java Native Interface (JNI) and the Java Debug Interface.

The JAVA_HOME Environment Variable

The most important directory in the JDK is the `bin` directory, because that directory has to be added to the path of your system. This allows you to call the Java executables from anywhere. Java executables are programs that run on your computer to compile, run and analyze Java code. It also allows other applications to call them without extra configurations steps needed. Most IDEs used for handling (writing, analyzing, compiling, and executing) Java code are written in Java, and they require knowing where the JDK is installed so that they can be run. This is done by declaring an environment variable named `JAVA_HOME` that points to the location of the JDK directory. To make the Java executables callable from any location within a system, you must add the `bin` directory to the system path. The next three sections explain how to do this on the three most common operating systems.

JAVA_HOME on Windows

To declare the `JAVA_HOME` environment variable on a Windows system, you need to open the dialog window for setting up system variables. On Windows systems, click the **Start** button. In the menu, there is a search box. In more recent versions, there is a search box on the horizontal toolbar; you can use this one too. Enter the word **environment** in there (the first three letters of the word should suffice to locate the option, though). Click the **Edit the system environment variables** option when it becomes available. These steps on Windows 10 are depicted in Figure 2-4.

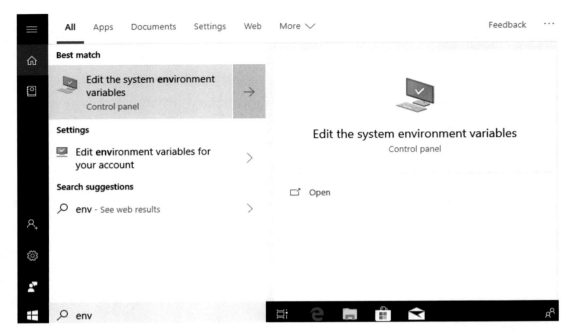

Figure 2-4. *Windows menu item to configure environment variables*

After clicking that menu item, the **System Properties** dialog window should open with the **Advanced** tab displayed, as shown in Figure 2-5.

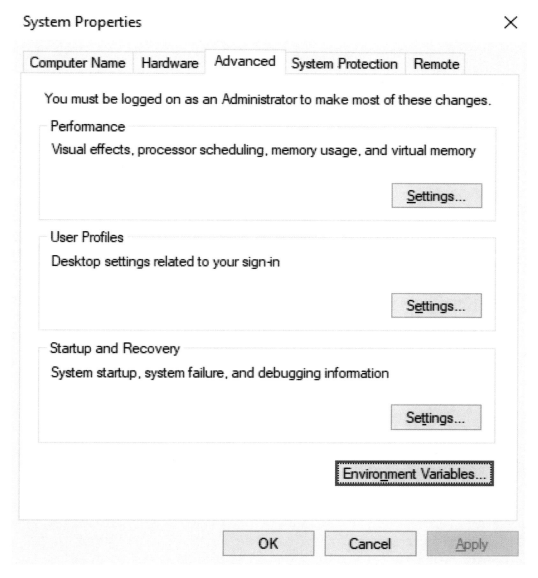

Figure 2-5. *First dialog window to set environment variables on Windows*

Click the **Environment Variables** button to open the dialog window of the same name, which is split into two sections: User variables and System variables. You are interested in **System variables** because that is where you declare JAVA_HOME. Just click the **New** button in that section, and a small **New System Variable** dialog window appears with two text fields; the top field requires you to enter the variable name—JAVA_HOME, in this case—and the bottom field requires you to enter the path (variable value)—the

JDK path in this case. Figure 2-6 shows the **Environment Variables** dialog window in the background and the **Edit System Variable** dialog window in the foreground (I had already created JAVA_HOME, so the dialog window shown is Edit System Variable instead of New System Variable).

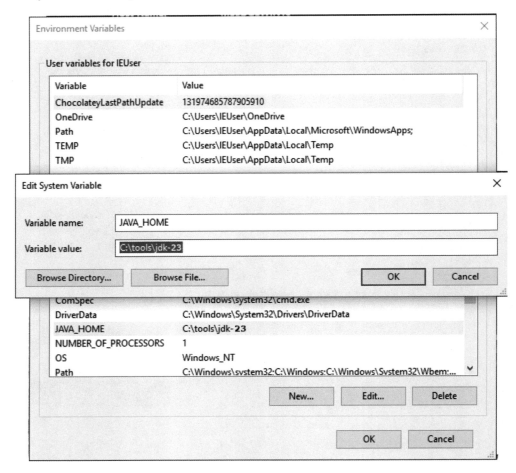

Figure 2-6. *Declaring JAVA_HOME as a system variable on Windows 10*

After declaring the JAVA_HOME variable, you need to add the executables to the system path. You do so by editing the Path variable. Select it from the **System variables** list in the **Environment Variables** dialog box, as shown on the left in Figure 2-7, and click the **Edit** button to open the **Edit environment variable** dialog (shown on the right). Starting in Windows 10, each part of the Path variable is shown on a different line, so you can add a new line and add %JAVA_HOME%\bin on it. This syntax is practical because it takes the location of the bin directory from whatever location the JAVA_HOME variable contains.

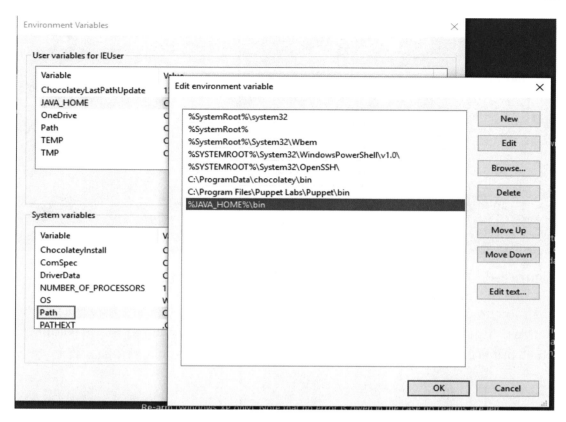

Figure 2-7. *Declaring the JDK executables directory as part of the system* Path *variable on Windows 10*

On older Windows systems, the contents of the Path are shown in a text field. So, you must add the %JAVA_HOME%\bin expression in the **Variable** text field and separate it from the existing content by using a semicolon (;).

No matter which Windows system you have, you can check that you set up everything correctly by opening **Command Prompt** (start typing the name in the search box to locate it easily) and executing the set command. This lists all the system variables and their values. JAVA_HOME and Path should be there with the desired values. For the setup proposed in this section, the output of executing set is depicted in Figure 2-8.

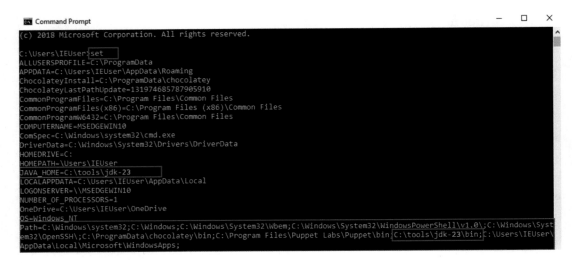

Figure 2-8. *Windows 10 system variables listed with the* `set` *command*

If you execute the previous command and see the expected output, you can now test your Java installation by executing `java -version` in the **Command Prompt** window, which prints the expected result, similar to the contents of Listing 2-1.

Listing 2-1. Java 23 Log for Execution of `java -version`

```
$ java -version
openjdk version "23" 2024-09-17
OpenJDK Runtime Environment (build 23+37-2369)
OpenJDK 64-Bit Server VM (build 23+37-2369, mixed mode, sharing)
```

JAVA_HOME on macOS

The location in which JDK is installed is `/Library/Java/JavaVirtualMachines/jdk-23.jdk/Contents/Home`. Your `JAVA_HOME` should point to this location. To do this for the current user, you can do the following:

- In the `/Users/{your.user}` directory (replace `{your.user}` with your actual system username), create a file named `.bash_profile`, if it doesn't exist already.

- In this file, write the following:

```
export JAVA_HOME=$(/usr/libexec/java_home -v23)
export PATH=$JAVA_HOME/bin:$PATH
```

If you use a different shell, just add the same two lines in its own configuration file.

On macOS, you can simultaneously install multiple Java versions. You can set which version is the one currently used on the system by obtaining the JDK location for the desired version by calling the `/usr/libexec/java_home` command and giving the Java version you are interested in as the argument. The result of executing the command is stored as a value for the `JAVA_HOME` variable.

On my system, I have JDK 8 to 23 installed. I can check the location for each JDK by executing the `/usr/libexec/java_home` command and providing each version as an argument. The commands and outputs for version 8 and 23 are depicted in Listing 2-2.

Listing 2-2. Java 8 and 23 Locations Obtained by Calling `/usr/libexec/java_home`

```
$ /usr/libexec/java_home -v23
 /Library/Java/JavaVirtualMachines/jdk-23.jdk/Contents/Home

$ /usr/libexec/java_home -v1.8
/Library/Java/JavaVirtualMachines/jdk1.8.0_381.jdk/Contents/Home
```

Tip   Manually installing Java and declaring the `JAVA_HOME` environment variable can be avoided by using SDKMAN.

The line `export PATH=$JAVA_HOME/bin:$PATH` adds the contents of the `bin` directory from the JDK location to the system patch. This means that I could open a terminal and execute any of the Java executables under it. For example, I could verify that the Java version set as default for my user is the expected one by executing `java -version`.

Depending on the version given as the argument, a different JDK location is returned. If you want to test the value of the `JAVA_HOME`, the echo command can help with that. Listing 2-3 depicts the outputs of the echo and `java -version` commands.

Listing 2-3. echo and `java` _HOME Value and Java Version Installed.

```
$ echo $JAVA_HOME
/Library/Java/JavaVirtualMachines/jdk-23.0.1/Contents/Home

$ java -version
openjdk version "23" 2024-09-17
OpenJDK Runtime Environment (build 23+37-2369)
OpenJDK 64-Bit Server VM (build 23+37-2369, mixed mode, sharing)
```

JAVA_HOME on Linux

Tip   If you are using Linux proficiently, you are either using a PPA or SDKMAN, so you can skip this section. However, if you like to control where the JDK is located and define your own environment variables, keep reading.

Linux systems are Unix-like operating systems. This is similar to macOS, which is based on Unix. Depending on your Linux distribution, installing Java can be done via the specific package manager or by directly downloading the JDK as a `*.tar.gz` archive from the official Oracle site.

If Java is installed using a package manager, the necessary executables are usually automatically placed in the system path at installation time. That is why this book covers only the cases where you do everything manually, and choose to install Java only for the current user in a location such as `/home/{your.user}/tools/jdk-23.jdk`, because covering package managers is not the object of the book.

After downloading the JDK archive from the Oracle site and unpacking it at `/home/{your.user}/tools/jdk-23.jdk`, you need to create a file named either `.bashrc` or `.bash_profile` in your user home directory. On some Linux distributions, the files might already exist, in which case you just need to edit them. Add the lines depicted in Listing 2-4.

Listing 2-4. Setting JAVA_HOME for the Current User in Linux

```
export JAVA_HOME=/home/{your.user}/tools/jdk-23.jdk
export PATH=$JAVA_HOME/bin:$PATH
```

As you can see, the syntax is similar to the macOS syntax. To check the location of the JDK and the Java version, the same commands presented in the macOS section are used.

Running Java Code

Before instructing you to install even more tools (Apache Maven, Git, etc.), let's run some Java code. Enhancements like JShell, introduced in Java 9, and unnamed classes and instance `main` methods, introduced in Java 21 and expanded in scope in future versions (even if still in preview), allow Java absolute beginners to run Java code directly without going through the compile phase, enabling them to get used to the syntax and get a "quick taste" of the language syntax.

Using JShell

Starting with Java 9, developers that want to test out the Java language can do so without the need to create a full-blown Java project. JShell is an interactive command-line tool for learning the Java programming language and prototyping Java code. So instead of writing your code in a class, compiling it, and executing the bytecode, you can just use JShell to directly execute statements.

JShell is quite late to the party, as scripting languages like Python and Node introduced similar utilities years ago, and JVM languages like Scala, Clojure, and Groovy followed in their footsteps. But better late than never.

JShell is a Read-Eval-Print Loop (REPL), which evaluates declarations, statements, and expressions as they are entered, and then it immediately shows the results. It is practical to try new ideas and techniques quickly and without the need to have a complete development environment, nor an entire context for the code to be executed in.

JShell is a standard component of the JDK. The executable to start it is in the `bin` directory located in the JDK installation directory. This means that all you have to do is open a terminal (Command Prompt in Windows) and type `jshell`. If the contents of the `bin` directory were added to the system path, you should see a welcome message containing the JDK version on your system. Also, the root of your terminal changes to `jshell>` to let you know you are now using `jshell`.

In Listing 2-5, jshell was started in verbose mode by calling jshell -v, which enables detailed feedback to be provided for all statements executed until the end of the session.

Listing 2-5. Output of Command jshell -v

```
$ jshell -v
|  Welcome to JShell -- Version 23
|  For an introduction type: /help intro

jshell>
```

If you are executing the commands as you are reading the book, go ahead and enter /help to view a list of all the available actions and commands. Assuming you are not, Listing 2-6 depicts the expected output.

Listing 2-6. Output of Command /help in jshell

```
jshell> /help
|  Type a Java language expression, statement, or declaration.
|  Or type one of the following commands:
|  /list [<name or id>|-all|-start]
|     list the source you have typed
|  /edit <name or id>
|     edit a source entry
|  /drop <name or id>
|     delete a source entry
|  /save [-all|-history|-start] <file>
|     Save snippet source to a file
...
|  /exit [<integer-expression-snippet>]
|     exit the jshell tool
...
```

In Java, values are assigned to groups of characters named **variables**. (More about how to choose them and use them in **Chapter 4**.) To begin using JShell, we'll declare a variable named six and assign the value 6 to it (*I know, smart right?*). The statement and the jshell logs are depicted in Listing 2-7.

Listing 2-7. Declaring a Variable Using `jshell`

```
jshell> int six = 6;
six ==> 6
|  created variable six : int
```

As you can see, the log message is clear and tells us that our command was executed successfully, and a variable of type `int` named `six` was created. The `six ==> 6` lets us know that value 6 was assigned to the variable that we just created.

You can create as many variables as you want and perform mathematical operations, string concatenations, and anything that you need to quickly execute. As long as the JShell session is not closed, the variables exist and can be used. Listing 2-8 depicts a few statements being executed with JShell and their results.

Listing 2-8. `jshell` Various Statements and Outputs

```
jshell> int six = 6
six ==> 6
|  modified variable six : int
|    update overwrote variable six : int
jshell> six = six + 1
six ==> 7
|  assigned to six : int
jshell> six +1
$14 ==> 8
|  created scratch variable $14 : int
jshell> System.out.println("Current val: " + six)
Current val: 7
```

The `$14 ==> 8` depicted in Listing 2-8 shows the value 8 being assigned to a variable named $14. This variable was created by `jshell`. When the result of a statement is not assigned to a variable named by the developer, `jshell` generates a scratch variable and its name is made of the $ (dollar) character and a number representing an internal index for that variable. It is not explicitly stated in the documentation, but from my observations while playing with `jshell`, the index value appears to be the number of the statement that lead to its creation.

Important   One of the most important building blocks of Java code is the **class**. Classes are pieces of code that model real-world objects and events. Classes contain two types of **members**: those modeling states, which are the class variables, also named **fields** or **properties**, and those modeling behaviors, named **methods**.

JDK provides a lot of classes that model the base components needed to create most applications. Classes are covered in more detail in **Chapter 3**. Even if some concepts seem foreign now, just be patient, and let them accumulate; they will make more sense later.

One of the most important JDK classes is `java.lang.String`, which is used to represent text objects. This class provides a rich set of methods that manipulate the value of a `String` variable. Listing 2-9 depicts a few of these methods being called on a declared variable of type `String`.

Listing 2-9. `jshell` Method Calling Examples with `String` Variable

```
jshell> String lyric = "twice as much ain't twice as good"
lyric ==> "twice as much ain't twice as good"
|  created variable lyric : String

jshell> lyric.toUpperCase()
$18 ==> "TWICE AS MUCH AIN'T TWICE AS GOOD"
|  created scratch variable $18 : String
jshell> lyric.length()
$20 ==> 33
|  created scratch variable $20 : int
```

The task of writing Java code in `jshell` using variables of JDK types might look complicated, because you do not know what method to call, right? `jshell` is quite helpful because it tells you when the method does not exist. When trying to call a method, you can press the **Tab** key to display a list of methods available. This is called **code completion**, and smart Java editors offer it too.

In Listing 2-10, you can see the error message printed by `jshell` when you try to call a method that does not exist and how to display and filter methods available for a certain type.

Listing 2-10. More `jshell` Method Calling Examples with `String` Variable

```
jshell> lyric.toupper()
|  Error:
|  cannot find symbol
|    symbol:   method toupper()
|  lyric.toupper()
|  ^-----------^

jshell> lyric.to   # <Tab>
toCharArray()    toLowerCase(     toString()        toUpperCase(
jshell> lyric.    # <Tab>
charAt(                 chars()                codePointAt(
codePointBefore(        codePointCount(        codePoints()
...
```

JShell is quite obvious in telling us that the `toupper()` method is not known for the `String` class.

When listing possible methods, methods ending in `()` require no arguments. The methods ending in `(` take none or more arguments and have more than one form. To view those forms, just write the method on your variable and press **Tab** again. Listing 2-11 depicts the multiple forms of the `indexOf` method.

Listing 2-11. `jshell` Listing All Forms of the `indexOf` Method in the `String` Class

```
jshell> lyric.indexOf(  # <Tab>
$1       $14      $18      $19      $2       $20      $5       $9        lyric    six

Signatures:
int String.indexOf(int ch)
int String.indexOf(int ch, int fromIndex)
int String.indexOf(String str)
int String.indexOf(String str, int fromIndex)

<press tab again to see documentation>
```

Right after the `lyric.indexOf(` line, `jshell` lists the variables that were created during the session, to give you an easy choice of existing arguments.

Anything you can write in a Java project, you can write in jshell as well. The advantage is that you can split your program in a sequence of statements, execute them instantly to check the result, and adjust as necessary. There are other things that jshell can do for you, the most important of which are covered in this book.

All variables you declared in a JShell session are listed by executing the /vars command. Listing 2-12 depicts the variables declared in the session for this chapter.

Listing 2-12. jshell> /vars Output Sample for a Small Coding Session (part one)

```
jshell> /vars
|    int $1 = 5
|    int $2 = 42
|    int $5 = 8
|    int $9 = 8
|    int six = 7
|    int $14 = 8
|    String lyric = "twice as much ain't twice as good"
|    String $18 = "TWICE AS MUCH AIN'T TWICE AS GOOD"
|    int $19 = 9
|    int $20 = 33
```

Now, since you've played enough with declaring variables and doing mathematical operations, it is time to write the most famous program of them all, the one that prints *Hello World!* in the console. Just open jshell and type the System.out.print("Hello World!") statement, like depicted in Listing 2-13.

Listing 2-13. jshell> /vars Output Sample for a Small Coding Session (part two)

```
jshell>
|  Welcome to JShell -- Version 23-ea
|  For an introduction type: /help intro

jshell> System.out.print("Hello World!")
Hello World!
```

Running Java Source Files Directly Using Java 21

Java 21, through JEP 445,[1] *Unnamed Classes and Instance Main Methods*, makes it easier for Java beginners to write their first programs without needing to understand language features designed for large programs. As the JEP title indicates, it does so by adding support for unnamed classes and instance `main` methods. What does this mean? Java 21 provides the ability to run Java code directly without needing to compile it explicitly (it is being done for you in memory), and a beginner can write Java code without having to use a dedicated IDE. JShell already provides this feature, but anything else than single-line commands is not practical.

Let's test that, shall we? In directory `chapter02/java21-sandbox` there is a file named `practice01.java`. Its contents are depicted in Listing 2-14.

Note   Oracle caused me a *chicken-and-egg* problem with the introduction of this feature. At this point in the book you haven't cloned the book repository yet, so you don't have the sources. For running the examples shown in this section and the next, you don't really need to have the sources anyway. You can create your own sandbox directory and create the files with the provided content. If you want to download the sources, you can temporarily jump to the **Installing Git** section.

Listing 2-14. Simple `main` Method in `practice01.java` File

```
void main() {
  System.out.println("Practice01: Hello World");
}
```

The method signature is very simple, and is different from the `main` methods you will see later in this book. This is a simplified dialect of the Java programming language targeted at total beginners. IntelliJ IDEA knows how to run this file, but if JEP 445 is still in preview status when you are reading this book, you will need to select an option for the project **Language level** that includes preview features. At the time of writing, this feature is a preview in Java version 21, which means running the file can be done only with the command shown in Listing 2-15.

---

[1] https://openjdk.org/jeps/445

Listing 2-15. java Command to Run the `practice01.java` File

```
> java --enable-preview --source 21 practice.java
# output
Note: practice.java uses preview features of Java SE 21.
Note: Recompile with -Xlint:preview for details.
Practice01: Hello World!
```

Listing 2-15 also shows the output produced by running the command. Normally in Java, methods must be enclosed in classes. However, the code in `practice01.java` does not require a `class` declaration; thus, it can be said that the `main()` method is actually part of an **unnamed** class. *Now the name of the JEP makes more sense, right?*

For Java code to be executed directly like this, there are a few rules to follow:

- The `package` statement is *not allowed.*

- There is no class definition and no constructor.

- The code in the file must be enclosed in an unnamed class, which cannot `extend` or `implement` another class or interface.

- A `main()` method must exist and is `static` by default (and `public`)—however, these two terms are omitted to avoid confusing a beginner with notions such as class and instance members.

- The file can declare only static members (fields and methods), and static methods can access only other static members.

- The `main()` method can have arguments, and they are passed over when executing the file.

These rules probably do not make sense to you right now, since most of the terms in this list are introduced in **Chapter 3**, but as an absolute beginner, it is not critical to know these rules yet. Feel free to come back to this section later if you need to. For now, let's see what other code we can run directly.

We can run Java code directly with arguments, as shown in Listing 2-16, which depicts the code in file `practice02.java`.

Listing 2-16. `main` Method with Arguments

```
void main(String... args) {
  if (args.length > 0) {
    System.out.print("Practice02: Hello " + args[0] + "\n");
  } else {
    System.out.println("Practice02: Hello World!");
  }
}
```

The code in `practice02.java` can be run with and without arguments. If an argument is provided, running the file produces output `Practice02: Hello {argument}`; otherwise it produces `Practice02: Hello World!`. Listing 2-17 shows running `practice02.java` with and without an argument.

Listing 2-17. Java command to run the `practice02.java` file

```
> java --enable-preview --source 21 practice02.java Mayer
# output
Practice02: Hello Mayer

> java --enable-preview --source 21 practice02.java
# output
Practice02: Hello World
```

There are two other files in the `java21-sandbox` directory. The `practice03.java` file contains a static variable. Its value is printed when the file is run without an argument. The `practice04.java` file contains an additional static method, aptly named `staticMethod`. This method is invoked in the `main` method and its result is printed when the file is run. Feel free to try them out.

This feature provides the opportunity to start writing Java code and running it immediately, to get familiar with the language syntax fast before jumping to advanced programming concepts.

The second preview of this feature is present in Java 22 under JEP 463,[2] *Implicitly Declared Classes and Instance Main Methods.* A different JEP was necessary to include feedback from the community. The implicitly declared classes mentioned in the JEP

---

[2] `https://openjdk.org/jeps/463`

title relax a few of the rules for Java directly executable files introduced in Java 21, as the main() method is considered implicitly enclosed in a class with a name decided by the system, and the main() method is no longer static. Anyway, there are a lot of details about the inner workings in this JEP that will make more sense after you have finished reading this book; for now, the only thing you need to know is that you can write simple Java program and execute them easily.

Running Java Source Files Directly Using Java 22

The improvements to support beginners' introduction to Java continue in Java 22, through JEP 458,[3] *Launch Multi-File Source-Code Programs*, which introduces the possibility to run actual Java files with proper Java syntax, not a simplified dialect for total beginners. In Java 22, people learning Java can write and run single-class programs and then expand them to include more features as their learning progresses.

As introduced in Chapter 1, most Java books for beginners start with the typical *Hello World!* example, shown in Listing 2-18.

Listing 2-18. TyTypical `HelloWorld` Java Example

```java
public class Practice01 {
    public static void main(String[] args) {
      System.out.println("Practice01: Hello World!");
    }
}
```

The code depicted in Listing 2-18 represents the content of the java22-sandbox/ Practice01.java file. You can run this file directly as shown in Listing 2-19.

Listing 2-19. Running a Java File Using Java 22

```
> java Practice01.java
# output
Practice01: Hello World!
```

---

[3] https://openjdk.org/jeps/458

Information   Notice that the `--enable-preview --source 22` options are not necessary, since this is not a preview feature.

In the previous section covering Java 21, the text to be printed was provided via a variable, or another method. In Java 22, the text can be provided using a method in another class. Listing 2-20 shows the contents of the HelloProvider class.

Listing 2-20. Class That Declares a Method That Returns Text

```java
public class HelloProvider {
  public static String get(){
    return "Hello World from HelloProvider!";
  }
}
```

This class is located in the java22-sandbox directory as well. Another class named Practice02 that invokes the get() method in the HelloProvider can be created in the same directory with the contents shown in Listing 2-21.

Listing 2-21. Class That Invokes HelloProvider.get()

```java
public class Practice02 {
  public static void main(String[] args) {
    System.out.println("Practice02: " + HelloProvider.get());
  }
}
```

This class has a main(..) method, thus the file can be run with the same command in Listing 2-19. The command and output is shown in Listing 2-22.

Listing 2-22. Running a Java File That Invokes a Method from a Different Class, from a Different File

```
> java Practice02.java
# output
Practice02: Hello World from HelloProvider!
```

Because the HelloProvider.java file is located in the same directory, Java can easily find it and use it. This proves that Java 22 can launch multiple Java files without the need to go through the compile phase.

And there is one thing more Java 22 can do. When wiring a Java project, you don't need to always write everything from scratch, because multiple libraries and frameworks in Java are publicly available that you can include in your project as a dependency and use them. Java libraries are collections of compiled classes that can be archived in files with the jar extension. When you run a class that references a class in a library, you need to tell Java where that library can be found. This practice is called *adding a library to the classpath* and is done by invoking the java. extension command with the -cp option and providing as an argument the location of the library.

Listing 2-23 shows the code of a class named Practice03 that invokes the HelloProvider.get() method but the HelloProvider class is loaded from a library on the classpath.

Listing 2-23. Class That Invokes HelloProvider.get() from a Library

```
public class Practice03 {
  public static void main(String[] args) {
    System.out.println("Practice03: " + lib.HelloProvider.get());
  }
}
```

To make it obvious that we are using the compiled and archived version of the HelloProvider class, the class definition includes the lib package, as shown in Listing 2-24.

Listing 2-24. Class That Invokes HelloProvider.get()

```
package lib;

public class HelloProvider {

  public static String get(){
    return "Hello World from HelloProvider in the lib jar!";
  }
}
```

You will learn how to compile classes and pack them in **Chapter 3**; for now, just use the provided jar for this example, which is located at java22-sandbox/lib/lib-provider.jar. The command to run the Practice03.java file and its output are shown in Listing 2-25.

Listing 2-25. Running a Java File That Invokes a Method from a Different Class, from a Library

```
> java -cp "lib/*" Practice03.java
# output
Practice03: Hello World from HelloProvider in the lib jar!
```

These features offers extension students and aspiring developers the opportunity to experiment with Java code without feeling overwhelmed by the number of tools they need to install and be somewhat familiar with just to print a message in the console.

Java 21 introduced the possibility of running a single Java file with a simplified Java dialect. The feature is still a preview when this chapter is being written, but it might be an official feature when Java 23 is released.

Java 22 added the possibility to run multiple Java files. The class containing the main(..) method can reference classes in other files, and it works as long as they are in the same directory with it, either at the same level or in nested directories. When a class is in a directory or in a nested directory structure, the class is considered to be in a package and thus the Java file must contain a package declaration. For example, let's consider the two Java files in Listing 2-26.

Listing 2-26. HelloProvider.java Java File in a Directory Hierarchy

The HelloProvider.java file is located under com/provider and is referenced in the Practice04.java file. The HelloProvider.java body starts with the package com.provider; statement (you will learn about packages in **Chapter 3**), as shown in Listing 2-27.

Listing 2-27. `HelloProvider.java` Contents

```java
package com.provider;

public class HelloProvider {

    public static String get(){
        return "Hello World from com.provider.HelloProvider!";
    }
}
```

When referencing it in the `Practice04.java` file, the package name must be used as shown in Listing 2-28.

Listing 2-28. `HelloProvider.java` Java File in a Directory Hierarchy

```java
class Practice04 {
  public static void main(String[] args) {
    System.out.println("Practice04: " + com.provider.HelloProvider.get());
  }
}
```

The command to run the `Practice04.java` file and its output are shown in Listing 2-29. Notice that no arguments are necessary to ensure that Java will find com/provider/HelloProvider.java.

Listing 2-29. Running a Java File That Invokes a Method from a Class in a Hierarchy of Directories

```
> java Practice04.java
# output
Practice04: Hello World from com.provider.HelloProvider!
```

Java 22 added the possibility to also use Java classes contained in libraries, and the in-memory compilation works as long as they are added to the classpath.

If the in-memory compilation fails because the Java syntax is incorrect, or dependencies cannot be found, in 99.99% of cases the error messages will help you fix the code. Let's examine a few very common errors. Look at the `Practice05.java` example depicted in Listing 2-30.

Listing 2-30. Java File with a Syntax Error

```
class Practice05 {
    public static void main(String[] args) {
        System.out.println("Practice05: Hello World!")
    }
}
```

Can you tell just by looking at it what the syntax error is? You probably can, but for the sake of this demonstration, try to run this file. The results are depicted in Listing 2-31.

Listing 2-31. Running a Java File with a Syntax Error

```
> java Practice05.java
#output
Practice05.java:3: error: ';' expected
        System.out.println("Practice05: Hello World!")
                                                      ^

1 error
error: compilation failed
```

As you can see, Java is telling you that it expects a semicolon (`;`) at the end of the `System.out.println(..)` statement on line 3. Feel free to play with this file or write your own to test various errors.

The `java22-sandbox` directory contains the file `Practice06.java`, which references a class that does not exist. This is more than a syntax error—it is a design error. The file contents are shown in Listing 2-32.

Listing 2-32. Java File That References a Class That Does Not Exist

```
class Practice06 {
    public static void main(String[] args) {
        System.out.println("Practice06: " + MockProvider.get());
    }
}
```

The error message is shown in Listing 2-33.

65

Listing 2-33. Running a Java File That References a Class That Does Not Exist

```
> java Practice06.java
#output
Practice06.java:3: error: cannot find symbol
        System.out.println("Practice06: " + MockProvider.get());
                                            ^
  symbol:   variable MockProvider
  location: class Practice06
1 error
error: compilation failed
```

Java identifies the line number where the error is (3) and reports that it cannot find symbol. This obviously means that it cannot find the class, so why does it say symbol? Well, Java is a programming language, and a language is composed of symbols. In Java not all symbols are classes, as you'll learn by reading this book.

The third type of error you might get occurs when there is a piece of text Java does not recognize, like the random sssssss text in the contents of the Practice07.java file depicted in Listing 2-34.

Listing 2-34. Java File That Contains a Piece of Random Text

```
class Practice07 {

  sssssss
  public static void main(String[] args) {
    System.out.println("Practice06: " + HelloProvider.get());
  }
}
```

Running the Practice07.java file causes the error depicted in Listing 2-35.

Listing 2-35. Running a Java File That Contains a Piece of Random Text

```
> java Practice07.java
#output
Practice07.java:3: error: <identifier> expected
    sssssss
           ^
```

```
1 error
error: compilation failed
```

As you can see, Java recognizes the foreign element that is not a piece of code and points you to the line, 3.

There are also errors that might happen when you run syntactically correct Java code, and you will learn about those further in the book.

Feel free to experiment with this way of running Java code. Use it when you quickly want to test a piece of code before including it in a bigger project, or to test the examples in the book this way. This topic must be kept short in this book, however, because the purpose of this book is for you to no longer be a Java absolute beginner by the end of it.

Installing Apache Maven

The source code for this book is organized in small projects that can be compiled and executed using Apache Maven. You can download Apache Maven and read more about it on its official page[4]. Apache Maven is a software project management and comprehension tool. It was chosen as a build tool for this book for the following reasons:

- Easy setup (XML is pretty much omnipresent nowadays)

- Its long-term relationship with Java

- Many companies use it

If you need one more reason to learn a build tool, here it is: for medium-sized and large projects, a build tool is a must-have because it facilitates the declaration, download, and upgrade of dependencies.

Installing Maven is quite easy. Just download it, unpack it somewhere, and declare the `M2_HOME` environment variable. Instructions on how to do this are available on the official site, or you can use SDKMAN.

Once you have Maven installed, you can check that it installed successfully and that it uses the JDK version you expect by opening a terminal (or Command Prompt on Windows) and executing `mvn -version`. The output should look pretty similar to the output in Listing 2-36.

---

[4] `https://maven.apache.org`

Listing 2-36. Output of Command mvn -version on macOS

```
Apache Maven 4.0.0-alpha-13 (0a6a5617fe5ef65c44f05903491e170d92cf37fc)
Maven home: /Users/iuliana/.sdkman/candidates/maven/current
Java version: 23-ea, vendor: Oracle Corporation, runtime: /Users/iuliana/.
sdkman/candidates/java/23.ea.5-open
Default locale: en_GB, platform encoding: UTF-8
OS name: "mac os x", version: "14.2.1", arch: "x86_64", family: "mac"
```

Important   If you are pursuing a career in Java development, knowing a build tool well is a valuable advantage. Most companies using Java have big projects, organized in interdependent modules that cannot be managed without a build tool. Apache Maven has been the de facto build tool for Java for a long time, so you might want to get familiar with it.

Installing Git

This is an optional section, but as a developer, being familiar with a versioning system is important, so here it is. To install Git on your system, just go to the official page[5] and download the installer. Open the installer and click **Next** until it completes the installation. This works for Windows and macOS (for macOS, you can use homebrew[6]). Yes, it is this easy; you do not need to do anything else. On Linux, it can be done using a PPA.

Just in case you need more guidance, here is a page with instructions on how to install Git for all operating systems: https://gist.github.com/derhuerst/1b15ff465 2a867391f03.

To test that Git was installed successfully on your system, open a terminal (Command Prompt in Windows) and run git --version to see the result that it is printed. It should be the version of Git that you just installed. The expected output should be similar to Listing 2-37.

---

[5] https://git-scm.com/downloads
[6] https://brew.sh

Listing 2-37. Output of Command `git -version` to Verify Git Installation

```
$ git --version
git version 2.44.0
```

Now that you have Git installed, you can get the sources for this book by cloning the official Git repository in a terminal or directly from the IDE.

Install a Java IDE

The editor that I recommend, based on my experience of more than ten years, is IntelliJ IDEA. It is produced by a company called JetBrains. You can download this IDE from their official site[7]. The Ultimate Edition expires after 30 days; beyond that, a paid license is required. There is also a Community Edition available that can be used without a license. For simple projects that facilitate learning Java, this version suffices.

After you download the IntelliJ IDEA archive, double-click it to install it. After that, start it and configure your plugins first. Click the **Plugins** menu item, and a list of plugins should appear on the right side of the window. Check out the list of plugins on the **Installed** tab (depicted in Figure 2-9).

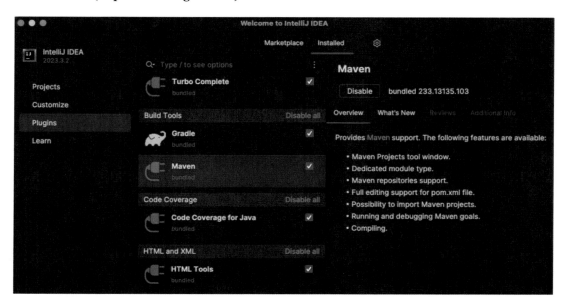

Figure 2-9. *IntelliJ IDEA Community Edition configure plugins dialog window*

---

[7] `https://www.jetbrains.com/idea/download/other.html`

Important   The plugins necessary for diverse styles of Java projects are enabled by default in IntelliJ IDEA. You can modify that list and disable the ones you do not need. This will reduce the amount of memory IntelliJ IDEA needs to function.

The Maven plugin is enabled by default; so is the Git plugin. This means your IDE is suitable for use right away, which in turn means that you need to get your hands on the sources for this book. There are three ways to get the sources for the book:

- Download the zipped package directly from GitHub.

- Clone the repository using a terminal (or Git Bash Shell in Windows) using the following command:

  ```
  $ git clone https://github.com/Apress/java-23-for-absolute-
  beginners.git
  ```

- Clone the project using IntelliJ IDEA.

Cloning from the command line or from IntelliJ IDEA does not require a GitHub user when the HTTPS URL of the repository is used. Figure 2-10 shows the two steps necessary to clone the GitHub project for this book.

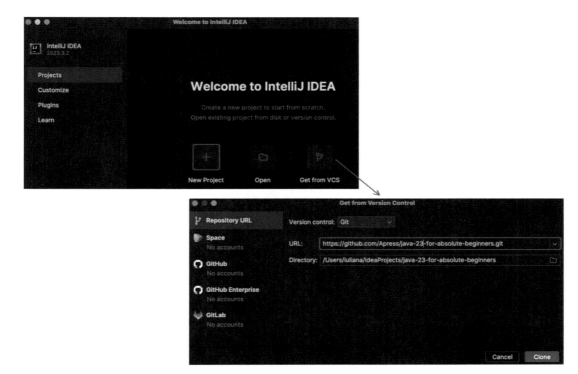

Figure 2-10. *IntelliJ IDEA Community Edition clone from VCS dialog windows*

When opening IntelliJ IDEA the first time, select the **Projects** menu item, then click the **Get from VCS** button. A new dialog window appears in which you can insert the repository URL and the location where the sources should be copied. After clicking the **Clone** button, the project will be copied, and IntelliJ IDEA will open it and figure out it uses Maven.

If you cloned the project using the command line, you can import it in IntelliJ IDEA using the **Open** button and selecting the directory created by the cloning operation.

Important   IntelliJ IDEA has its own internal Maven bundle. If you want to tell IntelliJ IDEA to use your local installation, just open the **Preferences** menu item, go to **Build, Execution, Deployment ➤ Build Tools ➤ Maven** section, and select the external Maven installation directory.

71

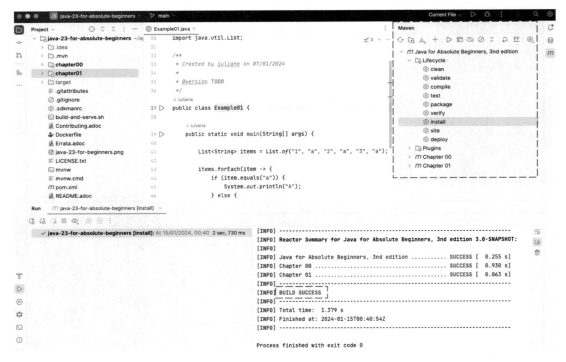

Figure 2-11. *IntelliJ IDEA Maven view*

It is expected a window to be opened at the bottom of the editor depicting the build progress and if the sources are ok this process should end with the message BUILD SUCCESS.

Important   If the build fails in IntelliJ IDEA, and you want to identify the problem, the first step is to run the build outside the IDE. You can run the build in a terminal (or Command Prompt on Windows) by executing mvn clean install. If the build passes in the terminal, the sources and your setup are correct and there is a problem with the editor configuration for sure.

The Maven build follows a specific life cycle to transform a Java project from sources to something that can be executed or deployed to an application server. Phases are executed in a specific order. Running a specific phase using the mvn {phase} command executes a number of steps called *goals,* each responsible for a specific task.

The `mvn clean install` command recommended previously executes the `clean` phase that deletes previously generated bytecode files and then executes the `install` phase that compiles Java files into bytecode, executes tests (if there are any), packs them up in Java Archives (jar files), and copies them to the local Maven repository. If you want to read more about Maven, check out the official site, but for the scope of this book, everything has been made really easy for you, as explained in **Chapter 3**.

Summary

If any of instructions are unclear to you (or I missed something), do not hesitate to use the Web to search for answers. All the software technologies introduced in this chapter are backed up by comprehensive official websites and by huge communities of developers eager to help. In the worst-case scenario, when you find nothing, you can always create an issue on the Apress GitHub official repository for this book, or drop me an e-mail. I'll do my best to support you if need be.

CHAPTER 3

Getting Your Feet Wet

This chapter covers the fundamental blocks and terms of the Java language. Although it could be considered yet another introductory chapter, it is quite important. The previous chapter left you with a complete development environment configured for writing Java code. It is time to make use of it. The following topics are covered in this chapter:

- Core syntax parts
- Java fundamental building blocks: packages, modules, and classes
- Creating a Java project with IntelliJ IDEA
- Compiling and executing Java code
- Packing a Java application into an executable jar
- Using Apache Maven

Core Syntax Parts

Writing Java code is easy, but before doing so, a few basic syntax rules are necessary. Let's analyze the code sample that started this book, reproduced in Listing 3-1.

Listing 3-1. The Java Beginner Code Sample a Smart Beginner Deserves

```java
package com.apress.ch.one.hw;

import java.util.List;

public class Example01 {
    public static void main(String[] args) {
        List<String> items = List.of("1", "a", "2", "a", "3", "a");
```

© Iuliana Cosmina 2024
I. Cosmina, *Java 23 for Absolute Beginners*, https://doi.org/10.1007/979-8-8688-1041-1_3

```
        items.forEach(item -> {
            if (item.equals("a")) {
                System.out.println("A");
            } else {
                System.out.println("Not A");
            }
        });
    }
}
```

The next list explains each line, or group of lines with the same purpose:

- `package com.apress.ch.one.hw;` is a package declaration. You can view this statement as an address of the class declared in the file.

- `;` (semicolon) is used to mark the end of a statement or declaration.

- `import java.util.List;` is an import statement. JDK provides a number of classes to use when writing code. Those classes are organized in packages too, and when you want to use one of them, you have to specify the class to use and its package, because two classes might have the same name but are declared in different packages. And when the compiler compiles your code, it needs to know exactly which class is needed.

- `public class Example01` is a class declaration statement. It contains an accessor (`public`), the type (`class`), and the name of the class (`Example01`). A class has a body that is wrapped between curly braces.

- `{ ... }` (curly braces) are used to group statements together into code blocks. Blocks do not require to be ended with a `;`. Blocks of code can represent a body of a class, a method, or just a few statements that have to be grouped together so the code looks better.

- `public static void main(String[] args)` is a method declaration statement. It contains an accessor (`public`), a reserved keyword (`static`) that will be explained later, the name of the method (`main`), and a section that declares parameters (`(String[] args)`).

- `List<String> items = List.of("1", "a", "2", "a", "3", "a");` is a statement declaring a variable named `items` of type `List<String>` and assigning the value returned by this statement to it: `List.of("1", "a", "2", "a", "3", "a")`.

- `items.forEach(...)` is a statement containing a function call on the `items` variable used to traverse all values in this list variable.

- `item -> { ... }` is a lambda expression. It declares a code block to be executed for each item in the list.

- `if (<condition>) { ... } else { ... }` is a decision statement. The block of code being executed is decided by evaluating the condition.

- `System.out.println(<text>);` is a statement used to print an argument passed to it.

It's too early in the book to start explaining everything in the previous list in detail, but the most important rule when writing Java code is that, except package declarations and import statements, all code must be within a block. Also, if a statement is not spread on multiple lines, it must end with ; (semicolon), because otherwise the code will not compile.

For writing more advanced Java classes, with code that solves a real problem, you must know and understand the building blocks of Java.

Java Fundamental Building Blocks: Packages, Modules, and Classes

---

Warning   This is a consistent introduction into Java as a platform. To write Java code confidently, you need to have a grasp of what happens under the hood, what the building blocks are, and the order in which you have to configure/write them. If you want, you can skip to the next section, "How to Determine the Structure of a Java Project," but in the same way some new drivers need a little knowledge of how the engine works before grabbing the driving wheel confidently, some people might feel more confident and in control when programming if they understand the mechanics a little. So, I wanted to make sure that anyone reading this book gets a proper start.

To write Java applications, a developer must be familiar with the Java building blocks of a Java program. Think about it like this: if you are trying to build a car, you have to learn what wheels are and where they are placed, right? This is what I'm trying to achieve for Java in this book: to explain all the components and their purpose.

The fundamental building block of Java is the **class**. There are other **object types** (like interfaces, enums, annotations, and records) in Java, but classes are the most important because they represent the templates for the objects making up an application. A class mainly contains **fields** and **methods**. When an object is created, the values of the fields define the state of the object, and the methods describe its behavior.

Important   The Java object is a model of a real-world object. So, if we choose to model a car in Java, we will choose to define fields that describe the car: manufacturer, modelName, productionYear, color, and speed. The methods of our car class describe what the car does. A car does mainly two things—accelerates and brakes—so any method should describe actions related to these two things.

Packages

When you are writing Java code, you are writing code to describe state and behavior of real-world items. The code must be organized in classes and other types that are used together to build an application.

All types are described in files with the .java extension. Object types are organized in **packages**. A package is a logical collection of types: some of them are visible outside the package, and some of them are not, depending on their scope.

Tip   To understand the way packages work, imagine a box containing other boxes. Those boxes might be filled with other boxes, or they might be filled with some items that are not boxes. For the sake of this example, let's say those items are Lego pieces. This analogy works well, because Java types can be composed in the same way as Lego pieces are.

Package names must be unique, and their name should follow a certain template. This template is usually defined by the company working on the project. Good practices say that to ensure unicity and meaning, you typically begin the name with your organization's Internet domain name in reverse order, then add various grouping criteria.

In this project, package names follow the template depicted here: `com.apress.bgn.[*]+`. This template begins with the reversed domain name for the publisher of this book, Apress (*www.apress.com*), then a term identifying the book is added (`bgn` is a shortcut for *beginner*), and the * replaces the number of the chapter the source (usually) matches.

Considering the previously introduced boxes and Legos analogy, the `com` package is the big box, containing the `apress` box. It could contain Legos too, but for this example it does not. The `apress` box represents the `com.apress` package and contains the `bgn` box.

The `bgn` represents the `com.apress.bgn` package box and contains boxes specific to each chapter, containing either other boxes and/or Legos. The Legos are the Java files, containing Java code. Figure 3-1 represents these boxes and Legos and the way they are nested.

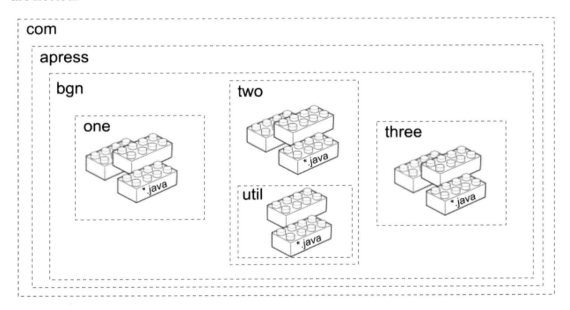

Figure 3-1. *Java packages with source code represented as nested boxes and Legos*

On your computer, a package is a hierarchy of directories. Each directory contains other directories and/or Java files. It all depends on your organizational skills and needs. This organization is important, because any Java object type can be identified uniquely using the package name and its own name. If we were to write a class named `HelloWorld` in a file named `HelloWorld.java` and put this file in package `com.apress.bgn.one`, `com.apress.bgn.one.HelloWorld` is the **fully qualified class name**, which acts as a unique identifier for this class. You can view the package name as an address of that class.

Starting with Java 5, inside each package a file named `package-info.java` can be created that contains a package declaration, package annotations, package comments, and Javadoc annotations. The comments are exported to the development documentation for that project, also known as **Javadoc**. (**Chapter 9** covers how to generate the project Javadoc using Maven.) The `package-info.java` file must reside under the last directory in the package. So, if we define a `com.apress.bgn.one` package, the overall structure and contents of the Java project looks like Figure 3-2.

Figure 3-2. *Java package contents*

The `package-info.java` contents could be similar to the contents of Listing 3-2.

Listing 3-2. `package-info.java` Sample Contents

```
/**
 * Contains classes used for reading information from various sources.
 * @author iuliana.cosmina
 * @version 3.0-SNAPSHOT
 */
package com.apress.bgn.one;
```

The files with .java extension containing type definitions are compiled into files with .class extension that are organized according to the same package structure and packaged into one or more **JAR**s (Java **Ar**chives).

When jar are hosted on a repository, such as The Maven Public Repository, they are also called **artifacts**. You can read more about jars here: https://docs.oracle.com/javase/8/docs/technotes/guides/jar/jarGuide.html.

For the previous example, if you were to unpack the jar that resulted after the compilation and linkage, you would see what's shown in Figure 3-3.

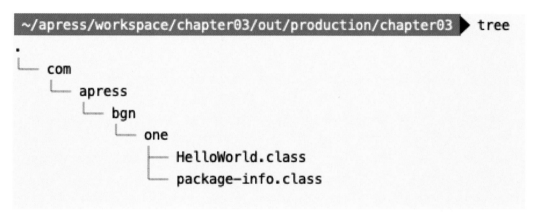

Figure 3-3. *Contents of a sample JAR*

The package-info.java file is compiled too, even if it only holds information about the package and no behavior or types.

Important   package-info.java files are not mandatory; packages can be defined without them. They are useful mostly for documentation purposes.

The contents of one package can span across multiple subprojects, meaning that if you have more than one subproject in your project, you can have the same package name in more than one subproject, containing different classes. A symbolic representation of this is depicted in Figure 3-4.

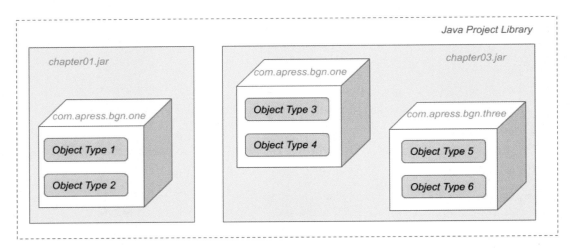

Figure 3-4. *Example of package contents that span across multiple JARs*

A **library** is a collection of jars containing classes used to implement a certain functionality. The most commonly used libraries are logging libraries like Log4J[1] and Logback[2]. For example, JUnit 5[3] is a very famous Java framework providing multiple classes that facilitate writing Java unit tests.

A moderately complex Java application references one or more libraries. To run the application, all its dependencies (all the JARs) must be on the **classpath**. What does this mean? It means that in order to run a Java application, a JDK, its dependencies (external jars), and the application jars are needed. Figure 3-5 depicts this quite clearly.

---

[1] https://logging.apache.org/log4j/3.x/
[2] https://logback.qos.ch/
[3] https://junit.org/junit5

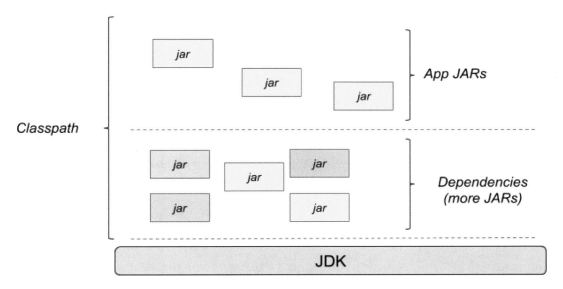

Figure 3-5. *Application classpath*

Warning   We are assuming here that the application is being run on the same environment where it was written, and so the JDK is used to run the application. Until JDK 11, any Java application could be run using the JRE. But starting with version 11, Java has become fully modular. This means a customized "JRE" distribution can be created only from the modules needed to run an application. Indirectly, this means that the resulting JRE contains a minimal number of JDK compiled classes.

The JARs that make up an application classpath are (obviously) not always independent of each other. For 21 years this organization style was enough, but in complex applications there were a lot of complications caused by

- Packages scattered in multiple jars(remember Figure 3-4?). This might lead to code duplication and circular dependencies.

- Transitive dependencies between jars, which sometimes lead to different versions of the same class being on the classpath. This might lead to unpredictable application behavior.

- Missing transitive dependencies and accessibility problems. This might lead to application crash.

All these problems are grouped under one name: **JAR Hell**[4]. This problem was resolved in Java 9 by introducing another level to organize packages: **modules**. Or at least that was the intention. However, the industry has been reluctant to adopt Java modules. As of this writing, although the majority of Java production applications are no longer stuck on Java 8, developers still avoid modules like the plague.

However, before you are introduced to modules, you should know about access modifiers. Java types and their members are declared with certain access rights within packages, and that is something quite important to understand before jumping to coding.

Access Modifiers

When declaring a type in Java—let's stick to the `class` for now, because it is the only one mentioned so far—you can configure its scope using **access modifiers**.

Access modifiers can be used to specify access to classes, and in this case we say that they are used at top-level. They also can be used to specify access to class members, and in this case they are used at member-level (We will not mention *nested classes* right now. We'll get there later in this chapter.

At top-level only two access modifiers can be used: public and none. A top-level class that is declared `public` must be defined in a Java file with the same name. Listing 3-3 depicts a class named Base that is defined in a file named `Base.java` located in package `com.apress.bgn.zero`.

Listing 3-3. Base Class

```
package com.apress.bgn.zero;

// top-level access modifier
public class Base {
  // code omitted
}
```

The contents of the class are not depicted for the moment and replaced with the `// code omitted` comment to stop you from losing focus. A public class is visible to all classes anywhere in the application. So, a different class in a different package can create an object of this type, as depicted in Listing 3-4.

---

[4] https://tech-read.com/2009/01/13/what-is-jar-hell

Listing 3-4. Creating an Object Using the Base Class

```
package com.apress.bgn.three;

import com.apress.bgn.zero.Base;

public class Main {
  public static void main(String... args) {
    // creating an object of type Base
    Base base = new Base();
  }
}
```

The line `Base base = new Base();` is where the object is created. The new keyword represents an operation called **instantiation** of a class, which means an object is created based on the specification described by the code that represents the `Base` class.

Important   A class is a template. Objects are created using this template and are called **instances**.

For now, just let this affirmation sink in: a public class is visible to all classes everywhere.

When no explicit access modifier is mentioned, it is said that the class is declared as **default** or that it is **package-private**. I know it seems confusing that there are two ways to talk about the lack of access modifiers, but because you might read other books or blog posts that refer to this situation, it is better to have all the possibilities listed here. This means if a class has no access modifier, the class can be used to create objects only by the classes defined in the same package. Its scope is limited to the package it is defined in. A class without an access modifier can be defined in any Java file, and it is not mandatory for the file name to coincide with the class name.

Important   When multiple classes are declared in the same file, the public class must have the same name as the file it is defined in, thus this is the class that names the file.

To test this, let's add a class named `HiddenBase` in the `Base.java` file introduced previously, as depicted in Listing 3-5.

Listing 3-5. Class with No Access Modifier

```
package com.apress.bgn.zero;

public class Base {
  // code omitted
}

class HiddenBase {
  // you cannot see me
}
```

Notice that the Base class is declared in the com.apress.bgn.zero package. If we try to create an object of type HiddenBase in a class declared within package com.apress. bgn.three (observe in a different package), the IDE will warn us by making the text red and refusing to provide any code completion. Furthermore, a tab listing the problems of the current file will be opened with an error message that is more than obvious, like depicted in Figure 3-6.

Figure 3-6. *Java class with no accessor modifier error*

> **Important**   For now, let this affirmation sink in as well: a class with no access modifier is visible to all classes (and other types) in the same package.

Inside a class the class members are defined: **fields** and **methods**. Aside from that, we can also define other Java types, which are referred to as being nested, but we'll cross that bridge when we come to it. At member-level two more modifiers can be applied, aside from the two previously mentioned: `private` and `protected`. At member-level the access modifiers have the following effect:

- `public`: Same as at top level, the member can be accessed from everywhere.

- `private`: -The member can be accessed only in the class where is declared.

- `protected`: The member can be accessed only in the package where the class containing it is declared or by any subclass of its class in another package.

- `none`: The member can be accessed only from within its own package.

The preceding rules might seem complicated, but once you start writing code, you'll get used to it. On the official Oracle documentation page, there is even a table with the visibility of members[5]. Table 3-1 provides a modified version.

Table 3-1. *Member-Level Accessors Scope*

Modifier	Class	Package	Subclass	World
public	Yes	Yes	Yes	Yes
protected	Yes	Yes	Yes	No
none (*default/package-private*)	Yes	Yes	No	No
private	Yes	No	No	No

---

[5] `https://docs.oracle.com/javase/tutorial/java/javaOO/accesscontrol.html`

To get an overall idea how that table applies to code, the class in Listing 3-6 is very helpful.

Listing 3-6. `PropProvider`, a Java Class with Members Decorated with Various Accessors

```
package com.apress.bgn.three.same;

public class PropProvider {
    public int publicProp;
    protected int protectedProp;
    /* default */ int defaultProp;
    private int privateProp;

    public PropProvider(){
        privateProp = 0;
    }
}
```

The class `PropProvider` declares four fields, each with a different access modifier. The field `privateProp` can only be modified within the body of this class. This means all other members of this class can read the value of this property and change it.

At this point in the book, only methods have been mentioned as being other types of members. But classes can be declared inside the body of another class. Such a class is called a **nested class** and has access to all the members of the class that is wrapped around it, including the private ones. The **Class** column (second column) in Table 3-1 covers the fields that are accessible to a class declared within another class (nested). Figure 3-7 depicts the modified `PropProvider` class that has an extra method added, named `printPrivate`. This method reads the value of the private field and prints it. A nested class named `LocalPropRequester` is declared as well, and the private field is shown being modified in this class (line 56).

```
   ⓒ PropProvider.java  ×
28        package com.apress.bgn.three.same;
29
30  ⊫  ⊟/**
31         * Table 3-1, column Class show in code
32      ⊟ */
33        public class PropProvider {
34            public int publicProp;
35            protected int protectedProp;
36            /* default */ int defaultProp;
37            private int privateProp;
38
39            // constructor
40      ⊟    public PropProvider(){
41                privateProp = 0;
42      ⊟    }
43
44            // method
45      ⊟    public void printPrivate(){
46                System.out.printf("Private member: %d ", privateProp);
47      ⊟    }
48
49            // nested class
50      ⊟    class LocalPropRequester {
51      ⊟        public LocalPropRequester() {
52                    PropProvider provider = new PropProvider();
53                    provider.publicProp = 1;
54                    provider.protectedProp = 2;
55                    provider.defaultProp =3;
56                    provider.privateProp = 4;
57      ⊟        }
58      ⊟    }
59      }
```

Figure 3-7. *Table 3-1 column **Class** accessors in Java code*

Figure 3-7 is a screenshot of how the Java code is viewed in IntelliJ IDEA. If any field is not accessible, it is displayed in red.

The third column in Table 3-1, the **Package** column, covers the fields that are accessible to a class declared in the same package as class PropProvider. Figure 3-8 depicts a class named PropRequester trying to modify all fields in class PropProvider. Notice the private field is shown in bright red. This means the field is not accessible, and IntelliJ IDEA makes that quite obvious.

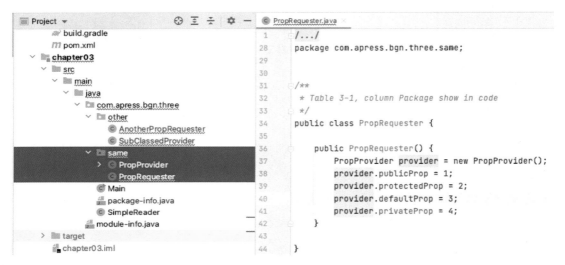

Figure 3-8. *Table 3-1 column **Package** accessors in Java code*

The fourth column in Table 3-1, the **Subclass** column, covers the fields that are accessible to a subclass of class PropProvider. A **subclass** inherits states and behavior from a class it derives from, which is called its **superclass**. The subclass is created using the extends keyword together with the superclass name. Figure 3-9 depicts a class named SubClassedProvider trying to modify all fields inherited from PropProvider. Notice the private field and the field without an accessor shown in bright red by IntelliJ IDEA. This means the fields are not accessible.

```
 38    /**
 31     * Table 3-1, column Subclass show in code
 32     */
 33    import com.apress.bgn.three.same.PropProvider;
 34
 35    /**
 36     * Table 3-1, column Subclass show in code
 37     */
 38    public class SubClassedProvider extends PropProvider {
 39
 40        public SubClassedProvider() {
 41            SubClassedProvider provider = new SubClassedProvider();
 42            provider.publicProp = 1;
 43            provider.protectedProp = 2;
 44            provider.defaultProp = 3;
 45            provider.privateProp = 4;
 46        }
 47
 48    }
```

Figure 3-9. *Table 3-1 column **Subclass** accessors in Java code*

Important   The field without an accessor is not accessible in the previous example, because the subclass is declared in a different package. If the subclass is moved in the same package, the rules from the **Package** column in Table 3-1 apply.

The final column in Table 3-1, the **World** column, applies to all classes outside the package where class PropProvider is declared, that are not subclasses of this class. Figure 3-10 depicts a class named AnotherPropRequester that tries to access all fields declared in PropProvider. As expected, only the public field is accessible, and the rest are shown in red.

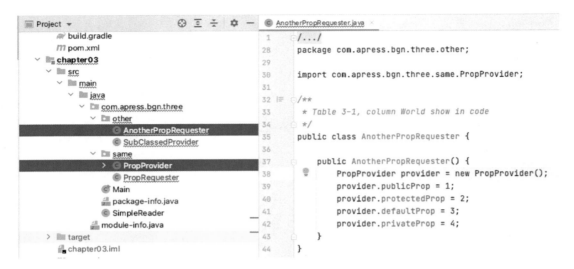

Figure 3-10. *Table 3-1 column **World** accessors in Java code*

Building the chapter03 subproject containing the AnotherPropRequester class using the Maven build tool fails. The error messages are displayed in Listing 3-7.

Listing 3-7. AnotherPropRequester Compile Errors

[ERROR] Failed to execute goal org.apache.maven.plugins:maven-compiler-plugin:3.8.1:compile (default-compile) on project chapter03: Compilation failure: Compilation failure:
[ERROR] ./java-23-for-absolute-beginners/chapter03/src/main/java/com/apress/bgn/three/other/AnotherPropRequester.java:[42,17] **protectedProp has protected access in com.apress.bgn.three.same.PropProvider**
[ERROR] ./java-23-for-absolute-beginners/chapter03/src/main/java/com/apress/bgn/three/other/AnotherPropRequester.java:[44,17] **defaultProp is not public in com.apress.bgn.three.same.PropProvider; cannot be accessed from outside package**
[ERROR] ./java-23-for-absolute-beginners/chapter03/src/main/java/com/apress/bgn/three/other/AnotherPropRequester.java:[46,17] **privateProp has private access in com.apress.bgn.three.same.PropProvider**

As demonstrated, build tools and editors are pretty good at letting you know when something is wrong in your Java code. Learn to use them well, trust them, and they will increase your productivity. *Sure, build tools and smart editors have occasional hiccups but not that many.*

You will probably come back to Table 3-1 once or twice after you start writing Java code. Everything covered in this section is still valid even after the introduction of modules. If you configure module access properly, that is.

Modules

Starting with Java 9 a new concept was introduced: `modules`.

Important   Build tools such as Maven or Gradle refer to subprojects as modules as well, but their purpose is different from that of the Java modules.

Java modules represent a more powerful mechanism to organize and aggregate packages. The implementation of this new concept took more than ten years. The discussion about modules started in 2005, and the hope was for them to be implemented for Java 7. Under the name **Project Jigsaw** ,an exploratory phase eventually started in 2008. Java developers hoped a modular JDK would be available with Java 8, but that did not happen.

Modules finally arrived in Java 9 after three years of work (and almost seven years of analysis). Supporting modules delayed the official release date of Java 9 to September 2017.

Note   The full history of the Jigsaw project can be found here: `https://openjdk.java.net/projects/jigsaw`

A **Java module** is a way to group packages and configure more-granulated access to package contents. A Java module is a uniquely named, reusable group of packages and resources (e.g., XML files and other types of non-Java files) described by a file named `module-info.java` , located at the root of the source directory. This file contains the following information:

- The module's name

- The module's dependencies (that is, other modules this module depends on)

- The packages the module explicitly makes available to other modules (all other packages in the module are implicitly unavailable to other modules)

- The services the module offers

- The services the module consumes

- To what other modules it allows reflection

- Native code

- Resources

- Configuration data

In theory, module naming resembles package naming and follows the reversed-domain-name convention. In practice, just make sure the module name does not contain any numbers and that it reveals clearly what its purpose is. The `module-info.java` file is compiled into a module descriptor, which is a file named `module-info.class` that is packed together with classes into a plain old JAR file.

The file is located at the root of the Java source directory, outside of any package. For the `chapter03` project introduced earlier, the `module-info.java` file is located in the `src/main/java` directory, at the same level with the `com` directory; the root of the `com.apress.bgn.three` package is shown in Figure 3-11.

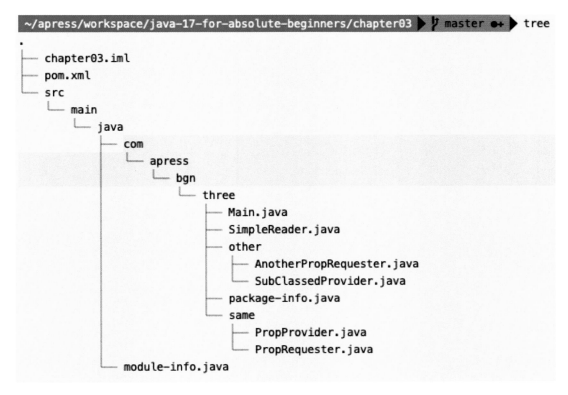

Figure 3-11. Location of the `module-info.java` file

As with any file with the `*.java` extension, the `module-info.java` file is compiled into a `*.class` file. As the module declaration is not a part of Java type declaration, `module` is not a Java keyword, so it can still be used when writing code for Java types (as a variable name, for example). For package the situation is different, as every Java type declaration must start with a package declaration. Just take a look at the `SimpleReader` class declared in Listing 3-8.

Listing 3-8. `SimpleReader` Class

```java
package com.apress.bgn.three;

public class SimpleReader {
    private String source;

    // code omitted
}
```

You can see the package declaration, but where is the module? Well, the module is an abstract concept, described by the `module-info.java` file. So, starting with Java 9, if you are configuring Java modules in your application, Figure 3-4 evolves into Figure 3-12.

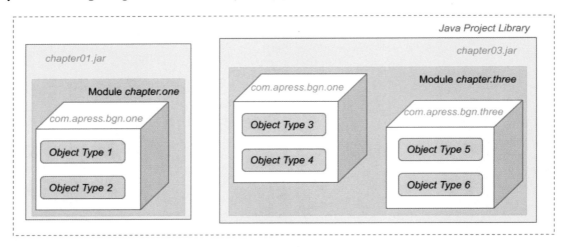

Figure 3-12. *Java modules represented visually*

A Java module is a way to logically group Java packages that belong together.

The introduction of modules allows for the JDK to be divided into modules too. The `java --list-modules` command lists all modules in your local JDK installation. Listing 3-9 depicts the output of this command executed on my personal computer, where currently JDK 23 is installed.

Listing 3-9. JDK 23 Modules

```
$ java --list-modules
java.base@23
java.compiler@23
java.datatransfer@23
java.desktop@23

# some output omitted
```

Each module name is followed by a version string, @23 in the previous listing, which means that the module belongs to Java version 23. So if a Java application does not require all modules, you can create a runtime with only the modules that it needs, which reduces the runtime's size. The tool to build a smaller runtime customized to an application's needs is called `jlink` and is part of the JDK executables. This allows for bigger levels of scalability and increased performance. How to use jlink is not a topic of this book. The focus of the book is learning the Java programming language, so the technical details of the Java platform will be kept to a minimum—just enough to start writing and executing code confidently.

There are multiple benefits of introducing modules that more experienced developers have been waiting for years to take advantage of. However, configuring modules for bigger and more complex projects is no walk in the park, and most software companies prefer to avoid configuring modules altogether.

The contents of the module-info.java file can be as simple as the name of the module and two brackets containing the body, as shown in Listing 3-10.

Listing 3-10. A Simple module-info.java Configuration

```
module chapter.three {
}
```

Advanced Module Configurations

A Java module declaration body contains one or more **directives** that are constructed using the keywords in Table 3-2. These directives represent access configurations and dependency requirements for the packages and classes contained in the modules.

Table 3-2. *Java Module Directives*

Directive	Purpose
requires	Specifies that the module depends on another module.
exports	One of the module's packages whose public types (and their nested public and protected types) should be accessible to code in all other modules.
exports ... to	Qualified version of the exports directive that enables specifying in a comma-separated list precisely which module's or modules' code can access the exported package.
open	Used at module-level declaration (open module mm {}) and allows reflective access to all module's packages. Java Reflection is the process of analyzing and modifying all the capabilities of a class at runtime, and it works on private types and members too. So before Java 9, nothing was really encapsulated.

(continued)

Table 3-2. (*continued*)

Directive	Purpose
opens	Used inside the body of a module's declaration to selectively configure access through reflection only to certain packages.
opens ... to	Qualified version of the opens directive that enables specifying in a comma-separated list precisely which module's or modules' code can access its packages reflectively.
uses	Specifies a service used by this module, making the module a *service consumer.* A service in this case represents the full name of an interface/abstract class that another module provides an implementation for.
provides ... with	Specifies that a module provides a service with a specific implementation, making the module a *service provider.*
transitive	Used together with requires to specify a dependency on another module and to ensure that other modules reading your module also read that dependency—known as *implied readability.*

Appendix A provides examples for all directives. For the purpose of learning the Java language, the only ones you really need to know are requires and exports, so those are the only two covered in this chapter. I will explain all directives in depth as soon as the context is appropriate for understanding them completely, and I will add analogies with real-world events and scenarios to make sure the idea comes through.

Importantly, *modules can depend on one another.* The project for this book consists of 13 modules, and most on them depend on module chapter.zero. This module contains the basic components used to build more complex components in the other modules. For example, classes inside module chapter.three need access to packages and classes in module chapter.zero. Declaring a module dependency is done using the requires directive, as depicted in Listing 3-11.

Listing 3-11. A Simple module-info.java Configuration

```
module chapter.three {
  requires chapter.zero;
}
```

The preceding dependency is an **explicit** one. But there are also **implicit** dependencies. For example, any module declared by a developer implicitly requires the JDK `java.base` module. This module contains the foundational APIs of the Java SE Platform, and no Java application could be written without it. This implicit directive ensures access to a minimal set of Java types, so basic Java code can be written. Listing 3-11 is equivalent to Listing 3-12.

Listing 3-12. A Simple `module-info.java` Configuration with an Explicit Directive of `requires java.base`

```
module chapter.three {
  requires java.base; // redundant directive

  requires chapter.zero;
}
```

Important   Declaring a module as required means that the module is required when the code is compiled (frequently referred to as *compile time*) and when the code is executed (frequently referred to as *runtime*). If a module is required only at runtime, the `requires static` keywords are used to declare the dependency. Just keep that in mind for now; it will make sense when we talk about web applications.

Now `chapter.three` depends on module `chapter.zero`. But does this mean `chapter.three` can access all `public` types (and their nested `public` and `protected` types) in the all the packages in module `chapter.zero`? If you are thinking that this is not enough, you are right. Just because a module depends on another, it does not mean it has access to the packages and classes it actually needs to. The required module must be configured to expose its *insides*. How can this be done? In our case, we need to make sure module `chapter.zero` gives access to the required packages. We can do so by customizing the `module-info.java` file for this module by adding the `exports` directive, followed by the necessary package names. Listing 3-13 depicts the `module-info.java` file for the `chapter.zero` module that exposes its single package.

Listing 3-13. The `module-info.java` Configuration File for the `chapter.`
zero Module

```
module chapter.zero {
  exports com.apress.bgn.zero;
}
```

Tip   Think about it like this: You are in your room cutting out Christmas
decorations, and you need a template for your decorations. Your roommate has all
the templates. But just because you need them doesn't mean they will magically
appear. You need to go and talk to your roommate. Needing your roommate's
assistance can be viewed as the *requires room-mate* directive. After talking to your
roommate, your roommate will probably say: *Sure, come in, they are on the desk!
Take as many as you need.* This can be considered the *exports all-templates-on-
desk* directive. The desk is probably a good analogy for a package.

Using the configuration in Listing 3-13, we have just given access to the `com.apress.`
`bgn.zero` package to any module configured with a `requires module.zero;` directive.
What if we do not want that? (Considering the previous tip, your roommate just left the
door to their room open, so anybody can enter and get those templates!)

What if we want to limit the access to module contents only to the `chapter.three`
module? (So, your roommate has to give their templates only to you.) This can be
done by adding the `to` keyword followed by the module name to clarify that only this
module is allowed to access the components. This is the qualified version of the `exports`
directive mentioned in Table 3-2.

Warning   If you were curious and you read the recommended **JAR Hell** article,
you noticed that one of the concerns of working with Java sources packed in jars
is security. The reason is that, even without access to Java sources, by adding
a Jar as a dependency to an application, objects can be inspected, extended,
and instantiated. So aside from providing a reliable configuration, better scaling,
integrity for the platform, and improved performance, the goal for introduction of
modules was in fact **better security**.

Listing 3-14 depicts the `module-info.java` file for the `chapter.zero` module that exposes its single package only to the `chapter.three` module.

Listing 3-14. Advanced `module-info.java` Configuration File for the `chapter.zero` Module

```
module chapter.zero {
  exports com.apress.bgn.zero to chapter.three;
}
```

More than one module can be specified to have access, by listing the desired modules separated by commas, as depicted in Listing 3-15.

Listing 3-15. Advanced `module-info.java` Configuration File for the `chapter.zero` Module with Multiple Modules

```
module chapter.zero {
  exports com.apress.bgn.zero to chapter.two, chapter.three;
}
```

The order of the modules is not important, and if there is a lot of them, you can place them on multiple lines. Just make sure to end the declaration with a `;` (semicolon).

This is all that can be presented about modules at this stage in the book, but fear not: all the other directives will be covered at the right time.

How to Determine the Structure of a Java Project

There are a few ways Java projects can be structured, and the choice is influenced by two things: project scope and the build tool used.

You might wonder why the project scope influences the project's structure. You might expect there should be a standard for this, right? Well, there is more than one standard, and that is dependent on the project scope. The reason for creating a Java project influences its size. If a project is small, it might not require you to split the sources into subprojects, and it might not need a build tool either, since build tools come with their own standard way of organizing a project. Let's start with the smallest Java project ever that should just print *Hello World!* to the console.

The HelloWorld! Project in IntelliJ IDEA

Since you installed IntelliJ IDEA, let's create a Java project and check what project structure the editor chooses for us. When you first open IntelliJ IDEA, you see a very simple dialog window, as shown in Figure 3-13.

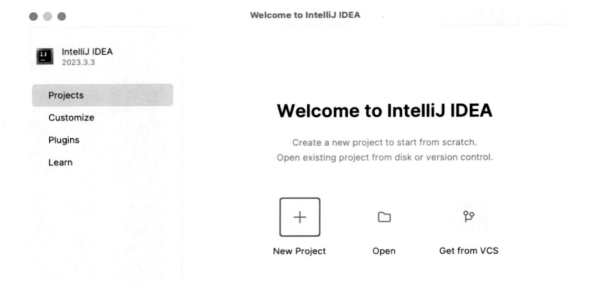

Figure 3-13. *IntelliJ IDEA first dialog window*

Select **New Project**. IntelliJ IDEA directs you to the project setup dialog window, where you can choose the name of the project, the programming language you want to use, and the build tool and automatically selects the system JDK. This dialog window is shown in Figure 3-14, with the default options for my computer.

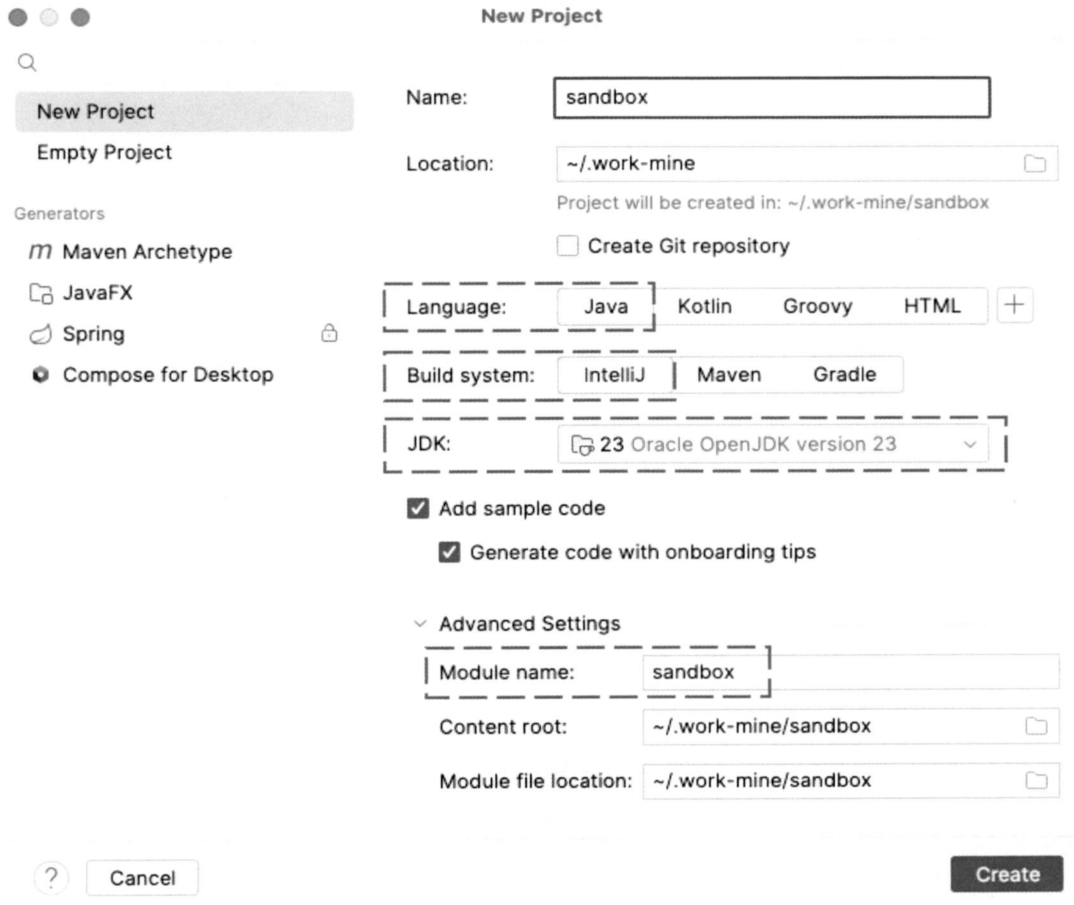

Figure 3-14. *IntelliJ IDEA dialog window for creating a Java project*

For purposes of creating this first Java project in IntelliJ IDEA, use sandbox for both the project name and the module name and then click **Create**.

The next window is the editor window, as shown in Figure 3-15, which is where you write your code. If you expand the sandbox node on the left (that section is called the *Project view*), you can see that the project is built using the JDK you have installed (in this case 23). A src directory is created to contain Java packages and class files. Inside the src directory, IntelliJ IDEA generates a default class file named Main.java containing a main(..) method with a simple body, as shown on the right in Figure 3-15.

IntelliJ IDEA assumes that you are a beginner and shows some onboarding tips in the code. You can turn them off by closing the notice on top of the Main.java class file.

Figure 3-15. *IntelliJ IDEA project view and default* `Main` *class*

Before writing code, let's check out what other project settings are available. IntelliJ IDEA provides you access to view and edit project properties through the **File ➤ Project Structure** menu item. If you click it, a Project Structure dialog window will open, similar to the one depicted in Figure 3-16.

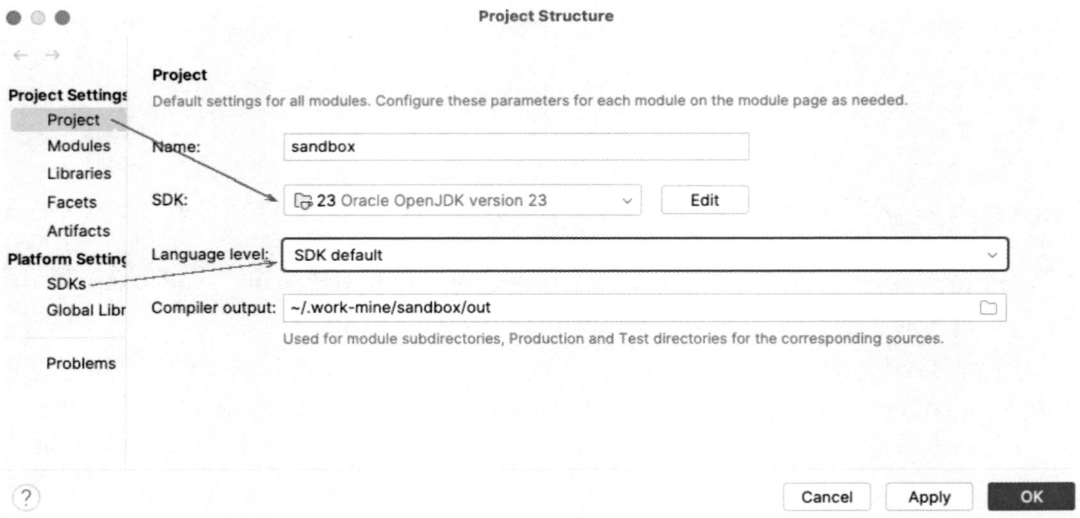

Figure 3-16. *IntelliJ IDEA Project Structure dialog window*

When the dialog window opens, the **Project Settings** section is open with the **Project** tab selected. In Figure 3-16 there are two arrows attracting your attention to the **SDK** field, which depicts the JDK version for a Java project, and the **Language level** field, which lists **SDK default**. At the time this chapter is being written, the default is the most recent version, JDK 23 EA. The most recent version of IntelliJ IDEA supports syntax and code completion for the latest official JDK release.

If you switch to the **Modules** tab under **Project Settings**, you will see the information depicted in Figure 3-17.

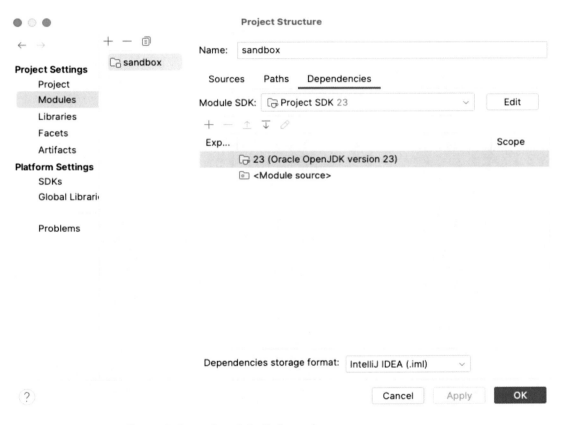

Figure 3-17. *IntelliJ IDEA project Modules tab*

Important   Aside from Java modules, which wrap together packages, a module is also a way to wrap together Java sources and resource files with a common purpose within a project. Before Oracle introduced the module concept as a way to modularize Java applications, the code making up these applications was already modularized by developers that needed to structure big projects in some practical way.

On the **Modules** tab, you can see how many parts (modules) a project has and the settings for each part. The sandbox project has one part, one module also named sandbox, and the source for this module is contained in the src directory. So if we want to write a class that prints *Hello World!*, the file called HelloWorld.java has to be placed under it. If you right-click on the src directory, the menu depicted in Figure 3-18 appears.

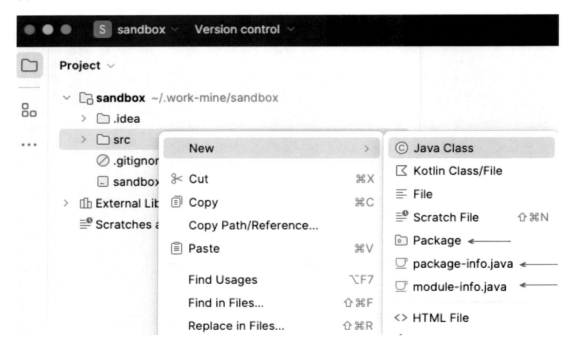

Figure 3-18.   IntelliJ IDEA context menu listing which Java objects can be created in the src directory

Aside from the **Java Class** option, the red arrows point to the other components that can be in the `src` directory. Let's go ahead and create our class. Click the **Java Class** menu option and in the dialog box that appears introduce the class name. Select **Class** from the list below the test field. Figure 3-19 shows all the Java types that you can create.

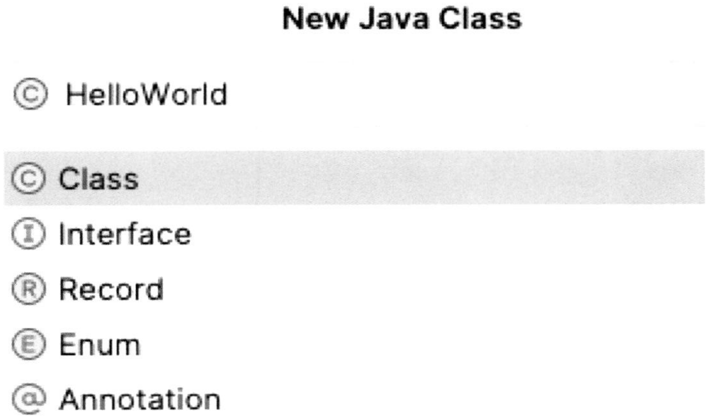

New Java Class

ⒸHelloWorld

ⒸClass
ⒾInterface
ⓇRecord
ⒺEnum
@Annotation

Figure 3-19. *IntelliJ IDEA dialog window to create a Java type*

As mentioned early in this chapter, the core building block of a Java application is the `class` but other types also exist in Java. The list in Figure 3-19 shows all five Java types. Each of them is explained in detail later in the book, so for now, notice that a file named `HelloWorld.java` was created under the `src` directory and the contents of that file are as simple as shown in Listing 3-16.

Listing 3-16. The `HelloWorld.java` Contents—the Body of an Empty Java Class

```
public class HelloWorld {

}
```

You have just created your first Java class, in your first very simple Java project. It does nothing yet. The class is compiled by selecting the **Build Project** option from the IntelliJ IDEA **Build** menu, as shown in Figure 3-20, or by pressing a combination of keys that differs for each operating system. Compiling the class produces the `HelloWorld.class` file, containing the bytecode. By default, IntelliJ IDEA stores compilation results into a directory named `out/production`. Figure 3-20 also partially show the result of compiling your project.

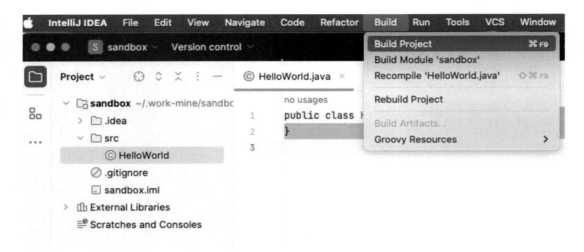

Figure 3-20. *How to compile a Java project in IntelliJ IDEA*

It is time to make the class print *Hello World!*. For that we need to add a special method to the class. Any Java desktop application has a special method named `main` that has to be declared in a top-level class. This method is called by the JRE to run the Java program/application, and I call it the *entry point*. Without such a method, a Java project is just a collection of classes that is not runnable, cannot be executed, and cannot perform a certain function.

Tip   Imagine it like this: it's like having a car, but you have no way of starting it, because the ignition lock cylinder is missing. For all intents and purposes, it is a car, but it cannot perform the main purpose of a car, which is to actually take you somewhere. You can imagine the `main` method as being the ignition lock cylinder, where the JRE will insert the key to get your application running. We'll add that method to the `HelloWorld` class next.

Because IntelliJ IDEA is an awesome editor, you can generate the `main` method by typing `psvm` and pressing the **Tab** key. The four letters represent the starting letter of all the components of the method declaration: **p**ublic, **s**tatic, **v**oid, and **m**ain.

The `HelloWorld` class with a `main` method that prints the text *Hello World!* is depicted in Listing 3-17.

Listing 3-17. The `HelloWorld` Class with the `main` Method

```
public class HelloWorld {
  public static void main(String... args) {
    System.out.println("Hello World");
  }
}
```

Now that we have a `main` method, we can execute (or run) the code. IntelliJ IDEA gives you two options:

- From the **Run** menu, choose the option **Run [ClassName]** (or press the key combination shown to the right of the option).

- Right-click the class body and select **Run [ClassName].main()** from the menu that appears.

Figure 3-21 depicts both menu items that you can use to execute the class, and the result of the execution.

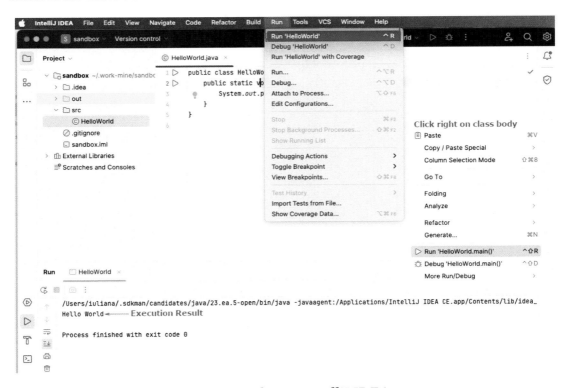

Figure 3-21. *How to execute a Java class in IntelliJ IDEA*

This is the most basic structure for a Java project. This project is so simple that it can also be compiled manually from the command line, so let's do that!

The HelloWorld! Project Compiled and Executed from the Command Line

You've probably noticed the **Terminal** button in your IntelliJ IDEA. If you click that button, inside the editor a terminal will open. On Windows, it will be a Command Prompt instance, and for Linux and macOS it will be the default shell. IntelliJ will open your terminal right into your project root. Here is what you have to do next:

- Enter the `src` directory by executing the following command: `cd src`. (`cd` is short for change directory.)

- Compile the `HelloWorld.java` file by executing `javac HelloWorld.java`. (`javac` is a JDK executable used to compile Java files, which IntelliJ IDEA calls in the background as well.)

- Run the resulting bytecode from the `HelloWorld.class` file by executing `java HelloWorld`.

Figure 3-22 depicts the execution of those commands in a terminal in IntelliJ IDEA.

Figure 3-22. *Manually compiling and running the HelloWorld class in a terminal inside IntelliJ IDEA*

Looks simple right? And it actually is that simple, because no packages or Java modules were defined. *But wait, is that possible?* Well, yes. If you did not define a package, the class is still part of an unnamed default package that is provided by default by the JSE platform for development of small, temporary, educational applications, like the one you are building now.

So let's make our project a little bit more complicated and add a named package for our class to be in.

Putting the HelloWorld Class in a Package

As pointed out previously in Figure 3-18, the context menu that opens when you right-click the src directory contains a **Package** option. So, right-click the src directory and select it. In the small dialog window that appears, enter the package name, com.sandbox. As shown in Figure 3-23, if the package you are trying to create already exists (as in my case), an error message is displayed in red.

Figure 3-23. *Creating duplicate package in IntelliJ IDEA*

Now we have a package, but the class is not in it. To get the class there, just click on it and drag it. Another dialog window will appear to confirm that this is what you really want to do, as depicted in Figure 3-24.

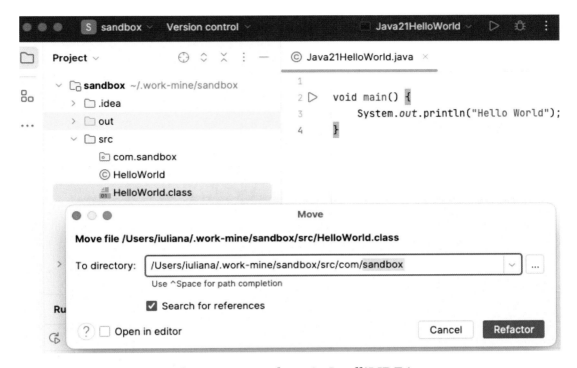

Figure 3-24. *Moving a class into a package in IntelliJ IDEA*

Click the **Refactor** button and look at what happens to the class. The class should now start with a `package com.sandbox;` declaration. If you rebuild your project and then look at the `production` directory, you will see something similar to what is depicted in Figure 3-25.

Figure 3-25. *New directory structure after adding the com.sandbox package*

Obviously, when compiling and executing the class manually, the package has to be taken into account, so the commands will change as shown in Listing 3-18.

Listing 3-18. Compiling and Executing the Package Version of HelloWorld.java File

```
~/sandbox/src/> javac com/sandbox/HelloWorld.java
~/sandbox/src/> java com/sandbox/HelloWorld
```

So what happens when modules are configured too? There is a default unnamed module, and all JARs, modular or not, and classes on the classpath will be contained in it. This default and unnamed module exports all packages and reads all other modules. Because it does not have a name, it cannot be required and read by named application modules. Thus, even if your small project seems to work with JDKs with versions 9 and above, it cannot be accessed by other modules, but it works because it can access others. (This ensures backward compatibility with older versions of the JDK.) That being said, let's add a module in our project as well.

Configuring the com.sandbox Module

Configuring a module is as easy as adding a `module-info.java` file under the `src` directory. Returning again to Figure 3-18, the `src` context menu contains a `module-info.java` option. Select that, and the IDE will generate the file for you. All is well and fine, and if you do not like the module name that was generated for you, you can change it. I changed it to `com.sandbox` to respect the module naming convention established by Oracle developers. The file is initially empty, as depicted in Listing 3-19.

Listing 3-19. The `com.sandbox` Module Configuration File

```
module com.sandbox {
}
```

What happens now that we have a module? Not much from the IDE's point of view. But if you want to compile a module manually, you have to know a few things. I compiled our module using the command in Listing 3-20.

Listing 3-20. Manually Compiling a Package Enclosed Within a Module

```
~/sandbox/src/> javac -d ../out/com.sandbox \
module-info.java \
com/sandbox/HelloWorld.java
```

Important   "\" (backslash) is a macOS/Linux separator. On Windows, either write the whole command on a single line or replace \ with ^ (caret).

The command in Listing 3-20 is built according to the template in Listing 3-21.

Listing 3-21. Template for Command to Manually Compile a Package Enclosed Within a Module

```
javac -d [destination location]/[module name] \
[source location]/module-info.java \
[java files...]
```

The -d [destination] determines where the results of the execution should be saved. The reason why the command line in Listing 3-20 specifies the output folder as /out/com.sandbox is to make it clear that com.sandbox is the enclosing module. Under this directory, we'll have the normal structure of the com.sandbox package. The contents of the out directory are depicted in Figure 3-26.

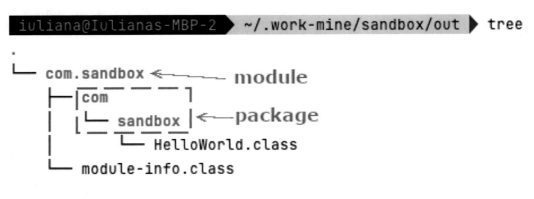

4 directories, 2 files

Figure 3-26. *Java module* com.sandbox *compiled manually*

As you have noticed in this example, the module does not really exist until we compile the sources, because a Java module is more of a logical mode of encapsulating packages described by the module-info.class descriptor. The only reason the com.sandbox directory was created is that we specified it as argument in the javac -d command.

Now that we've managed to compile a module, Listing 3-22 shows you how to run the HelloWorld class when it is enclosed in a module.

Listing 3-22. Manually Executing a Class Enclosed Within a Module

```
~/sandbox/> java --module-path out \
--module com.sandbox/com.sandbox.HelloWorld
Hello World!  # result
```

The previous command is built according to the template in Listing 3-23.

Listing 3-23. Template for Command to Manually Execute a Class Enclosed Within a Module

```
java --module-path [destination] \
--module [module name] /[package name].HelloWorld
```

The *Oracle Magazine* edition from September 2017 mentioned examples of naming Java modules for the first time. Although Oracle developers have decided that module names should follow the same rules as packages, to me this seems a little redundant, especially in complex projects where package names tend to become very long. Should you have module names just as long?

The truth is that people make the standards, and most times the practical becomes the standard. Since 2007, projects that have managed to embrace modules have chosen simpler, more practical module names. For example, the team that created the Spring Framework decided to name their modules `spring.core` instead of `org.springframework.core`, `spring.beans` instead of `org.springframework.beans`, and so on. So name your modules as you wish, as long as you avoid special characters and numbers.

Java Projects Using Build Tools, Mostly Maven

As introduced in Chapter 2, Apache Maven is a build automation tool used primarily for Java projects. Although Gradle is gaining ground, Maven is still one of the most commonly used build tools. Tools like Maven and Gradle are used to organize the source code of an application in interdependent project modules and configure a way to compile, validate, generate sources, test, and generate artifacts automatically. An *artifact* is a file, usually a JAR, that gets deployed to a Maven repository. A Maven *repository* is a location on an HDD where JARs get saved in a special directory structure.

Any discussion about build tools must start with Maven, because this build tool standardized a lot of the terms we use in development today. A project split into multiple subprojects can be downloaded from GitHub and built in the command line or imported into IntelliJ IDEA. This approach ensures that you get quality sources that can be compiled in one go. It is also practical, because I imagine you do not want to load a new project in IntelliJ IDEA every time you start reading a new chapter. Also, it makes it easier for me to maintain the sources and adapt them to a new JDK, and with Oracle releasing so often, I need to be able to do this quickly.

The project you will use to test the code written in this book, and to write your own code if you want to, is called java-23-for-absolute-beginners. It is a multimodule Maven project. The first level of the project is the java-23-for-absolute-beginners project, which has a configuration file named pom.xml. In this file, all dependencies and their versions are listed. The child projects, the ones on the second level, are the modules of this project. They are called *child* projects because they inherit those dependencies and modules from the parent project. In their configuration files, we can specify which dependencies are needed from the list defined in the parent.

These modules are actually a method of wrapping up together sources for each chapter, which is why these modules are named chapter00, chapter01, and so forth. If a project is big and needs a lot of code to be written, the code is split again in another level of modules. Module chapter05 is such a case and is configured as a parent for the projects underneath it. In Figure 3-27 you can see what this project looks like loaded in IntelliJ IDEA, and module chapter05 is expanded, so you can see the third level of modules. Each level is marked with the corresponding number.

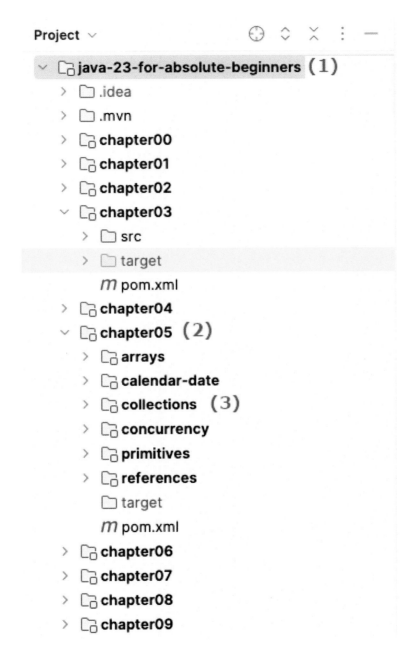

Figure 3-27. *Maven multilevel project structure*

If you have loaded the project into IntelliJ IDEA like you were taught in **Chapter 2**, you can make sure everything is working correctly by building it. Here's how you do it using the IntelliJ IDEA editor:

- In the upper right side, you should have a tab called *Maven*. If the subprojects are loaded like they are depicted in Figure 3-28, the project was loaded correctly.

- If the Maven tab is not visible, look for a label like the one marked with (1) and click it. Expand the `java-23-for-absolute-beginners` (root) node until you find the built task, marked with (2). If you double-click it and do not see any error in the view at the bottom of the editor, all your projects were built successfully. You should definitely see the BUILD SUCCESS (3) message.

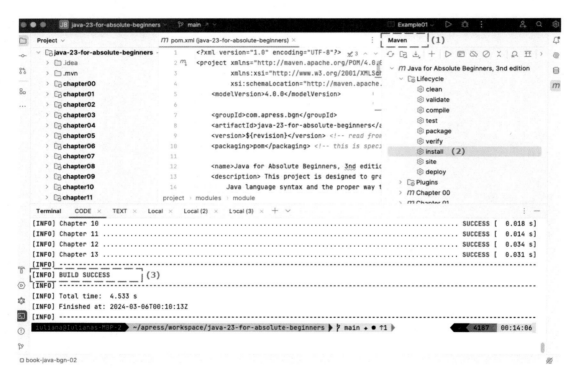

Figure 3-28. *Maven project view*

The second way to make sure the Maven project is working as expected is to build it from the command line. Open an IntelliJ IDEA terminal, and if you installed Maven on the system path as explained in **Chapter 2**, just type mvn and press **Enter**.

> **Important**   The main `pom.xml` file, located in the root of the project, has a default goal configured through the following line: `<defaultGoal>clean install</defaultGoal>`. It declares the two Maven execution phases required to build this project. Without this element in the configuration, to build the project, the two phases would be specified in the command (e.g., `mvn clean install`).

In the command line, you might see some warnings if JDK 23 is still unstable when this book reaches you, but as long as the execution ends with BUILD SUCCESSFUL, everything is all right.

Aside from the `sandbox` project, which is simple enough for you to create yourself, all the classes, modules, and packages mentioned in this section are part of this project. The `chapter00` and `chapter01` modules do not really contain classes specific to those chapters, but I needed them to be able to construct the Java module examples. IntelliJ IDEA sorts modules in alphabetical order, so the naming for the chapter modules was chosen this way so that they are listed in the normal order you should work with them.

Until now, this chapter has been focused on the building blocks of Java applications and we have created a class that prints *Hello World!* by following the instructions, but not all details were explained. Let's look at those now and even enrich the class with new details.

Explaining and Enriching the Hello World! Class

Previously, we wrote a class named `HelloWorld` in our `sandbox` project. This class is copied to the `chapter03` project, in package `com.apress.bgn.three.helloworld`. This chapter starts with a list of the main components of a class. The `HelloWorld` class contains a few of those elements that are explained in more detail in this section. In Figure 3-29, the `HelloWorld` class is depicted in the IntelliJ IDEA editor.

Figure 3-29. *The* `HelloWorld` *class in the* `java-23-for-absolute-beginners` *project*

The lines contain different statements that are explained in the following list, and the number of each line matches the number in the list:

1. **Package declaration**: When classes are part of a package, their code must start with this line that declares the package enclosing them. package is a reserved keyword in Java and cannot be used for anything else but declaring a package.

2. *Line left empty for easier viewing.*

3. **Class declaration**: This is the line where we declare our type:

   - It is public, so it can be seen from everywhere.

   - It is a class.

   - It is named HelloWorld.

   - It has a body enclosed in curly brackets, and the opening bracket is on this line. But it can be on the next one too, since empty spaces are ignored.

4. `main(..)` **method declaration**: In Java the method name and the number, type, and order of its parameters is referred to as the *method signature*. A method also has a **return type**, as in the type of result it returns. But there is also a special type that can be used

to declare that a method does not return anything. In the order of appearance, here is what every term of the main() method represents:

- public: This is the method accessor. The main method must be public, because otherwise JRE can't access it and call it.

  - static: Recall that the beginning of this chapter mentioned that a class has members (fields and methods). When an object of that class type is created, it has the fields and methods as declared by the class. The class is a template for creating objects. Because of the static keyword though, the main method is not associated with an object of a class type, but with the class itself. More details about this are provided in **Chapter 4**.

  - **void**: This keyword is used here to tell us that the main method does not return anything, so it's like a replacement for *no type*, because if nothing is returned, there is no need for a type.

  - String... args or String[] args: Methods are sometimes declared as receiving some input data, String[] args represents an array of text values. The three dots is another way to specify that a method can have more than one argument of the same type. (The varargs argument also has to be the only parameter for the method, or the last one; otherwise, resolving the arguments becomes an impossible job.) The three dots notation can be used only in a method argument, and are called *varargs*. It means you can pass in an array of parameters without explicitly creating the array. Arrays are sets of data of fixed length, and in mathematics they are known as *one-dimension matrix* or *vector*. String is the class representing text objects in Java. The [ ] means array and args is its name. But wait, we've run this method before and we did not need to provide anything! Well, it is not mandatory, but you'll see how you can give it arguments (values provided to the method that will be used by the code in its body) after this list.

5. System.out.println("HelloWorld!");: This statement is used for writing *Hello World!* in the console.

6. } is the closing bracket of the main method body.

7. *Line left empty for easier viewing.*

8. } is the closing bracket for the class body.

If we execute this class, we will see Hello World! printed in the console. You were shown earlier (in Figure 3-21) how to execute a class with a main(..) method in it. After executing a class that way, IntelliJ IDEA automatically saves the configuration for that execution in a *Run Configuration* and displays it in a drop-down list on the header of the IDE, located next to a triangular green button that can be clicked to execute that class, both of which options are ostentatiously pointed out to you in Figure 3-29.

Those two elements are really important, because they enable you to edit a run configuration and add arguments for the JVM and the main method. Let's first modify the main(..) method to do something with the arguments. The modified HelloWorld class is depicted in Listing 3-24.

Listing 3-24. Main Method with varargs

```
public class HelloWorld {
    public static void main(String... args) {
        System.out.println("Hello " + args[0] + "!");
    }
}
```

An important point to note is that arrays are accessed using indexes of their elements, and the counting starts in Java from 0. Consequently, the first member of an array can be found at 0, the second at 1, and so on. But arrays can be empty, so if no argument is provided when running the code in Listing 3-24, the execution of the program will crash and an explicit message similar to the one shown in Listing 3-25 will be printed (in red).

Listing 3-25. Empty Array Exception

```
Exception in thread "main" java.lang.ArrayIndexOutOfBoundsException: Index
0 out of bounds for length 0
at chapter.three/com.apress.bgn.three.helloworld.HelloWorld.
main(HelloWorld.java:5)
```

When a Java program ends because an error during execution time, we say that *an exception was thrown.*

When we try to access an empty array, or an element of an array that does not exist, the JVM throws an object of type ArrayIndexOutOfBoundsException containing the line where the failure happened and the index of the element we were trying to access. Exception objects are used by the JVM to notify developers of exceptional situations when a Java execution does not work as expected, and these objects contain details regarding where in the code it happened and what caused the problem.

The modification we did in Listing 3-25 will print the text value provided as an argument when executing the class. Let's modify the run configuration for this class and add an argument. Click the small drop-down arrow next to the **Run Configuration** name and a menu will appear, as shown in Figure 3-30. Click the **Edit Configurations** option and inspect the dialog window depicted to you, also shown in Figure 3-30.

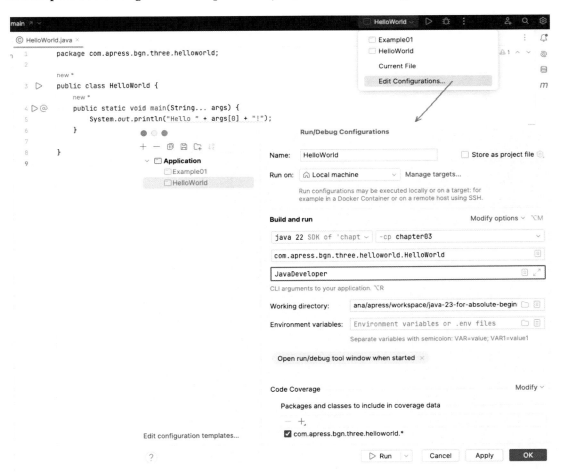

Figure 3-30. *Customizing a Run Configuration*

In Figure 3-30, the key elements are highlighted in light blue and gray. IntelliJ IDEA saves a few of your previous executions, including Maven build tasks, so you can run them again just with one click. In the left side of the **Run/Debug Configurations** dialog window, IntelliJ IDEA groups run configurations by their type. By default, the last run configuration is opened on the right side of the window, in this case the run configuration for the HelloWorld class. As you can see, there are a lot of options you can configure for an execution, and most of them have been automatically decided by the IDE. The program arguments or the arguments for the main() method are introduced in the text field surrounded in blue. In Figure 3-30 we introduced *JavaDeveloper*. So if you click the **Apply** button and then the **OK** button and then execute the class, in the console you now should see *Hello JavaDeveloper!* instead of *Hello World!*.

So, what else can we do with our class? Remember the code the book started with? Let's put it the main() method in this class. The code is depicted again in Listing 3-26.

Listing 3-26. A More Complex main Method

```
package com.apress.bgn.three.helloworld;

import java.util.List;

public class HelloWorld {
    public static void main(String... args) {
        //System.out.println("Hello " + args[0] + "!");
        List<String> items = List.of("1", "a", "2", "a", "3", "a");

        items.forEach(item -> {
            if (item.equals("a")) {
                System.out.println("A");
            } else {
                System.out.println("Not A");
            }
        });
    }
}
```

The import java.util.List; statement is the only type of statement that can exist between a package and a class declaration. This statement is telling the Java compiler that an object type java.util.List will be used in the program. The import keyword is followed by the fully qualified name of the type. A fully qualified name of a type is made of the package name (java.util), a dot (.), and the simple name of the type (List). Without it, the HelloWorld class will not compile. Try it by putting // in front of the statement—this will turn the line into a comment that is ignored by the compiler. You will see the editor complain by making any piece of code related to that list bright red.

The statement List<String> items = List.of("1", "a", "2", "a", "3", "a"); creates a list of text values. Creating lists this way was introduced in Java 9. Specifying what type of elements are in a list by using <E> was introduced in Java 5, and it's called **generics**. The elements in the list are then traversed by the forEach method, and each of them is tested to see if it is equal to the "*a*" character. The whole expression used to do this is called a **lambda expression** and this type of syntax was introduced in Java 8, together with the forEach method.

If you run the class now, in the console you should see a sequence of *A* and *Not A* printed, each on its own line, like shown in Listing 3-27.

Listing 3-27. Output of Running the Advanced HelloWorld Class

```
Not A
A
Not A
A
Not A
A
```

The code we have written until now uses quite a few types of objects to print some simple messages in the console. The List<E> object is used to hold a few String objects. The messages are printed using the println method that is called on the out object, which is a static field in the System class. And these are just the objects that are visible to you in the code. Under the hood, the List<E> elements are processed by a Consumer<E> object created on the spot that the lambda expression in Listing 3-26 hides for simplicity reasons, so that code can be expanded as shown in Listing 3-28.

Listing 3-28. A More Complex main Method Without Lambda Expressions

```java
package com.apress.bgn.three.helloworld;

import java.util.List;
import java.util.function.Consumer;

public class HelloWorld {
    public static void main(String... args) {
        List<String> items = List.of("1", "a", "2", "a", "3", "a");

        items.forEach(new Consumer<String>() {
            @Override
            public void accept(String item) {
                if (item.equals("a")) {
                    System.out.println("A");
                } else {
                    System.out.println("Not A");
                }
            }
        });
    }
}
```

Before ending this chapter, I would like to show you another neat thing. The contents of the forEach block can be written as a single line:

```java
+ items.forEach(item -> System.out.println(item.equals("a") ? "A" :
"Not A"));
```

And the previous line can be made even simpler by using something called a *method reference*. But more about that a little bit later in the book.

What you read in this chapter might look scary now, but I promise that this book introduces each concept in a clear context and compares the concepts with real-life objects and events so that you can understand them easily. And if that does not work, there are always more books, more blogs, and of course the official Oracle page for each JDK, which has quite good tutorials. Where there's a will, there's a way.

Important   Also, take advantage of your IDE! By clicking on any object type in the code while pressing the Control/Command key, the code of the object class is opened, enabling you to see how that class was written, and you can read the documentation for it directly in the editor. As an exercise, do this for the `forEach` method and the `System` class.

Most really smart editors have *keymaps*, groups of keys that when pressed together perform certain actions, like navigation, code generation, execution, and so on. Print the IntelliJ IDEA keymap reference and get comfortable with it. Your brains is very fast, and when coding, the aim is to type as fast as you think, if possible. :)

Summary

In this chapter you were introduced to the fundamental building blocks of a Java application. You were also taught how to use `jshell` to execute Java statements outside of the context of an application. You found out how you can manually compile and Java code that declared packages and modules.

Many of the things you did while following this chapter you will probably do daily if you get a job as a Java developer...except for the days that you will spend hunting and fixing bugs in existing code. You will probably spend a lot of time reading documentation too, because the JDK has a lot of classes, with fields and methods you can use to write an application. With each released version, things change, and you have to keep yourself up-to-date. The brain has limited capacity; no employer will ever expect you to know every JDK class and method, but work smart and keep this URL `https://docs.oracle.com/en/java/javase/23/docs/api/index.html` (or the one matching the JDK version used) always opened in your browser. When you have doubts about a JDK class or method, just read about it on the spot.

CHAPTER 4

Java Syntax

Languages are means of communication, verbal or written, between people. Whether they are natural or artificial, languages are made of terms and rules on how to use them to perform the task of communication. Programming languages are means of communication with a computer. The communication with a computer is a written communication. Basically, the developer defines some instructions to be executed and communicates them through an intermediary to the computer. If the computer understands the instructions, it performs the set of actions and, depending on the application type, returns some sort of reply to the developer.

In the Java language, the intermediary through which the developer communicates to the computer is the Java Virtual Machine. The set of programming rules that define how terms should be connected to produce an understandable unit of communication is called *syntax*. Java borrowed most of its syntax from another programming language called C++, which in turn has syntax based on the C language syntax. C syntax borrows elements and rules from other languages that preceded it, but in essence all these languages are based on the natural English language. Java got a little cryptic in version 8 because of the introduction of lambda expressions, but still, when writing a Java program, if you are naming your terms properly in the English language, the result should be a code that is easily readable, like a story.

A few details of Java syntax have been covered in **Chapter 2** and **Chapter 3**. Packages and modules were covered enough to give you a solid understanding of their purpose to avoid confusion regarding the organization of the project and avoid aimless fumbling through the code when trying to execute code mentioned in the book. But on other topics, the surface has been barely scratched. Thus, let's begin our deep dive into Java.

131

© Iuliana Cosmina 2024
I. Cosmina, *Java 23 for Absolute Beginners*, https://doi.org/10.1007/979-8-8688-1041-1_4

Base Rules of Writing Java Code

Before writing Java code, let's list a few rules that you should follow to make sure your code not only works but is easy to understand and thus maintain or extend. Listing 4-1 depicts the class we ended **Chapter 3** with and adds a few details.

Listing 4-1. The HelloWorld Class with Comments

```
01. package com.apress.bgn.four.basic;
02.
03. import java.util.List;
04.
05./**
06. * this is a JavaDoc comment
07. */
08. public class HelloWorld {
09.     public static void main(String... args) {
10.         //this is a one-line comment
11.         List<String> items = List.of("1", "a", "2", "a", "3", "a");
12.
13.         items.forEach(item -> {
14.             /* this is a
15.                 multi-line
16.             comment */
17.             if (item.equals("a")) {
18.                 System.out.println("A");
19.             } else {
20.                 System.out.println("Not A");
21.             }
22.         });
23.     }
24. }
```

Each section of the code gets its own section in this chapter. Let's start with the first line.

Package Declaration

A Java file always starts with the *package declaration* if the type declared in the file is declared within a package. The package name can contain letters and numbers, separated by dots. Each part matches a directory in the path to the type contained in it, as shown in **Chapter 3**. The package declaration should reveal the name of the application and the purpose of the classes in the package. Let's take the package naming used for the sources of this book: `com.apress.bgn.four.basic`. If we split the package name in pieces, this is the meaning of each piece:

- `com.apress` represents the domain of the application, or who owns the application in this case.

- `bgn` represents the scope of the code, in this case the book who it is written for: **beginners**.

- `four` represents the purpose of the classes: to be used with **Chapter 4**.

- `basic` represents a more refined level of the purpose for the classes: these classes are simple, used to depict basic Java notions.

A package name like the one introduced here that is made of more parts is called a **qualified package name**. It has a hierarchical structure, and package `com` is the root package. Assuming a type `MyType` is declared in this package, this type is referenced in classes in other packages using this import statement: `import com.MyType;`.

Package `apress` is a member of package `com` and is identified by a name composed of its own name prefixed by the enclosing package and a dot. Assuming a type `MyType` is declared in this package, this type is referenced in classes in other packages using this import statement: `import com.apress.MyType;`.

The same applies to package bgn, which is a member of package `apress` and its type members, and so on down the package tree.

Tip   You can imagine packages being the programming equivalent of Russian nesting Matryoshka dolls[1].

---

[1]https://en.wikipedia.org/wiki/Matryoshka_doll

Thus, a type is referenced in other types via its **fully qualified name**. The fully qualified name of a type is formed by prefixing the type name with the qualified name of the package and a dot. Figure 4-1 should make things pretty clear.

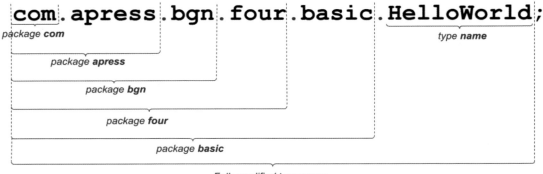

Figure 4-1. *Dissection of the fully qualified name of a Java type*

Import Section

After the package declaration, the *import section* follows. This section contains the fully qualified names of all classes, interfaces, and enums used within the file. Look at the code sample in Listing 4-2.

Listing 4-2. Small Code Snippet from the `java.lang.String` Class

```
package java.lang;

import java.io.ObjectStreamField;
import java.io.UnsupportedEncodingException;
import java.lang.annotation.Native;
import java.lang.invoke.MethodHandles;
import java.lang.constant.Constable;
import java.lang.constant.ConstantDesc;
import java.nio.charset.Charset;
import java.util.ArrayList;
// the rest of import statements omitted
```

```java
public final class String
        implements java.io.Serializable, Comparable<String>, CharSequence,
        Constable, ConstantDesc {

    private static final ObjectStreamField[] serialPersistentFields =
            new ObjectStreamField[0];

    // the rest of the code omitted
}
```

It is a snippet from the official Java `String` class. Every import statement represents a reference to the package and the name of a class used within the `String` class body.

Special import statements can be used to import static variables and static methods as well. The JDK includes a class used for mathematical processes. It contains static variables and methods that can be used by developers to implement code that solves mathematical problems. You can use its variables and methods without the need to create objects of this type, because static members do not belong to an object of a type, but to the type itself. Check out the code in Listing 4-3.

Listing 4-3. Using Static Imports for Members of Class `Math`

```java
package com.apress.bgn.four;

import static java.lang.Math.PI;
import static java.lang.Math.sqrt;

public class MathSample {
    public static void main(String... args) {
        System.out.println("PI value =" + PI);
        double result = sqrt(5.0);
        System.out.println("SQRT value =" + result);
    }
}
// output
// PI value =3.141592653589793
// SQRT value =2.23606797749979
```

By putting together `import` and `static` we can declare a fully qualified name of a class and the method or the variable we are interested in using in the code. This allows us to use the variable or method directly, without the name of the class it is being declared in. Without the static imports the code will have to be rewritten as shown in Listing 4-4.

Listing 4-4. Using Import of Class `Math`

```
package com.apress.bgn.four;

import java.lang.Math;

public class MathSample {
    public static void main(String... args) {
        System.out.println("PI value =" + Math.PI);
        double result = Math.sqrt(5.0);
        System.out.println("SQRT value =" + result);
    }
}
```

Important   Fully qualified names are powerful. Package names are unique within a module, but package names are not always unique within an application. Type names are not always unique within an application either. But fully qualified type names, formed by combining the two, are unique within an application.

Tip   You can also think about packages as home addresses and types as persons. Two persons can have the same address, but they can't have the same name. Two persons can have the same name and live at different addresses. This is how banks and other institutions identify individuals uniquely in the UK or US, for example.

Fully qualified names are not limited to import statements. When two types have the same name and both are used to declare a third type, the only way to be able to tell the compiler within a type body which you intend to use is to use the fully qualified name.

An example of this is shown in Listing 4-5, where a class Math from package com.apress. bgn.four.math is used within the body of a class where members of the java.lang.Math class are used too.

Listing 4-5. Using a Member of Class com.apress.bgn.four.math.Math

```
package com.apress.bgn.four.math;

import java.lang.Math;

public class Sample {
    public static void main(String... args) {
        System.out.println("PI value =" + Math.PI);

        System.out.println("My PI value= " + com.apress.bgn.four.math.
        Math.PI);
    }
}
// output
// PI value =3.141592653589793
// My PI value= 3.14
```

When more than one type is used from the same package, the type names can be replaced by an asterisk (*) that means any visible type from the package can be used in the code of the type being written. These are called *compact import statements.* Compacting imports is recommended when using multiple classes from the same package to write code, or multiple static variables and methods from the same class. When doing so, the import section of a file becomes verbose and difficult to read. This is where compacting comes to help. Compacting imports means replacing all classes from the same package, or variables and methods from the same class, with a wildcard so that only one import statement is needed. It works for static imports too. So the previous Sample class becomes class MathSample in Listing 4-6.

Listing 4-6. Using a Member of class java.lang.Math

```java
package com.apress.bgn.four;

import static java.lang.Math.*;

public class MathSample {
    public static void main(String... args) {
        System.out.println("PI value =" + PI);
        double result = sqrt(5.0);
        System.out.println("SQRT value =" + result);
    }
}
```

Java Grammar

The Java language is **case sensitive**, which means that we can write a piece of code like the one depicted in Listing 4-7 and the code compiles and executes successfully.

Listing 4-7. Java Code Proving Its Case Sensitivity

```java
package com.apress.bgn.four;

public class MultipleCaseVariables {
    public static void main(String... args) {
        int mynumber = 0;
        int myNumber = 1;
        int Mynumber = 2;
        int MYNUMBER = 3;
        System.out.println(mynumber);
        System.out.println(myNumber);
        System.out.println(Mynumber);
        System.out.println(MYNUMBER);
    }
}
```

All four variables are different, and the last four lines will print numbers 0 1 2 3. Obviously, you cannot declare two variables sharing the same name in the same context (e.g., in the body of a method), because you basically would be redeclaring the same variable. The Java compiler does not allow this. If you try to do this, your code will not compile, and even IntelliJ IDEA will try to make you see the error of your ways by underlining the code with red and showing you a relevant message, as shown on line 37 in Figure 4-2 where variable `mynumber` was declared twice.

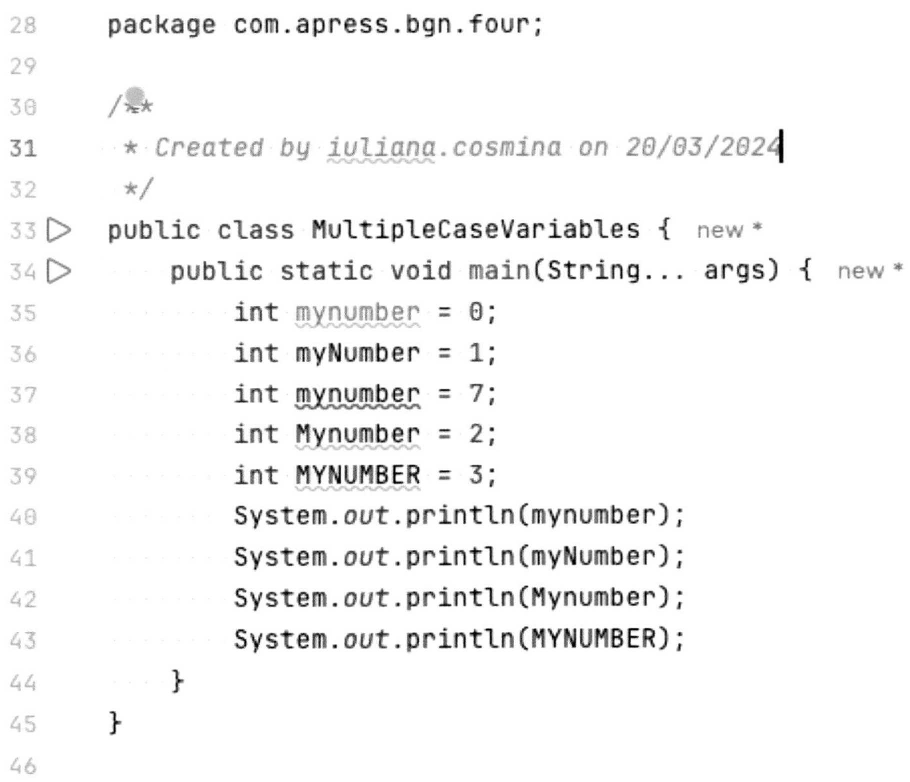

```
28      package com.apress.bgn.four;
29
30      /**
31       * Created by iuliana.cosmina on 20/03/2024
32       */
33 ▷    public class MultipleCaseVariables {  new *
34 ▷        public static void main(String... args) {  new *
35                int mynumber = 0;
36                int myNumber = 1;
37                int mynumber = 7;
38                int Mynumber = 2;
39                int MYNUMBER = 3;
40                System.out.println(mynumber);
41                System.out.println(myNumber);
42                System.out.println(Mynumber);
43                System.out.println(MYNUMBER);
44            }
45        }
46
```

Figure 4-2. *Same variable name used twice*

There is a set of **Java keywords** that can be used only for fixed and predefined purposes in the Java code. A few of them have already been introduced: `import`, `package`, `public`, `class`; the rest of them will be covered at the end of this chapter, with a short explanation for each of them in Tables 4-2, 4-3, and 4-4.

Important   Java keywords cannot be used as identifiers in code written by developers, so they cannot be used as names for variables, classes, interfaces, objects, and so on.

One or more types can be declared in a Java source file. Whether a `class`, `interface` (or `@interface`) or enum, the declaration of a type must be encased in curly brackets (`{}`). These are called **block delimiters.** `import` and `package` statements are not part of the type body. If you look back at the code in Listing 4-1, you will notice the brackets are used there to wrap up the following:

- Contents of a class, also called the body of the class (brackets in lines 08 and 23)

- Contents of a method, also called the body of a method (brackets in lines 09 and 22)

- A set of instructions to be executed together (brackets in lines 13 and 21)

Code lines are usually ended in Java by the semicolon (`;`) symbol or by the ASCII characters CR, or LF, or CR LF. These are called **line terminators**. Semicolons are used to terminate fully functioning statements, like the list declaration in line 11. When writing code on a small monitor, you might be forced to split that statement on two subsequent lines to keep the code readable. The semicolon at its end tells the compiler that the statement is correct only when taken all together. Look at Figure 4-3.

```
30    import java.util.List;
31      💡
32  >  /** Created by iuliana.cosmina on 20/03/2024 */
35 ▷   public class MultipleStatementsSample {  new *
36 ▷       public static void main(String... args) {  new *
37            List<String> items1 = List.of("1", "a", "2", "a", "3", "a");
38
39            List<String> item2 =
40                 List.of("1", "a", "2", "a", "3", "a");
41
42            List<String> items3 =
43                 List.of("1", "a", "2",
44                      "a", "3", "a");
45
46            List<String> badlist =̭;
47                 List.of("1", "a", "2", "a", "3", "a");
48        }
49    }
50
```

Figure 4-3. *Different statement samples*

The first three List declarations are equivalent. When declaring a List this way, you can even split its elements on multiple lines. The declaration on line 46, however, is written intentionally wrong. A semicolon is added in line 46, which ends the statement there. That statement is not valid, and when you try to compile that class, the compiler will complain about it by printing an exception saying Error:(13, 46) java: illegal start of expression.

If the message of the error seems not to fit the example, think about it like this: the problem for the compiler is not the wrongful termination of the statement, but the fact that after the equals (=) symbol, the compiler expects to find some sort of expression that will produce the value for the badList variable, but instead it finds nothing.

Java Identifiers and Variables

An **identifier** is the name you give to an item in your Java code: class, variable, method, and so forth. Identifiers must respect a few rules to allow the code to compile and also follow common-sense programming rules, called **Java coding conventions**. A few of them are listed here:

- An identifier cannot be one of the Java reserved words, or the code will not compile.

- An identifier cannot be a boolean literal (`true`, `false`) or the `null` literal, or the code will not compile.

- An identifier can be made of: letters, numbers, underscore (`_`), dollar sign (`$`).

- An identifier cannot start with a number.

- Starting with Java 9, a single underscore could no longer be used as an identifier, as it became a keyword. This is probably because in Java 7 numeric literals were introduced, and numbers with multiple digits can be written in a more readable way (e.g., `int i = 10_000;`).

- Starting with Java 21, a single underscore can now be used again as an identifier, but only for variables that hold values not used in the code. This behavior is inspired from the Golang programming language, and these variables are referred to as *unnamed variables*.

- Developers should declare their identifiers following **camel case** writing style, making sure each word or abbreviation in the middle of the identifier name begins with a capital letter (e.g., `StringBuilder`, `isAdult`).

A **variable** is a set of characters that can be associated with a value. It has a type, and based on it, the set of values that can be assigned to it are restricted to a certain interval, group of values, or just must follow a certain format defined by that type. For example, the item declared in line 11 in Listing 4-1 is a variable of type `List`, and the value associated with it is a list of values.

In Java there are three types of variables:

- **Fields** (also known as **properties**) are variables that are defined in class bodies outside of method bodies and that do not have the keyword `static` in front of them.

- **Local variables** are variables declared inside method bodies, and they are relevant only in that context.

- **Static variables** are variables declared inside class bodies with the keyword `static` in front of them. If they are declared as `public` they are accessible within the application wherever the enclosing type is (unless the module does not export the package where they are declared, that is).

Java Comments

Java comments refer to pieces of explanatory text that are not part of the code being executed and are ignored by the compiler. There are three ways to add comments within the code in Java, each of which has unique characters to declare them. All three types of comments were used in Listing 4-1, and the following list explains the purpose of each:

- `//` is used for single-line comments (line 10). Developers use this type of comment for adding `TODO` statements or explaining why a certain piece of code is needed. These comments are mostly intended for the team members working on the project.

- `/** ... */` JavaDoc comments are exported using special tools into the documentation of a project called JavaDoc API (lines 05 to 07). Developers use this type of comment to document their code. There are plugins for build tools that can extract the JavaDoc from a project as a website, which then can be hosted publicly to help other developers using your project.

- `/* ... */` is used for multiline comments (lines 14 to 16). Developers use this type of comment for adding `TODO` statements or for providing a lengthy explanation of why a certain piece of code is needed. These comments are mostly intended for the team members working on the project.

Java Types

In **Chapter 3** when introducing the Java building blocks, only the class was explained, to keep things simple. It was mentioned that there are other types in Java, and this section introduces all of them. Since classes are the most important, they must be covered first.

Classes

As mentioned in **Chapter 3**, classes are just templates for creating objects. Creating an object based on a **class** is called **instantiation**. The resulting object is referred to as an instance of that class. Instances are named objects because by default any class written by a developer implicitly extends class java.lang.Object, if no other superclass is declared. What this means is that in Java, there is a basic template for all classes and that is represented by the java.lang.Object class. Any class is by default an extension of this class, so the class declaration in Listing 4-8 is equivalent to the one in Listing 4-9.

Listing 4-8. Simple Sample Class Implicitly Extending the java.lang. Object Class

```
package com.apress.bgn.four.basic;

public class Sample {}
```

Listing 4-9. Simple Sample Class Explicitly Extending the java.lang. Object Class

```
package com.apress.bgn.four.basic;

public class Sample extends Object {}
```

Note   Notice how importing the java.lang package is not necessary, because the Object class being the root class of the Java hierarchy, all classes (including arrays) must have access to extend it. Thus, the java.lang package is implicitly imported.

Important   As mentioned in **Chapter 3**, the `java.base` module is added implicitly as required in any Java project that declares `module-info.java`. This module exports the `java.lang` package that contains the core components to writing Java code.

Tip   Every human being is defined by a DNA molecule containing 23 pairs of chromosomes. They declare the organs and limbs a human should have to look and function as a…human. You can view the `Object` class as the DNA molecule that declares all the components that a class should have to look and function as a class within a Java application.

The following sections introduce and explain the use of the other template types that can be used for creating objects in Java. To do so in context, we will create a family of templates for defining humans. Most Java tutorials use templates for vehicles or geometrical shapes. I want to model something that anybody can easily understand and relate to. The purpose of the following sections is to develop Java templates that can be used to model different types of people. The first Java template that was mentioned so far is the **class**, so let's continue with that.

Fields

The operation through which instances are created is called **instantiation**. To design a class that models a generic human, we should think about two things: human characteristics and human actions. So, what do all humans have in common? Well, a lot, but for the purpose of this section, let's choose three generic attributes: name, age, and height. These attributes map in a Java class to variables named **fields** or **properties**. The first version of the Human class is depicted in Listing 4-10.

Listing 4-10. Simple Human Class

```
package com.apress.bgn.four.base;

public class Human {
    String name;
    int age;
    float height;
}
```

In the previous code sample, the fields have different types, depending on what values should be associated with them. For example, the name can be associated with a text value, like "Alex," and texts are represented in Java by the String type. The age can be associated with numeric integer values, so it is of type int. And for the purpose of this section, the height of a person is considered a rational number like 1.9, so we use the special Java type for this kind of values: float.

So now we have a class modeling some basic attributes of a human. How do we use it? We need a main() method and we need to create an object of this type: we need to instantiate this class. In Listing 4-11 a human named "Alex" is created.

Listing 4-11. Simple Human Object Being Created

```
package com.apress.bgn.four.base;

public class BasicHumanDemo {
    public static void main(String... args) {
        Human human = new Human();
        human.name = "Alex";
        human.age = 40;
        human.height = 1.91f;
    }
}
```

To create a Human instance, we use the new keyword. After the new keyword we call a special method called a **constructor**. I've mentioned methods before, but this one is special. Some developers do not even consider a constructor to be a method. The most obvious reason for that is the constructor is not defined anywhere in the body of the Human class. So where is it coming from? It's a default constructor without parameters that is automatically generated by the compiler unless an explicit one is declared (with or without parameters). A class cannot exist without a constructor; otherwise, it cannot be instantiated, which is why the compiler generates one if none was explicitly declared. The default constructor, invokes super(), which in turn invokes the Object no argument constructor that initializes all fields with default values. This is tested by the code sample in Listing 4-12 (which includes the output).

Listing 4-12. Simple Human Object Being Created Without Setting Values or Its Fields

```
package com.apress.bgn.four.base;

public class BasicHumanDemo {
    public static void main(String... args) {
        Human human = new Human();
        System.out.println("name: " + human.name);
        System.out.println("age: " + human.age);
        System.out.println("height: " + human.height);
    }
}
// output
// name: null
// age:0
// height:0.0
```

Default values for the variable types are printed. Numeric variables were initialized with 0, and the `String` value was initialized with `null`. The reason for that is that the numeric types are primitive data types and `String` is an object data type. The `String` class is part of the `java.lang package` and is one of the predefined Java classes that is used to create objects of type `String`. It is a special data type that is used to represent text objects. We'll get deeper into data types in **Chapter 5**.

Class Variables

Aside from attributes that are specific to each human in particular, all humans have something in common: a lifespan (which we'll assume to be 100 years for the maximum value). It would be redundant to declare a field called lifespan, because it would have to be associated with the same value for all Human instances. So we will declare a field using the `static` keyword in the Human class, which will have the same value for all Human instances and that will be initialized only once. And we can go one step further as well and make sure that value never changes during the execution of the program by adding the `final` modifier in front of its declaration as well. This way we created a special type of variable called a **constant**.

Note   Java code conventions for constants specifies that their names should be all uppercase with words separated by underscores (_).

The new Human class is depicted in Listing 4-13.

Listing 4-13. Simple Human Class with a Constant Member

```
package com.apress.bgn.four.base;

public class Human {
    static final int LIFESPAN = 100;
    String name;
    int age;
    float height;
}
```

The LIFESPAN variable is also called a class variable because it is associated with the class, not with instances. *(And it was set to 100, which is a pretty optimistic value.)* This is made obvious by the code in Listing 4-14.

Listing 4-14. Code Sample Testing a Constant

```
package com.apress.bgn.four.base;

public class BasicHumanDemo {
    public static void main(String... args) {
        Human human = new Human();

        Human alex = new Human();
        alex.name = "Alex";
        alex.age = 40;
        alex.height = 1.91f;

        System.out.println("Alex's lifespan = " + alex.LIFESPAN);
        System.out.println("human's lifespan = " + human.LIFESPAN);
        System.out.println("Human lifespan = " + Human.LIFESPAN);
    }
}
```

```
/*
Alex's lifespan = 100
human's lifespan = 100
Human lifespan = 100
*/
```

Encapsulating Data

The class we defined makes no use of access modifiers on the fields, and this is not acceptable. Java is known as an **object-oriented programming language**, and thus code written in Java must respect the **principles of object-oriented programming (OOP).** Respecting these coding principles ensures that the written code is of good quality and totally aligns with the fundamental Java style.

Note   Starting with Java 8, the Java syntax has been modified—new types have been added, and internal changes have been made to the JDK to allow a more functional approach when writing code—but Java still remains mostly an OOP language.

One of the OOP principles is **encapsulation**, which refers to hiding the data implementation by restricting access to it using special methods called accessors (getters) and mutators (setters).

Usually, any field of a class should have private access, and access to it should be controlled by methods that can be intercepted, tested, and tracked to see where they were called. Using getters and setters is a common practice when working with objects, so most IDEs have a default option to generate them, including IntelliJ IDEA. As shown in Figure 4-4, just right-click inside the class body, select the **Generate** option to see all possibilities, and then select **Getter and Setter** to generate the methods for you.

Figure 4-4. *IntelliJ IDEA code generation menu:* ***Generate ➤ Getter and Setter*** *submenu*

After making the fields private and generating the getters and setters, the Human class now looks like the one depicted in Listing 4-15.

Listing 4-15. Simple Human Class with Getters and Setters

```java
package com.apress.bgn.four.base;

public class Human {
    static final int LIFESPAN = 100;

    private String name;
    private int age;
    private float height;

    public String getName() {
        return name;
    }

    public void setName(String name) {
        this.name = name;
    }

    public int getAge() {
        return age;
    }
}
```

```java
    public void setAge(int age) {
        this.age = age;
    }

    public float getHeight() {
        return height;
    }

    public void setHeight(float height) {
        this.height = height;
    }
}
```

After looking at Listing 4-15, you may be wondering what is the purpose of the `this` keyword. As the keyword name hints, it is a reference to the current object. So `this.` name is actually the value of the field name of the current object, also referred to as an **instance variable**. Inside the class body, this is used to access fields for the current objects when there are parameters in methods that have the same name. As you can see, the setters and getters that IntelliJ IDEA generates have parameters named exactly as the fields.

Getters are the simplest methods that are declared without any parameter, and they return the value of the field they are associated with. The coding convention for their names is to use the get prefix and the name of the field they access, with its first letter uppercased.

Setters are methods that return nothing and declare as a parameter a variable with the same type that needs to be associated to the field. Their names are made of the set prefix and the name of the field they access, with its first letter uppercased. When setters are generated by an editor, the parameter name matches the instance variable name, and the `this` keyword is needed to discern between the two in the context of the setter's body.

Figure 4-5 depicts the setter and getter for the name field.

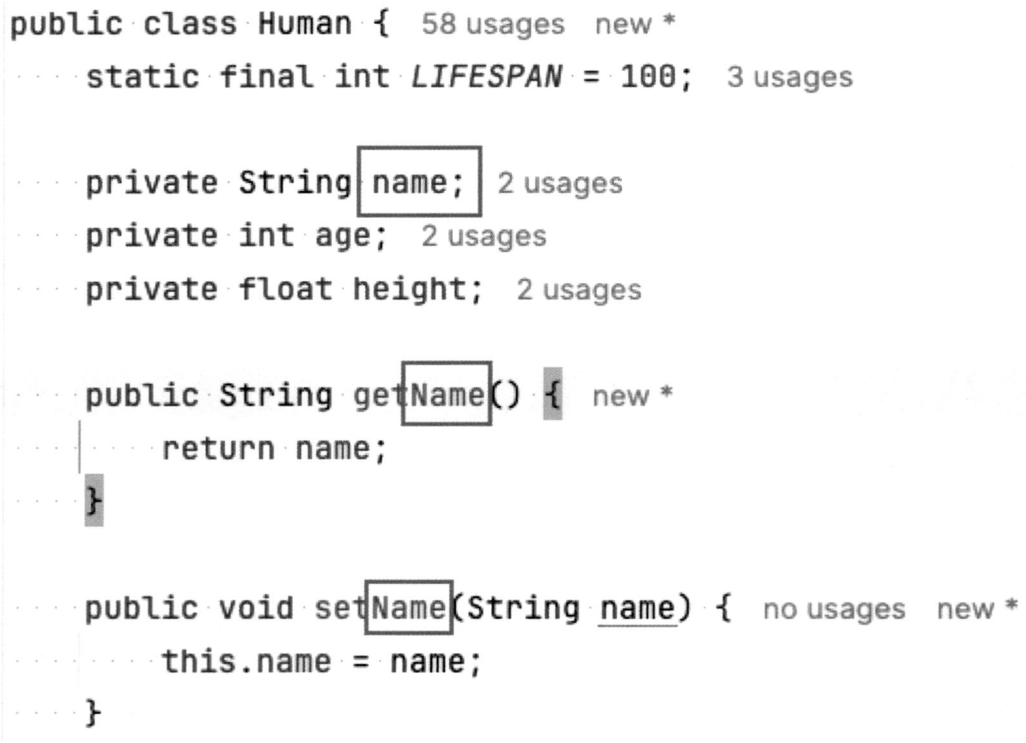

```
public class Human {   58 usages   new *
        static final int LIFESPAN = 100;   3 usages

        private String name;   2 usages
        private int age;   2 usages
        private float height;   2 usages

        public String getName() {   new *
            return name;
        }


        public void setName(String name) {   no usages   new *
                this.name = name;
        }
```

Figure 4-5. *Setter and getter methods used for the name field*

Since the fields are now private, when creating a Human instance, we have to use the setters to set the field values and the getters when accessing them. Therefore, our class BasicHumanDemo changes to the one depicted in Listing 4-16.

Listing 4-16. BasicHumanDemo Class Using Human Instance with Getters and Setters

```
package com.apress.bgn.four.base;

public class BasicHumanDemo {
    public static void main(String... args) {
        Human alex = new Human();
        alex.setName("Alex");
        alex.setAge(40);
        alex.setHeight(1.91f);
```

```
        System.out.println("name: " + alex.getName());
        System.out.println("age: " + alex.getAge());
        System.out.println("height: " + alex.getHeight());
    }
}
// output
// name: Alex
// age: 40
// height: 1.91
```

Most Java frameworks look for getters and setters within classes to initialize or read the values of an object's fields. Setters and getters are considered by most developers as **boilerplate code** (or just **boilerplate**), sections of code that are repeated in multiple places with little to no variation. This is why the Lombok[2] library was born—to generate them at runtime, so developers don't have to pollute their code with them. The Kotlin language removed them altogether.

Java did something similar in version 14 with the introduction of *records*. Records will be covered a little later in this chapter.

Methods

Since getters and setters are methods, it is time to start the discussion about methods too. A **method** is a block of code usually characterized by returned type, name, and parameters (when needed) that describes an action done by or on the object that makes use of the values of its fields and/or arguments provided. An abstract template of a Java method is depicted in Listing 4-17.

Listing 4-17. Method Declaration Template

```
[accessor] [returned type] [name]( type1 param1, type2 param2,...)
{
    // code
  [ [maybe] return val ]
}
```

---

[2] https://projectlombok.org

Following the template, let's create a method for the class Human that computes and prints how much time a human still has to live, by making use of their age and the LIFESPAN constant. Because the method does not return anything, the return type used will be void, a special type that tells the compiler that the method does not return anything (thus no return statement is present in the method body). The code of this method is depicted in Listing 4-18.

Listing 4-18. Human#computeAndPrintTtl Method with No Return Value

```java
package com.apress.bgn.four.base;

public class Human {
    static final int LIFESPAN = 100;
    private String name;
    private int age;
    private float height;

    /**
     * compute and prints time to live
     */
    public void computeAndPrintTtl() {
        int ttl = LIFESPAN - this.age;
        System.out.println("Time to live: " + ttl);
    }

    // some code omitted
}
```

The preceding method definition does not declare any parameters, so it can be invoked on a Human instance as depicted in Listing 4-19.

Listing 4-19. The computeAndPrintTtl() Method Invocation

```java
package com.apress.bgn.four.base;

public class BasicHumanDemo {
    public static void main(String... args) {
        Human alex = new Human();
        alex.setName("Alex");
```

```
        alex.setAge(40);
        alex.setHeight(1.91f);
        alex.computeAndPrintTtl();
    }
    // some code omitted
}
```

When the code in Listing 4-19 is executed, *Time to live: 60* is printed in the console.

The previous method can be modified to return the time to live value instead of printing it. The method must be modified to declare the type of the value being returned, and in this case the type is int, the same type of the value being computed inside the body of the method. The implementation is depicted in Listing 4-20.

Listing 4-20. The getTimeToLive() Method with Return Value

```
package com.apress.bgn.four.base;

public class Human {
    static final int LIFESPAN = 100;
    private String name;
    private int age;
    private float height;

    /**
     * @return time to live
     */
    public int getTimeToLive() {
        int ttl = LIFESPAN - this.age;
        return ttl;
    }

    // some code omitted
}
```

Calling the method will do nothing in this case, so we have to modify the code to save the returned value and print it, as depicted in Listing 4-21.

Listing 4-21. Using the getTimeToLive() Method

```
package com.apress.bgn.four.base;

public class BasicHumanDemo {
    public static void main(String... args) {
        Human alex = new Human();
        alex.setName("Alex");
        alex.setAge(40);
        alex.setHeight(1.91f);
        int timeToLive = alex.getTimeToLive();
        System.out.println("Time to live: " + timeToLive);
    }
    // some code omitted
}
```

Both methods introduced here declare no parameters, so they are called without providing any arguments. We won't cover methods with parameters, as the setters are more than obvious. Let's skip ahead to constructors.

Constructors

Now we've done it: we can no longer use alex.name in other classes without the compiler complaining about not being able to access that property. Also, calling all those setters just to set those properties is quite annoying, so we need to do something about that. Remember the implicit constructor? Developers can also declare constructors explicitly, and a class can have more than one. Constructors can be declared with parameters for each of the fields of interest. Listing 4-22 depicts a constructor for the Human class that initializes the class fields with the values of its parameters.

Listing 4-22. Human Class with Explicit Constructor

```
package com.apress.bgn.four.base;

public class Human {
    static final int LIFESPAN = 100;
    private String name;
    private int age;
    private float height;
```

```java
/**
 * Constructs a Human instance initialized with the given parameters.
 * @param name - the name for the Human instance
 * @param age - the age for the Human instance
 * @param height - the height for the Human instance
 */
public Human(String name, int age, float height) {
    this.name = name;
    this.age = age;
    this.height = height;
}

// some code omitted
}
```

A constructor does not require a `return` statement, even if the result of calling a constructor is the creation of an object. Constructors are different from methods in that way.

Note   By declaring an explicit constructor, the default constructor is no longer generated.

So creating a Human instance by calling the default constructor (as depicted in earlier code listings) does not work anymore. The code no longer compiles because the default constructor is no longer generated. To create a Human instance, we now have to call the new constructor and provide proper arguments in place of the parameters, having the correct types and respecting their declaration order. The default constructor invocation and the invocation of the custom constructor are shown in Listing 4-23.

Listing 4-23. Human Constructors

```java
Human human = new Human("John", 40, 1.91f);  // this works

Human human = new Human();  // this no longer works
```

But what if we do not want to be forced to set all fields using this constructor? We simply define another constructor with only the parameters we are interested in. Let's define a constructor that sets only the name and the age for a Human instance, as depicted in Listing 4-24.

Listing 4-24. Human Class with Explicit Constructors

```java
package com.apress.bgn.four.base;

public class Human {
    static final int LIFESPAN = 100;
    private String name;
    private int age;
    private float height;

    public Human(String name, int age) {
        this.name = name;
        this.age = age;
    }

    public Human(String name, int age, float height) {
        this.name = name;
        this.age = age;
        this.height = height;
    }

    // some code omitted
}
```

We've just stumbled upon another OOP principle called **polymorphism**. The term is Greek and translates to *one name, many forms*. Polymorphism applies to code design that has multiple methods all with the same name but slightly different signatures and functionality. It applies to constructors too. There are two basic types of polymorphism: **overriding**, also called *runtime polymorphism*, which we will cover a bit later with the coverage of the inheritance principle, and **overloading**, which is also referred to as *compile-time polymorphism*.

The second type of polymorphism applies to the constructors in Listing 4-24, because we have two of them, one with a different set of parameters that looks like it is an extension of the simpler one.

The second thing to notice in Listing 4-24 is that the two constructors contain two identical code lines. There is a commonsense programming principle named DRY, which is short for *Don't Repeat Yourself!* (DRY is also one of the clean coding principles.[3]) Obviously, the code in Listing 4-24 does not respect the DRY principle. So let's fix that by using the this keyword (introduced previously) in a new interesting way, shown in Listing 4-25.

Listing 4-25. Human Class with Better Custom Constructors

```
package com.apress.bgn.four.base;

public class Human {
    public static final int LIFESPAN = 100;
    private String name;
    private int age;
    private float height;

    public Human(String name, int age) {
        this.name = name;
        this.age = age;
    }

    public Human(String name, int age, float height) {
        this(name, age);
        this.height = height;
    }

    // some code omitted
}
```

The constructors can call each other by using this(...). This is pretty useful to avoid writing the same code twice, thus promoting code reusability.

So now both constructors provide the means to create Human instances. If we use the one that does not set the height, the height field will be implicitly initialized with the default value for type float (0.0).

---

[3] https://blog.aspiresys.pl/technology/top-9-principles-clean-code

Now our class is quite basic, and we could even say that it models a human in a quite abstract way. If we want to try to model humans with certain skill sets or abilities, we have to create new classes. Let's say we want to model musicians and actors. This means we need to create two new classes. The Musician class is depicted in Listing 4-26; getters and setters for the fields are skipped.

Listing 4-26. Musician Class

```
package com.apress.bgn.four.classes;

import java.util.List;

public class Musician {
    public static final int LIFESPAN = 100;
    private String name;
    private int age;
    private float height;
    private String musicSchool;
    private String genre;
    private List<String> songs;

// other code omitted
}
```

The Actor class is depicted in Listing 4-27; getters and setter for the fields are skipped.

Listing 4-27. Actor Class

```
package com.apress.bgn.four.classes;

import java.util.List;

public class Actor {
    static final int LIFESPAN = 100;
    private String name;
    private int age;
    private float height;
```

```
    private String actingSchool;
    private List<String> films;

    // other code omitted
}
```

As you can see, the two classes have more than a few common elements. As previously mentioned, one of the clean coding principles requires developers to avoid code duplication. This can be done by designing the classes by following two more OOP principles: **inheritance** (which was mentioned briefly) and **abstraction**.

Abstraction and Inheritance

Abstraction is an OOP principle that manages complexity. Abstraction is used to decompose complex implementations and define core parts that can be reused. In our case, common fields of classes Musician and Actor can be grouped in the Human class that we defined earlier in the chapter. The Human class can be viewed as an abstraction, because any human in this world is more than their name, age, and height. There is no need to ever create Human instances, because any human will be represented by something else, such as passion, purpose, and skill. A class that does not need to be instantiated, but just groups together fields and methods for other classes to inherit or provide a concrete implementation for is modelled in Java by an **abstract** class. Thus, the Human class is modified to make it abstract. Since we are abstracting this class, we'll make the LIFESPAN constant public to make it accessible from anywhere and make the getTimeToLive() method abstract to delegate its implementation to extending classes.

Important   When you declare at least one method as abstract, the class must be declared abstract too.

The class contents are shown in Listing 4-28.

Listing 4-28. Human Abstract Class

```
package com.apress.bgn.four.classes;

public abstract class Human {
    public static final int LIFESPAN = 100;
    private String name;
```

```java
    private int age;
    private float height;

    public Human(String name, int age) {
        this.name = name;
        this.age = age;
    }

    public Human(String name, int age, float height) {
        this(name, age);
        this.height = height;
    }

    /**
     * @return time to live
     */
    public abstract int getTimeToLive();

    // getters and setters omitted
}
```

An abstract method is a method missing the body, like the getTimeToLive() method declared in Listing 4-28. This means that within the Human class, there is no concrete implementation for this method, only a skeleton, a template. A concrete implementation for this method must be provided by the extending classes.

Oh, but wait, we kept the constructors! Why did we do that, if we are not allowed to use them anymore? And we aren't, as confirmed in Figure 4-6, which shows what IntelliJ IDEA does with the BasicHumanDemo class now.

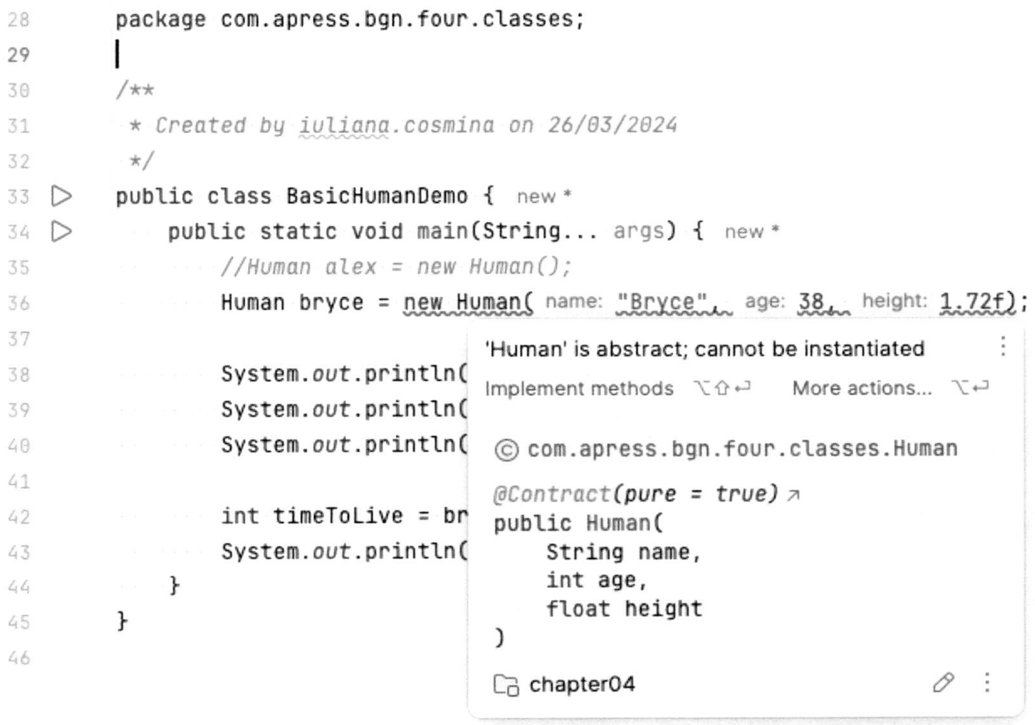

```
28      package com.apress.bgn.four.classes;
29      |
30      /**
31       * Created by iuliana.cosmina on 26/03/2024
32       */
33  ▷   public class BasicHumanDemo {  new *
34  ▷       public static void main(String... args) {  new *
35           //Human alex = new Human();
36           Human bryce = new Human( name: "Bryce",  age: 38,  height: 1.72f);
37
38           System.out.println(
39           System.out.println(
40           System.out.println(
41
42           int timeToLive = br
43           System.out.println(
44       }
45   }
46
```

'Human' is abstract; cannot be instantiated

Implement methods ⌥⇧↵   More actions... ⌥↵

ⓒ com.apress.bgn.four.classes.Human

```
@Contract(pure = true) ↗
public Human(
    String name,
    int age,
    float height
)
```

⌷ chapter04   ✎ ⋮

Figure 4-6. *Java compiler error when trying to instantiate an abstract class*

Yes, that is a compile error. Constructors can be kept, as they can help further in abstracting behavior. Classes Musician and Actor must be rewritten to extend the Human class. This is done by using the extends keyword when declaring the class and specifying the class to be extended, also called the **parent class** or **superclass.** The resulting class is called a **subclass**.

Important   When extending a class, the subclass inherits all the fields and concrete methods declared in the superclass. (Access to them is defined by access modifiers, covered in **Chapter 3**.) The exception are abstract methods, for which the subclass is forced to provide a concrete implementation—unless the subclass is abstract too, of course.

Important   The subclass must declare its own constructors that make use of the ones declared in the superclass. The constructors from the superclass are called using the keyword `super`. The same goes for methods and fields, unless they have an access modifier that prohibits access. Can you guess which one it is? It is `private`. A subclass cannot access private members of the superclass. If you did not know the answer, you might want to review **Chapter 3**.

Listing 4-29 depicts a version of the `Musician` class that is written by making use of abstraction and inheritance.

Listing 4-29. Musician Class That Extends Human

```
package com.apress.bgn.four.classes;

import java.util.List;

public class Musician extends Human {
    private String musicSchool;
    private String genre;
    private List<String> songs;

    public Musician(String name, int age, float height,
                    String musicSchool, String genre) {
        super(name, age, height);
        this.musicSchool = musicSchool;
        this.genre = genre;
    }

    @Override
    public int getTimeToLive() {
        return (LIFESPAN - getAge()) / 2;
    }

    // getters and setters omitted
}
```

The songs field was not used as a parameter in the constructor for simplicity reasons.

As you can see, the Musician constructor calls the constructor in the superclass to set the properties defined there, using the super(..) invocation. Also notice the full implementation provided for the getTimeToLive() method.

Note   Here is a fun fact about the super(..) invocation. Until version 21, in Java you were not allowed to put any other statement before this invocation, which made it difficult to use a constructor in a subclass to perform some initializations or validations before the actual construction of the instance.

For example, let's try to add a constructor without parameters for the Musician shown in Listing 4-29, that invokes the methods in a class named DataGenerator to generate random values use to populate fields inherited from the Human, and it does that right before calling super(..). Figure 4-7 shows the error that IntelliJ IDEA would show if the project were to be compiled with JDK 17.

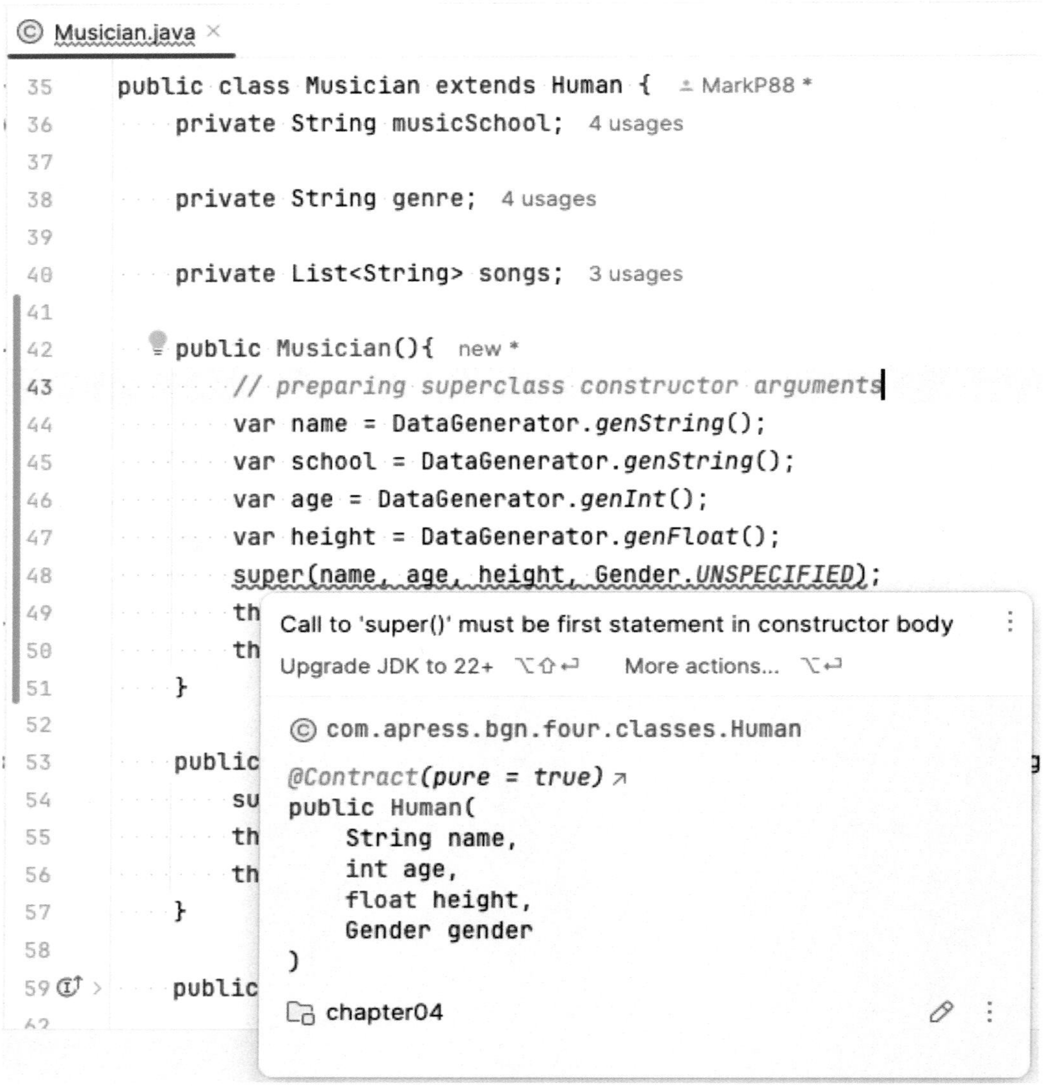

Figure 4-7. *IntelliJ IDEA compiling Java 22 sources with JDK 17, showing statements not allowed before the super(..) invocation*

The DataGenerator class is very simple and generates values based on a pseudo-random number generator (PRNG) instance. This instance is obtained by invoking RandomGenerator.of("SecureRandom"). The java.util.random.RandomGenerator interface was introduced in Java 17 to provide a common protocol for objects that generate random or (more typically) pseudo-random sequences of numbers (or Boolean values). Internally, an instance of `java.util.random.RandomGeneratorFactory` enables creation of various PRNGs, many of which are in the `jdk.random` package.

You can see the implementation of the data generator methods in class DataGenerator in Listing 4-30.

Listing 4-30. Data Generator Methods Using JDK 17 RandomGenerator

```java
package com.apress.bgn.four.classes;

import java.nio.charset.Charset;
import java.util.random.RandomGenerator;

public class DataGenerator {
    static RandomGenerator randomGenerator = RandomGenerator.
    of("SecureRandom");

    public static String genString() {
        byte[] array = new byte[7];
        randomGenerator.nextBytes(array);
        return new String(array, Charset.defaultCharset());
    }

    public static float genFloat() {
        return randomGenerator.nextFloat();
    }

    public static int genInt() {
        return randomGenerator.nextInt();
    }
}
```

The argument of the `RandomGenerator.of(String)` method is the algorithm name of the PRNG. The JDK contains many PRNG classes, which replace the `java.util.Random` class that has been part of the JDK since version 1.0. The `RandomGenerator` interface contains many methods, such as `nextLong()`, `nextInt()`, `nextDouble()`, `nextFloat()`, and `nextBoolean()`, to generate a random number of various primitive data types. Generating a `String` value is done by generating an array of bytes using `nextBytes(byte[])` and using it as an argument for the `String(byte[])` constructor.

Listing 4-31 shows how the new `Musician` constructor looks.

Listing 4-31. Constructor with Statements Before super(..) Invocation

```
package com.apress.bgn.four.classes;

import java.util.List;

public class Musician extends Human {
    private String musicSchool;
    private String genre;
    private List<String> songs;

    public Musician() {
        // -- preparing superclass constructor arguments
        var name = DataGenerator.genString();
        var school = DataGenerator.genString();
        var age = DataGenerator.genInt();
        var height = DataGenerator.genFloat();
        // ---
        super(name, age, height);
        this.musicSchool = DataGenerator.genString();
        this.genre = "undefined";
    }
    // other members omitted
}
```

The Actor class can be rewritten to extend the abstract Human class too. There is a proposal implementation in the sources for this book, but try to write your own before looking in the classes package.

Figure 4-8 depicts the Human class hierarchy as generated by IntelliJ IDEA. Methods are omitted to keep the image simple.

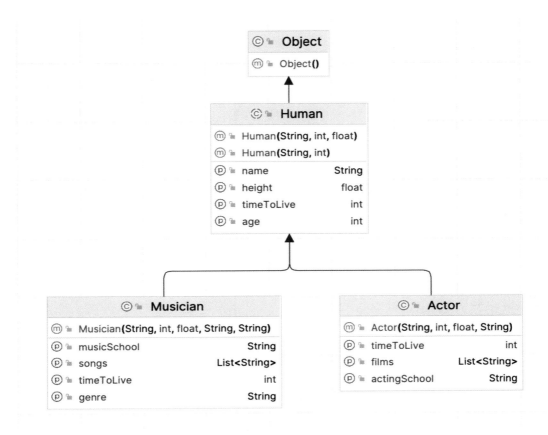

Figure 4-8. *UML diagram generated by IntelliJ IDEA*

The UML diagram clearly shows the members of each class, and the arrows point to the superclass. UML diagrams are useful tools in designing component hierarchies and defining logic of applications. If you want to read more about them, and the many types of UML diagrams that there are, there is plenty of information on the Internet freely available[4].

After covering so much about classes and how to create objects, we need to cover other important Java components that can be used to create even more detailed objects. Our Human class is missing quite a few attributes, such as gender. A field that models the gender of a person can only have values from a fixed set of values. It used to be limited to two, but in today's world we cannot limit the set of values for genders to two, so we will

---

[4] See, e.g., https://www.uml-diagrams.org

introduce a third, called UNSPECIFIED, that is to be used as a replacement for whatever a person identifies as. This means that we have to introduce a new class to represent gender that can only be instantiated thrice. This would be quite tricky to do with a typical class, which is why enums were introduced in Java version 1.5.

Enums

The enum type is a special class type. It is used to define a special type of class that can be instantiated only a fixed number of times. An enum declaration groups together all instances of that enum. All of them are constants. So the Gender enum can be defined as shown in Listing 4-32.

Listing 4-32. Gender Enum

```
package com.apress.bgn.four.classes;

public enum Gender {
    FEMALE,
    MALE,
    UNSPECIFIED
}
```

An enum cannot be instantiated externally. An enum is by default final, thus it cannot be extended. Remember how by default every class in Java implicitly extends class Object? Every enum in Java implicitly extends the abstract class java.lang. Enum<E>, and in doing so, every enum instance inherits special methods that are useful when writing code using enums.

Being a special type of class, an enum can have fields and a constructor that can only be private, as enum instances cannot be created externally. The private modifier is not needed explicitly, as the compiler knows what to do. Listing 4-33 shows the Gender enum implemented by adding an integer field that will be the numerical representation of each gender and a String field that will be the text representation. Of course, to access the enum properties, getters are needed.

Listing 4-33. A More Complex Gender Enum

```java
package com.apress.bgn.four.classes;

public enum Gender {
    FEMALE(1, "f"),
    MALE(2, "m"),
    UNSPECIFIED(3, "u");

    private int repr;
    private String descr;

    private Gender(int repr, String descr) {
        this.repr = repr;
        this.descr = descr;
    }

    public int getRepr() {
        return repr;
    }

    public String getDescr() {
        return descr;
    }
}
```

Warning   But wait, what would stop us from declaring setters as well and modifying the field values? Well, nothing. If that is what you need to do, you can do it, **but this is not a good practice** (it is actually really bad).

Enum instances should be constant. So, a correct enum design should not declare setters, and should make sure the values of the fields will never be changed by declaring them final. When we do so, the only way the fields are initialized is by calling the constructor, and since the constructor cannot be called externally, the integrity of our data is ensured. An example of a good enum design is depicted in Listing 4-34.

Listing 4-34. Proper Gender Enum

```java
package com.apress.bgn.four.classes;

public enum Gender {
    FEMALE(1, "f"),
    MALE(2, "m"),
    UNSPECIFIED(3, "u");

    private final int repr;
    private final String descr;

    private Gender(int repr, String descr) {
        this.repr = repr;
        this.descr = descr;
    }

    public int getRepr() {
        return repr;
    }

    public String getDescr() {
        return descr;
    }
}
```

Methods can be added to enums, and each instance can override them. So if we add a method called comment() to the Gender enum, every instance will inherit it. But the instance can override it, as depicted in Listing 4-35.

Listing 4-35. Code Sample Listing Enum Items Classes

```java
package com.apress.bgn.four.classes;

public enum Gender {
    FEMALE(1, "f"),
    MALE(2, "m"),
    UNSPECIFIED(3, "u") {
        @Override
```

```
        public String comment() {
            return "to be decided later: " + getRepr() + ", " + getDescr();
        }
    };

    private final int repr;
    private final String descr;

    Gender(int repr, String descr) {
        this.repr = repr;
        this.descr = descr;
    }

    // getters omitted

    public String comment() {
        return repr + ": " + descr;
    }
}
```

Important   So, how can an instance possibly override a method of its class type?
It can't. The UNSPECIFIED enum value is actually an instance of a class that
extends the Gender class and overrides the comment() method.

This can be easily proven by iterating over the enum values and printing the result
returned by the getClass() method, inherited from the Object class that returns the
runtime type of the object. To get all the instances of an enum, the class java.lang.
Enum<E>, which every enum extends implicitly, provides a method named values().
Listing 4-36 shows the code that does that and its output too.

Listing 4-36. Proper Gender Enum with Extra Method

```
package com.apress.bgn.four.classes;

public class BasicHumanDemo {
    public static void main(String... args) {
        for (Gender value : Gender.values()) {
            System.out.println(value.name() + ": " + value.getClass());
```

```
        System.out.println("\tcomment : " + value.comment());
      }
    }
}
// output expected in the console
/*
FEMALE: class com.apress.bgn.four.classes.Gender
    comment : 1: f
MALE: class com.apress.bgn.four.classes.Gender
    comment : 2: m
UNSPECIFIED: class com.apress.bgn.four.classes.Gender$1
    comment : to be decided later: 3, u
*/
```

Notice the value printed for the UNSPECIFIED element. The Gender$1 notation means that the compiler created an inner class by extending the original enum class and overriding the comment() method with the one provided in the declaration of the UNSPECIFIED element.

We're going to be playing with enums in future examples as well. Just remember that whenever you need to limit the implementation of a class to a fixed number of instances, or group related constants together, enums are the tools to use. Now that we have introduced enums, our Human class can have a field of type Gender, as depicted in Listing 4-37.

Listing 4-37. Human Class with a Gender Field

```
package com.apress.bgn.four.classes;

public abstract class Human {
    public static final int LIFESPAN = 100;
    protected String name;
    protected int age;
    protected float height;

    private Gender gender;
```

```java
    public Human(String name, int age, Gender gender) {
        this.name = name;
        this.age = age;
        this.gender = gender;
    }

    public Human(String name, int age, float height, Gender gender) {
        this(name, age, gender);
        this.height = height;
    }

    // other code omitted

    public Gender getGender() {
        return gender;
    }

    public void setGender(Gender gender) {
        this.gender = gender;
    }
}
```

In the previous sections **interfaces** were mentioned as one of the Java components used to create objects. It is high time we expand the subject.

Interfaces

Important   One of the most common job interview questions for prospective Java programmer is *What is the difference between an interface and an abstract class?* This section will provide you the most detailed answer to this question.

An **interface** is not a class, but it does help create classes. An interface is fully abstract, meaning that it has no fields, only abstract method definitions. I also like to call them *skeletons*. When a class is declared to implement an interface, unless the class is abstract, it must provide concrete implementations for all skeleton methods.

> **Important**   The name *skeleton method* is quite important in Java 8+ versions, because from this version on, interfaces are enriched so that `static`, `default`, and `private` methods can be part them.

Skeleton methods inside an interface are implicitly `public` and `abstract`, because skeleton methods must be abstract to force classes to provide implementations and must be public so that classes actually have access to do so.

The only methods with concrete implementation in an interface until Java 8 were `static` methods. In Java 8, *default* methods in interfaces were introduced. In Java 9 **private** methods in interfaces were introduced. The interfaces cannot be instantiated, because they do not have constructors.

Interfaces that declare no method definitions are called *marker* interfaces and have the purpose to mark classes for specific purposes. The most renown Java marker interface is `java.io.Serializable`, which marks objects that can be serialized, so their state can be saved to a binary file or another data source and sent over a network to be deserialized and used.

An interface can be declared in its own file as a top-level component or nested inside another component. There are two types of interfaces: *normal* interfaces and **annotations**.

The difference between abstract classes and interfaces and when one or the other should be used becomes relevant in the context of **inheritance**.

> **Important**   Java supports only single inheritance. This means a class can have only one superclass.

Single inheritance might seem like a limitation, but consider the following example. Let's modify the previous hierarchy and imagine a class named `Performer` that should extend classes `Musician` and `Actor`. If you need a real human that can be modeled by this class, think of David Duchovny, who is both an actor and a musician.

Figure 4-9 depicts the class hierarchy mentioned previously.

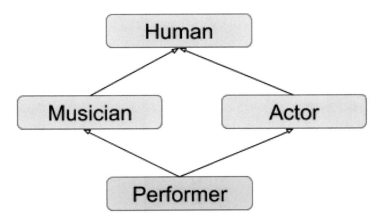

Figure 4-9. *Diamond class hierarchy*

This class hierarchy introduces something called the *diamond problem,* and the name is obviously inspired by the shape formed by the relationships between classes. What is actually wrong with the design? If both Musician and Actor extend Human and inherit all members from it, what will Performer inherit and from where? Because it obviously cannot inherit members of Human twice, that would make this class useless and invalid. And how could we discern between methods with the same signature? So what is the solution in Java? As you probably imagine, considering the focus of this section: interfaces. *(Well, sort of, because most times a combination of interfaces and a programming concept named* **composition** *is required.)*

What has to be done is to turn methods in classes Musician and Actor into method skeletons and transform those classes into interfaces. The behavior from the Musician class will be moved to a class called, let's say Guitarist, that will extend the Human class and implement the Musician interface. For the Actor class, something similar can be done, but I'll leave that as an exercise for you. The hierarchy in Figure 4-10 should provide some help.

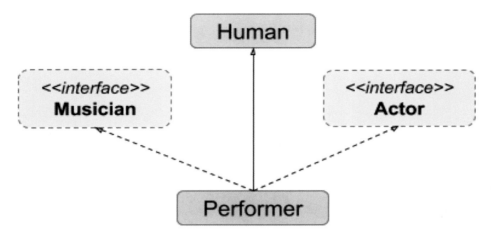

Figure 4-10. *Java hierarchy with interfaces for* Performer *class*

So the Musician interface contains only method skeletons mapping what a musician does. It does not go into detail to model how. The same goes for the Actor interface. In Listing 4-38, you can see the bodies of the two interfaces.

Listing 4-38. Musician and Actor Interfaces

```
package com.apress.bgn.four.interfaces;

import java.util.List;

interface Musician {
    String getMusicSchool();

    void setMusicSchool(String musicSchool);

    List<String> getSongs();

    void setSongs(List<String> songs);

    String getGenre();

    void setGenre(String genre);
}

interface Actor {
    String getActingSchool();

    void setActingSchool(String actingSchool);
```

```
    List<String> getFilms();

    void setFilms(List<String> films);

    void addFilm(String filmName);
}
```

As you can see, the fields have been removed because they cannot be part of the interfaces; only the method skeletons remain.

Note   In some of the code samples, more classes are declared in a single file that is named after the only public class in it. This choice was made because these classes have small bodies, and it made no sense to spread them into multiple files.

The Performer class is depicted in Listing 4-39.

Listing 4-39. Performer Class Implementing Two Interfaces

```
package com.apress.bgn.four.interfaces;

import com.apress.bgn.four.classes.Gender;
import com.apress.bgn.four.classes.Human;

import java.util.List;

public class Performer extends Human implements Musician, Actor {

    // fields specific to musician
    private String musicSchool;
    private String genre;
    private List<String> songs;

    // fields specific to actor
    private String actingSchool;
    private List<String> films;

    public Performer(String name, int age, float height, Gender gender) {
        super(name, age, height, gender);
    }
```

```java
    // from Human
    @Override
    public int getTimeToLive() {
        return (LIFESPAN - getAge()) / 2;
    }

    // from Musician
    @Override
    public String getMusicSchool() {
        return musicSchool;
    }

    // from Musician
    @Override
    public void setMusicSchool(String musicSchool) {
        this.musicSchool = musicSchool;
    }

    // from Actor
    @Override
    public String getActingSchool() {
        return actingSchool;
    }

    // from Actor
    @Override
    public void setActingSchool(String actingSchool) {
        this.actingSchool = actingSchool;
    }

    // other methods omitted
}
```

Important   What you must take from this example is that by using interfaces, multiple inheritance is possible in Java to some extent, and that **classes extend only one class and can implement one or more interfaces**.

There might be situations in which you need to write a class that implements multiple interfaces that might declare similar method skeletons. If the method skeletons have identical signatures, the solution is simple: only one implementation suffices. If the signatures differ enough, one implementation for each is necessary.

If the skeletons are similar enough to confuse the compiler, better avoid the inheritance and opt for solutions such as composition.

Inheritance applies to interfaces too. For example, both `Musician` and `Actor` interfaces can extend an interface named `Artist` that contains a template for behavior common to both. For example, we can combine the music school and acting school into a generic school and define the setters and getters for it as method skeletons. The `Artist` interface is depicted in Listing 4-40 together with `Musician`.

Listing 4-40. Artist and Musician Interfaces

```
package com.apress.bgn.four.interfaces;

import java.util.List;

interface Artist {
    String getSchool();

    void setSchool(String school);
}

interface Musician extends Artist {
    List<String> getSongs();

    void setSongs(List<String> songs);

    String getGenre();

    void setGenre(String genre);
}
```

Hopefully, you understood the idea of multiple inheritance and when it is appropriate to use classes and when to use interfaces in designing your applications, because it is high time to fulfil the promise made in the beginning of this section and list the differences between abstract classes and interfaces. You can find them in Table 4-1.

Table 4-1. *Differences Between Abstract Classes and Interfaces in Java*

Abstract Class	Interface
Can have nonabstract methods.	Can have only abstract, default, and private methods.
Single inheritance: a class can extend only one class.	Multiple inheritance: a class can implement more than one interface. Also, an interface can extend one or more interfaces.
Can have final, nonfinal, static, and nonstatic variables.	Can have only static and final fields.
Declared with **abstract class**.	Declared with **interface**.
Can extend another class using keyword **extends** and implement interfaces with keyword **implements**.	Can only extend other interfaces (one or more) using keyword **extends**.
Can have nonabstract, protected, or private members.	All members are by default abstract and public (except default and private methods).
If a class has an abstract method, it must be declared itself abstract.	(No correspondence.)

Default Methods in Interfaces

One problem with interfaces is that if you modify their bodies to add new methods, the code will stop compiling. To make it compile, you have to add a concrete implementation for the newly added interface method(s) in every class that implements that interface. This has been a pain for developers for many years. An interface is a contract that guarantees how a class will behave. When using third-party libraries in your project, you do so by designing your code to respect those contracts. When switching to a new version of a library, if that contract changes, your code will no longer compile.

Tip   This situation is very similar to Apple changing the charging ports for their computers and phones from one version to another. If you buy a new Mac and try to use your old charger, it won't fit.

Sure, a solution would be to declare the new methods in a new interface and then create new classes that implement both new and old interfaces (this is called **composition**, because the two interfaces are composed to represent a single contract). The methods exposed by an interface make up an application programming interface (API), and when developing applications, the aim is to design them to have stable APIs. This rule is described by a programming principle called Open-Closed Principle, which is one of the five SOLID Programming Principles [5]. This principle states that you should be able to extend a class without modifying it. Thus, modifying the interface that a class implements requires modifying the class too. So, modifying interfaces tends to lead to breaking this principle.

Aside from interfaces composition mentioned previously, in Java 8 a solution for this was introduced: **default methods**. Starting with Java 8, methods with a full implementation can be declared in interfaces as long as they are declared using the `default` keyword.

Let's consider the `Artist` interface. Any self-proclaimed artist should be able to create something, right? So an artist should have a creative nature. Given the world we are living in, I won't mention names, but some artists are actually products of the industry, so they are not creative themselves. So, the realization that we should have a method that tells us if an artist has a creative nature or not came after we decided our hierarchy depicted in Figure 4-11.

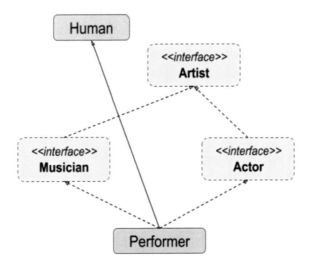

Figure 4-11. *Java hierarchy with more interfaces for* `Performer` *class*

---

[5] https://hackernoon.com/solid-principles-made-easy-67b1246bcdf

If we add a new abstract method to the `Artist` interface, the `Performer` class fails to compile. IntelliJ IDEA will make it really obvious that our application does not work anymore by showing a lot of things underlined in red, as depicted in Figure 4-12.

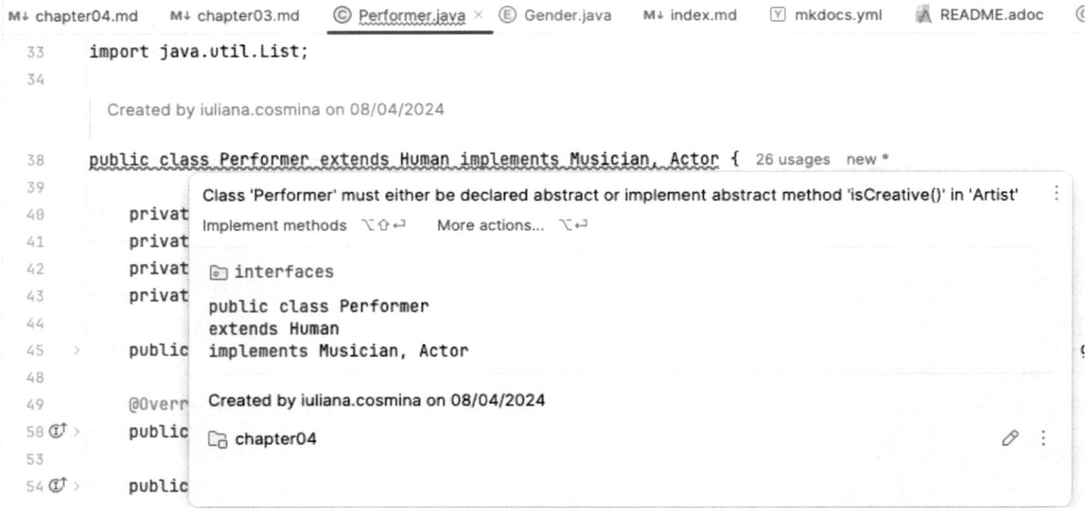

Figure 4-12. *Java broken hierarchy because of new method in interface*

The compiler errors that we see are caused by our decision to add a new abstract method named `isCreative` to the `Artist` interface, and if you hover your mouse cursor over the class declaration, you can even see why. Listing 4-41 depicts the abstract method breaking the code.

Listing 4-41. New Skeleton Method Added to the `Artist` Interface

```java
package com.apress.bgn.four.hierarchy;

public interface Artist {
    String getSchool();

    void setSchool(String school);

    boolean isCreative();
}
```

To get rid of the compiling errors, we'll transform the `isCreative` method skeleton into a `default` method that returns `true`, because every artist should be creative. Default methods are by default public, so they can be called on every object of a type implementing the interface where the method is declared. Listing 4-42 depicts the body of the default method.

Listing 4-42. New `default` Method Added to the `Artist` Interface

```java
package com.apress.bgn.four.hierarchy;

public interface Artist {
    String getSchool();

    void setSchool(String school);

    default boolean isCreative() {
        return true;
    }
}
```

Now the code should compile again. Default methods are pretty practical, as they allow the modification of the contract represented by an interface without enforcing modification of existing classes implementing that interface. This will ensure binary compatibility with code written for older versions of that interface.

Classes that implement an interface containing a default method can use the existing default implementation or provide a new implementation for default methods (can override them). To show this, the class named `MiliVanili` in Listing 4-43 provides a new implementation for the default method in the `Artist` interface.

Listing 4-43. Default Method Being Overridden in Class Implementing the `Artist` Interface

```java
package com.apress.bgn.four.hierarchy;

import java.util.List;

public class MiliVanili implements Artist {
```

```
@Override
public boolean isCreative() {
    return false; // dooh!
}

// other code omitted
}
```

Interfaces extending other interfaces can be written to do any of the following (for a little more clarity, the extended interface will be referred to as the super-interface):

- Declare their own abstract methods and default methods.

- Redeclare the default method from the super-interface as an abstract method, which forces classes extending this interface to provide an implementation.

- Redefine the default method from the super-interface.

- Declare a default method that provides an implementation for an abstract method from the super-interface.

Tip   Providing code samples for all these scenarios would be a bit too much for a Java absolute beginner book. If you are interested in seeing what the code looks like and testing the validity of these affirmations, check out the contents of the `com.ampress.bgn.four.interfaces.extensions` package.

Static Methods and Constants in Interfaces

From Java version 1 up to version 8, interfaces could only contain abstract methods and static constants. Interfaces changed in version 8, with the most important changes being the support for `default` and `private` methods.

Constants, or variables that never change once initialized, do not need an implementation, so it makes sense for developers to be allowed to declare them in an interface's body, right? Of course, you can do the same using enums, but sometimes you might want to keep related components together. In a previous example a LIFESPAN constant was declared in the Human class. Since any class implementing Artist will probably need the LIFESPAN for some calculation or another, we can move this constant in the Artist interface and use it in any class, as depicted in Listing 4-44.

Listing 4-44. The Constant LIFESPAN in the Artist Interface

```
package com.apress.bgn.four.hierarchy;

interface Artist {
    public static final int LIFESPAN = 100;

    // other code omitted
}

public class Performer extends Human implements Musician, Actor {

    @Override
    public int getTimeToLive() {
        return (LIFESPAN - getAge()) / 2;
    }

    // other code omitted
}
```

When declaring constants in interfaces, the three accessors public, static, and final are redundant, because they are implied. The explanation for each is quite simple:

- Interfaces cannot have mutable fields, so by default they have to be final.

- Since interfaces cannot be instantiated, they cannot have fields that will become properties on instances, so they have to be static.

- Since anything in an interface body must be accessible to implementing classes, they have to be public.

As for static methods in interfaces, they are usually utility methods that are specific to certain operations within the hierarchy the interface is part of. Let's add a static method that checks if the name provided as an argument is capitalized, and capitalizes it if it isn't.

The code is depicted in Listing 4-45, where the method capitalize is declared in the Artist interface and used in the Performer class.

Listing 4-45. Public Static Method in Interface

```
package com.apress.bgn.four.hierarchy;

interface Artist {
    public static String capitalize(String name) {
        Character c = name.charAt(0);
        if (Character.isLowerCase(c)) {
            Character upperC = Character.toUpperCase(c);
            name.replace(c, upperC);
        }
        return name;
    }

    // other code omitted
}

public class Performer extends Human implements Musician, Actor {

    public String getCapitalizedName() {
        return Artist.capitalize(this.name);
    }

    // other code omitted
}
```

In Java 8, any method with a body that was not declared as default had to be declared public and static, because of the reasons mentioned previously. If default or static methods share a lot of code, then a default or static method can group that code and have the others call it, right? The only problem appears when there is a need for that code to be private. That was not possible in Java 8, because everything in the body of an interface was public by default. But it became possible in Java 9.

Private Methods in Interfaces

Starting with Java 9, support for private and private static methods in interfaces was introduced. The reason behind this decision was (as you can probably imagine) to promote code reusability within interfaces and encapsulation of code that should not be shared across implementations of the interface. This means that the action performed by the default `isCreative()` method can be modified to also log an explanation for the returned value, by calling a `private` method. And just to make this example complete, let's add in a `private static` method printing the current system date, as shown in Listing 4-46.

Listing 4-46. New private Method Added to the Artist Interface

```java
package com.apress.bgn.four.hierarchy;

interface Artist {

  default boolean isCreative() {
    explain();
    return true;
  }

  private void explain() {
    log();
    System.out.println("A true artist has a creative nature.");
  }

  private static void log() {
    System.out.println("[LOG] checked creativity on: " + new Date());
  }

  /**
   * Yes this is allowed and you can run this. ;)
   */
  public static void main() {
    Artist artist =  new Performer("Myles Kennedy", 54, 1.8F, Gender.MALE);
    artist.isCreative();
  }
}
// output
//[LOG] checked creativity on: Wed May 08 17:45:15 BST 2024
//A true artist has a creative nature.
```

Here are a few last thoughts about private interface methods:

- Private methods are only accessible within the interfaces they are declared in, and thus should be written to contain sensitive code, which you do not want accessed by any other class or interface.

- Being private, they cannot be inherited, nor overridden.

- A consequence of this is that private methods cannot be abstract.

When doing development on a concrete project, you will find yourself using classes, interfaces, enums, and others. It is up to you how you design and organize your code. Just make sure to avoid repetition and keep it clean, uncoupled, and testable.

Records

The Java `record` is a special type of class with a clear syntax for defining immutable data-only classes. The Java compiler takes the code of your record and generates constructors, getters, and other specialized methods such as `toString()`, `hashCode()`, and `equals()`.

Information   The `hashCode()` and `equals()` specialized methods are defined in the `Object` class, and thus they are implicitly defined in every Java class. They are very important in establishing the identity of an instance and will be covered in **Chapter 5**, in the **Collections** section.

Java records were introduced in JDK 14 as a preview feature, long after similar types of constructs were introduced in other programming languages as C#, Scala, or Kotlin. Java developers avoided the hassle of writing a lot of boilerplate code by using libraries such as Lombok. Lombok was already mentioned in the **Encapsulating Data** section of this chapter, where some disadvantages of using it were listed too.

Lombok requires annotating classes with special annotations that tell its annotation processor to generate the desired bytecode at compile time. It works for generation of all the components now supported using Java records.

Listing 4-47 shows how the Human class would be written using Lombok.

Listing 4-47. Human Class—the Lombok Version

```
package com.apress.bgn.four.lombok;

import com.apress.bgn.four.classes.Gender;
import lombok.*;

@NoArgsConstructor
@AllArgsConstructor
@RequiredArgsConstructor
@ToString
@EqualsAndHashCode
public class Human {
    @Getter
    @Setter
    @NonNull
    private String name;

    @Getter
    @Setter
    @NonNull
    private int age;

    @Getter
    @Setter
    private float height;

    @Getter
    @Setter
    private Gender gender;
}
```

Another issue with Lombok is that it becomes unpredictable in a Java project using modules. Manipulating code at compile time to inject extra functionalities is a sensitive operation that requires access to JDK internals that might not be exported for security reasons. For example, when writing the previous edition of this book, compiling the project using Lombok didn't work because Lombok required access to class `com.sun.tools.javac.processing.JavacProcessingEnvironment` from module `jdk.compiler` that did not export the `com.sun.tools.javac.processing` package.

Without Lombok, the class in Listing 4-47 would have a lot more lines, because all the annotations in code snippets replace methods that the developer should write otherwise:

- `@NoArgsConstructor` tells Lombok to generate the bytecode for a default no-arguments constructor for the `Human` class.

- `@AllArgsConstructor` tells Lombok to generate the bytecode for a constructor requiring an argument for each field of the `Human` class.

- `@RequiredArgsConstructor` tells Lombok to generate the bytecode for a constructor requiring an argument for all required fields (the ones annotated with `@NotNull`).

- `@ToString` tells Lombok to generate the bytecode for the `toString()` method. The implementation of this method is decided by `Lombok` based on all the fields in the class.

- `@EqualsAndHashCode` tells Lombok to generate the bytecode for the `equals()` and `hashCode()` methods. The implementation of these methods is decided by Lombok based on all the fields in the class.

With the introduction of records, Lombok is no longer needed as long as the project is being compiled and run using JDK 15+. And you don't need your instances to be immutable. The classes generated by the JDK are immutable data-only classes, so there are no setters, but in the brave new world of reactivity, having immutable records is a must anyway. The `record` implementation of the Human class is shown in Listing 4-48 together with the code necessary to instantiate a Human.

Listing 4-48. Simple Human Record and Class Where Used

```
package com.apress.bgn.four.records;

import com.apress.bgn.four.classes.Gender;

record Human(String name, int age, float height, Gender gender) {
}

public class RecordDemo {

    public static void main(String... args) {
        Human john = new Human("John Mayer", 47, 1.9f, Gender.MALE);
```

```
        System.out.println("John as string: " + john);
        System.out.println("John's hashCode: " + john.hashCode());
        System.out.println("John's name: " + john.name());
    }
}
```

As you can see, records can be instantiated in the same way classes are, by calling a constructor using the new keyword. After all, records are just another type of classes. Also, since there is no need for setters, because the objects are immutable, getters don't make much sense either. So to access the property values, methods with the same name as the field are generated that return the field value. This can be confirmed by viewing the bytecode in the generated Human.class file using IntelliJ IDEA. Just look for this file in the chapter04/target/classes directory, select it, and from the menu select **View ➤ Show Bytecode**. A window should pop up with contents pretty similar to the ones shown in Figure 4-13.

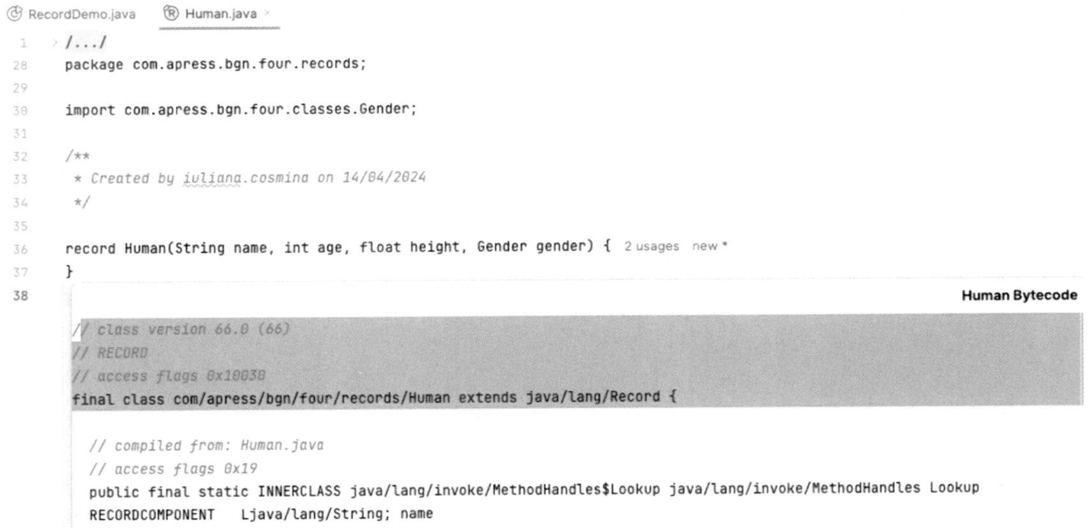

Figure 4-13. *Bytecode of the Human record*

From the bytecode we can figure out yet another important thing about records: the class being shown in the bytecode is final, thus records cannot be extended. Creation of sub-records is not possible. Also, all record classes implicitly extend class java.lang.Record.

Running the main(..) method in the RecordDemo class yields the results shown in Listing 4-49.

Listing 4-49. Results Printed by Execution of the RecordDemo Class

```
John as string: Human[name=John Mayer, age=44,height=1.9,gender=MALE]
John's hashCode: 1711330636
John's name: John Mayer
```

The toString() implementation of a record is decent enough. The values of the properties of the john instance can be read and understood easily.

Records can be customized. Nothing stops you from providing a custom implementation for the toString(), equals(), and hashCode() methods and providing various constructors in the record body, in the same way you would do it for a class. The only catch is that the constructor must call the default constructor of the record using the this keyword. Listing 4-50 shows a constructor being added that only requires name and age.

Listing 4-50. Simple Human Record with an Additional Constructor

```java
package com.apress.bgn.four.records;

import com.apress.bgn.four.classes.Gender;

record Human(String name, int age, float height, Gender gender) {

    public Human(String name, int age) {
        this(name, age, -0f, null);

    }
}
```

Since the default constructor and other methods generated for a record rely on the arguments of the record, no extra fields can be declared in a record's body. However, static variables and methods are supported. Figure 4-14 depicts a record with an extra constant and a field declared in its body (and the editor doesn't like the latter).

```
®  Human.java ×

 1    > /.../
28       package com.apress.bgn.four.records;

29

30       import com.apress.bgn.four.classes.Gender;

31

         Created by iuliana.cosmina on 14/04/2024

35       record Human(String name, int age, float height, Gender gender) {  2 usages  new *

36

37           public static final int LIFESPAN = 100;  no usages

38

39           private String notAllowedField;  no usages

40                          ┌─────────────────────────────────────────────────────────┐
41           public Human(St│  Instance field is not allowed in record              ⋮ │
42               this(name, │  Make 'notAllowedField' static  ⌥⇧↵    More actions...  ⌥↵│
43           }              │                                                          │
44       }                  │  © com.apress.bgn.four.records.Human                     │
45                          │  private String notAllowedField                          │
                           │                                                          │
                           │  ⌕ chapter04                                      ✎  ⋮  │
                           └─────────────────────────────────────────────────────────┘
```

Figure 4-14. *Record with constant and field*

Records are pretty practical when data immutability is a requirement, which is...most of the time (e.g., data transfer objects [DTOs] used to transfer data between software application subsystems). It can be done without records, but it requires a lot of effort from the developer—effort that old-school developers like me were doing whenever necessary. *You youngsters have no idea how easy you have it nowadays!*

Sealed Classes and Interfaces

Sealed classes and interfaces were a preview feature introduced in JDK 15 and finalized in Java 17. They were introduced to solve the problem of choosing the right scope modifier for developers' classes and interfaces and to allow them to control which code is responsible for implementing them, thus allowing for better security.

Security is always a concern, and for some projects, when classes need to be extended, making them public or protected is a risk. This is where the `sealed` modifier and its entire family should come in handy. It allows developers to `seal` a class to prevent it from being extended, except for a few subclasses declared using the `permits` keyword. Sure, the superclass seems to be doomed to be updated many times when new subclasses are added to the project, but it is an acceptable trade-off to have a better secured application. Taking this into consideration, let's seal a version of our RecordDemo class and permit only class Performer to extend it. Listing 4-51 depicts the two classes.

Listing 4-51. Sealed Class and Allowed Subclass

```java
// Human.java
package com.apress.bgn.four.sealed.one;

import com.apress.bgn.four.classes.Gender;

// Human.java
public sealed class Human
        permits Performer {
    protected String name;

    protected int age;

    protected float height;

    // other code omitted
}

// Performer.java
package com.apress.bgn.four.sealed.one;

import com.apress.bgn.four.classes.Gender;

public final class Performer extends Human {
    // other code omitted
}
```

If the extending classes are declared in the same source file, there is no need to list them after the permits keyword. If there are no extending classes outside the file, the permits keyword can be omitted altogether.

Classes allowed to extend sealed classes should be sealed or final themselves. If we need one of those classes to allow being extended by unknown classes, the non-sealed modifier allows that. Listing 4-52 shows the class Engineer that is declared non-sealed; of course, this class must be added to the list in the permits directive from the RecordDemo class.

Listing 4-52. non-sealed Class That Extends a sealed Class

```
package com.apress.bgn.four.sealed.one;

import com.apress.bgn.four.classes.Gender;

public non-sealed class Engineer extends Human {
    public Engineer(String name, int age, Gender gender) {
        super(name, age, gender);
    }

    public Engineer(String name, int age, float height, Gender gender) {
        super(name, age, height, gender);
    }
}
```

The sealed modifier can be applied to interfaces as well. The permits keyword specifies the classes that are permitted to implement the sealed interface.

Caution   You would expect the permits keyword to also support interfaces that extend the sealed interface, but in the current version of JDK it doesn't. *(You can try it if you want.)*

Important   The same rule applies for sealed interfaces as well: classes implementing a sealed interface are expected to be sealed, non-sealed, or final.

Listing 4-53 shows the sealed Mammal interface, which is implemented by the sealed Human class.

Listing 4-53. sealed Mammal Interface and the Sealed Human Class

```
package com.apress.bgn.four.sealed.two;

public sealed interface Mammal permits Human {
}
```

```
public sealed class Human
        implements Mammal
        permits Performer, Engineer {
    // rest of the code omitted
}
```

Important   A limitation of sealed classes and interfaces is that any subclasses and implementing classes need to be in the same module.

Also, in case it wasn't obvious, any classes present after the `permits` keyword must extend the sealed class/implement the sealed interface. If a class is specified after the `permits` keyword and does not extend the sealed class/implement the sealed interface, the compiler won't like it.

Sealed classes are a good for records, since records are by default final.

Hidden Classes

Hidden classes are an interesting feature for developers working on development frameworks such as Hibernate or Spring, because these frameworks generate code dynamically. The generated classes (or interfaces) cannot be used directly by the bytecode of other classes, since they are destined to be used only internally by the framework. Starting with Java 15, generating dynamic classes that are hidden has become an industry standard.

Hidden classes are not discoverable through a mechanism such as reflection[6]. They are generated dynamically by the framework, they have a short lifespan, and they are discarded when no longer needed, which leads to performance improvement of applications running on a JVM. Since hidden classes are undiscoverable, they cannot be used as a superclass, or as a type for fields or parameters. In case of error, by default, they do not show up in stack traces, but there are JVM options to show them.

Hidden classes are too advanced for a beginner's book, but if you are curious to learn more about them, there is an example in the code for this book—look at the class `HiddenClassDemo`.

---

[6]`https://www.oracle.com/technical-resources/articles/java/javareflection.html`

Annotation Types

An annotation is defined similarly to an interface, the only difference being that the `interface` keyword is preceded by the @ (at) sign. Annotation types are a form of interfaces, and most times are used as markers (look at the previous Lombok example). For example, you've probably noticed the @Override annotation. This annotation is placed on methods generated automatically by intelligent IDEs when classes extend classes or implement interfaces. Its declaration in the JDK is depicted in the code snippet in Listing 4-54.

Listing 4-54. The JDK @Override Declaration

```
package java.lang;

import java.lang.annotation.*;

/**
 * documentation omitted
 */
@Target(ElementType.METHOD)
@Retention(RetentionPolicy.SOURCE)
public @interface Override {
}
```

Annotations that do not declare any property are called **marker** or **informative** annotations. They are needed only to inform other classes in the application, or to inform developers of the purpose of the components they are placed on. They are not mandatory, and the code will compile without them.

Java 8 introduced an annotation named @FunctionalInterface. This annotation was placed on all Java interfaces containing exactly one abstract method, and that can be used in *lambda expressions*.

Lambda Expressions

Lambda expressions were also introduced in Java 8, and they represent a compact and practical way of writing code that was borrowed from languages like Groovy and Ruby. Listing 4-55 depicts the @FunctionalInterface declaration.

199

Listing 4-55. The JDK @FunctionalInterface Declaration

```
package java.lang;

import java.lang.annotation.*;

/**
 * documentation omitted
 */
@Documented
@Retention(RetentionPolicy.RUNTIME)
@Target(ElementType.TYPE)
public @interface FunctionalInterface {
}
```

Functional interfaces are interfaces that declare a single abstract method. Being the only method in the interface, the implementation can be provided on the spot, without the need to create a class to define a concrete implementation. Imagine the following scenario: we create an interface named Operation that contains a single method. We can provide an implementation for this interface by creating a class named Addition, or we can do it on the spot using a lambda expression. Listing 4-56 depicts the Operation interface, the Addition class, and a class named OperationDemo, showing the on-the-spot implementation being declared and used in the main(..) method.

Listing 4-56. Explicit Interface Implementation Compared to Lambda Expression

```
package com.apress.bgn.four.lambda;

@FunctionalInterface
interface Operation {
    int execute(int a, int b);
}

class Addition implements Operation {
    @Override
    public int execute(int a, int b) {
        return a + b;
    }
}
```

```java
public class OperationDemo {
    public static void main(String... args) {
        // using the Addition class
        Addition addition = new Addition();
        int result = addition.execute(2, 5);
        System.out.println("Result is " + result);

        // implementation on the spot using a Lambda Expression
        Operation addition2 = (a, b) -> a + b;
        int result2 = addition2.execute(2, 5);
        System.out.println("Lambda Result is " + result2);
    }
}
```

By using a lambda expression, class Addition is no longer needed, which leads to less and more readable code. Lambda expressions can be used for a lot of things, and we'll cover them more throughout the book whenever code can be written in a more practical way using them.

Note   The Operation instance can be replaced by Integer::sum, a construction named a method reference, introduced in Java 8. As the name indicates, this is a reference to the sum method in class Integer, also introduced in Java 8.

Exceptions

Exceptions are special Java classes that are used to intercept unexpected situations during the execution of a program, enabling the developer to implement the proper course of action based on the type of exception the compiler warns about or the type of exception that gets generated at runtime by the JVM. These classes are organized in a hierarchy that is depicted in Figure 4-15. Throwable is the root class of the hierarchy of classes used to represent unexpected situations in a Java application.

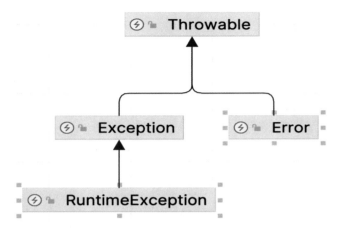

Figure 4-15. *Java exception hierarchy*

Exceptional situations in a Java application can happen for a myriad of reasons, but here are a few common reasons:

- Human error when writing the code

- Hardware issues (trying to read a file from a corrupted data disk)

- Missing resources (trying to read a file that does not exist)

Warning   Sloppy developers, when in doubt, tend to write code that always catches a Throwable. Obviously, you should try to avoid doing that, as class `Error` (a subclass of `Throwable`) is used to notify the developer that a situation the system cannot recover from has happened.

Let's start with a simple example. Listing 4-57 defines a method that calls itself (its technical name is **recursive**), but for purposes of demonstration it is designed badly to call itself forever and cause the JVM to run out of memory.

Listing 4-57. Bad Recursive Method

```
package com.apress.bgn.four.exceptions;

public class ExceptionsDemo {
    // bad method
    static int rec(int i) {
        return rec(i * i);
    }

    public static void main(String... args) {
        rec(1000);
        System.out.println("ALL DONE.");
    }
}
```

If we run the ExceptionsDemo class, *ALL DONE* is not printed. Instead, the program will end abnormally by throwing a StackOverflowError and mentioning the line where the problem is (in this case the line where the recursive method calls itself). The output is shown in Listing 4-58.

Listing 4-58. Console Output of ExceptionsDemo Execution

```
Exception in thread "main" java.lang.StackOverflowError at chapter.
four@3.0-SNAPSHOT/com.apress.bgn.four.exceptions.ExceptionsDemo.
rec(ExceptionsDemo.java:36)
at chapter.four@3.0-SNAPSHOT/com.apress.bgn.four.exceptions.ExceptionsDemo.
rec(ExceptionsDemo.java:36)
...
```

The StackOverflowError is indirectly a subclass of Error and is obviously caused by the defective recursive method that was called. Sure, we could modify the code to treat this exceptional situation and execute whatever has to be executed next, as shown in Listing 4-59.

Listing 4-59. Another Bad Recursive Method

```java
package com.apress.bgn.four.exceptions;

public class ExceptionsDemo {
    // other code omitted
    public static void main(String... args) {
        try {
            rec(1000);
        } catch (Throwable r) {
        }
        System.out.println("ALL DONE.");
    }
}
```

In the console only the *ALL DONE* message is printed, with no trace of the error. That is expected since we caught it and decided not to print any information about it.

Stop   This is a bad practice called **exception swallowing**—never do this!

Also, the system should not recover from this, as the result of any operation after an `Error` being thrown is unreliable.

Stop   This is why it is a very bad practice to catch a `Throwable`!

The `Exception` class is the superclass of all exceptions that can be caught and treated and from which the system can recover. Any subclasses of the `Exception` class that are not subclasses of `RuntimeException` are **checked exceptions**. These types of exceptions are known at compile time, because they are part of the methods declarations. Any method that is declared to throw a checked exception, when used in the code, either enforces the propagation of the exception further or requires the developer to write code to treat the exception.

The `RuntimeException` class is the superclass of exceptions that are thrown during the execution of the program, so the possibility of them being thrown is not known when the code is written. Consider the code sample in Listing 4-60.

Listing 4-60. Code Sample That Might Throw an Exception

```
package com.apress.bgn.four.exceptions;

import com.apress.bgn.four.hierarchy.Performer;

public class AnotherExceptionsDemo {
    public static void main(String... args) {
        Performer p = PerformerGenerator.get("Bryce");

        System.out.println("TTL: " + p.getTimeToLive());
    }
}
```

Let's suppose we do not have access to the code of the `PerformerGenerator` class, so we cannot see its code. We just know that calling the `get(..)` method with a name is supposed to return a `Performer` instance. So we write the code in Listing 4-60 and try to print the performer's time to live. What will happen if the p variable is not actually initialized with a proper object, because the `get("John")` call returns null? The outcome is depicted in Listing 4-61.

Listing 4-61. Console Output of `AnotherExceptionsDemo` Execution

```
Exception in thread"main"java.lang.NullPointerException:
Cannot invoke"com.apress.bgn.four.hierarchy.Performer.getTimeToLive()"
because "p" is null at chapter.four @3.0-SNAPSHOT/com.apress.bgn.four.
exceptions.AnotherExceptionsDemo.main(AnotherExceptionsDemo.java:40)
```

As you can see, the exception message telling you what is wrong is really explicit. More precise `NullPointerExceptions` messages are a feature introduced in Java 17.

Being smart developers, or a little paranoid, we'll prepare for this case. Depending on the requirements of the application, we can do any of the following three things.

Catch the exception, print an appropriate message, and exit the application

Catching an exception is done using a `try/catch` block. The syntax is pretty simple, and the behavior can be explained as follows: the JVM tries to execute the statements in the try block; if an exception is thrown that matches the type in the catch block declaration, the code in this block is executed. This is recommended when the rest of the code cannot be executed without a `Performer` instance, as depicted in Listing 4-62.

Listing 4-62. AnotherExceptionsDemo Version with Exception Handling Code

```java
package com.apress.bgn.four.exceptions;

import com.apress.bgn.four.hierarchy.Performer;

public class AnotherExceptionsDemo {
    public static void main(String... args) {
        Performer p = PerformerGenerator.get("Bryce");

        try {
            System.out.println("TTL: " + p.getTimeToLive());
        } catch (Exception e) {
            System.out.println("The performer was not initialized properly
            because of: " + e.getMessage());
        }
    }
}
```

The exception that was thrown here is of type `NullPointerException`, a class that extends `RuntimeException`, so a `try/catch` block is not mandatory. This type of exception is called an **unchecked exception** because the developer is not obligated to check for them. They are thrown during the execution of an application, and thus they are **runtime exceptions**. This means the compiler is not aware of the possibility of their being thrown and is not forcing the developer to write code to handle them.

Caution   The `NullPointerException` is the exception type Java beginner developers struggle with a lot because they do not have the *paranoia sense* developed well enough to always test objects with unknown origin before using them.

Throw an appropriate exception type

This option is suitable when there is a different class calling the problematic code, and that class will handle the exception appropriately, as depicted in Listing 4-63.

Listing 4-63. Code Sample That Wraps the Exception into a Custom Exception Type

```java
package com.apress.bgn.four.exceptions;

import com.apress.bgn.four.hierarchy.Performer;

public class ExtraCallerExceptionsDemo {
    public static void main(String... args) {
        Caller caller = new Caller();
        try {
            caller.printTTL("Bryce");
        } catch (EmptyPerformerException e) {
            System.out.println(e.getMessage());
        }
    }
}

class Caller {
    public void printTTL(String name) throws EmptyPerformerException {
        try {
            Performer p = PerformerGenerator.get(name);
            System.out.println("TTL: " + p.getTimeToLive());
        } catch (Exception e) {
            throw new EmptyPerformerException("There is no performer named
            " + name, e);  // wrapping happens here
        }
    }
}
```

```java
class EmptyPerformerException extends Exception {
    public EmptyPerformerException(String message, Throwable cause) {
        super(message, cause);
    }
}
```

Notice the EmptyPerformerException class. It is a simple custom class that extends the java.lang.Exception class, thus making it a checked exception. Checked exceptions are declared as explicitly being thrown by a method, as you can see in the first bold line in the code. In this case, when invoking that method, the compiler will force the developer to treat that exception or throw it forward. If the printTTL(..) method were to be declared without the throws EmptyPerformerException snippet, a compile-time error would be thrown and the code would not be executed. IntelliJ IDEA, being a very smart editor and using the JVM compiler to verify your code, will notify you that something is not okay in your code by underlining it with a red line. This situation is depicted in Figure 4-16, where the throws EmptyPerformerException was commented to show the compiler being totally not okay with the situation.

```
     ExtraCallerExceptionsDemo.java

30      import com.apress.bgn.four.hierarchy.Performer;
31
32      /**
33       * Created by iuliana.cosmina on 16/04/2024
34       */
35  ▷   public class ExtraCallerExceptionsDemo {  new *
36  ▷       public static void main(String... args) {  new *
37              Caller caller = new Caller();
38              try {
39                  caller.printTTL( name: "Bryce");
40              } catch (EmptyPerformerException  e) {
41                  System   Exception 'com.apress.bgn.four.exceptions.EmptyPerformerException' is never thrown in the corresponding try block
42              }            Delete catch for 'com.apress.bgn.four.exceptions.EmptyPerformerException'  ⌥⇧↵     More actions...  ⌥↵
43          }
44      }              ▣ com.apress.bgn.four.exceptions
45
46      class Caller { 3   class EmptyPerformerException
47          public void p   extends Exception
48              try {         ▢ chapter04                                                                          ✎
49                  Performer p = PerformerGenerator.get(name);
50                  System.out.println("TTL: " + p.getTimeToLive());
51              } catch (Exception e) {
52                  throw new EmptyPerformerException("There is no performer named " + name, e);
53              }
54          } 5 usages  new *        Unhandled exception: com.apress.bgn.four.exceptions.EmptyPerformerException     ⋮
55      }                           Add exception to method signature  ⌥⇧↵     More actions...  ⌥↵
56
57      class EmptyPerformerException extends Exce    ©  com.apress.bgn.four.exceptions.EmptyPerformerException
58          public EmptyPerformerException(String   public EmptyPerformerException(
59              super(message, cause);                   String message,
60          }                                            Throwable cause
61      }                                           )
62                                                  ▢ chapter04                                                  ✎  ⋮
63
```

Figure 4-16. *Compile errors caused by checked exception not being declared as being thrown by the* `printTTL(..)` *method*

Also, in the `main(..)` method, a `try/catch` block is required to catch and treat this type of exception, as shown in Listing 4-63. Or the `main(..)` method must be declared with `throws EmptyPerformerException`, to be allowed to pass the exception further, in this case to the JVM.

Tip   You can think of exceptions as being like the CO_2 bubbles in a frizzy drink: they tend to float up to the surface if not stopped by a filter. In Java the surface is represented by the JVM running the application. When the JVM encounters an exception, it stops running the application.

Notice in the line creating the `EmptyPerformerException` object that the original exception is provided as an argument, as per the constructor declaration. This is done so its message is not lost and can be used to debug the unexpected situation, since it will point directly to the problematic line.

Perform a dummy initialization

This option is suitable when the code following the problematic call does different things depending on the performer instance returned, as depicted in Listing 4-64.

Listing 4-64. Code Sample That Performs a Dummy Initialization

```java
package com.apress.bgn.four.exceptions;

import com.apress.bgn.four.hierarchy.Performer;
import com.apress.bgn.four.classes.Gender;

class DummyInitializer {

    public Performer getPerformer(String name) {
        Performer p = PerformerGenerator.get(name);
        try {
            System.out.println("Test if valid: " + p.getName());
        } catch (Exception e) {
            p = new Performer("Dummy", 0, 0.0f, Gender.UNSPECIFIED);
        }
        return p;
    }
}

public class DummyInitExceptionDemo {
    public static void main(String... args) {
        DummyInitializer initializer = new DummyInitializer();
        Performer p = initializer.getPerformer("Bryce");

        if ("Dummy".equals(p.getName())) { // different behavior based on
        performer name
            System.out.println("Nothing to do.");
```

```
        } else {
            System.out.println("TTL: " + p.getTimeToLive());
        }
    }
}
```

Notice here that the original exception is not used anywhere; it is being *swallowed*, and thus in case of trouble, the root cause of the problem is hidden. In applications where the original exception is not critical, a curated warning log message is printed to notify the developer that there was some behavior that should be noted.

Warning   Keep in mind that all the changes listed in this section apply to the code calling the `PerformerGenerator.get("Bryce")` method, because it is assumed that we cannot modify the contents of this class. If the class is accessible, the method can be modified to return an `Optional<Performer>`. More information about this type of object is presented in subsequent chapters.

---

try/catch Blocks

And since we are talking about exceptions, the `try`/`catch` block can be completed with a `finally` block. The contents of the `finally` block are almost always executed. If the exception does not match any of the types declared in the `catch` block (yes, more than one type can be declared in a `catch` block, as discussed later in the book.), the exception is thrown further, but the `finally` block is still executed. If the method returns normally, the `finally` block is executed. The only situation in which the `finally` block is not executed is when the program ends in an error.

Listing 4-65 is an enriched version of the code shown in Listing 4-63 that includes a `finally` block for the `Caller` example.

Listing 4-65. Code Sample That Shows a `finally` Block

```java
package com.apress.bgn.four.exceptions;

public class FinallyBlockDemo {

    public static void main(String... args) {
        try {
            Caller caller = new Caller();
            caller.printTTL("John");
        } catch (EmptyPerformerException e) {
            System.out.println("Cannot use an empty performer!");
        } finally {
            System.out.println("All went as expected!");
        }
    }
}
```

Later in this book, after your Java knowledge is more advanced, some examples will include code that will end in exceptional situations to provide the opportunity to expand the exceptions topic even further.

Generics

Up to this point in the chapter we have covered only object types and Java templates used for creating objects. But what if we need to design a class with functionality that applies to multiple types of objects? Since every class in Java extends the `Object` class, we could create a class with a method that receives a parameter of type `Object`, and in the method we could test the object type. It would be cumbersome, but it can be done, and will be covered later in the book. Fortunately, Java provides an easier way to design a class with functionality that applies to multiple types of objects.

Java 5 introduced the possibility to use a type as a parameter when creating an object. The classes that are developed to process other classes are called **generics**. There are a lot of examples for generics, but I will start with the one that I needed first when learning Java.

When writing Java applications, you will most likely need at some point to pair up values of different types. The simplest version of a `Pair` class that can hold a pair of instances of any type is shown in Listing 4-66.

Listing 4-66. Generic Class Pair<X,Y>

```
package com.apress.bgn.four.generics;

public class Pair<X, Y> {

    protected X x;
    protected Y y;

    private Pair(X x, Y y) {
        this.x = x;
        this.y = y;
    }

    public X x() {
        return x;
    }

    public Y y() {
        return y;
    }

    public void x(X x) {
        this.x = x;
    }

    public void y(Y y) {
        this.y = y;
    }

    public static <X, Y> Pair<X, Y> of(X x, Y y) {
        return new Pair<>(x, y);
    }

    @Override
    public String toString() {
        return "Pair{" + x.toString() + ", " + y.toString() + '}';
    }
}
```

We now have a generic Pair class declaration. X and Y represent any Java type in an application. The toString() method is inherited from the Object class and overridden in the Pair class to print the values of the fields.

The next step is to use the Pair class. To prove that the Pair class can be used to couple instances of any type, in Listing 4-67, the following pairs of objects are created:

- A pair of Performers that we can only assume they sing together since the variable is named duet.

- A pair of a Performer instance and a Double instance representing this performer's net worth; the variable is named netWorth.

- A pair of a String instance representing the genre of a performer and a Performer instance; the variable is named johnsGenre.

Listing 4-67. Using the Pair<X,Y> Generic Class

```
package com.apress.bgn.four.generics;

import com.apress.bgn.four.classes.Gender;
import com.apress.bgn.four.hierarchy.Performer;

public class GenericsDemo {

    public static void main(String... args) {
        Performer john = new Performer("John", 40, 1.91f, Gender.MALE);
        Performer jane = new Performer("Jane", 34, 1.591f, Gender.FEMALE);

        Pair<Performer, Performer> duet = Pair.of(john, jane);
        System.out.println(duet);

        Pair<Performer, Double> netWorth = Pair.of(john, 34_000_000.03);
        System.out.println(netWorth);

        Pair<String, Performer> johnsGenre = Pair.of("country-pop", john);
        System.out.println(johnsGenre);
    }
}
```

```
// output
/*
Pair { com.apress.bgn.four.hierarchy.Performer @1e80bfe8, com.apress.bgn.
four.hierarchy.Performer @66a29884}
Pair {com.apress.bgn.four.hierarchy.Performer@1e80bfe8, 3.400000003 E7}
Pair {country-pop, com.apress.bgn.four.hierarchy.Performer@1e80bfe8}
*/
```

The println(...) method expects its argument to be a String instance, and if it isn't, the toString() method will be called on the object given as the argument. If the toString() method was not overridden in a class extending Object, the one from the Object class will be called that returns the fully qualified name of the class and something called a **hashcode**, which is a numerical representation of the object.

There are a lot of generic classes in the JDK that you can use to write code, and some of them will be introduced in later chapters. This section is here just to introduce you to the typical generics syntax. This will help you to recognize generics easily and know how they are used.

var and the Diamond Operator

Java 10 introduced the var keyword to provide the capability to declare variables without their type, leaving the compiler to infer it. Languages like Python, Groovy, and JavaScript had provided this capability for years, and Java developers wanted it too.

It is not a big effort to write

```
String message = "random message"
```

instead of

```
var message = "random message" // infers String
```

But var becomes a lot more helpful when multilayered generic types are involved. For example, this statement:

```
HashMap<Long, Map<String, ? extends Performer>> performers = new
HashMap<Long, Map<String, ? extends Performer>>() ;
```

can be written as

```
var performers = new HashMap<Long, Map<String, ? extends Performer>>();
```

That same statement can be simplified by using the **diamond operator**, <>, introduced in Java 7. The diamond operator allows omitting the names of the generic types used when instantiating a variable if they can be inferred by the compiler from the declaration. So the previous example can also be written as follows:

```
HashMap<Long, Map<String, ? extends Performer>> performers3 = new
HashMap<>();
```

Important   A statement like `var performers = new HashMap<>();` is valid, but the compiler has no way of deciding the type of the instances that can be added to the `performers` map. So a statement like `performers.put(null, null);` is correct, since `null` does not have a type, but anything else, such as `performers.put("john", "mayer");`, will cause a compile error.

The `var` keyword can simplify the code being written in Java, but it has a long way to go. For now, it is being allowed only in the body of methods, indexes for enhanced loops, lambda expressions, constructors, and loop and initialization blocks. It cannot be used in class field declarations or constants. Thus, the compiler can infer the type only for local variables.

`var` cannot be used to declare variables that are not initialized, because this doesn't give the compiler any information about the type of the variable. So the `var list;` statement causes a compiler error, but `var list = new ArrayList<String>();` works just fine.

Important   Although `var` cannot be used as an identifier, this doesn't make it a reserved keyword. That is why a class field named `var` can be declared, for example. Since it replaces the type name of a variable, `var` is actually a **reserved type name**, and since using it depends on the context, you will find it in Table 4-4 containing Java contextual keywords.

Unnamed Patterns and Unnamed Variables

As mentioned earlier in the chapter, using the underscore (_) character as an identifier was supported up to JDK 8, was then removed in Java 9, and was reintroduced in Java 21 as a preview and as a feature in Java 22 but for purposes similar to the ones in Golang. For those unfamiliar with Golang, in Golang you must use any variable you declare, otherwise your code is invalid. A workaround for this in some cases is to use variables named _ (underscore). The _ identifier is used to denote an **unnamed variable** that is declared but never used.

There are a few situations in which this is useful. The most common is when using `Thread.sleep(..)` to pause the execution of a program. The `Thread.sleep(..)` method declaration includes a `throws java.lang.InterruptedException` that is rarely actually thrown if your code design is good, but since it is a checked exception, the compiler forces you to handle it. So most developers used to enclose this in a `try/catch` block that declares a named variable that is never used anywhere. Listing 4-68 shows two `try/catch` blocks, one pre-Java 22 with a named exception variable, and one since Java 22 with an unnamed variable.

Listing 4-68. Console Output for the Execution of `GenericsDemo`

```
// before Java 22
try {
    Thread.sleep(20);
} catch (InterruptedException e) {
    // nothing to do
}

// Java 22: unnamed variable
try {
    Thread.sleep(20);
} catch (InterruptedException _) {
}
```

You might think that this is not important, and you are right, but there is one consequence that I personally am very happy about: it makes the code more readable without adding extra verbiage, like a comment to explain why nothing is done with that exception. Also, the first `try/catch` block looks a lot like the exception-swallowing process previously described in the **Exceptions** section in this chapter, which I cautioned you should avoid. By using an _ as the variable name, I know just by looking at the code that this is not an exception I should worry about.

Another situation in which you might need an unnamed variable is when you need to iterate a collection and perform an operation that has nothing to do with the actual iterator (code that is also referred to as *code whose side effect is more important than its result*). You will learn about iterators and loops in **Chapter 7**.

Unnamed variables are also useful when declaring lambda expressions that need a formal parameter. However, unnamed variables are most useful when decomposing data types using patterns, to create `switch` statements with different branches based on the type of object. This will be covered in **Chapter 5** and **Chapter 7**. Unnamed variables will be used wherever necessary throughout the book.

Summary

This chapter introduced the most often used elements of the Java language. Hopefully, having read this chapter, not much you find in future code samples code will surprise you, so you can focus on learning the language properly. Do not worry if some things seem unclear at this point; they will become clearer later as your understanding of the Java language grows.

Here are the key takeaways from this chapter:

- Syntax mistakes prevent Java code from being transformed into executable code. This means *the code is not compiling*.

- Static variables can be used directly when *static import statements* are used. The same applies to static methods.

- Comments are ignored by the compiler, and there are three types of comments in Java.

- Classes, interfaces, and enums are Java components used to create objects.

- Enums are special types of classes that can be instantiated only a fixed number of times.

- Records are special types of classes used to create data-immutable objects.

- Abstract classes cannot be instantiated, even if they can have constructors.

- Interfaces could only contain skeleton (abstract) methods until Java version 8, when default methods were introduced.

- Private methods and private static methods are allowed in interfaces starting with Java 9.

- In Java there is no multiple inheritance using classes.

- Java identifiers must respect naming rules. A single underscore `_` is not an accepted Java identifier, unless is used to identify variables which are declared, but never used in various contexts (exception handling, loops, lambda expressions and patterns).

- Interfaces can extend other interfaces.

- Java defines a fixed number of *reserved keywords* that can be used only for specific purposes, and cannot be used as identifiers. The list of Java keywords tends to stay quite constant between Java versions. The reserved keywords are covered in the following section.

Java Keywords

As mentioned at the beginning of this chapter, there is a list of Java keywords that can be used only for their fixed and predefined purpose in the language. There are two types of keywords in Java: **reserved keywords** and **contextual keywords**. Reserved keywords (there are 51) cannot be used as identifiers: you cannot use them as names for variables, classes, interfaces, enums, or methods. Contextual keywords (there are 17) can be used as identifiers unless the context is related to their intended purpose, in which case they can't be used because it is too confusing for the compiler.

You can find the reserved keywords in Tables 4-2 and 4-3.[7]

---

[7] https://devopedia.org/race-condition-software

Table 4-2. *Java Reserved Keywords (Part 1)*

Keyword	Description
abstract	Used to declare a class or method as abstract—as in, any extending or implementing class must provide a concrete implementation.
assert	Used to test an assumption about your code. Introduced in Java 1.4, it is ignored by the JVM unless the program is run with the -ea option.
boolean byte char short int long float double	Primitive type names.
break	Statement used inside loops to terminate them immediately.
continue	Statement used inside loops to jump to the next iteration immediately.
switch	Statement used to test equality against a set of values known as cases.
case	Statement used to define case values in a switch statement.
default	Used to declare a default case within a switch statement. And starting with Java 8 it can be used to declare default methods in interfaces.
try catch finally throw throws	Keywords used in exception handling.
class interface enum	Keywords used to declare classes, interfaces, and enums.
extends implements	Keywords used in extending classes and implementing interfaces.
const	Not actually used in Java, a keyword borrowed from C, where it is used to declare constants, variables that are assigned a value that cannot be changed during the execution of the program.
final	The equivalent of the const keyword in Java. Anything defined with this modifier cannot change after a final initialization. A final class cannot be extended. A final method cannot be overridden. A final variable has the same value that was initialized with throughout the execution of the program. Any code written to modify final items will lead to a compiler error.

Table 4-3. *Java Reserved Keywords (Part 2)*

Keyword	Description

do
for
while
	Keywords used to create loops:
	do{..}
	while(condition)
	while(condition){..}
	for(initialization;condition;incrementation){..}

goto	Another keyword borrowed from C but currently not used in Java, because it can be replaced by labeled break and continue statements.
if else	Used to create conditional statements: if(condition) {..} else {..} else if (condition) {..}
import	Used to make classes and interfaces available in the current source code.
instanceof	Used to test instance types in conditional expressions.
native	Used to indicate that a method is implemented in native code using JNI (Java Native Interface).
new	Used to create Java instances.
package	Used to declare the package the class, interface, enum, annotation, or record is part of. It should be the first Java statement line.
public private protected	Access-level modifiers for Java items (templates, fields, or methods).
return	Used within a method to return to the code that invoked it. The method can also return a value to the calling code.
static	This modifier can be applied to variables, methods, blocks, and nested class. It declares an item that is shared between all instances of the class where declared.
stricfp	Used to restrict floating-point calculations to ensure portability. Added in Java 1.2.
super	Used inside a class to access members of the super class.

(continued)

Table 4-3. (*continued*)

Keyword	Description
this	Used to access members of the current object.
synchronized	Used to ensure that only one thread executes a block of code at any given time. This is used to avoid a problem named race condition.
transient	Used to mark data that should not be serialized.
volatile	Used to ensure that changes done to a variable value are accessible to all threads accessing it.
void	Used when declaring methods as a return type to indicate that the method does not return a value.
_ (underscore)	Can be used as an identifier prior to Java 9. Cannot be used as an identifier starting with Java 9 and up to Java 20. Starting with Java 21 it can be used as an identifier for unused (unnamed) variables.

You can find the contextual keywords in Table 4-4.

Table 4-4. *Java Contextual Keywords*

Keyword	Description
export module open opens provides requires to transitive uses with	Used in module-info.java to configure Java modules.
record	Keyword to declare Java records. It can be used as an identifier within the body of a Java class, interface, or enum.

(*continued*)

Table 4-4. (*continued*)

Keyword	Description
permits sealed non-sealed	Keywords used in the declaration of sealed classes and interfaces.
when	Keyword used to declare a guard expression in a `switch` block.
yield	Keyword used to declare a `yield` statement in a `switch` block.
var	Keyword introduced in Java 10 to replace the declared type of a variable method (or lambda expression) body when the type is obvious. `var` is a reserved type name. For example, `var` can be used as a field name or as a package name.

The following are a few important points to mention:

- `true` and `false` are boolean literals, but they are not reserved keywords. For example, `true` and `false` are valid package names.

- `null` is not a reserved keyword either. It is a literal used to represent a missing object. But it is a valid name for a package, for example.

Important   The keywords and many other details of the Java language are covered extensively in the Java Language Specification (JLS)[8], so if you are ever in doubt about the proper syntax of your Java code (or are just curious), browse through it. In the early days of my Java learning, when the Internet was smaller and not so helpful, the JLS saved me many times.

---

[8] https://docs.oracle.com/javase/specs/jls/se22/html/index.html

## CHAPTER 5

Data Types

Although we wrote a lot of code in the previous chapter, when designing classes, we used only the simplest data types, a few numeric ones and texts. In the JDK a lot of data types are declared for a multitude of purposes: for modeling calendar dates, for representing multiple types of numerics, and for manipulating texts, collections, data streams, files, database connections, and so on. Aside from the JDK, numerous libraries created by other parties are available that provide even more functionality. The data types provided by the JDK are fundamental types, the bricks every Java application is built from. Of course, depending on the type of application you are building, you might not need all of them. For example, I've never had the occasion to use the `java.util.logging.Logger` class. Most applications I have worked on were already set up by a different team when I came along, and they were using external libraries like `Log4j` or `Logback` or logging abstractions like SLF4J (covered in Chapter 9).

This chapter covers the basic Java data types that you will need to write about 80% of any Java application. Without further ado, let's begin.

Stack and Heap Memory

Java types can be split in two main categories: **primitive** types and **reference** types. Java code files and bytecode files are stored on the HDD. Java programs run on the JVM, which is launched as a process by executing the `java` executable. During execution, all data is stored in two different types of memory, stack and heap, which are allocated for a program's execution by the operating system.

The **stack** memory is used during execution (also referred to as *at runtime*) to store method primitive local variables and references to objects stored in the heap. A *stack* is also a data structure represented by a list of values that can be accessed only at one end, also called last-in, first-out (LIFO) order. The name fits, because every time a method gets called, a new block is created in the stack memory to hold local variables of the

© Iuliana Cosmina 2024
I. Cosmina, *Java 23 for Absolute Beginners*, https://doi.org/10.1007/979-8-8688-1041-1_5

method: primitives and references to other objects in the method. When the call ends, the block is removed (popped out) and new blocks are created for methods being called after that.

Important   A stack data structure is very similar to a stack of plates; you can only add or remove extra plates on the top. The first element in a stack is called the *head*. Operations performed on a stack have specific names: adding an element to the stack is called a *push* operation, inspecting the first element in the stack is called a *peek* or *top*, and extracting the first element in the stack, its head, is called a *pop*. A stack gets emptied by calling *pop* repeatedly until its size is zero.

Each JVM execution thread has its own stack memory, and its size can be specified using JVM parameter -Xss (or the equivalent and more explicit -XX:ThreadStackSize). If too many variables are allocated, or if the method being called is recursive and badly designed, the condition to return is never fulfilled and thus keeps invoking itself forever, and you will run into a java.lang.StackOverflowError. This means that there is no stack memory left, because every method call will cause a new block to be created on the stack. The size of the stack memory depends on the platform running the JVM: it is 1024KB for Unix-based systems (Linux and macOS), and for Windows, the size depends on the virtual memory. To check its size on your computer, just open a terminal or command prompt and run this command: java -XX:+PrintFlagsFinal -version. The command returns a list of JVM configurations referred to as *flags*. Some of them are used to configure the memory JVM is allowed to manage.

Listing 5-1 shows the command being executed on my macOS computer. The grep command filters the output for the criteria provided as an argument, thus resulting in a cleaner and scoped output.

Listing 5-1. Showing the Stack Size Default Values on macOS

```
> java -XX:+PrintFlagsFinal -version | grep ThreadStack
  #  Data Type  # Flag Name  #    = # Flag Value
    intx          ThreadStackSize  =    1024
```

The **heap** memory is used at runtime to allocate memory for objects and JRE classes. Objects are instances of JDK classes or developer-defined classes. Any object created with new will be stored inside the heap memory. Objects created inside the heap memory can be accessed by all threads of the application. Access and management of the heap memory are a little more complex and will be covered more in **Chapter 13**, which covers garbage collection. The -Xms and -Xmx JVM parameters are used to set the initial and maximum size of the heap memory for a Java program during execution. The heap size may vary depending on the number of objects created by the program, and if all heap memory allocated to a Java program is full, then a java.lang. OutOfMemoryError is thrown. The default size for the heap memory depends on the available physical memory of the computer running the JVM, and its minimum and maximum values and other additional data can be extracted from the output of the java -XX:+PrintFlagsFinal -version too.

Listing 5-2 shows the command being executed on my macOS computer, which has a total physical memory of 32GB. Again, the grep command filters the output for the criteria provided as an argument, thus resulting in a cleaner and scoped output.

Listing 5-2. Showing the Heap Size Default Values on macOS

```
> java -XX:+PrintFlagsFinal -version | grep HeapSize
#  Data Type  # Flag Name  #  = # Flag Value
   size_t MaxHeapSize        = 8589934592  # TODO make number bold
   size_t MinHeapSize        = 8388608     # TODO make number bold
```

Tip   You can find the complete list of JVM flags on the Oracle official site.[1] If you want more detailed explanations on how to use them, check out this blog:

https://www.codecentric.de/wissens-hub/blog?q=JVM%20flags

Important   Although it is probably too early to see the importance of this information, there are a lot of Java command-line options that you might find useful when working on real-world applications. Add this link to your must-have collection as well:

https://docs.oracle.com/en/java/javase/21/docs/specs/man/ java.html#java-command-line-argument-files

---

[1]https://www.oracle.com/java/technologies/javase/vmoptions-jsp.html

The java.lang.String class is the most-used class in the Java programming language. Because text values within an application might have the same value, for efficiency reasons this type of object is managed a little different within the heap. In the heap there is a special memory region named the **String Pool**, which is where all the String instances are stored by the JVM.

Note   The String Pool is mentioned here only because the following piece of code (which will be analyzed to explain how memory is managed in Java) contains a definition of a String instance, but the String Pool and other details about the String data type will be covered in detail a bit later in the chapter.

Let's consider the executable class in Listing 5-3 and examine how the memory is organized during its execution.

Listing 5-3. Code Sample Used to Discuss Memory Usage

```
01. package com.apress.bgn.five;
02.
03. import java.util.Date;
04.
05. public class PrimitivesDemo {
06.     void main() {
07.         int i = 5;
08.         int j = 7;
09.         Date d = new Date();
10.         int result = add(i, j);
11.         System.out.print(result);
12.         d = null;
13.     }
14.
15.     static int add(int a, int b) {
16.         String mess = new String("performing add ...");
17.         return a + b;
18.     }
19. }
```

As in the previous edition of this book, I have kept the example in Listing 5-3 because I think for a beginner it is easier to see the variable types, but local type inference and the var keyword have been introduced more than ten releases ago, so all examples from now on will make use of it. So the code in Listing 5-3 becomes the one in Listing 5-4.

Listing 5-4. Code Sample Used to Discuss Memory Usage (Using Type Inference)

```
01. package com.apress.bgn.five;
02.
03. import java.util.Date;
04.
05. public class PrimitivesDemo {
06.     void main() {
07.         var i = 5;
08.         var j = 7;
09.         var d = new Date();
10.         var result = add(i, j);
11.         System.out.print(result);
12.         d = null;
13.     }
14.
15.     static int add(int a, int b) {
16.         var mess = new String("performing add ...");
17.         return a + b;
18.     }
19. }
```

Just by looking at this code, can you figure out which variables are saved on the stack and which are saved on the heap? Let's go over the program line by line and see what is happening:

- As soon as the program starts, runtime classes that JVM needs are loaded in the heap memory.

- The main(..) method is discovered in line 06, so a stack memory is created to be used during the execution of this method.

- The primitive local variable in line 07, i=5, is created and stored in the stack memory of the main(..) method.

- The primitive local variable in line 08, j=7, is created and stored in the stack memory of the main(..) method. At this point the program memory can be depicted as shown in Figure 5-1.

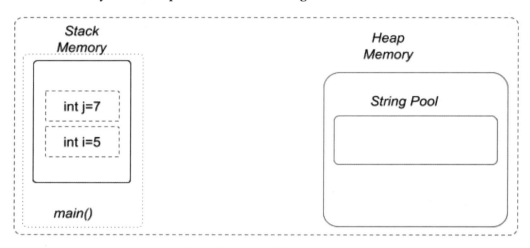

Java Runtime Memory

Figure 5-1. *Java stack and heap memory, after declaring two primitive variables*

- In line 09 an object of type java.util.Date is declared, so this object is created and stored in the heap memory and a reference named d is saved on the stack. At this point the program memory looks as depicted in Figure 5-2.

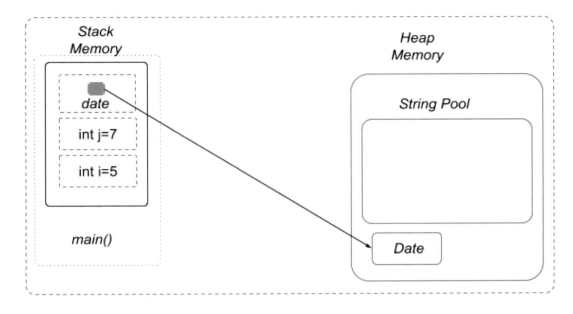

Java Runtime Memory

Figure 5-2. *Java stack and heap memory, after declaring two primitive variables and an object*

- In line 10 method add(..) is called with arguments i and j. This means their values will be copied into the local variables for this method named a and b and these two will be stored in the memory block for this method.

- Inside the add(..) method body, in line 16 a String instance is declared. So the String object is created in the heap memory, in the String Pool memory block, and the reference named mess is stored in the stack, in the memory block for this method. At this point the program memory looks as depicted in Figure 5-3.

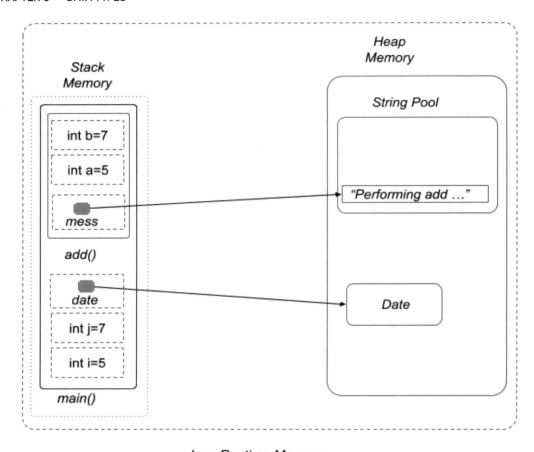

Java Runtime Memory

Figure 5-3. *Java stack and heap memory, after calling the add(..) method*

- Also in line 10, the result of the execution of method add(..) is stored into the local variable named result. At this point the add(..) method has finished its execution, so its stack block is discarded. Thus, we can conclude that variables that are stored on the stack exist for as long as the function that created them is running. In the stack memory of the main(..) method, the result variable is saved.

- In line 11, the print(..) method is called, but we'll skip the explanation for this line for simplicity reasons.

- In line 12, the d reference is being assigned a null value, which means the object of type Date is now only in the heap and not linked to the execution of the main(..) method in any way. In that line the JVM is instructed that that object is no longer needed and thus can be safely discarded, which means the space containing it can be collected and used to store other objects.

At this point the program memory looks as depicted in Figure 5-4.

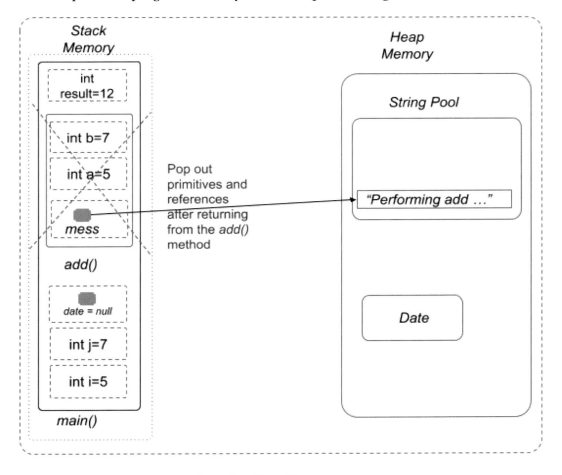

Java Runtime Memory

Figure 5-4. *Java stack and heap memory before the ending of the* main(..) *method execution*

Obviously, after the program execution ends, all memory contents are discarded.

From version to version, small changes have been introduced to the way Java does memory management (the algorithms deciding how and when space should be allocated and freed in the heap have been optimized), but the overall memory organization hasn't changed much over the years.

Important   When applying for a Java developer position, you will most likely be asked what the difference between stack and heap memory is. If this section did not clarify these two notions sufficiently for you, please feel free to consult additional resources, such as this very good article: `https://www.digitalocean.com/community/tutorials/java-heap-space-vs-stack-memory`.

Introduction to Java Data Types

As you have noticed in the previous example, the data types can be split in Java in two big groups based on where and how they are stored during execution: **primitive** types and **reference** types. Let's introduce them briefly and later explain their most important members.

Primitive Data Types

Primitive types are defined by the Java programming language as special types that do not have a supporting class and are named by their reserved keyword. Variables of these types are saved on the stack memory, and when values are assigned to them using the =(equals) operator, the value is actually copied. So if we declare two primitive variables of type int as in Listing 5-5, we end up with two variables, k and q, both having the same value: 42.

Listing 5-5. Code Sample Used to Discuss Primitives

```
package com.apress.bgn.five;

public class AnotherPrimitivesDemo {

    void main() {
        int k = 42;
        int q = k;
        System.out.println("k = " + k);
        System.out.println("q = " + q);
    }
}
```

When passed as arguments to other methods, the values of primitive values are copied and used without the initial variables being modified. Importantly, this means that in Java methods, *primitive arguments are passed by value.* This can be proved by creating a method to swap the values of two int variables. The code for the method and how to use it are depicted in Listing 5-6.

Listing 5-6. Code Sample Used to Show Primitives Are Passed by Value

```
package com.apress.bgn.five;

public class SwappingPrimitivesDemo {
    void main() {
        int k = 42;
        int q = 44;
        swap(k, q);
        System.out.println("k = " + k);
        System.out.println("q = " + q);
    }

    static void swap(int a, int b) {
        int temp = a;
        a = b;
        b = temp;
    }
}
```

So what do you think will get printed as values for k and q? If you thought the output is the same as the following, you are correct:

```
k = 42
q = 44
```

This happens because in Java passing arguments to a method is done through their value, which means for primitives, changing the formal parameter's value doesn't affect the actual parameter's (the method argument's) value. If you read the previous section, you can already imagine what happens on the stack. When the swap(..) method is called, a new stack memory block is created to save the values used by this method. During the execution of the method, the values might change, but if they are not returned and assigned to variables in the calling method, the values are lost when the method execution ends. Figure 5-5 depicts the changes that take place on the stack during the execution of the code in Listing 5-6.

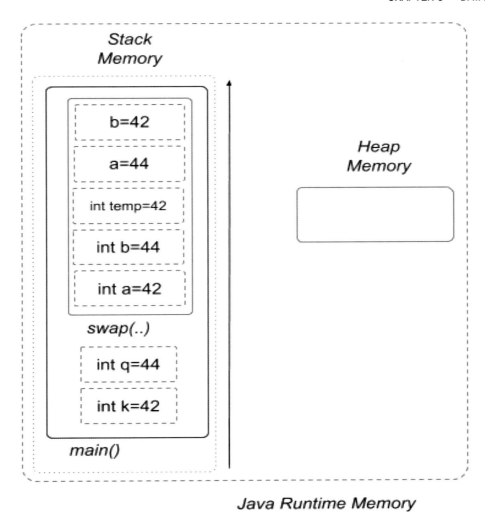

Figure 5-5. *Java passing primitive arguments by value*

Reference Data Types

There are six *reference types* in Java:

- Class types

- Interface types

- Enums

- Array types

- Records

- Annotations

Reference types are different from primitive types because they are instantiable (except interfaces and annotations). Instances (objects) of these types are created by calling constructors. Variables of these types are actually just references to objects stored in the heap. Because the references are stored on the stack as well, even if we modify the previous code to use references, the behavior will be the same.

Listing 5-7 introduces a class named IntContainer, with the only purpose to wrap int primitive values into objects.

Listing 5-7. Code Sample Used to Show IntContainer

```
package com.apress.bgn.five;

public class IntContainer {
    private int value;
    public IntContainer(int value) {
        this.value = value;
    }

    public int getValue() {
        return value;
    }
    public void setValue(int value) {
        this.value = value;
    }
}
```

Listing 5-8 shows the creation of two objects of this type and two references for them, and a new version of the swap method.

Listing 5-8. Code Sample Used to Show Swap of Two int Values Using a Reference Type

```java
package com.apress.bgn.five;

public class IntContainerDemo {

    void main() {
        IntContainer k = new IntContainer(42);
        IntContainer q = new IntContainer(44);
        swap(k,q);
        System.out.println("k = " + k.getValue());
        System.out.println("q = " + q.getValue());
    }

    static void swap(IntContainer a, IntContainer b) {
        IntContainer temp = a;
        a = b;
        b = temp;
    }
}
```

If we run the main(..) method, you will notice that we still get:

```
k = 42
q = 44
```

How can this be explained? Java still uses the same style of passing arguments, **by value**, only this time the value of the reference is the one passed.

Figure 5-6 depicts what is going on in the memory managed by the JVM for the execution of the previous code.

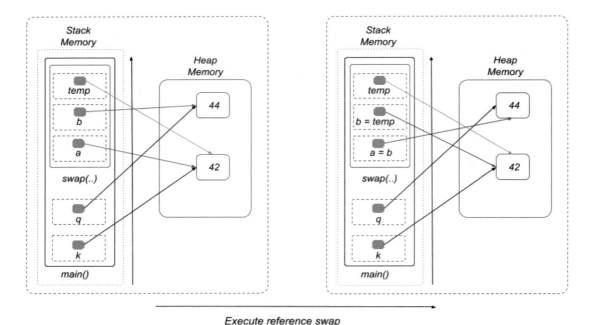

Execute reference swap

Figure 5-6. *Java passing reference arguments by value*

The references to the objects are interchanged in the body of the swap(..) method, but they have no effect on the k and q references, nor on the objects they point to in the heap.

Tip   If you use an intelligent Java editor like IntelliJ IDEA, it might even point you to the fact that something is wrong with this implementation by showing the a and b variables inside the swap method body in light gray, which means these two references are not used anywhere else.

To really exchange the values, we need to exchange the content of the objects, by using a new object. Look at the new version of the swap(..) method depicted in Listing 5-9.

Listing 5-9. Code Sample Used to Show Swap of Two int Values Using References That Actually Swap the Values

```
package com.apress.bgn.five;

public class ReferencesSwapDemo {

    void main() {
        IntContainer k = new IntContainer(42);
        IntContainer q = new IntContainer(44);
        swap(k,q);
        System.out.println("k = " + k.getValue());
        System.out.println("q = " + q.getValue());
    }
    static void swap(IntContainer a, IntContainer b) {
        IntContainer temp = new IntContainer(a.getValue());
        a.setValue(b.getValue());
        b.setValue(temp.getValue());
    }
}
```

By making use of setters and getters, we exchange the values of the objects, because the references are never modified inside the body of the method. Figure 5-7 depicts what happens within the memory during execution of the previous piece of code.

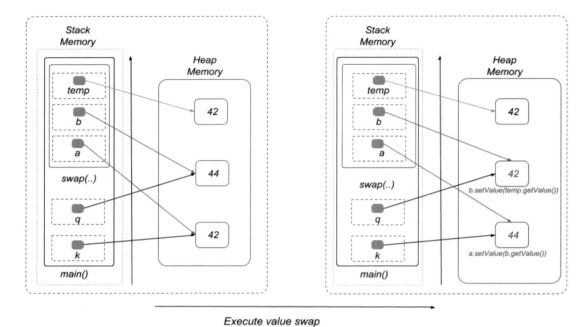

Execute value swap

Figure 5-7. *Java passing reference arguments by value, swapping object contents*

If you run the main() method in Listing 5-9, you will notice that the values of k and q are swapped:

```
k = 44
q = 42
```

Note   Maybe this example was introduced too early in this book, but it was important to show you as early as possible the major differences between primitive types and reference types. All the differences are listed in the **Summary**, but until then, let's explore the most-used data types in Java.

Java Primitive Types

Primitive types are the basic types of data in Java. Variables of this type can be created by directly assigning values of that type, so that they are not instantiated (which would be pretty difficult to do since these types are not backed up by a class). In Java there are eight types of primitive types: six types to represent numbers, one type to represent characters, and one type to represent boolean values. Primitive types are predefined into the Java language, and they have names that are reserved keywords. Primitive variables can have values only in the interval or dataset that is predefined for that type. When being declared as fields of a class, at instantiation time, a default value specific to the type is assigned to the field. Primitive values do not share state with other primitive values.

Most Java tutorials introduce the numeric types first and then the last two types, but we'll start with the non-numerics.

The **boolean** Type

Variables of this type can have only one of the two accepted values: `true` and `false`. If you have ever heard of boolean logic, this type should be familiar to you. In Java this type of value is used to set/unset flags and design execution flows. The values `true` and `false` are themselves boolean literals.

Important   The default value for a `boolean` variable is `false`.

Another observation about this type is that when a field is of type `boolean,` the getter for it has a different syntax: it is not prefixed with `get` but with `is`. Java IDEs respect this and generate the getters as expected. This prefix makes sense because boolean values are useful for modeling properties with only two values. For example, let's say we are writing a class to model a conversion process. A boolean field can be used to mark the process state as done or still in process. If the name of the field is `done`, a getter named `getDone()` would be pretty unintuitive, but one named `isDone()` would be quite intuitive.

Listing 5-10 depicts that class and also shows a `main()` method to test the default value of the done field.

Listing 5-10. Code Sample Used to Show Usage of `boolean` Fields

```
package com.apress.bgn.five;

public class ConvertProcessDemo {
    /* other fields and methods */
    private boolean done;
```

```
    public boolean isDone() {
        return done;
    }
    public void setDone(boolean done) {
        this.done = done;
    }
    void main() {
        ConvertProcessDemo cp = new ConvertProcessDemo();
        System.out.println("Default value = " + cp.isDone());
    }
}
```

And as expected, the output printed is

```
Default value = false
```

The boolean type is not compatible with any other primitive type, which means, for example, that assigning a boolean value to an int variable by simple assignment (using =) is not possible. Explicit conversion is not possible either. So writing something like

```
boolean f = false;
int fi = (int) f;
```

causes a compilation error like the one shown here:

> *javac chapter05/primitives/src/main/java/com/apress/bgn/five/*
> *PrimitivesDemo.java chapter05/primitives/src/main/java/com/apress/bgn/*
> *five/PrimitivesDemo.java:47: error: incompatible types: boolean cannot be*
> *converted to int*
> *   int fi = (int) f;*
> *   ^*

1 error

We'll be adding more information about this type in **Chapter 6**.

The char Type

The char type is used to represent characters. The values are 16-bit unsigned integers representing UTF-16 code units. The interval of the possible values for char variables is from \u0000 to \uffff inclusive, corresponding to the numbers from 0 to 65535.

This means that we can actually print the full set of values. Because the representation of the characters is numeric, we can convert int values from the previously mentioned interval to char values.

Listing 5-11 prints all the numeric values of the char interval and their matching characters.

Listing 5-11. Code Sample Used to Print All char Values

```
package com.apress.bgn.five;

import java.util.stream.IntStream;

public class CharListerDemo {
    void main() {
      IntStream.range(0, 65536)
              .forEach(i -> System.out.println("c[" + i + "]=" + (char) i));
    }
}
```

> **Important**   The last char value printed is 65535. The 65536 value is used just as an upper maximum value, because the IntStream.range(startInclusive, endExclusive) method returns a sequentially ordered IntStream from startInclusive (inclusive) to endExclusive (exclusive) by an incremental step of 1. This is a functional way to write code that manipulates a data set. The iterative way involves a for loop statement, which will be covered in detail in **Chapter 7**.

Depending on the operating system being used, some of the characters might not be supported. This means they won't be displayed, or they will be replaced with a bogus character. The same goes for whitespace characters.

If you think the interval dedicated to represent characters is too big, just scroll the console and you will understand why. The UTF-16 character set contains all numbers as characters, all separators, characters from Chinese and Arabic, and a lot more symbols.[2]

---

[2] https://www.fileformat.info/info/charset/UTF-16/list.htm

Numeric Primitive Types

In the code samples presented so far to introduce Java language basics, we mostly used variables of type int, but as previously mentioned, Java defines six numeric primitive types. Each of them has a specific internal representation on a certain number of bits, which obviously means they are bounded by a minimum value and a maximum value. There are four numeric types to represent integer values and two numeric types to represent real numbers. In Figure 5-8 you can see the integer types and the interval of the values for each of them.

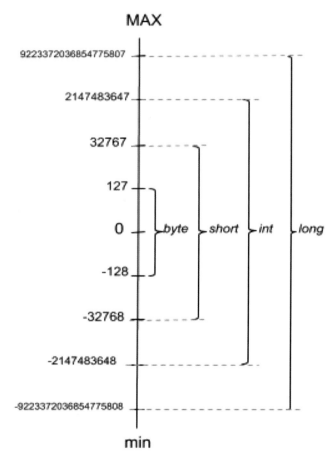

Figure 5-8. *Java numeric types*

Everything a computer processes is represented using bits of information; each bit can only have a value of 1 or 0, which is why it is called *binary representation*. Binary representation is not the focus of this book, but I'll explain it briefly because it is important. Why was binary representation chosen for our computers? Primarily because data (in memory and on hard disks) is stored using a series of ones (on) and zeros (off) binary representations; also, binary operations are really easy to do, and this makes computers very fast.

Let's take math for example. We widely use the decimal system, which is made of ten unique digits ranging from 0 to 9. Internally computers use a binary system, which uses only two digits: 0 and 1. To represent numbers greater than 1, we need more bits. So in a decimal system we have 0, 1, 2, 3, 4, 5, 6, 7, 8, 9, 10, 11, and so on. In a binary system to represent numbers, we have only two digits, so we have 0, 1, 10, 11, 100, 101, 110, 111, 1000, and so on. If you imagine a bit to be like a box in which you can put only ones and zeros, to represent numbers like a computer does, you need more and more ones and zeros as the numbers increase. As a bit can have only two values, the number of values to represent is defined by a power of 2. Just look at Figure 5-9.

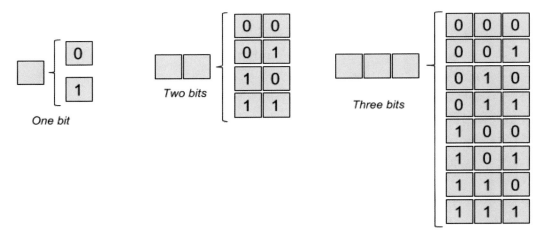

Figure 5-9. *Binary numeric representation*

So, on one bit we can represent two values, which is 2^1; on two bits we can represent four values, which is 2^2; and so on. So this is how we will refer to Java primitive numeric types representation boundaries, sometimes including a bit for the sign as well.

Java Integer Primitive Types

The following list contains the integer primitive types and their boundaries:

- byte is used to represent numbers between -2^7 and $2^7 - 1$ inclusive ([−128, 127]). The default value for a byte field is 0 and is represented on 8 bits.

- short is used to represent numbers between -2^{15} and $2^{15} - 1$ inclusive ([−32768, 32767]). The interval for this type is a superset of the byte interval, thus a byte value can be safely assigned to a short variable without the need for an explicit conversion. This applies to all types that have the interval a superset of the byte interval type. In the next code snippet, a byte value is assigned to a short variable, the code compiles, and when executed prints 23. The default value for a short field is 0 and is represented on 16 bits.

```
byte bv = 23;
short sbv = bv;
System.out.println("byte to short: " +   sbv);
```

- int is used to represent integer numbers between -2^{31} and $2^{31} - 1$ inclusive ([−2147483648, 2147483647]). The default value for an int field is 0 and is represented on 32 bits.

- long is used to represent integer numbers between -2^{63} and $2^{63} - 1$ inclusive ([−9223372036854775808, 9223372036854775807]). The default value for a long field is 0 and is represented on 64 bits.

Important   In practice, sometimes the need to work with integer numbers outside the interval long appears. For these situations, there is a special class (yes, a class, not a primitive type) in Java named BigInteger that allocates just as much memory as is needed to store a number of any size. Operations with BigInteger might be slow, but this is the trade-off to work with huge numbers.

Java Real Primitive Types

When it comes to arithmetic, aside from integer numbers we also have `real` numbers, which are quite useful because most prices and most arithmetic operations executed by programs do not result in an integer numbers. Real numbers contain a decimal point and decimals after it. To represent real numbers in Java, two primitive types are defined, called **floating-point types**: `float` and `double`.

- `float` is used to represent single-precision, 32-bit format IEEE 754 values as specified in IEEE Standard for Binary Floating-Point Arithmetic. The default value is 0.0. A floating-point variable can represent a wider range of numbers than a fixed-point variable of the same bit width, but at the cost of precision. Values of type `int` or `long` can be assigned to variables of type `float`. What is actually happening, and why the loss of precision? A number is represented as a floating-point number and an exponent, which is actually a power of 10. So when the floating-point number is multiplied by 10 at this exponent power, the initial number should result. Let's take the maximum long value and assign it to a float variable and check what is printed:

```
float maxLongF = Long.MAX_VALUE;
System.out.println("max long= " + Long.MAX_VALUE);
System.out.println("float max long= " + maxLongF);
```

`Long.MAX_VALUE` is a final static variable that has the maximum long value assigned to it: 9223372036854775807. The preceding code will print the following:

```
max long= 9223372036854775807
float max long= 9.223372E18
```

As you can see, the `maxLongF` number should be equal to 9223372036854775807, but because it is represented as a smaller number and a power of 10, precision is lost. If we were to reconstruct the integer number by multiplying 9.223372 by 10^18, the result would be 9223372000000000000. It's close, but not close enough. So what are the interval edges for `float`? Float is used to represent real numbers between 1.4E^–45 and 2^128 × 10^38.

- double is used to represent single-precision, 64-bit format IEEE 754 values as specified in IEEE Standard for Binary Floating-Point Arithmetic and is used to represent numbers between $4.9E^{-324}$ and $2^{127} \times 10^{308}$. The default value is 0.0.

Important   Values 0 and 0.0(double) are different in Java. To a normal user, they both mean zero, but in mathematics, the one with the decimal point is more precise. Still, in Java we are allowed to compare an int value to a float value, and if we compare 0 and 0.0, the result will be that they are equal. Also, positive zero and negative zero are considered equal; thus the result of the comparison 0.0==-0.0 is true.

Developers cannot define a primitive type, neither by defining it from scratch nor by extending an existing primitive type. Type names are *reserved Java keywords* that cannot be redefined by the developer. Java prohibits declaring fields, methods, or class names that are named as those types.

As you have noticed until now, a variable that we intend to use must be declared first and used later. When it is declared, a value can be associated as well. For primitive values, a number can be written in many ways. In Listing 5-12 you can see a few samples of how numeric values can be written when variables are initialized or assigned afterward.

Listing 5-12. Code Sample Used to Print Primitive Values in Multiple Ways

```
package com.apress.bgn.five;

public class NumericDemo {
    private byte b;
    private short s;
    private int i;
    private long l;
    private float f;
    private double d;

    void main() {
        NumericDemo nd = new NumericDemo();
```

```
        nd.b = 0b1100;
        System.out.println("Byte binary value: " + nd.b);

        nd.i = 42 ; // decimal case

        nd.i = 045 ; // octal case - base 8
        System.out.println("Int octal value: " + nd.i);

        nd.i = 0xcafe ; // hexadecimal case - base 16
        System.out.println("Int hexadecimal value: " + nd.i);

        nd.i = 0b10101010101010101010101010101011;
        System.out.println("Int binary value: " + nd.i);

        // Java 7 syntax
        nd.i = 0b1010_1010_1010_1010_1010_1010_1010_1011;
        System.out.println("Int binary value: " + nd.i);

        nd.l = 1000_000l; // equivalent to 1000_000L
        System.out.println("Long value: " + nd.l);

        nd.f = 5;
        System.out.println("Integer value assigned to a float variable: "
        + nd.f);

        nd.f = 2.5f; // equivalent to nd.f = 2.5F;
        System.out.println("Decimal value assigned to a float variable: "
        + nd.f);

        nd.d = 2.5d; // equivalent to nd.d = 2.5D;
        System.out.println("Decimal value assigned to a double variable: "
        + nd.f);
    }
}
// output
/**
 Byte binary value: 12
```

```
Int octal value: 37
Int hexadecimal value: 51966
Int binary value: -1431655765
Int binary value: -1431655765
Long value: 1000000
Integer value assigned to a float variable: 5.0
Decimal value assigned to a float variable: 2.5
Decimal value assigned to a double variable: 2.5
*/
```

As you can figure out from Listing 5-12, integer numbers can be represented in Java in four ways:

- **Decimal**: Base 10, written using digits 0 to 9.

- **Octal**: Base 8, written using digits 0 to 7 and prefixed by 0 (zero); this means number 8 is represented in octal as the 010 digits.

- **Hexadecimal**: Base 16, written using digits 0 to 9 and letters A to F, lowercase or uppercase and prefixed by 0x or 0X; this means that number 10 is represented in hexadecimal as 0x00A, number 11 as 0x00B, and so on until the letters in the set end, and 16 is represented as 0x010.

- **Binary**: Base 2, written using digits 0 and 1 and prefixed by 0b or 0B. This was already covered when explaining bits.

You can read more about numeric representation in a computer programming book, but unless you end up working on some project requiring you to do mathematical operations, you will seldom get to play with representations other than decimal.

Starting with Java 7, the _ (underscore) is permitted to be used when declaring numeric values to group together digits and increase clarity. Of course, there are some limitations, such us _ cannot be used

- At the start or end of a numeric value

- For byte values

- Next to digits or symbols representing the base (0b/0B for binary, 0 for octal, 0x/0X for hexadecimal)

- Next to the decimal point

The output of executing the code in Listing 5-12 is depicted in Listing 5-13.

Listing 5-13. Output from Executing the Code in Listing 5-12

```
Byte binary value: 12
Int octal value: 37
Int hexadecimal value: 51966
Int binary value: -1431655765
Int binary value: -1431655765
Long value: 1000000
Integer value assigned to a float variable: 5.0
Decimal value assigned to a float variable: 2.5
Decimal value assigned to a double variable: 2.5
```

As no formatting is done when the variables are printed, the values depicted in the console are in the decimal system.

For now, this is all that can be said about the primitive types. Each of the primitive types has a matching reference type defined within the JDK, which will be mentioned later in the chapter.

Java Reference Types

A short description of the Java reference types was provided earlier in the chapter to highlight the difference between primitive and reference types as early as possible. It is now time to expand that description and give some examples of the most-used JDK reference types when programming.

Objects or **instances** are created using the `new` keyword followed by the call of a constructor. The constructor is a special member of a class and is used to create an object by initializing all fields of the class with their default values, or values received as arguments. A class instance is created by calling the class constructor (one of them, because there might be more than one defined within the class). Consider the example in **Chapter 4** of the `Performer` class. To declare a reference to an object of type `Performer`, the following expression is used:

```
Performer human = new Performer("John", 40, 1.91f, Gender.MALE);
```

The interface reference types cannot be instantiated, but objects of class types that implement that interface can be assigned to references of that interface type. The hierarchy used in Chapter 4 is depicted in Figure 5-10.

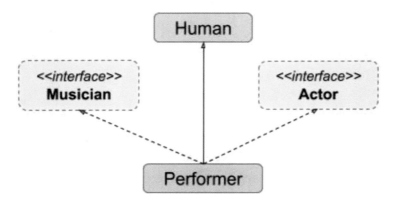

Figure 5-10. *Class and interface hierarchy*

Based on this hierarchy, the four statements in Listing 5-14 are valid; they compile, and the code can be executed successfully.

Listing 5-14. Code Sample Showing Different Reference Types

```
package com.apress.bgn.five;

import com.apress.bgn.four.classes.Gender;
import com.apress.bgn.four.hierarchy.*;

public class ReferencesDemo {

    void main() {
        Performer performer = new Performer("John", 40, 1.91f,
        Gender.MALE);
        Human human = new Performer("Jack", 40, 1.91f, Gender.MALE);
        Actor actor = new Performer("Jean", 40, 1.61f, Gender.UNSPECIFIED);
        Musician musician = new Performer("Jodie", 40, 1.81f, Gender.
        FEMALE);
    }
}
```

Listing 5-14 creates four objects of type `Performer` and assigns them to different reference types, including two interface reference types. If we were to inspect the stack and heap contents for the preceding method, we would find the scenario depicted in Figure 5-11.

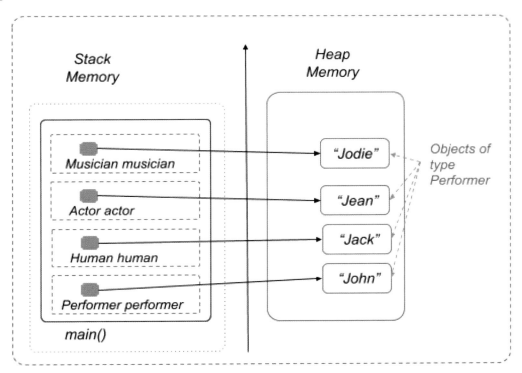

Figure 5-11. *Multiple reference types pointing to different objects in heap memory*

All the references in the previous example point to different objects in the heap, but having references of different types pointing to the same object is possible too, as shown in Listing 5-15.

Listing 5-15. Code Sample Showing Different Reference Types Pointing to the Same Object

```
package com.apress.bgn.five;

import com.apress.bgn.four.classes.Gender;
```

```
import com.apress.bgn.four.hierarchy.*;

public class ReferencesDemo {

    void main() {
        Performer john = new Performer("John", 47, 1.91f, Gender.MALE);
        Human human = john;
        Actor actor = john;
        Musician musician = john;
    }
}
```

In Listing 5-15, we've created only one object but multiple references to it, of different types. If we were to inspect the stack and heap contents again for the preceding method, we would find the scenario depicted in Figure 5-12.

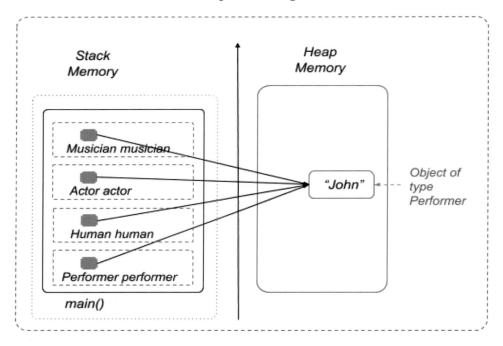

Figure 5-12. *Multiple reference types pointing to one object in heap memory*

References can only be of the type or super-type of an assigned object, so the assignments in Listing 5-16 will not compile.

Listing 5-16. Code Sample Showing Assignments Failing at Compile Time

```
package com.apress.bgn.five;

import com.apress.bgn.four.classes.Gender;
import com.apress.bgn.four.hierarchy.*;

public class BadReferencesDemo {

    void main() {
        Performer performer = new Performer("John", 47, 1.91f,
        Gender.MALE);
        Human human = performer;
        Actor actor = performer;
        Musician musician = performer;
        //these will not compile!!!
        performer = musician;
        //or
        performer = human;
        //or
        performer = actor;
    }
}
```

The reason for the error is that the methods are called on the reference type, so the object the reference is pointing to must have those methods. That is why the Java compiler complains, and that is why smart editors notify you by underlining the statement with a red line. The easiest way to fix the compiling errors in the previous example is an explicit cast (or conversion) to the Performer type. That silences the compiler, but it won't make the code runnable.

The easiest way to prove this is by creating a class named Fiddler that implements Musician and assign an instance of this class to a Performer reference. An explicit conversion of the Fiddler instance to Performer is necessary to trick the compiler into accepting this code as valid, as shown in the marked line in Listing 5-17.

Listing 5-17. Code Sample Showing Assignments Failing Runtime Time

```java
package com.apress.bgn.five;

import com.apress.bgn.four.classes.Gender;
import com.apress.bgn.four.hierarchy.*;

public class BadReferencesDemo {

    void main() {
        Musician fiddler = new Fiddler(true);
        Performer performer = (Performer) fiddler;
        System.out.println("Learned the skill at: " + performer.
        getSchool());
        System.out.println("Appeared in movies: " + performer.getFilms());
    }
}

class Fiddler implements Musician {
    private boolean ownsFiddle = false;

    public Fiddler(boolean ownsFiddle) {
        this.ownsFiddle = ownsFiddle;
    }

    @Override
    public String getSchool() {
        return "Irish Conservatory";
    }

// other methods omitted
}
```

The Fiddler instance was explicitly converted to Performer and the compiler accepted this, because it assumes we know what we are doing. The converted instance is then assigned to a reference of type Performer and then methods getSchool() and .getFilms() are called on it.

When running the code in Listing 5-17, you would expect the performer. getSchool() method to be executed correctly and "Learned the skill at: Irish Conservatory" to be printed in the console, because after all, class Fiddler implements

Musician and provides a concrete implementation for getSchool(). You would also expect an exception to be thrown when the next line is executed; calling performer.getFilms() is not possible since class Fiddler does not implement Actor and does not provide a concrete implementation for the getFilms() method.

But this is not how JVM does things. When running this code, an exception will be thrown exactly when executing the conversion line, because a Fiddler instance cannot be converted to a Performer instance. The message depicted in Listing 5-18 will be printed in red in the console.

Listing 5-18. Casting Exception Message

```
Exception in thread "main" java.lang.ClassCastException:
    class com.apress.bgn.five.Fiddler cannot be cast to class com.apress.
    bgn.four.hierarchy.Performer
        (com.apress.bgn.five.Fiddler is in module chapter.five.references
        of loader 'app';
         com.apress.bgn.four.hierarchy.Performer is in module chapter.
        four@3.0-SNAPSHOT of loader 'app')
    at chapter.five.references/com.apress.bgn.five.BadReferencesDemo.
    main(BadReferencesDemo.java:57)
```

Arrays

The new keyword can also be used to create arrays, in a similar way it is used to create objects. An **array** is a data structure that holds a group of values together. Its size is defined when created and cannot be changed. Each variable can be accessed using an index that starts from 0 and goes up to the length of the array-1. Arrays can hold primitive and reference values. Listing 5-19 contains a class with a declaration of an array field that groups together int values.

Listing 5-19. Class with int array Field

```
package com.apress.bgn.five;
import java.util.Arrays;

public class ArrayDemo {

    int array[];
```

```
    void main() {
        ArrayDemo ad = new ArrayDemo();
        System.out.println("array was initialized with " + Arrays.
        toString(ad.array));
    }
}
```

There are two ways to declare an array, depending on where the brackets are positioned—after the array name or after the array element types:

```
int array[];
int[] array;
```

Important   This is important to know because if you are ever interested in getting your Java knowledge certification[3], the exam might contain questions regarding the correct ways to declare arrays.

What do you think is the console output that results when the code in Listing 5-19 is executed? If you assumed that the ad.array field is initialized with null, and the message printed is *array was initialized with null*, you are quite right in your assumption.

Arrays are reference types, even when they contain elements of primitive types and thus when left to the JVM to initialize fields of this type with a default value, null will be used, as this is the typical default value for reference types. The null keyword was mentioned before, but let's emphasize its importance. The null keyword is used to represent a nonexistent value. A reference that is assigned this value does not have a concrete object assigned to it, meaning it does not point to an object in the heap. That is why when writing code, if an object is used (through its reference, of course) before being initialized, a NullPointerException is thrown. That is why developers test equality to null before using the object (or array).

---

[3] https://www.oracle.com/uk/education/certification/get-certified

The code snippet in Listing 5-19 could be written a little better to take into account the possibility of the array being null and to exit from the main(..) method gracefully using the return keyword, as shown in Listing 5-20.

Listing 5-20. Class with int array Field and Null Check

```
package com.apress.bgn.five;
import java.util.Arrays;

public class ArrayDemo {
    int[] array;

    void main() {
        var ad = new ArrayDemo();
        if (ad.array == null) {
            System.out.println("Array unusable. Nothing to do.");
            return;
        }
        System.out.println("array was initialized with " + Arrays.
        toString(ad.array));
    }
}
```

Information   When a method is declared to return nothing using the void keyword, a correct return from the method can be enforced by the return; statement without a value.

Why do we need the null keyword to mark something that does not exist yet? Because it is common practice in programming to declare a reference first and initialize it only when it is used for the first time. This is useful especially for objects that are big and require allocating a lot of memory. This programming technique is called **lazy loading**[4].

---

[4] https://en.wikipedia.org/wiki/Lazy_loading

Listing 5-21 depicts a more evolved version of the ArrayDemo class where the array field is initialized and a size is set for it.

Listing 5-21. Class with int array Field That Is Initialized Properly

```
01. package com.apress.bgn.five;
02. import java.util.Arrays;
03. public class InitializedArrayDemo {
04.
05.    int[] array = new int[2];
06.
07.    void main() {
08.          var ad = new InitializedArrayDemo();
09.          if (ad.array == null) {
10.               System.out.println("Array unusable. Nothing to do.");
11.               return;
12.          }
13.
14.          System.out.println(Arrays.toString(ad.array));
15.    }
16. }
```

The initialization of the array takes place in line 5. The size of the array is 2. The size of the array is given as a call, only instead of parentheses, square brackets are used, prefixed by the type of elements the array groups together. By setting the dimension of the array to 2, we are telling the JVM that two adjacent memory locations will have to be put aside (allocated) for this object, to store two int values in. Because no values were specified as the array contents, what do you think they will be filled with when the array is created? This is a simple one: the previous array is defined to be made of two int values, so when the array is initialized, the default value for the int type will be used.

Figure 5-13 depicts what happens in the stack and heap memory when the code in Listing 5-21 is executed.

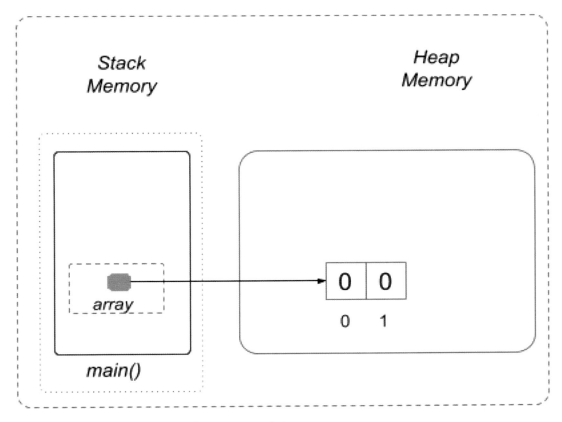

Figure 5-13. *Declaring an* int *array of size 2*

In line 14 of Listing 5-21, the Arrays.toString(..) utility method is used to convert our array to a String instance, which is computed by concatenating all String representations of the array element, separated by commas, and wrapping the results in square brackets. So the resulting console message is [0,0]

To put some values in an array, we have the following choices:

- Access the element directly and set the values:

```
array[0] = 5;
array[1] = 7;
//or
for (int i = 0; i < array.length; ++i) {
    array[i] = i;
}
```

- Initialize the array explicitly with the values we intend to store:

```
int[] another = {1,4,3,2};
```

Arrays can group references as well. Listing 5-22 depicts how a `Performer` array can be declared and used.

Listing 5-22. Class with `int` array Field That Is Initialized Properly

```
package com.apress.bgn.five;

import com.apress.bgn.four.classes.Gender;
import com.apress.bgn.four.hierarchy.Performer;

public class PerformerArrayDemo {

    void main() {
        Performer[] array = new Performer[2];
        for (int i = 0; i < array.length; ++i) {
            System.out.println("performer[" + i + "]= " + array[i] );
        }
        array[0] = new Performer("John", 40, 1.91f, Gender.MALE);
        array[1] = new Performer("Julianna", 35, 1.61f, Gender.FEMALE);
        for (int i = 0; i < array.length; ++i) {
            System.out.println("performer[" + i + "]= " + array[i].
            getName() );
        }
    }

}
```

Before explicit initialization, elements of the array are initialized with the default value for the `Performer` type. Since `Performer` is a reference type, that value is `null`.

Because depicting the memory contents makes it more obvious what happens with our array and objects, I give to you Figure 5-14.

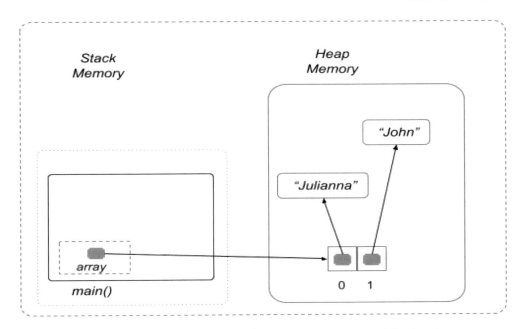

Figure 5-14. *Declaring an array of Performers Instances with size 2*

So yes, we actually have an array of references, and the object they point to can be changed during the program.

The last thing I need to cover here is that arrays can be multidimensional. If you studied advanced math you probably remember the *matrix* concept, which is a rectangular array arranged in rows and columns. In Java, you can model *matrices* by using arrays. If you want a simple matrix with rows and columns, you just define an array with two dimensions. A very simple example is depicted in Listing 5-23.

Listing 5-23. Class Modeling a Matrix Using a Two-Dimensional Array

```
package com.apress.bgn.five;

public class MatrixDemo {
    void main() {
        // bi-dimensional array: 2 rows, 2 columns
        int[][] intMatrix2 = new int[2][2];
        for (int i = 0; i < intMatrix2.length; ++i) {
```

```
            for (int j = 0; j < intMatrix2[i].length; ++j) {
                intMatrix2[i][j] = i + j;
                System.out.print(intMatrix2[i][j] + " ");
            }
            System.out.println();
        }
    }
}
//output
//0 1
//1 2
```

You can even go multidimensional and define as many coordinates as you want. Listing 5-24 shows how to model a cube by using a three-dimensional array.

Listing 5-24. Class Modeling a Cube Using a Three-Dimensional Array

```
package com.apress.bgn.five;

public class CubeDemo {

    void main() {
        // three-dimensional array with three coordinates
        int[][][] intMatrix3 = new int[2][2][2];
        for (int i = 0; i < intMatrix3.length; ++i) {
            for (int j = 0; j < intMatrix3[i].length; ++j) {
                for (int k = 0; k < intMatrix3[i][j].length; ++k) {
                    intMatrix3[i][j][k] = i + j + k;
                    System.out.print("["+i+", "+j+", " + k + "]");
                }
                System.out.println();
            }
            System.out.println();
        }
    }
}
```

```
/*
[0, 0, 0][0, 0, 1]
[0, 1, 0][0, 1, 1]

[1, 0, 0][1, 0, 1]
[1, 1, 0][1, 1, 1]
*/
```

When it comes to arrays, make them as big as you need them (and your computer memory allows), but make sure to initialize them and make sure in your code that you do not try to access indexes outside the allowed range. If the size of an array is N, then its last index is N – 1 and its first is 0. Try to access any index outside that range and an exception of type java.lang.ArrayIndexOutOfBoundsException will be thrown at runtime. So, the following code compiles, but the execution fails because of an exception being thrown:

```
int[] array = new int[2];
array[5] =7;
```

The exception message gives you a clear idea about *the err of your programming ways*:

```
Exception in thread "main" java.lang.ArrayIndexOutOfBoundsException: Index
5 out of bounds for length 2 at chapter.five.arrays/com.apress.bgn.five.
ArrayDemo.main(ArrayDemo.java:40)
```

For easier handling of arrays in Java, there is a special class: java.util.Arrays. This class provides utility methods to sort and compare arrays, to search elements, or to convert their contents to text or to a stream (as covered in **Chapter 8**) so that they can be printed without writing the tedious for loop used so far in the examples. Listing 5-25 depicts a few of these utility methods.

Listing 5-25. `java.util.Arrays` Useful Methods

```java
package com.apress.bgn.five;

import java.util.Arrays;

public class ArrayUtilitiesDemo {
    void main() {

        int[] array =  {4, 2};
        System.out.println(Arrays.toString(array));
        // or
        Arrays.stream(array).forEach(ai -> System.out.println(ai));
        // or using a method reference
        Arrays.stream(array).forEach(System.out::println);

        Arrays.sort(array);

        array = new int[]{4, 2, 1, 5, 7};
        int foundAt = Arrays.binarySearch(array, 5);
        System.out.println("Key found at: " + foundAt);
    }
}
// output
/*
[4, 2]
4
2
4
2
Key found at: 3
*/
```

The following list provides a short explanation of each statement in Listing 5-25:

- `int[] array = {4, 2}` is an array declaration and initialization. The new `int[]` is not required, as the compiler can figure out the type of elements from the declaration of the array and figure out the size of the array from the size of the set of values provided for initialization.

- `Arrays.toString(array)` returns a `String` representation of the contents of the specified array. The `String` representations of the elements are separated by commas, and the resulting string is enclosed in square brackets (`[]`).

- `Arrays.stream(array)` returns a sequential `IntStream` with the specified array as its source. Streams are covered in **Chapter 8**, and these classes provide methods to process elements one by one, without the need of a `for` loop. In Listing 5-25, the elements of the resulting stream are processed one by one using the `System.out.println(..)` method, which means they are printed one by one in the console.

- `Arrays.sort(array)` sorts the specified array into ascending numerical order. This method does not return a new sorted array, so the elements change positions within the original array. The algorithm used to perform the sorting is called **Dual-Pivot Quicksort** and is one of the most efficient sorting algorithms[5].

- `array = new int[]{4, 2, 1, 5, 7}` is a reinitialization of the array. This means a new array value is assigned to the `array` reference. So the declaration must specify the `new` keyword together with the type and the array size, unless a set of elements is used for the initialization, which is exactly the case of this statement, so the size is not mandatory.

- `Arrays.binarySearch(array, 5)` searches the array for the value provided as an argument (in this case, 5) and returns a value representing the position of the element in the array (ergo, its index). The algorithm used for the search is called **Binary Search** and works by splitting the array repeatedly in two parts until the element is found. This technique is called *divide et impera* (or **divide and conquer**), and it involves splitting a big problem into smaller problems repeatedly (recursively) until they can be easily solved. Of course, binary search on an array is most efficient when the array is sorted.

---

[5] `https://www.toptal.com/developers/sorting-algorithms`

Tip   Feel free to search the Web for the algorithms mentioned in this section; they are useful to understand when you need to develop your own solutions. **Chapter 7** will show you how to write code following a few simple and well-known algorithms.

The **String** Type

The next special Java data type on our list is String. Together with the primitive int, this is one of the most-used types in Java. String instances are used to model texts and perform all kinds of operations on them. The String type is a special type because objects of this type are given special treatment by the JVM. If you remember the first image with memory contents (Figure 5-1), the String object was allocated in the heap in a special place called the **String Pool**. In this section dedicated to it, this type will be covered in detail, and a lot of questions you might have had so far will hopefully be answered.

Until now String variables were declared in this book as depicted in Listing 5-26.

Listing 5-26. A Few String Statements Used in This Book

```
package com.apress.bgn.five;

public class SimpleStringDemo {
    public static void main(String... args) {
01.         String text1 = null;
02.
03.         String text21 = "two";
04.         String text22 = "two";
05.         String text23 = new String ("two");
06.
07.         String piece1 = "t";
08.         String piece2 = "wo";
09.         String text24 = piece1 + piece2;
10.
```

```
11.         char[] twoCh = {'t', 'w', 'o'};
12.         String text25 = new String(twoCh);
    }
}
```

As you can see, each one of the lines 03, 04, 05, 09, and 12 define a String object with the same content, *two*. I intentionally did this for reasons that will become obvious soon enough. In real life applications, especially in this big-data hype period, applications handle a lot of data, most of it in text form. So being able to compress the data and reuse it would reduce the memory consumption. Reducing memory access attempts increases speed by reducing processing, which in turn will reduce costs.

String variables can be initialized with text values directly (lines 03 and 04). In this case the JVM looks first in the String Pool for a String object with the same value. If found, the new String variable is initialized with a reference to it. If not found, memory is allocated, the text value is written to it, and the new String variable is initialized with a reference to it.

In line 05, the constructor of the class String is used to create a String object. Notice the new keyword is being used. This means that allocation for memory to store the text provided as a parameter is being explicitly requested.

Before continuing this section, we have to make a quick detour and mention what **object equality** means in Java. Objects are handled in Java using references to their memory location. The == (double equals) operator compares memory locations the references point to, so two objects are equal if and only if they are stored in the same memory address. That is why objects should be compared using the equals(..) method. This is a special method inherited from the Object class, but each class must provide its own implementation that is truly relevant to its own structure. As expected, the equals(..) implementation in the Object class defaults to the == behavior.

Think about two red balls with the same diameter and same color, made of the same material. They are identical, which translates to Java as being equal, but they are not the same ball; they were just created using the same specifications. If you take two random kids, like Jim and Jane, each can play with their own ball. But if Jim and Jane play with the same ball, just throwing it from one to the other, this is pretty similar to equality of references in Java. Figure 5-15 is an abstract representation of this situation.

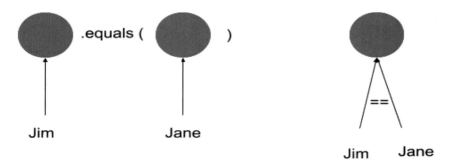

Figure 5-15. *Showing the difference between* equals(..) *and* == *using red balls*

Listing 5-27 depicts a simple version of the Ball class and an executable code sample that creates two separate ball objects and compares them, but also creates a single ball to test equality of references. Since Jim and Jane could be considered references to a ball, the code was written as such.

Listing 5-27. Code Sample Showing Differences Between equals(..) and == on bale References

```
package com.apress.bgn.five;

import java.util.Objects;

public class EqualsDemo {
    void main() {
        var jim = new Ball(10, "red", "rubber");
        var jane = new Ball(10, "red", "rubber");

        System.out.println("-- Playing with different balls -- ");
        System.out.println("Jim and Jane have equal balls? A:" + jim.
        equals(jane));
        System.out.println("Jim and Jane have the same ball? A:" + (jim
        == jane));

        System.out.println("-- Playing with the same ball -- ");
        var  extra = new Ball(10, "red", "rubber");
        jim= extra;
        jane = extra;
```

```
        System.out.println("Jim and Jane have equal balls? A:" + jim.
        equals(jane));
        System.out.println("Jim and Jane have the same ball? A:" + (jim
        == jane));
    }
}

class Ball {
    int diameter;
    String color;
    String material;

    public Ball(int diameter, String color, String material) {
        this.diameter = diameter;
        this.color = color;
        this.material = material;
    }

    @Override
    public boolean equals(Object o) {
        if (this == o) return true;
        if (o == null || getClass() != o.getClass()) return false;
        Ball ball = (Ball) o;
        return diameter == ball.diameter && Objects.equals(color, ball.
        color) && Objects.equals(material, ball.material);
    }

    // other code omitted
}
// output
/*
 -- Playing with different balls --
Jim and Jane have equal balls? A:true
Jim and Jane have the same ball? A:false
-- Playing with the same ball --
Jim and Jane have equal balls? A:true
Jim and Jane have the same ball? A:true
 */
```

Listing 5-27 points out pretty well the difference between the == operator and the equals(..) method on references: the == operator tests references equality, and the equals(..) method tests the equality of the objects those references point to.

Note   Of course, the equals(..) method implementation introduced here is naive, because the nullability and comparison with an object of a different type should be taken into consideration. And there is also the hashCode() method, which must be implemented when equals(..) is, because otherwise your classes won't function correctly with some collection classes that will be covered later in this chapter. For now, I really hope the difference between object equality and reference equality is clear, so that the rest of the String section makes sense.

That ends our object equality detour.

In Java, String instances are *immutable*, which means they cannot be changed once created. The String class is also declared final, so developers cannot extend it. There are multiple reasons why String instances are immutable in Java, some of which are related to security of applications, but those reasons are too advanced to cover in this book. In this section the focus is on the most obvious reason.

Since String instances cannot be changed once created, the JVM can reuse existing values that were already allocated to form new String values, without consuming additional memory. This process is called *interning*. One copy of each text value (literal) is saved into the previously mentioned special memory region called the String Pool. When a new String variable is created and a value is assigned to it, the JVM first searches the pool for a String of equal value. If found, a reference to this memory address will be returned, without allocating additional memory. If not found, it'll be added to the pool and its reference will be returned. This being said, considering the sample code in Listing 5-26 (the one before the equality detour), we expect text21 and text22 variables to point to the same String object in the pool, which means references are equal too.

Listing 5-28 depicts code that tests this assumption.

Listing 5-28. Code Sample Showing Differences Between equals(..) and == on String References (Scenario1: equal references, equal objects)

```java
package com.apress.bgn.five;

public class SimpleStringDemo {
    void main() {
        String text21 = "two";
        String text22 = "two";

        if (text21 == text22) {
            System.out.println("Equal References");
        } else {
            System.out.println("Different References");
        }
        if (text21.equals(text22)) {
            System.out.println("Equal Objects");
        } else {
            System.out.println("Different Objects");
        }
    }
}
```

When running the code in Listing 5-28, the following will be printed in the console, proving the previous affirmations and the existence of the String Pool:

```
Equal References
Equal Objects
```

In Figure 5-16 you can see an abstract representation of the memory contents when the previous code is executed.

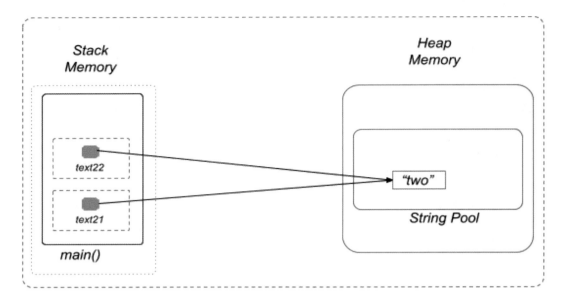

Java Runtime Memory

Figure 5-16. *Abstract representation of the String Pool area created in the heap memory*

When a new `String` object is created using the new operator, the JVM will allocate new memory for the new object and store it in the heap, so the String Pool won't be used. This results in every `String` object created like this having its own memory region with its own address.

Warning   It should be obvious at this point that using `String` constructors (there are more than one) to create `String` objects is in fact equivalent to wasting memory.

Because of the existence of the string pool if we were to compare variable `text22` and variable `text23` from the initial code sample (Listing 5-26), we would expect their references to be different, but the objects should be equal. Listing 5-29 depicts code that tests this assumption.

Listing 5-29. Code Sample Showing Differences Between equals(..) and == on String References (Scenario2: different references, equal objects)

```java
package com.apress.bgn.five;

public class SimpleStringDemo {
    void main() {
        String text22 = "two";
        String text23 = new String ("two");

        if (text22 == text23) {
            System.out.println("Equal References");
        } else {
            System.out.println("Different References");
        }
        if (text22.equals(text23)) {
            System.out.println("Equal Objects");
        } else {
            System.out.println("Different Objects");
        }
    }
}
```

When running the code in Listing 5-29, the following will be printed in the console, proving everything in the assumption was correct:

```
Different References
Equal Objects
```

I leave it up to you to imagine how the stack and heap memory looks for the previous example.

Tip   If you want to check if you understood memory management and Strings correctly, you are welcome to draw your own picture and send it to me (the author) for a review and a technical discussion.

> **Important**   The *String Pool* had a default size of 1009 entries until Java 6. Starting with this version, its size can be modified using the `-XX:StringTableSize` command-line option. Since the size varies from one Java version to another and the memory available to the program, my recommendation is just to run `java -XX:+PrintFlagsFinal -version` and look for `StringTableSize` in the returned output to get the real size of the String Pool on your machine.

In Listing 5-26, lines 11 and 12 depict how a `String` instance can be created from a `char[3]` array. Until Java 8, internally that was the initial representation for `String` values—arrays of characters. A character is represented on 2 bytes, which means a lot of memory was consumed for `Strings`. In Java 9, a new representation was introduced called Compact `String`, which uses `byte[]` or `char[]` depending on the content. This means that the memory consumed by a `String` processing application is significantly lower starting with Java 9.

The `String` class provides a huge set of methods to manipulate strings. Over the years it received many improvements, like better optimization possibilities, multiline blocks, and new practical methods of text transformations. A lot of `String` utility methods were missing from the JDK over the years, and developers used libraries like Apache Commons Lang[6] to avoid writing their own. After Java 8 a few modifications have been added that make external libraries unnecessary. The following section lists and explains the most interesting and useful of them that a beginner should be aware of.

Useful String Methods Added After Java 8

All the useful `String` methods added after Java 8 are demonstrated in class `com.apress.bgn.five.NewAgeStringDemo`, which won't be fully depicted in the book to keep it to an acceptable size. The following list briefly describes the most useful methods added to the `String` class after Java 8.

In Java 11:

- `strip()`: Returns a string whose value is this string, with all leading and trailing whitespace removed.

---

[6] https://commons.apache.org/proper/commons-lang

- `stripLeading()`: Returns a string whose value is this string, with all leading whitespace removed.

- `stripTrailing()`: Returns a string whose value is this string, with all trailing whitespace removed.

- `isBlank()`: Returns `true` if the string is empty or contains only whitespace codepoints, otherwise returns `false`.

- `lines()`: Returns a stream of lines extracted from this string, separated by line terminators.

- `repeat(int count)`: Returns a string whose value is the concatenation of this string repeated `count` times.

In Java 12:

- `indent(int n)`: Adjusts the indentation of each line of this string based on the value of n, and normalizes line-termination characters.

In Java 15:

- `String formatted(Object templateReference)`: Formats using this string as the format string, and the supplied arguments. This method is an equivalent to `String.format(stringReference, templateReference)` introduced in Java 1.5, a static method in the `String` class that required the processed string to be provided as an argument.

In Java 21:

- `int indexOf(int ch, int beginIndex, int endIndex)`: Returns the index within this string of the first occurrence of the specified character, starting the search at `beginIndex` and stopping before `endIndex`.

- `int indexOf(String str, int beginIndex, int endIndex)`: Returns the index of the first occurrence of the specified substring within the specified index range of this string (equivalent of `s.substring(beginIndex, endIndex).indexOf(str) + beginIndex`).

- String[] splitWithDelimiters(String regex, int limit):
  Splits this string around matches of the given regular expression and
  returns both the strings and the matching delimiters (the pattern will
  be applied at most limit-1 times).

Escaping Characters

There are special characters that cannot be part of a String value. As you have probably
noticed, String values are defined between double quotes ("sample"), and this makes
the " (double quote) character unusable as a value. To be able to use it as a String value
or part of one, it has to be *escaped*. Another special character that is not allowed to be
part of a String value is \ (backslash). Figure 5-17 shows how IntelliJ IDEA informs you
with its squiggly red line that you cannot use those characters in the content of a String
value. It also shows how you can escape those characters to make them usable.

```
BadStringDemo.java ×
  1   > /.../
 28     package com.apress.bgn.five;
 29
 30     /**
 31      * Created by iuliana.cosmina on 28/04/2024
 32      */
 33  ▷  public class BadStringDemo {  new *
 34  ▷      public static void main() {  new *
 35            String text332 = "Special "_character"_;
 36            String text331 = "Special \" character" ;
 37
 38            String text341 = "Special \_character" ;
 39            String text342= "Special \\ character" ;
 40
 41            String text351 = "Special \a character" ;
 42            String text352 = "Special \\a character" ;
 43
 44        }
 45    }
 46
```

Figure 5-17. *Code samples with special characters*

To escape those characters, a backlash must be inserted before them. So a single \
is not allowed to be part of a String value, but two of them together are, which tells the
compiler that the String value contains a \ character:

```
System.out.println(" Example using \\.")
//Prints
 Example using \.
```

The \a special character in Figure 5-17 is not allowed in a String value because the \
is used to construct escape sequences, but \a is not an escape sequence.

The ' (single quote) must be escaped as well when used as a character value.

```
char quote = '\'';
```

There are several Java escape sequences that can be used in String values to get a
certain effect, the most important of which are listed in Table 5-1.

Table 5-1. *Java Escape Sequences*

Escape Sequence	Effect
\n	Create a new line (often called the newline character).
\t	Create a tab character.
\b	Create a backspace character (which might delete the preceding character, depending on the output device).
\r	Return to the start of the line (but do not make a new line, the equivalent of the Home key on the keyboard).
\f	Form feed (move to the top of the next page for printers).
\s	Create a space character.
\	Line terminator.

Information   The full list of characters that need to be escaped in String
values can be found in the Java Language Specification documentation here:
`https://docs.oracle.com/javase/specs/jls/se23/html/jls-3.`
`html#jls-3.10.7`

Important   According to the JLS, it is a compile-time error if the character following a backslash in an escape sequence is not a \ or an ASCII b, s, t, n, f, r, ", ', 0, 1, 2, 3, 4, 5, 6, or 7.

The newline \n and the tab \t character are used quite often in programming to properly format console output. If we declare a String instance like the following:

```
String perf = "The singers performing tonight are: \n\t Paolo Nutini \n\t
Seth MacFarlane\n\t John Mayer";
```

When printed in the console, the text will be formatted and will look like this:

```
The singers performing tonight are:
    Paolo Nutini
    Seth MacFarlane
    John Mayer
```

Text Blocks

In JDK 15, support for text blocks was introduced, which means instead of splitting a big String value into multiple smaller values written on multiple lines and concatenating them to keep the code readable, you can now declare a single block of text and assign it to a String reference.

Before Java 15, if you wanted to declare a multiline string value, you had a few options, which included concatenations, explicit line terminators, and delimiters. A few of these options are depicted in Listing 5-30. Depending on the solution you are building, you can choose any of them; a discussion about the efficiency and drawbacks of each is out of scope for this book.

Listing 5-30. Multiline Java String Value Before JDK 15

```
package com.apress.bgn.five;

import java.io.PrintWriter;
import java.io.StringWriter;
```

```java
public class MultiLineDemo {
    void main() {
        // this statement extracts the newline character specific to the
        // operating system
        String newLineCh = System.getProperty("line.separator");

        // method 1: simple concatenation using the '+' operator
        String multilineStr = "line one of the text block" +
                newLineCh +
                "line two of the text block" +
                newLineCh +
                "last line of the text block" ;

        // or method 2 using `String#concat(..)` method
        multilineStr = "line one of the text block"
                .concat(newLineCh)
                .concat("line two of the text block")
                .concat(newLineCh)
                .concat("last line of the text block") ;

        // or method 3 using `String.join` utility method
        multilineStr = String.join("line one of the text block" ,
                newLineCh ,
                "line two of the text block" ,
                newLineCh ,
                "last line of the text block");

        // or method 4 using a StringBuffer instance
        multilineStr = new StringBuffer("line one of the text block")
                .append(newLineCh)
                .append("line two of the text block")
                .append(newLineCh)
                .append("last line of the text block").toString();
```

```
        // or method 5 using a StringBuilder instance
        multilineStr = new StringBuilder("line one of the text block")
                .append(newLineCh)
                .append("line two of the text block")
                .append(newLineCh)
                .append("last line of the text block").toString();

        // or method 5 using a StringWriter instance
        StringWriter stringWriter = new StringWriter();
        stringWriter.write("line one of the text block");
        stringWriter.write(newLineCh);
        stringWriter.write("line two of the text block");
        stringWriter.write(newLineCh);
        stringWriter.write("last line of the text block");
        multilineStr = stringWriter.toString();

        // or method 6 using a StringWriter and PrintWriter instance
        stringWriter = new StringWriter();
        PrintWriter printWriter = new PrintWriter(stringWriter);
        printWriter.println("line one of the text block");
        printWriter.println("line two of the text block");
        printWriter.println("last line of the text block");
        multilineStr = stringWriter.toString();

        System.out.println(multilineStr);
    }
}
```

Important   `StringBuffer` represents a thread-safe, mutable sequence of characters. This means any action on a `StringBuffer` is executed after single access is ensured. This is why using `StringBuffer` to concatenate strings is slower than using `StringBuilder`, which is its non-thread-safe equivalent. So when designing your code, unless there is a risk that your string concatenation block will be executed by multiple threads in parallel, go with `StringBuilder`.

In JDK 15, support for declaring text blocks was added, which enables programmers to embed multiline texts in the code exactly as they are without modifying them to add line terminators, delimiters, or concatenation operators. A text block is thus an alternative form of Java `String` representation that starts with three double-quote characters followed by a line terminator and ends with three double-quote characters. So the previous multiline text can be written with the new syntax as shown here:

```
String multilineStr = """
        line one of the text block
        line two of the text block
        last line of the text block
    """;
```

The new syntax is designed only for declaring multiline texts, so it cannot be used to declare single-line texts. Doing so will result in a compile error. The same will happen if the starting three double-quote characters are followed by text instead of the expected line terminator. Figure 5-18 depicts two wrong ways to declare multiline text blocks, and the explanation provided by the IDE.

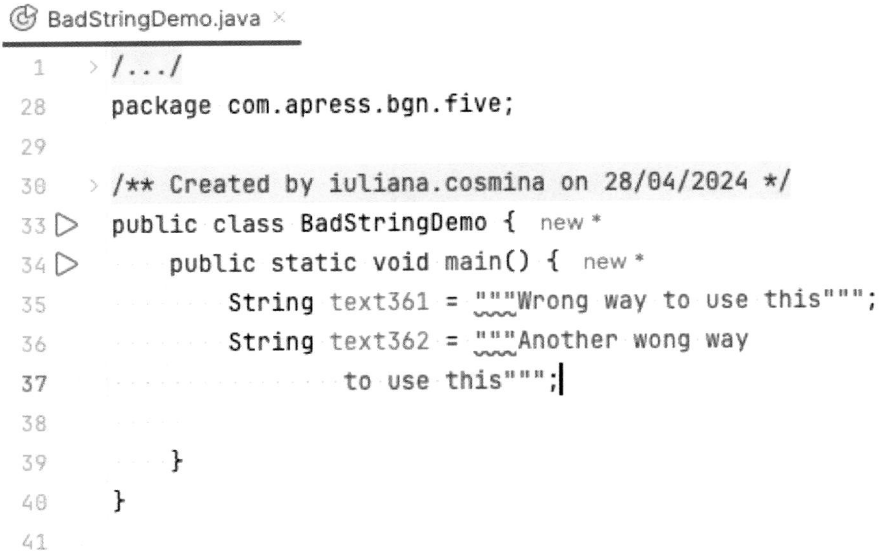

Figure 5-18. Invalid syntax for declaring multiline texts

The following are a few items to note about the syntax:

- The " (double quote) does not need to be escaped in a multiline text block, unless three of them are grouped together within the value. In this case the compiler might be a little confused as to where the text block ends, so in this case at least one of them must be escaped.

- When the lines that make the text block need to be indented, either spaces or tabs should be used; using them both might lead to unpredictable results (e.g., irregular indentation can break a YAML configuration).

- Text blocks support two extra escape sequences: \<line-terminator> and \s. Both are described next.

The first escape sequence, \<line-terminator>, suppresses the inclusion of an implicit newline character. For example, a text block declared as shown previously is equivalent to the following:

```
String multilineStr = "line one of the text block" + "\n" +
                      "line two of the text block" + "\n" +
                      "last line of the text block" + "\n" ;
```

If the last line is not needed, there are two options. First, the text block can have the terminator specified inline with the last line of text:

```
String multilineStr = """
    line one of the text block
    line two of the text block
    last line of the text block""";
```

But this is not recommended since it might affect indentation. The recommended way is to use the \<line-terminator> escape character since this better frames the text block and allows the closing delimiter to manage indentation.

```
String multilineStr = """
        line one of the text block
        line two of the text block
        last line of the text block\
    """;
```

The other escape sequence supported by text blocks, \s, translates to space. This is useful when we want some spaces at end of the lines in the text block:

```
String multilineStr = """
        line one of the text block\s
        line two of the text block\s
        last line of the text block\
    """;
```

The official Oracle documentation includes a section dedicated to the new multiline blocks added in JDK 15. If you ever need more information, that is the best place to look[7].

String Concatenation

Java does not have a way to embed variables in strings to be resolved at runtime. Most developers can work around this problem by using various string concatenation and formatter methods. Class `com.apress.bgn.five.PseudoTemplatesDemo` demonstrates all these methods. You can see its code in Listing 5-31, together with comments indicating the drawbacks of using each method.

Listing 5-31. Java Code Workarounds for Lack of Embedded Variables

```
package com.apress.bgn.five;

import com.apress.bgn.four.classes.Musician;
import java.text.MessageFormat;

public class PseudoTemplatesDemo {
    void main() {
        var bryce = new Musician("Bryce", 38, 1.72f, "High School Rock",
        "Metal");
```

---

[7]https://docs.oracle.com/en/java/javase/23/text-blocks/index.
html#new-escape-sequences

```java
// hard to read
// concatenation using +
var introduction = "My name is " + bryce.getName() +"  and I am "
        + bryce.getAge() +" years old.";
System.out.println("[using '+'] -> " + introduction);

// still hard to read
// concatenation using String#concat
introduction = "My name is ".concat(bryce.getName()).
concat("  and I am ")
        .concat(String.valueOf(bryce.getAge())).concat
        (" years old.");
System.out.println("[using 'concat(..)'] -> " + introduction);

// verbose, hard to read as well
// concatenation using StringBuilder
// similar approach to using StringBuffer
introduction = new StringBuilder("My name is ").append(bryce.
getName()).append("  and I am ")
        .append(bryce.getAge() ).append(" years old.").toString();
System.out.println("[using 'StringBuilder#append(..)' ] -> " +
introduction);

// numbber of arguments mismatch
// concatenation using String.format
introduction = String.format("My name is %s and I am %d years
old.", bryce.getName() , bryce.getAge());
System.out.println("[using `String.format(..)`] -> " +
introduction);

// number of arguments mismatch
// concatenation using MessageFormat.format
introduction = MessageFormat.format("My name is {0} and I am {1}
years old.", bryce.getName() , bryce.getAge());
System.out.println("[using 'MessageFormat.format(..)'] -> " +
introduction);
```

```
// Java 15
// concatenation using String#formatted
introduction = introduction.formatted(bryce.getName() , bryce.
getAge());
System.out.println("[using 'String#formatted(..)']:  -> " +
introduction);
    }
}
```

Embedded variables resolved at runtime, also known as *string interpolation*, is a concept that Java finally implemented via preview JEP 430 in Java 21, and continued the work in Java 22 via JEP 459[8], but it was finally dropped in Java 23. Most languages implement string interpolation in the following way:

- Evaluate expression/variable

- Convert to String if needed

- Insert resulting String into the original String literal

While string interpolation is extremely helpful, it has a few drawbacks:

- Replacing the result of the interpolation would create an invalid overall string literal without validation, which opens up the possibility of SQL injections.

- And invalid JSON, if the test being processed is in this format.

- The results need to be validated or secured, especially when interacting with other systems.

Java designers wanted to improve on this, but the way they chose to do it did not have developers rejoice about it, so string iterpolation is not included in Java 23.

Wrapper Classes for Primitive Types

As mentioned in the **Primitive Data Types** section of this chapter, each primitive type has a corresponding reference type. Before covering each of them and why they are needed, check out Table 5-2.

---

[8] https://openjdk.org/jeps/459

Table 5-2. *Java Primitive Types and Equivalent Reference Types*

Primitive Type	Reference Type
char	java.lang.Character
boolean	java.lang.Boolean
byte	java.lang.Byte
short	java.lang.Short
int	java.lang.Integer
long	java.lang.Long
float	java.lang.Float
double	java.lang.Double

The Java wrapper classes wrap a value of the primitive type with the same name. In addition, these classes provide methods for converting primitive values to String and vice versa, as well as constants and methods that are useful when dealing with primitive types that need to be treated as objects. The numeric wrapper classes are related in that all of them extend the Number class, as depicted in Figure 5-19.

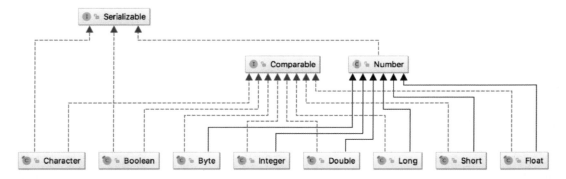

Figure 5-19. *Java primitive and equivalent reference types*

The code samples in this section will use mostly the Integer class, but the other numeric wrapper classes can be used in a similar way. Converting a primitive value to its equivalent reference is called **boxing**; the reverse process is called **unboxing**. JVM does these conversions automatically in most situations; the term **autoboxing** was introduced to refer to the process of boxing, while for some reason automatic unboxing is still called **unboxing**.

The code sample depicted in Listing 5-32 contains a few operations with `Integer` and int values.

Listing 5-32. Autoboxing and Unboxing in Action

```java
package com.apress.bgn.five;

public class WrapperDemo {
    void main() {
        // upper interval boundary for int
        Integer max = Integer.MAX_VALUE;
        System.out.println(max);

        //autoboxing Integer -> int
        int pmax = max;

        //autoboxing int -> Integer
        Integer io = 10;

        //creating primitive utility method
        //exception is thrown, if string is not a number
        int i1 = Integer.parseInt("11");

        //exception is thrown, if string is not a number
        Integer i3 = Integer.valueOf("12");

        //convert int into to String
        String s0 = Integer.toString(13);

        //convert int to float
        float f0 = Integer.valueOf(14).floatValue();

        //creating string with binary representation of number 9 (1001)
        String s1 = Integer.toBinaryString(9);

        //introduced in Java 1.8
        Integer i4 = Integer.parseUnsignedInt("+15");
```

```
        //method to add to integers
        int sum = Integer.sum(2, 3);

        //method to get the bigger value
        int maximum = Integer.max(2, 7);
    }
}
```

The Character and Boolean types are a little different, because these types are not numeric, so they cannot be converted to any numeric values. They cannot be converted one to another either. Oracle provides good documentation for its classes, so if you are curious about using these two types, check out the official JDK API documentation[9].

Date/Time API

Many applications make use of calendar date types to print the current date, deadlines, and birthdays. No matter what application you decide to build, you will most likely need to use calendar dates. Until Java 8, the main class to model a calendar date was `java.util.Date`. There are a few problems with this class and others involved in handling calendar dates. But before we get into those problems, take a look at Listing 5-33 and check out how we can get the current date, create a custom date, and print certain details.

Listing 5-33. `java.util.Date` Code Sample

```
package com.apress.bgn.five;

import java.text.ParseException;
import java.text.SimpleDateFormat;
import java.util.Date;

public class DateDemo {
    public static void main() {
        SimpleDateFormat sdf = new SimpleDateFormat("dd-MM-yyyy");
        Date currentDate = new Date();
        System.out.println("Today: " + sdf.format(currentDate));
```

---

[9] https://docs.oracle.com/en/java/javase/23/docs/api/index.html

```
//deprecated since 1.1
Date johnBirthday = new Date(77, 9, 16);
System.out.println("John's Birthday: " + sdf.format(johnBirthday));

int day = johnBirthday.getDay();
System.out.println("Day: " + day);
int month = johnBirthday.getMonth() + 1;
System.out.println("Month: " + month);
int year = johnBirthday.getYear();
System.out.println("Year:" + year");

        try {
            Date johnBirthday2 = sdf.parse("16-10-1977");
        } catch (ParseException e) {
            e.printStackTrace();
        }
    }
}
//output
/*
Today: 18-05-2024
John's Birthday: 16-10-1977
Day: 0
Month: 10
Year: 77
*/
```

Retrieving the current date on your system is simple; just call the default constructor of the Date class:

```
Date currentDate = new Date();
```

The contents of currentDate can be displayed directly, but usually an instance of java.text.SimpleDateFormat is used to format the date to a pattern that is country specific or just more readable. The formatter can also be used to convert a String with that specific format intro a Date instance. Of course, if the text does not match the pattern of the formatter, a specific exception will be thrown (type java.text.ParseException):

```
try {
```

```
    Date johnBirthday = sdf.parse("16-10-1977");
} catch (ParseException e) {
    // do something with the exception
}
```

To create a Date instance from the numbers representing a date (year, month, and day), a constructor that takes those values as arguments can be used. That constructor, however, has been deprecated since Java 1.1, so some developers prefer to use the sdf.parse(..) method instead. The constructor has a few particularities regarding its arguments:

- The year argument must be the year value – 1900.

- The months are counted from 0, so the month provided as an argument must be the month we want – 1.

The code to construct a Date instance from the numeric values for year, month, and day is depicted below:

```
//deprecated since 1.1
Date johnBirthday = new Date(77, 9, 16);
System.out.println("John's Birthday: " + sdf.format(johnBirthday));
//it prints: John's Birthday: 16-10-1977
```

If we want to extract the year, month, and day of the month from the date, there are methods for that, but again a peculiarity exists: the method to extract the day of the month is named getDate(). Also keep in mind that since months are numbered from 0 to 11, to get the real month value you have to add 1 to the result returned by getMonth(). Listing 5-34 shows the code to create a Date instance, extract the day, month, and year, and then print them.

Listing 5-34. Printing Components of a Calendar Date

```
package com.apress.bgn.five;

import java.text.ParseException;
import java.text.SimpleDateFormat;
import java.util.Date;

public class PrintDateDemo {
    void main() {
```

```java
    try {
        SimpleDateFormat sdf = new SimpleDateFormat("dd-MM-yyyy");
        Date johnBirthday = sdf.parse("16-10-1977");
        System.out.println("John's Birthday: " + sdf.
        format(johnBirthday));

        //day of the month
        int day = johnBirthday.getDate();
        System.out.println("Day: " + day);

        int month = johnBirthday.getMonth() + 1;
        System.out.println("Month: " +"month);

        int year = johnBirthday.getYear();
        System.out.println("Year: " +"year);

    } catch (ParseException e) {
        e.printStackTrace();
    }
    }
}
//output
/*
John's Birthday: 16-10-1977
Day: 16
Month: 10
Year: 77
*/
```

Warning   The `java.util.Date` class has two methods that can be easily confused: the `getDate()` method returns the day of the month of a `Date` object, whereas the `getDay()` method returns the day of the week of a `Date` object.

Both are deprecated as of JDK version 1.1, and better, less confusing ways to extract that information are presented later in this section.

If you inspect the demo classes of this section in the IntelliJ IDEA editor, you will notice that some constructors and methods are written with a strikethrough font. This means that they are deprecated and might be removed in future versions of Java, and thus they should not be used. This is why there is another way to achieve all of the previous results: by using the java.util.Calendar class. The code to do the same as in Listing 5-34 but using the Calendar class is depicted in Listing 5-35.

Listing 5-35. Code Sample for Handling Calendar Dates Using the Calendar Class

```
package com.apress.bgn.five;

import java.text.SimpleDateFormat;
import java.util.Calendar;
import java.util.Date;
import java.util.GregorianCalendar;

public class CalendarDateDemo {
    void main() {
        SimpleDateFormat sdf = new SimpleDateFormat("dd-MM-yyyy");
        Calendar calendar = new GregorianCalendar();
        Date currentDate = calendar.getTime();
        System.out.println("Today: "+ sdf.format(currentDate));

        calendar.set(1977, 9, 16);
        Date johnBirthday = calendar.getTime();
        System.out.println("John's Birthday: "+ sdf.format(johnBirthday));

        int day = calendar.get(Calendar.DAY_OF_MONTH);
        System.out.println("Day: "+ day);
        int month = calendar.get(Calendar.MONTH);
        System.out.println("Month: "+ month);
        int year = calendar.get(Calendar.YEAR);
        System.out.println("Year: "+ year);
    }
}
// output
/*
```

```
Today: 18-05-2024
John's Birthday: 16-10-1977
Day: 16
Month: 9
Year: 1977
*/
```

Unfortunately some of the peculiarities mentioned earlier remain, as the central class for representing dates is still `java.util.Date`, but at least we are not using deprecated methods anymore.

The `java.util.Date` class and the `java.text.SimpleDateFormat` class are not thread-safe, so in complex applications with multiple execution threads, developers must synchronize access to those type of objects explicitly. Objects of those types are not immutable, and working with time zones is a pain. This is the main reason why Java 8 introduced a new API to model calendar date operations that is better designed to make date instances thread-safe and immutable.

The central classes for the API are `java.time.LocalDate` and `java.time.LocalDateTime`, used to model calendar dates and calendar dates with time, respectively. Listing 5-36 shows how to get the current date and how to create a custom date with the new API.

Listing 5-36. Code Sample for Handling Calendar Dates Using the New DateTime API, Introduced in JDK 8

```java
package com.apress.bgn.five;

import java.time.LocalDate;
import java.time.LocalDateTime;
import java.time.Month;

public class NewCalendarDateDemo {
    void main() {
        var currentTime = LocalDateTime.now();
      System.out.println("Current DateTime: " + currentTime);
      LocalDate today = currentTime.toLocalDate();
      System.out.println("Today: " + today);
```

```
        var johnBd = LocalDate.of(1977, Month.OCTOBER, 16);
        System.out.println("John's Birthday: " + johnBd);

        int day = johnBd.getDayOfMonth();
        System.out.println("Day: " + johnBd.getDayOfWeek());
        int month = johnBd.getMonthValue();

        System.out.println("Month: " +  johnBd.getMonth());
        int year = johnBd.getYear();
        System.out.println("Year: " + year);
    }
}
//output
/*
Current DateTime: 2024-05-18T00:28:35.873773
Today: 2024-05-18
John's Birthday: 1977-10-16
Day: 16, SUNDAY
Month: 10, OCTOBER
Year: 1977
*/
```

To get the current date and time, a static method named `now()` is called, which returns an instance of type `LocalDateTime`. This instance can be used to get the current date by calling `toLocalDate()`, which returns the current date as an instance of type `LocalDate`. This class has a `toString()` method that prints the formatted date according to the default locale set on the system.

To create a custom date, the actual year and day of month can be used as arguments, and the month can be specified using one of the values of the `java.time.Month` enum.

Extracting information regarding a date can be done easily by calling methods with intuitive names. Just look at the `getDayOfMonth()` and `getDayOfWeek()` methods in Listing 5-36. Their names reflect exactly what data they are returning.

As you can see, classes `LocalDate` and `LocalDateTime` simplify the development where time zones are not required. Working with time zones is quite an advanced subject, so it won't be covered within this book.

Collections

One of the most important family of types in JDK is the collections family, which you will probably use a lot. Classes and interfaces in the collections family are used to model common data collections such as sets, lists, and maps. All the classes are stored under package java.util and can be split into two categories: tuples and collections of key/value pairs.

The tuples are unidimensional sets of data: if the values are unique, any class implementing the java.util.Set<E> interface should be used to model them, if not any class implementing the java.util.List<E> interface should be used. For collections of key/value pair classes, java.util.Map<K,V> should be implemented.

Starting with Java version 1.5, collections have become generic, which allows developers more precision and security when working with them. Before Java 1.5, collections could contain any type of objects. Developers can still write code like that, as depicted in Listing 5-37.

Listing 5-37. Code Using Collections Up to Java 1.5

```java
package com.apress.bgn.five;

import com.apress.bgn.four.classes.Gender;
import com.apress.bgn.four.hierarchy.Performer;

import java.util.ArrayList;
import java.util.List;

public class CollectionsBasicDemo {
  void main() {
    List objList = new ArrayList();
    objList.add("temp");
    objList.add(Integer.valueOf(5));
    objList.add(new Performer("John", 40, 1.91f, Gender.MALE));
  }
}
```

You probably do not see any problem with this (the compiler sure doesn't), but when you iterate this list, it is quite difficult to determine which objects you are handling, at least not without complicated code analyzing the type of each object. This was mentioned before at the end of **Chapter 4** when generics were introduced. The code to iterate the list and process the elements differently based on their type is depicted in Listing 5-38, just to show you why this is a bad idea and bad practice in this day and age of Java.

Listing 5-38. More Code Using Collections Up to Java 1.5

```java
package com.apress.bgn.five;

import com.apress.bgn.four.classes.Gender;
import com.apress.bgn.four.hierarchy.Performer;

import java.util.ArrayList;
import java.util.List;

public class CollectionsBasicDemo {
  void main() {
    List objList = new ArrayList();
    objList.add("temp");
    objList.add(Integer.valueOf(5));
    objList.add(new Performer("John", 40, 1.91f, Gender.MALE));

    for (Object obj : objList) {
      if (obj instanceof String) {
        System.out.println("String object = " + obj.toString());
      } else if (obj instanceof Integer) {
        Integer i = (Integer)obj;
        System.out.println("Integer object = " + i.intValue());
      } else {
        Performer p = (Performer) obj;
        System.out.println("Performer object = " + p.getName());
      }
    }
  }
}
```

Maybe this is not clear to you now, but to be able to use the contents of the list, you have to know exactly all the types of the objects that were put in the list. This might be doable when you are working alone on a project, but in a bigger project, when multiple developers are involved, this can get messy really fast.

This is where **generics** come to help. Generics help define at compile time what types of objects should be put into a collection, and thus if the wrong object type is added to the collection, the code no longer compiles. Both lists and sets implement the same interface, `java.util.Collection<E>`, which means their API is almost the same. The simplified hierarchy of collection interfaces and classes most used in programming is depicted in Figure 5-20.

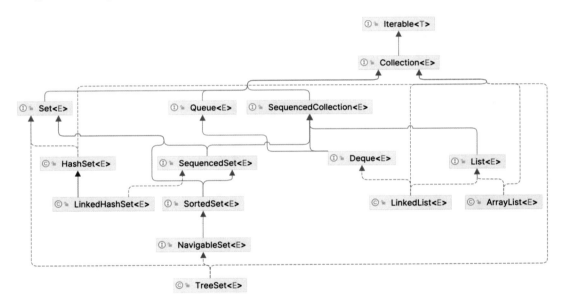

Figure 5-20. *Collection hierarchy*

Listing 5-39 depicts the creation of a `List` of `String` values, and the loop statement needed to traverse it and print its elements.

Listing 5-39. Code Using Collections Starting with Java 1.5

```
package com.apress.bgn.five;

import java.util.ArrayList;
import java.util.List;
```

```java
public class GenericListDemo {
    public static void main() {
        List<String> stringList = new ArrayList<>();
        stringList.add("one");
        stringList.add("two");
        stringList.add("three");

        for (String s : stringList) {
            System.out.println(s);
        }
    }
}
```

A List<E> contains an unsorted collection of nonunique data, null elements included. In Listing 5-39 we declared a reference of type List<E> and an object of type ArrayList<E>. We did this because as all implementations have the same API, we could easily switch ArrayList<E> with LinkedList<E> and the code will still work:

```java
List<String> stringList = new ArrayList<String>();
stringList = new LinkedList<String>();
```

Important   Declaring abstract references is a good programming practice because it increases the flexibility of your code.

The syntax in the previous examples is pre-Java 1.7. In Java 1.7 the <> (diamond operator) was introduced. This allowed more simplification of collections initializations, because it required declaring the type of the elements in the list only in the reference declaration. So the two lines in the previous code snippet become

```java
List<String> stringList = new ArrayList<>();
stringList = new LinkedList<>();
```

Starting with Java 1.5, every new Java version has added changes to the collection framework. Java 1.8 added support for lambda expressions by adding a default method named `forEach` in the `java.lang.Iterable<E>` interface (see Figure 5-20), which is extended by the `java.lang.Collection<E>` interface. So the code to print all the values in the list, like we did previously using a `for` loop, can be replaced with

```
stringList.forEach(element -> System.out.println(element));
```

In Java 9, yet another improvement was introduced: factory methods for collections. Our collection was populated with elements by repeatedly calling `add(..)`, which is a little redundant, especially since we have the full collection of elements we want to put in the list. That is why in Java 9 methods to create collection objects in one line of code were introduced, as shown in the following example:

```
List<String> stringList = List.of("one", "two", "three");
```

The resulting `List<E>` is an immutable collection: it can no longer be modified, meaning elements cannot be added to it or removed from it.

Java 10 added support for local variable type inference, which means that we no longer have to explicitly specify the reference type, because it will be automatically inferred based on the object type. So the following declaration:

```
List<String> stringList = List.of("one", "two", "three");
```

becomes

```
var stringList = List.of("one", "two", "three");
```

Until Java 21, the collections framework lacked a collection type that represents a sequence of elements with a defined encounter order. It also lacked a uniform set of operations that apply across such collections. For example, `List<E>` and `Deque<E>` both define an encounter order, but their common supertype is `Collection<E>`, which does not. Similarly, `Set<E>` does not define an encounter order, and subtypes such as `HashSet<E>` do not define one, but subtypes such as `SortedSet<E>` and `LinkedHashSet<E>` do. Java 21 introduced the `SequencedCollection<E>` interface defining a collection with a well-defined encounter order that supports operations at both ends, and that is reversible.

Of course, the chance to access a collection at both ends was possible before Java 21, but that required invoking `get(..)` and `add(..)` methods with the specific indexes.

The new methods provide a simple way to write code using ordered collections, and the simpler code is also easier to read.

Listing 5-40 depicts the methods declared by the SequencedCollection<E> interface, invoked on an ArrayList<E> instance, and where it applies, a comment shows the invoked methods to do the same thing before Java 21.

Listing 5-40. SequencedCollection<E> Methods Example

```java
package com.apress.bgn.five;

import java.util.ArrayList;
import java.util.List;
import java.util.stream.IntStream;
import static java.lang.System.out;

public class GenericListDemo {
    void main() {
        List<String> list = new ArrayList<>();
        list.add("one");
        list.add("two");
        list.add("three");

        var reversed = list.reversed();
        out.println("[after reversed()]:" +reversed);
        out.println("----------------------------------------------------");

        out.println("[first element]: " + list.getFirst()); // list.get(0)
        out.println("[last element]: " + list.getLast());    // list.get(list.
        size()-1)
        out.println("----------------------------------------------------");

        out.println("[original list]: " + list);
        list.addFirst("zero");                               // list.add(0, "zero");
        out.println("[after addFirst(..)]: " + list);
        list.removeFirst();                                  // list.remove(0);
        out.println("[after removeFirst(..)]: " + list);
        out.println("----------------------------------------------------");

        list.addLast("four");                                // list.add("four");
```

```
        out.println("[after addLast(..)]: " + list);
        list.removeLast();                          //list.remove(list.size()-1);
        out.println("[after removeLast(..)]" +list);
    }
}
```

Similar code can be written with Set<E>, HashSet<E>, and TreeSet<E>, and similar methods exist for this family of classes as well.

Important   Collections is a common topic in interviews for Java entry-level jobs, so if you apply for such a job, don't be surprised if you are asked what the difference is between a List<E> and a Set<E>.

When working with Set<E> implementations, you have to make sure the objects added to the set have equals(..) and hashCode() implemented correctly. The reason for this is that Set<E> models the mathematical *set* abstraction that allows no duplicate elements.

The equals(..) method indicates whether the object passed as an argument is "equal to" the current instance. The default implementation provided by the Object class considers two objects to be equal if they are stored in the same memory location.

The hashCode(..) method returns an integer representation of the object memory address, obtained via *hashing*[10]. The default implementation provided by the Object class returns a random integer that is unique for each instance. This value might change between several executions of the application. This method is useful when objects are used as keys in hash tables, because it optimizes retrieving elements from them. If you want to learn more about hash tables, the Internet is your oyster; as for Java, a hash table can be modeled by an instance of java.util.HashMap<K,V>.

---

[10] https://www.developer.com/java/hashing-java

As per the official documentation, if two objects are equal, then calling `hashCode()` on each of them must yield the same result. But it is not a must for two unequal objects to have different hashCodes) values.

With the preceding details in mind, the `Ball` class introduced earlier (Listing 5-27) will be used to create some ball instances and add them into a `Set<E>`. The code sample in Listing 5-41 shows a version of the `Ball` class containing proper implementations for the `equals(..)` and `hashCode()` methods.

Listing 5-41. Basic `equals(..)` and `hashCode()` Implementations

```java
package com.apress.bgn.five;
import java.util.HashSet;
import java.util.Set;

import static java.lang.System.out;

public class SetDemo {

    void main() {
        Set<Ball> ballSet = new HashSet<>();
        ballSet.add(new Ball(2, "RED", "rubber"));
        ballSet.add(new Ball(4, "BLUE", "cotton"));

        out.println("Set size: " +  ballSet.size());
        Ball duplicate = new Ball(2, "RED", "rubber");
        boolean wasAdded = ballSet.add(duplicate);
        if(!wasAdded) {
            out.println("Duplicate ball not added to the set. ");
            out.println("Set size: " +  ballSet.size());
        }
    }
}

class Ball {
    private int diameter;
    private String color;
    private String material;

    @Override
```

```java
    public boolean equals(Object o) {
        if (this == o) return true;
        if (o == null || getClass() != o.getClass()) return false;
        Ball ball = (Ball) o;
        return diameter == ball.diameter &&
                color.equals(ball.color) &&
                material.equals(ball.material);
    }

    @Override
    public int hashCode() {
        int result = 17 * diameter;
        result = 31 * result + (color == null ? 0 : color.hashCode());
        result = 31 * result + (material == null ? 0 : material.hashCode());
        return result;
    }
    // other code omitted
}
// output
//Set size: 2
//Duplicate ball not added to the set.
//Set size: 2
```

Before Java 1.7 developers had to write equals(..) and hashCode() implementations similar to the ones in Listing 5-41 for all classes that might have been used in a Set<E> or as a key in a Map<K,V>. The implementations had to be based on the values of the most important fields in the class; 17 and 31 are just two random integers used to compute the value returned by hashCode().

In Java 1.7 class java.util.Objects was introduced, providing utility methods to make implementing equals(..) and hashCode() easier. Listing 5-42 depicts equals(..) and hashCode() implementations after Java 1.7.

Listing 5-42. Basic equals(..) and hashCode() Implementations After Java 1.7

```java
package com.apress.bgn.five;
import java.util.HashSet;
import java.util.Objects;
```

```java
import java.util.Set;

import static java.lang.System.out;

public class SetDemo {

    void main() {
        Set<Ball> ballSet = new HashSet<>();
        ballSet.add(new Ball(2, "RED", "rubber"));
        ballSet.add(new Ball(4, "BLUE", "cotton"));

        out.println("Set size: " + ballSet.size());
        Ball duplicate = new Ball(2, "RED", "rubber");
        boolean wasAdded = ballSet.add(duplicate);
        if(!wasAdded) {
            out.println("Duplicate ball not added to the set. ");
            out.println("Set size: " + ballSet.size());
        }
    }
}

class Ball {
    private int diameter;
    private String color;
    private String material;

  @Override
  public boolean equals(Object o) {
    if (this == o) return true;
    if (o == null || getClass() != o.getClass()) return false;
    Ball ball = (Ball) o;
    return diameter == ball.diameter &&
            Objects.equals(color, ball.color) &&
            Objects.equals(material, ball.material);
  }

  @Override
  public int hashCode() {
    return Objects.hash(diameter, color, material);
```

```
    }
      // other code omitted
}
// output
//Set size: 2
//Duplicate ball not added to the set.
//Set size: 2
```

Starting with Java 14, things became even simpler because now a class like `Ball` can be written as a record, as depicted in Listing 5-43.

Listing 5-43. Class `Ball` Written As a Record to Avoid Implementing `equals(..)` and `hashCode()`

```
package com.apress.bgn.five;
import java.util.HashSet;
import java.util.Objects;
import java.util.Set;

import static java.lang.System.out;

public class SetDemo {

  void main() {
    // same as Listing 5-42
  }
}

record Ball(int diameter, String colour, String material) {}
// output
//Set size: 2
//Duplicate ball not added to the set.
//Set size: 2
```

Executing the code Listing 5-43 yields the same result as the code in Listing 5-42, thus proving that the `equals(..)` method generated by the Java compiler is valid.

`Map<K,V>` implementations come with a few differences because they model collections of key/value pairs. The simplified hierarchy of map interfaces and classes most used in programming is depicted in Figure 5-21.

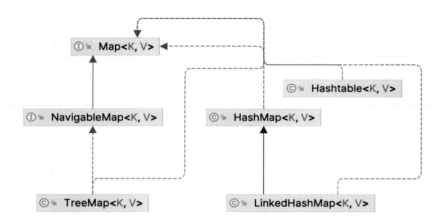

Figure 5-21. *Map hierarchy*

The code in Listing 5-44 depicts the creation and initialization of a map that uses keys of type Ball and values of type Integer. You can imagine this map instance to represent the number of identical balls in a bucket.

Listing 5-44. Map<Ball, Integer> Code Sample

```
package com.apress.bgn.five;

import java.util.HashMap;
import java.util.Map;

public class MapDemo {
    void main(String... args) {
        Map<Ball, Integer> ballMap = new HashMap<Ball, Integer>();
        ballMap.put(new Ball(2, "RED", "rubber"), 5);
        ballMap.put(new Ball(4, "BLUE", "cotton"), 7);

        for (Map.Entry<Ball, Integer> entry : ballMap.entrySet()) {
            System.out.println(entry.getKey() + ": " + entry.getValue());
        }
    }
}
```

```
//output
/*
Ball[diameter=2, colour=RED, material=rubber]: 5
Ball[diameter=4, colour=BLUE, material=cotton]: 7
*/
```

As you can notice from the `for` loop, you can infer that a map is actually a collection of `Map.Entry<K, V>` elements. Moving ahead to the Java 1.7 syntax, the declaration of the map becomes simpler by applying the `<>` (diamond) operator:

```
Map<Ball, Integer> ballMap = new HashMap<>();
```

Moving further to Java 1.8, traversal and printing values in a map become more practical as well, because of the introduction of the `forEach(..)` method and lambda expressions:

```
ballMap.forEach((k,v) -> System.out.println(k + ": " + v));
```

And in Java 9, declaring and populating a map becomes easier too:

```
Map<Ball, Integer> ballMap = Map.of(new Ball(2, "RED", "rubber"), 5, new
Ball(4, "BLUE", "cotton"), 7);
```

Java 10 adds in `var` to simplify the declaration even more:

```
var ballMap = Map.of(new Ball(2, "RED", "rubber"), 5, new Ball(4, "BLUE",
"cotton"), 7);
```

Another thing that needs to be mentioned before ending this section is what happens when a key/pair value is added to the map and the key already exists. As you probably expect, the existing key/pair in the map is overwritten. Before Java 8, writing code to prevent this situation when a set of values is lost required checking if the key is present, and if not present only then adding the new key-pair, as depicted in Listing 5-45.

Listing 5-45. Preventing Key/Pair Overwriting Before Java 8

```
package com.apress.bgn.five;

import java.util.HashMap;
import java.util.Map;
```

```java
public class MapDemo {
    void main(String... args) {
        Map<Ball, Integer> ballMap = new HashMap<>();
        Ball redBall = new Ball(2, "RED", "rubber");

        ballMap.put( redBall, 5);
        ballMap.put(new Ball(4, "BLUE", "cotton"), 7);

         //ballMap.put( redBall, 3); // this overrides entry <redBall, 5>

        if(!ballMap.containsKey(redBall)) {
            ballMap.put(redBall, 3);
        }

        for (Map.Entry<Ball, Integer> entry : ballMap.entrySet()) {
            System.out.println(entry.getKey() + ": " + entry.getValue());
        }
    }
}
```

In Java 8 a practical set of utility methods was added to the Map<K,V> interface to simplify code written using maps, including the method putIfAbsent(..) depicted in Listing 5-46, which replaces the statement marked in Listing 5-45.

Listing 5-46. Preventing Key-Pair Overwriting After Java 8

```java
package com.apress.bgn.five;

import java.util.HashMap;
import java.util.Map;

public class MapDemo {
    void main(String... args) {
        Map<Ball, Integer> ballMap = new HashMap<>();
        Ball redBall = new Ball(2, "RED", "rubber");

        ballMap.put( redBall, 5);
        ballMap.put(new Ball(4, "BLUE", "cotton"), 7);

        ballMap.putIfAbsent(redBall, 3);
```

```
        for (Map.Entry<Ball, Integer> entry : ballMap.entrySet()) {
            System.out.println(entry.getKey() + ": " + entry.getValue());
        }
    }
}
```

The JDK classes for working with collections cover a wide range of functionality, like sorting, searching, merging collections, intersections, conversions to/from arrays, and so on. As the book advances, the context of the code samples will widen, and we will be able to use collections to solve real-life problems.

Concurrency-Specific Types

Previously in the book it was mentioned from time to time that a Java program can run multiple threads in parallel. The abstract concept to support that is referred to as **executing multiple threads**. There are a few Java-specific types used to implement parallel processing, and this section introduces them to you.

Classic Thread Creation (Before Java 21)

By default, when a Java program is executed, a thread is created for the code that is called from the main(..) method. A few other utility threads are created and executed in parallel for JVM-related things. These threads can be accessed easily by using static utility methods defined in the java.lang.Thread class. The code in Listing 5-47 does just that, extracts the references to the Thread instances and prints their name to the console.

Listing 5-47. Preventing Key/Pair Overwriting After Java 8

```
package com.apress.bgn.five;

public class ListJvmThreads {
    void main() {
        var threadSet = Thread.getAllStackTraces().keySet();
        var threadArray = threadSet.toArray(new Thread[threadSet.size()]);
        for (int i = 0; i < threadArray.length; ++i) {
            System.out.println("thread name: " + threadArray[i].getName());
        }
    }
}
```

```
// output
/*
```
thread name: main
```
thread name: Signal Dispatcher
thread name: Common-Cleaner
thread name: Monitor Ctrl-Break
thread name: Reference Handler
thread name: Notification Thread
thread name: Finalizer
 */
```

The output shown in Listing 5-47 was produced when running the code on JDK 23.ea, on a macOS computer, in IntelliJ IDEA. The threads listed have the following responsibilities:

- main executes the developer-written code. The developer can write code to start its own threads from the main thread.

- Reference Handler takes unused objects and adds them to a queue to be evicted.

- Finalizer is a low-priority JVM thread that executes the finalize() method of each object in a queue waiting to be evicted from memory. This method can be overwritten by developers explicitly to free resources linked to objects about to be evicted.

- Common-Cleaner is a low-priority JVM thread that is in charge of lightweight cleanup of objects without using finalization.

- Monitor Ctrl-Break is a thread created by IntelliJ IDEA, since the code is executed using this editor that probably watches the execution and picks up the output so it can display it.

- Signal Dispatcher handles native signals sent by an operating system to the JVM.

- Notification Thread handles notifications sent by an operating system to the JVM.

Except for main, Monitor Ctrl-Break (which is not a JVM application thread) and Common-Cleaner, all the other three are system threads that ensure the JVM collaborates with the operating system. Except for main, all other threads are called **daemon threads**.

They have low priority, and they provide services to **user threads**, which is what the main thread is. These are the only two types of threads in Java.

The developer can write code to start its own threads from the main thread. A thread is the smallest unit of processing that can be scheduled. The simplest way to create a custom thread is to create a class that extends the Thread class. The Thread class implements an interface named Runnable that declares a single method named run(). The Thread class declares a method named start(). When this method is called, the body of the run() method is executed in a separate execution thread than the one calling start().

Note   The internals of thread management is much more complicated, so this section just scratches the surface.

Thus, when extending the Thread class or implementing the Runnable interface directly, the run() method must be overridden.

The example in Listing 5-48 depicts a class named RandomDurationThread and the main() method used to run a few instances of it. The content of the run() method pauses the execution at random times by calling the Thread.sleep(..) utility method. The body of the method is wrapped in two lines of code that print the name of the thread, a starting message and an ending message. The Thread.sleep(..) ensures that each thread execution has a different duration, so that we can clearly see they are executed in parallel.

Listing 5-48. Code Sample Declaring Threads with Random Execution Durations by Extending the Thread Class

```
package com.apress.bgn.five;

class RandomDurationThread extends Thread {

  @Override
  public void run() {
    System.out.println(this.getName()+ " started...");
    for (int i = 0; i < 10; ++i) {
      try {
        Thread.sleep(i * 10);
```

```
      } catch (InterruptedException _) {}
    }
    System.out.println(this.getName() +" ended.");
  }
}

public class MultipleUserThreadsDemo {
  void main() {
    for (int i = 0; i < 10; ++i) {
      new RandomDurationThread().start();
    }
  }
}
```

The main method in class MultipleUserThreadsDemo creates multiple threads that are instances of RandomDurationThread and starts them. Ten instances of class RandomDurationThread are created, and the start() method is called for each of them. When the previous code is executed, a log similar to the one depicted in Listing 5-49 should be seen in the console.

Listing 5-49. Output from Running the Code in Listing 5-48

```
Thread-5 started...

Thread-0 started...
Thread-3 started...
Thread-6 started...
Thread-8 started...
Thread-4 started...
Thread-2 started...
Thread-7 started...
Thread-9 started...
Thread-1 started...
Thread-3 ended.
Thread-6 ended.
Thread-0 ended.
Thread-4 ended.
```

Thread-8 ended.

Thread-5 ended.

Thread-1 ended.

Thread-7 ended.

Thread-2 ended.

Thread-9 ended.

As is obvious from this output, the threads start and end in a random order.

Another way to create threads is by creating a class that implements the Runnable interface. This is useful when we want to extend another class. Or, considering that the Runnable declares a single method, lambda expressions can be used too. Listing 5-50 shows the equivalent Runnable implementation of the RandomDurationThread class and the class used to create threads using the RandomDurationRunnable class.

Listing 5-50. Code Sample Declaring Threads with Random Execution Durations by Implementing the Runnable Interface

```
package com.apress.bgn.five;

class RandomDurationRunnable  implements  Runnable{
    @Override
    public void run() {
        System.out.println(Thread.currentThread().getName() +"
        started...");

        for (int i = 0; i < 10; ++i) {
            try {
                Thread.sleep(i * 10);
            } catch (InterruptedException _) {}
        }
        System.out.println(Thread.currentThread().getName() +" ended.");
    }
}

public class RunnableDemo {
    void main() {
        for (int i = 0; i < 10; ++i) {
            new Thread(new RandomDurationRunnable()).start();
```

```
        }
    }
}
```

Because we no longer have access to the name of the thread, to print it, we must use another utility method, Thread.currentThread(), to retrieve a reference to the current thread in execution so we can get its name.

The Thread class provides a constructor with a parameter of type Runnable, which means it can be called with any argument of a type that implements Runnable.

Running the code in Listing 5-50 produces an output just as random as the output in Listing 5-49.

It was previously mentioned this particular case is a good candidate for using lambda expressions, because Runnable can be implemented on the spot. This means the RandomDurationRunnable class in Listing 5-50 is not necessary, as depicted in Listing 5-51.

Listing 5-51. Code Sample to Run Multiple Threads in Parallel Using Lambda Expressions

```java
package com.apress.bgn.five;

import static java.lang.Thread.currentThread;
import static java.lang.Thread.sleep;

public class LambdaThreadsDemo {
    void main() {
        for (int i = 0; i < 10; ++i) {
            new Thread(
                    //Runnable implemented on the spot
                    () -> {
                        System.out.println(Thread.currentThread().getName()
                        +" started...");
                        for (int j = 0; j < 10; ++j) {
                            try {
                                sleep(j * 10);
                            } catch (InterruptedException _) { }
```

```
            }
            System.out.println(Thread.currentThread().getName()
            +" ended.");
        }).start();
    }
  }
}
```

Java provides thread management classes that can create and manage threads, so the developer mustn't declare the threads explicitly. One such interface is `java.util.concurrent.ExecutorService`. Java provides implementing classes that can be instantiated, and the instances can be configured to run a big number of threads in parallel in a **thread pool**. A thread pool is a group of preconstructed platform threads that are reused when they become available. Some thread pools have a fixed number of threads, while others create new threads as needed. Most times, though, you won't need to go too much into detail, and can just rely on factory methods provided by the `java.util.concurrent.Executors` utility class.

Listing 5-52 shows an example of using the `Executors.newFixedThreadPool(..)` method to create a thread pool instance used to manage 100 instances of `java.util.concurrent.Callable<V>`. The `Callable<V>` interface is a concurrency Java type used to model a task that returns a result and may throw an exception. `Callable<V>` is similar to `java.lang.Runnable` in that they are both supposed to be implemented by classes whose instances are executed on a thread.

Listing 5-52. Code Sample to Run Multiple Threads in Parallel Using an `Executor`

```
package com.apress.bgn.five;

import java.util.ArrayList;
import java.util.concurrent.Callable;
import java.util.concurrent.Executors;

public class FixedThreadPoolDemo {
    void main() {
        var rdc = new RandomDurationCallable();
        try (var executor = Executors.newFixedThreadPool(10)) {
```

319

```
            var assignments = new ArrayList<RandomDurationCallable>();
            for (int i = 0; i < 100; i++) {
                assignments.add(rdc);
            }
            try {executor.invokeAll(assignments);} catch
            (InterruptedException _) {}
        }
    }
}

class RandomDurationCallable  implements Callable<Boolean>  {
    @Override
    public Boolean call() {
        System.out.println(Thread.currentThread().getName() +"
        started...");
        for (int i = 0; i < 10; ++i) {
            try {
                Thread.sleep(i * 10);
            } catch (InterruptedException _) {}
        }
        System.out.println(Thread.currentThread().getName() +" ended.");
        return true; // assume done
    }
}
// output
/*
pool-1-thread-4 started...
pool-1-thread-7 started...
pool-1-thread-10 started...
pool-1-thread-1 started...
...
pool-1-thread-1 ended.
pool-1-thread-9 ended.
pool-1-thread-9 started...
pool-1-thread-1 started...
```

```
pool-1-thread-7 ended.
...
 */
```

When running this class, the thread names are printed in the console, and the names are specific to the execution mechanism, as in each thread name is named following this template: `pool-1-thread-{thread_index}`. This makes it obvious that threads are reused to execute the code declared by the `RandomDurationCallable` class, as the `{thread_index}` appears more than once for threads being started and ended.

The concurrency framework is a subject too advanced for this book, but if this section has made you so curious you want to know more, you can have a look at this Oracle Concurrency tutorial.[11]

Java 21 Threads New Syntax and Virtual Threads

It is said often in the Java world that a JVM thread maps to an OS thread. In the code, when the `start()` method of a `Thread` object is invoked, a **platform thread** is created and linked to an OS thread. The platform thread remains linked to the OS thread for the platform thread's entire lifetime, which means the number of threads available to the Java application depends on the number of available OS threads, which in turn depends on the architecture of the CPU. This means that creating multiple Java threads that do extensive work might actually overload the CPU and freeze your computer, unless the threads are managed by a thread pooling mechanism, like mentioned at the end of the previous section, **Classic Thread Creation (Before Java 21)**.

Java 21 improved the Java concurrency model not only by revamping the existing code for creating threads but also by introducing **virtual threads**. Virtual threads are not linked to OS threads. Their code executes in an OS thread, but it does so through an engine managing **carrier threads** that ensures when a virtual thread is blocked, the OS thread can be released until the virtual thread can resume its execution. For this reason, virtual threads are lightweight threads that dramatically reduce the effort of writing, maintaining, and observing high-throughput concurrent applications. They are obviously meant to be used for compact simple operations that spend most of the time blocked, often waiting for I/O operations to complete. So virtual threads are suitable for applications that require a large number of concurrent tasks.

---

[11] https://docs.oracle.com/javase/tutorial/essential/concurrency/index.html

Before going into more detail about virtual threads, let's take a look at the change in syntax for creating platform threads. The listings in the previous section showed how to extend the Thread class and implement the Runnable interface to create threads. Listing 5-53 shows the new way to create threads introduced in Java 21, by invoking Thread.ofPlatform() to create a platform thread.

Listing 5-53. Code Sample to Run Multiple Threads Created with Thread. ofPlatform()

```
package com.apress.bgn.five;

public class MultipleUserThreadsJava21Demo {
    void main() {
        for (int i = 0; i < 10; ++i) {
            var rdt = new RandomDurationRunnable();
            Thread.ofPlatform().name("rdt " + i).start(rdt);
        }
    }
}
// output
/*
rdt 4 started...
rdt 6 started...
...
rdt 1 ended.
redt 0 ended.
...
*/
```

Since the RandomDurationRunnable implementation contains very simple processing, it is suitable to be run in a virtual thread. Changing the code in Listing 5-53 to create virtual threads is as simple as replacing Thread.ofPlatform() with Thread. ofVirtual(), as shown in Listing 5-54. The java.lang.VirtualThread class extends java.lang.Thread and, as such, is the latest addition to the hierarchy (see Figure 5-22) of components for writing Java code destined to be run in parallel.

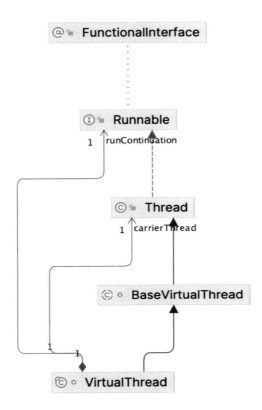

Figure 5-22. *Thread classes hierarchy*

Listing 5-54. Code Sample to Run Multiple Threads Created with `Thread.ofVirtual()`

```
package com.apress.bgn.five;

public class VirtualThreadsDemo {
  void main() {
    for (int i = 0; i < 1000; ++i) {
      var rdt = new RandomDurationRunnable();
      Thread.ofVirtual().name("rdt " + i).start(rdt);
    }
  }
}
```

Because virtual threads are so lightweight, you can create and run a lot of them. Notice that the VirtualThreadsDemo creates and runs 1000 threads, and does so in record time. Also, virtual threads allow programming in the familiar, sequential thread-per-request style. Sequential code is not only easier to write and read but also easier to debug since we can use a debugger to trace the program flow step by step, and stack traces reflect the expected call stack. Because of this coding style, they are also easier to debug.

Important   Virtual threads are lightweight, short-lived, and have shallow call stacks, so there is no need to pool them. If you need a thread, just create one.

Virtual threads are designed to model a *single task* rather than a mechanism for running tasks.

Virtual threads are transparently suspended/resumed when they block. The Blocking API throughout the JDK has been retrofitted to be aware of virtual threads.

Runnable instances can be replaced with lambda expressions and other methods in the Thread class to configure, create, and start virtual and platform threads. Threads can be created as unstarted, and the body of the run() method can be provided when invoking the start(..) method. Listing 5-55 shows a few ways to create, name, and start platform and virtual threads using syntax supported starting with Java 21.

Listing 5-55. Java 21 Syntax for Creating and Starting Platform and Virtual Threads

```
package com.apress.bgn.five;
import static java.lang.System.out;

public class NewTheadSyntax21Demo {
  void main() {
    // Os Thread
    Thread.ofPlatform()
            .name("Thread-P")
            .start(() -> out.println(" >> Hi, I am " + Thread.
            currentThread().getName() + " and I am an Platform thread! "));
```

```
    // Virtual thread
    Thread.startVirtualThread(() -> out.println(" >> Hi, I am " + Thread.
    currentThread()+" and I am a Virtual thread!"));

    // using VirtualThreadBuilder 'under the bonnet'
    Thread.ofVirtual()
            .name("Thread-V1")
            .start(() -> out.println(" >> Hi, I am " + Thread.
            currentThread().getName()+" and I am also a Virtual thread! "));

    // or creating it unstarted
    Thread vt = Thread.ofVirtual()
            .name("Thread-V2")
            .unstarted(() -> out.println(" >> Hi, I am " +      Thread.
            currentThread().getName()+" and I am also a Virtual
            thread! "));
    vt.start();

    try {
      Thread.sleep(2000); // making sure 'main' thread finishes
      execution last
    } catch (InterruptedException _) {}
  }
}
// output
/**
 >> Hi, I am Thread-P and I am an Platform thread!
 >> Hi, I am VirtualThread[#30]/runnable@ForkJoinPool-1-worker-1 and
    I am a Virtual thread!
 >> Hi, I am Thread-V2 and I am also a Virtual thread!
 >> Hi, I am Thread-V1 and I am also a Virtual thread!
 */
```

Note   Notice the Thread.sleep(2000); statement that pauses the main thread to allow for the threads started by it to finish execution. Without it, the main thread might exit before one of the threads has even started, or ended, and thus won't be able to print its message. Feel free to comment the statement and run the program a few times.

One of the virtual threads is not configured with a custom name, so printing its name yields nothing. However, we can print the string representation of the thread using Thread.currentThread() and it yields VirtualThread[#30]/runnable@ ForkJoinPool-1-worker-1. This output is made of three parts:

- VirtualThread[#30]: Identifies the virtual thread in execution.

- runnable: Identifies the instance used to create the thread, in this case a java.lang.Runnable instance.

- @ForkJoinPool-1-worker-1: Identifies the carrier thread on which the virtual thread executes.

Although virtual threads are not supposed to be pooled, a builder method was introduced in the Executors utility class that creates an Executor instance that starts a new virtual thread for each task, and the threads are put into an unbounded pool. This allows us to separate thread management and creation from the rest of the application if needed. Starting with Java 19, the java.util.concurrent.ExecutorService interface extends java.lang.AutoCloseable that models instances that hold on to a resource until its close() method is invoked. This is important because this means we can use the virtual thread executor in a construction referred to as **try-with-resources**. In **Chapter 4** you were introduced to the exception data type, and in order to catch exceptions try-catch-finally blocks were used. try-with-resources wraps around instances that hold on to resources, to tell the JVM to release them at the end of the execution block, and if exceptions are thrown during the execution of the block, they can be caught too. Listing 5-56 shows an example of using Executors. newVirtualThreadPerTaskExecutor() to create an ExecutorService that manages a pool of virtual threads.

Listing 5-56. Using `Executors.newVirtualThreadPerTaskExecutor()` to Manage an Unbounded Pool of Virtual Threads

```
package com.apress.bgn.five;

import java.util.ArrayList;
import java.util.concurrent.*;
import java.util.random.RandomGenerator;

import org.slf4j.Logger;
import org.slf4j.LoggerFactory;

import static com.apress.bgn.five.VirtualThreadsExecutorDemo.log;

public class VirtualThreadsExecutorDemo {
    public static final Logger log = LoggerFactory.getLogger(VirtualThreads
    ExecutorDemo.class);
    public static RandomGenerator RND = RandomGenerator.of("SecureRandom");

    void main() {
        try (ExecutorService executor = Executors.
        newVirtualThreadPerTaskExecutor()) {
            var tasks = new ArrayList<MyTask>();
            for (int i = 0; i < 1_000; i++) {
                tasks.add(new MyTask());
            }

            long time = System.currentTimeMillis();
            var futures = executor.invokeAll(tasks);

            long sum = 0;
            for (Future<Integer> future : futures) {
                sum += future.get();
            }

            time = System.currentTimeMillis() - time;
            log.info(">> Virtual threads: sum = " + sum+ ", time = " + time
            + " ms");
```

```
        } catch (ExecutionException | InterruptedException e) {
            throw new RuntimeException("Failed to execute tasks", e);
        }
    }
}

class MyTask implements Callable<Integer> {

    @Override
    public Integer call() {
        var pause = VirtualThreadsExecutorDemo.RND.nextInt(0, 1000);
        log.info("Thread.currentThread()} produces " + pause);
        return pause;
    }
}
```

Between Java 21 and Java 23 releases, no more development has been done on virtual threads, but it is expected some development will be done until Java 25, since Netflix have already started finding bugs. If you are interested, take a peek at this article: `https://netflixtechblog.com/java-21-virtual-threads-dude-wheres-my-lock-3052540e231d`.

Note   The VirtualThreadsExecutorDemo uses a different way to print messages in the console called logging, which is explained in detail in **Chapter 9**. This approach was chosen to show more details about the execution threads without having to write the complex code to do so.

Asynchronous Programming Using CompletableFuture<T>

Most applications that make use of threads need them to work together in parallel, but synchronize to exchange data when required. This can be resolved using **asynchronous programming**. In Java there is a hierarchy of components with the java.util.concurrent. Future<V> interface at the top that are used to model the result of an asynchronous computation. By using classes in this hierarchy, we can start a thread and tell it what to do when the data arrives. This action that is triggered by data arrival is called a **callback action**.

The java.util.concurrent.CompletableFuture<T> class, introduced in Java 8, implements Future<V> and is one of the most-used classes to write asynchronous code in Java because it provides a big set of convenience methods for creating, chaining, and combining multiple Future<V> instances. It also has a very comprehensive exception handling support.

Listing 5-57 shows a few simple ways to use CompletableFuture<T>.

Listing 5-57. Simple Examples of CompletableFuture<T> Usage

```
package com.apress.bgn.five;

import java.util.concurrent.CompletableFuture;
import java.util.concurrent.ExecutionException;

public class AsynchronousDemo {

    void main() throws ExecutionException, InterruptedException {
        CompletableFuture.runAsync(
                    () -> System.out.println(Thread.currentThread().
                    getName() +" async run (1)") // Runnable as lambda
                ).get(); // Block and wait for the future to complete

        var result1 = CompletableFuture.supplyAsync(() ->  Thread.
        currentThread().getName() + " async run (2)" // Supplier<String>
        as lambda
            ).get(); // Block and wait for the future to complete
        System.out.println(result1);

        var result2 = CompletableFuture.supplyAsync(() ->  Thread.
        currentThread().getName()+ " async run (3)" // Supplier<String>
        as lambda
            ).thenApply(String::toUpperCase) // apply transformation
            to result
                .get(); // Block and wait for the future to complete
        System.out.println(result2);

        CompletableFuture.supplyAsync(() ->  Thread.currentThread().
        getName() + " async run (4)" // Supplier<String> as lambda
            ).thenAccept(System.out::println); //  Consumer<T> processes
            the result when received
```

```
        var result3 = CompletableFuture.supplyAsync(() ->  Thread.
        currentThread().getName()+ "  async run (5)" // Supplier<String>
        as lambda
                ).thenApplyAsync(s -> Thread.currentThread().getName() +
                " thenApplyAsync : " + s) // apply async transformation
                to result
                .get(); // Block and wait for the future to complete
        System.out.println(result3);

        var result4 = CompletableFuture.supplyAsync(() -> {
            if (System.currentTimeMillis()%2 ==0) {
                throw new IllegalStateException("No can do!");
            }
            return Thread.currentThread().getName() + " async run (6)";
        }).exceptionally(ex -> {
                System.err.println(ex.getMessage());
                return "There be dragons!";
        })
            .get(); // Block and wait for the future to complete
        System.out.println(result4);
        try {
            Thread.sleep(2000); // making sure 'main' thread finishes
            execution last
        } catch (InterruptedException _) {}
    }
}
```

For each example, the Thread.currentThread().getName() invocation is used as part of the String returned so that it is obvious that the thread on which the body of a CompletableFuture<T> executes is a different one than the main thread.

Asynchronous programming using CompletableFuture<T> is useful enough, but the Oracle team decided it could do better.

Structured Concurrency

In Java 19, through JEP 428[12] a new API for simplifying concurrent programming was introduced. This API simplifies multithreaded programming for **structured concurrency**. The work continued in Java 21[13] , Java 22 and Java 23 (JEP `https://openjdk.org/jeps/480`), but when this chapter is being written this is still a preview feature.

Structured concurrency treats multiple tasks running in different threads as a single unit of work, thereby streamlining error handling and cancellation, improving reliability, and enhancing observability. The simplest way to explain structured concurrency is to compare it to typical methods' invocation. If method A invokes method B, then the execution of method B must finish before the execution of method A can continue, but both methods execute in the same thread. Structured concurrency means having the same behavior for virtual threads: if virtual thread A creates virtual thread B, the execution of thread B should take place within the execution time of thread A. Structured concurrency brings an order to thread execution, a way to create dependency relationships between virtual threads' executions using readable code that hides the complexity of concurrency and synchronization.

The main class of the structured concurrency API is `StructuredTaskScope<T>` in the `java.util.concurrent` package. This class enables you to coordinate a group of concurrent subtasks as a unit. Out of the box, in Java there are two extensions of this class, `ShutdownOnSuccess<T>` and `ShutdownOnFailure`, both of which are declared as static nested in the `StructuredTaskScope<T>` body, but developers can write their own versions by extending this class.

The `ShutdownOnSuccess<T>` instance is suitable for situations in which the success of at least one subtask in a task set is enough to consider the execution a success. This is also known as the **invoke any** pattern. The `ShutdownOnSuccess<T>` instance captures the result of the first subtask **to complete successfully**, then it invokes the shutdown method to interrupt unfinished threads and wake up the owner.

Listing 5-58 shows how to use `ShutdownOnSuccess<T>` to generate a random `Integer` value using two subtasks: one that uses a generator and one that returns a constant. This approach ensures that one subtask will most likely be dropped.

---

[12] `https://openjdk.org/jeps/428`
[13] `https://openjdk.org/jeps/453`

Listing 5-58. Simple Example of ShutdownOnSuccess<Integer> Task Usage

```java
package com.apress.bgn.five;

import com.apress.bgn.four.classes.DataGenerator;

import java.time.Duration;
import java.time.Instant;
import java.util.concurrent.ExecutionException;

import static java.util.concurrent.StructuredTaskScope.*;
import static java.lang.System.out;

public class StructuredConcurrencyDemoOne {
  void main() {
    var start = Instant.now();
    try (var scope = new ShutdownOnSuccess<Integer>()) {
      Subtask<Integer> task1 = scope.fork(() -> DataGenerator.genInt());
      Subtask<Integer> task2 =  scope.fork(() -> 2);

      scope.join();
      out.println("task1: " + task1.state() + ", result : " + (task1.
      state() == Subtask.State.SUCCESS ? task1.get() : "Not Available")  +
              "\ntask2: " + task2.state()+ ",  result : " + (task2.state()
              == Subtask.State.SUCCESS ? task2.get() : "Not Available")
      );
      out.println("Execution time : " + Duration.between(start, Instant.
      now()).toMillis() + " ms");
      out.println("Task result: " + scope.result());

    } catch (InterruptedException | ExecutionException e) {
      throw new RuntimeException(e);
    }
  }
}

// output
/*
```

```
task1: UNAVAILABLE, result : Not Available
task2: SUCCESS, result : 2

Execution time : 30ms
Task result: 2
 */
```

The join() method waits for a subtask started in this task scope to complete successfully, and it stops waiting when one of the following happens:

- All threads finish

- A subtask completes successfully

- The current thread is interrupted

- The shutdown() method is invoked directly to shut down the owner task

Notice in the output of Listing 5-58 that we can inspect the subtask states. If the subtask state is Subtask.State.SUCCESS, the result of the subtask can be accessed, and it becomes the result of the owner task. Although not shown here, subtasks that get abandoned end up in state Subtask.State.UNAVAILABLE. Subtasks that end up with an exception being thrown, or time out, end up in state Subtask.State.FAILED.

ShutdownOnFailure is suitable for situations in which the success of all subtasks is necessary to consider the execution a success. This is also known as the **invoke all** pattern. The ShutdownOnFailure instance captures the result of the first subtask **to complete abnormally**, then it invokes the shutdown method to interrupt unfinished threads and wake up the owner.

Listing 5-59 shows how to use ShutdownOnFailure to generate a list of random Integer values using two subtasks: one that uses a generator and one that returns a constant. This approach ensures that one subtask will most likely be dropped.

Listing 5-59. Simple Example of ShutdownOnFailure Task Usage

```
package com.apress.bgn.five;

import java.time.Duration;
import java.time.Instant;
import java.util.ArrayList;
import java.util.List;
```

```
import java.util.concurrent.TimeoutException;
import java.util.stream.Collectors;

import static com.apress.bgn.five.VirtualThreadsExecutorDemo.RND;

import static java.util.concurrent.StructuredTaskScope.*;
import static java.lang.System.out;

public class StructuredConcurrencyDemoTwo {

  void main() {
    var d = new StructuredConcurrencyDemoTwo();
    List<Subtask<Integer>> subtasks = new ArrayList<>();
    var start = Instant.now();
    try (var scope = new ShutdownOnFailure()) {
      for (int i = 0; i < 10; i++) {
        subtasks.add(scope.fork(() -> d.genValue()));
      }

      scope.joinUntil(Instant.now().plusSeconds(5));
      scope.throwIfFailed(t -> new IllegalStateException(("Well this
      sucks!  " + t.getMessage())));

      // if all subtasks complete successfully
      var result = subtasks.stream()
            .map(Subtask::get)
            .collect(Collectors.toList());
      out.println("All results: " + result);
    } catch (InterruptedException | TimeoutException |
    IllegalStateException e) {
      System.err.println("Some tasks have failed. " + e.getMessage());
      subtasks.forEach(t -> out.println(
              "task "  + subtasks.indexOf(t)  + " " + t.state() +
              ", result : " + (t.state() == Subtask.State.SUCCESS ?
              t.get() : "Not Available")
          )
      );
    }
```

```
  out.println("Execution time : " + Duration.between(start, Instant.
  now()).toMillis() + " ms");
}

Integer genValue() throws InterruptedException {
  var generatedVal = RND.nextInt();
  if(generatedVal % 11 ==0) {
    throw new IllegalStateException("This value is bad, bad bad...");
  }
  return generatedVal;
}
}
// output
// all success
/*
All results: [-1992358099, 1997495937, 1711128236, -1859724079, 1177627696,
1839477352, -1031424090, 1759698562, -186490484, -73552283]
Execution time : 371ms
*/
// or some failures
/*
..
task6: SUCCESS, result : 930381003
task7: FAILED, result : Not Available
task8: SUCCESS, result : -1545203690
...
Execution time : 409ms
 */
```

This example is similar to the one in Listing 5-58, but the behavior is different. The genValue() method was introduced to randomly throw an exception when the randomly generated number divides perfectly by 11, causing some of the subtasks to fail. The number 11 is complex enough that sometimes it happens for the exception not to be thrown at all, which makes all the subtasks to execute successfully.

Instead of the join() method, we've used joinUntil(..) that takes a java.time. Instant argument that represents the allowed execution time, which in this case is 5 seconds from the current system time. If executing the task takes longer than that, the execution fails and an IllegalStateException is thrown.

The throwIfFailed(..) method throws the exception produced by the given exception supplying the function if a subtask failed. When this is used, if any subtask failed with an exception, then the function is invoked, with the exception of the first subtask to fail. In this example we include the subtask exception message in the exception returned by the function. The exception returned by the function is thrown. This method does nothing if no subtasks failed. There is a version of this method that takes no argument, and in this case a java.util.concurrent.ExecutionException is thrown that is wrapped around the exception of the first subtask to fail.

Another thing that is worth mentioning is the special catch block. This type of catch block was introduced in Java 7 to reduce the duplicated code caused by the necessity of handling multiple exceptions:

```
} catch (InterruptedException | TimeoutException |
IllegalStateException e)  {
    // handle the exception
}
```

Before Java 7 the same block would have been written as follows:

```
} catch (InterruptedException e) {
    // handle the exception
} catch (TimeoutException e) {
    // handle the exception
} catch (IllegalStateException e) {
    // handle the exception
}
```

Even if there was support for executing subtasks concurrently in Java, provided by the java.util.concurrent.ExecutorService API introduced in Java 5, the new structured concurrency API helps developers write more readable code, which is easier to debug too and adds in the bonus of eliminating common risks arising from cancellation and shutdown, such as thread leaks and cancellation delays.

Summary

In this chapter you learned how memory for a Java program is administered by the JVM and the basics of the most-used Java data types. A few important details that should remain with you from this chapter are listed here:

- There are two type of memory managed by the JVM: stack and heap.

- The difference between primitive and reference types.

- Primitive values are stored in the stack memory, and object values are stored in the heap.

- There are eight primitive data types in Java: `boolean`, `char`, `short`, `byte`, `int`, `long`, `float`, `double`.

- References can only be of the super-type of an assigned object.

- The size of an array is defined when it is created, and it cannot be changed afterward.

- In Java, `String` instances are *immutable*, which means they cannot be changed once created.

- If calendar dates need to be handled, use the new DateTime API.

- `null` is useful and powerful.

- Collections can group object types together in tuples or key/value pairs.

- Classic concurrency in Java is fun in small doses.

- Virtual threads are one of the most useful features introduced in Java 21.

- Structured concurrency allows you to write code to execute tasks in parallel without needing to write any thread management code.

Some examples in this chapter might seem complicated, but do not be discouraged. It is difficult to explain certain concepts without providing working code that you can execute, test, and even modify yourself. Unfortunately, this requires the use of concepts that will be introduced in later chapters (such as `for` and `if` statements). Just make a note of every concept that it is not clear now and the page number, and return to this chapter after you have read about the concept in detail later in the book.

CHAPTER 6

Operators

The previous chapters have covered basic concepts of Java programming. You learned how to organize your code, how your files should be named, and which data types you can use, depending on the problem you are trying to solve. You also learned how to declare fields, variables, and methods and how they are stored in memory, to help you design your solutions so that the resource consumption will be optimal.

In this chapter you will learn how to combine your declared variables by using operators. Most Java operators are the same operators that you know from math, but because programming involves other types than numeric, Java includes extra operators with specific purposes. Table 6-1 lists all Java operators along with their category and their scope.

Table 6-1. *Java Operators*

Category	Operator	Scope
casting	(type)	Explicit type conversion.
unary, postfix	expr++, expr--	Post increment/decrement.
unary, prefix	++expr, --expr	Pre increment/decrement.
unary	+expr, -expr	Sign.
unary, logical	!	Negation.
unary, bitwise	~	Bitwise complement. Performs a bit-by-bit reversal of an integer value.
multiplicative, binary	*, /, %	For numeric types: multiply, divide, divide and return remainder.

(*continued*)

© Iuliana Cosmina 2024
I. Cosmina, *Java 23 for Absolute Beginners*, https://doi.org/10.1007/979-8-8688-1041-1_6

Table 6-1. (*continued*)

Category	Operator	Scope
additive, binary	+, -	For numeric types: addition, subtraction. + is used for `String` concatenation as well.
bit shifting, binary	>>, >>, >>>	For numeric types: multiply and divide by a power of two, signed, and unsigned.
conditional, relational	`instanceof`	Test whether the object is an instance of the specified type (class or subclass or interface).
conditional, relational	==, !=, <, >, <=, >=	Equals, differs from, lesser than, greater than, less than or equals, greater than or equals.
AND, binary	&	Bitwise logical AND.
exclusive OR, binary	^	Bitwise logical XOR.
inclusive OR, binary	|	Bitwise logical OR.
conditional, logical AND	&&	Logical AND.
conditional, logical OR	||	Logical OR.
conditional, ternary	? :	Also called the *Elvis operator*.
assignment	=, +=, -=, *=, /= %=, &=, ^=, <<= >>=, >>>= , |=	Simple assignments, combined assignments.

Let's start this chapter with the most common operator in programming: the assignment operator, =.

The Assignment Operator

The = (assignment) operator is the most-used operator in programming, as nothing can be done without it. Any variable that you create, regardless of the type, primitive or reference, has to be given a value at some point in the program. Setting of a value using the assignment operator is quite simple: specify a variable name on the left side of the = (equal) operator and specify a value on the right side. The only condition for an assignment to work is that the value must match the type of the variable.

To test this operator, you can use JShell; just make sure you start it in verbose mode (-v) so that you can see the effect of your assignments. The statements executed for this chapter are shown in Listing 6-1.

Listing 6-1. Using jshell to Play with the Assignment Operator

```
 jshell -v
|  Welcome to JShell -- Version 23-ea
|  For an introduction type: /help intro

jshell>int i = 0;
i ==> 0
|  created variable i : int

jshell> i = -4
i ==> -4
|  assigned to i : int

jshell> String sample = "text"
sample ==> "text"
|  created variable sample : String

jshell> List<String> list = new ArrayList<>()
list ==> []
|  created variable list : List<String>

jshell>  list = new LinkedList<>()
list ==> []
|  assigned to list : List<String>
```

In Listing 6-1, we declared primitive and reference values and assigned and reassigned values to them. Assignment of values with types that mismatch the initial type is not permitted. In the code sample in Listing 6-2, we are trying to assign a text value to a variable that was previously declared as having the int type.

Listing 6-2. More `jshell` Play with the Assignment Operator

```
jshell> i = -5
i ==> -5
|  assigned to i : int

jshell> i = "you are not allowed"
|  Error:
|  incompatible types: java.lang.String cannot be converted to int
|  i = "you are not allowed";
|      ^-------------------^
```

Introduction of type inference in JDK 10 does not affect this, and the type of the variable will be inferred depending on the type of the first value assigned. Obviously, this means you cannot declare a variable using the `var` keyword without specifying an initial value. This excludes the `null` value, as it has no type. This can be forced, though, by casting the `null` value to the type we are interested in, as shown in Listing 6-3.

Listing 6-3. `jshell` Failed Variable Declaration

```
jshell> var j
|  Error:
|  cannot infer type for local variable j
|    (cannot use 'var' on variable without initializer)
|  var j;
|  ^----^
jshell> var j =5
j ==> 5
|  created variable j : int
jshell> var sample2 = "bubulina";
sample2 ==> "bubulina"
|  created variable sample2 : String

// this does not work, obviously
jshell> var funny = null;
|  Error:
|  cannot infer type for local variable funny
|    (variable initializer is 'null')
```

```
|  var funny = null;
|  ^---------------^

// yes, this actually works !
jshell> var funny = (Integer) null;
funny ==> null
|  created variable funny : Integer
```

Explicit Type Conversion: (*typem*) and `instanceof`

These two operators are covered together because it is easier to provide code samples pretty similar to what you might need to write for real scenarios.

As previously mentioned in this book, it is better to keep the reference type as generic as possible to allow for changing of the concrete implementation without breaking the code. This is called **type polymorphism**. Type polymorphism is the provision of a single interface to entities of different types or the use of a single symbol to represent multiple different types.

Sometimes we might need to group objects together but execute different code depending on their types. Recall the `Performer` hierarchy presented in Chapter 5 (depicted in Figure 5-10). We're going to make use of these types here to show you how to use these operators. If you do not want to go back to the previous chapter to remember the hierarchy, Figure 6-1 shows it again, but with a twist: it adds an extra class named `Graphician` that implements interface `Artist` and extends class `Human`.

Note   The implementation of the `Graphician` class is not relevant for this chapter, so it won't be detailed here, but you can find it in the project attached to this book.

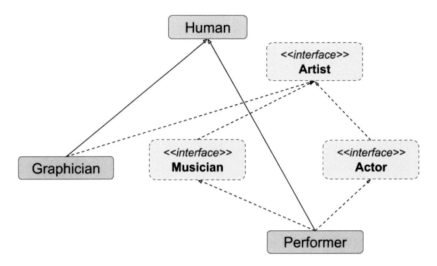

Figure 6-1. *The Human hierarchy*

In Listing 6-4, an object of type Musician and one of type Graphician are created and then added into a list containing references of type Artist. We can do this because both types implement the interface Artist. The code in Listing 6-4 shows a few classes in this hierarchy being used to create objects, added to the same list and then extracted from it and have their type tested.

Listing 6-4. Code Sample Showing instanceof and (type)

```
package com.apress.bgn.six;

import com.apress.bgn.four.classes.Gender;
import com.apress.bgn.four.hierarchy.Artist;
import com.apress.bgn.four.hierarchy.Musician;
import com.apress.bgn.four.hierarchy.Performer;

import java.util.ArrayList;
import java.util.List;

import static java.lang.System.out;

public class OperatorDemo {
    public static void main() {
        List<Artist> artists = new ArrayList<>();
```

```java
Musician john = new Performer("John", 47, 1.91f, Gender.MALE);
List<String> songs = List.of("Gravity");
john.setSongs(songs);
artists.add(john);

Graphician diana = new Graphician("Diana", 23, 1.62f, Gender.
FEMALE, "macOs");
artists.add(diana);

for (Artist artist : artists) {
    if (artist instanceof Musician) {    // (*)
        Musician musician = (Musician) artist; // (**)
        out.println("Songs: " + musician.getSongs());
    } else {
        out.println("Other Type: " +  artist.getClass());
    }
}
}
}
// output
/*
Songs: Gravity
Other Type: class com.apress.bgn.six.Graphician
 */
```

The line marked with (*) at the end shows how to use the instanceof operator. This operator is used to test whether the object is an instance of the specified type (class, superclass, or interface). It is used in writing conditions to decide which code block should be executed.

The line marked with (**) does an explicit conversion of a reference, also known as a *cast* operation. Since the instanceof operator helps figure out that the object the reference points to is of type Musician, we can now convert the reference to the proper type so methods of class Musician can be called.

Notice how the instanceof operator is used to test the type however, to use the reference an explicit conversion needs to be written.

Type Patterns

Starting with Java 14 the `instanceof` operator was enriched to include conversion, which allows for a clearer and simpler syntax, as depicted in Listing 6-5.

Listing 6-5. Java 14 New `instanceof` Syntax

```
for (Artist artist : artists) {
    if (artist instanceof Musician musician) {
        out.println("Songs: " + musician.getSongs());
    } else {
        out.println("Other Type: " + artist.getClass());
    }
}
```

The `musician` variable is called a **pattern variable**; it is final and declared and initialized at the same place. Its scope is limited to the `if` block—if you try to use it in the `else` block, the compiler will object. Using `instanceof` this way is referred to as a **type pattern**.

But what happens if an explicit conversion fails? To find out, we will try to convert the previously declared `Graphician` reference to `Musician`. The following line can be added to Listing 6-5 and it won't stop the code from compiling:

```
Musician fake = (Musician) diana;
```

The `Graphician` class has no relation to the `Musician` type, so the code will not run. A special exception will be thrown in the console to tell you what is wrong. The error message printed in the console will be quite explicit and is depicted in the next log snippet:

```
Exception in thread "main" java.lang.ClassCastException:
    class com.apress.bgn.six.Graphician cannot be cast to class com.apress.
    bgn.four.hierarchy.Musician
        (com.apress.bgn.six.Graphician is in module chapter.six of
        loader 'app';
        com.apress.bgn.four.hierarchy.Musician is in module chapter.
        four@3.0-SNAPSHOT of loader 'app')
    at chapter.six/com.apress.bgn.six.OperatorDemo.main(OperatorDemo.
    java:75)
```

The message clearly states that the two types are not compatible, and it includes the package and module names.

The situation in which the instanceof operator is most useful is in equals(..) methods. **Chapter 5** introduced the equals(..) and hashCode() methods when discussing object equality. IntelliJ IDEA can generate these two methods for you. Just right-click inside the class body and select the **Generate** option to see all possibilities, and then select **equals() and hashCode** to generate the methods for you. The menu is depicted in Figure 6-2.

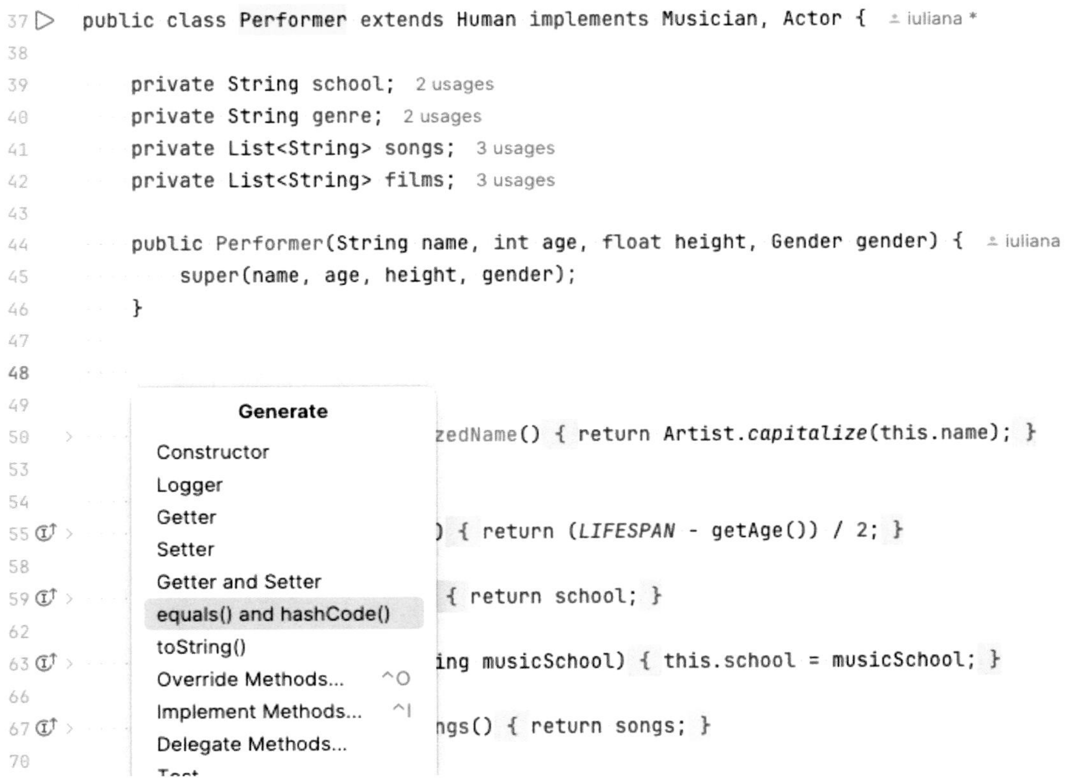

```
37 ▷   public class Performer extends Human implements Musician, Actor {   ≛ iuliana *
38
39         private String school;   2 usages
40         private String genre;   2 usages
41         private List<String> songs;   3 usages
42         private List<String> films;   3 usages
43
44         public Performer(String name, int age, float height, Gender gender) {   ≛ iuliana
45             super(name, age, height, gender);
46         }
47
48
49                          Generate
50    >                                              zedName() { return Artist.capitalize(this.name); }
                      Constructor
53
                      Logger
54
                      Getter
55 ⓣ >                                              ) { return (LIFESPAN - getAge()) / 2; }
                      Setter
58
                      Getter and Setter
59 ⓣ >                                              { return school; }
                      equals() and hashCode()
62
                      toString()
63 ⓣ >                                              ing musicSchool) { this.school = musicSchool; }
                      Override Methods...        ^O
66
                      Implement Methods...       ^I
67 ⓣ >                                              ngs() { return songs; }
                      Delegate Methods...
70
                      Test
```

Figure 6-2. *IntelliJ IDEA code generation menu:* ***Generate > equals() and hashCode()*** *submenu*

Listing 6-6 shows the IntelliJ IDEA–generated equals(..) and hashCode() methods.

Listing 6-6. equals(..) and hashCode() Generated Methods for Class
Performer

```java
package com.apress.bgn.four.hierarchy;

import com.apress.bgn.four.classes.Gender;

import java.util.List;
import java.util.Objects;

public class Performer extends Human implements Musician, Actor {

    private String school;
    private String genre;
    private List<String> songs;
    private List<String> films;

    public Performer(String name, int age, float height, Gender gender) {
        super(name, age, height, gender);
    }

    @Override
    public boolean equals(Object o) {
        if (this == o) return true;
        if (o == null || getClass() != o.getClass()) return false;
        Performer other = (Performer) o;
        return Objects.equals(school, other.school)
                && Objects.equals(genre, other.genre)
                && Objects.equals(songs, other.songs)
                && Objects.equals(films, other.films);
    }

    @Override
    public int hashCode() {
        return Objects.hash(school, genre, songs, films);
    }
    // other code omitted
}
```

Look at the equals(..) method. Before checking field equality, it checks that the type of the argument is equal to the type of the instance being compared to: getClass() != o.getClass(). This works, but another way to write this comparison would be !(o instanceof Performer). But we still have cast the o argument before doing field comparison. We had to do this before Java 14. After Java 14, we can rewrite the equals(..) method as shown in Listing 6-7.

Listing 6-7. equals(..) Using instanceof Starting with Java 14

```
    @Override
public boolean equals(Object o) {
    if (this == o) return true;
    if (o == null || !(o instanceof Performer)) return false;

    return (o instanceof Performer other)
            && Objects.equals(school, other.school)
            && Objects.equals(genre, other.genre)
            && Objects.equals(songs, other.songs)
            && Objects.equals(films, other.films);
}
```

Note   The work of incorporating pattern matching for instanceof started in Java 14, when it was introduced as a preview, and was finalized in Java 16 through JEP 394[1].

Another situation where the pattern matching for instanceof is useful is in switch expressions, which will be covered in **Chapter 7**.

Record Patterns

Starting with JDK 19, the instanceof operator works with records too. The record patterns feature was completed and released officially in Java 21, through JEP 440[2]. **Record patterns** help not only with record type identification but deconstruction as well.

---

[1] https://openjdk.org/jeps/394
[2] https://openjdk.org/jeps/440

Record instances are immutable data carriers. The data they carry is referred to as **components**. The data is accessed using the built-in component accessor methods.

To show a few common ways record patterns could be used, we need a few record classes. Let's start with the very simple example in Listing 6-8.

Listing 6-8. Record Patterns Example

```
package com.apress.bgn.six;

record FullName (String firstName, String lastName){ }

public class RecordPatternsDemo {
    void main() {
        Object john = new FullName("John", "Mayer");

        /*1*/
        if (john instanceof FullName full) {
            System.out.println("FullName: " + full);
        }

        /*2*/
        if (john instanceof FullName(String firstName, String lastName)) {
            System.out.println("[Deconstruction] FirstName: " + firstName);
            System.out.println("[Deconstruction] LastName: " + lastName);
        }
    }
}
// output
/*
FullName: FullName[firstName=John, lastName=Mayer]
[Deconstruction] FirstName: John
[Deconstruction] LastName: Mayer
 */
```

In Listing 6-8 we declared a very simple record named FullName that contains two fields.

The first statement (marked with /*1*/) looks like a normal type check and conversion, very similar to a type pattern usage. The second statement (marked with /*2*/) is a record pattern example that deconstructs the instance into its components,

350

which are used independently without being encapsulated into a record instance. This works for nested records too. If we declare a `PersonRecord` record that has a `FullName` component, we can use a nested record pattern like shown in Listing 6-9.

Listing 6-9. Nested Record Pattern Example

```
package com.apress.bgn.six;

record FullName (String firstName, String lastName){ }

record PersonRecord (FullName fullName, Integer age) {}

public class RecordPatternsDemo {
    void main() {
        Object john = new FullName("John", "Mayer");
        Object johnRecord = new PersonRecord((FullName) john, 47);

        if (johnRecord instanceof PersonRecord(FullName(var firstName,
        String lastName), var age)) {
            System.out.println("[Nested] FirstName: " + firstName);
            System.out.println("[Nested] LastName: " + lastName);
            System.out.println("[Nested] Age: " + age);
        }
    }
}
// output
/*
[Nested] FirstName: John
[Nested] LastName: Mayer
[Nested] Age: 47
 */
```

With nested record patterns, we can decompose nested records and use their components individually too.

Note   *Nested records* is just another way to refer to **record composition**.

It also works with generics. The code in Listing 6-10 shows using a record pattern to decompose a generic type.

Listing 6-10. Decomposing a Generic Type Wrapper

```java
package com.apress.bgn.six;

record FullName (String firstName, String lastName){ }

record PersonRecord (FullName fullName, Integer age) {}

record WrapperBeing<T>(T t, String description) { }

public class RecordPatternsDemo {
    void main() {
        Object john = new FullName("John", "Mayer");
        WrapperBeing<PersonRecord> wrapper = new
        WrapperBeing<>((PersonRecord) johnRecord, "is mise Iain");

        if (wrapper instanceof WrapperBeing<PersonRecord>(var personRecord,
        var description)) {
            System.out.println("[Generics] PersonRecord: " + personRecord);
            System.out.println("[Generics] Description: " + description);
        }
    }
}
// output
/*
[Generics] PersonRecord: PersonRecord[fullName=FullName[firstName=John,
lastName=Mayer], age=47]
[Generics] Description: is mise Iain
 */
```

You've already noticed that some examples in this section use var instead of the actual component type. As long as some parameters have their types, so that the compiler can identify the correct pattern, all works as intended.

When decomposing nested records, you might not always be interested in using all the components. This is where _ (underscore), the unnamed variable, comes in. For example, when decomposing the johnRecord instance, you would just be interested in extracting the lastName component, so you could write something like this:

```
if (johnRecord instanceof PersonRecord (FullName
    (var _, String lastName), var _)) {
    System.out.println("[Unnamed Variable] LastName: " + lastName);
}
```

And that's about it, except for usage in switch expressions, which will be covered in **Chapter 7**.

Primitive Patterns

Explicit conversion is not limited to reference types—it works for primitives too. **Chapter 5** mentioned that any variable of a type with values in a smaller interval can be converted to a type with a bigger interval without explicit conversion. The reverse is possible too, by using explicit conversion, but if the value is too big, bits will be lost and the value will be...unexpected. Just look at the examples of conversions between byte and int depicted in Listing 6-11.

Listing 6-11. jshell Conversions Examples

```
jshell> byte b = 2;
b ==> 2
|  created variable b : byte

jshell> int i = 10;
i ==> 10
|  modified variable i : int
|    update overwrote variable i : int

jshell> i = b
i ==> 2
|  assigned to i : int
```

```
jshell> b = i
|  Error:  \\ <1>
|  incompatible types: possible lossy conversion from int to byte
|  b = i
|      ^

jshell> b = (byte) i
b ==> 2
|  assigned to b : byte

jshell> i = 300_000
i ==> 300000
|  assigned to i : int
```

jshell> b = (byte) i
b ==> -32 // oops! value outside of byte interval
| assigned to b : byte

Important   As a rule, just use explicit conversion to widen the scope of a variable, not to narrow it, as narrowing it can lead to exceptions or loss of precision.

The accompanying note is a good recommendation, but what if the value you are working with is provided by a generator component that you have no control over? Should you test the value against all the numerical types of interval boundaries to see what is the proper type to convert it to? It is doable, sure, but tedious. Java 23 introduces a preview feature that makes things easier. As this section is being written, this feature has just been introduced, but it has been a request from developers for years: primitive types in patterns, or the ability to use instanceof with primitive types.

Note   Another thing developers have been requesting for years is the ability to use primitive types in collections, so maybe that is on the way too.

Chapter 5 introduced primitive data types, most of which are numeric types limited to certain intervals and representations. The only way to check if a numeric value is a byte, short, int, or long is to check the value against the margins of the interval for

each type or attempt a conversion and check if an exception was thrown. Without the
check, a conversion of an int value to a byte might work, but with some potential loss
of precision. It would be nice if we could test if a value can be converted to a certain type
and convert it in one go, right? Well, this is one of the features previewed by JEP 455[3].

Listing 6-12 shows an example that generates a random long value based on the
current system time; this value is then checked and, if possible, converted to any
numeric type.

Listing 6-12. Using instanceof with Primitive Types

```
package com.apress.bgn.six;

public class PrimitivePatternsDemo {
    void main() {
        var generated = genVal();

        if (generated instanceof byte b){
            System.out.println("byte val = " + b);
        }
        if (generated instanceof short s){
            System.out.println("short val = " + s);
        }
        if (generated instanceof char c){
            System.out.println("char val = " + c);
        }
        if (generated instanceof int i) {
            System.out.println("int val = " + i);
        }
        if (generated instanceof long l) {
            System.out.println("long val = " + l);
        }
        if (generated instanceof float f) {
            System.out.println("float val = " + f);
        }
    }
```

---

[3] https://openjdk.org/jeps/455

```java
    static long genVal() {
        var t = System.currentTimeMillis();
        if (t % 3 == 0) {
            byte bv = Byte.MAX_VALUE;
            return bv;
        } else if (t % 5 == 0) {
            short sbv = Short.MAX_VALUE;
            return sbv;
        } else if (t % 7 == 0) {
            long lv = Long.MAX_VALUE;
            return lv;
        } else {
            return Integer.MAX_VALUE;
        }
    }
}
// output for Integer.MAX_VALUE
/*
int val = 2147483647
long val = 2147483647
*/
// output for Byte.MAX_VALUE
/*
byte val = 127
short val = 127
char val = []  # invisible character here: DEL
int val = 127
long val = 127
float val = 127.0
*/
// output for Short.MAX_VALUE;
/*
short val = 32767
char val = 翿
int val = 32767
```

```
long val = 32767
float val = 32767.0
*/
// output for Long.MAX_VALUE;
// long val = 9223372036854775807
```

Notice that when the value returned by the genVal() function is the upper interval for the int type, it can only be converted safely to int and long. Since converting it to any types with values in intervals the value is outside of (byte, short, char, float) comes with a loss precision, the instanceof operator returns false and the conversion is not done.

Note   This feature is very useful, and I expect it to be officially released by Java 25, the next next LTS version. In case that does not happen, I will keep the sources, but comment them to avoid compiling failures.

Numerical Operators

This section groups together all operators that are mostly used on numerical types. The numerical operators you know from math: +, -, /, *. Comparators are found in programming too, but they can be combined to obtain different effects.

Unary Operators

Unary operators require only one operand, and they affect the variable they are applied to.

Incrementors and Decrementors

In Java (and some other programming languages) there are unary operators named **incrementors** (++) and **decrementors** (--). These operators are placed before or after a variable to increase or decrease its value by 1. They are usually used in loops as counters, to condition the termination of the loop. When they are placed before the variable, they are called **prefixed**, and when they are placed after it, they are called **postfixed**.

When incrementors and decrementors are prefixed, the operation is executed on the variable before the variable is used in the next statement. This means that in Listing 6-13, the value of the i variable will be incremented and then assigned to j.

Listing 6-13. Prefixed Incrementor Example

```
package com.apress.bgn.six;

import static java.lang.System.out;

public class UnaryOperatorsDemo {
    void main() {
        int i = 1;
        int j = ++i;
        out.println("j is " + j+ ", i is " + i);
    }
}
// output
// j is 2, i is 2
```

The expected result of the code in Listing 6-13 is that j equals 2, because the value of the i variable is modified to 2 before it is assigned to j.

When incrementors and decrementors are postfixed, the operation is executed on the variable after the variable is used in the next statement. This means that in the code in Listing 6-14, the value of i first is assigned to j and then incremented.

Listing 6-14. Postfixed Incrementor Example

```
package com.apress.bgn.six;

import static java.lang.System.out;

public class UnaryOperatorsDemo {
    void main() {
        int i = 1;
        int j = i++;
        out.println("j is " + j+ ", i is " + i);
    }
}
```

```
// output
// j is 1, i is 2
```

The expected result of the code in Listing 6-14 is that j equals 1, because the value of the i variable is modified to 2 after it is assigned to j.

The decrementor operator can be used in the same way, the only difference being that the variable is decreased by 1.

Tip   Try to modify the `UnaryOperatorsDemo` class to use the `--` operator instead.

Sign Operators

Mathematical operator + (plus) can be used on a single operator to indicate that a number is positive (this operator is quite redundant and mostly never used). So, basically

```
int i = 3;
```

is the same as

```
int i = +3;
```

Mathematical operator - (minus) can be used to declare negative numbers:

```
[jshell> int i = -3
i ==> -3
| created variable i : int
```

Or it can be used to negate an expression:

```
[jshell> int i = -3
i ==> -3
| created variable i : int
[jshell> int j = -( i + 4 )
j ==> -1
| created variable j : int
```

As you can see in the previous example, the result of (i + 4) is 1, because i = -3, but because of the - operator in front of the parentheses, the final result that is assigned to the j variable is -1.

Negation Operator

There is one more unary operator, and its role is to negate variables. Operator ! (bang or exclamation mark) applies to boolean variables and is used to negate them. So true becomes false and false becomes true, as shown in the next code snippet:

```
[jshell> boolean t = true
t ==> true
| created variable t : boolean
[jshell> boolean f = !t
f ==> false
| created variable f : boolean
[jshell> boolean t2 = !f
t2 ==> true
| created variable t2 : boolean
```

Binary Operators

There are quite a few binary operators, and some of them can even be combined to perform new operations. This section starts with the ones you probably know from math.

The + (Plus/Addition/Concatenation) Operator

The + (plus) operator is used to add two numeric variables, as shown in the statements from Listing 6-15.

Listing 6-15. Adding Numeric Values in jshell

```
jshell> int i = 4
i ==> 4
|  created variable i : int

jshell> int j = 6
j ==> 6
```

```
|  created variable j : int

jshell> int k = i + j
k ==> 10
|  created variable k : int

jshell> int i = i + 2
i ==> 6
|  modified variable i : int
|    update overwrote variable i : int
```

The last statement, int i = i + 2, has the effect of incrementing the value of i with 2, and as you can see, it has a little redundancy. That statement can be written without referring to i twice, because its effect is to increase the value of i with 2. This can be done by using the += operator, which is composed of the assignment operator and the addition operator. The optimal statement is i += 2.

The + operator can also be used to concatenate String instances, or to concatenate String instances with other types. The JVM decides how to use the + operator depending on the context. For example, try to guess the output of the code in Listing 6-16 at runtime.

Listing 6-16. Concatenating String and int Values

```
package com.apress.bgn.six;

import static java.lang.System.out;

public class ConcatenationDemo {
    void main(){
        int i1 = 0;
        int i2 = 1;
        int i3 = 2;
        out.println(i1 + i2 + i3);
        out.println("Result1 = " + (i1 + i2) + i3);
        out.println("Result2 = " + i1 + i2 + i3);
        out.println("Result3 = " + (i1 + i2 + i3));
    }
}
```

So how did the guessing go? Executing the code displays the following in the console:

```
1. 3
2. Result1 = 12
3. Result2 = 012
4. Result3 = 3
```

The explanation for each line in this output is provided here:

- Line 1: All operands are of type `int`, so JVM adds the terms as `int` values, and the `out.println` method prints this result.

- Line 2: Parentheses isolate the addition of two terms, `(i1 + i2)`, so the JVM executes the addition between the parentheses as a normal addition between two `int` values. But after that, we are left with `"Result1 = " + 1 + i3`, and this operation includes a `String` operand, which means the `+` operator must be used as a concatenation operator, since adding a number with a text value does not work otherwise.

- Line 3: We have three `int` operands and a `String` operand, and thus the JVM decides that the context of the operation cannot be numeric, so it chooses concatenation.

- Line 4: Similar to the case in line 2, the parentheses ensure that the context of the operation is numeric, and thus the three operands are added.

This is a typical example to show how JVM decides the context for operations involving the `+` operator that you might find in other Java tutorials as well. The `int` variables can be replaced with `float` or `double` and the behavior will be similar.

Concatenation works with reference types too, since any Java type is by default an extension of `Object` and thus can be converted to `String`, by calling its `toString()` method. Listing 6-17 shows the concatenation between a `String` and a `Performer` instance.

Listing 6-17. Concatenating String and Performer Values

```
package com.apress.bgn.six;

import com.apress.bgn.four.classes.Gender;
import com.apress.bgn.four.hierarchy.Musician;
import com.apress.bgn.four.hierarchy.Performer;

import static java.lang.System.out;

public class ReferenceConcatenationDemo {
    void main() {
        Musician john = new Performer("John", 43, 1.91f, Gender.MALE);

        out.println("Singer: " + john);
        // or convert explicitly
        out.println("Singer: " + john.toString());
    }
}
// output
//Singer: Performer{name='John', age=43, height=1.91, gender=MALE}
//Singer: Performer{name='John', age=43, height=1.91, gender=MALE}
```

The - (Minus) Operator

Mathematical operator - (minus) is used to subtract two variables or subtract a value from a variable. Listing 6-18 shows how this operator and the -= operator (composed of the assignment operator and the subtraction operator) are used.

Listing 6-18. Subtracting Numeric Values in jshell

```
jshell> int i = 4
i ==> 4
|  created variable i : int

jshell> int j = 2
j ==> 2
|  created variable j : int
```

```
jshell> int k = i - j
k ==> 2
|  created variable k : int

jshell> int i = 4
i ==> 4
|  modified variable i : int
|     update overwrote variable i : int

jshell> i  = i - 3
i ==> 1
|  assigned to i : int

jshell> int i = 4
i ==> 4
|  modified variable i : int
|     update overwrote variable i : int

jshell> i -=3
$7 ==> 1
|  created scratch variable $7 : int
```

The * (Multiply) Operator

The * (multiply) operator is used to multiply two variables or to multiply a value with a variable. It can be used in similar statements as + and -, and there is also a composed operator, *=, that can be used to multiply the value of a variable and assign it on the spot. In Listing 6-19, you can see this operator in action.

Listing 6-19. Multiplying Numeric Values in jshell

```
jshell>  int i = 4
i ==> 4
|  created variable i : int

jshell> int j = 2
j ==> 2
|  created variable j : int
```

```
jshell> int k = i * j
k ==> 8
|  created variable k : int

jshell> int i = 4
i ==> 4
|  modified variable i : int
|    update overwrote variable i : int

jshell> i  = i * 3
i ==> 12
|  assigned to i : int

jshell> int i = 4
i ==> 4
|  modified variable i : int
|    update overwrote variable i : int

jshell>  i *= 3
$7 ==> 12
|  created scratch variable $7 : int
```

The / (Divide) Operator

The / (divide) operator is used to divide two variables or to divide a value by a variable. It can be used in similar statements as + and -, and there is a composed operator, /=, that can be used to divide the value of a variable and assign it on the spot.

The result of a division is named **quotient**, and it is assigned to the variable on the left side of the assignment operator, =. When the operands are integers, the result is an integer too, and the remainder is discarded. In Listing 6-20, you can see this operator in action.

Listing 6-20. Dividing Numeric Values in jshell

```
jshell> int i = 4
i ==> 4
|  created variable i : int
```

```
jshell> int j = 2
j ==> 2
|  created variable j : int

jshell> int k = i / j
k ==> 2
|  created variable k : int

jshell> int i = 4
i ==> 4
|  modified variable i : int
|     update overwrote variable i : int

jshell> int i = i / 3
i ==> 1
|  modified variable i : int
|     update overwrote variable i : int

jshell> int i = 4
i ==> 4
|  modified variable i : int
|     update overwrote variable i : int

jshell> i /= 3
$7 ==> 1
|  created scratch variable $7 : int

# you obviously cannot divide by zero, dooh!
jshell> i /= 0
|  Exception java.lang.ArithmeticException: / by zero
|        at (#3:1)
```

The % (Modulus) Operator

The % (modulus) operator is used to divide two variables, but the result is the remainder of the division. The operation is called **modularization**. There is also a composed operator, %=, that can be used to divide the value of a variable and assign the remainder on the spot. In Listing 6-21, you can see this operator in action.

Listing 6-21. Modulus Numeric Values in `jshell`

```
jshell> int i = 4
i ==> 4
|  created variable i : int

jshell> int j = 3
j ==> 3
|  created variable j : int

jshell> int k = i % j
k ==> 1
|  created variable k : int

jshell> int i = 4
i ==> 4
|  modified variable i : int
|    update overwrote variable i : int

jshell> i = i % 3
i ==> 1
|  assigned to i : int

jshell> int i = 4
i ==> 4
|  modified variable i : int
|    update overwrote variable i : int

jshell> i %= 3
$7 ==> 1
|  created scratch variable $7 : int

# modularization is essentially a division, so yet again, nope!
jshell> i %= 0
|  Exception java.lang.ArithmeticException: / by zero
|        at (#5:1)
```

The modulus operator returns the remainder, but what happens when the operands are real numbers? The short answer is that operations with floating-point numbers are tricky. The result depends on the digits after the decimal point and the operand used for the division. Look at Listing 6-22.

Listing 6-22. Modulus Numeric Operations with Floating-Point Numbers in jshell

```
jshell> double d = 5.28d
d ==> 5.28
|  created variable d : double

jshell> d / 2
$2 ==> 2.64
|  created scratch variable $2 : double

jshell> d % 2
$4 ==> 1.2800000000000002
|  created scratch variable $4 : double
```

The explanation for the previous result is loss of precision because of how floating-point numbers are represented internally.

Also, if the remainder is a real number with an infinite number of decimals after the decimal point, representing it is not possible, so some rounding is necessary. This is shown in Listing 6-23.

Listing 6-23. Loss of Precision in jshell for a Remainder with an Infinite Number of Decimals After the Decimal Point

```
jshell> float f = 1.9f
f ==> 1.9
|  created variable f : float

jshell> float g = 0.4f
g ==> 0.4
|  created variable g : float

jshell> float h = f % g
h ==> 0.29999995      # remainder
|  created variable h : float
```

368

The reminder returned in jshell is 0.29999995, which can be rounded to 0.3 for some cases. However, rounding can be dangerous when the data is used for sensitive operations, such as determining the volume of a tumor for a robot to operate on, or the perfect trajectory for a rocket to be sent to Mars.

Warning   Rounding of floating-point numbers is problematic because it causes a loss of precision.

The loss of precision when working with floating-point numbers is not a Java problem, since operations with floating-point numbers are supported according to the rules of the IEEE 754 (IEEE Standard for Floating-Point Arithmetic)[4] arithmetic.

If a project needs mathematical operations with a better precision, the java.lang. Math class provides methods for different types of rounding and other types of floating-point number operations.

Relational Operators

In certain cases, when designing the solution for a problem, you need to introduce conditions to drive and control the execution flow. Conditions require the evaluation of a comparison between two terms using a **comparison** operator. In this section all comparison operators used in Java are described and code samples are be provided. Let's proceed.

The == (Equals) Operator

The == (equals) operator tests equality of terms. Because in Java a single = is used to assign values, == was introduced to test equality and avoid confusion. This operator is very often used to control execution flows. Controlling execution flows is the topic of **Chapter 7**, but to show how the == operator should be used, a few simple code samples involving control statements such as if and for are introduced in this chapter.

In Listing 6-24, you can see an example of testing the == comparator in searching value 2 in an array. If the value is found, the index where it was found is printed in the console.

---

[4]https://en.wikipedia.org/wiki/IEEE_754

Listing 6-24. Example of Using the == Operator to Test a Value in an Array

```
package com.apress.bgn.six;

import static java.lang.System.out;

public class ComparisonOperatorsDemo {
    void main(){
        int[] values = {1, 7, 9, 2, 6,};
        for (int i = 0; i < values.length; ++i) {
            if (values[i] == 2) {
                out.println("Found 2 at index: " + i);
            }
        }
    }
}
// output
// Found 2 at index: 3
```

The condition in the marked line is evaluated, and the result is a boolean value. When the result is `false`, nothing is done, but if the result is `true`, the index is printed. Because the result is of type `boolean`, if you make a mistake and use = instead of ==, the code will not compile. So you must be extra careful when comparing boolean values. The code in Listing 6-25 compiles and runs, but it doesn't work as expected.

Listing 6-25. Example of an Unexpected Initialization of a Boolean Variable Instead of an Evaluation of Its Value

```
package com.apress.bgn.six;

import static java.lang.System.out;

public class BadAssignementDemo {
    void main() {
        boolean testVal = false;

        if(testVal = true) {
            out.println("TestVal got initialized incorrectly!");
```

```
        } else {
            out.println("TestVal is false? " + (testVal == false));
        }
    }
}
// output
//TestVal got initialized incorrectly!
```

The == operator works just fine for primitives. For reference types, you need to use the equals() method, which was covered at the beginning of **Chapter 5** when explaining the difference between stack and heap memory.

The Other Comparison Operators

The other comparison operators work only on primitive types. Since there is not that much to say about each of them individually, this section covers them all.

- != tests inequality of terms. It is the opposite of the == operator. This operator also works on reference types, but it compares reference values instead the objects themselves, exactly as ==.

Tip   As an exercise, modify the example in Listing 6-24 to print a message when the array element value is different from 2.

- < (less than) and <= (less than or equal with) have the same purpose as you probably learned in math class: < tests if the item on the left of the operator is less than the one on the right, and <= tests if the item on the left of the operator is less or equal to the one on the right. The <= operator cannot be used on reference types.

- > and >= also have the same purpose as you probably learned in math class: > tests if the item on the left of the operator is greater than the one on the right, and >= tests if the item on the left of the operator is greater than or equal to the one on the right. The >= operator cannot be used on reference types.

Almost all numeric operators can be used on variables of different types, as they are automatically converted to the type that has a wider interval representation. The code in Listing 6-26 reflects a few situations, but in practice you might need to make even more dubious things that do not always abide to the commonsense rules of programming, nor follow good practices. Just try to avoid doing that if you can, though!

Listing 6-26. Different Primitive Types Comparison Examples

```java
package com.apress.bgn.six;

import static java.lang.System.out;

public class MixedOperationsDemo {
    void main() {
        byte b = 1;
        short s = 2;
        int i = 3;
        long l = 4;

        float f = 5;
        double d = 6;
        int ii = 6;

        double resd = l + d;
        long resl = s + 3;
        //etc

        if (b <= s) {
            out.println("byte val < short val");
        }
        if (i >= b) {
            out.println("int val >= byte val");
        }
        if (l > b) {
            out.println("long val > byte val");
        }
        if(d > i) {
            out.println("double val > byte val");
        }
```

```
            if(i == i) {
                out.println("double val == int val");
            }
        }
}
// output
/*
byte val < short val
int val >= byte val
long val > byte val
double val > byte val
double val == int val
*/
```

Just make sure that if you are ever in a situation where you need to make shady things *(nonoptimal code constructs)* like these, test a lot and think your conversions well, especially when floating-point types are involved. This is because (for example) the piece of code in Listing 6-27 can have quite unexpected results.

Listing 6-27. Unexpected Comparison Results with Floating-Point Numbers

```
package com.apress.bgn.six;

import static java.lang.System.out;

public class BadDecimalPointDemo {
    void main(){
        float f1 = 2.2f;
        float f2 = 2.0f;
        float f3 = f1 * f2;
        if (f3 == 4.4) {
            out.println("expected float value of 4.4");
        } else {
            out.println("!! unexpected value of " + f3);
        }
    }
}
```

If you expected the message *expected float value of 4.4* to be printed in the console, you will be quite surprised.

Any IEEE 754 floating-point number representation will present issues, because some numbers that appear to have a fixed number of decimals in the decimal system actually have an infinite number of decimals in the binary system. So obviously we cannot compare floats and doubles using ==. One of the solutions that is easiest to implement is to use the compare method provided by the wrapper class, in this case `Float.compare(..)`, as shown in Listing 6-28.

Listing 6-28. Correct Comparison Results with `Float.compare`

```java
package com.apress.bgn.six;

import static java.lang.System.out;

public class GoodDecimalPointDemo {
    void main(){
        float f1 = 2.2f;
        float f2 = 2.0f;
        float f3 = f1 * f2;
        if (Float.compare(f3,4.4f) == 0) {
            out.println("expected float value of 4.4");
        } else {
            out.println("!!unexpected value of " + f3);
        }
    }
}
```

Using the previous example, the expected message is now printed in the console: *expected float value of 4.4.*

Bitwise Operators

In Java there are a few operators that are used at the bit level to manipulate variables of numerical types. Bitwise operators are used to change individual bits in an operand. Bitwise operations are faster and usually use less CPU processing power because of the reduced use of resources. They are most useful in programming visual applications (e.g., games) where color, mouse clicks, and movements should be quickly determined to ensure a satisfactory experience.

Bitwise (~) NOT

Operator ~ is sort of a binary **negator**. It performs a bit-by-bit reversal of an integer value. This affects all bits used to represent the value. So if we declare

```
byte b1 = 10;
```

the binary representation is 00001010.

The Integer class provides a method named toBinaryString(), which can be used to print the binary representation of the previously defined variable, but it won't print all the bits, because the method doesn't know on how many bits we want the representation on. So we need to use a special String method to format the output. The method depicted in Listing 6-29 can be used to print the b1 value in binary on 8 bits, exactly as mentioned previously.

Listing 6-29. Method Used to Print Each Bit of a byte Value

```
import static java.lang.System.out;
//...
public static void print8Bits(byte arg) {
    out.println("decimal:" + arg);
    String str = String.format("%8s", Integer.toBinaryString(arg)).
replace(' ', '0');
    out.println("binary:" + str);
}
```

If we apply the ~ operator on the b1 value, the binary value that results is 11110101. In case you did not notice, this value is out of the byte interval range and thus is converted to int automatically. This is how negative numbers are represented internally in Java, which according to the Java Language Specification is a representation called **2's complement**. (This will be covered toward the end of the chapter.)

So the result will be -11, as displayed by the code in Listing 6-30.

Listing 6-30. Testing the ~ Bitwise Negator Operator

```
package com.apress.bgn.six;

import static java.lang.System.out;

public class BitwiseDemo {
    void main(){
        byte b1 = 10;
        print8Bits(b1);
        byte b2 = (byte) ~b1;
        print8Bits(b2);
    }

    // print8Bits method omitted
}
// output
/*
decimal:10
binary:00001010
decimal:-11
binary:11111111111111111111111111110101
 */
```

Notice the statement byte b2 = (byte) ~b1 in Listing 6-30. The bitwise complement expression operator requires an operand that is convertible to a primitive integral type, or a compile-time error occurs. Internally, Java uses one or more bytes to represent values. The ~ operator converts its operand to the int type, so it can use 32 bits when doing the complement operation; this is needed to avoid loss of precision. That is why an explicit cast to byte is needed in the previous example.

And because everything is clearer with images, in Figure 6-3 you can see the effect of the ~ operator on the bits of the b1 variable, in parallel with its value.

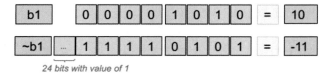

Figure 6-3. *The effect of the ~ negator operator on every bit of a byte value*

Bitwise (&) AND

The bitwise AND operator, represented by &, compares two numbers bit by bit. If the bits on identical positions have the value of 1, the bit in the result will be 1. The code sample in Listing 6-31 depicts the result of the & operator.

Listing 6-31. Testing the & Bitwise AND Operator

```
package com.apress.bgn.six;

import static java.lang.System.out;

public class BitwiseDemo {
    void main(){
        byte b1 = 117;
        print8Bits(b1);
        byte b2 = 95;
        print8Bits(b2);
        byte result  = (byte) (b1 & b2);
        print8Bits(result);
    }

    // print8Bits method omitted
}
// output
/*
decimal:117
binary:01110101
decimal:95
binary:01011111
decimal:85
binary:01010101
 */
```

The effect of the & operator can be seen better in Figure 6-4. The 01010101 value is the binary representation of decimal number 85.

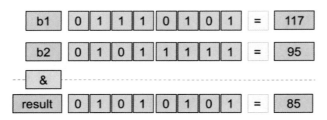

Figure 6-4. *The effect of the & operator on every bit*

Also, for practical reasons the composed operator &= is available in Java, so that the bitwise AND operation can be done on the same variable to which the result is assigned, as shown next. The advantage of this is that the result is automatically converted to byte, so no explicit conversion is required.

```
jshell> byte b1 = 117
b1 ==> 117
|  created variable b1 : byte

jshell> b1 &= 95
$2 ==> 85
|  created scratch variable $2 : byte
```

Bitwise Inclusive (I) OR

The bitwise OR operator (also known as inclusive OR), represented by I (pipe), compares two numbers bit by bit, and if at least one of the bits is 1, the bit in the result is set to 1. The code in Listing 6-32 depicts the result of the I operator.

Listing 6-32. Testing the I Bitwise OR Operator

```
package com.apress.bgn.six;

import static java.lang.System.out;

public class BitwiseDemo {
    void main(){
        byte b1 = 117;
        print8Bits(b1);
        byte b2 = 95;
        print8Bits(b2);
```

```
        byte result  = (byte) (b1 | b2);
        print8Bits(result);
    }

    // print8Bits method omitted
}
// output
/*
decimal:117
binary:01110101
decimal:95
binary:01011111
decimal:127
binary:01111111
 */
```

The effect of the | operator can be seen better in Figure 6-5. The 01111111 value is the binary representation of number 127.

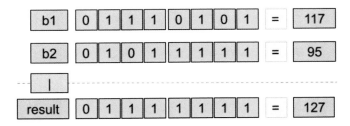

Figure 6-5. *The effect of the | operator on every bit*

Also, for practical reasons the composed operator |= is available in Java, so that the bitwise inclusive OR operation can be done on the same variable to which the result is assigned, as shown next. The advantage of this is that the result is automatically converted to byte, so no explicit conversion is required.

```
jshell>  byte b1 = 117
b1 ==> 117
|  created variable b1 : byte

jshell> b1 |= 95
$2 ==> 127
|  created scratch variable $2 : byte
```

Bitwise Exclusive (^) OR

The bitwise exclusive OR (or XOR) operator, ^, compares two numbers bit by bit, and if the values of the bits are different, the bit in the result is set to 1. The code sample in Listing 6-33 depicts the result of the ^ operator.

Listing 6-33. Testing the ^ Bitwise XOR Operator

```
package com.apress.bgn.six;

import static java.lang.System.out;

public class BitwiseDemo {
    void main(){
        byte b1 = 117;
        print8Bits(b1);
        byte b2 = 95;
        print8Bits(b2);
        byte result  = (byte) (b1 ^ b2);
        print8Bits(result);
    }

    // print8Bits method omitted
}
// output
/*
decimal:117
binary:01110101
decimal:95
binary:01011111
decimal:42
binary:00101010
 */
```

The effect of the ^ operator can be seen better in Figure 6-5. The 00101010 value is the binary representation of number 42.

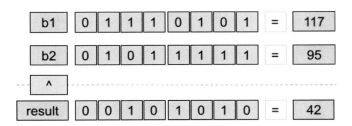

Figure 6-6. *The effect of the ^ operator on every bit*

Also, for practical reasons the composed operator ^= is available in Java, so that the bitwise exclusive OR operation can be done on the same variable to which the result is assigned, as shown next. The advantage of this is that the result is automatically converted to byte, so no explicit conversion is required.

```
jshell> byte b1 = 117
b1 ==> 117
|  created variable b1 : byte

jshell> b1 ^= 95
$2 ==> 42
|  created scratch variable $2 : byte
```

Logical Operators

When designing conditions for controlling the flow of the execution of a program, sometimes there is need to write complex conditions—composed conditions constructed from multiple expressions. There are four operators that can be used to construct complex conditions. Two of them are bitwise operations that can be reused &(AND) and |(OR), but they require evaluation of all the parts of the condition. The other operators &&(AND) and ||(OR) have the exact effect as the previously mentioned ones, but the difference is they do not require evaluation of all the expression, which is why they are also called *shortcut operators*. To explain the behavior of these operators, we'll use a typical example.

In Listing 6-34 we declare a list of ten terms (some of them null) and a method to generate a random index, used to select an item from the list. Then we test the selected element from the list to see if it is not null and equal to an expected value. If both conditions are true, then a message is printed in the console.

Listing 6-34. Testing the & Operator to Control the Execution Flow

```java
package com.apress.bgn.six;

import java.util.ArrayList;
import java.util.List;
import java.util.Random;
import static java.lang.System.out;

public class LogicalOperatorsDemo {

    static List<String> terms = new ArrayList<>() {{
        add("Rose");
        add(null);
        add("River");
        add("Clara");
        add("Vastra");
        add("Psi");
        add("Cas");
        add(null);
        add("Nardhole");
        add("Strax");
    }};

    void main() {
        for (int i = 0; i < 20; ++i) {
            int index = getRandomIndex(terms.size());
            String term = terms.get(index);
            out.println("Generated index: " + index);
            if (term != null & term.equals("Rose")) {
                out.println("Rose was found");
            }
        }
    }
}
```

```
    private static int getRandomIndex(int listSize) {
        var r = new Random();
        return r.nextInt(listSize);
    }
}
```

To make sure we get the expected result, we repeat the operation of selecting a random element from the list 20 times. As you can probably notice in the marked line, the bitwise & is used to compose the two expressions. You would expect the text *Rose was found* to be printed in the console only if the value of the term variable is not null and is equal to Rose. But when the preceding code is run, this gets printed:

```
Exception in thread "main" java.lang.NullPointerException: Cannot invoke
"String.equals(Object)" because "term" is null
    at chapter.six@3.0-SNAPSHOT/com.apress.bgn.six.LogicalOperatorsDemo.
main(LogicalOperatorsDemo.java:65)
```

This is because both expressions are evaluated. But think about it! If the term variable is null, should we even evaluate its equality to Rose, especially since calling a method on a null object causes a runtime error? Obviously not, which is why the & operator is not suitable for this case. If the term variable is null, it fails the first condition and there is no point in evaluating the second, so enter the && shortcut operator, which does exactly this. This works because when using the logical AND operator, if the first expression is evaluated to false, it does not really matter what the second expression is evaluated to—the result will always be false. So, we can correct previous code sample as shown in Listing 6-35.

Listing 6-35. Testing the && Operator to Control the Execution Flow

```
package com.apress.bgn.six;
// imports omitted

public class LogicalOperatorsDemo {
    static List<String> terms = new ArrayList<>() {{ /* list elements
omitted*/ }};

    void main() {
        for (int i = 0; i < 20; ++i) {
            int index = getRandomIndex(terms.size());
```

```
            String term = terms.get(index);
            out.println("Generated index: " + index);
            if (term != null && term.equals("Rose")) {
                out.println("Rose was found");
            }
        }
    }
    // getRandomIndex method omitted
}
```

When the code is executed, no exception will be thrown, because if the term variable is null, the second expression is not evaluated. Thus, this code is technically more efficient because it evaluates fewer conditions, but it is also designed better because it avoids failures.

Now let's modify the code sample in Listing 6-35 to print a message if we find a null or if we find Rose. For this an OR operator is needed, so we'll try first to use the bitwise version, as shown in Listing 6-36.

Listing 6-36. Testing the | Operator to Control the Execution Flow

```
for (int i = 0; i < 20; ++i) {
    int index = getRandomIndex(terms.size());
    String term = terms.get(index);
    out.println("Generated index: " + index);
    if (term == null | term.equals("Rose")) {
        out.println("null or Rose was found");
    }
}
```

If we run the code in Listing 6-36, a NullPointerException will be thrown when the random index happens to match the index of a null element in the list. This is because the | operator requires both expressions to be evaluated, so if term is null, calling term.equals(..) will cause the exception to be thrown.

To make sure the code works as expected, the | operator must be replaced with ||, which shortcuts the condition and does not evaluate the second expression in it, except if the evaluation result of the first condition is false. This works because when using the logical OR operator, if the first expression evaluates to true, it does not really matter what the second expression evaluates to: the result will always be true. I'll leave this as an exercise for you.

Conditions can be made up from more than one expression and more than one operator, whether it is && or ||. The code in Listing 6-37 depicts a few complex conditions.

Listing 6-37. Testing the || Operator to Control the Execution Flow

```
package com.apress.bgn.six;
// imports omitted

public class ComplexConditionsDemo {
    static List<String> terms = new ArrayList<>() {{ /* list elements
omitted*/ }};

    void main(){
        for (int i = 0; i < 20; ++i) {
            int rnd = getRandomIndex(terms.size());
            if (rnd == 0 || rnd == 1 || rnd <= 3) {
                out.println("rnd}: this works...");
            }
            if (rnd > 3 && rnd <=6 || rnd < 3 && rnd > 0) {
                out.println("rnd}: this works too...");
            }
        }
    }
}
```

Beware of conditions that become too complex; make sure you cover that piece of code with a lot of tests. When writing complex conditions, it is possible that some expressions become redundant, and IntelliJ IDEA and other smart editors display warnings of dead code on expressions that are redundant and unused to help the developer improve the design of the code.

Shift Operators

The *shift operators* are operators working at the bit level. Because moving bits around is a sensitive operation, the requirement of these operands is for arguments to be integers. The operand to the left of the operator is the number that will be shifted, and the operand to the right of the operator is the number of bits that will be shifted.

There are three shift operators in Java, and each of them can be composed with the assignment operator to do the shifting and assign the result to the original variable on the spot. This section analyzes all shift operators with simple examples and images to make them clear.

The << Shift Left Operator

As its name indicates, given a number represented in binary, this operator is used to shift bits to the left. The code in Listing 6-38 shows the << shift left operator in action.

Listing 6-38. Testing the << Operator

```
package com.apress.bgn.six;
// imports omitted

public class ShiftDemo {
    void main(){
        byte b1 = 12;
        print8Bits(b1);
        byte b2 = (byte) (b1 << 3);
        print8Bits(b2);
    }
    // print8Bits method omitted
}
// output
/*
decimal:12
binary:00001100
decimal:96
binary:01100000
 */
```

When bits are shifted to the left, the remaining positions are filled with 0. Also, the number becomes bigger, and the new value is its old value multiplied with 2^N, where N is the second operand.

The code in Listing 6-38 can be written as b1 <<= 3, using the composed operator, without the need to declare another variable. The result is 12 * 2^3. The bits are shifted as displayed in Figure 6-7.

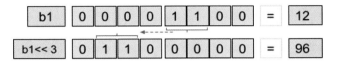

Figure 6-7. *The effect of the << operator*

Warning   Shifting operators promote `byte` values to `int`, to avoid loss of precision. In Listing 6-38, the number of bits to shift was small enough to result in a value inside the `byte` type interval. That is why explicit conversion to `byte` works and the result is still valid. This is not always possible, as you will see further in this section.

The >> Shift Right Operator

As its name indicates, given a number represented in binary, this operator is used to shift bits to the right. The code in Listing 6-39 shows the >> shift right operator *in action*.

Listing 6-39. Testing the >> Operator

```
package com.apress.bgn.six;
// imports omitted

public class ShiftDemo {
    void main(){
        byte b1 = 96;
        print8Bits(b1);
        byte b2 = (byte) (b1 >> 3);
        print8Bits(b2);
    }
```

```
    // print8Bits method omitted
}
// output
/*
decimal:96
binary:01100000
decimal:12
binary:00001100
 */
```

When bits are shifted to the right, the remaining positions are filled with 0 if the number is positive. If the number is negative, the remaining positions are replaced with 1. This is done to preserve the sign of the number. Also, the number becomes smaller, and the new value is its old value divided by 2^N, where N is the second operand.

The code in Listing 6-39 can be written as b1 >>= 3, using the composed operator, without the need to declare another variable. So, the result is 12 * 2^3. The bits are shifted as displayed in Figure 6-8.

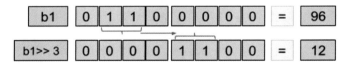

Figure 6-8. *The effect of the >> operator*

Figure 6-8 and Listing 6-39 both show the shift right operator applied to a positive number. When it comes to negative numbers, things get complicated, because negative numbers are represented internally as 2's complement. This means that, to get the representation of a negative number, we get the representation of the positive number, flip the bits, and then add 1. Figure 6-9, depicts the process of obtaining the internal representation of -7, starting from the representation of 7.

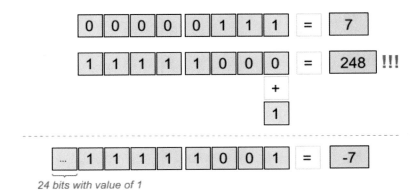

Figure 6-9. *Representing negative numbers internally in 2's complement*

The -7 value in 2's complement representation is out of the byte range, so internally negative numbers are represented as integers. This means that the print8Bits(..) method needs to be replaced with a version that prints all 32 bits of an int value. Listing 6-40 shows the >> unsigned shift right operator applied to a negative number.

Listing 6-40. Testing the >> Operator with Negative Numbers

```
package com.apress.bgn.six;
// imports omitted

public class ShiftDemo {
    void main(){
        out.println( " -- ");
        int i1 = -96;
        print32Bits(i1);
        int i2 =  i1 >> 3;
        print32Bits(i2);
    }

    public static void print32Bits(int arg) {
        out.println("decimal:" + arg);
        String str = arg > 0 ?
                String.format("%32s", Integer.toBinaryString(arg)).
                replace(' ', '0') :
                String.format("%32s", Integer.toBinaryString(arg)).
                replace(' ', '1') ;
```

```
        out.println("binary: " + str);
    }
}
// output
/*
decimal:-96
binary:11111111111111111111111110100000
decimal:-12
binary:11111111111111111111111111110100
 */
```

An advantage of 2's complement representation is that arithmetic operations are identical for signed and unsigned operators, which means half the circuitry is required in the CPU's arithmetic logic unit.

Information   A peculiar thing about 2's complement representation is that `Integer.MAX_VALUE` and `Integer.MIN_VALUE` are represented in the same way, because when an integer addition overflows, then the result is the low-order bits of the mathematical sum as represented in some sufficiently large 2's-complement format.

The >>> Unsigned Shift Right Operator

The >>> unsigned shift right operator is also called *logical shift*. Given a number represented in binary, this operator is used to shift bits to the right, and the remaining positions are replaced with 0, regardless of whether the value is positive or negative. This is why the result will always be a positive number.

Listing 6-41 shows the >>> operator in action on a negative value.

Listing 6-41. Testing the >>> Operator with Negative Values

```
package com.apress.bgn.six;
// imports omitted

public class ShiftDemo {
    void main(){
```

```
        System.out.println( " -- ");
        int i1 = -16;
        print32Bits(i1);
        int i2 = i1 >>> 1;
        print32Bits(i2);
    }
    // print32Bits method omitted
}
// output
/*
decimal:-16
binary:11111111111111111111111111110000
decimal:2147483640
binary:01111111111111111111111111111000
 */
```

The code in Listing 6-41 can be written as i1 >>>= 1, using the composed operator, without the need to declare another variable. The result is a very big positive number. The bits are shifted as displayed in Figure 6-10.

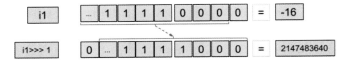

Figure 6-10. *The effect of the >>> operator on a negative value*

As with all bitwise operators, shift operators promote char, byte, or short type variables to int, which is why an explicit conversion is necessary. As you have probably noticed, shifting bits on negative numbers is tricky, because it is quite easy for the resulting number to be outside the interval of allowed values for a type, and an explicit conversion can lead to loss of precision or even serious anomalies. So why use them? Because they are fast. Just make sure to test intensively when using shift operators.

The Elvis Operator

The *Elvis operator* (? :) is the only ternary operator in Java. Its function is equivalent to a Java method that evaluates a condition and, depending on the outcome, returns a value. The template of the Elvis operator is depicted here:

```
variable = (condition) ? val1 : val2
```

The method equivalent to this operator is depicted in Listing 6-42.

Listing 6-42. The Elvis Operator Equivalent Method

```
variable = methodName(..);

type methodName(..) {
    if (condition) {
        return val1;
    } else {
        return val2;
    }
}
```

The reason this operator is named the *Elvis operator* is that, with a little imagination, the question mark resembles Elvis Presley's hair and the colon resembles eyes. The Elvis operator can be easily tested in jshell, as depicted in Listing 6-43.

Listing 6-43. The Elvis Operator Example in JShell

```
jshell> int a = 4
a ==> 4
|  created variable a : int

jshell> int result = a > 4 ? 3 : 1;
result ==> 1
|  created variable result : int

jshell> String a2 = "test"
a2 ==> "test"
|  created variable a2 : String
```

392

```
jshell> var a3 = a2.length() > 3 ? "hello": "bye-bye"
a3 ==> "hello"
|  created variable a3 : String
```

This operator is quite practical when you have a simple `if` statement that contains only one expression per branch, because using this operator enables you to compact the whole thing in one expression, one line of code. Just make sure when using it that the readability of the code is improved. From a performance point of view, there is no difference between an `if` statement and the equivalent Elvis operator expression. Another advantage of using the Elvis operator is that the expression can be used to initialize a variable.

Summary

In this chapter you learned the following:

- Java has a lot of operators, simple and composed.

- Java has the capability of converting instances of one type to another in the same statement where the check of the conversion is possible using `instanceof`. This is done via type, record, and primitive patterns.

- Bitwise operators are fast, but dangerous.

- Negative numbers are represented internally in 2's complement.

- The + operator does different things in different contexts.

- Java has a ternary operator that accepts three operands: a boolean expression and two objects of the same type. The result of the evaluation of the boolean expression decides which operand is the result of the statement.

The purpose of this chapter was just to make you familiar with all the operators that will be used throughout the book, to help you understand the provided solutions and even design and write your own.

CHAPTER 7

Controlling the Flow

The previous chapters have covered ways to create statements, and what operators to use depending on the operand types. Sometimes in the previous chapters elements of logic were added to make the code runnable for you, and this chapter is dedicated to explaining in detail how you can manipulate the execution of your code (that is, control the flow) using fundamental programming conditional and repetitive statements. The suite of steps to solve a problem and their order of execution is called an algorithm. Computer programs are solutions to a problem modelling algorithms. A algorithm can be represented using flowcharts.

Most of the programming we did up to this chapter contained declaration and printing statements, simple one-step statements. Take a look at the piece of code in Listing 7-1.

Listing 7-1. Java Code Made of a Few Statements

```
package com.apress.bgn.seven;

public class Main {
    void main() {
        String text = "sample";
        System.out.println(text);
    }
}
```

If we were to design a flowchart for it, the schema would be simple and linear, no decision and no repetition, as depicted in Figure 7-1.

© Iuliana Cosmina 2024
I. Cosmina, *Java 23 for Absolute Beginners*, https://doi.org/10.1007/979-8-8688-1041-1_7

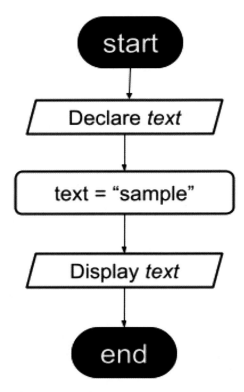

Figure 7-1. *Simple flowchart sample*

Resolving real-world problems often requires a more complicated logic than that, so more complicated statements are necessary. Before getting into that, let's analyze the components of a flowchart, because we will make use of flowcharts a lot during this chapter. Table 7-1 depicts and identifies all flowchart elements and explains their purpose.

Table 7-1. *Flowchart Elements*

Shape	Name	Scope
	Terminal	Indicates the beginning or end of a program, and contains a text relevant to its scope.
	Flowline	Indicates the flow of the program and the order of operations.
	Input/output	Indicates declaration of variables and outputting values.
	Process	Simple process statement: assignment, change of values, and so on.
	Decision	Shows a conditional operation that will decide a certain path of execution.
	Predefined process	Indicates a process defined elsewhere.
	On-page connector	Indicates the continuation of the flow on the same page. This element is usually labeled.
	Off-page connector	Indicates the continuation of the flow on a different page. This element is usually labeled.
	Comment (or annotation)	Used when a flow or an element requires extra explanation.

The flowchart elements presented in Table 7-1 are pretty standard, and you will probably find very similar elements used in any programming course or tutorial. After this consistent introduction, the second getting into it.

`if-else` Statement

The simplest decisional flow statement in Java is the `if-else` statement (probably in other languages as well). You've seen the `if-else` statement being used in code samples in the previous chapters; there was no way to avoid it, because providing runnable code that encourages you to write your own is an important goal of this book. In this section the focus will be strictly on this type of statement.

Let's imagine this scenario: We run a Java program with a numeric argument provided by the user. If the number is even, we print EVEN in the console; otherwise, we print ODD. The flowchart matching this scenario is depicted in Figure 7-2.

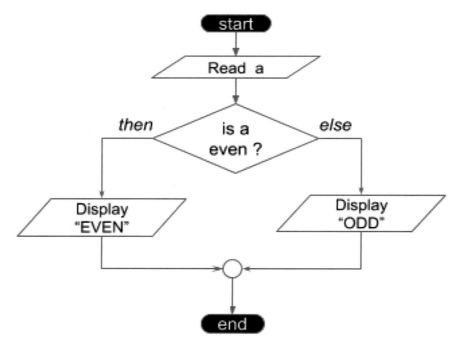

Figure 7-2. *if-else flowchart sample*

The condition is evaluated to a boolean value: if the result is true the statement corresponding to the if branch is executed, and if the result is false, the statement corresponding to the else branch is executed.

The Java code that implements the process described by this flowchart is depicted in Listing 7-2.

Listing 7-2. Java Code with if-else Statement

```
package com.apress.bgn.seven;

public class IfElseFlowDemo {
    void main(String... args){
        int a = Integer.parseInt(args[0]);
        if (a % 2 == 0) { // is even
            //Display EVEN
```

```
        System.out.println("EVEN");
    } else {
        //Display ODD
        System.out.println("ODD");
    }
  }
}
```

To run this class with different arguments, you have to create an IntelliJ IDEA launcher and add your argument into the `Program arguments` text field, as explained at the beginning of this book. Each Java statement in Listing 7-2 is paired with a comment matching the flowchart element, to make the implementation obvious.

Note that both branches of an `if` statement are not mandatory. The `else` branch is not always necessary. Sometimes you just want to print something if a value matches a condition, and you are not interested in what happens otherwise. For example, given a user-provided argument, we just want to print a message if the number is negative, but we are not interested in printing or doing anything else if the number is positive. The flowchart for that is depicted in Figure 7-3.

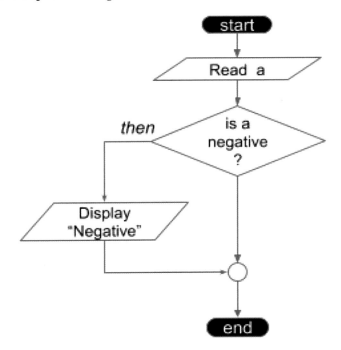

Figure 7-3. *if flowchart sample, missing the* else *branch*

The Java code matching this flowchart is depicted in Listing 7-3.

Listing 7-3. Java Code with `if` Statements

```
package com.apress.bgn.seven;

public class IfFlowDemo {
    public static void main(String... args) {
        int a = Integer.parseInt(args[0]);

        if (a < 0) {
            System.out.println("Negative");
        }
    }
}
```

In the same way as the statement can be made simple, we can link more `if-else` statements together if needed. Let's consider the following example: the user inserts a number from 1 to 12, and we have to print the season of the month corresponding to that number. The flowchart presented in Figure 7-4 fits the scenario.

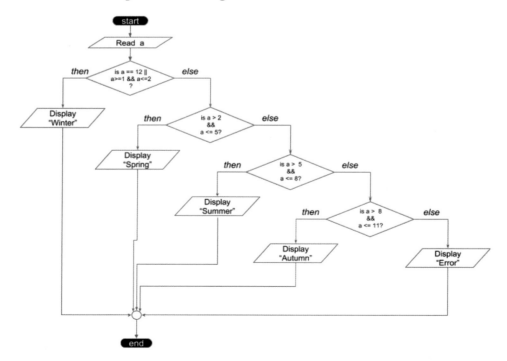

Figure 7-4. *Complex if-else flowchart sample*

> **Important**   When the code block for `if` or `else` contains a single statement, the curly brackets are not mandatory. Most developers keep them for code clarity, and to help IDEs indent the code properly.

Looks complicated, right? Wait until you see the code, which is depicted in Listing 7-4.

Listing 7-4. Java Code with a Lot of `if-else` Statements

```java
package com.apress.bgn.seven;

public class SeasonsDemo {
    void main(String... args) {
        int a = Integer.parseInt(args[0]);
        if(a == 12 || (a>=1 && a<= 2)) {
            System.out.println("Winter");
        } else {
            if (a>2 && a <= 5 ) {
                System.out.println("Spring");
            } else {
                if (a>5 && a <= 8 ) {
                    System.out.println("Summer");
                } else {
                    if (a>8 && a <= 11 ) {
                        System.out.println("Autumn");
                    } else {
                        System.out.println("Error");
                    }
                }
            }
        }
    }
}
```

It looks ugly, right? Fortunately, Java provides a way to simplify it, especially because it really makes no sense to have so many else blocks that only contain another if statement. The simplified code connects the else statements with the contained if(s) statements. The code ends up looking like Listing 7-5.

Listing 7-5. Java Code with Compacted if-else Statements

```java
package com.apress.bgn.seven;

public class CompactedSeasonDemo {
    void main(String... args) {
        int a = Integer.parseInt(args[0]);
        if (a == 12 || (a >= 1 && a <= 2)) {
            System.out.println("Winter");
        } else if (a > 2 && a <= 5) {
            System.out.println("Spring");
        } else if (a > 5 && a <= 8) {
            System.out.println("Summer");
        } else if (a > 8 && a <= 11) {
            System.out.println("Autumn");
        } else {
            System.out.println("Error");
        }
    }
}
```

Any argument provided by the user that is not in the [1,12] range will cause the program to print *Error*. You can test it for yourself by modifying your IntelliJ IDEA launcher. The elements to focus on are underlined in Figure 7-5.

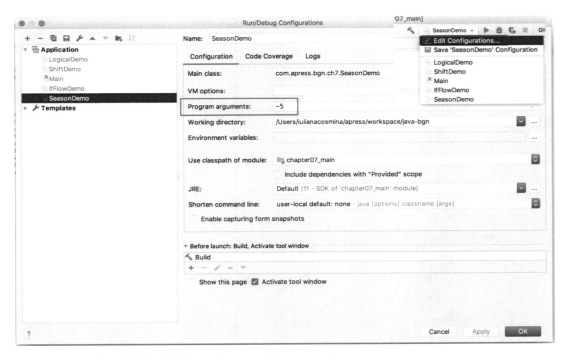

Figure 7-5. *IntelliJ IDEA launcher and parameters*

switch

When a solution requires different actions for a fixed set of values, the `if` statement
might get more complex. In this case the more suitable statement is the `switch`
statement or a `switch` expression.

The Classic `switch` Statement

The original `switch` statement, which we will refer to as the **classic switch** statement, has
been part of the Java language since its conception.

Let's look at the code in Listing 7-6 first, and then check what more can be improved.

Listing 7-6. Java Code with Detailed `switch` Statement

```java
package com.apress.bgn.seven.switchst;

import static java.lang.System.out;

public class SeasonSwitchDemo {
    void main(String... args) {
        //Read a
        int a = Integer.parseInt(args[0]);

        var season = "";
        switch (a) {
            case 1:
                season = "Winter";
                break;
            case 2:
                season = "Winter";
                break;
            case 3:
                season = "Spring";
                break;
            case 4:
                season = "Spring";
                break;
            case 5:
                season = "Spring";
                break;
            case 6:
                season = "Summer";
                break;
            case 7:
                season = "Summer";
                break;
            case 8:
                season = "Summer";
                break;
```

```
        case 9:
            season = "Autumn";
            break;
        case 10:
            season = "Autumn";
            break;
        case 11:
            season = "Autumn";
            break;
        case 12:
            season = "Winter";
            break;
        default:
            out.println("Error");
        }
    out.println(">> Result: " + season);
    }
}
```

That does not look very practical, at least not for this scenario. The general template of the classic switch statement is depicted in Listing 7-7.

Listing 7-7. General Template of the switch Statement

```
switch ([onvar]) {
    case [option]:
        [statement;]
        break;
    ...
    default:
        [statement;]
}
```

The terms in square brackets are detailed in the list here:

- [onvar]: The variable that is tested against the case statements to select a statement. It can be of any primitive type, enumerations, and (starting with Java 7) String. Clearly the switch statement is not limited by conditions evaluated to boolean results, which allows for a lot of flexibility.

- case [option]: A value the variable mentioned previously is matched upon to make a decision regarding the statement to execute (a case, as the keyword states).

- [statement]: A statement or a group of statements to execute when [onvar] == [option]. Considering that there is no else branch, we have to make sure that only the statement(s) corresponding to the first match is executed, which is where the break; statement comes in. The break; statement stops the current execution path and moves the execution point to the next statement outside the statement that contains it. Without break; statements the behavior switches to fall-through, which means every case statement after the match is executed until a break; is found. Without it, after the first match, all subsequent cases are traversed and statements corresponding to them will be executed.

  - If we execute the program in Listing 7-6 and provide the number 7 as an argument, the text *Summer* will be printed.

  - If the break statements for case 7 and 8 are commented, the output changes to *Autumn*.

- default [statement;]: A statement that is executed when no match on a case has been found; the default case does not need a break statement. If the program in Listing 7-6 is run with any number outside the [1-12] interval, *Error* will be printed, because the default statement will be executed.

Now that you understand how switch works, let's see how we can reduce the previous statement. The months example is suitable here because it can be modified further to show how the switch statement can be simplified when a single statement should be executed for multiple cases. In our code, writing each assignment statement three times is a little redundant. There are also a lot of break; statements. There are two ways in which the previous switch statement can be improved.

The first way of simplifying the switch statement in Listing 7-6 is by grouping together the cases that return the same value, as shown in Listing 7-8.

Listing 7-8. Simplified switch Statement

```
package com.apress.bgn.seven.switchst;

import static java.lang.System.out;

public class SimplifiedSwitchDemo {
    void main(String... args){
        //Read a
        int a = Integer.parseInt(args[0]);

        var season = "";
        switch (a) {
            case 1:
            case 2:
            case 12:
                season = "winter";
                break;
            case 3:
            case 4:
            case 5:
                season = "Spring";
                break;
            case 6:
            case 7:
            case 8:
                season = "Summer";
                break;
            case 9:
            case 10:
```

```
            case 11:
                season = "Autumn";
                break;
            default:
                out.println("Error");
        }
        out.println(">> Result: " + season);
    }
}
```

The grouping in this case represents the alignment of the cases that require the same statement to be executed. This still looks a little weird, but it reduces the statement repetition a little. The behavior in the previous case is possible because each `case` statement without a `break` statement is followed by the next `case` statement. This is also called a **fall-through condition**. The second way of simplifying the `switch` statement in Listing 7-6 is to use a `switch` expression, described next.

The `switch` Expression

Java 12 introduced the `switch` expression. Continuing our months example, the `switch` expression returns the season directly instead of storing it in a variable, and this allows for a simpler syntax, as depicted in Listing 7-9.

Listing 7-9. `switch` Expression Example

```
import static java.lang.System.out;

public class ExpessionSwitchDemo {
    void main(String... args) {
        //Read a
        int a = Integer.parseInt(args[0]);

        String season = switch (a) {
            case 1 -> "Winter";
            case 2 -> "Winter";
            case 3 -> "Spring";
            case 4 -> "Spring";
            case 5 -> "Spring";
```

```
            case 6 -> "Summer";
            case 7 -> "Summer";
            case 8 -> "Summer";
            case 9 -> "Autumn";
            case 10 -> "Autumn";
            case 11 -> "Autumn";
            case 12 -> "winter";
            default -> "Error";
        };
        out.println(season);
    }
}
```

The switch expression was introduced as a way to treat a switch statement as an expression, evaluate it to a single value, and thus use it in statements.

The switch expression does not require break; statements to prevent fall-through. When blocks of code are executed following a match with a case value, the value is returned using the yield statement, introduced in Java 13. The code in Listing 7-10 shows a different version of the switch expression, where case values that require the same result are grouped using a , (comma), an extra System.out.println(..) is added to show the yield usage, and the returned value is provided as an argument to a System.out.println() method, to be printed directly.

Listing 7-10. switch Expression Example Using yield Statements

```
package com.apress.bgn.seven.switchst;

import static java.lang.System.out;

public class AnotherSwitchExpressionDemo {
    void main(String... args) {
        //Read a
        int a = Integer.parseInt(args[0]);

        out.println( switch (a) {
            case 1, 2, 12 -> {
                System.out.println("One of 1,2,12 is tested.");
                yield "Winter";
            }
```

409

```
        case 3,4,5 -> {
            System.out.println("One of 3,4,5 is tested.");
            yield "Spring";
        }
        case 6,7,8 -> {
            System.out.println("One of 6,7,8 is tested.");
            yield "Summer";
        }
        case 9,10,11 -> {
            System.out.println("One of 9,10,11 is tested.");
            yield "Autumn";
        }
        default ->
                throw new IllegalStateException("Unexpected value");
    });
  }
}
```

Before Java 7, the switch statement supported only Integer and enum options. In Java 7, the switch statement started supporting String options.

switch with String Options

To rewrite the switch statement in Listing 7-8 using String options, we must modify the code a bit, and instead of converting the program argument to Integer, we'll just treat it as a String and require it to be the name of a month. This version of the code is depicted in Listing 7-11.

Listing 7-11. switch Statement Using String Values

```
package com.apress.bgn.seven.switchst;

import static java.lang.System.out;

public class StringSwitchSeasonDemo {
    void main(String... args) {
        //Read a
        String a = args[0];
```

```java
        var season = "";
    switch (a) {
        case "January":
        case "February":
        case "December":
            season = "winter";
            break;
        case "March":
        case "April":
        case "May":
            season = "Spring";
            break;
        case "June":
        case "July":
        case "August":
            season = "Summer";
            break;
        case "September":
        case "October":
        case "November":
            season = "Autumn";
            break;
        default:
            out.println("Error");
    }
    out.println(">> Result: " + season);
    }
}
```

The switch expression supports String values as well. The main problem with switch supporting String values is that there is always a possibility of unexpected behavior, because the equals(..) method, which is case sensitive, is used to find a match.

The example in Listing 7-11 can be modified to ask the user for a text representing the month. The switch statement is used to decide the season to print, and unless the text in the case options matches the text introduced by the user exactly, the text printed is *Error*. Also, since the switch expression was mentioned, the code changes shown in Listing 7-12.

Listing 7-12. switch Expression Using String Values

```
package com.apress.bgn.seven.switchst;

import static java.lang.System.out;

public class StringSwitchSeasonDemo {
    void main(String... args) {
        //Read a
        String a = args[0];
        var season = "";
        switch (a) {
            case "January", "February", "December" -> season = "Winter";
            case "March", "April", "May" -> season = "Spring";
            case "June", "July", "August" -> season = "Summer";
            case "September", "October", "November" -> season = "Autumn";
            default -> out.println("Error");
        }
        out.println(season);
    }
}
```

If we run the previous program with lowercase argument january, winter will be printed in the console. If we run it with January or null, *Error* will be printed in the console.

switch with enum Options

Before support for String values, switch statements supported enum values. This is practical when the values are grouped into a fixed set, such as the names of the months in a year. By using enums, support for String values can be achieved. The user introduces the month as a text value. This value is converted to uppercase and used to extract the corresponding enum value. This allows for support of String values that are not case sensitive in a switch statement. The code in Listing 7-13 shows such an implementation.

Listing 7-13. switch Statement Using enum Values

```java
package com.apress.bgn.seven.switchst;

import static java.lang.System.out;

public class EnumSwitchDemo {
    enum Month {
        JANUARY, FEBRUARY, MARCH, APRIL, MAY, JUNE, JULY, AUGUST,
        SEPTEMBER, OCTOBER, NOVEMBER, DECEMBER
    }

    void main(String... args) {
        //Read a
        String a = args[0];
        try {
            Month month = Month.valueOf(a.toUpperCase());
            var season = "";
            switch (month) {
                case JANUARY:
                case FEBRUARY:
                case DECEMBER:
                    season = "Winter";
                    break;
                case MARCH:
                case APRIL:
                case MAY:
                    season = "Spring";
                    break;
                case JUNE:
                case JULY:
                case AUGUST:
                    season = "Summer";
                    break;
                case SEPTEMBER:
                case OCTOBER:
                case NOVEMBER:
```

```
                season = "Autumn";
                break;
        }
        out.println(season);
    } catch(IllegalArgumentException iae) {
        out.println("Unrecognized enum value: " + a );
    }
  }
}
```

By using enums, the same season is returned for january, January, JANuary, and other case variation. This is because of the way the code was designed, of course. Also, no default option is needed, because an exception is thrown if an enum value cannot be found matching the user-provided data before the switch expression is evaluated.

The switch expression equivalent of the code in Listing 7-13 is shown in Listing 7-14.

Listing 7-14. switch Expression Using enum Values

```
package com.apress.bgn.seven.switchst;

import static java.lang.System.out;

public class EnumSwitchExprDemo {
    enum Month {
        JANUARY, FEBRUARY, MARCH, APRIL, MAY, JUNE, JULY, AUGUST,
        SEPTEMBER, OCTOBER, NOVEMBER, DECEMBER
    }

    void main(String... args) {
        String a = args[0];
        try {
            Month month = Month.valueOf(a.toUpperCase());
            out.println(switch(month) {
                case JANUARY, FEBRUARY, DECEMBER -> "Winter";
                case MARCH , APRIL, MAY -> "Spring";
                case JUNE, JULY, AUGUST -> "Summer";
                case SEPTEMBER, OCTOBER, NOVEMBER -> "Autumn";
            });
```

```
    } catch(IllegalArgumentException iae) {
        out.println("Unrecognized enum value: " + a );        }
  }
}
```

In practice, depending on the solution you are trying to develop, you might decide to use a combination of if and switch statements. Unfortunately, because of the switch statement's peculiar logic and its flexible number of options, drawing a flowchart for the switch statement is difficult, but nevertheless I've tried, and it's depicted in Figure 7-6.

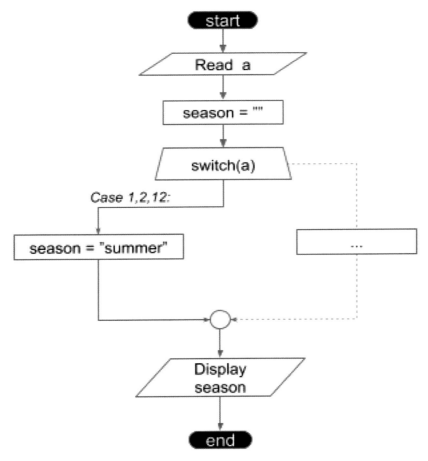

Figure 7-6. *The switch statement flowchart*

So what should you use, the switch statement or the switch expression? The answer is pretty easy to determine. The classic switch statement comes with a few drawbacks:

- Accidental fall-through, if you forget to add a break; the execution will continue to the next clause.

- Variables are scoped to the entire switch statement, which means a variable name cannot be reused in two different case clauses.

  The default clause is not required, and thus somebody reading the code might be confused as to what should be done with values that do not match the switch options, and whether the default clause was omitted intentionally or just forgotten.

The switch expression does not have any of these drawbacks and has a few other advantages:

- break; is not necessary, because there is no default fall-through.

- There is no need for a default clause with enums when all enum values are used as options, and if not all values are used but there is no default clause, the compiler will complain about it through an error.

- Instead of falling through by listing multiple labels, they can be comma-separated.

- Options can be of any type. *For real.* (Check out the FloatSwitchExprDemo class in the book repo to see an example, or feel free to write your own with a type of your choice.)

Which one would you use?

Caution   Keep in mind that the switch expression must return a value or throw an exception, and you cannot use a return statement to exit a switch expression. The classic switch statement, however, allows using the return statement in its clause.

Pattern Matching for `switch`

Chapter 6 introduced the `instanceof` operator to check the type of an instance and perform a certain operation based on it. This meant, however, that in the case where an object could have multiple types, you would end up with a construction similar to the one shown in Listing 7-15.

Listing 7-15. `if` Statement Checking Multiple Types for an Object

```
if (obj instanceof type1 t1) {
    //do something with t1
} else  if (obj instanceof type2 t2) {
    //do something with t2
} else if (...) {

} else {
    // action when type is none of the above
}
```

The code in Listing 7-15 gets the job done and is not wrong in any way, but it is tedious to write and it looks bad. Putting all those conditions in a `switch` expression would be nice, wouldn't it? Well, we can, starting with Java 21.

The `switch` expression is powerful and practical, but it does not come close to the similar constructs in other languages (e.g., the `when` construct in Kotlin)—at least it didn't until Java 17, when pattern matching for `switch` was introduced as a feature preview. The pattern matching for `switch` feature matured and was released in Java 21. Extending pattern matching to `switch` allows an expression to be tested against a number of patterns, each with a specific action, so that complex data-oriented queries can be expressed concisely and safely. This means, starting with Java 21, we can write code similar to shown in Listing 7-16.

Listing 7-16. `switch` Statement Checking Multiple Types for an Object

```
package com.apress.bgn.seven.pattern;

import com.apress.bgn.four.classes.Gender;
import com.apress.bgn.four.hierarchy.MiliVanili;
import com.apress.bgn.four.hierarchy.Performer;
import com.apress.bgn.six.Graphician;
```

```java
import java.util.List;
import static java.lang.System.out;

public class PatternDemo {

    void main(){
        Object obj = genRandomInstance();

        var res = switch (obj) { /* (*) */
            case Performer p -> "Performed in: " + p.getFilms();
            case MiliVanili m -> "Creativity " + (m.isCreative() ? "found"
            : "not found");
            case Graphician g -> "Prefers " + g.getFavoriteOs();
            case Painter p -> "Style: " + p.getStyle();
            default -> "something else";
        };
        out.println(res);
    }

    static Object genRandomInstance(){
      var t = System.currentTimeMillis();

      if (t % 3 == 0 ) {
        return new Painter("Pablo Picasso", "Cubism", "School of Fine Arts
        Barcelona");
      } else if (t % 5 == 0 ) {
        return new Performer("Sean", 94, 1.88f, Gender.MALE, List.of("James
        Bond"));
      } else if (t % 11 == 0) {
        return new MiliVanili();
      } else if (t % 17 == 0) {
        return new Graphician("Diana", 23, 1.62f, Gender.FEMALE, "macOs");
      } else  if (t % 23== 0) {
        return "random text";
      } else  if (t % 31== 0) {
        return Integer.MAX_VALUE;
      }
```

```
        return null;
    }
}
```

The genRandomInstance() method is included in the example to show the possible types of the object being tested. Repeated runs of the program in Listing 7-16 will generate a different output based on the current system time. Notice that the switch expression (and statement) supporting objects of any types to be tested allows the case labels to work with patterns instead of just constants. Running the code a few times might generate an object of each type, but you might notice that sometimes a NullPointerException exception with the following message is thrown:

```
Exception in thread "main" java.lang.NullPointerException
    at java.base/java.util.Objects.requireNonNull(Objects.java:220)
    at chapter.seven/com.apress.bgn.seven.pattern.PatternDemo.
main(PatternDemo.java:47)
```

So what gives? If you open the PatternDemo.java file in an editor, you will notice that the line where the exception is thrown is the first line of the switch expression (the line marked with (*) in the example). This happens because the expression evaluates to null. To avoid this, we could test for null before evaluating the switch expression, but that would add extra code. The good news is that pattern matching for switch supports null values as an option too. So we can rewrite the switch expression to include a null option and return a string for this scenario, and *voila*, no more exceptions are thrown (see Listing 7-17); instead, when the genRandomInstance() method returns null, the *no object* text is printed in the console.

Listing 7-17. switch Statement Checking Multiple Types for an Object and Handling null Values

```
package com.apress.bgn.seven.pattern;

import com.apress.bgn.four.classes.Gender;
import com.apress.bgn.four.hierarchy.MiliVanili;
import com.apress.bgn.four.hierarchy.Performer;
import com.apress.bgn.six.Graphician;
```

```java
import java.util.List;
import static java.lang.System.out;

public class PatternDemo {

    void main(){
        Object obj = genRandomInstance();

        var res = switch (obj) {
            case null -> "no object";
            case Performer p -> "Performed in: " + p.getFilms();
            case MiliVanili m -> "Creativity " + (m.isCreative() ? "found"
            : "not found");
            case Graphician g -> "Prefers " + g.getFavoriteOs();
            case Painter p -> "Style: " + p.getStyle();
            default -> "something else";
        };
        out.println(res);
    }

    // method genRandomInstance() omitted
}
```

An interesting thing happens when a switch statement or expression has options in a sealed hierarchy. You might not have noticed (unless you wrote some of the code in this chapter yourself), but when writing a switch statement or expression, unless the options are part of a fixed set, such as enum, the compiler always forces you to add a default option. This is not the case for the types in a sealed hierarchy—*can you guess why?*

The answer is quite simple: since interfaces and classes declare which other interfaces and classes are implementing them, the set of types becomes known at compile time, so it is possible by using the root of the hierarchy as a reference type for a generated instance to write a switch statement or expression that does not require a default option. Also, because all the types are part of the same hierarchy, the most specific types must come first in the list of options.

Considering the sealed hierarchy introduced in **Chapter 4**, which has sealed interface com.apress.bgn.four.sealed.two.Mammal at the root, we could write a switch expression like the one shown in Listing 7-18.

Listing 7-18. switch Expression Checking Multiple Types from a sealed Hierarchy for an Object

```
// sealed hierarchy from Chapter 4
package com.apress.bgn.four.sealed.two;

public sealed interface Mammal permits Human { }
public sealed class Human implements Mammal permits Performer,
Engineer { ... }
public non-sealed class  Engineer extends Human {...}
public final class Performer  extends Human { ... }

// testing class
package com.apress.bgn.seven.sealed;

import com.apress.bgn.four.classes.Gender;
import com.apress.bgn.four.sealed.two.Engineer;
import com.apress.bgn.four.sealed.two.Human;
import com.apress.bgn.four.sealed.two.Mammal;
import com.apress.bgn.four.sealed.two.Performer;

public class SealedHierachyDemo {

  void main(){
    var obj = genRandomInstance();

    switch (obj) {
      case Engineer e -> System.out.println(e);
      case Performer p -> System.out.println(p);
      case Human h -> System.out.println(h);
    }
  }

  public static Mammal genRandomInstance(){
    var t = System.currentTimeMillis();

    if (t % 3 == 0 ) {
      return new Engineer("Juan", 41, Gender.MALE);
    } else if (t % 5 == 0 ) {
```

421

```
      return new Human("Om", 41, Gender.MALE);
    }
    return new Performer("Ada", 209, Gender.FEMALE);
  }
}
```

Record Patterns for `switch`

JDK 21 also introduced **record patterns**, which, beside normal type matching and automatic conversion, introduced the capability of deconstructing records, as shown in **Chapter 6**. By using record patterns, not only can record types be used as options for the `switch` statements and expressions, but the options can be deconstruction expressions. Listing 7-19 shows a piece of code that shows a `switch` expression using various deconstructed record patterns as options.

Listing 7-19. `switch` Statement Checking Multiple Record Types for an Object

```
package com.apress.bgn.seven.pattern;

import static java.lang.System.out;

record FullName (String firstName, String lastName){}
record PersonRecord (FullName fullName, Integer age) {}
record WrapperBeing<T>(T t, String description) {}

public class RecordPatternDemo {

    void main(){
        Object obj = genRandomRecordInstance();

        switch (obj) {
            case null -> out.println("no record");
            case FullName(String fn, String ln) -> out.println("FullName
            record: " + fn +" " + ln);
            case PersonRecord(FullName(var fn, String _), var age) -> out.
            println("Person record " + fn +"  of age " + age);
            default -> out.println("something else");
        }
    }
```

```
public static Object genRandomRecordInstance(){
    var t = System.currentTimeMillis();

    if (t % 3 == 0 ) {
        return new FullName("John", "Doe");
    } else if (t % 5 == 0 ) {
        return new PersonRecord(new FullName("John", "Doe"), 42);
    } else if (t % 11 == 0) {
        return new WrapperBeing<>(new PersonRecord(new FullName("John",
        "Doe"), 42), "is mise");
    }
    return null;
}
}
```

Looping Statements

Sometimes in programming, we need repetitive steps that involve the same variables. To write the same statement over and over again to get the job done would be ridiculous. Let's take the example of sorting an array of integer values. The most popular algorithm to do this, and the one that is taught first in programming courses because it is simple, is called *Bubble Sort*. The algorithm compares the elements of an array two by two, and if they are not in the correct order, it swaps them. It goes over the array again and again until no more swaps are needed. The effects of the algorithm are depicted in Figure 7-7.

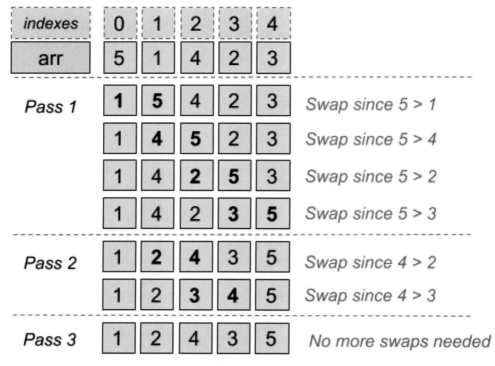

Figure 7-7. *Bubble Sort algorithm phases and effect*

This algorithm performs two types of loops: one iterates each element of the array using indexes. The second one repeats this traversal until no swaps are necessary. In Java this algorithm can be written in more than one way using different looping statements. But we'll get there; let's take it slow.

There are three types of looping statements in Java:

- `for` statement

- `while` statement

- `do-while` statement

The for looping statement is the most used, but while and do-while have their uses as well.

for Statement

The for statement is recommended for iterating on objects such as arrays and collections that can be counted. For example, traversing an array and printing each one of its values is as simple as depicted in Listing 7-20.

Listing 7-20. for Statement traversing an array

```
package com.apress.bgn.seven.forloop;
import static java.lang.System.out;

public class ForLoopBasicDemo {
  void main() {
    int[] arr = {5, 1, 4, 2, 3};
    for (int i = 0; i < arr.length; ++i) {
      out.println("arr[" +i +"] = " + arr[i]);
    }
  }
}
```

Based on the Listing 7-20 example, a flowchart for the for statement can be drawn as depicted in Figure 7-8.

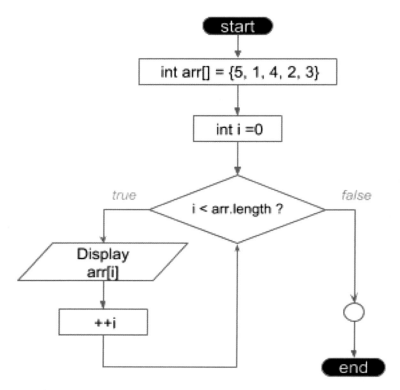

Figure 7-8. *The for statement flowchart*

The code snippet in Listing 7-21 depicts the for loop template.

Listing 7-21. The for Loop Template

```
for ([init_expr]; [condition];[step]){
    [code_block]
}
```

Each of the terms between square brackets have a specific purpose that is explained in the following list:

- [init_expr]: The initialization expression that is used to set the initial value of the counter used by this loop. It ends with ; and is not mandatory, as the declaration and initialization can be done outside the statement, especially if we are interested in using the counter variable later in the code and outside the statement. The code in Listing 7-20 can be very well written as shown in Listing 7-22.

Listing 7-22. The for Loop with Termination Condition and Counter
Modification Expression

```java
package com.apress.bgn.seven.forloop;
import static java.lang.System.out;

public class AnotherForLoopBasicDemo {

    void main(){
        int[] arr = {5, 1, 4, 2, 3};
        int i = 0;
        for (; i < arr.length; ++i) {
            out.println("arr[" +i +"] = " + arr[i]);
        }
        out.println("Loop exited with index: " + i);
    }
}
```

- [condition]: The termination condition of the loop. As long as this
  condition is evaluated to true, the loop will continue executing. The
  condition ends with ; and, funny enough, it is not mandatory either,
  as the termination condition can be placed inside the code to be
  executed repeatedly by the loop. So the code in Listing 7-22 can be
  modified further as shown in Listing 7-23.

Listing 7-23. The for Loop with Only Counter Modification Statement

```java
package com.apress.bgn.seven.forloop;
import static java.lang.System.out;

public class AndAnotherForLoopDemo {
    void main() {
        int[] arr = {5, 1, 4, 2, 3};
        int i = 0;
        for (; ; ++i) {
            if (i >= arr.length) {
                break;
            }
```

```
            out.println("arr[" +i +"] = " + arr[i]);
        }
        out.println("Loop exited with index: " + i);
    }
}
```

- [step]: The step expression, or increment, that increases the counter on every step of the loop. Being the last term, it does not end in ;. As you probably already expected, it is not mandatory either, as nothing stops the developer from manipulating the counter inside the code block. So the code in Listing 7-23 can also be written as shown in Listing 7-24.

Listing 7-24. The for Loop with No Initialization, Condition, or Counter Modification Expression

```
package com.apress.bgn.seven.forloop;

import static java.lang.System.out;

public class YeyAnotherForLoopDemo {
    void main() {
        int[] arr = {5, 1, 4, 2, 3};
        int i = 0;
        for (; ;) {
            if (i >= arr.length) {
                break;
            }
            out.println("arr[" +i +"] = " + arr[i]);
            ++i;
        }
        out.println("Loop exited with index: " + i);
    }
}
```

Another way to get creative with the `for` loop is to merge the modification of the counter and termination condition into a single condition. The code depicted in Listing 7-25 has the same effect as all examples shown so far in this section.

Listing 7-25. The `for` Loop with Counter Modification in Termination Condition

```
package com.apress.bgn.seven.forloop;

import static java.lang.System.out;

public class LastForLoopDemo {
    public static void main(String... args) {
        int[] arr = {5, 1, 4, 2, 3};
        int i = -1;
        for (; i++ < arr.length -1;) {
            out.println("arr[" +i +"] = " + arr[i]);
        }
        out.println("Loop exited with index: " + i);
    }
}
```

Also note that the step expression does not really have to be an incrementation. It can be any expression that modifies the value of the counter. Instead of ++i or i++, you can use i= i+1 or i=i+3, or even decrementation if the array or collection is traversed starting with a bigger index toward a lower one.

Note   Any mathematical operations that keep the counter within the boundaries of the type and within the collection boundaries can be used safely.

- [code_block]: A block of code that is executed repeatedly, in every step of the loop. If there is no exit condition within this code, this block of code will be executed as many times as the counter passes the termination condition.

Important   When the code block contains a single statement, the curly brackets are not mandatory, but most developers keep them for code clarity and to help IDEs indent the code properly.

Warning   As mentioned, the initialization expression, the termination condition, and the iteration expression are optional, which means the following is a valid `for` statement:

```
for ( ; ; ) {
    \\ statement(s) here
}
```

Caution   Just be careful when using the `for` statement like that. The code block must contain a termination condition to avoid an *infinite loop*.

This is the basic form of the `for` looping statement, but in Java there are other ways to iterate a group of values. Let's say that instead of an array we have to iterate over a list, as depicted in Listing 7-26.

Listing 7-26. The `for` Loop over a list

```
package com.apress.bgn.seven.forloop;

import java.util.List;
import static java.lang.System.out;

public class ListLoopDemo {
    void main() {
        var list = List.of(5, 1, 4, 2, 3);
        for (int j = 0; j < list.size(); ++j) {
            out.println("list[ " +j +"] = " + list.get(j));
        }
    }
}
```

The code in Listing 7-26 seems somehow impractical because of the multiple invocations of list methods, which is why `List<E>` instances can be traversed with a different type of `for` statement that was known as `forEach` until Java 8. You will see immediately why, but first let's see the `forEach` in action in Listing 7-27.

Listing 7-27. The forEach Loop over a List<E>

```
package com.apress.bgn.seven.forloop;

import java.util.List;
import static java.lang.System.out;

public class ForEachLoopDemo {
  void main() {
    var list = List.of(5, 1, 4, 2, 3);
    for (Integer item : list) {
      out.println(item);
    }
  }
}
```

This type of for statement is also referenced as having enhanced syntax and executes the code block for each item in the collection used in its expression. This means that it works on any implementation of the Collection<E> interface, and it works on arrays too. So the code examples presented until now can also be written as depicted in Listing 7-28.

Listing 7-28. The forEach Loop over an Array

```
package com.apress.bgn.seven.forloop;
import static java.lang.System.out;

public class ArrayForEachDemo {

    void main(){
        int[] arr = {5, 1, 4, 2, 3};
        for (int item : arr) {
            out.println(item);
        }
    }
}
```

Clearly the best part in this case is that we no longer need a termination condition or counter at all. Starting with Java 8, the name forEach can no longer be used for the for statement with enhanced syntax, because the forEach default method was added to all Collection<E> implementations, so now it is just being called "enhanced for". Combine the forEach default method with lambda expressions, and the code to print the elements of a list becomes the one in Listing 7-29.

Listing 7-29. The forEach Method Used to Loop over a List<E>

```
package com.apress.bgn.seven.forloop;
import java.util.List;
import static java.lang.System.out;

public class ForLoopDemo {
  void main(){
    var list = List.of(5, 1, 4, 2, 3);
    list.forEach(item -> out.println(item));
    //or using method reference
    list.forEach(out::println);
  }
}
```

Pretty neat, right? But wait, there's more: it works on arrays too, but a small conversion to a suitable implementation of java.util.stream.BaseStream is necessary first. This is provided by the Arrays utility class, which was enriched in Java 8 with methods to support lambda expressions. So the code with the arr array written so far can be written starting in Java 8 as shown in Listing 7-30.

Listing 7-30. The forEach Method Used to Loop over an Array

```
package com.apress.bgn.seven.forloop;
import static java.lang.System.out;

public class ForLoopDemo {
  void main(){
    int[] arr = {5, 1, 4, 2, 3};
    Arrays.stream(arr).forEach(out::println);
  }
}
```

432

Another way to traverse an array without using an index variable is by using java.util.stream.IntStream.range(..), as shown in Listing 7-31. The range(startInclusive, endExclusive) method returns a sequential ordered IntStream from startInclusive (inclusive) to endExclusive (exclusive) by an incremental step of 1.

Listing 7-31. Loop over an Array Using IntStream.range(startInclusive, endExclusive)

```
package com.apress.bgn.seven.forloop;
import java.util.stream.IntStream;
import static java.lang.System.out;

public class ForLoopDemo {
  void main(){
    int[] arr = {5, 1, 4, 2, 3};
    IntStream.range(0, arr.length).forEach(out::println);
  }
}
```

In Java 21, all the preceding examples will compile and execute just fine, so use whatever syntax you prefer most when writing your solutions.

while Statement

The main difference between a while statement and a for statement is that a while statement does not require executing a fixed number of steps, so a counter is not always needed. The number of repetitions a while statement executes depends only on how many times the continuation condition that controls this number is evaluated to true. The generic template for this statement is depicted in Listing 7-32.

Listing 7-32. The while Statement Template

```
while ([eval(condition)] == true) {
    [code_block]
}
```

A while statement does not really require an initialization statement either. If needed, it can be inside the while code block, or outside it. The while statement can replace the for statement, but the advantage of the for statement is that it encapsulates the initialization, the termination condition, and the modification of the counter in a single block, so it is more concise. The array traversal code sample can be rewritten using the while statement, as depicted in Listing 7-33.

Listing 7-33. The while Statement Used to Loop over an Array

```
package com.apress.bgn.seven.whileloop;

import static java.lang.System.out;

public class WhileLoopDemo {

    void main(){
        int[] arr = {5, 1, 4, 2, 3};
        int i = 0;
        while(i < arr.length) {
            out.println("arr[" +i +"] = " + arr[i]);
            ++i;
        }
    }
}
```

As you can see, the declaration and initialization of the counter variable int i = 0; is done outside the while code block. The incrementation of the counter is done inside the code block to be repeated. At this point, if we design the flowchart for this scenario, it will look the same as the one for the for statement depicted in Figure 7-8.

As incredible as it sounds, the [condition] is not mandatory either, as it can be replaced directly with true, but in that case you have to make sure there is an exit condition inside the block of code that will definitely be executed; otherwise, the execution will most likely end with an error, since the JVM will not allow an infinite loop. This condition must be placed at the beginning of the block of code, to prevent the execution of the useful logic in a situation where it shouldn't be executed. For our simple example, clearly we do not want to call System.out.println for an element with an index outside the array range, as depicted in Listing 7-34.

Listing 7-34. The while Statement Used to Loop over an Array, Without a Continuation Expression

```
package com.apress.bgn.seven.whileloop;
import static java.lang.System.out;

public class AnotherWhileLoopDemo {

    void main(){
        int[] arr = {5, 1, 4, 2, 3};
        int i=0;
        while(true){
            if (i >= arr.length) {
                break;
            }
            out.println("arr[" +i +"] = " + arr[i]);
            ++i;
        }
    }
}
```

The while statement is best used when we are working with a resource that is not always online. Let's say we are using a remote database for our application that is in a network that is unstable. Instead of giving up trying to save our data after the first timeout, we could try until we succeed, right? This can be done by using a while statement, which will keep trying to initialize a connection object in its code block. The code looks roughly as depicted in Listing 7-35.

Listing 7-35. The while Statement Used to Repeatedly Try to Obtain a Database Connection

```
package com.apress.bgn.seven.whileloop;

import java.sql.Connection;
import java.sql.DriverManager;
import java.sql.ResultSet;
import java.sql.Statement;
import static java.lang.System.out;
```

```java
public class WhileConnectionTester {

    void main()throws Exception {
        Connection con = null;
        while (con == null) {
            try {
                con = DriverManager.getConnection(
                        "jdbc:mysql://localhost:3306/mysql",
                        "root", "mypass");
            } catch (Exception e) {
                out.println("Connection refused. Retrying in 5
                seconds ...");
                Thread.sleep(5000);
            }
        }
        // con != null, do the thing
        Statement stmt = con.createStatement();
        ResultSet rs = stmt.executeQuery("select * from user");
        while (rs.next()) {
            out.println(rs.getString(1) + " " + rs.getString(2));
        }
        con.close();
    }
}
// output
// maybe
// Connection refused. Retrying in 5 seconds ...
// definitely
/*
% root
localhost mysql.infoschema
localhost mysql.session
localhost mysql.sys
localhost root
*/
```

The problem with this code is that it will run forever if there is no database to connect to. If we want to give up trying after a certain time, we have to introduce a variable counting the number of tries and exit the loop using a break; statement, as shown in Listing 7-36.

Listing 7-36. The while Statement Used to Repeatedly Try to Obtain a Database Connection Until the Number of Tries Expires

```
package com.apress.bgn.seven.whileloop;

import java.sql.Connection;
import java.sql.DriverManager;
import static java.lang.System.out;

public class AnotherWhileConnectionTester {
    public static final int MAX_TRIES = 10;
    void main() throws Exception {
        var cntTries = 0;
        Connection con = null;
        while (con == null && cntTries < MAX_TRIES) {
            try {
                con = DriverManager.getConnection(
                        "jdbc:mysql://localhost:3306/mysql",
                        "root", "mypass");
            } catch (Exception e) {
                ++cntTries;
                out.println("Connection refused. Retrying in 5
                seconds ...");
                Thread.sleep(5000);
            }
        }
        if (con != null) {
            // con != null, do the thing
            var stmt = con.createStatement();
            var rs = stmt.executeQuery("select * from user");
            while (rs.next()) {
                out.println(rs.getString(1) + " " + rs.getString(2));
            }
```

```
                con.close();
        } else {
            out.println("Could not connect!");
        }
    }
}
// output when no db
// Connection refused. Retrying in 5 seconds ... (10 times)
// Could not connect!
```

Important   As a rule of thumb, always make sure there is an exit condition when using looping statements.

Since we've now covered all the statements needed to implement the Bubble Sort algorithm depicted in Figure 7-7, let's see what the code looks like. Be aware that this algorithm can be written in many ways, but the following code best matches the explanation provided earlier: while there are elements in the array that are not in the proper order, the array is traversed again and again and adjacent elements are swapped to fit the desired order (ascending, in this case). The simplest version of the Bubble Sort algorithm is depicted in Listing 7-37.

Listing 7-37. The Simplest Version of the Bubble Sort Algorithm

```
package com.apress.bgn.seven.whileloop;

import java.util.Arrays;

import static java.lang.System.out;

public class BubbleSortDemo {
    public static final int[] arr = {5, 1, 4, 2, 3};

    void main() {
            boolean swapped = true;
            while (swapped) {
                swapped = false;
```

```
            for (int i = 0; i < arr.length - 1; ++i) {
                if (arr[i] > arr[i + 1]) {
                    int temp = arr[i];
                    arr[i] = arr[i + 1];
                    arr[i + 1] = temp;
                    swapped = true;
                }
            }
        }
        Arrays.stream(arr).forEach(out::println);
    }
}
// output
/*
1
2
3
4
5
*/
```

do-while Statement

The do-while statement is similar to the while statement, with one difference: the continuation condition is evaluated after executing the code block. This causes the code block to be executed at least once, which is useful to show a menu, for example, unless there is a condition embedded in it that prevents it. The generic template for this statement is depicted in the Listing 7-38.

Listing 7-38. The do-while Statement Template

```
do {
    [code_block]
} while ([eval(condition)] == true)
```

Most times statements while and do-while can be easily interchanged with minimum or no changes of the logic of the code block. For example, traversing an array and printing the values of its elements can be written using do-while as well, without changing the code block at all. In Figure 7-9 you can see the two implementations side by side, with the while statement on the left and do-while on the right. Each condition is made obvious by setting a breakpoint on each line.

```
WhileLoopDemo.java ×                                    DoWhileLoopDemo.java ×
 1   > /.../                          △ 1 ✓ 3 ∧ ∨   1   > /.../
28   package com.apress.bgn.seven.whileloop;        28   package com.apress.bgn.seven;
29                                                   29
30   import static java.lang.System.out;            30   import static java.lang.System.out;
31                                                   31
32   /**                                             32   /**
33    * Created by iuliana.cosmina on 22/06/2024     33    * Created by iuliana.cosmina on 22/06/2024
34    */                                             34    */
35 ▷ public class WhileLoopDemo {  new *             35 ▷ public class DoWhileLoopDemo {  new *
36                                                   36
37 ▷     void main(){  new *                         37 ▷     void main(){  new *
38           int[] arr = {5, 1, 4, 2, 3};            38 ⦿       int[] arr = {5, 4, 1, 3, 2};
39           int i = 0;                              39           int i = 0;
●          while(i < arr.length) {                  40           do {
41               out.println(STR."arr[\{i}] = \{arr[i]}");  41               out.println(STR."arr[\{i}] = \{arr[i]}");
42               ++i;                                42               ++i;
43           }                                       ●          } while (i < arr.length);
44       }                                           44       }
45   }                                               45   }
46                                                   46
```

Figure 7-9. *while and do-while implementation for printing elements of an array*

The flowcharts for these two examples are quite different, however, and reveal the different logic of the two statements. You can compare them by taking a look at Figure 7-10.

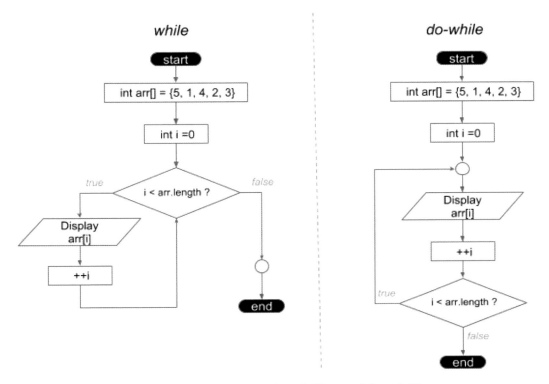

Figure 7-10. *Comparison of flowcharts for* while *and* do-while *statements*

In the examples in Figure 7-9, if the array is empty, the do-while statement causes an ArrayIndexOutOfBoundsException exception to be thrown, because the contents of the code block are executed. The index value is equal to the array length (zero), so the block should not be executed. However, because the condition is evaluated after the code block, there's no way to know that. In Figure 7-11 you can see the previous code sample modified to run with an empty array and the output of each side by side.

```
WhileLoopDemo.java ×
1   > /.../
28    package com.apress.bgn.seven.whileloop;
29
30    import static java.lang.System.out;
31
32    /** Created by iuliana.cosmina on 22/06/2024 */
35 ▷ public class WhileLoopDemo {  new *
36
37 ▷     void main(){  new *
38         int[] arr = new int[0]; //{5, 1, 4, 2, 3};
39         int i = 0;
40         while(i < arr.length) {
41             out.println(STR."arr[\{i}] = \{arr[i]}");
42             ++i;
43         }
44     }
45   }
```

```
Run    WhileLoopDemo ×
/Users/iuliana/.sdkman/candidates/java/23.ea.18-open/bin/java ...

Process finished with exit code 0
```

```
DoWhileLoopDemo.java ×
1   > /.../
28    package com.apress.bgn.seven;
29
30    import static java.lang.System.out;
31
32    /** Created by iuliana.cosmina on 22/06/2024 */
35 ▷ public class DoWhileLoopDemo {  new *
36
37 ▷     void main(){  new *
38         int[] arr = new int[0]; //{5, 4, 1, 3, 2};
39         int i = 0;
40         do {
41             out.println(STR."arr[\{i}] = \{arr[i]}");
42             ++i;
●        } while (i < arr.length);
44     }
45   }
```

```
Run    DoWhileLoopDemo ×
/Users/iuliana/.sdkman/candidates/java/23.ea.18-open/bin/java ...
Exception in thread "main" java.lang.ArrayIndexOutOfBoundsException Create breakpoint : Index 0 out of bounds for length 0
    at chapter.seven/com.apress.bgn.seven.DoWhileLoopDemo.main(DoWhileLoopDemo.java:41)

Process finished with exit code 1
```

***Figure 7-11.** while and do-while implementation for printing elements of an empty array*

To fix the do-while implementation to have the same behavior as the while implementation, the code block execution must be conditioned by the array having at least one element. Code Listing 7-39 shows one way to do it.

Listing 7-39. do-while Statement Implementation That Works Correctly for an Empty Array Too

```
package com.apress.bgn.seven.dowhileloop;
import static java.lang.System.out;

public class DoWhileLoopDemo {

  void main(){
    int[] arr = new int[0]; //{5, 4, 1, 3, 2};
    int i = 0;
    do {
      if(arr.length >=1) {
        out.println("arr[" +i +"] = " + arr[i]);
        ++i;
      }
    } while (i < arr.length);
  }
}
```

Tip The do-while statement works best when the code block must be executed at least once; otherwise we evaluate the condition once unnecessarily.

The Bubble Sort algorithm introduced earlier is a good example where while and do-while statements can be used interchangeably with no extra code modifications.

Since it has been mentioned that there is more than one way to write this algorithm, the Listing in 7-40 shows an improved version that not only uses do-while, but decreases the size of the array being traversed each time. This is possible because (according to Figure 7-7) after each traversal, the last index of the array holds the biggest number of the subset being traversed.

Listing 7-40. Optimized Version of the Bubble Sort Algorithm Using `do-while` Statement

```java
package com.apress.bgn.seven.dowhileloop;
import java.util.Arrays;
import static java.lang.System.out;

public class BubbleSortDemo {
    public static final int[] arr = {5, 1, 4, 2, 3};

    void main(){
        boolean swapped;
        do {
            swapped = false;
            for (int i = 0, n = arr.length -1; i < n - 1; ++i, --n) {
                if (arr[i] > arr[i + 1]) {
                    int temp = arr[i];
                    arr[i] = arr[i + 1];
                    arr[i + 1] = temp;
                    swapped = true;
                }
            }
        } while (swapped);
        Arrays.stream(arr).forEach(out::println);
    }
}
```

Important   The initialization and the step expressions in the `for` statement allow for multiple terms separated by `,`. So the following code is valid and works just fine:

```java
for (int j = 0, k =2; j < 10; ++j, ++k) {
    out.println("composed indexes: [" +j + ", " + k + "]");
}
```

Remember the code sample in Listing 7-35 that was trying to connect to a database that was in an unstable network? When while was used, the execution started by testing to see if the connection was not null, but the connection was not even initialized with a valid value yet. It's illogical to perform that test, right? See the snippet shown in Listing 7-41.

Listing 7-41. while Implementation to Check Connection to a Database

```
Connection con = null;
while (con == null) {
    try {
        con = DriverManager.getConnection(
                "jdbc:mysql://localhost:3306/mysql", "root", "mypass");
    // some code omitted
```

This implementation, although functional, is a bit redundant, and the logic is not really following best programming practices. A do-while implementation is most suitable because it avoids the initial testing if the con instance is null, when there is no way it could be otherwise. One variant of writing the code is depicted in Listing 7-42.

Listing 7-42. do-while Implementation to Check Connection to a Database

```
package com.apress.bgn.seven.dowhileloop;

import java.sql.Connection;
import java.sql.DriverManager;
import static java.lang.System.out;

public class DoWhileConnectionTester {
    public static final int MAX_TRIES = 10;

    void main() throws Exception {
        int cntTries = 0;
        Connection con = null;
        do {
            try {
                con = DriverManager.getConnection(
                        "jdbc:mysql://localhost:3306/mysql",
                        "root", "mypass");
```

445

```java
        } catch (Exception e) {
            ++cntTries;
            out.println("Connection refused. Retrying in 5
            seconds ...");
            Thread.sleep(5000);
        }
    } while (con == null && cntTries < MAX_TRIES);

    if (con != null) {
        var stmt = con.createStatement();
        var rs = stmt.executeQuery("select * from user");
        while (rs.next()) {
            out.println(rs.getString(1) + " " + rs.getString(2));
        }
        con.close();
    } else {
        out.println("Could not connect!");
    }
  }
}
```

Sure, skipping the evaluation of the condition a single time is not a big optimization, but in a big application, every little optimization counts.

Breaking Loops and Skipping Steps

As promised in the discussion of the previous examples that exited a loop using the break; statement, this section adds more details. There are three statements that we can use to manipulate the behavior of a loop:

- break: Exits the loop and, if accompanied by a label, breaks the loop that is labeled with it; this is useful when we have more nested loops, because we can break from any of the nested loops, not just the one containing the statement.

- continue: Skips the execution of any code after it and continues with the next step.

- return: Exits a method, so if the loop or a switch statement is within the body of a method, it can be used to exit the loop as well.

Warning   As for best practices, usage of return statements to exit a method should not be abused, as they might make the execution flow difficult to follow.

---

break Statement

The break statement can be used only within switch, for, while, and do-while statements. You have already seen how it can be used within the switch statement, so let's look at how to use it in the other three statements. Breaking out of a for, while, or do-while loop can be done using the break statement, but it must be controlled by an exit condition, otherwise no step will be executed. In Listing 7-43, we print only the first three elements in an array, even if the for loop is designed to traverse all of them. If we get the index equal to 3, we exit the loop.

Listing 7-43. Breaking Out of a for Loop

```
package com.apress.bgn.seven.forloop;
import static java.lang.System.out;

public class BreakingForDemo {
    public static final int[] arr = {5, 1, 4, 2, 3};

    void main(){
        for (int i = 0; i < arr.length ; ++i) {
            if (i == 3) {
                out.println("Bye bye!");
                break;
            }
            out.println("arr[" +i +"] = " + arr[i]);
        }
    }
}
```

If we have a case of nested loops, a label can be used to decide the looping statement to break out of. As an example, in Listing 7-44 we have three nested for loops, and we exit the middle loop when all indexes are equal.

Listing 7-44. Breaking Out of a Nested for Loop

```java
package com.apress.bgn.seven.forloop;
import static java.lang.System.out;

public class BreakingNestedForLoopDemo {
    public static final int[] arr = {5, 1, 4, 2, 3};

    void main(){
        for (int i = 0; i < 2; ++i) {
            HERE: for (int j = 0; j < 2; ++j) {
                for (int k = 0; k < 2; ++k) {
                    if (i == j && j == k) {
                        break HERE;
                    }
                    out.println("(i, j, k) = (" +i + ", " + j + ",
                    " + k +")");
                }
            }
        }
    }
}
```

The label used in Listing 7-44 is named HERE and it is declared in front of the for statement that is exited when the condition is fulfilled. The same label follows the break statement. Writing label names with all all-caps letters is considered a best practice in development, as it avoids confusing labels with variables or class names when reading the code.

To make sure this works, you can take a look in the console. You should see that some combinations of (i, j, k), including the one with i = j = k, are missing. The output is listed here:

```
(i, j, k) = (1,0,0)
(i, j, k) = (1,0,1)
(i, j, k) = (1,1,0)
```

Caution   Breaking loops with labels is very much frowned upon in software development, which is a tame way to say **it is a bad practice**, since it causes a code jump and makes the execution flow more difficult to follow. So if you have no choice but to do it, make sure your labels are visible.

Tip   Depending on the solution you are building, you might be able to avoid using breaking with labels by wrapping the nested loops inside a method and using a `return` statement to break out of the loop, as you will be shown a little bit later in this chapter.

continue Statement

The `continue` statement does not break a loop, but it can be used to skip certain steps based on a condition. Essentially, the `continue` statement stops the execution of the current step of the loop and moves to the next one, so you could say that this statement continues the loop. Let's continue experimenting with the array traversal example, but let's skip the step of printing the elements with odd indexes by using the `continue` statement. The code is shown in Listing 7-45.

Listing 7-45. Skipping Printing Elements with Odd Indexes Using a `for` Loop and `continue` Statement

```
package com.apress.bgn.seven.forloop;
import static java.lang.System.out;

public class ContinueForDemo {
    public static final int[] arr = {5, 1, 4, 2, 3};

    void main(){
        for (int i = 0; i < arr.length; ++i) {
            if (i % 2 != 0) {
                continue;
            }
            out.println("arr[" +i +"] = " + arr[i]);
        }
    }
}
```

Obviously, this statement must be conditioned—otherwise, the loop will just iterate uselessly.

The continue statement can be used with labels too. Let's take a similar example to the three for nested loops used earlier, but this time, when the k index is equal to 1, nothing is printed, and we skip to the next step of the loop enclosing the k loop. The code is shown in Listing 7-46.

Listing 7-46. Skipping Printing Elements with Odd Indexes Using a for Loop and Labeled continue Statement

```java
package com.apress.bgn.seven.forloop;
import static java.lang.System.out;
/**
 * Created by iuliana.cosmina on 23/06/2024
 */
public class ContinueNestedForLoopDemo {
    public static final int[] arr = {5, 1, 4, 2, 3};

    void main(){
        for (int i = 0; i < 3; ++i) {
            HERE: for (int j = 0; j < 3; ++j) {
                for (int k = 0; k < 3; ++k) {
                    if (k == 1) {
                        continue HERE;
                    }
                    out.println("(i, j, k) = (" +i + ", " + j + ",
                    " + k +")");
                }
            }
        }
    }
}
```

To make sure this works, you can take a look in the console and see what combinations are printed. The expected output is listed here, which clearly shows that no combination with k = 1 or k = 2 is printed:

```
(i, j, k) = (0,0,0)
(i, j, k) = (0,1,0)
(i, j, k) = (0,2,0)
(i, j, k) = (1,0,0)
(i, j, k) = (1,1,0)
(i, j, k) = (1,2,0)
(i, j, k) = (2,0,0)
(i, j, k) = (2,1,0)
(i, j, k) = (2,2,0)
```

> **Important**   The usage of labels to break out of loops is frowned upon in the Java community, because jumping to a label resembles the goto statement that can be found in certain old-school programming languages.

> **Note**   goto is a Java reserved keyword, because this statement used to exist in the first version of Java. Using jumping makes code less readable since the execution flow becomes more difficult to follow, less testable and promotes bad design. This is why goto was removed in later Java versions, but any need of such operation can be implemented break and continue statements.

return Statement

The return statement is an easy one to understand: as already mentioned, it can be used to exit the execution of a method body. If the method returns a value, the return statement is accompanied by the value returned. The return statement can be used to exit any of the statements mentioned in this section. It can represent quite a smart way to shortcut the execution of a method, as the execution of the current method stops and processing continues from the point in the code that called the method.

Let's look at a few examples. The code in Listing 7-47 shows a method that searches for the first even element in an array. If found, the method returns its index; otherwise, it returns -1.

Listing 7-47. Skipping Printing Elements with Odd Indexes Using a `for` Loop and `continue` Statement

```java
package com.apress.bgn.seven;
import static java.lang.System.out;

public class ReturnDemo {
    public static final int[] arr = {5, 1, 4, 2, 3};

    void main() {
        int foundIdx = findEvenUsingFor(arr);

        if (foundIdx != -1) {
            out.println("First even is at: " + foundIdx);
        }
    }

    public static int findEvenUsingFor(int ... arr) {
        for (int i = 0; i < arr.length; ++i) {
            if (arr[i] %2 == 0) {
                return i;
            }
        }
        return -1;
    }
}
```

The same method can be written using a `while` statement, but the purpose of the return statement is the same. The code is shown in Listing 7-48.

Listing 7-48. Finding an Even Number Using the `while` Statement

```java
// enclosing class omitted
public static int findEvenUsingWhile(int ... arr) {
    int i = 0;
    while (i < arr.length) {
```

```
        if (arr[i] % 2 == 0) {
            return i;
        }
        ++i;
    }
    return -1;
}
```

As you can see, the `return` statement can be used in any situation in which you want to terminate the execution of a method if a condition is met.

Controlling the Flow Using **try-catch** Constructions

Exceptions and `try-catch` statements have been mentioned before in this book, but not as tools to control flow execution. Before we skip to explanations and examples, let's first discuss the general template of a `try-catch-finally` statement. This template is shown in Listing 7-49.

Listing 7-49. `try-catch-finally` Statement Template

```
try {
    [code_block]
} catch ([exception_block]} {
    [handling_code_block]
} finally {
    [cleanup_code_block]
}
```

The components of the template are explained in the following list:

- `[code_block]`: The code block to execute.

- `[exception_block]`: A declaration or more of an exception type for the instances that can be thrown by the `[code_block]`.

- [handling_code_block]: An exception being thrown marks an unexpected situation that must be handled. Once the exception is caught, this piece of code is executed to treat it, either by trying to return the system to a normal state or by logging details about the cause of the exception.

- [cleanup_code_block]: If needed, this block of code is used to release resources or set objects to null so that they are eligible for collection. When present, this block of code is executed regardless of whether an exception is thrown or not.

Now that you know how a try-catch-finally statement works, you can probably imagine how to use it to control the execution flow. Within the [code_block] you can explicitly throw exceptions and decide how they are treated.

Considering the array that we have been using until now, we'll design our piece of code based on it again. Listing 7-50 shows a piece of code that throws an exception when an even value is found.

Listing 7-50. Controlling Flow Using Exceptions

```
package com.apress.bgn.seven.ex;
import java.util.Arrays;

import static java.lang.System.out;

public class ExceptionFlowDemo {
    public static final int[] arr = {5, 1, 4, 2, 3};

    void main(){
        try {
            checkNotEven(arr);
            out.println("Not found, all good!");
        } catch (EvenException e) {
            out.println(e.getMessage());
        } finally {
            out.println("Cleaning up arr");
            Arrays.fill(arr, 0);
        }
    }
}
```

```java
    public static int checkNotEven(int... arr) throws EvenException {
        for (int i = 0; i < arr.length; ++i) {
            if (arr[i] % 2 == 0) {
                throw new EvenException("Did not expect an even number
                at " + i);
            }
        }
        return -1;
    }
}

class EvenException extends Exception{
    public EvenException(String message) {
        super(message);
    }
}
// output
//Did not expect an even number at 2
//Cleaning up arr
```

The EvenException type is a custom exception type written for this specific example. Notice the output of this snippet. As you can see, by throwing an exception, we've directed the execution to the handling code, so *Not found, all good!* is not printed. Because there is a `finally` block that was executed as well, we get the *Cleaning up arr* message in the console too.

You also can mix and match: use different types of exceptions and include multiple `catch` blocks—whatever you need to solve your problem. At a previous company I worked for we had a piece of code that validated a document and threw different types of exceptions depending on the validation check that failed, and in the `finally` block we had code that converted the error object to PDF. The code looked similar to that in Listing 7-51.

Listing 7-51. Code Sample Showing a `try-catch-finally` Block with Multiple catch Statements

```
ErrorContainter errorContainer = new ErrorContainter();
try {
    validate(report);
} catch (FileNotFoundException | NotParsable e) {
    errorContainer.addBadFileError(e);
} catch (InvestmentMaxException e) {
    errorContainer.addInvestmentError(e);
} catch (CreditIncompatibilityException e) {
    errorContainer.addIncompatibilityError(e);
} finally {
    if (errorContainer.isEmpty()) {
        printValidationPassedDocument();
    } else {
        printValidationFailedDocument(errorContainer);
    }
}
```

The code in the `finally` code block was complex and totally not recommended to be in there. However, sometimes in the real world, the solutions do not always respect best practices, or even commonsense practices. When dealing with legacy code, you might find yourself in the position of having to write functional but crappy code that solves the client's problem—because sure, programming is awesome, but in the eyes of some managers, results are more important...quicker results even more so. If you are lucky enough to get a job at a company that is looking to build the code in the future or hand it to other team members, you might actually end up with a manager who favors best practices. Just remember to do your best and document everything properly, and you'll be fine.

`try-catch-finally` blocks are quite powerful. They are a useful construction for directing execution flow and printing useful information about the overall status of the application and the source of an eventual problem. When designed properly, exception handling can increase the quality and readability of your code. There are a few rules to follow when designing exception handling:

- Try to avoid multiple catch blocks, unless they are used to treat different types of exceptions differently.

- Group together similar types of exceptions that are treated the same way by using the | (pipe) symbol. Support for this was added in Java 7.

- Be careful when catching exceptions with related types. The first catch statement that matches an exception type handles the exception, so superclasses should be lower in the catch list. The compiler will even get really upset if the order is not correct, as shown in Figure 7-12.

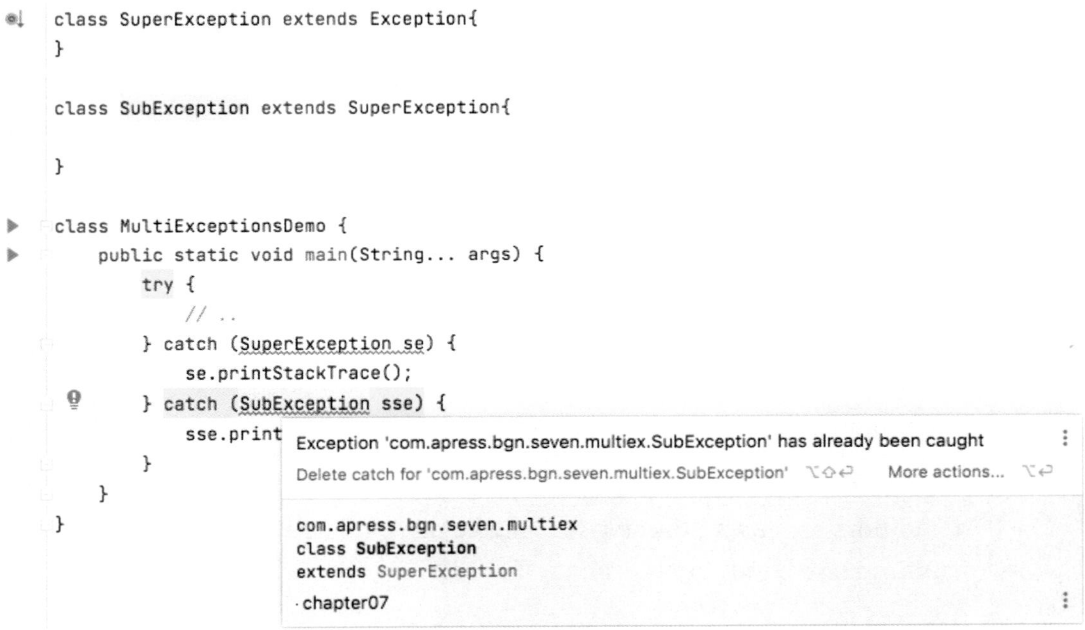

```
class SuperException extends Exception{
}

class SubException extends SuperException{

}

class MultiExceptionsDemo {
    public static void main(String... args) {
        try {
            // ..
        } catch (SuperException se) {
            se.printStackTrace();
        } catch (SubException sse) {
            sse.print
        }
    }
}
```

Exception 'com.apress.bgn.seven.multiex.SubException' has already been caught

Delete catch for 'com.apress.bgn.seven.multiex.SubException'   ⌥⇧↵   More actions...   ⌥↵

com.apress.bgn.seven.multiex
class **SubException**
extends SuperException
· chapter07

Figure 7-12. *IntelliJ IDEA compile error and message showing the wrong order of exception types in a* try-catch *block*

And of course, you should also respect the basic rules of avoiding exception swallowing and catching Throwable that were mentioned earlier in the book.

Summary

This chapter covered one of the most important aspects of development: how to design your solutions, and the logic of it. You've also been introduced to flowcharts and their components as tools for deciding how to write your code and how to control execution paths. And finally, you've learned which statements to use and when, and a few Java best practices for using them, so that you will be able to design the most suitable solutions to solve your problems. Java provides the following:

- Both simple and more complex ways to write `if` statements

- A `switch` statement that works with any primitive type, enumerations, and (starting with Java 7) `String` instances

- A `switch` expression that returns a value and that can be used to write more complex statements

- Use of pattern matching and record patterns in `switch` expressions and statements

- A few ways to write `for` statements

- Use of `forEach` methods and streams to traverse a collection of values

- A `while` statement, used when a step must be repeated until a condition is met

- A `do-while` statement, used when a step must be repeated until a condition is met, and the step is repeated at least once, because the continuation condition is evaluated after it

- Manipulation of loop behavior by using statements such as `break`, `continue`, and `return`

- Control of the execution flow by using `try-catch-finally` constructions

CHAPTER 8

The Stream API

The noun *stream* has more than one meaning, as defined on Dictionary.com:

1. a body of water flowing in a channel or watercourse, as a river, rivulet, or brook

2. a steady current in water, as in a river or the ocean

3. any flow of water or other liquid or fluid

4. a current or flow of air, gas, or the like

5. a beam or trail of light

6. a continuous flow or succession of anything

7. prevailing direction; drift

8. *Digital Technology*

   a. a flow of data, as an audio broadcast, a movie, or live video, transmitted smoothly and continuously from a source to a computer, mobile device, etc.

   b. livestream

When it comes to the term *stream* in the context of programming, the definitions in the preceding list that are closest to what a stream is are numbers 6 and 8a. Indeed, in programming, a stream is a sequence of objects from a source that supports aggregate operations (operations that accumulate all values in a stream). In your mind, you might be thinking the more appropriate term is *collection*. Well…not quite. This chapter will make the distinction clear.

459

© Iuliana Cosmina 2024
I. Cosmina, *Java 23 for Absolute Beginners*, https://doi.org/10.1007/979-8-8688-1041-1_8

Introduction to Streams

Consider a really big collection of songs that we want to analyze and find all songs with duration of at least 300 seconds. For these songs, we want to save the names in a list and sort them in decreasing order of their duration. Assuming we already have the songs in a list, the code looks like Listing 8-1.

Listing 8-1. Java Code Made of a Few Statements

```java
// non-relevant code omitted

List<Song> songList = loadSongs();
List<Song> resultedSongs = new ArrayList<>();

//find all songs with duration of at least 300 seconds
for (Song song: songList) {
    if (song.getDuration() >= 300) {
        resultedSongs.add(song);
    }
}

Collections.sort(resultedSongs, new Comparator<Song>(){
    public int compare(Song s1, Song s2){
        return s2.getDuration().compareTo(s1.getDuration());
    }
});

System.out.println(resultedSongs);
List<String> finalList0 = new ArrayList<>();
for (Song song: resultedSongs) {
    finalList0.add(song.getTitle()); // only the song title is required
}
System.out.println("Before Java 8: " + finalList0);
```

One of the problems with this code is that processing large collections is not very efficient. Also, we are traversing lists over and over again and performing checks to get to a final result. Wouldn't it be more efficient if we could execute all those operations on every element one by one, without repeated traversals? It would be, and it is possible to do so starting with Java 8.

The new **Stream** abstraction introduced in Java 8 represents a sequence of elements that can be processed sequentially or in parallel and supports aggregate operations. Because of the latest evolutions in hardware development, CPUs have become more powerful and more complex, containing multiple cores that can process information in parallel. To make use of these hardware capabilities, in Java, the Fork Join Framework was introduced. And in Java 8, the Stream API was introduced to support parallel data processing, without the boilerplate code of defining and synchronizing threads.

The central interface of the Stream API is `java.util.stream.BaseStream`. Any object with stream capabilities is of a type that extends this interface. A stream does not store elements itself, because it is not a data structure; it is just used to compute elements and serve them on demand to an operation or a set of aggregate operations.

Aggregate operations are special methods in the Stream API with the following characteristics:

- They support behavior as parameters. Most aggregate operations support lambda expressions as parameters.

- They use internal iteration. Internal iteration does not go over the elements sequentially, thus taking advantage of parallel computing. Internal iteration splits a problem into subproblems, solves them simultaneously, then combines the results.

- They process the elements from a stream, not directly from the stream origin.

Serving the elements in a sequence involves an internal automatic iteration. Operations that return a stream can be chained in a pipeline, and are called **intermediate operations**. Operations process elements of a stream and return the result as a stream to the next operation in the pipeline. Operations that return a result that is not a stream are called **terminal operations** and are normally present at the end of a pipeline. As a quick example before getting deeper into using streams, the code in Listing 8-1 is rewritten as depicted in Listing 8-2, and it is called a **stream pipeline**.

Listing 8-2. Code in Listing 8-1 Rewritten with Streams

```
List<String> finalList = songList.stream()
    .filter(s -> s.getDuration() >= 300)
    .sorted(Comparator.comparing(Song::getDuration).reversed())
    .map(Song::getTitle)
    .collect(Collectors.toList());
System.out.println(finalList);
```

Yes, programming with streams is awesome, both expressive and efficient. The *Stream API* concept allows developers to transform collections into streams, write code to process the data in parallel, and then get the results into a new collection.

Working with streams is quite a sensitive way of programming, and it is recommended to design the code taking every possibility in mind. NullPointerException is one of the most common exceptions to be thrown in Java.

In Java 8, the class Optional<T> was introduced to avoid this type of exception. Stream<E> instances are used to store an infinite instance of type T, while Optional<T> is an instance that might or might not contain an instance of type T. Because both of these implementations are basically wrappers for other types, they will be covered together.

Note For practical reasons, this chapter refers to Stream<E> instances as **streams**, in a similar manner that List<E> instances are referred to as **lists**, Collection<E> instances as **collections**, and many more.

Important You might notice that the term **function** was introduced and is used to refer to the behavior provided as an argument to stream operations. This is because working with streams allows for Java code to be written in *functional programming* style. As mentioned at the beginning of this book, Java is an object-oriented programming (OOP) language, and the object is its core term. In functional programming the core term is **pure function** and code is written by composing pure functions, which allows programmers to avoid shared state, take advantage of immutable data, and thus avoid side effects of processing contamination.

Tip   If you want to learn more about functional programming in Java, there are quite a few good books about it[1], but if you want to learn more about it as a programming paradigm, I gladly recommend you to check out this[2] blog entry.

Pure functions are software analogues of mathematical functions and have the following properties:

- Pure functions return identical values for identical arguments. The implementation does not involve any random value, or non-final global variables that might cause a different value to be returned for the same arguments. Pure functions must produce consistent results.

- The return value of the function depends only on the input parameters passed to the function.

- Pure functions have no side effects (no mutation of local static variables, non-local variables, mutable reference arguments, or input/output streams).

The combination of streams, pure functions, and lambda expressions facilitates writing Java **declarative code**. In this chapter we leave behind the typical object-oriented **imperative coding style**, where each step of the algorithm is declared one after the other and the flow is controlled by `boolean` conditions. Instead, we start designing the chain of pure functions applied to elements of streams.

Creating Streams

Before having fun and optimizing our code using streams, let's see how we can create them. To create a stream we obviously need a **source**. That source can be anything: a collection (list, set, or map), an array, or I/O resources used as input (such as files, databases, or anything that can be transformed into a sequence of instances).

---

[1] https://medium.com/javarevisited/5-best-java-functional-programming-books-for-beginners-and-experienced-programmers-4daecd159756

[2] https://medium.com/javascript-scene/master-the-javascript-interview-what-is-functional-programming-7f218c68b3a0

> **Important**   A stream does not modify its source, so multiple stream instances can be created from the same source and used for different operations.

The biggest difference between collections and streams is that the elements emitted by the stream are consumed by the operations and thus the stream cannot be used more than once. However, the bad code in Listing 8-3 is accepted by the Java compiler.

Listing 8-3. Bad Code: Attempting to Reuse a Stream

```
int[] arr = { 50, 10, 250, 100};
IntStream intStream = Arrays.stream(arr);

intStream.forEach(System.out::println);
intStream.forEach(System.out::println);
```

However, an `IllegalStateException` is thrown at runtime when we try traversing the stream a second time:

```
Streams cannot be recycled: stream has already been operated upon or closed
java.lang.IllegalStateException: stream has already been operated upon
or closed
    at java.base/java.util.stream.AbstractPipeline.sourceStageSpliterator(A
bstractPipeline.java:311)
    at java.base/java.util.stream.IntPipeline$Head.forEach(IntPipeline.
java:617)
    at chapter.eigth/com.apress.bgn.eight.StreamRecyclingDemo.
main(StreamRecyclingDemo.java:45)
```

So if you need to process the elements of a stream twice, you have to re-create it from the source again.

Creating Streams from Collections

The code snippet previously presented in Listing 8-2 depicts one method of creating a stream from a list. Starting with Java 8, all collection interfaces and classes were enriched with default methods that return streams. In Listing 8-4, we take a list of integers and transform it into a stream by calling the `stream()` method. After the stream is created, we traverse it using the forEach(..) method to print the values in the stream, and the name of the execution thread this code is executed on. Why the thread name, you ask? You will see shortly.

Listing 8-4. Creating a Stream of Integer Values from a List of Integers

```
package com.apress.bgn.eight;

import java.util.List;
import static java.lang.System.out;

public class IntegerStreamDemo {
    void main() {
        List<Integer> bigList = List.of(50, 10, 250, 100/* ...*/);

        bigList.stream().forEach(i ->
            out.println(Thread.currentThread().getName() +": " + i));
    }
}
```

The code in Listing 8-4 creates a stream of integer elements. The Stream<E> interface exposes a set of methods that each Stream<E> implementation provides a concrete implementation for. The most used is the forEach(..) method that iterates over the elements in the stream. The forEach(..) method requires a parameter of type java. util.function.Consumer<T>.

Important   A **consumer** is what we call in this book an inline implementation of the java.util.function.Consumer<T> functional interface. This interface declares a unique abstract method that a class implementing it has to provide a concrete implementation for. This interface is annotated with @FunctionalInterface for this same reason. The method is named accept(T t) and is referred to as a **functional method**. It takes an element of type T as argument, processes it, and returns nothing (void). For this reason, consumer functions are suitable for the end of a functional pipeline.

This consumer method is called for each element in the stream. The implementing class is basically declared inline, by only mentioning the body of the method. The JVM does the rest, because of the magic of lambda expressions. Without them, you would have to write code like the one in Listing 8-5.

Listing 8-5. Expanded Declaration of a Consumer

```java
package com.apress.bgn.eight;

import java.util.List;
import java.util.function.Consumer;
import static java.lang.System.out;

public class IntegerStreamDemo {
    void main() {
        List<Integer> bigList = List.of(50, 10, 250, 100/* ...*/);

        bigList.stream().forEach(
            new Consumer<Integer>() {
                @Override
                public void accept(Integer i) {
                    out.println(STR."\{Thread.currentThread().
                    getName()}: \{i}");
                }
            });
    }
}
// output
/*
main: 50
main: 10
main: 250
main: 100
...
 */
```

Again, this is the way the code had to be written before lambda expressions were introduced in Java 8. When classes implement interfaces this way, inline, using a syntax that looks a lot like a constructor call using the interface type, they are called **anonymous classes** because they don't have a name, and they are used exactly where declared. Lambda expressions simplified this process a lot, but only for interfaces that define one single method, the interfaces named **functional interfaces**. These interfaces were annotated with @FunctionalInterface annotation starting with Java 8. In the previous example the code prints the thread name and the value of the element.

Each number is prefixed with main, which means that all integers in the stream are processed sequentially by the same thread, the main thread of the application.

Tip   For practical reasons, for collections there is no need to invoke stream() when a sequential stream is needed only for traversal, because the forEach(..) method defined for them does the job just as well. So the preceding code can be reduced to this:

```
bigList.forEach(i ->
    System.out.println(Thread.currentThread().getName() +
    ": " + i
));
```

The name of the thread was printed because there is another way to create a stream, by calling the parallelStream() method. The only difference is that the returned stream is a parallel stream. This means that each element of the stream is processed on a different thread, which in turn means the implementation of Consumer<T> must be thread-safe and not contain code that involves instances that are not meant to be shared among threads. The code to print the value of a stream element does not affect the value of the element returned by the stream, nor other external objects, so it is safe to parallelize.

Listing 8-6 depicts the use of parallelStream() instead of stream() to create a stream and print the elements of the stream using the same Consumer<T> implementation. The output is depicted at the bottom of the snippet.

Listing 8-6. Creating a Parallel Stream of Integer Values from a List of Integers

```java
package com.apress.bgn.eight;

import java.util.List;
import java.util.function.Consumer;
import static java.lang.System.out;

public class IntegerStreamDemo {
    void main() {
        List<Integer> bigList = List.of(50, 10, 250, 100/* ...*/);

        bigList.parallelStream()
            .forEach(i ->
                    out.println(Thread.currentThread().getName()
                    + ": " + i)
            );
    }
}
// sample output
/*
main: 83
ForkJoinPool.commonPool-worker-1: 23
main: 33
ForkJoinPool.commonPool-worker-1: 45
ForkJoinPool.commonPool-worker-2: 50
main: 67...
 */
```

The first thing you will notice is the thread name: we no longer have only one, but a lot of them all named ForkJoinPool.commonPool-worker-. The main thread still prints some values, but the other threads do some of the work too, and the order (or more like, the disorder) of the printed values makes it clear that the threads run in parallel. The threads have similar names that make it obvious that they are all part of the same *thread pool.* A thread pool is created by the JVM in this case to contain a few thread instances used to process all elements in the stream in parallel, and this concept was introduced in **Chapter 5**. The advantage of using a thread pool is that the threads can be reused, so no new thread instances need to be created, and this optimizes the execution time a little.

If you look at the number associated to each thread (the number at the end of the thread name), you can see that the numbers sometimes repeat. This basically means the same thread is reused to process another stream element.

Tip   Performance improvements when using `parallelStream()` have been and still are up for debate in the Java world. For simple examples, creating a thread pool and managing the threads is clearly a waste of CPU and memory. So unless you have a specific problem that can be resolved more efficiently using parallel execution and a fast CPU with multiple cores, you probably won't need `parallelStream()`.

Caution   The Stream API is the preferred way to process large data sets in parallel. The process is assumed to be a fairly complex function, so virtual threads are not supposed to be used for stream parallel processing, since they are lightweight threads that process compact simple operations.

Creating Streams from Arrays

For the previous code samples, the source for our streams is represented by a `List<E>` instance. The same syntax is used with `Set<E>` instances as well.

But streams can be created from arrays as well, as the example shown in Listing 8-7 demonstrates.

Listing 8-7. Creating a Stream of Integer Values from an Array of Integers

```
package com.apress.bgn.eight;
import java.util.Arrays;
import static java.lang.System.out;

public class ArrayStreamDemo {
    void main() {
        int[] arr = { 50, 10, 250, 100 /* ... */};
```

```
        Arrays.stream(arr).forEach(
                i -> out.println(Thread.currentThread().getName() + ": " + i)
        );
    }
}
```

The static method `stream(int[] array)` was added to the `java.util.Arrays` in Java 1.8 and is used in Listing 8-7 to create a stream of primitives.

For arrays that contain objects, the method called is `stream(T[] array)`, where T is a generic type that replaces any reference type (also added in Java 1.8). Streams generated from arrays can be parallelized, by calling the same `parallel()` method.

The novelty with arrays is that a stream can be created from a part of the array, by specifying the start and the end indexes for the array chunk. The code in Listing 8-8 shows the creation of a stream from a part of the array and the output of printing the elements of the resulting stream using a simple consumer.

Listing 8-8. Creating a Stream of Integer Values from a part of an Array of Integers

```
package com.apress.bgn.eight;
import java.util.Arrays;
import static java.lang.System.out;

public class ArrayStreamDemo {
    void main() {
        int[] arr = { 50, 10, 250, 100 /* ... */};

        Arrays.stream(arr, 3,6).forEach(
                i -> System.out.println(Thread.currentThread().getName() +
                ": " + i)
        );
    }
}
// output
/*
main: 100
main: 23
main: 45
*/
```

Creating Empty Streams

When writing Java code, a good practice is to write methods that return objects and to avoid returning null. This reduces the possibility of NullPointerExceptions being thrown. When methods return streams, the preferred way is to return an empty stream. This can be done by calling the static Stream.empty() method provided by the Stream<T> interface.

The code snippet in Listing 8-9 depicts a method that takes a list of Song instances as an argument and returns a stream using it as a source. If the list is null or empty, an empty stream is returned. The resulting stream is traversed in the main(..) method, without additional verification. If the stream is empty, nothing will be printed.

Listing 8-9. Creating a empty streams

```
package com.apress.bgn.eight;

import com.apress.bgn.eight.util.Song;
import com.apress.bgn.eight.util.StreamMediaLoader;
import java.util.List;
import java.util.stream.Stream;
import static java.lang.System.out;

public class SongStreamDemo {
    void main(){
        out.println(" -- Testing 'getAsStream(..)' method with null -- ");
        getAsStream(null).forEach(out::println);

        out.println(" -- Testing 'getAsStream(..)' method with empty
        list --");
        getAsStream(List.of()).forEach(out::println);

        out.println(" -- Testing 'getAsStream(..)' method with a
        list -- ");
                        getAsStream(StreamMediaLoader.
                        loadSongsAsList()).forEach(out::println);
    }
```

```java
    public static Stream<Song> getAsStream(List<Song> songList) {
        if(songList == null || songList.isEmpty()) {
            return Stream.empty();
        } else {
            return songList.stream();
        }
    }
}
// output
/*
 -- Testing 'getAsStream(..)' method with null --
 -- Testing 'getAsStream(..)' method with empty list --
 -- Testing 'getAsStream(..)' method with a list --
 Song {
    id=1
    singer=John Mayer
    title=New Light
    duration=206
    audioType=FLAC
}
 ...
 */
```

Running the code in Listing 8-9 results in the first two messages being printed one after the other with nothing in between, since the stream returned by the method is empty.

Creating Finite Streams

Aside from creating streams from actual sources, streams can be created on the spot by calling stream utility methods like Stream.generate() or Stream.builder().

The builder() method should be used when building a limited stream with a fixed set of known values. This method returns an instance of java.util.stream.Stream.Builder<T>, an internal interface that declares a default method named add(T t) that needs to be called to add the elements of the stream. To create the Stream<T> instance, its build() method must be called last. The add(T t) method returns a reference to the

Builder<T> instance, so it can be chained with any other methods of this interface. The code in Listing 8-10 is a sample of how the builder() method can be used to create a finite stream of various values.

Listing 8-10. Creating Streams from Finite Sets of Values

```java
package com.apress.bgn.eight;
import com.apress.bgn.eight.util.AudioType;
import com.apress.bgn.eight.util.Song;

import java.util.List;
import java.util.stream.Stream;

public class FiniteStreamsDemo {
    void main() {
        Stream<Integer> built = Stream.<Integer>builder()
                .add(50).add(10).add(250)
                .build();

        Stream<String> lyrics = Stream.<String>builder()
                .add("In a world where people never meet,")
                .add("They fall in love looking at some screen")
                .add("And love can only be one-sided")
                .add("Bitter, burning unrequited.")
                .build();

        Stream<Song> songs = Stream.<Song>builder()
                .add (new Song("John Mayer", "New Light", 206,
                AudioType.FLAC))
                .add (new Song("Ben Barnes", "You find me", 420,
                AudioType.FLAC))
                .build();

        Stream data = Stream.builder() // compiler warns about raw use of
                                       //      parameterized class 'Stream'
                .add("Vultures")
                .add(3)
```

```
                .add(List.of("aa"))
                .build();
    }
}
```

Because the `Builder<T>` interface is a generic one, it is mandatory to specify a type argument, as the type of the elements in the stream. Also, the `builder()` method is generic and requires the type to be provided as a parameter in front of it, right before being called. If no type is specified, the default `Object` is used, and instances of any type can be added to the stream (as shown in the fourth stream declaration in Listing 8-10). However, the compiler warns about *raw use of parameterized class 'Stream'*.

To create a stream, there is another method named `generate(..)`. This method requires an argument of type `java.util.function.Supplier<T>`.

Important   A **supplier** is what we call in this book an inline implementation of the `java.util.function.Supplier<T>` functional interface. This interface requires a concrete implementation to be provided for its single method named `get()`. This method should return the element to be added to the stream.

So if we want to generate a stream of integers, a proper implementation for `get()` should return a random integer. The expanded code is depicted in Listing 8-11. Lambda expressions are not used to make it clear that the `generate(..)` method receives as a parameter a `Supplier<Integer>` instance created on the spot.

Listing 8-11. Creating Stream Using a Supplier

```
package com.apress.bgn.eight;
import java.util.function.Supplier;
import java.util.random.RandomGenerator;
import java.util.stream.Stream;

public class FiniteStreamsDemo {
    static RandomGenerator randomGenerator = RandomGenerator.
    of("SecureRandom");
    void main() {
        Stream<Integer> generated = Stream.generate(
```

```
            new Supplier<Integer>() {
                @Override
                public Integer get() {
                    return randomGenerator.nextInt(300) + 1;
                }
            }).limit(15);
    }
}
```

The limit(15) method limits the number of elements generated by the supplier to 15; otherwise the generated stream would be infinite. The code in Listing 8-11 can be simplified by using Lambda expressions as depicted in Listing 8-12.

Listing 8-12. Creating Stream Using a Supplier and Lambda Expressions

```
package com.apress.bgn.eight;
import java.util.function.Supplier;
import java.util.random.RandomGenerator;
import java.util.stream.Stream;

public class FiniteStreamsDemo {
    static RandomGenerator randomGenerator = RandomGenerator.
    of("SecureRandom");
    void main() {
        Stream<Integer> generated = Stream.generate(
                () -> randomGenerator.nextInt(300) + 1
        ).limit(15);
    }
}
```

If Supplier<Integer>.get() always returns the same number, no matter how useless such a stream might be, the previous declaration becomes

```
Stream<Integer> generated = Stream.generate( () -> 5 ).limit(15);
```

If more control is needed over the elements emitted by a Stream<T> instance, the iterate(..) method can be used. There are two versions of this method, one added in Java 8 and one in Java 9. Using either version of this method is like having a for statement generate the entries for the stream.

The Java 8 version of the `iterate(..)` method is used to generate an infinite stream. This version of the method receives as arguments an initial value called a `seed` and an iteration `step`.

The Java 9 version of the `iterate(..)` method is used to generate a finite stream. This version of the method receives as arguments an initial value called a `seed`, a `predicate` that determines when the iteration should stop, and an iteration `step`.

Important   A *predicate* is an inline implementation of the functional interface `java.util.function.Predicate<T>`, which declares a single method named `test(T t)` that returns a boolean value. The implementation of this method should test its single argument of type T against a condition and return `true` if the condition is fulfilled and `false` if not.

Important   The iteration step is an inline implementation of the functional interface `java.util.function.UnaryOperator<T>` used to represent an operation on a single operand that produces a result of the same type as its operand.

In the following example, stream elements are generated starting from 0, using a step of 5, and they are generated as long as the values are lesser than 50, as defined by the predicate:

```
Stream<Integer> iterated = Stream.iterate(0, i -> i < 50 , i -> i + 5);
```

Similar to the `for` statement, without the predicate, you would be calling the version of this method introduced in Java 8, and in this case the `limit(..)` method must be used to make sure the stream is finite.

```
Stream<Integer> iterated = Stream.iterate(0, i -> i + 5).limit(15);
```

In Java 9, beside the `limit(..)` method, another way to control the numbers of values in a stream is the `takeWhile(..)` method. This method takes the longest set of elements from the original stream that match the predicate received as an argument, starting with the first element. This works fine for ordered streams, but if the stream is unordered, the result is any set of elements that matches the predicate, including an empty one.

To explain the different streams that result by calling `takeWhile(..)`, the concept of **order** for streams has to be discussed first.

The expression **encounter order** represents the order in which a `Stream<T>` instance encounters data. The encounter order of a stream is defined by the source and intermediate operations. For example, if an array is used as a source, the encounter order of the stream is defined by the ordering in the array. If a list is used as a source, the encounter order is the list's iteration order. If a set is used as a source, then there is no encounter order, because a set is inherently unordered.

Each intermediate operation in a stream pipeline acts on the encounter order, and the effects are as follows:

- An encounter order could be imposed on the output. For example, the `sorted()` operation imposes an encounter order on an unordered stream.

- The encounter order is preserved. Some operations like `filter(..)` might drop a few elements, but the original order is unaffected.

- The encounter order is destroyed. For example, the `sorted()` operation imposes an encounter order on an ordered stream, replacing the existing one.

Collector operations preserve encounter order if accumulating elements into a container with an encounter order. Sequential and parallel streams have the same properties with respect to ordering.

Listing 8-13 shows two usages of the `takeWhile(Predicate<? super T> predicate)` method.

Listing 8-13. Creating a Stream Using a Supplier and the `takeWhile(..)` Method

```
package com.apress.bgn.eight;

import java.util.stream.Stream;
import static java.lang.System.out;

public class FiniteStreamsDemo {
    void main() {
        // (1)
        Stream<Integer> orderedStream = List.of( 3, 6, 9, 11, 12, 13, 15).
        stream();
```

```
Stream<Integer> result = orderedStream.takeWhile(s -> s % 3 == 0);
result.forEach(s -> out.print(s + " "));
// output: 3 6 9

// (2)
Stream<Integer> unorderedStream = Set.of(3, 6, 9, 2, 4, 8, 12, 36,
18, 42, 11, 13).stream();
result = unorderedStream.parallel().takeWhile(s -> s % 3 == 0);
result.forEach(s -> out.print(s + " "));
// output (maybe): 3 12 36
    }
}
```

The first code chunk uses takeWhile(..) on an ordered stream of integers and returns a stream with elements that divide by 3. The resulting stream contains the elements *3 6 9* because this is the first set of elements that match the given predicate.

If takeWhile(..) is called on an unordered stream, as depicted in the second code chunk, the result will be unpredictable. The result might be *3 6 9* or *12 36 18 42*, as the result is a subset of any elements matching the predicate. Also, since the order is not fixed, the code chunk might end up printing *6 3 9*, or *9 3 6*, and so on. So the result of takeWhile(..) on an unordered stream is **nondeterministic**.

The takeWhile(..) method is the "sister" of the dropWhile(..) method, also introduced in Java 9. As its name indicates, dropWhile(..) does exactly the reverse of what takeWhile(..) does: it returns, for an ordered stream, a new stream consisting of elements after dropping the longest set of elements that matches the predicate. For an unordered stream, there is only chaos, because any subset of elements matching the predicate can be dropped, including the empty stream. Listing 8-14 shows two usages of the dropWhile(..) method.

Listing 8-14. Creating Stream Using a Supplier and the dropWhile(..) Method

```
package com.apress.bgn.eight;

import java.util.stream.Stream;
import static java.lang.System.out;
```

```
public class FiniteStreamsDemo {
    void main() {
        List.of( 3, 6, 9, 11, 12, 13, 15).stream()
            .dropWhile(s -> s % 3 == 0 )
            .forEach(s -> out.print(STR."\{s} "));
        // output: 11 12 13 15

        Set.of(3, 6, 9, 2, 4, 8, 12, 36, 18, 42, 11, 13).stream()
            .parallel()
            .dropWhile(s -> s % 3 == 0 ).forEach(s -> out.print(STR."\
            {s} "));
        // output (maybe): 2 4 8 12 36 18 42 11 13
    }
}
```

If these two operations are applied to parallel streams, the only thing that changes is the order in which the elements are printed, but the result sets will contain the same elements.

Streams of Primitives and Streams of Strings

When we first created a stream of primitives, we used an int[] array as a source. However, streams of primitives can be created in many ways, because the Stream API contains more interfaces with default methods to make programming with streams practical. In Figure 8-1 you can see the hierarchy of the Stream API interfaces.

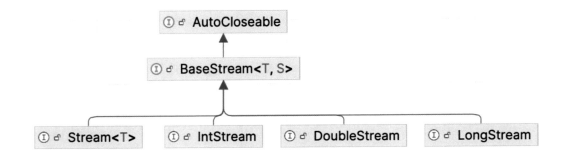

Figure 8-1. *Stream API interfaces*

As you probably imagine after looking at Figure 8-1, the `IntStream` interface can be used to create primitive streams of integers. This interface exposes many methods to do so, some of them inherited from `BaseStream<T,S>`. An `IntStream` instance can be created from a few values specified on the spot, either by using the `builder()`, `generate(..)`, or `iterate(..)` method or by using the of `range*(..)` methods as depicted in Listing 8-15.

Listing 8-15. Creating `IntStream` Instances Using Various Methods

```
package com.apress.bgn.eight;
import java.util.Random;
import java.util.stream.IntStream;

public class NumericStreamsDemo {

    void main(){
        var intStream0 = IntStream.builder().add(0).add(1).add(2).add(5).
        build();
        var intStream1 = IntStream.of(0,1,2,3,4,5);

        var intStream2 = IntStream.range(0, 10);
        var intStream3 = IntStream.rangeClosed(0, 10);

        Random random = new Random();
        IntStream intStream4 = random.ints(5);
    }
}
```

An `IntStream` instance can be created by giving the start and end of an interval as arguments to the `range(..)` and `rangeClosed(..)` methods. Both of them generate elements for the stream with a step of 1, only the last one includes the upper range of the interval as a value.

Also in Java 1.8, the `java.util.Random` class was enriched with a method named `ints(..)` that generates a stream of random integers. It declares a single argument that represents the number of elements to be generated and put in the stream, but there is a form of this method without the argument that generates an infinite stream.

All the methods mentioned for `IntStream` can be used to generate `LongStream` instances, as equivalent methods are defined in this interface as well.

For DoubleStream there are no range methods, but there is of(..) a, builder(), generate(..), and so on. Also, the java.util.Random class was enriched in Java 1.8 with the doubles(..) method that generates a stream of random double values. It declares a single argument that represents the number of elements to be generated and put in the stream, but there is a form of this method without the argument that generates an infinite stream. Listing 8-16 depicts a few ways of creating streams of doubles.

Listing 8-16. Creating Numeric Stream Instances Using Various Methods

```
package com.apress.bgn.eight;

import java.util.Random;
import java.util.stream.DoubleStream;

public class NumericStreamsDemo {
    void main() {
        DoubleStream doubleStream0 = DoubleStream.of(1, 2 , 2.3, 3.4,
        4.5, 6);

        Random random = new Random();
        DoubleStream doubleStream1 = random.doubles(3);

        DoubleStream doubleStream2 = DoubleStream.iterate(2.5, d -> d =
        d + 0.2).limit(10);
    }
}
```

For streams of char values, there is no special interface, but IntStream can be used just fine:

```
IntStream intStream = IntStream.of('a','b','c','d');
intStream.forEach(c -> System.out.println((char) c));
```

Another way to create a stream of char values is to use a String instance as a stream source:

```
IntStream charStream = "sample".chars();
charStream.forEach(c -> System.out.println((char) c));
```

In Java 8, `java.util.regex.Pattern` was enriched with stream-specific methods too; as a class used to process `String` instances, it is the proper place to add these methods. A `Pattern` instance is useful for splitting an existing `String` instance and returning the pieces as a stream using the `splitAsStream(..)` method:

```
Stream<String> stringStream = Pattern.compile(" ")
    .splitAsStream("live your life");
```

The contents of a file can also be returned as a stream of strings using the `Files.lines(..)` utility method:

```
String inputPath = "chapter08/src/main/resources/songs.csv";
Stream<String> stringStream = Files.lines(Path.of(inputPath));
```

The sections so far have shown you how to create all types of streams; the next sections will show you how to use them to process data.

Important   If you feel the need to associate stream instances with real objects to make sense of them, I recommend the following: imagine a finite stream (like one created from a collection) as the water dripping from a mug when inclined. The water in the mug will end eventually, but while the water drips, it forms a stream. An infinite stream is like a river that has a fountainhead: it flows continuously *(unless a serious drought dries the river, of course).*

Short Introduction to Optional<T>

The `java.util.Optional<T>` instances are the Schrödinger[3] boxes of the Java language. They are very useful because they can be used as a return type for methods to avoid returning a `null` value, and cause either a possible `NullPointerException` to be thrown or the developer using the method to write extra code to treat the possibility of an exception being thrown. `Optional<T>` instances can be created in a similar way to streams.

---

[3] `https://en.wikipedia.org/wiki/Schr%C3%B6dinger%27s_cat`

There is an empty() method for creating an optional value of any type that does not contain anything:

```
Optional<Song> empty = Optional.empty();
```

There is an of() method used to wrap an existing object into an Optional<T> instance:

```
Optional<Long> value = Optional.of(5L);
```

Considering that these type of instances are designed not to allow null values, the way the Optional<T> instance was created previously, stops us from writing something like this:

```
Song song = null;
Optional<Song> nonNullable = Optional.of(song);
```

The compiler doesn't mind, but at runtime when the code is executed, a NullPointerException will be thrown. Still, if we really need an Optional<T> instance to permit null values, it is possible: a utility method named ofNullable(T t) was introduced in Java 9 just for that purpose:

```
Song song = null;
Optional<Song> nullable = Optional.ofNullable(song);
```

Now that we have Optional<T> instances, what can use them, as shown in the code in Listing 8-17.

Listing 8-17. Code Showing the Necessity of Optional<T>

```
package com.apress.bgn.eight;

import com.apress.bgn.eight.util.MediaLoader;
import com.apress.bgn.eight.util.Song;

import java.util.List;
import static java.lang.System.out;

public class NonOptionalDemo {
    void main() {
        List<Song> songs = MediaLoader.loadSongs();
        Song song = findFirst(songs, "B.B. King");
```

```
        if(song != null && song.getSinger().equals("The Thrill Is Gone")) {
            out.println("Good stuff!");
        } else {
            out.println("not found!");
        }
    }

    public static Song findFirst(List<Song> songs, String singer) {
        for (Song song: songs) {
            if (singer.equals(song.getSinger())) {
                return song;
            }
        }
        return null;
    }
}
```

The findFirst(..) method looks for the first song in the list that has the singer equal to "B.B. King"; returns it and prints a message if found, and another message if not. Notice the nullability test and iteration of the list. In Java 8, both of them are no longer necessary. Listing 8-18 depicts the code in Listing 8-17 redesigned to use Optional<T>.

Listing 8-18. Code Showing the Necessity of Optional<T>

```
package com.apress.bgn.eight;
// import statements omitted

public class OptionalDemo {
    void main() {
        List<Song> songs = MediaLoader.loadSongs();
        Optional<Song> opt = songs.stream()
                .filter(s -> "B.B. King".equals(s.getSinger()))
                .findFirst();
        opt.ifPresent(r -> out.println(r.getTitle()));
    }
}
```

If the `Optional<T>` instance is not empty, the song title will be printed; otherwise, nothing will be printed and the code will continue from that point on without an exception being thrown. But what if we want to print something when the `Optional<T>` instance is empty? In Java 11, we can do something about that, because a method named `isEmpty()` was introduced to test the `Optional<T>` instance contents, as demonstrated in Listing 8-19.

Listing 8-19. Code Showing Usage of `Optional.isEmpty()`

```
package com.apress.bgn.eight;
// import statements omitted

public class OptionalDemo {
    void main() {
        Optional<Song> opt1 = songs.stream()
                .filter(s -> "B.B. King".equals(s.getSinger()))
                .findFirst();
        if(opt1.isEmpty()) {
            out.println("Not found!");
        }
    }
}
```

But wait, this is a little bit...not right. Can't we just have a method to call on an `Optional<T>` instance to get the exact behavior as an `if-else` statement? Yes, that is possible starting with Java 9; the `ifPresentOrElse(..)` method takes as arguments a `Consumer<T>` instance to process the contents of the `Optional<T>` instance when it is not empty and a `Runnable` instance to execute when the `Optional<T>` instance is empty, as shown in Listing 8-20.

Listing 8-20. Code Showing Usage of `Optional.ifPresentOrElse(..)`

```
package com.apress.bgn.eight;
// import statements omitted

public class OptionalDemo {
    void main() {
        List<Song> songs = MediaLoader.loadSongs();
        Optional<Song> opt2 = songs.stream()
```

```
                    .filter(ss -> "B.B. King".equals(ss.getSinger())).findFirst();
        opt2.ifPresentOrElse(
                    r -> out.println(r.getTitle()),
                    () -> out.println("Not found!")) ;
    }
}
```

If the Optional<T> instance is not empty, its contents can be extracted by calling the get() method, as shown in Listing 8-21.

Listing 8-21. Code Showing Usage of Optional.get()

```
package com.apress.bgn.eight;
// import statements omitted

public class OptionalDemo {
    void main() {
        List<Song> songs = MediaLoader.loadSongs();
        Optional<Song> opt3 = songs.stream()
                    .filter(ss -> "Rob Thomas".equals(ss.getSinger()))
                    .findFirst();
        out.println("Found Song " + opt3.get());
    }
}
```

The previous code does not print anything when the desired object is not found, because the Optional<T> instance is empty. But if we want to print a default value, for example, we can do that as well by using a method named orElse(..), as shown in Listing 8-22.

Listing 8-22. Code Showing Usage of Optional.orElse(..)

```
package com.apress.bgn.eight;
// import statements omitted

public class OptionalDemo {
    void main() {
        List<Song> songs = MediaLoader.loadSongs();
        Optional<Song> opt4 = songs.stream()
```

```
                .filter(ss -> "B.B. King".equals(ss.getSinger()))
                .findFirst();
        opt4.ifPresent(r -> out.println(r.getTitle()));

        Song defaultSong = new Song();
        defaultSong.setTitle("Untitled");
        Song s = opt4.orElse(defaultSong);
        out.println("Found: " + s.getTitle());
    }
}
```

The orElse(T t) method receives as an argument an instance of the type wrapped by Optional<T>. There is another version of it that takes a Supplier<T> instance that returns an object of the required type. The snippet using that method is shown here:

```
Song fromSupplier =
    opt4.orElseGet(() -> new Song("None", "Untitled", 0, null));
System.out.println("Found: " + fromSupplier.getTitle());
```

If we were interested in throwing a specific exception when the Optional<T> instance is empty, there is a method for that as well, named orElseThrow(..), as shown in Listing 8-23.

Listing 8-23. Code Showing Usage of Optional.orElseThrow(..)

```
package com.apress.bgn.eight;
// import statements omitted

public class OptionalDemo {
    void main() {
        List<Song> songs = MediaLoader.loadSongs();
        Optional<Song> opt5 = songs.stream()
                .filter(st -> "B.B. King".equals(st.getSinger()))
                .findFirst();
        Song song = opt5.orElseThrow(IllegalArgumentException::new);
    }
}
```

487

As you probably noticed in the previous code samples, `Optional<T>` and `Stream<T>` instances can be combined to write practical code to solve complex solutions. There are a lot of methods that can be applied to `Optional<T>` and `Stream<T>` instances as well, so the next sections will introduce them for streams and randomly make reference to `Optional<T>` as well.

How to Use Streams Like a Pro

After creating a stream, the next thing is to process the data on the stream. Before taking a deep dive into advanced stream usage, let's recapitulate the core concepts:

- The result of that processing can be another stream, which can be further processed as many times as needed. There are quite a few methods to use to process a stream and return the result as another stream. These methods are called **intermediate operations**.

- The methods that do not return a stream but actual data structures, or nothing, are named **terminal operations**.

All these are defined in the `Stream<T>` interface, and they are used to define a **stream pipeline**.

The key feature of streams is that the processing of data using streams occurs only when the terminal operation is initiated, which means the elements from sources are consumed only as needed. So you could say that the whole stream process is actually **lazy**. Lazy loading of source elements and processing them only when needed allows significant optimizations.

After the previous affirmations, you've probably realized that the `forEach(..)` method that was used a lot previously to print values from the streams is actually a terminal operation. But there are quite a few other terminal operations, and a few of them—the ones you'll most likely need for the most commons implementations—will be used in the examples in the rest of the chapter.

This chapter started with an example that processes a stream of Song instances, but the Song class was not shown. You can see its fields in Listing 8-24.

Listing 8-24. Fields of Class Song

```
package com.apress.bgn.eight;

public class Song implements Comparable<Song> {
    private Long id;
    private String singer;
    private String title;
    private Integer duration;
    private AudioType audioType;

    //getters and setters and other methods omitted
}
```

AudioType is an enum containing the types of audio files and is depicted in Listing 8-25.

Listing 8-25. AudioType Enum

```
package com.apress.bgn.eight;

public enum AudioType {
    MP3, FLAC, OGG, AAC, M4A, WMA
}
```

Having identified the data type that will be used on the following stream examples, the data is presented next. In the example in Listing 8-26, the data is contained in a file named songs.csv. The .csv extension denotes a *comma separated file*, and each Song instance matches a line in the file. Each line contains all the property values of each Song instance, separated by columns. The order of the values must match the order of the constructor arguments. Other separators can be used, but semicolons are used here for practical reasons (which is the default supported by the library reading the data).

Listing 8-26. Song Entries (Sample) in the songs.csv File

```
01;John Mayer;New Light;206;FLAC
02;John Mayer;My Stupid Mouth;225;M4A
...
28;Mike Shinoda;Crossing A Line;248;MP3
19;John Mayer;Helpless;249;MP3
```

Each line in the file will be transformed into a Song instance by using classes in a library named JSefa[4]. This library is not the focus of this discussion, but if you are interested, you can use the link in the footnote to get more details from the official site.

Now you are ready to start playing with streams.

Terminal Functions forEach and forEachOrdered

Assuming the songs stream will provide all Song instances declared in Listing 8-26, let's first print all the elements in the stream. The code in Listing 8-27 prints all Song instances on a Stream<Song> instance using a simple consumer.

Listing 8-27. Using a Stream to Print Song Instances

```
package com.apress.bgn.eight;

import com.apress.bgn.eight.util.Song;
import com.apress.bgn.eight.util.StreamMediaLoader;

import java.util.stream.Stream;
import static java.lang.System.out;

public class MediaStreamTester {
    public static void main(String... args) {
        Stream<Song> songs = StreamMediaLoader.loadSongs();
        songs.forEach(song -> out.println(song));
    }
}
```

Method references, introduced in Java 8, are a shortcut for cases when a lambda expression does nothing else than call a method, so the method can be referenced by name directly. So this line:

```
songs.forEach(song -> System.out.println(song));
```

becomes

```
songs.forEach(System.out::println);
```

---

[4] http://jsefa.sourceforge.net

The forEach(..) method receives an instance of Consumer<T> as an argument. In the two previous examples, the implementation of the accept() method contained only a call to System.out.println(song), and that is why the code is so compact, because method references can be used. But if the implementation of this method needs to contain more statements, then the compact code previously written would not be possible (unless a method reference is introduced). Instead of printing the songs directly, let's first change to uppercase the singer's name, as depicted in Listing 8-28.

Listing 8-28. Using a Consumer Anonymous Class to Print Song Instances

```
package com.apress.bgn.eight;
// import statements omitted

public class MediaStreamTester {
    void main(){
        Stream<Song> songs = StreamMediaLoader.loadSongs();
        songs.forEach(new Consumer<Song>() {
            @Override
            public void accept(Song song) {
                song.setSinger(song.getSinger().toUpperCase());
                out.println(song);
            }
        });
    }
}
```

It can be simplified using lambda expressions, but since the method body has two lines, it still looks bad. So, a different way to do it is to declare a consumer field and use lambda expression to call its accept(..) method for every song, as depicted in Listing 8-29.

Listing 8-29. Using a Consumer Instance to Print Song Instances

```
package com.apress.bgn.eight;
// import statements omitted

public class MediaStreamTester {
    public static Consumer<Song> myConsumer = song -> {
```

```
        song.setSinger(song.getSinger().toUpperCase());
        out.println(song);
    };

    void main(){
        Stream<Song> songs = StreamMediaLoader.loadSongs();
        songs.forEach(song -> myConsumer.accept(song));
    }
}
```

The sister function forEachOrdered(..) does the same thing as forEach(..), with one little difference to ensure that the elements on the stream will be processed in encounter order, if such order is defined for the stream, even if the stream is a parallel one. So basically the following second and third lines will print the songs in the same order:

```
import static java.lang.System.out;
...
songs.forEach(out::println);
songs.parallel().forEachOrdered(out::println); // underline function or
make it bold
```

Intermediate Operation **filter** and Terminal Operation **toArray**

In the following example, we will select all MP3 songs and save them to an array. Selecting all MP3 songs is done using the filter(..) method. This method receives an argument of type Predicate<T>, which is used to define a condition that the elements of the stream must pass to be put into the array that results by calling the terminal method named toArray(..).

The toArray(..) method receives an argument of type IntFunction<A[]>. This type of function is also called a *generator* and takes an integer as an argument and generates an array of that size. In most cases the most suitable generator is an array constructor reference.

The code to filter the MP3 entries and put them into an array of type Song[] is depicted in Listing 8-30.

Listing 8-30. Using `filter(..)` to Select Songs from a Stream

```
package com.apress.bgn.eight;
// import statements omitted

public class MediaStreamTester {

    void main(){
        Stream<Song> songs = StreamMediaLoader.loadSongs();
        Song[] sarray = songs.filter(s -> s.getAudioType() == AudioType.
        MP3).toArray(Song[]::new); // array constructor reference
        Arrays.stream(sarray).forEach(out::println);
    }
}
```

Intermediate Operations `map` and `flatMap` and Terminal Operation `collect`

In the following example we will process all the songs and calculate the duration in minutes. To do this, we will use the `map(..)` method to call a pure function for each song instance emitted by the stream that returns the duration in minutes. This will result in a new stream of `Integer` values. All its elements will be added to a `List<Integer>` instance using the `collect(..)` method. This method accumulates the elements as they are processed into a `Collection<Integer>` instance. Listing 8-31 shows these methods being used.

Listing 8-31. Using `map(..)` and `collect(..)` Methods

```
package com.apress.bgn.eight;
// import statements omitted

public class MediaStreamTester {
    public static int processDuration(Song song) {
        int secs = song.getDuration();
        return secs/60;
    }
```

```
    void main(){
        Stream<Song> songs = StreamMediaLoader.loadSongs();

        List<Integer> durationAsMinutes = songs
                .map(SongTransformer::processDuration) // method reference
                .collect(Collectors.toList());

        durationAsMinutes.forEach(out::println);
    }
}
```

The map(..) method receives an argument of type Function<T,R> (T input type, R result type), which is basically a reference to a function to apply on each element of the stream. The function we applied in the previous example takes a song element from the stream, gets its duration and transforms it into minutes, and returns it. The code in Listing 8-31 can be rewritten as depicted in Listing 8-32, where the method processDuration is declared as a field of type Function<T,R> and the Collection<Integer> instance is replaced by the .toList() method for a simplified syntax.

Listing 8-32. Using a Function<T,R> Instance to Process Stream Elements

```
package com.apress.bgn.eight;
// import statements omitted

public class MediaStreamTester {
    public static Function<Song, Integer> processDuration = song -> song.
getDuration()/60;

    void main(){
        Stream<Song> songs = StreamMediaLoader.loadSongs();

        List<Integer> durationAsMinutes = songs
                .map(processDuration)
                .toList();

        durationAsMinutes.forEach(out::println);
    }
}
```

The first generic type of the Function<T,R> instance is the type of the processed element, and the second is the type of the result.

A version of the filter(..) method mentioned in the previous section is defined for the Optional<T> type as well and can be used to avoid writing complicated if statements, together with the map(..) method. Let's assume we have a Song instance and we want to check if it is more than three minutes long and less than ten minutes long. Instead of writing an if statement with two conditions connected by an AND operator, we can use an Optional<Song> instance and those two methods to do the same, as shown in Listing 8-33.

Listing 8-33. Using filter(..) and map(..) to Avoid Writing if Statements

```
package com.apress.bgn.eight;
// import statements omitted

public class MediaStreamTester {

    void main(){
        Song song0 = new Song("Ben Barnes", "You find me", 420,
        AudioType.FLAC);
        if(isMoreThan3MinsAndLessThenTen(song0)) {
            out.println("This song is just right!");
        }
    }

    public static boolean isMoreThan3MinsAndLessThenTen(Song song) {
        return Optional.ofNullable(song).map(SongTransformer::
        processDuration)
                .filter(d -> d >= 3)
                .filter(d -> d <= 10)
                .isPresent();
    }
}
```

> **Caution**   The implementation in Listing 8-33 might not be ideal when it comes to performance—the two `filter()` invocations could be one, after all—but code like that can be written if you wish. Just make sure to read the documentation properly before abusing stream operations.

So the `map(..)` method is quite powerful, but it has a small flaw. If we take a look at its signature in the `Stream.java` file, this is what we will see:

```
<R> Stream<R> map(Function<? super T, ? extends R> mapper);
```

So if the `map(..)` function applied to each element in the stream returns a stream with the result, which is placed into another stream that contains all results, the `collect(...)` method is actually called on a `Stream<Stream<R>>` instance.

The same goes for `Optional<T>`; the terminal method will be called on an `<Optional<Optional<T>>` instance. When the objects are simple, like the Song instances used in this chapter's code samples, the `map(..)` method works quite well, but if the objects in the original stream are more complex, such as a `List<List<T>>` instance, things *might* get complicated.

The easiest way to show the effects of the `flatMap(..)` method is to apply it on a `List<List>` instance. Let's take a look at the example in Listing 8-34.

Listing 8-34. Using `flatMap(..)` to Unwrap Stream Elements

```java
package com.apress.bgn.eight;
// import statements omitted

public class MoreStreamsDemo {
    public static Function<Song, Integer> processDuration = song -> song.
    getDuration()/60;

    void main(){
        List<List<Integer>> testList = List.of (List.of(2,3), List.of(4,5),
        List.of(6,7));
        System.out.println(processList(testList));
    }
```

```
    public static List<Integer> processList( List<List<Integer>> list) {
    List<Integer> result = list
            .stream()
            .flatMap(Collection::stream)
            .collect(Collectors.toList());
    return result;
  }
}
```

The flatMap(..) method receives as an argument a reference to a method that takes a collection and transforms it into a stream, which is the simplest way to create a Stream<Stream<Integer>> instance. The flatMap(..) method does its magic and the result is transformed into Stream<Integer>, and the elements are then collected by the collect(..) method into a List<Integer> instance. The operation of removing the useless stream wrapper is called *flattening*. If it is still not obvious what is happening, Figure 8-2 should make things clearer.

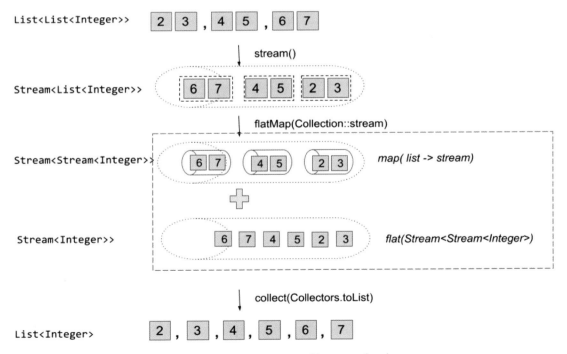

Figure 8-2. *Visual depiction of the effects of* flatMap(..)

In the code sample in Listing 8-34, using the map(..) method doesn't yield the expected result. If the flatMap(..) method is replaced with map(..), the final result is not a List<Integer> instance, but a List<Stream<Integer>> instance. IntelliJ IDEA is smart enough to figure it out, and it provides the appropriate message to help you choose the right method to call, as depicted in Figure 8-3.

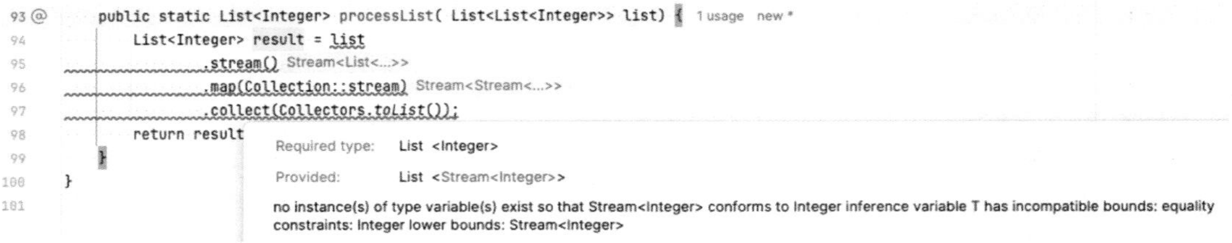

```
93 @        public static List<Integer> processList( List<List<Integer>> list) {  1 usage   new *
94              List<Integer> result = list
95                  .stream()  Stream<List<...>>
96                      .map(Collection::stream)  Stream<Stream<...>>
97                          .collect(Collectors.toList());
98              return result
                                 Required type:    List <Integer>
99          }
100    }                         Provided:         List <Stream<Integer>>
101                              no instance(s) of type variable(s) exist so that Stream<Integer> conforms to Integer inference variable T has incompatible bounds: equality
                                 constraints: Integer lower bounds: Stream<Integer>
```

Figure 8-3. *IntelliJ IDEA error message when* map(..) *is used instead of* flatMap(..)

Another way to see the effect of the flatMap(..) method is to write an even simpler example with Optional<T>. Let's say we need a function that transforms a String value into an Integer value. If the String value is not a valid number, we want to avoid returning null. This means that our function must take a String value and return Optional<Integer>. The code shown in Listing 8-35 contains an explicit flattening and a flattening done with flatMap(..).

Listing 8-35. Flattening of an Optional<Optional<T>> Instance

```
package com.apress.bgn.eight;
// import statements omitted

public class MoreStreamsDemo {

    void main(){
        // explicit flattening
        Optional<String> strO = Optional.of("42");
        Optional<Optional<Integer>> resIntO = strO.map(toIntOpt);
        Optional<Integer> desiredResO = resIntO.orElse(Optional.empty());
        out.println("finally: " + desiredResO.get());
```

```
    // flatMap(..) flattening
    Optional<String> str1 = Optional.of("42");
    Optional<Integer> desiredRes1 = str1.flatMap(toIntOpt);
    out.println("boom: " + desiredRes1.get());
}

public static Function<String, Optional<Integer>> toIntOpt = str -> {
    try {
        return Optional.of(Integer.parseInt(str));
    } catch (NumberFormatException e) {
        return Optional.empty();
    }
};
}
```

So yes, there is a slight difference between map(..) and flatMap(..), and although in most cases you will use map(..), it is good to know that flatMap(..) exists too.

Intermediate Operation **sorted** and Terminal Operation **findFirst**

As the name indicates, the sorted() method has something to do with sorting: element ordering. When called on a stream, it creates another stream with all the elements of the initial stream, but sorted in their natural order. If the type of elements on the stream is not comparable (i.e., the type does not implement java.lang.Comparable<T>), a java.lang.ClassCastException is thrown. And since we are going to use sorted() to get a stream of sorted elements, we will use findFirst() to get the first element in the stream. This method returns an Optional<T> instance, because the stream might be empty and thus there is no first element. This means to get the value, the get() method must be called. For the situation where the stream might be empty, the orElse(..) or orElseGet(..) method can be used to return a default value in case of the missing first element. The code in Listing 8-36 depicts both situations.

Listing 8-36. Extracting the First Element in an Ordered Stream

```java
package com.apress.bgn.eight;
// import statements omitted

public class MoreStreamsDemo {
    public static Function<Song, Integer> processDuration = song -> song.
    getDuration()/60;

    void main(){
        // non-empty stream, result 'ever'
        List<String> pieces = List.of("some","of", "us", "we're", "hardly",
        "ever", "here");
        String first0 = pieces.stream().sorted().findFirst().get();
        out.println("First from sorted list: " + first0);

        // empty stream, result 'none'
        pieces = List.of();
        String first1 = pieces.stream().sorted().findFirst().
        orElse("none");
        out.println("First from sorted list: " + first1);
    }
}
```

Intermediate Operation **distinct** and Terminal Operation **count**

The distinct() method takes a stream and generates a stream with all the distinct elements of the original stream. And since in the examples in this book we couple intermediary and terminal operations, let's use count(), which counts the elements of the stream. A small example is depicted in Listing 8-37.

Listing 8-37. Counting Elements of a Stream, After Removing Duplicate Elements

```
package com.apress.bgn.eight;
// import statements omitted

public class MoreStreamsDemo {

    void main(){
        pieces = List.of("as","long", "as", "there", "is", "you", "there",
        "is", "me");
        long count = pieces.stream().distinct().count();
        out.println("Elements in the stream: " + count);
    }
}
// output
// Elements in the stream: 6
```

As shown in the output of Listing 8-37, when run, the code prints *Elements in the stream: 6*, because after removing the duplicate terms of *as*, *there*, and *is*, we are left with six terms. If the initial stream is empty, the `count()` method returns 0 (zero).

Intermediate Operation `limit` and Terminal Operations `min` and `max`

The `limit(..)` method was used previously in this chapter to transform an infinite stream into a finite one. Because `limit(..)` transforms a stream into another, it clearly is an intermediate function. The terminal methods covered in this section model two mathematical functions:

- Calculating the minimum of the elements in the stream: `min(..)`
- Calculating the maximum of the elements in the stream: `max(..)`

The type of elements in the stream must implement `java.util.Comparator<T>`; otherwise, a minimum value and maximum value cannot be calculated. Using the `limit(..)`, `min(..)`, and `max(..)` functions together is depicted in Listing 8-38.

Listing 8-38. Computing the Maximum and Minimum Values in a Stream

```
package com.apress.bgn.eight;
// import statements omitted

public class MoreStreamsDemo {

    void main(){
        out.println("Listing 8-38. Computing the maximum and minimum value
        in a stream.");
        Stream<Integer> ints0 = Stream.of(5,2,7,9,8,1,12,7,2);
        ints0.limit(4).min(Integer::compareTo)
                .ifPresent(min -> out.println("Min is: " + min));
        // Prints "Min is: 2"

        Stream<Integer> ints1 = Stream.of(5,2,7,9,8,1,12,7,2);
        ints1.limit(4).max(Integer::compareTo)
                .ifPresent(max -> out.println("Max is: " + max));
        // Prints "Max is: 9"
    }
}
```

Terminal Operations sum and reduce

Let's consider the scenario in which we have a finite stream of Song values and we want to calculate the sum of their durations. There are two stream terminator methods that can be used to do this: the sum(..) method and the reduce(..) method. The code to do this is depicted in Listing 8-39.

Listing 8-39. Adding the Elements of a Stream

```
package com.apress.bgn.eight;
import com.apress.bgn.eight.util.Song;
import com.apress.bgn.eight.util.StreamMediaLoader;
import static java.lang.System.out;

public class MediaStreamTester {
```

```
    void main(){
        var songs = StreamMediaLoader.loadSongs();
        Integer totalDuration0 = songs
                .mapToInt(Song::getDuration)
                .sum();
        out.println("Total duration: " + totalDuration0);

        songs = StreamMediaLoader.loadSongs();
        Integer totalDuration1 = songs
                .mapToInt(Song::getDuration)
                .reduce(0, (a, b) -> a + b);
        out.println("Total duration: " + totalDuration1);
    }
}
// both statements output
// Total duration: 5466
```

The version of the reduce(..) operation takes two arguments:

- The **identity** argument represents the initial result of the reduction and the default result if there are no elements in the stream.

- The **accumulator** function takes two parameters that the operation is applied on to get a partial result (in this case, it is the addition of those two elements).

The reduce(..) operation accumulator is an instance of java.util.function. BinaryOperator<T> that represents an operation upon two operands of the same type, producing a result of the same type as the operands. On an IntStream instance, like the one returned by the mapToInt(..) operation, the reduce(..) operation accumulator is an instance of java.util.function.IntBinaryOperator, which is a custom function that takes two int arguments and returns an int result.

Essentially, every time an element of the stream is processed, the accumulator returns a new value, which in this case is the result of adding the processed element with the previous partial result. If the result of the process is a collection, the accumulator's result is a collection, so every time a stream element is processed, a new collection is created. This is pretty inefficient, so in scenarios where collections are involved, the collect(..) operation is more suitable.

Intermediate Operation peek

The peek() function is special, because it doesn't affect a stream in any way; it does not consume stream elements. The peek() function returns a stream consisting of the elements of the stream it is called on, while also performing the operation specified by its Consumer<T> argument on each element. This means that this function can be used to debug stream operations using logging statements that print information at runtime.

Let's take our stream of Song instances, filter them by their duration, select all of them with duration > 300 seconds, and then get their titles and collect them in a list. The code to do this is depicted in Listing 8-40.

Listing 8-40. Calling peek(..) on Stream Elements

```
package com.apress.bgn.eight;
// import statements omitted

public class MediaStreamTester {

    void main(){
        var songs = StreamMediaLoader.loadSongs();
        List<String> result = songs.filter(s -> s.getDuration() > 300)
                .peek(e -> out.println("\t Filtered value: " + e))
                .map(Song::getTitle)
                .peek(e -> out.println("\t Mapped value: " + e))
                .toList();
    }
}
```

In Listing 8-40, before the map(..) call, a peek(..) call is introduced to check if the filtered elements are the ones we expect. Another peek(..) call is introduced after to inspect the mapped value.

Intermediate Operation **skip** and Terminal Operations **findAny, anyMatch, allMatch,** and **noneMatch**

These are the last operations that will be discussed in this chapter, so they were coupled all together because the skip(..) operation might affect the result of the others when applied together.

The findAny() method returns either an Optimal<T> instance that contains some element of the stream or an empty Optimal<T> instance when the stream is empty.

Caution   The behavior of findAny() is explicitly nondeterministic; it is free to select any element in the stream. Its behavior is the same as findFirst() when applied to an unordered stream.

Since findAny() is nondeterministic, its result is unpredictable, so applying it to a parallel stream is the same as applying it to a sequential stream. The findAny() operation is applied to a parallel Song stream in Listing 8-41.

Listing 8-41. Example Using findAny() on a Parallel Stream

```
package com.apress.bgn.eight;
// import statements omitted

public class MediaStreamTester {

    void main(){
      var songs = StreamMediaLoader.loadSongs();
      Optional<Song> optSong = songs.parallel().findAny();
      optSong.ifPresent(out::println);
    }
}
// sample output
/*
Song {
    id=13
    singer=George Michael
    title=Fastlove
    duration=306
    audioType=MP3
}
 */
```

The anyMatch(..) method receives an argument of type Predicate<T> and returns a boolean true value if there is any element in the stream that matches the predicate; it returns false otherwise. It works on parallel streams as well. The code in Listing 8-42 returns true if any of the songs in our stream has a title containing the word Paper.

Listing 8-42. Example Using anyMatch(..)

```
package com.apress.bgn.eight;
// import statements omitted

public class MediaStreamTester {

    void main(){
      var songs = StreamMediaLoader.loadSongs();
      boolean b0 = songs.anyMatch(s -> s.getTitle().contains("Paper"));
      out.println("Are there songs with title containing 'Paper'? " + b0);
    }
}
// output
// Are there songs with title containing 'Paper'? true
```

As you can see, the code in Listing 8-42 prints true, because there is a song in that stream named Paper Dolls. But if we want to change that result, all we have to do is skip the first six elements from processing in the original stream, by calling skip(6) as depicted in Listing 8-43. Yes, this method works on parallel streams as well.

Listing 8-43. Example Using skip(..) and anyMatch(..)

```
package com.apress.bgn.eight;
// import statements omitted

public class MediaStreamTester {

    void main(){
      var songs = StreamMediaLoader.loadSongs();
      boolean b1 = songs.parallel()
              .skip(6)
              .anyMatch(s -> s.getTitle().contains("Paper"));
```

```
        out.println("Are there songs with title containing `Paper`? " + b1);
    }
}
// output
// Are there songs with title containing `Paper` false
```

If the first six elements in the original stream are not processed, the code in Listing 8-43 returns false. There is another function that analyzes all elements of a stream to check if they all match a single predicate, and that method is named allMatch(..). In Listing 8-44, we check if all Song instances have duration longer than 300 seconds. The function returns a boolean value, and the value is true if all Song instances match the predicate and false otherwise. For the dataset used in the examples for this chapter, the expected result is a false value, because not all our Song instances have the duration field value greater than 300.

Listing 8-44. Showing What allMatch(..) Can Do

```
package com.apress.bgn.eight;
// import statements omitted

public class MediaStreamTester {

    void main(){
      var songs = StreamMediaLoader.loadSongs();
      boolean b2 = songs.allMatch(s -> s.getDuration() > 300);
     out.println("Are all songs longer than 5 minutes? " + b2);
    }
}
// output
// Are all songs longer than 5 minutes? false
```

The "sister" of this function is a function named noneMatch(..) that does exactly the opposite thing: takes a predicate as an argument and returns a boolean value as well, but the value is true if none of the stream elements match the predicate provided as an argument, and false otherwise. In Listing 8-45 we use the noneMatch(..) method to check if there is no Song instance with duration > 300, and we expect the result to be false as well.

Listing 8-45. Showing What noneMatch(..) Can Do

```
package com.apress.bgn.eight;
// import statements omitted

public class MediaStreamTester {

    void main(){
        var songs = StreamMediaLoader.loadSongs();
        boolean b3 = songs.noneMatch(s -> s.getDuration() > 300);
        out.println("Are all songs shorter than 5 minutes? " + b3);
    }
}
// output
// Are all songs shorter than 5 minutes? false
```

Intermediate Operation gather

Let's assume we want to reduce the stream of songs we have been playing with so far by keeping only one song for each singer. There is no stream operation that does this, so we need to design a component that defines songs' equality based on the singer and use it together with map(..) and distinct(..) as shown in Listing 8-46.

Listing 8-46. Stream Complex Operation for Creating a Stream Containing Only One Song per Singer

```
package com.apress.bgn.eight;

import com.apress.bgn.eight.util.Song;
import com.apress.bgn.eight.util.StreamMediaLoader;

import java.util.HashSet;
import java.util.Objects;

import static java.lang.System.out;
```

```
public class NoStreamGathererDemo {

  record DistinctBySinger(Song song) {

    @Override public boolean equals(Object obj) {
      return obj instanceof DistinctBySinger(Song other)
              && Objects.equals(song.getSinger(), other.getSinger());
    }

    @Override public int hashCode() {
      return song == null ? 0 : song.getSinger().hashCode();
    }
  }

  void main(){
    var songs = StreamMediaLoader.loadSongs();
    var reducedSongs = songs.map(DistinctBySinger::new)
            .distinct()
            .map(DistinctBySinger::song)
            .peek(out::println);
    var songList = reducedSongs.toList();
    out.println(songList.size() + " == " + new HashSet<>(songList).size());
  }
}
```

Just because it is practical to do so, we've defined the `DistinctBySinger` instance to be a record, but this does not do much to simplify the stream pipeline. A better solution to simplify the stream pipeline would be to have—instead of two `map(..)` calls and one `distinct(..)` call—a single call to a method we pass a `DistinctBySinger` instance to.

The `gather(..)` method, introduced in Java 22 as a preview feature, returns a stream consisting of the results of applying the given `java.util.stream.Gatherer<T, A, R>` instance. This operation has been introduced to provide support for more complex stream intermediary operations by applying a user-defined entity called a **gatherer**. The `gather(..)` operation allows developers to build efficient, parallel-ready streams that implement almost any intermediate operation. A gatherer is very powerful and has the following capabilities:

- Transform elements in a one-to-one, one-to-many, many-to-one, or many-to-many fashion.

- Track previously seen elements to influence the transformation of later elements.

- Short-circuit to transform infinite streams to finite streams.

- Apply different transformations based on conditions, and create more elements as a result of processing one from the initial stream.

These capabilities translate into being able to group elements in batches, deduplicate consecutively similar elements, gradually accumulate elements, or gradually reorder them.

As you can see, a gatherer can do a lot of things, and this is because the gatherer is actually made of four functions that work together:

- An **initializer** function: Can be used to provide an object that maintains private state while processing stream elements.

- An **integrator** function: Integrates a new element from the input stream, possibly inspecting the private state object and possibly emitting elements to the output stream.

- A **combiner** function: Can be used evaluate the gatherer in parallel when the input stream is marked as parallel.

- A **finisher** function: Can be invoked when there are no more input elements to consume. This function can inspect the private state object and, possibly, emit additional output elements.

There would be a lot more things to say about gatherers, but let's mix some practice with the theory, shall we?

Creating a Custom Gatherer

Gatherer<T, A, R> is an interface that developers must implement to create their own custom gatherer. So, to rewrite the code in Listing 8-46 to replace the two map(..) calls and one distinct(..) call with a call of gather(..), we need to implement the DistinctBySinger record to implement the Gatherer<T, A, R> interface. This type of processing does not require a *combiner*, since we are not interested in running the gatherer in parallel, and does not require a *finisher*, since we are interested in the resulting stream. So the code in Listing 8-46 becomes the code in Listing 8-47.

Listing 8-47. Stream Complex Operation for Creating a Stream Containing Only One Song per Singer Using a Gatherer

```
package com.apress.bgn.eight;

import com.apress.bgn.eight.util.Song;
import com.apress.bgn.eight.util.StreamMediaLoader;

import java.util.ArrayList;
import java.util.HashSet;
import java.util.List;
import java.util.function.Supplier;
import java.util.stream.Gatherer;

import static java.lang.System.out;

public class CustomGathererDemo {

  record DistinctBySinger() implements Gatherer<Song, Set<String>, Song> {

    @Override
    public Supplier<Set<String>> initializer() {
      return () -> new HashSet<>();
    }

    @Override
    public Integrator<Set<String>, Song, Song> integrator() {
      return Integrator.of((singersList, element, downstream) -> {
        if (singersList.add(element.getSinger())) {
          // emit the current integer downstream, if singer was added
          // to the set
          downstream.push(element);
        }
```

```
        // Return true to continue processing stream elements
        return true;
    });
  }
}

void main(){
    var songs = StreamMediaLoader.loadSongs();
    var reducedSongs = songs.gather(new DistinctBySinger())
            .peek(out::println);
    var songList = reducedSongs.toList();
    out.println(songList.size() + " == " + new HashSet<>(songList).
    size());
  }
}
```

The following list explains the components of Listing 8-47:

- The three types used as parameters when implementing the
  Gatherer<T, A, R> represent the following:

  - T: The type of input elements to the gatherer operation. In this
    case the original stream contains Song instances that are the
    input to the gatherer operation.

  - A: The potential mutable state type of the gatherer operation. In
    this case the type is Set<String> because we are going to use this
    string to keep track of the distinct singer names.

  - R: The type of output elements from the gatherer operation. In
    this case the type is also Song.

- The initializer() function is optional, but in this scenario we need
  it to initialize the Set<String> instance that will hold the values that
  determine the output of the gatherer.

- The integrator() function is mandatory, since a gatherer would not
  be a gatherer without the ability to integrate(*gather*) the provided
  elements. To make it easy to create an integrator function the JDK
  provides two factory methods:

- • Gatherer.Integrator.of(Gatherer.Integrator): The method used in this example, it receives elements, processes them, and optionally sends incremental results downstream. Our integrator function does exactly this using the Set<String> instance as an internal state for the gatherer: it attempts to add the element singer name to the set, and if that succeeds it pushes the element downstream.

- • Gatherer.Integrator.ofGreedy(Gatherer.Greedy): As its name indicates, this method consumes all the input and may only relay that the downstream does not want more elements.

- • The class that implements Gatherer<T, A, R> is instantiated and the instance is passed as an argument to the gather(..) method.

Selecting songs with distinct singers does not allow for parallel processing, because having multiple sets storing distinct singers does not ensure that the songs emitted downstream all have distinct singers. A use case that is suitable for parallel processing is finding the longest duration for a song in a stream. This use case is also suitable for short-circuiting the gatherer and stopping processing if a duration has been found that is above a custom limit. And since we only expect one element to be returned, a finisher is also suitable.

The LongestSong gatherer and its usage are shown in Listing 8-48.

Listing 8-48. Stream Custom Gatherer for Computing the Longest Duration of a Song in a Stream

```
package com.apress.bgn.eight;
// import statements omitted

public class LongestSongDemo {

  record LongestSong(int limit) implements Gatherer<Song, List<Integer>,
  Integer> {
    @Override
    public Supplier<List<Integer>> initializer() {
      return () -> new ArrayList<>(1);
    }
```

```java
    @Override
    public Integrator<List<Integer>, Song, Integer> integrator() {
      return Integrator.of((max, element, downstream) -> {
        if (max.isEmpty()) max.addFirst(element.getDuration());
        else if (element.getDuration() > max.getFirst()) max.set(0,
        element.getDuration());
        // "short-circuit": emit the current duration downstream
        // and return false to stop processing stream elements
        if (element.getDuration() >= limit) {
          downstream.push(element.getDuration());
          return false;
        }
        // Return true to continue processing stream elements
        return true;
      });
    }

    @Override
    public BinaryOperator<List<Integer>> combiner() {
      return (left, right) -> {
        if (left.isEmpty()) return right;
        if (right.isEmpty()) return left;

        int leftVal = left.getFirst();
        int rightVal = right.getFirst();
        if (leftVal > rightVal) return left;
        else return right;
      };
    }

    @Override
    public BiConsumer<List<Integer>, Downstream<? super Integer>>
    finisher() {
      // Emit the largest integer, if there is one, downstream
      return (max, downstream) -> {
        if (!max.isEmpty()) {
          downstream.push(max.getFirst());
```

```
        }
      };
    }
  }

  void main(){
    var songs = StreamMediaLoader.loadSongs();
    var longestDuration = songs.gather(new LongestSong(360)).findFirst().
    orElse(-1);
    out.println("Longest duration: " + longestDuration + " seconds");
  }
}
```

In this example we use the initializer to declare an ArrayList<Integer> instance with a capacity of only one Integer, as it is meant to store the longest song duration the gatherer has encountered so far.

The integrator compares the stream element duration with the value stored in the ArrayList<Integer> instance, and if it is greater than the stored value, it replaces it. Also, if the value is greater than the limit passed as an argument when instantiating the LongestSong(limit) instance, the gatherer just stops processing stream elements.

When the gatherer is run in parallel, the combinator merges two private state objects using the provided implementation. In this case the list containing the larger value is returned. This might remind you of the merge phase of the divide-and-conquer algorithm mentioned in **Chapter 5**.

The finisher function is a lambda expression that contains two parameters: the gatherer private state and the downstream where to push the value contained within it. In this example, the finisher function pushes the value contained in the private state object.

The result of running the code in Listing 4-48 is *Longest duration: 372 seconds*. This happens because the integrator encounters the 372 value that is bigger than 360 and stops processing stream elements. If the limit is set higher or lower and the code is run again, the returned duration will be different.

The two custom gatherers introduced were created by implementing Gatherer<T, A, R>, but gatherers can be created using Gatherer.of(..) factory methods too. For example, the code in Listing 8-48 can be written as shown in Listing 8-49.

Listing 8-49. Stream Custom Gatherer for Computing the Longest Duration of a
Song in a Stream Created Using a Factory Method

```java
package com.apress.bgn.eight;
// import statements omitted

public class LongestSongFactoryDemo {
  static Gatherer<Song, List<Integer>, Integer>  LONGEST_SONG(int limit) {
    return Gatherer.of(
            () -> new ArrayList<>(1),
            Gatherer.Integrator.of(
                    (max, element, downstream) -> {
                      if (max.isEmpty()) max.addFirst(element.
                      getDuration());
                      else if (element.getDuration() > max.getFirst()) max.
                      set(0, element.getDuration());

                      if (element.getDuration() >= limit) {
                        downstream.push(element.getDuration());
                        return false;
                      }
                      return true;
                    }),
            (left, right) -> {
              if (left.isEmpty()) return right;
              if (right.isEmpty()) return left;

              int leftVal = left.getFirst();
              int rightVal = right.getFirst();
              if (leftVal > rightVal) return left;
              else return right;
            },
            (max, downstream) -> {
              if (!max.isEmpty()) {
                downstream.push(max.getFirst());
              }
            }
```

```
    );
  }

  void main(){
    var songs = StreamMediaLoader.loadSongs();
    var longestDuration = songs
            .gather(LONGEST_SONG(360))
            .findFirst().orElse(-1);
    out.println("Longest duration: " + longestDuration + " seconds");
  }
}
```

Built-In Gatherers

To make development easier, the JDK comes with a few built-in gatherers declared in the java.util.stream.Gatherers class. They are listed in this section with examples for each:

- windowFixed(int windowSize): Returns a gatherer that gathers elements into windows (many-to-many)—encounter-ordered groups of elements—of a fixed size that is passed as an argument.

```
Stream.generate(() ->  randomGenerator.nextInt(300) + 1)
        .gather(Gatherers.windowFixed(3))
        .limit(2).forEach(e ->out.println(e));
// output sample
// [158, 284, 287]
// [60, 79, 203]
```

- windowSliding(int windowSize): Returns a gatherer that gathers elements into windows (many-to-many) - as the name points to, each subsequent window includes the elements of the window before it, except the first element and adds the next element in the stream.

```
Stream.generate(() ->  randomGenerator.nextInt(300) + 1)
        .gather(Gatherers.windowSliding(3))
        .limit(3).forEach(e ->out.println(e));
// output sample
```

517

```
// [286, 92, 96]
// [92, 96, 130]
// [96, 130, 32]
```

- fold(Supplier<R> initial, BiFunction<? super R, ? super T, ? extends R> folder): Returns a gatherer that gathers elements into a single element (many-to-one) using the function provided as an argument. The initial supplier provides a value to be emitted in case the source stream is empty.

```
Stream.of(1,2,3,4,5,6,7,8,9)
        .gather(
                Gatherers.fold(
                        () -> "",
                        (result, element) -> {
                                if (result.equals("")) return
                                element.toString();
                                return result + ";" +element;
                        }
                )
        )
        .findFirst().ifPresent(out::println);
// output
// 1;2;3;4;5;6;7;8;9
```

- scan(Supplier<R> initial, BiFunction<? super R, ? super T, ? extends R> scanner): Returns a one-to-one gatherer that produces downstream elements by starting with an initial value produced by the provided supplier, then applying the provided function to the current value and the next input element.

```
Stream.of(0,1,1,2,3,5,8,13,21,34,55,89,144)
        .gather(Gatherers.scan(() -> 0, Integer::sum))
              .forEach(de -> out.print(de +" "));
// output
// 0 1 2 4 7 12 20 33 54 88 143 232 376
```

- mapConcurrent(final int maxConcurrency, final Function<?
  super T, ? extends R> mapper): Returns a one-to-one gatherer
  that produces downstream elements concurrently for each of
  the elements of the input stream, up to the limit specified by
  maxConcurrency. This gatherer preserves the ordering of the stream.
  The following example applies a function named *triple* concurrently
  to the elements of the input stream, to produce an output stream.
  The triple(..) function also prints the thread executing the
  function. This makes it obvious that the gatherer returned by
  mapConcurrent(..) runs the function concurrently using virtual
  threads.

```
Function<Integer, Integer> triple = integer -> {
    out.println("Thread.currentThread()} - " + integer);
    return integer * 3;
};
Stream.of(1,2,3,4,5,6,7,8,9,10,11,12,13,14,15,16,17,18,19,20,21,2
2,23,24,25)
        .gather(Gatherers.mapConcurrent(5, triple))
        .limit(10)
        .forEach(de -> out.print(de + " "));
// output
// 0 1 2 4 7 12 20 33 54 88 143 232 376
```

As you can see, the Stream Gatherers API enhances the Stream API with new built-
in intermediate operations and the capability to define custom gatherers that provide
support for solving more complex tasks.

Note   The Stream Gatherers API is a Java 22 preview feature. It is still a preview
feature in Java 23, with plans for development to be completed in Java 24. Since it
is quite a useful one, it surely won't be dropped, but there might be some changes
between the API described in this book and the final version released by Oracle. If
that happens, I, the author of this book, will make sure the code is updated in the
repo and a notice will be added in the errata.

Debugging Stream Pipelines

As mentioned previously, the peek(..) method can be used for light debugging, more like logging the changes that happen on stream elements between one stream method call and another. Another simple way to debug code written with streams is to implement predicates, consumers, and suppliers and add logging statements in their main methods.

These simple methods are not always enough, especially when that code is part of a big application that numerous users access simultaneously. The methods might also be tedious to implement, because logging statements must be added during development and then removed before putting the application in production, to avoid polluting the application logs and (maybe) slowing it down.

A more advanced way to debug streams is provided by the IntelliJ IDEA editor, which includes a specialized plugin for stream debugging named Java Stream Debugger[5].

Tip   If you are reading this book and are not using IntelliJ IDEA as an editor to test the code, you can skip this section and research a Stream API debugger plugin for the editor of your choice. This book is focused of the Java language mostly, and this section is just added here for convenience.

To use the Java Stream Debugger, you must place a breakpoint on the line where a stream processing chain is defined. In Figure 8-4 you can see a piece of code representing the processing of a stream of Song instances being executed in debug mode and a breakpoint pausing the execution in line 44. When the execution is paused, you can open the stream debugger view by clicking the button with three vertical points (in the toolbar at the top of the Debug window) and selecting **Trace Current Stream Chain** from the menu that opens.

---

[5] https://plugins.jetbrains.com/plugin/9696-java-stream-debugger?platform=hootsuite

Figure 8-4. *Starting the Java Stream Debugger*

A popup window will appear that has a tab for each operation of the stream processing. In Figure 8-5 you can see the tabs and their methods underlined and linked to each other.

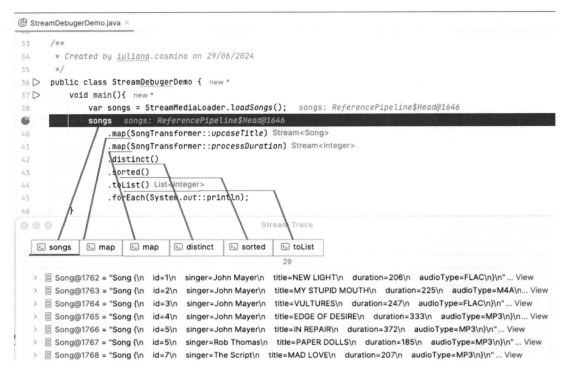

Figure 8-5. *The Java Stream Debugger window*

In the operation tabs, the text box on the left contains the elements on the original stream. The text box on the right contains the resulting stream with its elements. The following images in the chapter show tabs for various operations. For operations that reduce the number of elements or change their order, there are lines from one set of elements to the other. The first `map(..)` method transforms the song titles to their uppercase version. The second `map(..)` method transforms the duration of the songs in minutes and returns a stream of integers.

The `distinct(..)` method produces a new stream that contains only the distinct elements in the previous one, and this operation's effect is depicted quite nicely in the debugger and in Figure 8-6.

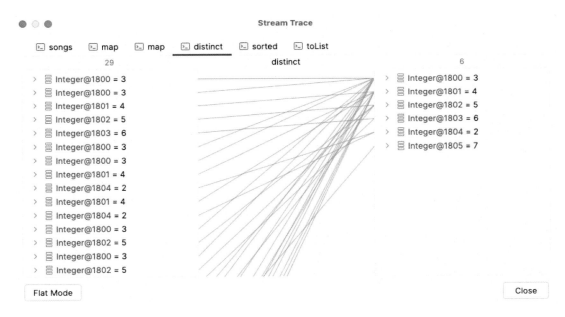

Figure 8-6. *The* `distinct()` *operation in the IntelliJ IDEA Java Stream Debugger*

The next operation is `sorted()`, which sorts the entries on the stream returned by the `distinct()` operation. The reordering of the elements and adding them to a new stream is depicted in the debugger also and in Figure 8-7.

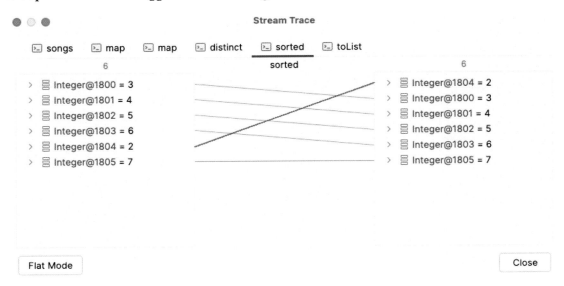

Figure 8-7. *The* `sorted()` *operation in the IntelliJ IDEA Java Stream Debugger*

After inspecting the results in the debugger, even if you want to continue the execution, this won't be possible, because all elements in the original stream and the resulting ones were actually consumed by the debugger, so the following exception will be printed in the console:

```
Exception in thread "main" java.lang.IllegalStateException:
    stream has already been operated upon or closed
    at java.base/java.util.stream.AbstractPipeline.<init>(AbstractPipeline.
    java:201)
    at java.base/java.util.stream.ReferencePipeline.<init>(ReferencePipeli
    ne.java:98)
    at java.base/java.util.stream.ReferencePipeline$StatelessOp.<init>(Refe
    rencePipeline.java:820)
    at java.base/java.util.stream.ReferencePipeline$3.<init>(ReferencePipel
    ine.java:206)
    at java.base/java.util.stream.ReferencePipeline.map(ReferencePipeline.
    java:205)
    at chapter.eigth/com.apress.bgn.eight.StreamDebugerDemo.
    main(StreamDebugerDemo.java:40)
```

A gatherer is just another operation, so if the code is modified to add a gatherer, another tab will appear in the debugger named gather, as shown in Figure 8-8.

Figure 8-8. *The gather(..) operation in the IntelliJ IDEA Java Stream Debugger*

Debugging stream pipelines using the IntelliJ IDEA Java Stream Debugger plugin is practical for simple enough examples, and is most useful when you are just learning to use the Stream API. After learning how to design your solutions using the Stream API, `peek(..)` will probably be all you need.

Summary

After reading this chapter and running the provided code samples, it should be obvious why the Stream API is so awesome. Personally, I like four things best:

- More compact and simple code can be written to solve problems without losing readability (`if` statements and loops can be avoided),

- Parallel processing of data is possible without the boilerplate code required before Java 8, as long as the performance angle is taken into consideration.

- Code can be written in functional programming style.

- Complex processing can be implemented using gatherers.

Also, the Stream API is a more declarative way of programming, as most stream methods take arguments of type `Consumer<T>`, `Predicate<T>`, `Supplier<T>`, `Function<T>`, and so on, that declare what should be done for each stream element, but the methods are not explicitly called unless there are elements on the stream.

This chapter also covered how to use `Optional<T>` instances to avoid `NullPointerExceptions` and writing `if` statements.

Having finished reading this chapter, you should have a pretty good idea about the following:

- How to create sequential and parallel streams from collections

- What empty streams are useful for

- These stream-related terms:

    - sequence of elements

    - predicate

    - consumer

- supplier

- gatherer

- method reference

- source

- aggregate operations

- intermediate operation

- terminal operation

- pipelining

- internal automatic iterations

- How to create and use `Optional<T>` instances

- How to use built-in gatherers

- How to implement custom gatherers

- How to debug stream pipelines

CHAPTER 9

Debugging, Testing, and Documenting

Development work requires you to not only design the solution for a problem and write the code for it but also test it to make sure your solution solves the problem. **Testing** involves making sure every component making up your solution behaves as expected in both expected and unexpected situations.

The most practical way to test code is to inspect values of intermediary variables by **logging** them and printing them in the console in specific situations.

When a solution is complex, **debugging** provides the opportunity to pause the execution and inspect the state of the variables. Debugging sometimes involves **break points** and requires an integrated development environment (IDE). Break points, as the name says, are points where the application pauses its execution and inspection of variables is performed.

After making sure your solution fits the requirements, you have to document it, especially if the problem that is being solved is one that requires complex code to solve it. Or if your solution might be a prerequisite for other applications, it is your responsibility to explain to other developers how to use it.

This chapter will cover a few ways to do all these testing, debugging, and documenting activities, because these are key talents for a developer.

© Iuliana Cosmina 2024
I. Cosmina, *Java 23 for Absolute Beginners*, https://doi.org/10.1007/979-8-8688-1041-1_9

Debugging

Debugging is a process of finding and resolving defects or problems within a computer program. There are several debugging tactics and, depending on the complexity of an application, one or more can be used. A list of those techniques is noted here:

- Logging intermediary states of objects involved in the process and analyzing log files

- Interactive debugging using breakpoints to pause the execution of the program and inspect intermediary states of objects involved in the process

- Testing

- Monitoring at the application or system level

- Analysis of memory dumps item profiling, a form of dynamic program analysis that measures the memory occupied by a program, or CPU used, duration of method calls, and so on.

Let's start with the simplest way of debugging: *logging*.

Logging

In the real world, logging is the destructive (at least for mother nature) process of cutting down and processing trees to produce timber. In software programming **logging** means writing log files that can be later used to identify problems in code. The simplest way to log information is to use the `System.out.print*(..)` method family, as depicted in Figure 9-1.

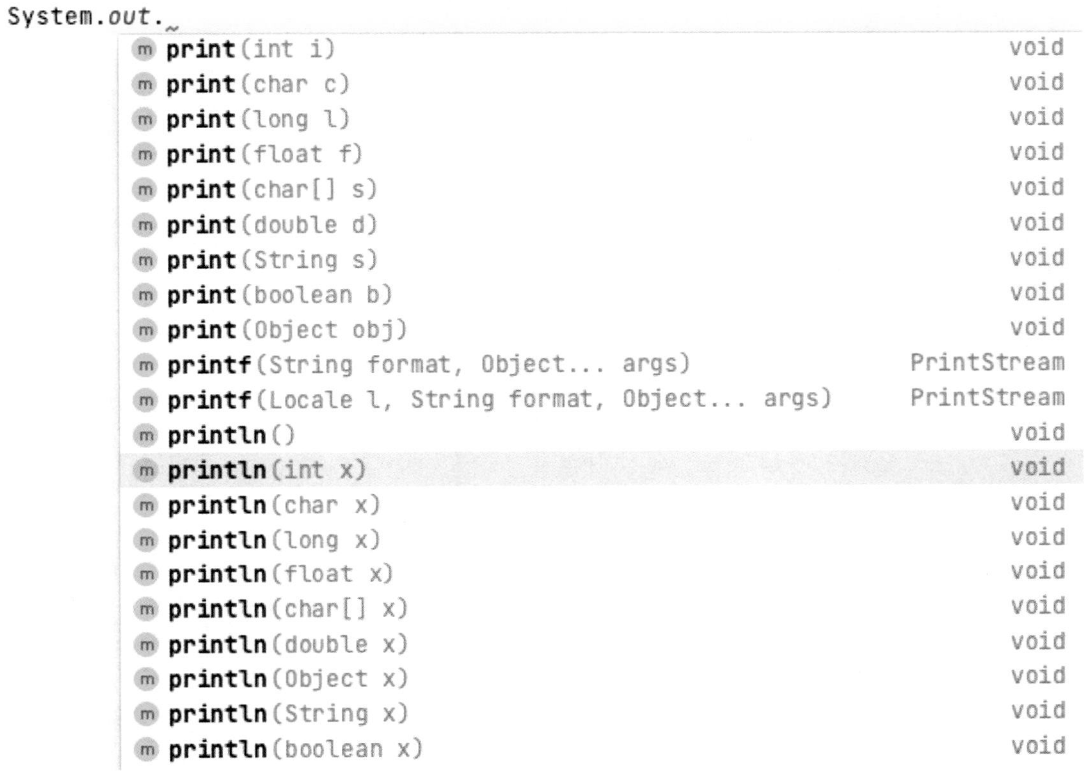

```
System.out._
        m print(int i)                                      void
        m print(char c)                                     void
        m print(long l)                                     void
        m print(float f)                                    void
        m print(char[] s)                                   void
        m print(double d)                                   void
        m print(String s)                                   void
        m print(boolean b)                                  void
        m print(Object obj)                                 void
        m printf(String format, Object... args)      PrintStream
        m printf(Locale l, String format, Object... args)  PrintStream
        m println()                                         void
        m println(int x)                                    void
        m println(char x)                                   void
        m println(long x)                                   void
        m println(float x)                                  void
        m println(char[] x)                                 void
        m println(double x)                                 void
        m println(Object x)                                 void
        m println(String x)                                 void
        m println(boolean x)                                void
```

Figure 9-1. *System.out.print*(..) method family*

The examples in this chapter use a hierarchy of classes that provide methods to sort integer arrays. The class hierarchy is depicted in Figure 9-2.

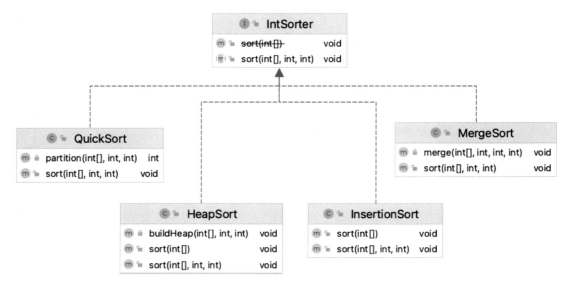

Figure 9-2. *The Sorting Classes Hierarchy*

In Listing 9-1, the MergeSort class contents are modified to add System.out.
print(..) statements to log the steps of the algorithm. **MergeSort** is the name of a
sorting algorithm that provides better performance than Bubble Sort (introduced in
Chapter 7). MergeSort describes sorting an array as the following suite of steps:

1. Split the array in two halves.

2. Split each half again until the resulting array is one that can be
    sorted easily.

3. Merge the sorted arrays repeatedly until the result is a single
    sorted array.

This approach of splitting the array repeatedly until sorting becomes a manageable
operation is called **divide et impera,** also known as **divide and conquer** (previously
introduced in **Chapter 5**. There are more algorithms that follow the same approach for
solving a problem, and MergeSort is only the first of them that will be covered in this
book. In Figure 9-3, you can see what happens in every step of a MergeSort algorithm.

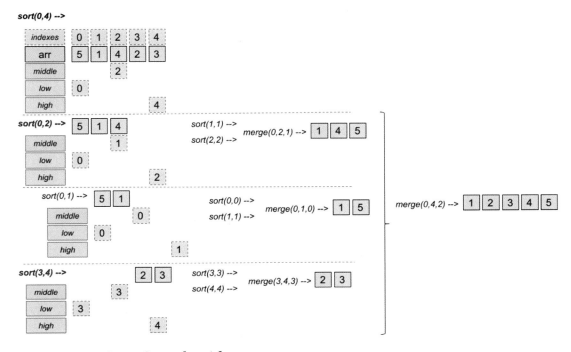

Figure 9-3. *Merge Sort algorithm steps*

In each step of the algorithm, the middle index of the array is identified. Then the `sort(..)` method is called for the arrays split in the middle by that index. This continues until there is no middle index, because the array has a single element. That is when the `merge(..)` method is called, which merges pieces of the array and also sorts them during the merging.

Figure 9-3 depicts the algorithm in a pretty similar way to the output that will be generated by the `System.out.print(..)` statements. Since it was mentioned that this algorithm is based on the divide-and-conquer method, Figure 9-4 better shows the order of the operations.

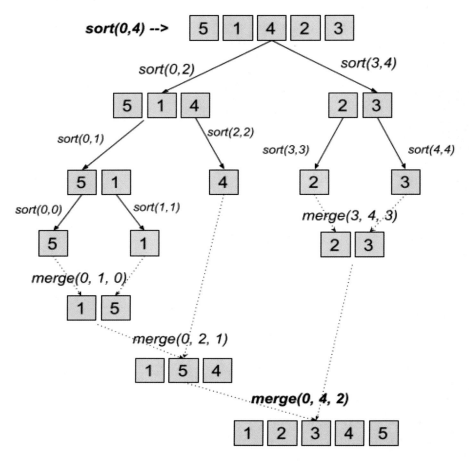

Figure 9-4. *Merge Sort algorithm steps shown as a tree*

To write the code that models the Merge-Sort algorithm, we need to write the two methods: sort(array, low, high) and merge(array, low, high, middle). The proposed implementation is going to be depicted in the next section, with the appropriate logging.

Logging with System.out.print

The code for the Merge-Sort algorithm requires a lot of steps and a lot of variables to refer to all the indexes used to arrange our elements in the proper order. To make sure our solution is properly implemented, it would be useful to see the values each method is called with and the array pieces that are being handled. We can do this by simply adding a few System.out.print statements. To keep things even simpler, we'll use import static java.lang.System.out;, which allows us to write out.println as shown in Listing 9-1.

Listing 9-1. Merge-Sort Proposed Implementation with Logging Using out. print Statements

```
package com.apress.bgn.nine.algs;
import static java.lang.System.out;

public class MergeSort implements IntSorter {

    public void sort(int[] arr, int low, int high) {
        out.print("Call sort of [low,high]: [" + low + ", " + high + "] ");
        for (int i = low; i <= high; ++i) {
            out.print(arr[i] + " ");
        }
        out.println();

        if (low < high) {
            var middle = (low + high) / 2;

            //sort lower half of the interval
            sort(arr, low, middle);
            //sort upper half of the interval
            sort(arr, middle + 1, high);

            // merge the two intervals
            merge(arr, low, high, middle);
        }
    }

    private void merge(int[] arr, int low, int high, int middle) {
        var leftLength = middle - low + 1;
        var rightLength = high - middle;

        var left = new int[leftLength];
        var right = new int[rightLength];
```

```
    for (int i = 0; i < leftLength; ++i) {
        left[i] = arr[low + i];
    }
    for (int i = 0; i < rightLength; ++i) {
        right[i] = arr[middle + 1 + i];
    }

    var i = 0;
    var j = 0;

    var k = low;
    while (i < leftLength && j < rightLength) {
        if (left[i] <= right[j]) {
            arr[k] = left[i++];
        } else {
            arr[k] = right[j++];
        }
        k++;
    }

    while (i < leftLength) {
        arr[k++] = left[i++];
    }

    while (j < rightLength) {
        arr[k++] = right[j++];
    }
    out.print("Called merge of [low, high, middle]: " + low + ", " +
    high + ", " + middle + "]");
    for (int z = low; z <= high; ++z) {
        out.print(arr[z] + " ");
    }
    out.println();
    }
}
```

A combination of out.print(..) and out.println(..) statements format the output to show the progress of the algorithm. To test the output, we need a class containing a main(..) method to execute the algorithm, something similar to the one depicted in Listing 9-2.

Listing 9-2. Main Class to Execute the Merge-Sort Proposed Implementation

```
package com.apress.bgn.nine;

import com.apress.bgn.nine.algs.IntSorter;
import com.apress.bgn.nine.algs.MergeSort;

import java.util.Arrays;
import static java.lang.System.out;

public class SortingDemo {
    void main(){
        int[] arr = {5,1,4,2,3};

        IntSorter mergeSort = new MergeSort();
        mergeSort.sort(arr, 0, arr.length - 1);

        out.print("Sorted: ");
        Arrays.stream(arr).forEach(i -> out.print(i + " "));
    }
}
```

If we run the class in Listing 9-2, the arguments provided to methods sort(..) and merge(..) are printed in the console, as are the values being sorted and the array pieces being merged. The output should look like the one depicted in Listing 9-3.

Listing 9-3. Values Printed During Execution of the Merge-Sort Proposed Implementation

```
Call sort of [low,high]: [0 4] 5 1 4 2 3
Call sort of [low,high]: [0 2] 5 1 4
Call sort of [low,high]: [0 1] 5 1
Call sort of [low,high]: [0 0] 5
Call sort of [low,high]: [1 1] 1
Called merge of [low, high, middle]: [0 1 0]) 1 5
```

```
Call sort of [low,high]: [2 2] 4
Called merge of [low, high, middle]: [0 2 1]) 1 4 5
Call sort of [low,high]: [3 4] 2 3
Call sort of [low,high]: [3 3] 2
Call sort of [low,high]: [4 4] 3
Called merge of [low, high, middle]: [3 4 3]) 2 3
Called merge of [low, high, middle]: [0 4 2]) 1 2 3 4 5
Sorted: 1 2 3 4 5
```

You can see that the console output matches the algorithm steps depicted in Figure 9-3, so that output is clearly proof that the solution works as expected.

Although all seems well, there is a problem with this code: every time the sort(..) method is called, those printing statements are executed.

Caution   If the sorting is just a step of a more complex solution, the output is not really necessary and can even pollute the output of the bigger solution. Also, if the array is quite big, printing that output could affect the performance of the overall solution.

So a different approach should be considered, one that could be customized and that includes the option to choose whether or not to print the output. This is where logging libraries come in.

Logging with JUL

JUL is the name of the logging back end provided by the JDK and is an acronym for java.util.logging. The JDK provides its own logger classes that are grouped under this package. A Logger instance is used to write messages. The Logger instance should be provided a name when it is created. Log messages are printed by calling specialized methods that print messages at different levels. For the JUL module, the levels and their scope are listed here, but other logging libraries have similar logging levels:

- OFF: Used to turn off all logging

- SEVERE: Highest level message, indicates a serious failure

- WARNING: Indicates that this message is being printed because of a potential problem

- INFO: Indicates that this is an informational message

- CONFIG: Indicates that this is a message containing configuration information

- FINE: Indicates that this is a message providing tracing information

- FINER: Indicates that this is a fairly detailed tracing message

- FINEST: Indicates that this is a very detailed tracing message

- ALL: Indicates all log messages should be printed

Loggers can be configured using .xml (Extensible Markup Language) or .properties files, and their output can be directed to external files. For the code sample introduced previously, all out.print statements in the MergeSort class are replaced with logging statements. Listing 9-4 depicts the MergeSort class with logging statements.

Listing 9-4. MergeSort Implementation with JUL Logging Statements

```
package com.apress.bgn.algs;

import java.util.logging.Logger;

public class MergeSort implements IntSorter {
    private static final Logger log = Logger.getLogger(MergeSort.class.
    getName());

    public void sort(int[] arr, int low, int high) {
        var sb = new StringBuilder("Call sort of ")
                .append("[low,high]: [")
                .append(low).append(" ").append(high)
                .append("] ");
        for (var i = low; i <= high; ++i) {
            sb.append(arr[i]).append(" ");
        }
        log.info(sb.toString());
```

```
    if (low < high) {

        var middle = (low + high) / 2;

        //sort lower half of the interval
        sort(arr, low, middle);
        //sort upper half of the interval
        sort(arr, middle + 1, high);

        // merge the two intervals
        merge(arr, low, high, middle);
    }
}

private void merge(int[] arr, int low, int high, int middle) {
    var leftLength = middle - low + 1;
    var rightLength = high - middle;

    var left = new int[leftLength];
    var right = new int[rightLength];

    for (int i = 0; i < leftLength; ++i) {
        left[i] = arr[low + i];
    }
    for (int i = 0; i < rightLength; ++i) {
        right[i] = arr[middle + 1 + i];
    }

    var i = 0;
    var j = 0;

    var k = low;
    while (i < leftLength && j < rightLength) {
        if (left[i] <= right[j]) {
            arr[k] = left[i++];
        } else {
            arr[k] = right[j++];
        }
        k++;
    }
```

```
        while (i < leftLength) {
          arr[k++] = left[i++];
        }

        while (j < rightLength) {
          arr[k++] = right[j++];
        }
        var sb = new StringBuilder("Called merge of [low, high,
        middle]: [")
                .append(low).append(" ").append(high).append(" ")
                .append(middle)
                .append("]) ");
        for (var z = low; z <= high; ++z) {
            sb.append(arr[z]).append(" ");
        }
        log.info(sb.toString());
    }
}
```

A `StringBuilder` instance is introduced to construct longer messages before writing them with `log.info([message])`, which is equivalent to calling `log.log(Level.INFO, [message]);`. Listing 9-5 depicts the main class to run the algorithm.

Listing 9-5. Main Class to Run the MergeSort Proposed Implementation with JUL Logging Statements

```
package com.apress.bgn.nine;

import com.apress.bgn.algs.IntSorter;
import com.apress.bgn.algs.MergeSort;

import java.io.FileInputStream;
import java.io.IOException;
import java.util.Arrays;
import java.util.logging.Level;
import java.util.logging.LogManager;
import java.util.logging.Logger;
```

```java
public class SortingJulDemo {
    private static final Logger log = Logger.getLogger(SortingJulDemo.
    class.getName());

    static {
        try {
            LogManager logManager = LogManager.getLogManager();
            logManager.readConfiguration(new FileInputStream("./chapter09/
            logging-jul/src/main/resources/logging.properties"));
        } catch (IOException exception) {
            log.log(Level.SEVERE, "Error in loading configuration",
            exception);
        }
    }

    void main(){
        int[] arr = {5,1,4,2,3};

        final StringBuilder sb = new StringBuilder("Sorting  an array with
        merge sort: ");
        Arrays.stream(arr).forEach(i -> sb.append(i).append(" "));
        log.info(sb.toString());

        IntSorter mergeSort = new MergeSort();
        mergeSort.sort(arr, 0, arr.length - 1);

        final StringBuilder sb2 = new StringBuilder("Sorted: ");
        Arrays.stream(arr).forEach(i -> sb2.append(i).append( " "));
        log.info(sb2.toString());
    }
}
```

There are not many log statements in this class. The body of the class starts with the declaration and initialization of the Logger instance. The instance is not created by calling the constructor, but obtained by calling the getLogger(..) static method declared in the Logger class. This method looks for a Logger instance with the name provided as an argument and, if found, returns that instance; otherwise, it creates an instance with that name and returns it. In this example the name of the Logger instance is the fully qualified class name, obtained by calling SortingJulDemo.class.getName().

Right after this statement, there is a `static` block used to configure the logger from the `logging.properties` file. The contents of this file are shown in Listing 9-6.

Listing 9-6. Properties Used to Configure the JUL Logger Declared in the `logging.properties` File

```
handlers=java.util.logging.ConsoleHandler
java.util.logging.ConsoleHandler.level=ALL
java.util.logging.ConsoleHandler.formatter=java.util.logging.
SimpleFormatter
java.util.logging.SimpleFormatter.format=[%1$tF %1$tT] [%4$-4s] %5$s %n
```

This file contains a list of values in the format `propertyName=propertyValue`, which represents the configuration for the JUL logger. Their values specify the following:

- The class used to print the log messages: `java.util.logging.ConsoleHandler` prints messages in the console.

- The class used to format the log messages: `java.util.logging.SimpleFormatter`

- A template for printing log messages: `[%1$tF %1$tT] [%4$-4s] %5$s %n`

- The levels of the log messages that are printed, which in this case includes all levels of log messages because of the `ALL` value.

The `Logger` instance is created by calling the static method `Logger.getLogger(..)`. The recommended practice is for the logger to be named as the class it is logging messages for. Without any additional configuration, every message printed with `log.info(..)` is printed prefixed with the full system date, full class name, and method name in front of it. As you can imagine the result is quite verbose, and this is why the `logging.properties` file comes in handy and the `LogManager` configured from it. The `LogManager` reads the configuration that customizes the `Logger` instance.

Running the `SortingJulDemo` produces the output shown in Listing 9-7.

Listing 9-7. Values Printed During Execution of the MergeSort Proposed
Implementation When Logging Using JUL with a Custom Configuration

```
[2024-06-30 01:20:40] [INFO] Sorting  an array with merge sort: 5 1 4 2 3
[2024-06-30 01:20:40] [INFO] Call sort of [low,high]: [0 4] 5 1 4 2 3
[2024-06-30 01:20:40] [INFO] Call sort of [low,high]: [0 2] 5 1 4
[2024-06-30 01:20:40] [INFO] Call sort of [low,high]: [0 1] 5 1
[2024-06-30 01:20:40] [INFO] Call sort of [low,high]: [0 0] 5
[2024-06-30 01:20:40] [INFO] Call sort of [low,high]: [1 1] 1
[2024-06-30 01:20:40] [INFO] Called merge of [low, high, middle]:
[0 1 0]) 1 5
[2024-06-30 01:20:40] [INFO] Call sort of [low,high]: [2 2] 4
[2024-06-30 01:20:40] [INFO] Called merge of [low, high, middle]:
[0 2 1]) 1 4 5
[2024-06-30 01:20:40] [INFO] Call sort of [low,high]: [3 4] 2 3
[2024-06-30 01:20:40] [INFO] Call sort of [low,high]: [3 3] 2
[2024-06-30 01:20:40] [INFO] Call sort of [low,high]: [4 4] 3
[2024-06-30 01:20:40] [INFO] Called merge of [low, high, middle]:
[3 4 3]) 2 3
[2024-06-30 01:20:40] [INFO] Called merge of [low, high, middle]: [0 4 2])
1 2 3 4 5
[2024-06-30 01:20:40] [INFO] Sorted: 1 2 3 4 5
```

Without the static initialization block that customizes how log messages are
shown, the default class used to specify where the log messages are printed is `java.
util.logging.ConsoleHandler` and the `java.util.logging.SimpleFormatter` class
is configured with a default format that is quite verbose, declared by `jdk.internal.
logger.SimpleConsoleLogger.Formatting.DEFAULT_FORMAT`. The value of this constant
is `%1$tb %1$td, %1$tY %1$tl:%1$tM:%1$tS %1$Tp %2$s%n%4$s:  %5$s%6$s%n`, which
makes the logger prefix the log messages with a line containing the system date and time
formatted in a readable manner, the full class name and the method name, and a new line
containing the log level. The default configuration is typically loaded from the properties
file `conf/logging.properties` in the Java installation directory, by the `LogManager`[1].

---

[1] https://docs.oracle.com/en/java/javase/23/docs/api/java.logging/java/util/logging/
LogManager.html#readConfiguration()

To test this, just comment the `static` initialization block and run the
`SortingJulDemo` class. The log messages in the console are now printed as depicted in
Listing 9-8.

Listing 9-8. Values Printed During Execution of the MergeSort Proposed
Implementation When Logging Using JUL with the Default Configuration

```
Jun 30, 2024 1:26:54 AM com.apress.bgn.nine.SortingJulDemo main
                      INFO: Sorting  an array with merge sort: 5 1 4 2 3
Jun 30, 2024 1:26:54 AM com.apress.bgn.nine.algs.MergeSort sort
                      INFO: Call sort of [low,high]: [0 4] 5 1 4 2 3
# some logs omitted
Jun 30, 2024 1:26:54 AM com.apress.bgn.nine.algs.MergeSort merge
                      INFO: Called merge of [low, high, middle]:
                      [0 1 0]) 1 5
Jun 30, 2024 1:26:54 AM com.apress.bgn.nine.algs.MergeSort sort
                      INFO: Call sort of [low,high]: [2 2] 4
# some logs omitted
Jun 30, 2024 1:26:54 AM com.apress.bgn.nine.algs.MergeSort merge
                      INFO: Called merge of [low, high, middle]: [0 4 2])
                      1 2 3 4 5
Jun 30, 2024 1:26:54 AM com.apress.bgn.nine.SortingJulDemo main
                      INFO: Sorted: 1 2 3 4 5
# some logs omitted
```

Beside the `SimpleFormatter` class, another class that can be used to format log
messages is `XMLFormatter`, which formats the messages as XML. The XML format of
writing data is defined by a set of rules for encoding the data that is both human-
readable and machine-readable. Also, the set of rules makes it easy to validate and
find errors[2]. Since for XML it makes no sense for the messages to be written to the
console, the `FileHandler` class should be used to direct the log messages to a file. The
modifications to be added to the configuration file are depicted in Listing 9-9.

---

[2]`https://en.wikipedia.org/wiki/XML`

Listing 9-9. Values Printed During the Execution of the Merge-Sort Proposed Implementation When Logging Using JUL with a Custom Configuration

```
handlers=java.util.logging.FileHandler
java.util.logging.FileHandler.pattern=chapter09/out/chapter09-log.xml
.level=ALL
java.util.logging.ConsoleHandler.formatter=java.util.logging.XMLFormatter
```

Using the configuration file with the contents shown in Listing 9-9 when running the SortingJulDemo class, a file named chapter09-log.xml is generated under chapter09/out and contains entries that look like those depicted in Listing 9-10.

Listing 9-10. Logging Messages As XML

```
<?xml version="1.0" encoding="UTF-8" standalone="no"?>
<!DOCTYPE log SYSTEM "logger.dtd">
<log>
  <record>
    <date>2024-06-30T00:30:58.777397Z</date>
    <millis>1719707458777</millis>
    <nanos>397000</nanos>
    <sequence>0</sequence>
    <logger>com.apress.bgn.nine.SortingJulDemo</logger>
    <level>INFO</level>
    <class>com.apress.bgn.nine.SortingJulDemo</class>
    <method>main</method>
    <thread>1</thread>
    <message>Sorting  an array with merge sort: 5 1 4 2 3 </message>
  </record>
  <!-- other log messages omitted-->
</log>
```

The logging output can also be customized by providing a custom class, the only condition being that the class extends the java.util.logging.Formatter class, or any of its JDK subclasses.

In the previous code samples, only log.info(..) calls were used, because the code is quite basic; there is little room for anything unexpected to happen (there are no external resources involved that might be unavailable). The code can be modified to allow the user to insert the elements of the array. Code to treat the case when the user does not provide any data and code to treat the case when user inserts bad data should be added to the class. For example, if the user does not provide any data, a SEVERE log message should be printed, and the application should terminate. If the user introduces invalid data, the valid data should be used and a warning should be printed for elements that are not integers. This means that the SortingJulDemo class changes as depicted in Listing 9-11.

Listing 9-11. SortingJulDemo Using an Array of Elements Provided As Argument for the main(..) Method

```
package com.apress.bgn.nine;
// imports omitted

public class SortingJulDemo {
    private static final Logger log = Logger.getLogger(SortingJulDemo.
    class.getName());

    // logging config omitted

    void main(){
      if (args.length == 0) {
        log.severe("No data to sort!");
        return;
      }
      int[] arr = getInts(args);

      final StringBuilder sb = new StringBuilder("Sorting  an array with
      merge sort: ");
      Arrays.stream(arr).forEach(i -> sb.append(i).append(" "));
      log.info(sb.toString());

      IntSorter mergeSort = new MergeSort();
      mergeSort.sort(arr, 0, arr.length - 1);

      final StringBuilder sb2 = new StringBuilder("Sorted: ");
      Arrays.stream(arr).forEach(i -> sb2.append(i).append( " "));
      log.info(sb2.toString());
    }
```

```java
/**
 * Transforms a String[] to an int[] array
 * @param args
 * @return an array of integers
 */
private static int[] getInts(String[] args) {
  List<Integer> list = new ArrayList<>();
  for (String arg : args) {
    try {
      int toInt = Integer.parseInt(arg);
      list.add(toInt);
    } catch (NumberFormatException nfe) {
      log.warning("Element " + arg +" is not an integer and cannot be
      added to the array!");
    }
  }
  int[] arr = new int[list.size()];

  int j = 0;
  for (Integer elem : list) {
    arr[j++] = elem;
  }
  return arr;
  }
}
```

As you can see, the arr array is no longer hard-coded in the main(..) method, but the values that this method receives as arguments become the array to be sorted and are converted from String values to int values by the getInts(..) method. The person executing this program can provide the arguments from the command line, but because we are using IntelliJ IDEA, there is an easier way to do that. If you now run the program without providing any arguments, this is what will be printed in the console:

```
[2021-06-06 12:16:14] [SEVERE] No data to sort!
```

The execution stops right there, because there is nothing to sort. Since you've probably run this class a few times, IntelliJ IDEA probably created a launcher configuration for you that you can customize and provide arguments for the execution. Take a look at Figure 9-5 and try to edit your configuration as depicted there by adding the recommended values as program arguments.

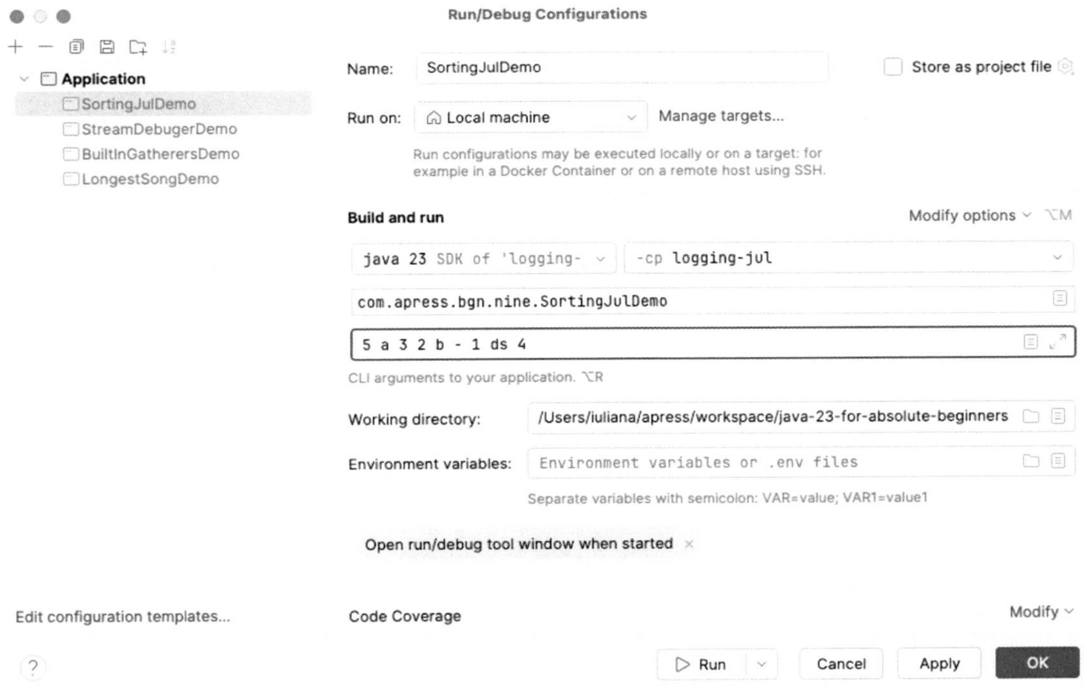

Figure 9-5. *IntelliJ IDEA launcher for the* `SortingJulDemo` *class*

Running this version of the `SortingJulDemo` class with the default console logging configured produces a few extra log messages, as depicted in Listing 9-12.

Listing 9-12. Logging Messages of Level `WARNING` Shown During Execution of the New Version of `SortingJulDemo`

```
[2021-06-06 12:21:35] [WARNING] Element a is not an integer and cannot be
added to the array! # <1>
[2021-06-06 12:21:35] [WARNING] Element b is not an integer and cannot be
added to the array! # <2>
```

```
[2021-06-06 12:21:35] [WARNING] Element - is not an integer and cannot be
added to the array! # <3>
[2021-06-06 12:21:35] [WARNING] Element ds is not an integer and cannot be
added to the array! # <4>
[2021-06-06 12:21:35] [INFO] Sorting an array with merge sort: 5 3 2 1 4
[2021-06-06 12:21:35] [INFO] Call sort of [low,high]: [0 4] 5 3 2 1 4
# other log messages omitted
```

As mentioned in the previous section, writing logs can affect performance in some cases. When the application is running in a production system, we might want to refine the logging configuration to filter out less important log messages and keep only those that notify us of a risk of a problem. The previous configuration examples included the following configuration line that enables all log messages to be printed:

```
java.util.logging.ConsoleHandler.level=ALL
```

Or the more general format that works for any `java.util.logging.Handler` subclass:

```
.level=ALL
```

If the value of this property is changed to `OFF`, nothing will be printed. The log levels have integer values assigned to them, and those values can be used to compare the severity of the messages. As a rule, if you configure a certain level of messages, more severe messages will be printed as well. So if we set that property to `INFO`, `WARNING` messages will be printed as well. The values for the severity levels of messages are defined in the `java.util.logging.Level` class, and if you open that class in your editor, you can see the integer values assigned to each of them as depicted in Listing 9-13.

Listing 9-13. The Integer Values Specific to the Log Levels

```java
package java.util.logging;
// import statements omitted

public class Level implements java.io.Serializable {

    public static final Level OFF = new Level("OFF",Integer.MAX_VALUE,
    defaultBundle);
    public static final Level SEVERE = new Level("SEVERE",1000,
    defaultBundle);
```

```
    public static final Level WARNING = new Level("WARNING", 900,
    defaultBundle);
    public static final Level INFO = new Level("INFO", 800, defaultBundle);
    public static final Level CONFIG = new Level("CONFIG", 700,
    defaultBundle);
    public static final Level FINE = new Level("FINE", 500, defaultBundle);
    public static final Level FINER = new Level("FINER", 400,
    defaultBundle);
    public static final Level FINEST = new Level("FINEST", 300,
    defaultBundle);
    public static final Level ALL = new Level("ALL", Integer.MIN_VALUE,
    defaultBundle);
    // other comments and code omitted
}
```

In the previous configuration, by changing `.level=ALL` to `.level=WARNING`, we would expect to see all log messages of levels WARNING and SEVERE. Running the SortingJulDemo class with the previous arguments, we should see only the WARNING level messages, as depicted in Listing 9-14.

Listing 9-14. Only Logging Messages of Level WARNING Being Shown During Execution of SortingJulDemo

```
[2021-06-06 17:12:29] [WARNING] Element a is not an integer and cannot be
added to the array!
[2021-06-06 17:12:29] [WARNING] Element b is not an integer and cannot be
added to the array!
[2021-06-06 17:12:29] [WARNING] Element - is not an integer and cannot be
added to the array!
[2021-06-06 17:12:29] [WARNING] Element ds is not an integer and cannot be
added to the array!
```

Other ways to define log messaging formatting exist: system properties can be used or, programmatically, a formatter can be instantiated and set on a Logger instance. The choice really depends on the specifics of the application. This topic won't be covered in the book, however, so if you are interested in reading more about Java logging with JUL, I recommend the tutorial referenced in the footnote[3]. The reason JUL isn't covered further here is that JUL is known for its weak performance compared to other logging libraries. Another thing you have to take into account is that if the application you are building is a complex one, with a lot of dependencies, these dependencies might use different logging libraries—how do you configure and use them all? This is where a logging facade proves useful. The next section will show you how to use the most renown Java logging facade: **SLF4J**.

Logging with SLF4J and Logback

The most renown Java logging facade is SLF4J (Simple Logging Facade for Java)[4], which serves as a logging abstraction for various logging frameworks. This means that if you use the SLF4J interfaces and classes in your code, behind the scenes all the work will be done by a concrete logging implementation found in the classpath. The best part? You can change the logging implementation at any time and your code will still compile and execute correctly, with no need to change anything in it.

In the logging code samples covered thus far in this chapter, the code is tied to JUL; if we want for some reason to change the logging library, we need to change the existing code as well. The first step is to change our code to use the SLF4J API.

Note   As a reminder, an application programming interface (API) describes the publicly available components of a library: interfaces, classes, methods, and so forth.

Another advantage of using SLF4J is that the configuration is read automatically if the logging configuration file is on the classpath. This means the `LogManager` initialization block that we needed for JUL is not needed for SLF4J, as long as the configuration file is named according to the standard of the concrete logging implementation used. This section starts with the transformation of the main `SortingJulDemo` class in Listing 9-5 to the `SortingLogbackDemo` class shown in Listing 9-15, by replacing JUL configuration and log statements with SLF4J-specific ones.

---

[3] `https://www.vogella.com/tutorials/Logging/article.html`
[4] `https://www.slf4j.org`

Listing 9-15. The SortingLogbackDemo Class

```
package com.apress.bgn.nine;

import org.slf4j.Logger;
import org.slf4j.LoggerFactory;
// other imports omitted

public class SortingLogbackDemo {

    private static final Logger log = LoggerFactory.
    getLogger(SortingLogbackDemo.class);

    public static void main(String... args) {
        if (args.length == 0) {
            log.error("No data to sort!");
            return;
        }
        int[] arr = getInts(args);

        final StringBuilder sb = new StringBuilder ("Sorting an array with
        merge sort: ");
        Arrays.stream(arr).forEach(i -> sb.append(i).append(" "));
        log.debug(sb.toString());

        IntSorter mergeSort = new MergeSort();
        mergeSort.sort(arr, 0, arr.length - 1);

        final StringBuilder sb2 = new StringBuilder("Sorted: ");
        Arrays.stream(arr).forEach(i -> sb2.append(i).append( " "));
        log.info(sb2.toString());
    }

    // getInts method omitted
}
```

SLF4J defines an API that maps to the concrete implementation provided by a logging library that hasn't been mentioned yet. The SLF4J log statements look pretty similar, but the log levels are a little different than JUL's log levels. The following list explains the most common SLF4J log statements:

551

- `log.error(..)` is used for logging messages at the ERROR level; usually these messages are used when there is a critical failure of the application and normal execution cannot continue. There is more than one form for this method, and exceptions and objects can be passed as arguments to it so that the state of the application at the moment of the failure can be assessed.

- `log.warn(..)` is used for logging messages at the WARN level; usually these messages are printed to notify that the application is not functioning normally and there might be reason to worry. As with `log.error(..)`, there is more than one form of `log.warn(..)`, and exceptions and objects can be passed as arguments to better assess the current state of the application.

- `log.info(..)` is used for logging messages at the INFO level; this type of message is informational, to let the user know that everything is okay and working as expected.

- `log.debug(..)` is used for logging messages at the DEBUG level; usually these messages are used to print intermediary states of the application, to check that things are going as expected and, in case of a failure, to trace the evolution of the application objects.

- `log.trace(..)` is used for logging messages at the TRACE level; this type of message is informational and of very low importance.

The concrete logging implementation used for this example is called Logback[5], which I chose for the first edition of this book because, at the time, it was the only library that worked with SLF4J after modules were introduced in Java 9. Logback was viewed as the successor of Apache Log4j[6], another popular logging implementation.

---

[5] https://logback.qos.ch
[6] https://logging.apache.org/log4j

Info   Fun fact: Log4j, SLF4j, and Logback were all founded by the same person: Ceki Gülcü. He is currently working on the latter two. As for Log4j, it was replaced by Apache Log4j 2, an upgrade that provides significant improvements over its predecessor. Currently, Log4j 2 version 3 is under development, so when it comes to logging, developers have quite a few decent options to choose from.

Logback implements SLF4J natively, so there is no need to add another bridge library, and it is faster, as the Logback internals have been rewritten to perform faster on critical execution points. After modifying our classes to use SLF4J, we simply have to add Logback as a dependency of our application and add a configuration file under the src/main/resources directory. The configuration file can be written in XML or Groovy, and the standard requires it to be named logback.xml. Listing 9-16 depicts the contents of this file for this section's example.

Listing 9-16. Contents of the logback.xml Configuration File

```xml
<?xml version="1.0" encoding="UTF-8"?>
<configuration>
    <appender name="console" class="ch.qos.logback.core.ConsoleAppender">
        <encoder>
            <pattern>%d{HH:mm:ss.SSS} %-5level %logger{5} -
            %msg%n</pattern>
        </encoder>
    </appender>
    <logger name="com.apress.bgn.nine" level="debug"/>
    <root level="info">
        <appender-ref ref="console" />
    </root>
</configuration>
```

The ch.qos.logback.core.ConsoleAppender class writes log messages in the console, and the <pattern> element value defines the format of the log messages. Logback can format fully qualified class names by shortening up package names to their initials, thus it allows for compact logging without losing details. This makes Logback one of the favorite logging implementations of the Java development world at the moment. The package names, if they are made up of more than one part, are reduced to the first letter of each part. The logging calls in the MergeSort class were all replaced with log.debug(..) because these messages are intermediary and not really informational, just samples of the state of the objects used by the application during the execution of the process. The general logging level of the application can be set using a <root> element to the desired level, but different logging levels can be set for classes or packages or subsets of packages using <logger> elements.

Using the previous configuration running the SortingLogbackDemo class yields the output shown in Listing 9-17.

Listing 9-17. Log Messages Printed by SLF4J + Logback

```
16:25:41.178 WARN  c.a.b.n.SortingLogbackDemo - Element a is not an integer
and cannot be added to the array!
16:25:41.182 WARN  c.a.b.n.SortingLogbackDemo - Element b is not an integer
and cannot be added to the array!
16:25:41.182 WARN  c.a.b.n.SortingLogbackDemo - Element - is not an integer
and cannot be added to the array!
16:25:41.182 WARN  c.a.b.n.SortingLogbackDemo - Element ds is not an
integer and cannot be added to the array!
16:25:41.183 DEBUG c.a.b.n.SortingLogbackDemo - Sorting  an array with
merge sort: 5 3 2 1 4
16:25:41.185 DEBUG c.a.b.n.a.MergeSort - Call sort of : [0 4] 5 3 2 1 4
# log statements omitted
16:25:41.185 DEBUG c.a.b.n.a.MergeSort - Called merge of: [0 1 0],) 3 5
# log statements omitted
16:25:41.185 DEBUG c.a.b.n.a.MergeSort - Called merge of: [0 4 2],)
1 2 3 4 5
16:25:41.186 INFO  c.a.b.n.SortingLogbackDemo - Sorted: 1 2 3 4 5
```

As you can see, the fully qualified class name com.apress.bgn.nine. SortingLogbackDemo was shortened to c.a.b.n.SortingLogbackDemo. The configuration file can be provided to the program as a VM argument (an argument the JVM will use when running your class), which means the logging format can be configured externally. When launching the class, just use -Dlogback. configurationFile=\temp\ext-logback.xml as a VM argument if you want to provide a different log file.

Logback can direct output to a file as well; simply add a configuration using the `ch.qos.logback.core.FileAppender` class and direct the output to the file by adding an `<appender>` element in the `<root>` configuration. A configuration sample is depicted in Listing 9-18.

Listing 9-18. Logback Configuration to Direct Log Messages to a File

```xml
<?xml version="1.0" encoding="UTF-8"?>
<configuration>
    <appender name="file" class="ch.qos.logback.core.FileAppender">
        <file>chapter09/logging-slf4j/out/output.log</file>
        <append>true</append>
        <encoder>
            <pattern>%d{HH:mm:ss.SSS} %-5level %logger{5} -
            %msg%n</pattern>
        </encoder>
    </appender>
    <appender name="console" class="ch.qos.logback.core.ConsoleAppender">
        <encoder>
            <charset>UTF-8</charset>
            <pattern>%d{HH:mm:ss.SSS} %-5level %logger{5} -
            %msg%n</pattern>
        </encoder>
    </appender>
    <logger name="com.apress.bgn.nine" level="debug"/>
    <root level="info">
        <appender-ref ref="file"/>
        <appender-ref ref="console" />
    </root>
</configuration>
```

In the previous example, the original configuration was kept so that log messages are also printed in the console, thus proving that log messages can be directed to two destinations at once.

What if the log file becomes too big and cannot be opened? There's an approach for that. A class named `ch.qos.logback.core.rolling.RollingFileAppender` can be configured to write a file up to a configured limit in size and then start another file. The `RollingFileAppender` class requires two arguments:

- An instance of a type that implements `ch.qos.logback.core.rolling.RollingPolicy`, which provides functionality to write a new log file (an operation also called *rollover*)

- An instance of a type that implements `ch.qos.logback.core.rolling.TriggeringPolicy`, which configures the conditions under which the rollover will happen

Also, a single instance of a type that implements both of the interfaces can be used to configure the logger. Rolling over a log file means that the log file is renamed according to the configuration—usually the last date the file was accessed is added to its name, and a new log file is created, with the log file name configured (and without a date suffix, to make it clear this is the file logs are currently dumped in). Such a Logback configuration is depicted in Listing 9-19.

Listing 9-19. Logback Configuration to Direct Log Messages to a File of a Reasonable Limit

```xml
<?xml version="1.0" encoding="UTF-8"?>
<configuration scan="true">

    <appender name="r_file" class="ch.qos.logback.core.rolling.
    RollingFileAppender">
        <file>chapter09/logging-slf4j/out/output.log</file>
        <rollingPolicy class="ch.qos.logback.core.rolling.
        TimeBasedRollingPolicy">
            <fileNamePattern>chapter09/logging-slf4j/out/output_%d
            {yyyy-MM-dd}.%i.log</fileNamePattern>

            <timeBasedFileNamingAndTriggeringPolicy class="ch.qos.logback.
            core.rolling.SizeAndTimeBasedFNATP">
                <maxFileSize>10MB</maxFileSize>
            </timeBasedFileNamingAndTriggeringPolicy>
```

```xml
        <maxHistory>30</maxHistory>
    </rollingPolicy>

    <encoder>
        <charset>UTF-8</charset>
        <pattern>%d{HH:mm:ss.SSS} %-5level %logger{5} -
        %msg%n</pattern>
    </encoder>
</appender>

<appender name="console" class="ch.qos.logback.core.ConsoleAppender">
    <encoder>
        <pattern>%d{HH:mm:ss.SSS} %-5level %logger{5} -
        %msg%n</pattern>
    </encoder>
</appender>

<logger name="com.apress.bgn.nine" level="info"/>

<root level="info">
    <appender-ref ref="r_file"/>
    <appender-ref ref="console" />
</root>
</configuration>
```

The configuration in Listing 9-19 includes the following elements:

- The `<file>` element configures the location and the name of the
  log file.

- The `<rollingPolicy>` element configures the name the log
  file will receive when log messages will no longer be written in
  it, using the `<fileNamePattern>` element. For example, in the
  previous configuration the `output.log` file will be renamed to
  `output_2020-07-22.log`, and then a new `output.log` file will be
  created for the next day the application is running.

- The `<timeBasedFileNamingAndTriggeringPolicy>` element
  configures when the new log file should be created and how big
  the `output.log` file should be before a new file is created. The
  configured size in the previous example is 10MB. If a log file gets
  bigger than 10MB before the end of the day, the file is renamed to
  `output_2018-07-22.1.log`. An index is added to the name and a new
  `output.log` file is created.

- The `<maxHistory>` element configures the lifespan of a log file, and in
  this example it is 30 days.

Logging is a powerful tool when used properly. When not used properly, it can easily
lead to performance problems. Also, logging everything is not really useful, because
looking for a problem in a big logging file is like looking for a needle in a haystack.

Another thing worth noticing in Listing 9-19 is that `StringBuilder` instances
are used to construct big log messages that are to be printed at a certain level. What
happens if logging for that level is disabled via configuration? If you guessed that time
and memory is consumed creating those messages, even if they are not logged, you
are right. So, what do we do? The creators of SLF4J have thought of this as well and
added methods to test if a certain logging level is enabled and statements creating
elaborate log messages can be encapsulated in an `if` statement. This being said, the
`SortingLogbackDemo.main(..)` method can be made more effective by rewriting it as
shown in Listing 9-20.

Listing 9-20. Logging Efficiently in Class `SortingLogbackDemo`

```
package com.apress.bgn.nine;
// import statements omitted

public class SortingLogbackDemo {

    private static final Logger log = LoggerFactory.getLogger
    (SortingLogbackDemo.class);

    public static void main(String... args) {
        if (args.length == 0) {
            log.error("No data to sort!");
            return;
```

```
        }
        int[] arr = getInts(args);

        if (log.isDebugEnabled()) {
            var sb = new StringBuilder("Sorting  an array with merge
            sort: ");
            Arrays.stream(arr).forEach(i -> sb.append(i).append(" "));
            log.debug(sb.toString());
        }

        IntSorter mergeSort = new MergeSort();
        mergeSort.sort(arr, 0, arr.length - 1);

        if (log.isInfoEnabled()) {
            var sb2 = new StringBuilder("Sorted: ");
            Arrays.stream(arr).forEach(i -> sb2.append(i).append(" "));
            log.info(sb2.toString());
        }
    }
}
```

In Listing 9-20, if the SLF4J configuration for the com.apress.bgn.nine package is set to info, the message starting with *Sorting an array with merge sort:* is no longer created, nor printed, because log.isDebugEnabled() returns false, so the code enclosed in the if statement is no longer executed. The Logger class contains if<Level>Enabled() methods for any logger level.

This concludes the discussion of logging within the scope of this book. Just keep in mind that you should use logging moderately, pay very close attention when you decide to log messages in loops, and for big application always use a logging facade; in Java, for 99% of projects this facade is SLF4J.

Debug Using Assertions

Another way to debug your code is to use assertions. As introduced in the **Chapter 4** section about Java keywords, the assert reserved keyword is used to write an assertion statement, which is just a test of your assumptions about the program execution. In the previous examples in this chapter, we had the user provide the input for our sorting program, so in order for our program to do the right thing, it is assumed that the user will provide the proper input, which means an array with size greater than 1, because there is no point to run the algorithm for a single number. So what does this assertion look like in the code? The answer is depicted in Listing 9-21.

Listing 9-21. Asserting the Size of User-Provided Array

```
package com.apress.bgn.nine;

import com.apress.bgn.algs.QuickSort;
import java.util.Arrays;
import static com.apress.bgn.nine.SortingLogbackDemo.getInts;
import static java.lang.System.out;

public class AssertionDemo {

    void main(String... args){
        int[] arr = getInts(args);

        assert arr.length > 1;

        var mergeSort = new QuickSort();
        mergeSort.sort(arr, 0, arr.length - 1);

        final StringBuilder sb2 = new StringBuilder("Sorted: ");
        Arrays.stream(arr).forEach(i -> sb2.append(i).append(" "));
        out.println(sb2);
    }
}
```

Running the code in Listing 9-21 without providing any arguments to the program is possible, even though we have an assertion statement in it. As expected, the code does nothing because there is no array to be sorted. The reason the code runs despite the assertion is that all assertions need to be enabled using a VM argument: -ea. To specify this argument, you can add it to the command when executing from the command line, but you also can use the editor by adding the argument in the VM options text box of the IntelliJ IDEA launcher, as depicted in Figure 9-6.

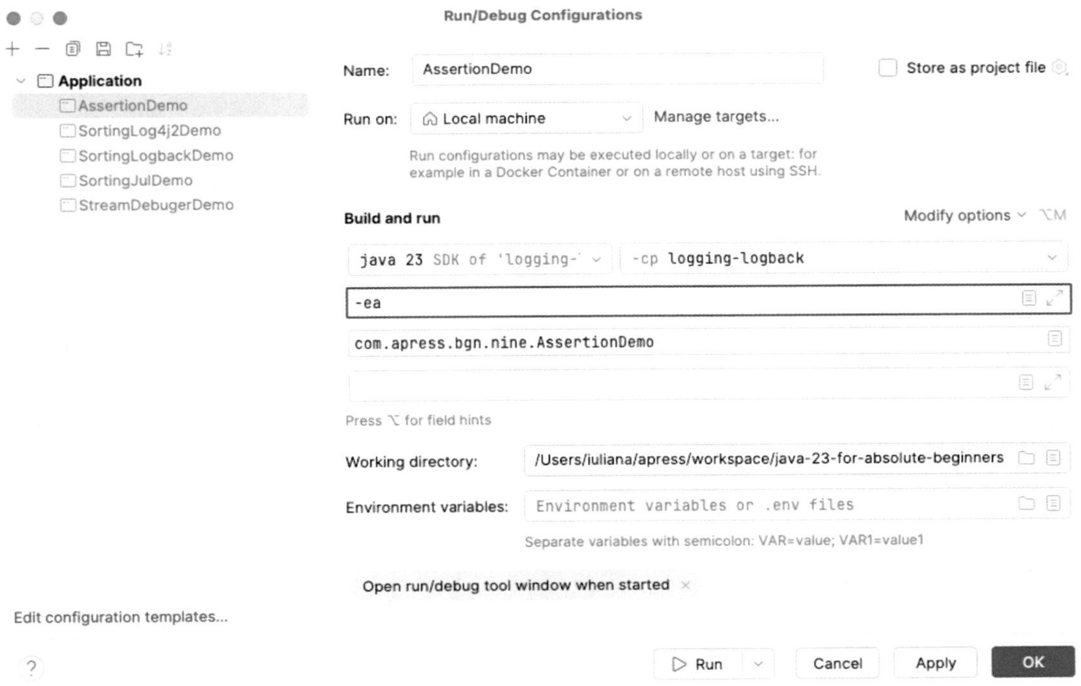

Figure 9-6. *IntelliJ IDEA launcher for the* `AssertionDemo` *class with the* `-ea` *VM argument set*

When assertions are enabled, running the code in Listing 9-21 ends with a `java.lang.AssertionError` being thrown because the expression of the assertions is evaluated to `false`, since obviously the value of `arr.length` is clearly not greater than 1 when no argument is provided.

Assertions have two forms, one simple and one more complex. The simple form of an expression has just the expression to evaluate, the assumption to test:

```
assertion [expression];
```

In this case, the `java.lang.AssertionError` being thrown just prints the line where the assumption is asserted for the current run of the program, together with the module and the full classname:

```
Exception in thread "main" java.lang.AssertionError
    at chapter.nine.logback@3.0-SNAPSHOT/com.apress.bgn.nine.AssertionDemo.
    main(AssertionDemo.java:46)
```

The more complex form of an assertion adds another expression to be evaluated or a value to be used in the stack to tell the user which assumption was wrong:

```
assertion [expression1] : [expression2];
```

So if we replace

```
assert arr.length > 1;
```

with

```
assert arr.length > 1 : "Not enough data to sort!";
```

when the `java.lang.AssertionError` is thrown, now it also depicts the *Not enough data to sort!* message, which makes it clear why the assertion statement is preventing the rest of the code from being executed:

Exception in thread "main" java.lang.AssertionError: Not enough data to sort!
*   at chapter.nine.logback@3.0-SNAPSHOT/com.apress.bgn.nine.AssertionDemo.main(AssertionDemo.java:46)*

Or we could just print the size of the array:

```
assert arr.length > 1 : arr.length;
```

Or both:

```
assert arr.length > 1 : "Not enough data to sort! Number of values: " +
arr.length;
```

Assertions can be used before and after the piece of code that needs to be debugged. In the previous case, the assertion was used as a precondition of the execution, because the failure of the assertion prevents code from being executed.

Assertions can also be used as post conditions, to test the outcome of executing a piece of code.

In the previous code snippet, the assertion was used to test the correctness of the user-provided input. In situations like this, the restriction of a valid input should be obeyed, whether assertions are enabled or not. Sure, if our array is empty or contains just a single element, this is not a problem, as the algorithm is not executed and this does not lead to a technical failure.

There are a few rules to obey, or things to look for, when writing code using assertions, and they are listed here:

- **Assertions should not be used to check the correctness of arguments provided to public methods**. Correctness of arguments should be tested in the code, and a proper RuntimeException should be thrown. Validating public methods' arguments should not be avoidable.

Caution   Unfortunately, to keep this introduction to assertions simple, the previous code samples showing how assertions work break this rule. After all, the presence of valid arguments for the main(..) method is checked using an assertion.

- **Assertions should not be used to do work that is required for your application to run properly**. The main reason for this is that assertions are disabled by default, and having them disabled leads to that code not being executed, so the rest of the application will actually not function properly because of the missing code. Assuming no arguments are provided to the main(..) method in the previous example, an assertion could be used to initialize the array being processed with a default value. But that doesn't mean you should! Code like the next line is bad, because disabling assertions removes the initialization of the array with a default value:

```
assert arr.length > 1 : arr = new int[]{1, 2, 3};
```

- **For performance reasons, do not use expressions that are expensive to evaluate in assertions.** Even if assertions are disabled by default, imagine that somebody enables them by mistake on a production application, which could be quite unfortunate if some of those assertions are expensive to evaluate. The next assertion breaks all three rules: initializes the array with a default value if none is supplied, but only after waiting five minutes.

```
Function<Long, int[]> sleepFiveMinsThenInit  =  aLong ->  {
    try {Thread.sleep(Duration.ofMinutes(aLong).toMillis()); }
catch (InterruptedException _) {}
    return new int[]{1, 2, 3};
};
assert arr.length > 1 : sleepFiveMinsThenInit.apply(5L);
```

- Assertions are a simple but powerful feature. They can be used to detect bugs early in the development life cycle, when they are easy to fix, and they simplify debugging and improve quality. Just make sure to stick to the preceding three rules if you use them.

Step-By-Step Debugging

If you do not want to write log messages or use assertions, but you still want to inspect values of variables during the execution of a program, there is a way to do that using an IDE, as mentioned in previous chapters: pause the execution using breakpoints and use the IDE to inspect variable contents or execute simple statements to check if your program is performing as expected.

A **breakpoint** is a mark set on an executable line of code (not a comment line or an empty line, and not a declaration) To set a breakpoint in IntelliJ IDEA, either click the gutter area on the line you are interested in or select the line and choose from the **Run** menu the option **Toggle Line Breakpoint**. When a breakpoint is in place, a red bubble appears on the line in the gutter section. Figure 9-7 shows a few breakpoints set in IntelliJ IDEA.

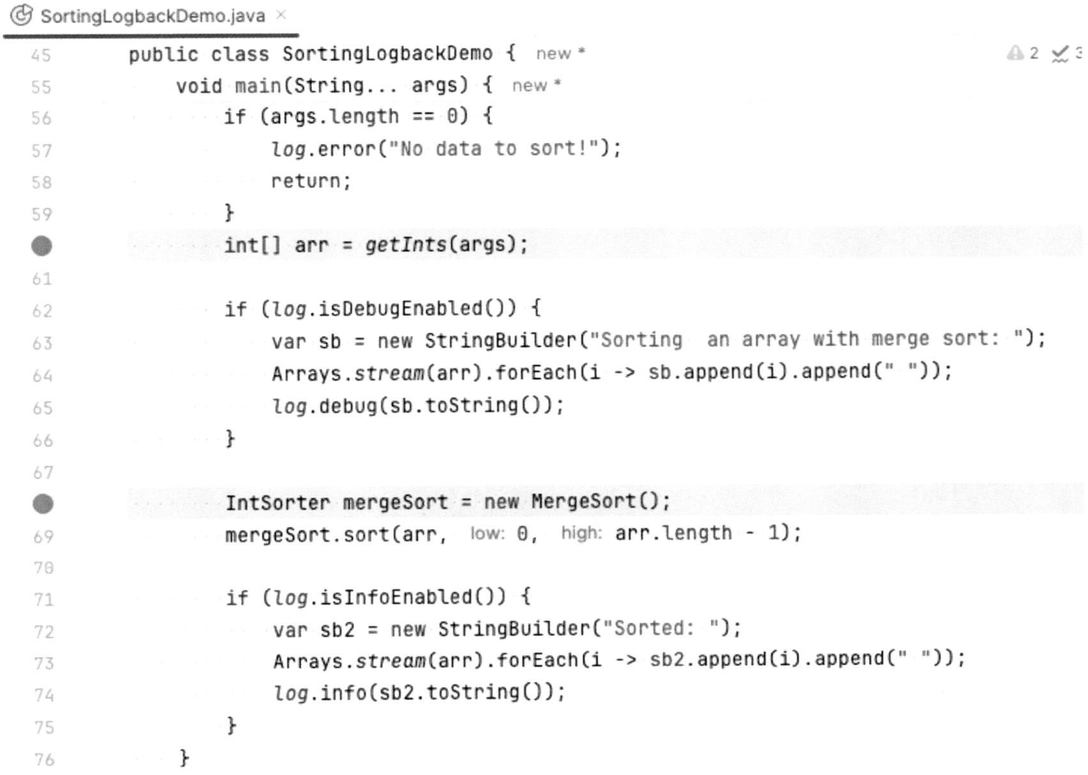

```
    SortingLogbackDemo.java ×

45      public class SortingLogbackDemo {  new *                                    ⚠ 2 ✓ 3
55          void main(String... args) {  new *
56              if (args.length == 0) {
57                  log.error("No data to sort!");
58                  return;
59              }
●               int[] arr = getInts(args);
61
62              if (log.isDebugEnabled()) {
63                  var sb = new StringBuilder("Sorting  an array with merge sort: ");
64                  Arrays.stream(arr).forEach(i -> sb.append(i).append(" "));
65                  log.debug(sb.toString());
66              }
67
●               IntSorter mergeSort = new MergeSort();
69              mergeSort.sort(arr,  low: 0,   high: arr.length - 1);
70
71              if (log.isInfoEnabled()) {
72                  var sb2 = new StringBuilder("Sorted: ");
73                  Arrays.stream(arr).forEach(i -> sb2.append(i).append(" "));
74                  log.info(sb2.toString());
75              }
76          }
```

Figure 9-7. *IntelliJ IDEA breakpoints*

Once the breakpoints are in place, when the application runs in debug mode, it will pause on each of the marked lines. During the pause, you can continue the execution step by step, inspect values of the variables, and even evaluate expressions in the context of the running application. IntelliJ IDEA is very helpful with this, as it shows you the contents of every variable in each line of the code currently being executed. In Figure 9-8 the SortingLogbackDemo class is running in debug mode and is paused during execution using breakpoints.

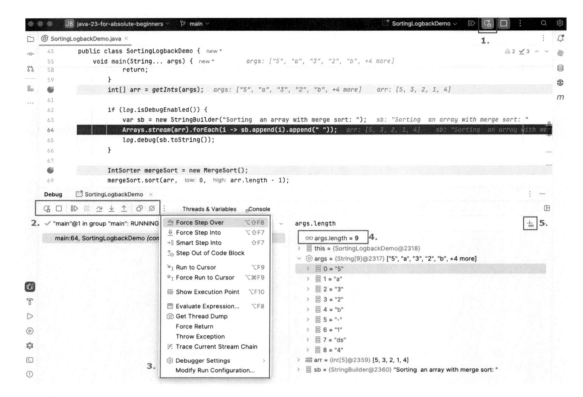

Figure 9-8. *IntelliJ IDEA* `SortingLogbackDemo` *class paused during execution*

To run an application in debug mode, instead of starting the launcher normally, start it by clicking the green bug-shaped button with a curved arrow (marked with a red **1.** in Figure 9-8) next to the green triangle-shaped button that is used to run the application normally.

The application runs and stops at the first line marked with a breakpoint, enabling the developer to inspect the values of the variables on that line, as shown in the upper half of Figure 9-8. From that point, the developer can also do the following in the **Debug** section at the bottom of Figure 9-8:

- Continue the execution until the next breakpoint by clicking the green triangle-shaped button (left toolbar, marked in Figure 9-8 with **2.**).

- Stop the execution by clicking the red square-shaped button (left toolbar).

- Disable all breakpoints by clicking the button with a red bubble cut diagonally (left toolbar).

- Continue execution to the next line of code by clicking the button with a thin black arrow with a 90-degree angle (left toolbar).

- Continue execution by entering the method in the current line of code by clicking the button with a thin black arrow oriented down with an underscore at its tip (left toolbar).

Important   The **Force Step Into** and **Step Out of Code Block** options in the **Debug** menu marked in Figure 9-8 with **3.** are used to step over and step into methods provided by third-party libraries. IntelliJ IDEA tries to find source code for those methods. If it can't find source code, then it might show you an auto-generated stub based on the bytecode/library. The thin black arrows in the section marked with **2.** Only allow debugging of the current project code.

- Continue execution by stepping out of the current method by choosing the **Step Out of Code Block** option from the drop-down menu marked in Figure 9-8 with **3.**

- Continue the execution to the line pointed at by the cursor by choosing the **Run to Cursor** option from the drop-down menu marked in Figure 9-8 with **3.**

- Evaluate your own expressions by adding them to the **Watches** section marked in Figure 9-8 with 4, by using the button marked with 5. The only condition is that the expressions only use variables that are accessible in the context of the breakpoint line. E.g. are part of the same method body, or class body and the accessor is not important, private fields can be inspected too.

Another way to evaluate expression in the context of the application currently running is to right-click the file where your execution is currently paused and, from the context menu that opens, select the option **Evaluate Expression**. A dialog window opens where you can write complex expressions and then click **Evaluate** to evaluate them on the spot, as depicted in Figure 9-9.

Figure 9-9. *IntelliJ IDEA expression evaluation during debugging session*

Most Java smart editors provide means to run a Java application in debug mode; just make sure to clean up your Watches (or equivalent) section from time to time. If the expressions added in the Watches section are expensive to evaluate, they might affect the performance of the application. Also, be aware of expressions that use streams, since these might make the application fail, as proven in **Chapter 8**.

Inspect a Running Application Using Java Tools

Aside from the executables to compile Java code and execute or package Java bytecode, the JDK provides a set of utility executables that can be used to debug and inspect the state of a running Java application. This section covers the most useful of them. Without further ado, let's do this!

jps

A running Java application has a unique process id entifier also referred to as *PID* or *process id*. This is how an operating system keeps track of all applications running in parallel at the same. You can see the process ids in utilities such as **Process Explorer** in Windows and **Activity Monitor** in macOS, but if you are comfortable enough working in the console, you might prefer using the **jps** (short for Java Virtual Machine Process Status Tool) executable provided by the JDK because it focuses only on Java processes.

When calling jps from the console, all Java process ids will be listed, together with the main class name or some details that are exposed by the API that will help you identify the application running. This is useful when an application crashes but the process remains in a hanging state. This can be painful when the application uses resources such as files or network ports, because it might block them and prevent you from using them. When executing jps on my computer (I have a Mac) these are the Java processes I see running:

```
> jps
73397 SortingLogbackDemo
72196 RemoteMavenServer40
73396 Launcher
73814 Jps
59103 Main
60935
```

As you can see, jps includes itself in the output, because it is also a Java process. The other processes are as follows (not in order of the output):

- Process 73397 is the execution of the SortingLogbackDemo class.

- Process 73396 is a launcher application that IntelliJ IDEA uses to start the execution of the SortingLogbackDemo class.

- Process 60935 does not have any description, but at this point I can identify the process myself, because I know I have IntelliJ IDEA opened, which is itself a Java application.

- Process 59103 is also IntelliJ IDEA, as you will see in the next section.

- Process 72196 is also IntelliJ IDEA, because I have it configured to build my sources using Maven.

The advantage of being able to know the process ids is that you can kill them when they end up hanging and blocking resources. Let's assume that the process started because the execution of SortingLogbackDemo ended up hanging. To kill a process, all operating systems provide a version of the kill command. For macOS and Linux you should execute the following:

```
kill -9 [process_id]
```

For this example, if I call kill -9 73397 and then call jps, I can see that the SortingLogbackDemo process is no longer listed:

```
> jps
72196 RemoteMavenServer40
73396 Launcher
60935
59103 Main
74029 Jps
```

Warning   The kill -9 command is not always suitable, especially if the process you are trying to kill uses resources that need to be safely released. Also, the command used as an example here works on Linux and macOS systems, not on Windows; on Windows, depending if you use Command Prompt or PowerShell, you might need to use taskkill or Stop-Process.

I still have the Launcher process, but that is a child process of IntelliJ IDEA, so there is no point in killing it, because the next time that I run a main class in the IDE, the process will be started again.

jps is quite a simple tool and is particularly useful when you have doubts about a Java application being alive or not on a remote machine that you can access only via a terminal. So it's good to know it exists.

jcmd

The **jcmd** executable is another JDK utility that can be useful. You can use it to send diagnostic command requests to the JVM that can help to troubleshoot and diagnose the JVM and running Java applications. It must be used on the same machine where the

JVM is running, and the result of calling it without any arguments is that it shows all Java processes currently running on the machine, including itself. Beside the process ids, jcmd also displays the command used to start their execution:

```
> jcmd
74152 chapter.nine.logback/com.apress.bgn.nine.SortingLogbackDemo 5 a 3 2
b - 1 ds 4
74158 jdk.jcmd/sun.tools.jcmd.JCmd
59103 com.intellij.idea.Main
72196 com.intellij.maven.server.m40.RemoteMavenServer40
74151 org.jetbrains.jps.cmdline.Launcher ... # rest of the details omitted
```

When jcmd is run with a Java process id and the text help as an argument, it displays all additional commands you can use on that process. This will work if the application is currently running and not paused using a breakpoint. The SortingLogbackDemo class is currently paused when I am writing this since its execution lasts too little time for the jcmd to be used. Another Java process, created for running the BigSortingSlf4jDemo class that sorts an array of 100,000,000 randomly generated numbers, is used as an example to produce the output depicted in Listing 9-22.

Listing 9-22. The Output of jcmd [pid] help on a Java Process Doing Some Serious Work

```
> jcmd 74152 help
74152:
The following commands are available:
Compiler.CodeHeap_Analytics
Compiler.codecache
Compiler.codelist
# other Compiler.* options omitted
GC.class_histogram
GC.finalizer_info
GC.heap_dump
GC.heap_info
GC.run
GC.run_finalization
JFR.check
```

```
JFR.configure
# other JFR.* options omitted
JVMTI.agent_load
JVMTI.data_dump
ManagementAgent.start
ManagementAgent.start_local
ManagementAgent.status
ManagementAgent.stop
Thread.dump_to_file
Thread.print
VM.cds
VM.class_hierarchy
# other VM.* options omitted
help
```

It is not the objective of this book to cover all the command options, as they are quite advanced features of Java, but you should have a basic idea of the scope of each command. As an example, Listing 9-23 shows the output of calling jcmd 51301 GC.heap_info.

Listing 9-23. The Output of jcmd [pid] GC.heap_info on a Java Process Doing Some Serious Work

```
> jcmd 74828 GC.heap_info
74828:
 garbage-first heap   total reserved 8388608K, committed 1368064K, used
460069K [0x0000000600000000, 0x0000000800000000)
  region size 4096K, 2 young (8192K), 1 survivors (4096K)
 Metaspace       used 6551K, committed 6848K, reserved 1114112K
  class space    used 887K, committed 1024K, reserved 1048576K
```

Recall from **Chapter 5** the different types of memory used by the JVM, and that **heap** is the memory where all the objects used by an application are stored. This command prints the heap details, including how much of it is used, how much is reserved, the region size, and so on. All these details will be covered in more detail in **Chapter 13**.

jconsole

jconsole is a JDK utility that can be used to inspect various JVM statistics in its very basic GUI. To use jconsole, you just have to start it from the command line and connect it to a Java application that is already running. This application is quite useful, as it can monitor both local and remote JVMs. It can also monitor and manage an application. The application must expose a port for jconsole to connect to.

To start a Java application and expose a port for an external application, simply start the application with the following VM parameters:

```
-agentlib:jdwp=transport=dt_socket,server=y,suspend=y,address=1044
```

The transport=dt_socket parameter instructs the JVM that the debugger connections will be made through a socket. The address=1044 parameter informs the JVM that the port number will be 1044. The port number can be any port higher than 1024, because those are restricted by the operating system. The suspend=y parameter instructs the JVM to suspend execution until a debugger such as jconsole is connected to it. To avoid that, suspend=n should be used.

For our simple example and considering that we will use jconsole to debug a Java application on the same machine, we do not need all those parameters. We just need to start jconsole from the command line and look in the *Local Processes* section and identify the Java process we are interested in debugging.

In Figure 9-10 you can see the first jconsole dialog window.

Figure 9-10. *jconsole first dialog window*

When the process is running locally, it can be easily identified because it will be named using the module and the fully qualified main class name. For an application as simple as ours, we need to make a few tweaks to make sure that we can actually see a few statistics with jconsole during the run of the application. A few Thread.sleep(..) statements were added to pause the execution enough for jconsole to connect. Also, we'll use quite a big array of data to make sure the statistics are relevant. The BigSortingSlf4jDemo class is depicted in Listing 9-24.

Listing 9-24. The Contents of the BigSortingDemo Class

```java
package com.apress.bgn.nine;
// import statements omitted

public class BigSortingDemo {
    private static final Logger log = LoggerFactory.
    getLogger(BigSortingDemo.class);
    static RandomGenerator randomGenerator = RandomGenerator.
    of("SecureRandom");

    void main() throws InterruptedException {
        Thread.sleep(3000);

        // We are using this stream of ints to generate a huge array and a
        // huge log file. Be patient, the execution will take a while.
        var intStream = IntStream.generate(() -> randomGenerator.
        nextInt(350) + 1).limit(100_000_000);

        int[] arr =  intStream.toArray();

        if (log.isDebugEnabled()) {
            final StringBuilder sb = new StringBuilder("Sorting  an array
            with merge sort: ");
            Arrays.stream(arr).forEach(i -> sb.append(i).append(" "));
            log.debug(sb.toString());
        }
        Thread.sleep(3000);

        var mergeSort = new MergeSort();
        mergeSort.sort(arr, 0, arr.length - 1);

        if (log.isInfoEnabled()) {
            final StringBuilder sb2 = new StringBuilder("Sorted: ");
            Arrays.stream(arr).forEach(i -> sb2.append(i).append(" "));
            log.info(sb2.toString());
        }
    }
}
```

With this modification, the class can be executed normally and connect jconsole to it. After a successful connection, a window like the one shown in Figure 9-11 opens, displaying graphs of the JVM memory consumption, number of live threads, number of classes loaded, and CPU usage.

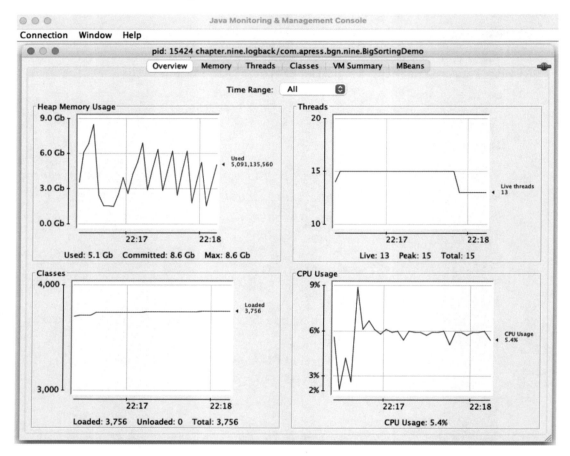

Figure 9-11. jconsole *statistics window*

There is a tab for each of these statistics that provides more information, and in the case of a more complex application, this information can be used to improve performance, identify potential problems, and even estimate application behavior for desired cases. For our small application, the jconsole graphs do not reveal much, but if you really want to see valuable statistics, use jconsole to monitor IntelliJ IDEA during development or while running some code.

Information   The more advanced version of `jconsole` is called VisualVM. It used to be part of the JDK, but it was removed in Java 8, after which it became an independent project. When this chapter is being written, there is no version available for Java 23, so it won't be covered in this book, but feel free to give it a try.[7]

Using JDK Mission Control

JDK Mission Control (JMC) is an advanced Oracle application for debugging and analyzing JVM statistics for a running application. Its official description states *JDK Mission Control (JMC)[8] is an advanced set of tools for managing, monitoring, profiling, and troubleshooting Java applications.*

Similar to the previous tools discussed, this utility identifies the Java processes currently running and provides the option to check out how much memory they require at specific times during execution, how many threads are running in parallel at a given moment in time, the classes loaded by the JVM, and how much CPU processing power is required to run a Java application. JMC has a friendlier interface than JConsole and one of its most important components is the Java Flight Recorder (JFR) that can be used to record all JVM activity while the application is running. All data collected during a custom time of the execution is useful to diagnose and profile the application.

Although JMC is one of the Oracle tools, it is no longer shipped as part of the JDK, so you have to download it from the JMC official page and install the version suitable for your operating system.

To inspect the application while it is running, we open JMC and then select the process that we recognize as the one running the `BigSortingDemo` main class based on the same rule as before. We look for a process name containing the module name and the fully classified class name, right-click it, and select **Start JMX Console**. You should see something similar to the image depicted in Figure 9-12.

---

[7] https://visualvm.github.io
[8] https://docs.oracle.com/en/java/java-components/jdk-mission-control

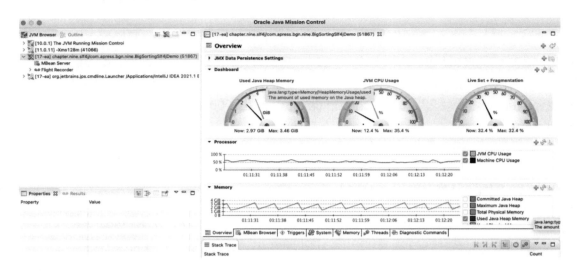

Figure 9-12. *JMC JMX Console*

As you probably noticed, the interface is definitely more friendly, and the provided statistics are definitely more detailed. Using JMC, everything that happens with the application and JVM during a run can be recorded and analyzed later, even if the application has stopped running since. The **Memory** tab provides a lot of information regarding the memory used by the application, including what types of objects are occupying it.

Recording detailed information about a Java process requires it to be started with -XX:+UnlockCommercialFeatures -XX:+FlightRecorder. OpenJDK and early access JDKs do not have commercial features or Flight Recorder. These are part of the Oracle JDK, designed to be used only commercially and require a paid subscription.

The JMC subject is too advanced and wide for this chapter (probably an entire book could be written about its usage and how to interpret the statistics), so we'll stop here. If you have an Oracle JDK subscription and want to learn more about using JMC, Oracle provides very good resources for that.

Accessing the Java Process API

Java 9 came with a lot of other improvements besides the Jigsaw modules (introduced in **Chapter 3**), one of which was a new and improved Java Process API, which allows you to start native operating system processes, retrieve information about them, and manage them. The ability to manipulate processes existed in previous versions of Java, but it was quite rudimentary. Listing 9-25 shows how a process was created before Java 5.

Listing 9-25. Creating a Process Using Pre-Java 5 API

```
package com.apress.bgn.nine;
// import section omitted

public class ProcessCreationDemo {
    private static final Logger log =
            LoggerFactory.getLogger(ProcessCreationDemo.class);

    public static void main(String[] args){
        try {
            Process exec = Runtime.getRuntime()
                    .exec(new String[] { "/bin/sh", "-c", "echo Java home:
                    $JAVA_HOME" });
            exec.waitFor();
            InputStream is = exec.getInputStream();
            StringBuilder textBuilder = new StringBuilder();
            try (Reader reader = new BufferedReader(new
            InputStreamReader(is, StandardCharsets.UTF_8))) {
                int c = 0;
                while ((c = reader.read()) != -1) {
                    textBuilder.append((char) c);
                }
            }
            log.info("Process output -> {}", textBuilder.toString());
            log.info("Process result: {}", exec.exitValue());
        } catch (Exception e) {
            log.error("Process execution failed: {}", e.getMessage(), e);
        }
    }
}
// output
// INFO  c.a.b.n.ProcessCreationDemo - Process output -> Java home: /Users/
iuliana/.sdkman/candidates/java/current
// INFO  c.a.b.n.ProcessCreationDemo - Process result: 0
```

Intercepting output of the started process was a pain, and a `BufferedReader` instance had to be wrapped around the `InputStream` instance connected to the normal output of the process. In Java 5, a class named `ProcessBuilder` was introduced in the `java.lang` package to create operating system processes using an improved API, however considerable improvements of the Java Process API landed only with the release of Java 9.

The Java 9 Process API made things a little more practical. It has at its core a few classes and interfaces, all having names that start with `Process`. What we've done so far with Java executables can be directly done by writing Java code. The interface that provides an API to access native processes is named `ProcessHandle` and is part of the core Java `java.lang` package. Similar to the `Thread` class, there is a static method named `current` to call on this interface to retrieve the `ProcessHandle` instance of the current running process. Once we have this, we can use its methods to access more process details. The `ProcessHandle` provides several static utility methods to access native processes. Java code can be written to list all processes running on a computer, and they can be sorted based on various criteria. The code in Listing 9-26 lists all processes that were created by running the `java` command.

Listing 9-26. Listing All java Processes Using Java 9 Process API

```
package com.apress.bgn.nine;
// import section omitted

public class ProcessListingDemo {
    private static final Logger log = LoggerFactory.
    getLogger(ProcessListingDemo.class);

    public static void main(String[] args){
        Optional<String> currUser = ProcessHandle.current().info().user();

        ProcessHandle.allProcesses().filter(ph -> ph.info().user().
        equals(currUser) && ph.info().commandLine().isPresent())
                .filter(ph -> ph.info().commandLine().get().
                contains("java"))
                .forEach(p -> {
```

```
                    log.info("PID: " + p.pid());
                    p.info().arguments().ifPresent(s -> Arrays.stream(s).
                    forEach(a -> log.info("   arg: {}", a)));
                    p.info().command().ifPresent(c -> log.info("\t Command:
                    {}", c));
                });
    }
}
```

The code in Listing 9-26 extracts the user from the current running process by obtaining its handle and calling info() to obtain an instance of ProcessHandle. Info, an interface that declares a set of methods that are implemented by the ProcessHandleImpl.Info class to access snapshot information about the process as the command and arguments that were used to create the process. The output of running the code in Listing 9-26 is printed in the console and might look pretty similar to the output listed in Listing 9-27 (except, you know, different user, different processes).

Listing 9-27. Partial Output Produced by Running the Code in Listing 9-26

INFO c.a.b.n.ProcessListingDemo - PID: 30750

```
INFO  c.a.b.n.ProcessListingDemo -    arg: -classpath
INFO  c.a.b.n.ProcessListingDemo -    arg: /Users/iuliana/apress/
workspace/java-23-for-absolute-beginners/chapter09/process-api/target/
classes:...*.jar
INFO  c.a.b.n.ProcessListingDemo -    arg: com.apress.bgn.nine.
ProcessListingDemo # TODO underline
INFO  c.a.b.n.ProcessListingDemo -    Command: /Users/iuliana/.sdkman/
candidates/java/current/bin/java

INFO  c.a.b.n.ProcessListingDemo - PID: 30733
INFO  c.a.b.n.ProcessListingDemo -    arg: -Xmx700m
INFO  c.a.b.n.ProcessListingDemo -    arg: -Djava.awt.headless=true
INFO  c.a.b.n.ProcessListingDemo -    arg: -Djna.boot.library.path=/Users/
iuliana/Applications/IntelliJ IDEA Ultimate 2024.2 EAP.app/Contents/lib/
jna/amd64
INFO  c.a.b.n.ProcessListingDemo -    arg: -Djna.nosys=true
INFO  c.a.b.n.ProcessListingDemo -    arg: -Djna.noclasspath=true
```

```
INFO  c.a.b.n.ProcessListingDemo -      arg: --add-opens
INFO  c.a.b.n.ProcessListingDemo -      arg: jdk.compiler/com.sun.tools.
javac.api=ALL-UNNAMED
INFO  c.a.b.n.ProcessListingDemo -      arg: --add-opens
INFO  c.a.b.n.ProcessListingDemo -      arg: jdk.compiler/com.sun.tools.
javac.util=ALL-UNNAMED
...
INFO  c.a.b.n.ProcessListingDemo -      arg: org.jetbrains.jps.cmdline.
Launcher
INFO  c.a.b.n.ProcessListingDemo -      arg: /Users/iuliana/Applications/
IntelliJ IDEA Ultimate 2024.2 EAP.app/.../*.jar
INFO  c.a.b.n.ProcessListingDemo -      arg: org.jetbrains.jps.cmdline.
BuildMain
INFO  c.a.b.n.ProcessListingDemo -      arg: 127.0.0.1
INFO  c.a.b.n.ProcessListingDemo -      arg: 59887
INFO  c.a.b.n.ProcessListingDemo -      arg: 07840096-15db-47c9-8f08-9640af
37397b
INFO  c.a.b.n.ProcessListingDemo -      arg: /Users/iuliana/Library/Caches/
JetBrains/IntelliJIdea2024.2/compile-server
INFO  c.a.b.n.ProcessListingDemo -      Command: /Users/iuliana/.sdkman/
candidates/java/current/bin/java
# other output omitted
```

> **Note**   The log in Listing 9-27 lists only the IntelliJ IDEA launcher used to run the
> `ProcessListingDemo` class and the process spawned to run it, but the output
> could be much longer. Some arguments were skipped all together, as it is quite
> useless to waste pages of the book with logs that you can produce yourself.
> Nevertheless, some depiction of the log format was necessary in you choose not to
> run the code yourself.

The code sample in Listing 9-26 showed you roughly how to access native processes
and print information about them. Using the improved Java Process API, we can create
new processes and start commands of the underlying operating system. For example,
we can create a process that prints the value of the JAVA_HOME environment variable, and

capture the output to display it in the IntelliJ IDEA console, as depicted in
Listing 9-28. (This code works on macOS and Linux; for Windows the equivalent
PowerShell command should be used.)

Listing 9-28. Java Sample Code to Create a Process

```
package com.apress.bgn.nine;
// other import statements omitted
import java.util.concurrent.CompletableFuture;
import java.util.concurrent.ExecutionException;

public class NewApiProcessCreationDemo {
    private static final Logger log = LoggerFactory.getLogger(NewApiProcess
    CreationDemo.class);

    public static void main(String... args) throws IOException,
    InterruptedException, ExecutionException {
        ProcessBuilder processBuilder = new ProcessBuilder();
        processBuilder.command("/bin/sh", "-c", "echo Java home:
        $JAVA_HOME");
        processBuilder.inheritIO();

        Process process = processBuilder.start();
        CompletableFuture<Process> future = process.onExit();
        int result = future.get().exitValue();
        log.info("Process result: " + result);

        CompletableFuture<ProcessHandle> futureHandle = process.toHandle().
        onExit();
        ProcessHandle processHandle = futureHandle.get();
        log.info("Process ID: {}", processHandle.pid());
        ProcessHandle.Info info = processHandle.info();
        info.arguments().ifPresent(s -> Arrays.stream(s).forEach(a ->
        log.info("   arg: {}", a)));
        info.command().ifPresent(c -> log.info("\t Command: {}", c));
    }
}
```

New processes can be created by using instances of ProcessBuilder, which receive as arguments a list of commands and arguments for them. The class has many constructors and methods with different signatures that can be used to create and start processes easily.

The inheritIO() method is used to set the source and destination for the subprocess standard I/O to be the same as the current process. This means the process output is printed directly in the console, without the need of reading it using an InputStream instance.

The onExit() method in the Process class returns a CompletableFuture<Process> that can be used to access the process at the end of its execution to retrieve the exit value of the process. For a process terminating normally, the value should be 0 (zero).

The onExit() method in the ProcessHandle class returns a CompletableFuture<P rocessHandle> that can be used to access the process, can be used to wait for process termination, and possibly trigger dependent actions.

When a Java program creates a process, that process becomes a child of the process that created it. To be able to list all children processes, we need to make sure they last a while, because once terminated they obviously no longer exist. The code sample in Listing 9-29 creates three identical processes, each of them executing three Linux shell commands.

Listing 9-29. Java Sample Code to Create Three Processes

```
package com.apress.bgn.nine;
//import statements omitted

public class ThreeProcessesDemo {
    private static final Logger log =
            LoggerFactory.getLogger(ThreeProcessesDemo.class);

    public static void main(String... args) {
        try {
            List<ProcessBuilder> builders = List.of(
                    new ProcessBuilder("/bin/sh", "-c",
                            "echo \"start...\" ; sleep 3; echo \"done.\"").
                            inheritIO(),
                    new ProcessBuilder("/bin/sh", "-c",
```

```
                    "echo \"start...\" ; sleep 3; echo \"done.\"").
                    inheritIO(),
            new ProcessBuilder("/bin/sh", "-c",
                    "echo \"start...\" ; sleep 3; echo \"done.\"").
                    inheritIO()
        );
        builders.parallelStream().forEach(pbs -> {
            try {
                pbs.start();
            } catch (Exception e) {
                log.error("Oops, could not start process!", e);
            }
        });
        ProcessHandle ph = ProcessHandle.current();
        ph.children().forEach(pc -> {
            log.info("Child PID: {}", pc.pid());
            pc.parent().ifPresent(parent ->
                    log.info(" Parent PID: {}", parent.pid()));
        });
        System.out.println("Press any key to exit!");
        System.in.read();
    } catch (Exception e) {
        log.error("Failed to create three processes: {}",
        e.getMessage(), e);
    }
  }
}
```

As you can see, we have grouped the ProcessBuilder instances in a list and processed the instances using a parallel stream to make sure that all processes were started almost at the same time. We printed the results of each of them after termination, to make sure all were executed correctly. The children() method returns a stream containing ProcessHandle instances corresponding to the processes started by the current Java process.

The parent() method was called for each child ProcessHandle instance to obtain the ProcessHandle corresponding to the process that created it, if there is one. When running the code in Listing 9-29, you should see in the console an output similar to what is depicted in the Listing 9-30. (*If you run it on macOS or Linux, that is. Windows will probably have no idea what it is being asked to do.*)

Listing 9-30. Output of a Java Application That Creates Three Processes

```
start...
start...
start...
INFO  c.a.b.n.ThreeProcessesDemo - Child PID: 31033
INFO  c.a.b.n.ThreeProcessesDemo -  Parent PID: 31032
INFO  c.a.b.n.ThreeProcessesDemo - Child PID: 31035
INFO  c.a.b.n.ThreeProcessesDemo -  Parent PID: 31032
INFO  c.a.b.n.ThreeProcessesDemo - Child PID: 31034
INFO  c.a.b.n.ThreeProcessesDemo -  Parent PID: 31032
Press any key to exit!
done.
done.
done.
```

In the past, developers who needed to work with processes on a more advanced level needed to resort to native code. The improved Java Process API provides a lot more control over running and spawned processes, so if you ever need it, now you know it exists. You can find a full list of the Java Process API improvements added in Java 9 on the official Oracle page.[9]

Testing

Debugging is a part of a software process named **testing** and involves identifying and correcting code errors as early as possible in the development cycle. In software development, avoiding technical errors is not enough. Testing an application means much more than that. There is even an organization that provides great materials for training and certifications for software testers. The **International Software Testing Qualifications Board (ISTQB)** is a software testing qualification certification organization that operates internationally. It established a syllabus and a hierarchy of

---

[9] https://docs.oracle.com/javase/9/core/process-api1.htm

qualifications and guidelines for software testing[10]. If you think you are more interested in software testing, then you should look into getting an ISTQB certification.

The ISTQB definition of testing is "the process consisting of all lifecycle activities, both static and dynamic, concerned with planning, preparation and evaluation of software and related work products to determine that they satisfy specified requirements to demonstrate that they are fit for purpose and to detect defects."

The ISTQB definition is a technical, academic definition. The definition I propose is "the process of verifying that an implementation does what it is supposed to, in the amount of time it is expected to, with an acceptable resources consumption."

Important   Testing is an essential part of the development process and should start as early as possible, because the effort of fixing a defect grows exponentially with the time it takes to be discovered. You can read more about the disadvantages of testing late in Robert Martin's book *Clean Code: A Handbook of Agile Software Craftsmanship*, specifically in Chapter 9, "Testing."

During the development phase, aside from writing the actual solution, you can also write code to test your solution. You can run those tests either manually or by using a build tool when you build your project. When writing your code, in addition to thinking about how you can write it so that the solution solves the problem, you should think about how to test the solution. This approach is named **Test Driven Development (TDD)**, a programming paradigm that states that you should think about how to test your solution before implementing it, because if it is difficult to test, it probably will be difficult to implement, maintain in the long run, and extend to solve related problems.

The simplest tests you can write are called **unit tests**, which are very simple methods that test small units of functionality. If you can't easily write unit tests for your design, it might be rotten. Unit tests are the first line of defense against failures. If unit tests fail, the foundation of your solution is bad.

The tests that span across multiple components, testing the communication between units of functionality and the results of their interactions against expected results, are called **integration tests**.

The last type of tests a developer should write are **regression tests**, which are run periodically to make sure that code that was previously tested still performs correctly

---

[10] https://www.istqb.org/about-us/why-istqb

after it was changed. This type of test is crucial for big projects where code is written by a considerable number of developers, because sometimes dependencies among components are not obvious and code that one developer wrote might break somebody else's code.

To stay within the scope of this book, this section will show you how to write only the simple unit tests, using a Java framework named Junit, and describe a few typical testing components you can build to set up a context for the unit tests. Thus, as my Scottish colleagues say: *Let's get cracking!*

Test Code Location

As you probably remember, **Chapter 3** explained the java-bgn project structure. The discussion about tests must start with the structure of the lowest-level project's modules, the ones that contain the source code and tests. In Figure 9-13 you can see the structure of the module containing the sources and test code for the module used in this section.

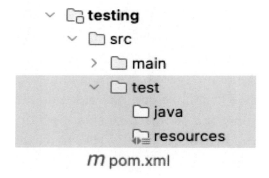

Figure 9-13. *The Maven module structure*

The src directory contains all code and resources of the project. The contents are split into two directories, main and test.

- The main directory contains the source code and the application configuration files, split into two directories (not displayed in Figure 9-13). The java directory contains the Java source code, and the resources directory contains configuration files, nonexecutable text files (which can be written according to various formats, such as XML, SQL, CSV, etc.), media files, PDFs, and so forth. When the application is built and packed into a jar (or war or ear), only the files in the `java` directory are taken onto account; the `*.class` files together with the configuration files are packed.

- The `test` directory contains code used to test the source code in the `src` directory. The Java files are kept under the `java` directory, and the `resources` directory contains configuration files needed to build a test context. The classes in the `test` directory are part of the project and have access to the classes declared in the `main` directory as described by accessors in **Chapter 3**. However, the contents of the `test` directory are not part of the project that will be delivered to a client. They exist just to help test the application during development. The files in the `test/resources` directory usually override configuration files in the `main/resources` directory to provide an isolated, smaller execution context for the test classes.

Building an Application to Test

For the examples in this section, we will build a simple application that uses an embedded Apache Derby[11] database to store data. This will be the production database. For the test environment, the database will be replaced with various pseudo-constructions that will mimic the database behavior.

The application is quite rudimentary. An `AccountService` implementation takes data from the input and uses it to manage `Account` instances. The `Account` class is a very abstract and unrealistic implementation of a banking account. It has a `holder` field, which is the account owner, an `accountNumber` field, and an `amount` field. The `AccountService` implementation uses an `AccountRepo` implementation to perform all related database operations with `Account` instances using an implementation of `DBConnection`. The classes and interfaces that make up this simple application and the relationships between them are depicted in Figure 9-14.

---

[11] `https://db.apache.org/derby`

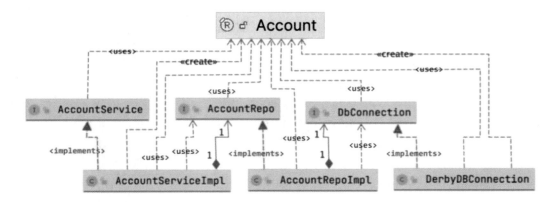

Figure 9-14. *Simple account management application components (as shown in IntelliJ IDEA)*

The implementation of these classes is not relevant for this section, but if you are curious, you can find the full code in the official repository of this book. So let's start testing. The easiest way would be to write a main class and perform some account operations. However, it is useless to do that once the application is in production, since testing new features on it comes with risks of data corruption. Also, production databases are usually hosted on costly products, such as Oracle RDBMS (Oracle Relational Database Management System) or Microsoft SQL Server. They are not really appropriate for development, or testing. The intention is to run tests automatically during an automated build, so in-memory databases or implementations that can be instantiated are more suitable. So let's start by testing the AccountRepoImpl class.

Introducing JUnit

JUnit is undoubtedly the most-used testing framework in the Java development world. At the end of 2017, JUnit 5[12] was released, which is the next generation of this framework. It comes with a new engine, is compatible with Java 9+, and includes a lot of lambda-based functionalities. JUnit 5 provides annotations to mark test methods for automated execution, annotations for initialization and destruction of a test context, and utility methods to practically implement test methods. There are multiple JUnit 5 annotations that you can use[13], but five of them and a utility class represent the core of the JUnit

---

[12] https://junit.org/junit5
[13] https://junit.org/junit5/docs/current/user-guide/#writing-tests-annotations

framework, and this is the best place to start to learn testing. The following list describes each of the five Junit 5 annotations (all of which are from package `org.junit.jupiter.api`) and the utility class, to build a general picture of how JUnit can be used to test your application:

- `@BeforeAll` is used on a nonprivate static method that returns `void` which is used to initialize objects and variables to be used by all test methods in the current class. This method will be called only once, before all test methods in the class, so test methods should not modify these objects because their state is shared, and modification might affect the test results. Eventually, the static fields to be initialized by the annotated method can be declared `final`, so once initialized, they can no longer be changed. More than one method annotated with `@BeforeAll` can be declared in a test class, but what would be the point?

- `@AfterAll` is the counterpart of `@BeforeAll`. It is also used to annotate nonprivate static methods that return `void`, and their purpose is to destroy the context the test methods were run in and perform cleanup actions.

- `@BeforeEach` is used on nonprivate, nonstatic methods that return `void`, and methods annotated with it are executed before every method annotated with `@Test`. These methods can be used to further customize the test context, to populate objects with values that will be used to test assertions in the test methods.

- `@AfterEach` is used on nonprivate, nonstatic methods that return `void`, and methods annotated with it are executed after every method annotated with `@Test`.

- `@Test` is used on nonprivate, nonstatic methods that return `void`, and the method annotated with it is a test method. A test class can have one or more test methods, depending on the class that is being tested.

- Utility class `org.junit.jupiter.api.Assertions` provides a set of methods that support asserting conditions in tests.

Another noteworthy annotation is @DisplayName, which is declared in the same package as all the others and is used to name the test in a more pleasant way. The test name is displayed by the IDE and in the resulting reports created by the build tool.

The PseudoTest class, shown in Listing 9-31, is a simple test class that shows the effect of the annotations introduced so far.

Listing 9-31. PseudoTest Class Using JUnit Annotations

```java
package com.apress.bgn.nine;

// some import statements omitted
import org.junit.jupiter.api.*;
import static org.junit.jupiter.api.Assertions.assertFalse;
import static org.junit.jupiter.api.Assertions.assertTrue;

public class PseudoTest {
    private static final Logger log = LoggerFactory.
    getLogger(PseudoTest.class);

    @BeforeAll
    static void loadCtx() {
        log.info("Loading general test context.");
    }

    @BeforeEach
    void setUp(){
        log.info("Prepare  single test context.");
    }

    @Test
    @DisplayName("test one")
    void testOne() {
        log.info("Executing test one.");
        assertTrue(true);
    }

    @Test
    @DisplayName("test two")
    void testTwo() {
```

```
        log.info("Executing test two.");
        assertFalse(false);
    }

    @AfterEach
    void tearDown(){
        log.info("Destroy  single test context.");
    }

    @AfterAll
    static void unloadCtx(){
        log.info("UnLoading general test context.");
    }
}
```

Keeping in mind the information that you now have about these annotations, you should be able to infer the order of the log messages, because by default, JUnit Jupiter tests are run sequentially in a single thread. So when running the class, you could see output something like this:

```
INFO  c.a.b.n.PseudoTest - Loading general test context.
INFO  c.a.b.n.PseudoTest - Prepare  single test context.
INFO  c.a.b.n.PseudoTest - Executing test one.
INFO  c.a.b.n.PseudoTest - Destroy  single test context.
INFO  c.a.b.n.PseudoTest - Prepare  single test context.
INFO  c.a.b.n.PseudoTest - Executing test two.
INFO  c.a.b.n.PseudoTest - Destroy  single test context.
INFO  c.a.b.n.PseudoTest - UnLoading general test context.
```

Enabling parallel execution of tests is possible by adding a file named junit-platform.properties under test\resources that contains the following properties:

```
junit.jupiter.execution.parallel.enabled = true
junit.jupiter.execution.parallel.mode.default = concurrent
junit.jupiter.execution.parallel.mode.classes.default = same_thread
```

Notice the junit.jupiter.execution.parallel.enabled property is set to true. The previous set of properties represents the configuration parameters to execute top-level classes sequentially but their methods in parallel. More configuration examples are provided in the official JUnit documentation.

Note   Parallel execution might lead to test failures if your test suite was designed with an order for the test methods executions in mind.

Maven runs all tests in a project as part of the build when executing mvn test, and there are options to run test classes separately. Most Java smart editors like IntelliJ IDEA provide you with an option to run tests too; you can run entire classes, run just one method, run a specific package, or even run in debug mode and use breakpoints. Figure 9-15 shows the menu option to run a test class in IntelliJ IDEA, accessed by right-clicking the PseudoTest class to open the context menu.

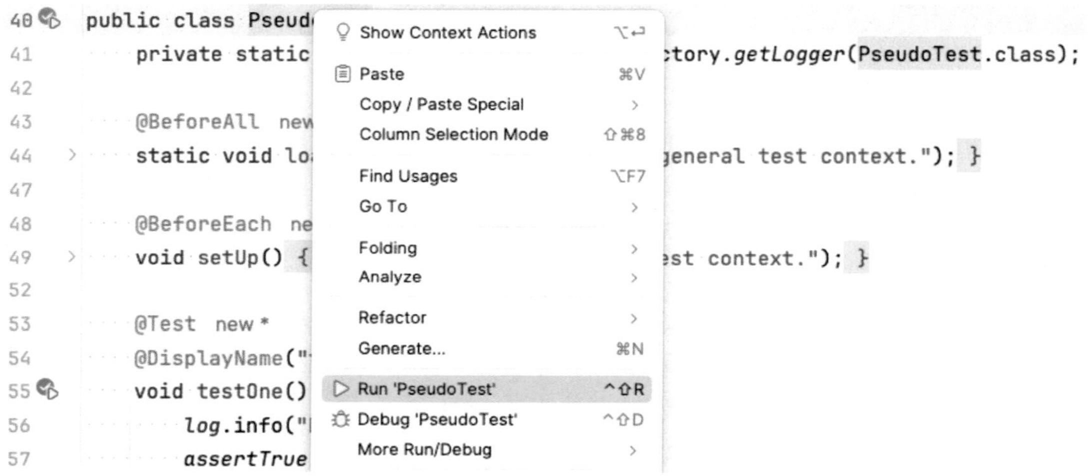

```
40 ⬡  public class Pseud┌─────────────────────────────────────────┐
41       private static │ 💡 Show Context Actions        ⌥↵ │story.getLogger(PseudoTest.class);
42                      │ 📋 Paste                      ⌘V │
43       @BeforeAll  new│    Copy / Paste Special        > │
44  >    static void lo │    Column Selection Mode     ⇧⌘8 │general test context."); }
47                      │    Find Usages                ⌥F7 │
48       @BeforeEach  ne│    Go To                       > │
49  >    void setUp() { │    Folding                     > │st context."); }
52                      │    Analyze                     > │
53       @Test  new *   │    Refactor                    > │
54       @DisplayName(" │    Generate...                ⌘N │
55 ⬡     void testOne() │ ▷ Run 'PseudoTest'           ^⇧R │
56          log.info(" │ ⚙ Debug 'PseudoTest'         ^⇧D │
57          assertTrue │    More Run/Debug              > │
                        └─────────────────────────────────────────┘
```

Figure 9-15. *IntelliJ IDEA menu for running unit tests*

After selecting **Run 'PseudoTest'**, the test class is executed. A launcher is created so that you can launch it from the typical launch menu as well. Test classes can be executed in debug mode, and breakpoints can be used too. When executing the PseudoTest class, even if the test methods are run in parallel, the output is consistent with the order of the methods matching the annotation specifications mentioned previously. To make sure that test methods are executed in parallel, the logger is configured to print the thread id as well. Sample output is depicted in Listing 9-32.

Listing 9-32. Output of the Execution of `PseudoTest`

```
[1-worker-1] INFO  c.a.b.n.PseudoTest - Loading general test context.
[1-worker-3] INFO  c.a.b.n.PseudoTest - Prepare  single test context.
[1-worker-2] INFO  c.a.b.n.PseudoTest - Prepare  single test context.
[1-worker-2] INFO  c.a.b.n.PseudoTest - Executing test one.
[1-worker-3] INFO  c.a.b.n.PseudoTest - Executing test two.
[1-worker-2] INFO  c.a.b.n.PseudoTest - Destroy  single test context.
[1-worker-3] INFO  c.a.b.n.PseudoTest - Destroy  single test context.
[1-worker-1] INFO  c.a.b.n.PseudoTest - UnLoading general test context.
```

The `testOne()` method in Listing 9-31 contains the statement `assertTrue(true);`, which is included to show you how assertion methods look like. The `true` value is replaced with a condition in a real test. The same goes for the `assertFalse(false);` assertion in method `textTwo()`.

That's about all the space we can dedicate to JUnit in this book. My recommendation is to look more into it, because a developer can write code, but a good developer knows how to make sure it works as well.

Using Fakes

Using **fakes** is a way for us to simulate objects and method functionality in our code without actually depending on a real object or method. The code written to implement such an object has simplified functionality of the one deployed in production.

To test the `AccountRepoImpl` class, we have to replace the `DerbyDBConnection` instance with a `FakeDBConnection` instance that is not backed up by a database, but by something simpler and more accessible, like a `Map<?,?>`. The `DerbyDBConnection` uses `java.sql.Connection` and other classes in that package to perform data operations on the Derby database.

The `FakeDBConnection` class will implement the `DBConnection` interface so that it can be passed to an `AccountRepoImpl` and all its methods will be called on it.

The rule of thumb when writing tests and test supporting classes is to put them in the same packages with the objects tested or replaced, but in the `test/java` directory. This is because test classes must access the classes being tested, without extra configurations needed in the module-info.java file. Supporting classes to test the application classes using fakes are declared in the com.apress.bgn.nine.fake package.

Another rule of thumb when writing tests is to write a method to test the correct outcome of the method being tested, and to write a method to test the incorrect behavior. In unexpected cases, with unexpected data, your application will behave in unexpected ways, so although this seems paradoxical, you have to expect the unexpected and write tests for it.

The AccountRepoImpl class implements the basic methods to persist or delete an Account instance to/from the database. The implementation is depicted in Listing 9-33.

Listing 9-33. The AccountRepoImpl Implementation

```
package com.apress.bgn.nine.repo;

import com.apress.bgn.nine.Account;
import com.apress.bgn.nine.db.DbConnection;

import java.util.List;
import java.util.Optional;

public class AccountRepoImpl  implements AccountRepo {

    private DbConnection conn;

    public AccountRepoImpl(DbConnection conn) {
        this.conn = conn;
    }

    @Override
    public Account save(Account account) {
        var dbAcc = conn.findByHolder(account.holder());
        if(dbAcc == null) {
            return conn.insert(account);
        }
        return conn.update(account);
    }

    @Override
```

```java
public Optional<Account> findOne(String holder) {
    var acc = conn.findByHolder(holder);
    if(acc != null) {
        return Optional.of(acc);
    }
    return Optional.empty();
}

@Override
public List<Account> findAll() {
    return conn.findAll();
}

@Override
public int deleteByHolder(String holder) {
    var acc = conn.findByHolder(holder);
    conn.delete(holder);
    if(acc != null) {
        return 0;
    }
    return 1;
}
}
```

The deleteByHolder(..) method in the AccountRepoImpl class is used to delete
an account. If the entry is present, it deletes it and returns 0; otherwise it returns 1. The
deleteByHolder(..) method is depicted in Listing 9-34.

To test this class, we need to provide a DbConnection implementation that simulates
a connection to a database. This is where the previously mentioned FakeDBConnection
comes in, the code for which is also shown in Listing 9-34.

Listing 9-34. The FakeDBConnection Implementation

```java
package com.apress.bgn.nine.fake.db;

import com.apress.bgn.nine.Account;
import com.apress.bgn.nine.db.DBException;
```

```java
import com.apress.bgn.nine.db.DbConnection;
import java.util.*;

public class FakeDBConnection implements DbConnection {
    /**
     * pseudo-database {@code Map<holder, Account>}
     */
    Map<String, Account> database = new HashMap<>();

    @Override
    public void connect() {
        // no implementation needed
    }

    @Override
    public Account insert(Account account) {
        if (database.containsKey(account.holder())) {
            throw new DBException("Could not insert " + account);
        }
        database.put(account.holder(), account);
        return account;
    }

    @Override
    public Account findByHolder(String holder) {
        return database.get(holder);
    }

    @Override
    public List<Account> findAll() {
        return new ArrayList<>(database.values());
    }

    @Override
    public Account update(Account account) {
        if (!database.containsKey(account.holder())) {
            throw new DBException("Could not find account for " + account.
            holder());
        }
        database.put(account.holder(), account);
```

```java
        return account;
    }

    @Override
    public void delete(String holder) {
        database.remove(holder);
    }

    @Override
    public void disconnect() {
        // no implementation needed
    }
}
```

The FakeDBConnection behaves exactly like a connection object that can be used to save entries to a database, search for them, or delete them, only instead of a database it is backed up by a Map<String, Account>. The map key will be the holder's name, because in our database the holder name is used as a unique identifier for an Account entry in the table. Now that we have the fake object, we can test that our AccountRepoImpl behaves as expected. Because of practical reasons, only one method will be tested in this section, but the full code is available on the official GitHub repo for this book.

Listing 9-35 shows a test class that tests methods that verify the behavior of the findOne(..) method. It contains a positive test method when there is an entry matching the criteria and a negative test method when there isn't.

Listing 9-35. The FakeAccountRepoTest Test Class

```java
package com.apress.bgn.nine;
// other import statements omitted

import static org.junit.jupiter.api.Assertions.*;

public class FakeAccountRepoTest {
    private static final Logger log = LoggerFactory.
getLogger(FakeAccountRepoTest.class);
    private static DbConnection conn;

    private AccountRepo repo;

    @BeforeAll
```

```java
static void prepare() {
    conn = new FakeDBConnection();
}

@BeforeEach
public void setUp(){
    repo = new AccountRepoImpl(conn);

    // inserting an entry so we can test update/findOne
    repo.save(new Account("Pedala", 200, "2345"));
}

@Test
public void testFindOneExisting(){
    Optional<Account> expected = repo.findOne("Pedala");
    assertTrue(expected.isPresent());
}

@Test
public void testFindOneNonExisting(){
    Optional<Account> expected = repo.findOne("Dorel");
    assertFalse(expected.isPresent());
}

@Test
public void testFindAll(){
    assertEquals(1, repo.findAll().size());
}

@Test
public void testInsert(){
    Account expected = new Account("Gigi", 100, "12345");
    Account actual = repo.save(expected);

    assertEquals(expected, actual);
}

@Test
```

```java
public void testUpdate(){
    Account existing = conn.findByHolder("Pedala");
    int originalSum = existing.sum();
    var upAcc = new Account(existing.holder(), originalSum -50,
    existing.number());
    Account actual = repo.save(upAcc);

    assertEquals(upAcc.sum(),actual.sum());
}

@Test
public void testDeleteExisting(){
    assertEquals( 0, repo.deleteByHolder("Pedala"));
}

@Test
public void testDeleteNonExisting(){
    assertEquals( 1, repo.deleteByHolder("NotExisting"));
}

@AfterEach
void tearDown(){
    // delete the entry
    repo.deleteByHolder("Pedala");
}

@AfterAll
public static void cleanUp(){
    conn = null;
    log.info("All done!");
}
}
```

Notice how we are creating exactly one entry that is added to our fake database.

Now that we are sure the repository class does its job properly, the next one to test is AccountServiceImpl. To test this class, we will look into a different approach. Fakes are useful, but writing one for a class with complex functionality can be quite costly. So what are the alternatives? There are a few. In the next section, we'll look at stubs.

Using Stubs

Stubs are a type of fake that quietly fake behavior and can return a predefined expected value. An instance of AccountServiceImpl uses an instance of AccountRepo to retrieve data from the database or save data to a database. When writing unit tests for this class, each test method must cover the functionality from a method in a service class, so that we can write a stub class to simulate the behavior of AccountRepo. For the AccountServiceImpl instance to be able to use it, the stub must implement AccountRepo. In this section the tests will cover the method createAccount(..) because this method can fail in many ways. Thus, more than one test method can be written for it. Listing 9-36 shows the createAccount(..) method.

Listing 9-36. The AccountServiceImpl#createAccount(..) Method

```
package com.apress.bgn.nine.service;
// import statements omitted

public class AccountServiceImpl implements AccountService {

    AccountRepo repo;

    public AccountServiceImpl(AccountRepo repo) {
        this.repo = repo;
    }

    @Override
    public Account createAccount(String holder, String accountNumber,
    String amount) {
        int intAmount;
        try {
            intAmount = Integer.parseInt(amount);
        } catch (NumberFormatException nfe) {
            throw new InvalidDataException("Could not create account with
            invalid amount!");
        }
```

```
    if (accountNumber == null || accountNumber.length() < 5 ||
    intAmount < 0) {
        throw new InvalidDataException("Could not create account with
        invalid account number!");
    }

    Optional<Account> existing = repo.findOne(holder);
    if (existing.isPresent()) {
        throw new AccountCreationException("Account already exists for
        holder " + holder);
    }
    Account acc = new Account(holder, intAmount, accountNumber);
    return repo.save(acc);
}
// other methods omitted
}
```

The createAccount(..) method takes as parameters the holder name, the number
of the account to be created, and the initial amount. All of these parameters are provided
as String instances intentionally, so that the method body contains a little bit of logic
that requires serious testing. Let's analyze the behavior of the createAccount(..)
method and make a list with all possible returned values and returned exceptions:

- If the amount is not a number, an InvalidDataException is thrown.
  (InvalidDataException is a custom type of exception created
  specifically for this project, which is not relevant at the moment.)

- If the accountNumber argument is null, an InvalidDataException
  is thrown.

- If the accountNumber argument has less than five characters, an
  InvalidDataException is thrown.

- If the amount argument converted to a number is negative, an
  InvalidDataException is thrown.

- If the account for the holder argument already exists, an
  AccountCreationException is thrown.

- If all the inputs are valid and there is no account for the holder
  argument, an Account instance is created, saved to the database, and
  the result is returned.

If we were to be really obsessive about testing, we would have to write a test scenario
for all those cases. In the software world, there is something called **test coverage**, which
is a process that determines whether test cases cover application code and how much
of it. The result is a percentage value, and companies usually define a test coverage
percentage[14] that represents a warranty of quality for the application. Before showing the
test methods for the createAccount(..) method, take a look at Listing 9-37 that shows
the repo stub code.

Listing 9-37. The AccountRepoStub Class

```
package com.apress.bgn.nine.service.stub;
//other import statement
public class AccountRepoStub implements AccountRepo {

    private Integer option = 0;

    public synchronized void set(int val) {
        option = val;
    }

    @Override
    public Account save(Account account) {
        return account;
    }

    @Override
    public Optional<Account> findOne(String holder) {
        if (option == 0) {
            return Optional.of(new Account(holder, 100, "22446677"));
        }
```

---

[14] https://martinfowler.com/bliki/TestCoverage.html

```java
        return Optional.empty();
    }

    @Override
    public List<Account> findAll() {
        return List.of(new Account("sample", 100, "22446677"));
    }

    @Override
    public int deleteByHolder(String holder) {
        return option;
    }
}
```

The `option` field can be used to change behavior of the stub to cover more test cases. As we have one stub repository, this means tests might fail when run in parallel, but for this example with this basic stub, it works.

There are two ways to write tests using JUnit, depending on the `assert*(..)` statements used. Listing 9-38 shows two negative test methods that validate the behavior when an invalid amount is provided as an argument.

Listing 9-38. The `AccountServiceTest` Unit Test Class Using a Stub Repo

```java
package com.apress.bgn.nine.service;
// import statements omitted

public class AccountServiceTest {
    private static AccountRepoStub repo;
    private AccountService service;

    @BeforeAll
    public static void prepare() {
        repo = new AccountRepoStub();
    }

    @BeforeEach
    public void setUp() {
        service = new AccountServiceImpl(repo);
    }
```

```java
@Test
public void testNonNumericAmountVersionOne() {
    assertThrows(InvalidDataException.class,
            () -> {
                service.createAccount("Gigi", "223311", "2I00");
            });
}

@Test
public void testNonNumericAmountVersionTwo() {
    InvalidDataException expected = assertThrows(
            InvalidDataException.class, () -> {
                service.createAccount("Gigi", "223311", "2I00");
            }
    );
    assertEquals("Could not create account with invalid amount!",
    expected.getMessage());
}

@AfterEach
public void tearDown() {
  repo.set(0);
}

@AfterAll
public static void destroy() {
  repo = null;
}
}
```

The testNonNumericAmountVersionOne() method makes use of assertThrows(..),
which receives two parameters: the type of exception expected to be thrown when the
second parameter of type Executable is executed. Executable is a functional interface
defined in the org.junit.jupiter.api.function package that can be used in a lambda
expression to get the compact test that you see in Listing 9-38.

The `testNonNumericAmountVersionTwo()` method saves the result of the `assertThrows(..)` call, which allows for the message of the exception to be tested as well, to make sure that the execution flow worked exactly as expected.

Similar methods can be written to test all other service methods. The `AccountServiceTest` class hosted on the repository for this book depicts a few other testing methods. Feel free to add your own methods to cover your own situations.

The next section introduces the last test technique covered in this chapter: writing tests using mocks.

Using Mocks

Mocks are objects that register calls they receive. During execution of a test, using assert utility methods, the assumption that all expected actions were performed on mocks are tested. Thankfully, code for mocks does not have to be written by the developer, because there are three well-known libraries that provide the type of classes needed to test using mocks: Mockito[15], JMock[16], and EasyMock[17]. Also, if you ever need to mock static methods—the most common reason being bad design (which is beyond your power to fix)—there is PowerMock[18].

Using mocks, you can jump directly to writing the tests. Listing 9-39 shows two tests for the `createAccount(..)` method that focus on the repository class actually calling its methods, because the repository class is the one being replaced with a mock.

Listing 9-39. The `AccountServiceTest` Unit Test Class Using a Mock Repo

```
package com.apress.bgn.nine.mock;
// other import statements omitted
import org.junit.jupiter.api.extension.ExtendWith;
import org.mockito.Mock;
import org.mockito.junit.jupiter.MockitoExtension;
import static org.junit.jupiter.api.Assertions.*;
import static org.mockito.ArgumentMatchers.any;
import static org.mockito.Mockito.when;
```

---

[15] https://site.mockito.org
[16] http://jmock.org
[17] https://easymock.org
[18] https://powermock.github.io

```java
@ExtendWith(MockitoExtension.class)
public class AccountServiceTest {
    public AccountService service;

    @Mock
    public AccountRepo mockRepo;

    @BeforeEach
    public void checkMocks() {
        assertNotNull(mockRepo);
        service = new AccountServiceImpl(mockRepo);
    }

    @Test
    public void testCreateAccount() {
        Account expected = new Account("Gigi", 2100, "223311");
        when(mockRepo.findOne("Gigi")).thenReturn(Optional.empty());
        when(mockRepo.save(any(Account.class))).thenReturn(expected);

        Account result = service.createAccount("Gigi", "223311", "2100");
        assertEquals(expected, result);
    }

    @Test
    public void testCreateAccountAlreadyExists() {
        Account expected = new Account("Gigi", 2100, "223311");
        when(mockRepo.findOne("Gigi")).thenReturn(Optional.of(expected));

        assertThrows(AccountCreationException.class,
                () -> service.createAccount("Gigi", "223311", "2100"));
    }
}
```

The tests are quite self-explanatory, and the Mockito utility methods' names make it easy to understand what is actually happening during a test execution. Wait, you might ask, how are the mocks created and injected? Who does that?

The @ExtendWith(MockitoExtension.class) annotation is necessary for JUnit 5 tests to support Mockito annotations. Without it, annotations like @InjectMocks and @Mock have no effect on the code.

The @Mock annotation is used on references to mocks created by Mockito. The preferred way to work with mocks is to specify a reference of an interface type that is implemented by the real object type and the mock that will be created for the test scenario. But @Mock can be placed on a concrete type reference as well, and the created mock will be a subclass of that class.

The @InjectMocks annotation is used on the object to be tested, so that Mockito knows to create this object and inject mocks instead of the dependencies.

This is all you need to know to start using Mockito mocks in your test. Declaring the objects to be replaced with mocks and the object to be injected in is the only setup a class containing unit tests using mocks needs.

The body of test methods using mocks has a typical structure as well. The first line must declare objects and variables passed as arguments to the method called on the object being tested or passed as arguments to Mockito utility methods that declare what mocks take as arguments and what they return. The next line establishes the behavior of the mock when its methods are called by the object to be tested.

The following two lines depict this for the findOne(..) method. The first line creates an account object. The second line defines the behavior of the mock. When mockRepo.findOne("Gigi") will be called, then the previously created account instance will be returned wrapped in an Optional<T> instance.

```
Account expected = new Account("Gigi", 2100, "223311");
when(mockRepo.findOne("Gigi")).thenReturn(Optional.of(expected));
```

There are many other libraries to make writing tests as effortless as possible for developers, and big frameworks like Spring provide their own testing library to help developers write tests for applications using this framework. Build tools like Ant, Maven, and Gradle can be used to automatically run the tests when the project is built and generate useful reports related to the failures.

Using Maven, the project can be built by calling mvn clean install in the console. All test classes declared in the test module are picked up automatically if they are named *Test.java. When writing tests, and not changing application code, you can just run the tests only, by calling mvn test. This is a configuration that can be changed by configuring the Maven Surefire Testing Plugin configured in the pom.xml file.

In a Maven project, tests are run by the maven-surefire-plugin. The Maven test results are saved in TXT and XML format and the files are located in the target/surefire-reports directory. The test results can be grouped into an HTML report by adding the maven-surefire-report-plugin to the project configuration and configuring it to run during the test phase. This is practical since it causes the report to be generated by running mvn clean install or mvn test. The report is represented by a file named surefire-report.html located in the target/site directory.

To have the report generated, the build has to run fully, so the maven-surefire-plugin is configured to continue testing, not to stop at the first failure, by setting testFailureIgnore to true, as shown in Listing 9-40.

Listing 9-40. The maven-surefire-plugin Being Configured to Ignore Test Failures

```
<build>
    <plugins>
        <plugin>
            <groupId>org.apache.maven.plugins</groupId>
            <artifactId>maven-surefire-plugin</artifactId>
            <dependencies>
                <dependency>
                    <groupId>org.junit.jupiter</groupId>
                    <artifactId>junit-jupiter-engine</artifactId>
                    <version>${jupiter.junit.version}</version>
                </dependency>
            </dependencies>
            <configuration>
                <testFailureIgnore>true</testFailureIgnore>
            </configuration>
        </plugin>
    </plugins>
<build>
```

For the following example, a test failure was introduced intentionally, and the report is generated. You can see the first part of the generated report in Figure 9-16.

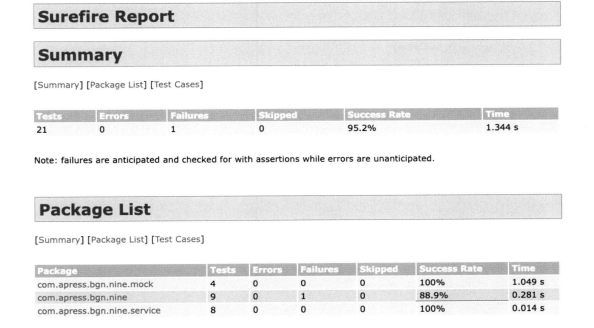

Figure 9-16. *The Maven test report with a test failure (part 1)*

The first part of the report shows the percentage of failed tests, the package in which they are located, and the name of the test class. The second part of the report, shown in Figure 9-17, shows the details of the failure.

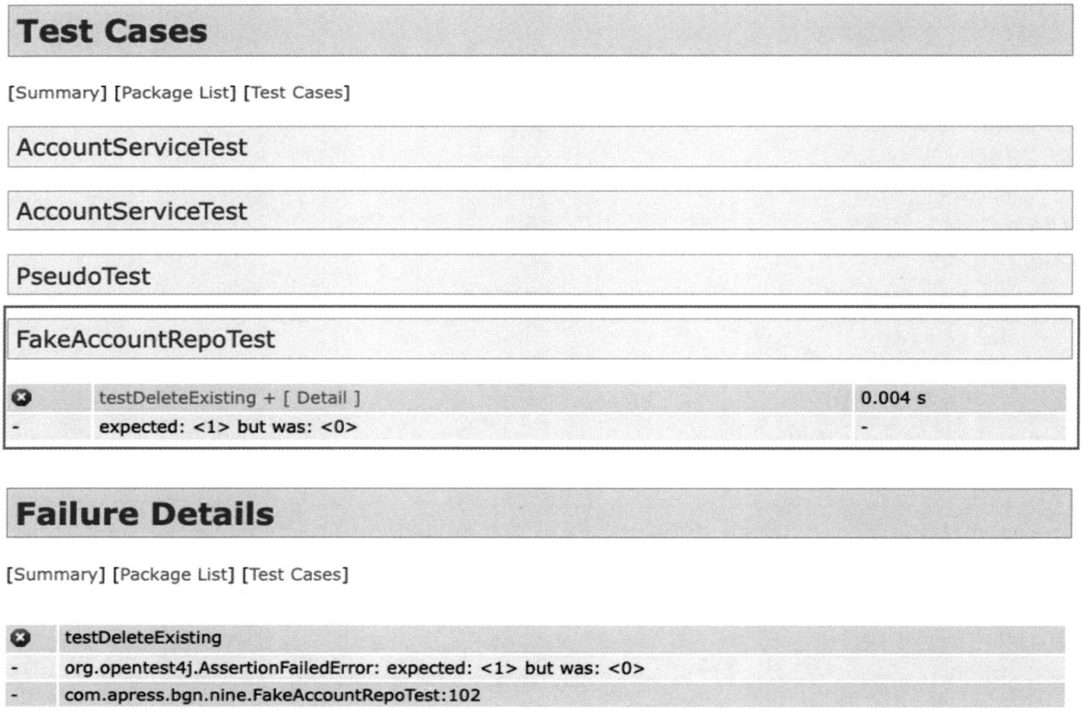

Test Cases

[Summary] [Package List] [Test Cases]

AccountServiceTest

AccountServiceTest

PseudoTest

FakeAccountRepoTest

⊗	testDeleteExisting + [Detail]	0.004 s
-	expected: <1> but was: <0>	-

Failure Details

[Summary] [Package List] [Test Cases]

⊗	testDeleteExisting
-	org.opentest4j.AssertionFailedError: expected: <1> but was: <0>
-	com.apress.bgn.nine.FakeAccountRepoTest:102

Figure 9-17. *The Maven test report with a test failure (part 2)*

Upon fixing the test, the report becomes simpler, and the last two sections are not generated, as depicted in Figure 9-18.

Surefire Report

Summary

[Summary] [Package List] [Test Cases]

Tests	Errors	Failures	Skipped	Success Rate	Time
21	0	0	0	100%	1.923 s

Note: failures are anticipated and checked for with assertions while errors are unanticipated.

Package List

[Summary] [Package List] [Test Cases]

Package	Tests	Errors	Failures	Skipped	Success Rate	Time
com.apress.bgn.nine.mock	4	0	0	0	100%	1.533 s
com.apress.bgn.nine	9	0	0	0	100%	0.373 s
com.apress.bgn.nine.service	8	0	0	0	100%	0.017 s

Figure 9-18. *The Maven test report with no test failures and typical Maven-generated site styling*

Information   In the first edition of this book, I used Gradle to build this project. Because of various incompatibilities with newer versions of Java and the difficulty of configuration, I dropped it in favor of Maven, which is widely used and pretty stable. Unfortunately, generating test reports requires multiple Maven plugins and the reports are not as pretty.

Important   As a conclusion of this section, remember this: no matter how good a development team is, without a great testing team, the resulting application might actually be far away from an acceptable quality standard. So if you ever interview with a company that does not have a dedicated testing team, or a company with a culture that compromises in techniques such as code review and writing tests, think twice before accepting that job.

Documenting

In the software world there is a joke about documentation that might not be to everybody's liking, but it is worth a mention: *Documentation is like sex. When it's good, it's really, really good. And when it's bad, it's still better than nothing.*

A commonsense rule and best practice of programming is to write code that is self-explanatory, which lessens the need to write much documentation. Basically, if you need to write too much documentation, you're programming wrong. There are many ways to make your code self-explanatory to obviate the need to write lots of documentation, such as using meaningful names for classes and variables and respecting the language code conventions. However, when you are building a set of classes that will be used by other developers, you need to provide some documentation for the main APIs. If your solution requires a very complicated algorithm to be written, you might want to add comments about it here and there, although in this case, proper technical documentation with schemas and diagrams should be written too.

Recall that in **Chapter 3** I introduced the different types of comments and promised to provide more details regarding Javadoc comments in this chapter. We've reached that point. Javadoc block comments, also called *documentation comments*, can be found associated with a public class, interface, method body, public field, and sometimes even protected or private components if really necessary. Javadoc comments contain special tags that link documented elements together or mark the different types of information. Javadoc comments and their associated code can be processed by Javadoc tools, extracted, and wrapped together into an HTML site, which is called the Javadoc API of the project. The Maven configuration of this project declares a few reporting plugins and among them `maven-site-plugin` that is configured to wrap together all reports into a static site for the project that can be found under `target/site`.

Important   The project site is generated by executing `mvn site`.

Smart editors can download and access documentation of a project and display it when the developer tries to write code using the documented components, so good code documentation considerably increases the speed of the development process. Let's start with a few examples of Javadoc comments, to explain the most important tags used.

Whenever we create a class or interface, we should add Javadoc comments to explain its purpose, identify the version of the application in which the class or interface was added, and eventually link some existing resources. The "Logging" section early in this chapter introduced the IntSorter hierarchy (see Figure 9-1), a hierarchy of classes implementing the IntSorter interface that provide implementations of different sorting algorithms. When other developers use these classes, they might want to add a customized algorithm to the IntSorter hierarchy. Some information about the IntSorter interface would help them a lot in designing a proper solution. Listing 9-41 shows a Javadoc comment added to the IntSorter interface.

Listing 9-41. The Documentation Comment on the IntSorter Interface

```
package com.apress.bgn.nine.algs;
/**
 * Interface {@code IntSorter} is an interface that needs to be implemented
 * by classes that provide a method to sort an array of {@code int}
   values. <p>
 *
 * {@code int[]} was chosen as a type because int values are sortable
   efficiently ({@link Comparable})
 *
 * <pre>
 *     You can use any implementation like this:
 *       {@snippet id="highlighting" lang="java" :
 *         IntSorter mergeSort = new MergeSort(); // @highlight
           type=highlighted
 *       mergeSort.sort(arr,0,arr.length-1);
 *     }
 *     where {@code arr} is an {@code int[]}
 * </pre>
 * @author Iuliana Cosmina
 * @since 1.0
 */
public interface IntSorter {
    // interface body omitted
}
```

In the Javadoc comments, HTML tags can be used to format information. In the code in Listing 9-41, a `<p>` element is used to make sure the comment will consist of two paragraphs instead of one.

The `@author` tag, introduced in JDK 1.0, is useful when the development team is quite big, because if you end up working with somebody else's code, you know who to consult in case issues appear.

The `@since` tag is used to identify the version of the application in which this interface was added. For an application that has had a long development and release cycle, this tag can be used to mark elements (methods, classes, fields, etc.) of a specific version, so that a developer using the codebase of your application knows when elements were added and, in case of a rollback to a previous version, will know where in their application compile-time errors might appear.

The best example of using the `@since` tag is the Java official Javadoc. Let's focus on the `String` class. It was introduced in Java version 1.0, but more constructors and methods were added to it with every Java version being released. Each of the constructors and methods is marked with the specific versions. Listing 9-42 depicts code snippets and documentation comments that prove the previous affirmation.

Listing 9-42. The Documentation Comments in the `String` Class

```
package java.lang;
// import statements omitted

/**
 * // omitted
 * @since    1.0
 */
public final class String
        implements java.io.Serializable, Comparable<String>, CharSequence,
        Constable, ConstantDesc {
  /**
   * ...
   * @since  1.1
   */
```

```java
public String(byte[] bytes, int offset, int length, String charsetName)
        throws UnsupportedEncodingException {
  this(lookupCharset(charsetName), bytes, checkBoundsOffCount(offset,
  length, bytes.length), length);
}

/**
 * ...
 * @since  1.4
 */
public boolean contentEquals(StringBuffer sb) {
  // method body omitted
}

/**
 * ...
 * @since  1.5
 */
public String(int[] codePoints, int offset, int count) {
  // method body omitted
}

/**
 * ...
 * @since  1.6
 */
public String(byte[] bytes, int offset, int length, Charset charset) {
  // method body omitted
}

/**
 * ...
 * @since 1.8
 */
public static String join(CharSequence delimiter, CharSequence... 
elements) {
  // method body omitted
}
```

```java
/**
 * ...
 * @since 9
 */
@Override
public IntStream codePoints() {
  // method body omitted
}

/**
 * ...
 * @since 11
 */
public String strip() {
  // method body omitted
}

/**
 * ...
 * @since 12
 */
public String indent(int n) {
  // method body omitted
}

/**
 * ...
 * @since 15
 */
public String stripIndent() {
  // method body omitted
}
}
```

In the IntSorter example in Listing 9-41, you might have noticed the @code tag. This tag was introduced in Java 1.5 and is used to display text in code form by using a special font and escaping symbols that might break the HTML syntax (e.g., < or >).

The @link tag was added in Java 1.2 and is used to insert a navigable link to relevant documentation.

The @snippet tag was introduced in Java 18 to easily integrate code snippets into documentation. It provides a lot of attributes to support documentation text formatting that enables developers to make important pieces in their code *pop*. As just mentioned, adding code snippets was possible before Java 18 with the @code annotation, but it was quite limited, as it treated the code like normal text.

Listing 9-43 shows an even better documented version of the IntSorter interface, which contains documentation comments for the methods so that developers implementing it know how its methods should be used.

Listing 9-43. The Documentation Comments for Methods in the IntSorter Interface

```
package com.apress.bgn.nine.algs;
/**
 * Interface {@code IntSorter} is an interface that needs to be implemented
 * by classes that provide a method to sort an array of {@code int}
   values. <p>
 *
 * {@code int[]} was chosen as a type because int values are sortable
   efficiently ({@link Comparable})
 *
 * <pre>
 *     You can use any implementation like this:
 *       {@snippet id="highlighting" lang="java" :
         IntSorter mergeSort = new MergeSort(); // @highlight
         type=highlighted
         mergeSort.sort(arr,0,arr.length-1);
 *     }
 *     where {@code arr} is an {@code int[]}
 * </pre>
 *
 * @author Iuliana Cosmina
 * @since 1.0
 */
```

```java
public interface IntSorter {

  /**
   * Sorts {@code arr}
   *
   * @param arr int array to be sorted
   * @param low lower limit of the interval to be sorted
   * @param high higher limit of the interval to be sorted
   */
  void sort(int[] arr, int low, int high);

  /**
   * Implement this method to provide a sorting solution that does not
   * require pivots.
   * @deprecated As of version 0.1, because the
   *                {@link #sort(int[], int, int) ()} should be used
   * instead.<p>
   * To be removed in version 3.0.
   * @param arr int array to be sorted
   */
  @Deprecated (since= "0.1", forRemoval = true)
  default void sort(int[] arr) {
    System.out.println("Do not use this! This is deprecated!!");
  }
}
```

The IntelliJ IDEA editor (and other smart editors) can generate small pieces of Javadoc for you. Once you have declared a class or method body that you want to document, type /** and press **Enter**. The generated block of comments contains entries for everything that can be inferred from the component's declaration. The following list describes the most common:

- One or more @param tags together with the parameter names. The developer simply needs to add extra documentation to explain their purpose.

- If the method returns a value of a type different from void, a @return tag is generated. Documentation must be provided by the developer to explain what the result represents, and if there are special cases when a certain value is returned.

- If the methods declare an exception to be thrown, a @throws tag is generated together with the exception type, and the developer's job is to explain when and why that type of exception is thrown.

Listing 9-44 depicts a snippet from the Optional<T> class containing the filter(..) method and its documentation comments.

Listing 9-44. The Documentation Comments for Optional<T>#filter(..) Method

```
/**
 * ...
 * @param predicate the predicate to apply to a value, if present
 * @return an {@code Optional} describing the value of this
 *         {@code Optional}, if a value is present and the value
           matches the
 *         given predicate, otherwise an empty {@code Optional}
 * @throws NullPointerException if the predicate is {@code null}
 */
public Optional<T> filter(Predicate<? super T> predicate) {
  Objects.requireNonNull(predicate);
  if (isEmpty()) {
    return this;
  } else {
    return predicate.test(value) ? this : empty();
  }
}
```

The @link tag can be used to create a documentation link to a class page, or a method in that class or interface, a method documentation section, a field, or even an external web page. Listing 9-45, depicts a class implementing IntSorter. Its documentation comment contains a link to the abstract method in the IntSorter interface.

Listing 9-45. The Documentation Comments for `Optional<T>#filter(..)` Method (@link)

```
package com.apress.bgn.nine.algs;

/**
 * The {@code InsertionSort} class contains a single method that is a
concrete implementation of {@link IntSorter#sort(int[])}.<p>
 * Instances of this class can be used to sort an {@code int[] } array
using the insertion-sort algorithm.
 *
 * @author Iuliana Cosmina
 * since 1.0
 * @see IntSorter
 */
public class InsertionSort implements IntSorter {
    // class body omitted
}
```

The @see tag is a simple alternative to @link that is used to direct developers' attention to documentation specific to the element this tag references.

The @deprecated tag is used to add text to explain the reasons for deprecation, the version in which the component is due to be removed, and what to use instead. Javadoc generation tools will take the text for this tag, use italic font for its display, and add it to the main description of the component (class, field, method, etc.).

Beside this tag, the @Deprecated annotation was introduced in Java 1.5. Annotating a component with it should discourage developers from using it. The advantage of this annotation is that compilers pick it up and issue warnings when a deprecated component is used or overridden in nondeprecated code. This annotation can be used on any Java language component, including modules.

Smart Java IDEs, like IntelliJ IDEA, are aware of the @deprecated tag and the @Deprecated annotation and show deprecated components in strikethrough format to warn the developer not to use them. The Maven `maven-compiler-plugin` responsible for compiling Java source code provides a configuration option to show or hide deprecation warnings. All these are depicted in Figure 9-19.

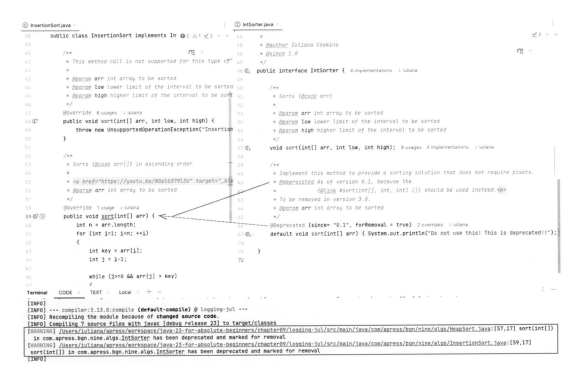

Figure 9-19. *IntelliJ IDEA recognizes the @deprecated tag. Maven build is configured to show deprecation warnings*

This section has introduced you to the most-used tags when writing Javadoc comments. If you want to check out the complete list, you can find it on the official Javadoc page[19]. Javadoc documentation is also a wide subject that could provide material for an entire book. We are just scratching the surface in this section and covering the basics so that you have a good understanding of it.

Information   The Maven plugin configuration for generating the site for a project is an advanced subject, not suitable for this book. However, Maven plugins have been mentioned by name, and some comments have been added in the pom.xml files to explain their purpose and their configuration, if you are curious about these details.

---

[19] https://www.oracle.com/java/technologies/javase/javadoc-tool.html

To generate the HTML site for the `logging-jul` module, open the Maven project view, navigate to the **chapter09:logging-jul -> Lifecycle** node, and under it you will find the `site` phase, as depicted in Figure 9-20.

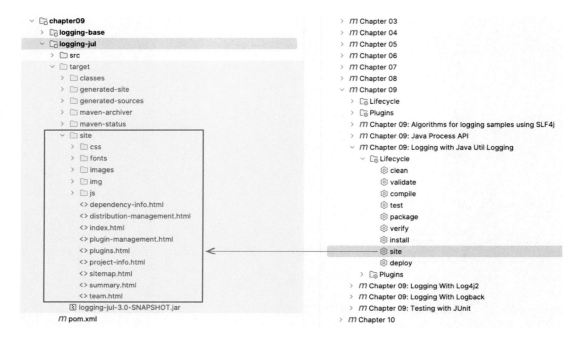

Figure 9-20. *The Maven `site` phase and the result for the `logging-jul` module*

Double-clicking this phase in the IDE is the same as executing `mvn site` in the console. It triggers the execution of the Maven site generation phase and all the phases it depends on, and the result of the build is a directory named `site`, located under the `target` directory. It contains a static site and its starting page is named `index.html`. The site is quite simple, since a default configuration was used. Right-click that file to open a context menu, select **Open in Browser**, and select your preferred browser.

The main page of the project depicts information from the `pom.xml` file, such as the project name, description, and so forth. In the navigation pane on the left side of the page, expand the **Project Reports** menu item and select **Javadoc**. Clicking that directs you to the project Javadoc page, as shown in Figure 9-21. If you think the page resembles the JDK official Javadoc page, you are not imagining it; the same Doclet API was used to generate the official one as well.

Figure 9-21. *The Maven project site and the main Javadoc site for the* `logging-jul` *module*

The documentation is not particularly rich, but it is usable.

It was previously mentioned that Javadoc documentation, when present, is picked up by IntelliJ IDEA and other smart editors and depicted on the spot, while the developer uses the documented components in the code. Smarter editors, when selecting a class, method name, interface method, and so on, provide some kind of combination of keys that include F1, that the developer must press, so that the documentation is depicted in a pop-up window. In IntelliJ IDEA, just click an element and press **F1** and the Javadoc documentation is shown in a pop-up window, formatted quite nicely, like depicted in Figure 9-22.

Figure 9-22. *Javadoc information depicted in IntelliJ IDEA*

You can view Javadoc information in a smart editor for any dependency of your project (including JDK classes) as long as the code is open source and the module exports the appropriate packages.

In Java 9 the Doclet API for generating Javadoc received an upgrade and a facelift. Before Java 9, developers complained about the performance issues of the old version, the cryptic API, the lack of support, and the shallowness of it overall. In Java 9 most of the problems were resolved. The detailed description and list of improvements can be found on the JEP 221 page[20]. Improvements continued in Java 18 with the introduction of the @snippet annotation, and in Java 23 by enabling Javadoc documentation comments to be written in Markdown[21] rather than in a mixture of HTML and Javadoc @-tags[22]. Figure 9-23 shows side by side the same Javadoc comments written in the classic way (left) and written using Markdown.

---

[20] https://openjdk.org/jeps/221
[21] https://www.markdownguide.org
[22] https://openjdk.org/jeps/467

Figure 9-23. *Javadoc classic (left) and Markdown (supported starting with Java 23 for class* QuickSort

Figure 9-24 shows the generated documentation for the Javadoc comments in the QuickSort class shown in Figure 9-23.

Class QuickSort

java.lang.Object
   com.apress.bgn.algs.QuickSort

All Implemented Interfaces:
  IntSorter

---

public class **QuickSort**
extends Object
implements IntSorter

The QuickSort class contains a single method that is a concrete implementation of IntSorter.sort(int[], int, int).

Instances of this class can be used to sort an int[] array using the quick-sort algorithm. Quicksort is an efficient, general-purpose, *divide-and-conquer* sorting algorithm.

Author:
  Iuliana Cosmina since 1.0

See Also:
  IntSorter

Constructor Summary

Constructors

Constructor	Description
QuickSort()	

Method Summary

All Methods	Instance Methods	Concrete Methods

Modifier and Type	Method	Description
void	sort(int[] arr, int low, int high)	How it works

Figure 9-24. *QuickSort documentation*

Documentation is valuable and can make development practical and pleasant when it is really good. So when writing code, document it as you would expect the dependencies of your project to be. You might have heard of the expression **RTFM**, which is an abbreviation for **Read The F%ing Manual!**. This expression is used quite a lot in software by experienced developers when working with newbie developers. The problem is, what can you do when there is no manual? Most companies on a deadline might have the tendency to allocate little or no time to documenting a project, so this section was added to this book to emphasize the importance of good documentation in software development, and to teach you how to write your documentation while you write your code, because you might not have time to do it afterward.

Summary

This chapter has covered important development tools and techniques to help you write production-worthy Java code. Having read this chapter, you should have a good basis for understanding of how to accomplish the following:

- Configure and use logging in a Java application

- Log messages in the console

- Log messages to a file

- Use Java logging

- Use a logging facade (and appreciate why it is recommended)

- Configure and use SLF4J with Logback

- Program using assertions

- Debug step by step using IntelliJ IDEA

- Monitor and inspect JVM statistics while an application is running using various JDK tools such as `jps`, `jcmd`, `jconsole`, and `jmc`

- Use the Process API to monitor and create processes

- Test an application using JUnit

- Write tests using fakes

- Write tests using mocks

- Write tests using stubs

- Write Javadoc comments to document a Java application and generate documentation in HTML format using Maven

## CHAPTER 10

Making Your Application Interactive

So far in the book, input data for our Java programs was provided via arrays or variables that were initialized inside the code or via program arguments. In real life, however, most applications require interaction with the user. The user can be provided access by entering a username and a password, and the user is sometimes required to type in details to confirm their identity or to instruct the application what to do. Java supports multiple methods for user input to be read. In this chapter, we will be covering a few ways to build interactive Java applications that take their input a variety of sources.

As introduced in previous chapters, JShell is a Java command-line interface (CLI) shell that enables developers to test variable declarations and one-line statements. Other CLI shells like `bash` and terminals like Command Prompt from Windows can be used to issue commands to programs in the form of successive lines of text.

Reading User Data from the Command Line

This section is dedicated to reading user input from the command line, whether it is the IntelliJ IDEA console, or whether if the program is run from an executable jar from any terminal specific to an operating system. In the JDK there are two classes that can be used to read user data from the command line, `java.util.Scanner` and `java.io.Console`, and this section will cover them both in detail. But first, let's start with the basics: using `System.in` to read user data.

© Iuliana Cosmina 2024
I. Cosmina, *Java 23 for Absolute Beginners*, https://doi.org/10.1007/979-8-8688-1041-1_10

Using `System.in`

Before introducing logging in **Chapter 9** to print data in the console, methods under `System.out` were used in the code samples for this book. There is also a counterpart utility object named `System.in` that is used to read data from the console, data that a user of the program introduces to control the application flow. You might have noticed that until now, all Java programs, when executed, would start, process the data, execute the declared statements, and then terminate, exiting gracefully or with an exception when something went wrong. The simplest and most common way to pass decision of termination to the user is to end the `main()` method with a call to `System.in.read()`. This method reads the next byte of data from the input stream, and the program is paused until the user introduces a value; as the value is returned, we can even save it and print it. Listing 10-1 shows the code to read user input using `System.in.read`.

Listing 10-1. Reading a Value Provided by the User in the Console

```
package com.apress.bgn;
import java.io.IOException;

import static java.lang.System.out;
import static java.lang.System.in;

public class ReadingFormStdinDemo {
    public static void main(String... args) throws IOException {
        out.print("Press any key to terminate:");
        byte[] b = new byte[3];
        int read = in.read(b);
        for (int i = 0; i < b.length; ++i) {
            out.println(b[i]);
        }
        out.println("Key pressed: " + read);
    }
}
```

The user input is saved in the byte[] b array; its size is arbitrary. You can type anything you want. Only the first three bytes will be kept in the array. However, this way of reading information is not really useful, is it? Take a look at the following snippet, which depicts the previous code being executed and random text being inserted:

```
Press any key to terminate: ini mini miny moo.  # inserted text
32
105
110
Key pressed: 3
```

Using System.in to interact with a java application.

Using `java.util.Scanner`

The System.in variable is of type java.io.InputStream, which is a JDK special type extended by all classes representing an input stream of bytes. (You will learn more about the class InputStream in **Chapter 11**.) This means that System.in can be wrapped in any java.io.Reader extension (also discussed in **Chapter 11**), so bytes can be read as readable data. The one that is really important is a class named Scanner from package java.util. An instance of this type can be created by calling its constructor and providing System.in as an argument. The Scanner class provides a lot of next*() methods that can be used to read almost any type from the console. In Figure 10-1 you can see the next*() methods list.

ⓜ **next** ()	String
ⓜ **next** (String pattern)	String
ⓜ **next** (Pattern pattern)	String
ⓜ **nextInt** ()	int
ⓜ **nextByte** ()	byte
ⓜ **nextBigDecimal** ()	BigDecimal
ⓜ **nextBigInteger** ()	BigInteger
ⓜ **nextBigInteger** (int radix)	BigInteger
ⓜ **nextBoolean** ()	boolean
ⓜ **nextByte** (int radix)	byte
ⓜ **nextDouble** ()	double
ⓜ **nextFloat** ()	float
ⓜ **nextInt** (int radix)	int
ⓜ **nextLine** ()	String
ⓜ **nextLong** ()	long
ⓜ **nextLong** (int radix)	long
ⓜ **nextShort** ()	short
ⓜ **nextShort** (int radix)	short
ⓜ **hasNext** ()	boolean
ⓜ **hasNext** (String pattern)	boolean
ⓜ **hasNext** (Pattern pattern)	boolean
ⓜ **hasNextBigDecimal** ()	boolean

Figure 10-1. *Scanner methods for reading various types of data*

The advantage of using Scanner to read data from the console is that the values read are automatically converted to the proper types, when possible; when not possible, a java.util.InputMismatchException is thrown.

The code in Listing 10-2 is designed so that you can select the type of value you want to read by inserting text and then the value. The appropriate method of the Scanner instance is called to read the value.

Listing 10-2. Reading a Value Provided by the User in the Console Using `java.util.Scanner`

```java
package com.apress.bgn;

import java.math.BigInteger;
import java.util.ArrayList;
import java.util.List;
import java.util.Scanner;

import static java.lang.System.out;

public class ReadingFromStdinUsingScannerDemo {
    public static final String EXIT = "exit";
    public static final String HELP = "help";
    public static final String BYTE = "byte";
    public static final String SHORT = "short";
    public static final String INT = "int";
    public static final String BOOLEAN = "bool";
    public static final String DOUBLE = "double";
    public static final String LINE = "line";
    public static final String BIGINT = "bigint";
    public static final String TEXT = "text";
    public static final String LONGS = "longs";

    public static void main(String... args) {
        Scanner sc = new Scanner(System.in);
        var help = getHelpString();
        out.println(help);

        String input;
        do {
            out.print("Enter option: ");
            input = sc.nextLine();

            switch (input) {
                case HELP:
                    out.println(help);
                    break;
```

```
        case EXIT:
            out.println("Hope you had fun. Buh-bye!");
            break;
        case BYTE:
            byte b = sc.nextByte();
            out.println("Nice byte there: " + b);
            sc.nextLine();
            break;
        case SHORT:
            short s = sc.nextShort();
            out.println("Nice short there: " + s);
            sc.nextLine();
            break;
        case INT:
            int i = sc.nextInt();
            out.println("Nice int there: " + i);
            sc.nextLine();
            break;
        case BOOLEAN:
            boolean bool = sc.nextBoolean();
            out.println("Nice boolean there: " + bool);
            sc.nextLine();
            break;
        case DOUBLE:
            double d = sc.nextDouble();
            out.println("Nice double there: " + d);
            sc.nextLine();
            break;
        case LINE:
            String line = sc.nextLine();
            out.println("Nice line of text there: " + line);
            break;
        case BIGINT:
            BigInteger bi = sc.nextBigInteger();
            out.println("Nice big integer there: " + bi);
            sc.nextLine();
```

```
                break;
            case TEXT:
                String text = sc.next();
                out.println("Nice text there: " + text);
                sc.nextLine();
                break;
            default:
                out.println("No idea what you want bruh!");
        }

    } while (!input.equalsIgnoreCase(EXIT));
}

private static String getHelpString() {
    return """
            This application helps you test various usage of Scanner.
            Enter type to be read next:\
            \n\t help >  displays this help\
            \n\t exit >  leave the application\
            \n\t byte > read a byte\
            \n\t short > read a short\
            \n\t int > read an int\
            \n\t bool > read a boolean\
            \n\t double > read a double\
            \n\t line > read a line of text\
            \n\t bigint > read a BigInteger\
            \n\t text > read a text value""";
    }
}
```

As you probably noticed in Listing 10-2, most scanner methods are called together with the nextLine() method. This is because every input you provide is made of the actual token and a newline character (the **<Enter>** pressed to end your input), and before you can enter your next value, you need to take that character from the stream as well.

Listing 10-3 depicts the code in Listing 10-2 being used to read a few user values.

Listing 10-3. Running the ReadingFromStdinUsingScannerDemo Class

This application helps you test various usage of Scanner. Enter type to be
read next:
        help > displays this help
        exit > leave the application
        byte > read a byte
        short > read a short
        int > read an int
        bool > read a boolean
        double > read a double
        line > read a line of text
        bigint > read a BigInteger
        text > read a text value
Enter option: byte
12
Nice byte there: 12
Enter option: bool
true
Nice boolean there: true
Enter option: line
some of us are hardly ever here
Nice line of text there: some of us are hardly ever here
Enter option: text
john
Nice text there: john
Enter option: text
the rest of us are made to disappear...
Nice text there: the
Enter option: double
4.2
Nice double there: 4.2
Enter option: int
AAAA
Exception in thread "main" java.util.InputMismatchException
    at java.base/java.util.Scanner.throwFor(Scanner.java:939)

at java.base/java.util.Scanner.next(Scanner.java:1594)

at java.base/java.util.Scanner.nextInt(Scanner.java:2258)

at java.base/java.util.Scanner.nextInt(Scanner.java:2212)

ReadingUsingConsoleDemo

at chapter.ten.scanner/com.apress.bgn.ten.ReadingFromStdinUsingScanner

Demo.main(ReadingFromStdinUsingScannerDemo.java:80)

The output that is highlighted in Listing 10-3 represents the test case for the `next()` method. This method should be used to read a single `String` token. The next token gets converted to a `String` instance, and obviously the token ends when a whitespace is encountered. That is why in the example the only read text ends up being: *the*. In the last case in the example, the expected option is an integer value, but *AAAA* is entered, and that is why the exception is thrown.

When you need to repeatedly read the same type of values from the console, you can peek at the value you want to read and check it before reading it to avoid the `InputMismatchException` being thrown. For this particular scenario, each of the `next*()` methods has a pair of methods named `hasNext*()`. To show an example how these methods can be used, let's add an option to the code in Listing 10-3 to be able to read a list of `Long` values, as depicted in Listing 10-4.

Listing 10-4. Using `java.util.Scanner` to Read a List of `long` Values

```
//...
public static final String LONGS = "longs";
//...
    String input;
    do {
        System.out.print("Enter option: ");
        input = sc.nextLine();
        switch (input) {
            case LONGS:
                List<Long> longList = new ArrayList<>();
                while (sc.hasNextLong()) {
                    longList.add(sc.nextLong());
                }
                System.out.println("Nice long list there: " + longList);
```

```
                // else all done
                sc.nextLine();
                sc.nextLine();
                break;
            default:
                System.out.println("No idea what you want bruh!");
        }
    } while (!input.equalsIgnoreCase(EXIT));
//...
```

Although it seems weird, we need to call the nextLine() method twice in a row: once for the character that cannot be converted to long, so that the while loop ends, and once for the newline character, so that the next read is the type of the following read value.

There are a few other methods in the Scanner class that can be used to filter the input and read only desired tokens, but the methods listed in this section are the ones you will use the most.

Using `java.io.Console`

The java.io.Console class was introduced in Java version 1.6, one version later than Scanner, and provides methods to access the character-based console device, if any, associated with the current Java Virtual Machine. Thus, the methods of class java. io.Console can also be used to write to the console, not only read user input. If the JVM is started from a background process or a Java editor, the console will not be available, as the editor redirects the standard input and output streams to its own window. That is why if we write code using Console, we can only test it by running the class or jar from a terminal, by calling

```
java ReadingUsingConsoleDemo.class
```

or

```
java -jar using-console-1.0-SNAPSHOT.jar
```

The console of a JVM, if available, is represented in the code by a single instance of class Console that can be obtained by calling System.console(). In Figure 10-2 you can see the methods that can be called on the Console instance.

```
ⓜ printf(String format, Object... args)                    Console
ⓜ readLine()                                                 String
ⓜ readLine(String fmt, Object... args)                      String
ⓜ readPassword()                                             char[]
ⓜ readPassword(String fmt, Object... args)                  char[]
ⓜ charset()                                                 Charset
ⓜ flush()                                                       void
ⓜ isTerminal()                                               boolean
ⓜ reader()                                                    Reader
ⓜ writer()                                                PrintWriter
ⓜ format(String fmt, Object... args)                        Console
ⓜ equals(Object obj)                                        boolean
Press ↵ to insert, → to replace  Next Tip
```

Figure 10-2. Console methods for reading various types of data

Obviously, the read*(..) methods are for reading user input from the console and printf(..) and format(..) are for printing text in the console. The special case here are the two readPassword(..) methods that allow for text to be read from the console, but not depicted while it is being written. This means that a Java application supporting authentication can be written without any actual user interface. Listing 10-5 depicts sample code to see all that in action.

Listing 10-5. Using java.io.Console to Read and Write Values

```
package com.apress.bgn.ten;

import java.io.Console;
import java.util.Calendar;
import java.util.GregorianCalendar;
import static java.lang.System.err;

public class ReadingUsingConsoleDemo {
    public static void main(String[] args) {
        Console console = System.console();
        if (console == null) {
            err.println("No console found.");
        } else {
```

```
        console.writer().print("Hello there! (reply to salute)\n");
        console.flush();
        String hello = console.readLine();
        console.printf("You replied with: '" + hello + "'\n");

        Calendar calendar = new GregorianCalendar();
        console.format("Today is : %1$tm %1$te,%1$tY\n", calendar);
        char[] passwordChar = console.readPassword("Please provide
                            password: ");
        String password =  new String(passwordChar);
        console.printf("Your password starts with '" + password.
        charAt(0) + "' and ends with '" + password.charAt(password.
        length()-1) + "'\n");
    }
  }
}
```

In the code sample in Listing 10-5, I intentionally used various methods to read
and write data using the console to show you how they should be used. The console.
writer() method returns an instance of java.io.PrintWriter that can be used to print
messages to the console. The catch is that the messages are not printed until console.
flush() is called. This means that more messages can be queued up by the java.
io.PrintWriter instance and printed only when flush() is called or when its internal
buffer is full.

The console.format(..) method is called to print a formatted message; in this
case a Calendar instance is used to extract the current date and print it according to
the following template: dd mm,yyyy (defined by the argument %1$tm %1$te,%1$tY).
Templates accepted by the Console methods that use formatters are defined in class
java.util.Formatter.

Important   To avoid creating new OS console windows when running code, most
IDEs, including IntelliJ IDEA, use "windowless Java." Since there is no window,
there is no console for the user to access and insert data. So, applications using
java.io.Console must be executed in the command line.

The easiest way to run a Java application using `Console` is to configure the Maven `maven-jar-plugin` to create an executable jar with the main class to be executed being `ReadingUsingConsoleDemo`. The jar produced by Maven can be found here: `/chapter10/using-console/target/using-console-3.0-SNAPSHOT.jar`. If you want to follow along, open a terminal in IntelliJ IDEA by clicking the **Terminal** button and then go to the `target` directory. Once there, execute `java -jar using-console-3.0-SNAPSHOT.jar` and have fun. In Listing 10-6 you can see the entries I used to test the program.

Listing 10-6. Running the Class `ReadingUsingConsoleDemo`

```
Hello there! (reply to salute)
hi
You replied with: 'hi'
Today is : 07 7,2024
Please provide password:
Your password starts with 'g' and ends with 'a'
```

This section has introduced all that is worth covering about using the console, since once you are working on a real production-ready project, you might never need to use it.

Building Applications Using Swing

Swing is a graphical user interface (GUI) widget toolkit for Java. It has been part of the JDK since version 1.2 and was developed to provide more pleasant-looking and practical components for building user applications with complex interfaces. Swing offers all types of buttons, progress bars, selectable lists, and so on. Swing is based on an early version of the **Abstract Window Toolkit (AWT)**, which is the original Java GUI widget toolkit. AWT is pretty basic and has a set of GUI components that are available on any platform. This means that AWT is portable, but this does not imply that AWT code written on one platform will actually work on another, because of the platform-specific limitations. AWT components depend on the native OS equivalent components, which is why they are called *heavyweight* components. In Figure 10-3 you can see a simple Java AWT application.

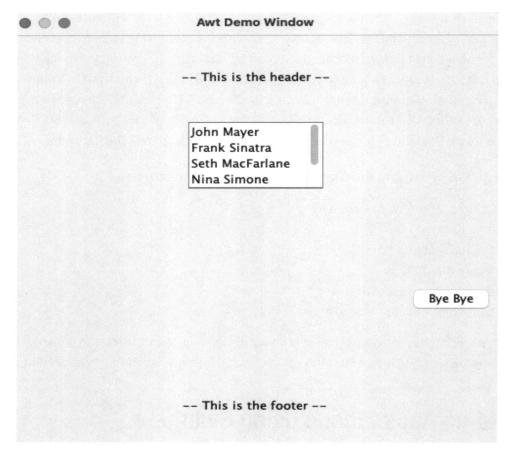

Figure 10-3. *Simple Java AWT application*

The application is a simple window that contains a list, a text area, and a button. The theme, also called *look and feel*, of the application is the same as that of the operating system it was built on—macOS in the examples in this chapter. The theme cannot be changed because AWT taps into the OS native GUI. If you run the same code on a Windows machine, the window will look different because it will use the Windows theme.

Swing components are built in Java and follow the AWT model, but they provide a pluggable look and feel. Swing is implemented entirely in Java and includes all features of AWT, but they are no longer dependent on the native GUI; this is why they are called *lightweight* components. Swing provides everything AWT does and also extends the set of components with higher-level ones such as tree views, list boxes, and tabbed panes. The look-and-feel and the theme are both pluggable and can be easily changed. This obviously means that Swing applications are more portable than AWS applications, and also means that writing applications with a more-complex design and components that are not platform-specific is possible. From the time Swing was introduced as an alternative to AWT, a lot more development has been done on it.

When web applications took flight, their UI was pretty basic, because browsers had quite limited capabilities. AWT was introduced to build Java web applications, called **applets**, that looked better, and they were also dynamic. Java applets were small applications that were launched from the browser and then executed within the JVM installed on the user's operating system in a process separate from the browser itself. That is why an applet can be run in a frame of the web page, in a new application window, or in stand-alone tools designed for testing applets. Java applets used the GUI from the operating system, which made them prettier than the bulky initial look of HTML at the time. Java applets are now deprecated and were removed in Java 11.

As for Java desktop applications written in Swing or AWT, they are rarely used anymore; you might learn how to build one in a programming class, but otherwise they are quite...antique. Nevertheless, some institutions and companies still use legacy applications that are built with Swing. For example, I have seen Swing applications used by restaurants to manage tables and orders, and I think most supermarkets use Swing applications to manage shopping items. This section exists in this book not only because you might end up working on maintaining such applications, in which case it is good to know the basics, but also because Swing is still a part of the JDK. All Swing components (AWT too) are part of the `java.desktop` module. So if you want to use Swing components, you have to declare a dependence on this module. Listing 10-7 shows a configuration snippet in which the module of our project that uses Swing declares its dependency on the `java.desktop` module by using the `requires` directive in its `module-info.java` file.

Listing 10-7. Module Configuration for the `using-swing` Project

```
module chapter.ten.swing {
    requires java.desktop;
}
```

The application depicted in Figure 10-3 was built using AWT. This section will cover building something similar in Swing and adding more components to it. The main class of any Swing application is named JFrame, and instances of this type are used to create windows with borders and a title. The code in Listing 10-8 does just that.

Listing 10-8. Basic Swing Demo Class

```
package com.apress.bgn.ten;

import javax.swing.*;
import java.awt.*;

public class BasicSwingDemo extends JFrame {

    public static void main(String... args) {
        BasicSwingDemo swingDemo = new BasicSwingDemo();
        swingDemo.setTitle("Swing Demo Window");
        swingDemo.setSize(new Dimension(500,500));

        swingDemo.setVisible(true);
    }
}
```

The code in Listing 10-8 creates an instance of javax.swing.JFrame, sets a title for it, and sets a size so that when the window is created we can actually see something. To actually display the window, setVisible(true) must be called on the JFrame instance. Running the previous code displays a window like the one shown in Figure 10-4.

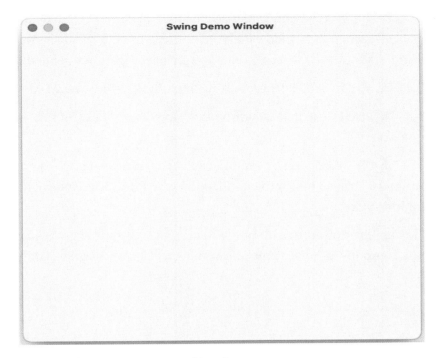

Figure 10-4. *Simple Java Swing application*

By default, the window is positioned in the upper left corner of your main monitor, but you can change that by using some Swing components to compute a position relative to the screen size. Determining the size and position of a Swing window relative to screen size is limited only by the amount of math you are willing to get into.

At this moment, if we close the displayed window, the application keeps running. By default, closing the window just makes it invisible by calling `setVisible(false)`. If we want to change the default behavior to exiting the application, we have to change the default operation that is done when closing. This can be easily done by adding the following line of code after creating the `JFrame` instance:

```
swingDemo.setDefaultCloseOperation(JFrame.EXIT_ON_CLOSE);
```

The JFrame.EXIT_ON_CLOSE constant is part of a set of constants that define application behavior when the window is closed. JFrame.EXIT_ON_CLOSE is used to declare that the application should exit when the window is closed. The other related options are

- DO_NOTHING_ON_CLOSE: Does nothing, including closing the window.

- HIDE_ON_CLOSE: The default option that causes setVisible(false) to be called.

- DISPOSE_ON_CLOSE: An application can have more than one window; this option is used to exit the application when the last displayable window is closed.

Most Swing applications are written by extending the JFrame class to gain more control over its component, so the preceding code can also be written as depicted in Listing 10-9.

Listing 10-9. Swing Application That Exits When Closed

```
package com.apress.bgn.ten;

import javax.swing.*;
import java.awt.*;

public class ExitingSwingDemo extends JFrame {

    public static void main(String... args) {
        ExitingSwingDemo swingDemo = new ExitingSwingDemo();
        swingDemo.setDefaultCloseOperation(JFrame.EXIT_ON_CLOSE);
        swingDemo.setTitle("Swing Demo Window");
        swingDemo.setSize(new Dimension(500,500));

        swingDemo.setVisible(true);
    }
}
```

Now that we have a window, let's start adding components, because changing the look and feel is pointless if we do not have more components so that we can notice the change. Each Swing application has at least one JFrame that is the root, the parent of all other windows, because windows can be created by using the JDialog class as well. JDialog is the main class for creating a dialog window, a special type of window that contains mostly a message and buttons to select options. Developers can use this class to create custom dialog windows or use JOptionPane class methods to create a variety of dialog windows.

Back to adding components to a JFrame instance: components are added to a JFrame by adding them to its container. A reference to the JFrame container can be retrieved by calling getContentPane(). The default content pane is a simple intermediate container that inherits from JComponent, which extends java.awt.Container (Swing being an extension of AWT, most of its components are AWT extensions). For JFrame the default content pane is actually an instance of JPanel. This class has a field of type java.awt.LayoutManager that defines how other components are arranged in a JPanel. The default content pane of a JFrame instance uses a java.awt.BorderLayout as its layout manager, which splits a pane in five regions: EAST, WEST, NORTH, SOUTH, and CENTER. Each of the zones can be referred by a constant with a matching name defined in the BorderLayout.

So if we would like to add an exit button to our application, we could add it to the SOUTH region by writing the code depicted in Listing 10-10.

Listing 10-10. Swing Application Using BorderLayout to Arrange Components

```
package com.apress.bgn.ten;

import javax.swing.*;
import java.awt.*;
import java.awt.event.ActionEvent;
import java.awt.event.ActionListener;

public class LayeredSwingDemo extends JFrame {
    private JPanel mainPanel;
    private JButton exitButton;

    public LayeredSwingDemo(String title) {
        super(title);
        mainPanel = (JPanel) this.getContentPane();
        exitButton = new JButton("Bye Bye!");
        exitButton.addActionListener(new ActionListener() {
            @Override
            public void actionPerformed(ActionEvent e) {
                System.exit(0);
            }
```

```
        });
        mainPanel.add(exitButton, BorderLayout.SOUTH);
    }

    public static void main(String... args) {
        LayeredSwingDemo swingDemo = new LayeredSwingDemo("Swing Demo
        Window");
        swingDemo.setDefaultCloseOperation(JFrame.DO_NOTHING_ON_CLOSE);
        swingDemo.setSize(new Dimension(500, 500));
        swingDemo.setVisible(true);
    }
}
```

In Figure 10-5 you can see the modified application. We've added an exit button in the SOUTH area of the content pane and underlined the overall region arrangement of the BorderLayout.

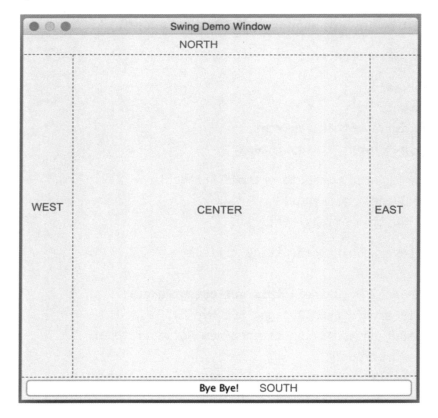

Figure 10-5. *Border layout zones*

Also, because the new button has to be the only way to exit our application, the

```
setDefaultCloseOperation(JFrame.EXIT_ON_CLOSE);
```

was replaced with

```
setDefaultCloseOperation(JFrame.DO_NOTHING_ON_CLOSE);
```

and an `java.awt.event.ActionListener` instance was attached to the button, so that it could record the event of the button being clicked and react accordingly, in this case by exiting the application.

Most Swing components support listeners that can be defined to capture events performed on the object by the user and react in a certain way. As we can see, the button expands and fills the entire space of the region, because it inherits the dimension of the region. To avoid that, the button should be put in another container, and that container should use a different layout: `FlowLayout`. As the name implies, this layout allows for Swing components to be added in a directional flow, as in a paragraph. Adjustments can be made similar to text formatting in text documents, and constants are defined for components being aligned: in the center (CENTER), left-justified (LEFT), and so on. Continuing the previous example, we will wrap the `exitButton` in another `JPanel` that will make use of the `FlowLayout`.

Listing 10-11 shows how `FlowLayout` can be used to place a button in the right corner of the `JFrame` instance.

Listing 10-11. Swing Application Using `BorderLayout` and `FlowLayout` to Arrange Components

```
public LayeredSwingDemo(String title) {
        super(title);
        mainPanel = (JPanel) this.getContentPane();
        exitButton = new JButton("Bye Bye!");
        exitButton.addActionListener(e -> System.exit(0));
        JPanel exitPanel = new JPanel();
        FlowLayout flowLayout = new FlowLayout();
        flowLayout.setAlignment(FlowLayout.RIGHT);
        exitPanel.setLayout(flowLayout);
        exitPanel.setComponentOrientation(ComponentOrientation.RIGHT_
        TO_LEFT);
```

```
        exitPanel.add(exitButton);
        mainPanel.add(exitPanel, BorderLayout.SOUTH);
    }
...
```

There are more layouts available in the JDK, but for now let's complete the application by adding a list with a number of entries. We'll also add a listener to it, so that when an element is clicked, its value is added to a text area added to the center of the frame.

A Swing list can be created by instantiating the JList<E> class. This will create an object that displays a list of objects and allows the user to select one or more items. The Swing JList<E> class contains a field of type ListModel<E> that manages the data contents displayed by the list. After each object is created and has elements added to it, the object is associated with an index. When the user selects an object, the index can be used for processing as well. In the snippet shown in Listing 10-12, the JList<E> object is declared and initialized and a ListSelectionListener is associated with it to define the action to perform when an element from the list is selected. In our case the element's value must be added to a JTextArea.

Listing 10-12. Swing Application Using Layouts and JTextArea to Arrange Components

```
private static String[] data = {"John Mayer", "Frank Sinatra",
    "Seth MacFarlane", "Nina Simone", "BB King", "Peggy Lee"};
private JList<String> list;
private JTextArea textArea;
...
    textArea = new JTextArea(50, 10);
    //NORTH
    list = new JList<>(data);
    list.addListSelectionListener(new ListSelectionListener() {
        @Override
        public void valueChanged(ListSelectionEvent e) {
            if (!e.getValueIsAdjusting()) {
                textArea.append(list.getSelectedValue() + "\n");
            }
        }
    }
```

```
});
mainPanel.add(list, BorderLayout.NORTH);
//CENTER
JScrollPane txtPanel = new JScrollPane(textArea);
textArea.setBackground(Color.LIGHT_GRAY);
mainPanel.add(txtPanel, BorderLayout.CENTER);
```

• • •

When a user clicks a list element, two things happen: the previous element is deselected, and the one that was clicked is selected, so the selected element changes. The getValueIsAdjusting() method returns whether this is one in a series of multiple events (selection events, click events, whatever is supported), where changes are still being made, and we test if this method returns false to check that the selection has been already made, so we can get the value of the current selected element and add it to the text area.

The JTextArea instance is added to a JScrollPane instance that allows for the textArea contents to still be visible as it fills with text by providing a scrollbar or two, depending on the configuration. The JScrollPane can be wrapped around a list with too many items as well, to make sure all of them are accessible. Also, as we are not interested in user-provided input via the text area, the setEditable(false); method is called.

Now that we have a more complex application, it is time to play with the look and feel of the application. Until now, we've used the default theme, provided by the underlying operating system. Using Swing, the look and feel can be configured as one of the defaults supported by the JDK, or extra custom ones can be used that are provided as dependencies in the project classpath, or developers can create their own. To specify a look and feel explicitly, the following line of code must be added in the main method, before any Swing component is created:

```
UIManager.setLookAndFeel(..).
```

This method receives as a parameter a String value representing the fully qualified name of the look-and-feel subclass. This class must extend the abstract javax.Swing.LookAndFeel. Although not necessary, you could specify explicitly that you want to use the native GUI by calling

```
UIManager.setLookAndFeel(UIManager.getCrossPlatformLookAndFeelClassName());
```

Knowing this, let's do something interesting. The UIManager class contains utility methods and nested classes used to manage look and feel for Swing applications. One of these methods is getInstalledLookAndFeels(), which extracts the list of supported look-and-feel implementations and returns them as a LookAndFeelInfo[]. With this in mind, let's do the following: list all the supported look-and-feel implementations, add them to our list, and apply each when a user selects it. Unfortunately, as Swing is rarely used these days, there are not that many custom look-and-feel implementations that we could use in our application, so the only thing to do is to work with what the JDK has. The code in Listing 10-13 initializes the data array with the look-and-feel fully qualified class names.

Listing 10-13. Code Sample to Initialize the List of Supported Look-and-Feel Implementations

```
...
    public static void main(String... args) throws Exception {
        UIManager.setLookAndFeel(UIManager.
        getCrossPlatformLookAndFeelClassName());
        UIManager.LookAndFeelInfo[] looks = UIManager.
                                            getInstalledLookAndFeels();
        data = new String[looks.length];
        int i =0;
        for (UIManager.LookAndFeelInfo look : looks) {
            data[i++] = look.getClassName();
        }
        SwingDemo swingDemo = new SwingDemo("Swing Demo Window");
        swingDemo.setDefaultCloseOperation(JFrame.DO_NOTHING_ON_CLOSE);
        swingDemo.setSize(new Dimension(500, 500));
        swingDemo.setVisible(true);
    }
...
```

Now the ListSelectionListener implementation becomes a little complicated, because after selecting a new look-and-feel class, we have to call repaint() on the JFrame instance to apply the new look and feel, so we'll take the declaration out into its own class and provide the SwingDemo object as an argument, so that repaint() can be called on it, inside the valueChanged(..) method. The code snippet is depicted in Listing 10-14.

Listing 10-14. Code Sample Showing repaint() Being Called

```
private class LFListener implements ListSelectionListener {
    private JFrame parent;
    public LFListener(JFrame swingDemo) {
        parent = swingDemo;
    }
    @Override
    public void valueChanged(ListSelectionEvent e) {
        if (!e.getValueIsAdjusting()) {
            textArea.append(list.getSelectedValue() + "\n");
            try {
                UIManager.setLookAndFeel(list.getSelectedValue());
                Thread.sleep(1000);
                parent.repaint();
            } catch (Exception ee) {
                System.err.println(" Could not set look and feel! ");
            }
        }
    }
}
```

If we run the modified program and select each item in the list one by one, we should see the window look change a little bit. In Figure 10-6 you can see all the windows side by side; the differences are barely noticeable, but they are there.

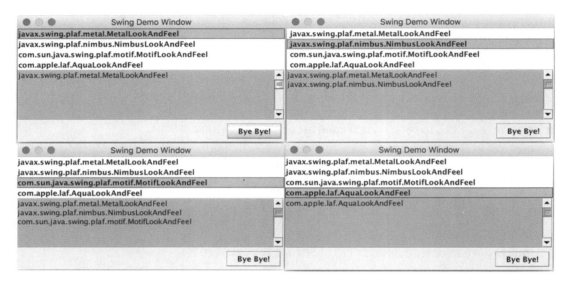

Figure 10-6. *Different look and feel provided by the JDK*

This is what you can do with Swing components with a few lines of code. There are a lot more components in the Swing library, but again, Swing is not used that much anymore. As the focus nowadays is on mobile and web applications, we'll end this section here. If you ever need to create or maintain a Swing application, Oracle provides quite an extensive tutorial, with a lot of examples, that you can directly copy and paste and adapt to your necessities[1].

Introducing JavaFX

JavaFX Script was a scripting language designed by Sun Microsystems, forming part of the JavaFX family of technologies on the Java platform. It was released shortly after JDK 6 in December 2008, and for a while developers expected it would be dropped because it really did not catch on that much, being a totally different language.

After acquiring Sun Microsystems, Oracle decided to keep JavaFX Script, and they transformed into the JavaFX library, which is a set of graphics and media packages that can be used by developers to design, create, test, debug, and deploy rich client applications that operate consistently across diverse platforms, including mobile ones. JavaFX was intended to replace Swing as the main GUI library of the JDK, but both Swing

---

[1] https://docs.oracle.com/javase/tutorial/uiswing/examples/layout/index.html

and JavaFX have been part of all JDK versions until 10. This changed in JDK 11. Starting with JDK 11, JavaFX became available only as a separate module, and that module became part of the OpenJDK under the OpenJFX project[2].

JavaFX is a Java library that is used to develop desktop applications as well as Rich Internet Applications (RIAs). JavaFX is still not used as much as Oracle hoped, but separating it from the JDK allowed it to transform into an actual competitor for the other existing GUI toolkits on the market, like Eclipse SWT[3] and Google Web Toolkit (GWT)[4].

After its exclusion from the JDK, JavaFX has evolved on its own, keeping itself in sync with the Java versions being released. At the moment when this chapter is being written, there is a JavaFX 23 version available for download[5]. The official documentation is good enough to get you started.

Information   The project for this book is built using Maven, and this makes things very practical, because the Maven configuration ensures that the necessary dependencies are added to the classpath without too much of a fuss.

JavaFX code is currently normal Java code, so no more scripting. JavaFX components are defined under a list of `java.fx` modules. In the configuration snippet shown in Listing 10-15, you can see that the module of our project that uses JavaFX declares its dependency on a few `java.fx` modules by using the `requires` directive in its `module-info.java` file.

Listing 10-15. Configuration Sample for a Project Using `java.fx` Modules

```
module chapter.ten.javafx {
    requires javafx.base;
    requires javafx.graphics;
    requires javafx.controls;
    opens com.apress.bgn.ten to javafx.graphics;
}
```

---

[2] https://openjfx.io
[3] https://www.eclipse.org/swt
[4] https://www.gwtproject.org
[5] https://jdk.java.net/javafx23

The JavaFX application launcher uses reflection to launch an application, so we need to open the com.apress.bgn.ten package to allow reflection using the opens directive. Without that directive a java.lang.IllegalAccessException is thrown and the application does not start:

The easiest application to start with is a simple window that has just a closing option. The code to display a plain square window is depicted in Listing 10-16.

Listing 10-16. Simple JavaFX Application

```
package com.apress.bgn.ten;

import javafx.application.Application;
import javafx.scene.Scene;
import javafx.scene.layout.StackPane;
import javafx.stage.Stage;

public class JavaFxDemo extends Application {
    public static void main(String... args) {
        launch(args);
    }

    @Override
    public void start(Stage primaryStage) {
        primaryStage.setTitle("JavaFX Demo Window!");
        var root = new StackPane();
        primaryStage.setScene(new Scene(root, 500, 500));
        primaryStage.show();
    }
}
```

The first thing you need to know is that the main class of the application must extend the javafx.application.Application class, because this is the entry point for a JavaFX application. This is required because JavaFX applications are run by a new performance graphics engine named **Prism** that sits on top of the JVM. Aside from Prism, JavaFX comes with its own windowing system named **Glass**, a media engine and a web engine. They are not exposed publicly; the only thing available to developers is the JavaFX API that provides access to any components you might need to build applications with fancy interfaces. All these engines are tied together by the **Quantum** toolkit, which is the interface between these engines and the layer above in the stack. The Quantum toolkit manages execution threads and rendering.

The `launch(..)` method is a static method in the `Application` class that is used to launch a stand-alone application. It is usually called from the main method and can be called only once; otherwise, a `java.lang.IllegalStateException` will be thrown. The `launch(..)` method does not return until the application is exited, by closing all windows or calling `Platform.exit()`. The `launch(..)` method creates a JavaFxDemo instance, calls the `init()` method on it, and then calls `start(..)`. The `start(..)` method is declared abstract in the `Application` class, so the developer is forced to provide a concrete implementation.

A JavaFX application is built using components defined under the `javafx.scene` package and has a hierarchical organization. The core class of the `javafx.scene` package is `javafx.scene.Node`, which is the root of the `Scene` hierarchy. Classes in this hierarchy provide implementations for all the visual elements of the application's user interface. Because all of them have `Node` as a root class, visual elements are called *nodes*, which makes an application *a scene graph of nodes*, and the initial node of this graph is called a *root*. Each node has a unique identifier, a style class, and a bounding volume, and except the root node, each node in the graph has a single parent and zero or more children. Besides that, a node has the following properties:

- Effects, such as blurs and shadow, which are useful when you hover with your mouse cursor over the interface, to make sure you click the right component

- Opacity

- Transformations for changing visual state or position

- Event handlers, similar to listeners in Swing, used to define reaction on mouse, key, and input methods

- Application-specific state

The scene graph simplifies building rich interfaces a lot, and because it also includes primitive graphics such as rectangles, text, images, and media. Animating various graphics can be accomplished by the animation APIs from package `javax.animation`. If you are interested in finding out more about what's under the hood of JavaFX, check out the information at Dev.Java[6]. The focus of this book is more on *how to do things* than on *how they work*, so reading that additional article might help you with the design of your future solutions.

We've started again with a simple window. The first step is to add a button for quitting the application. As rendering a JavaFX application involves a rendering engine, this means it has to shut down gracefully, so calling System.exit(0) is not a preferred option. The contents of the start(..) method must call a special JavaFX method to close the application gracefully. The code is shown in Listing 10-17.

Listing 10-17. Simple JavaFX Application with a Button

```java
package com.apress.bgn.ten;

// other 'javafx' import statements omitted
import javafx.scene.control.Button;

public class JavaFxDemo extends Application {

    void main() {
        launch();
    }

    @Override
    public void start(Stage primaryStage) {
        primaryStage.setTitle("Java FX Button Demo!");

        var btn = new Button();
        btn.setText("Bye bye! ");
        btn.setOnAction(new EventHandler<ActionEvent>() {
            @Override
            public void handle(ActionEvent event) {
                Platform.exit();
            }
        });
        //btn.setOnAction(_ -> Platform.exit());
```

---

[6] https://dev.java/learn/javafx/structure

```
        var root = new StackPane();
        root.getChildren().addAll(new Rectangle(100,100, Color.PINK), btn);
        primaryStage.setScene(new Scene(root, 300, 300));
        primaryStage.show();
    }
}
```

Running the JavaFxDemo class causes the window depicted in Figure 10-7 to pop up on your screen, and if you click the Bye bye! Button, the application will be gracefully closed because of the Platform.exit() call.

Figure 10-7. *JavaFX window demo*

The button and the pink rectangle are added to an instance of StackPane that lays out its children in a back-to-front stack. The children are sized to fill the StackPane instance, unless their size is already fixed, and by default they are centered. JavaFX supports arranging nodes in a window in a manner similar to Swing, but Java FX provides a few layout panes that support several different styles of layouts. The equivalent of a JPanel with BorderLayout manager in JavaFX is a built-in layout named

BorderPane. The BorderPane provides five regions in which to place your nodes, with distribution similar to BorderLayout, but different names. Listing 10-18 shows the code to place our button in the bottom region in the right corner.

Listing 10-18. Simple JavaFX Application with a Properly Positioned Button

```
package com.apress.bgn.ten;

// other 'javafx' import statements omitted
import javafx.scene.layout.HBox;

public class PannedJavaFxDemo extends Application {
    void main() {
        launch();
    }

    @Override
    public void start(Stage primaryStage) {
        primaryStage.setTitle("Java FX Demo Window!");

        var exitButton = new Button();
        exitButton.setText("Bye bye! ");
        exitButton.setOnAction(_ -> Platform.exit());

        var borderPane = new BorderPane();
        var box = new HBox();
        box.setPadding(new Insets(10, 12, 10, 12));
        box.setSpacing(10);
        box.setAlignment(Pos.BASELINE_RIGHT);
        box.setStyle("-fx-background-color: #85929e;");
        box.getChildren().add(exitButton);
        borderPane.setBottom(box);

        var root = new StackPane();
        root.getChildren().add(borderPane);
        primaryStage.setScene(new Scene(root, 500, 500));
        primaryStage.show();
    }
}
```

Running the PannedJavaFxDemo class causes the window depicted in Figure 10-8 to pop up on your screen; the figure has been modified to show the regions of a BorderPane.

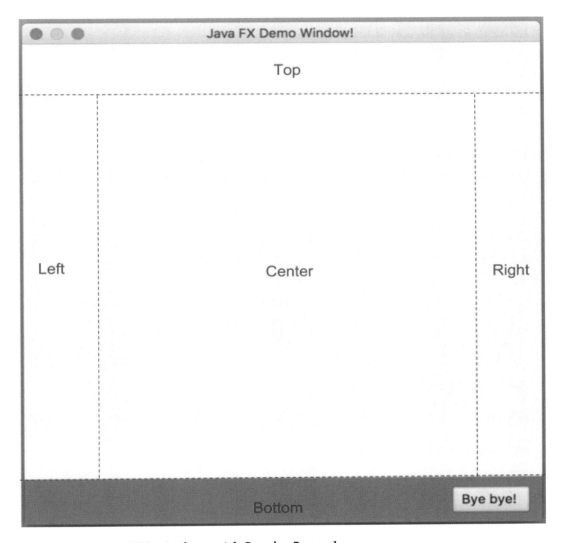

Figure 10-8. *JavaFX window with* BorderPane *demo*

As you can see, the approach to decide where our button should be located is similar to the approach in Swing, with a few differences. The BorderPane has five regions named: Top, Bottom, Center, Left, and Right. To place a node in each of those regions, a set*(..) method for each of them has been defined: setTop(..), setBottom(..),

setCenter(..), setLeft(..), and setRight(..). To further customize the position
of the node, it should be placed in an HBox node, another JavaFX element that can be
customized quite extensively. As you can see from the code in Listing 10-18, we are setting
the background using CSS style elements. We customize the space between nodes in it
and the borders of the containing node by using an instance of class Insets, and
we customize the alignment of the contained nodes by calling box.setAlignment
(Pos.BASELINE_RIGHT). There are many more things that HBox supports, so what you
can do with a box is limited (mostly) only by your imagination.

So besides *making pretty code* in Listing 10-18, we did the following: the root node
became parent to a BorderPane node; in the bottom region of the BorderPane, a HBox
was added; and this HBox instance became parent for a Button. As you can see, this
organization is hierarchic, with the button being the last node in the hierarchy.

We also avoided using a layer pane, by styling the HBox node properly.

It is time to add the last functionality to our application: the text area and the list
with selectable elements. On being selected, the value is added to the text area. Creating
a text area in JavaFX is simple. The class has a pretty obvious name: TextArea. We can
directly add the node in the center region of the BorderPane because the JavaFX text area
is scrollable by default. So there is no need to put it in a ScrollPane, although the class
does exist in the javafx.scene.control package and is useful to display nodes inside it
that make a form that is bigger than the window size. The three lines of code in
Listing 10-19 create a node of type TextArea, declare it to not be editable, and add it to
the center region of the BorderPane.

Listing 10-19. Creating and Configuring a JavaFX TextArea

```
import javafx.scene.control.TextArea;
...
var textArea = new TextArea();
textArea.setEditable(false);
borderPane.setCenter(textArea);
```

The next functionality to add is the list. The list is a little more complicated, but also
a lot more fun to work with, because by using JavaFX there is a lot you can do with a list.
The class that needs to be instantiated to create a list object is named ComboBox<T>. This
class is just one of a bigger family of classes used to create lists, the root class being the

abstract class `ComboBoxBase<T>`. The choice of the proper implementation depends on the desired behavior of the list, such as whether we want support for single selection or multiple selection and whether or not we want the list to be editable. In our case, the `ComboBox<T>` class matches the following requirements: we need a noneditable list that supports single element section. A `ComboBox<T>` has a `valueProperty()` method that returns the current user input. The user input can be based on a selection from a drop-down list or the input manually provided by the user when the list is editable. Listing 10-20 shows how to add a list to the top section of the `BorderPane` and add a listener to record the selected value and save it the `TextArea` that we previously declared.

Listing 10-20. Creating and Configuring a JavaFX `ComboBox`

```
import javafx.scene.control.ComboBox;
...
private static String data = {"John Mayer", "Frank Sinatra",
        "Seth MacFarlane", "Nina Simone", "BB King", "Peggy Lee"};
...
ComboBox<String> comboBox = new ComboBox<>();
comboBox.getItems().addAll(data);
borderPane.setTop(comboBox);

comboBox.valueProperty().addListener(
    new ChangeListener<String>() {
    @Override
    public void changed(ObservableValue<? extends String> observable,
    String oldValue, String newValue) {
        textArea.appendText(newValue + "\n");
    }
});
```

The `ComboBox<T>` value field is an `ObservableValue<T>` instance. The listener is added to this instance and it is notified anytime its value changes and its `changed(..)` method is called. As you can see, the `changed(..)` method receives as an argument the the value previously selected in the list as well, because maybe we have some logic that requires both.

In AWT and Swing there was not much that you could do with a list visually. You had the default look and feel and that was that. JavaFX supports more visual customization for nodes, as it even supports CSS. That is why in the next section we'll make our ComboBox<T> list interesting. In Java FX each entry in a list is a cell that can be drawn differently. To do that, we have to add a CellFactory<T> to this class, which will create for each item in a list an instance of ListCell<T>.

If a CellFactory<T> is not specified, the cells will be created with the default style. Listing 10-21 shows the code to customize a ComboBox<T>.

Listing 10-21. Creating and Customizing Colors of Cells of a JavaFX ComboBox

```java
comboBox.setCellFactory(
    new Callback<>() {
        @Override
        public ListCell<String> call(ListView<String> param) {
            return new ListCell<>() {
            {
                super.setPrefWidth(200);
            }

            @Override
            public void updateItem(String item, boolean empty) {
                super.updateItem(item, empty);
                if (item != null) {
                    setText(item);
                    if (item.contains("John") || item.contains("BB")) {
                        setTextFill(Color.RED);
                    } else if (item.contains("Frank") || item.
                    contains("Peggy")) {
                        setTextFill(Color.GREEN);
                    } else if (item.contains("Seth")) {
                        setTextFill(Color.BLUE);
                    } else {
                        setTextFill(Color.BLACK);
                    }
```

```
            } else {
                setText(null);
            }
        }
    };
}
});
```

The javafx.util.Callback interface is a practical utility interface that can be used every time a callback is needed after a certain action. In this case, after a String value is added to the ListView of the ComboBox<T> node (ListView as the name says is the visual, the façade type of a ComboBox<T> , that displays a horizontal or vertical list of items), a cell is created and some piece of logic is inserted there to decide the color of the text depicted in the cell based on its value.

Inside the ListCell<T> declaration there is a block of code that seems out of place:

```
{
    super.setPrefWidth(200);
}
```

The previous block is an interesting way to call a method from the parent class inside the declaration of an anonymous class. The setPrefWidth(200) method is called here to make sure all the ListCell<T> instances will have the same size. The logic in the updateItem(..) method is quite obvious, and thus does not need any extended explanation. The result of adding the cell factory can be viewed in Figure 10-9.

Figure 10-9. JavaFX colored ComboBox demo

Internationalization

Interactive applications are usually created to be deployed on more than one server
and available 24/7 and in multiple locations. As not all of us speak the same language,
the key to convince people to become your clients and use your application is to build
it in multiple languages. The process of designing an application so that it meets
user needs in multiple countries and easily adapts to satisfy those needs is called

internationalization. For example, take the initial Google page. Depending on the location where it is accessed, it changes language according to that area. When you create an account, you can select the language you prefer. This does not mean that Google has built a web application for each region; rather, it's a single web application that displays text in different languages depending on the location of the user. Internationalization should always be taken into consideration in the design phase of an application, because adding it later is quite difficult. We have not built a web application yet (we will in the next section), so we will internationalize the JavaFX application that we have built so far in this chapter.

When you start reading about internationalization you might notice that files or directories containing the internationalization property files are named *i18n*, which is because there are 18 letters between *i* and *n* in the English alphabet.

Internationalization is based on locale. **Locale** is the term given to a combination of language and region. The application locale is what decides which internationalization file will be used to customize the application. The locale concept is implemented in Java by the `java.util.Locale` class, and a `Locale` instance represents a geographical, political, or cultural region. When an application depends on the locale, we say that it is *locale-sensitive*, as most applications are nowadays. Selecting a locale can be something a user has to do as well. Each `Locale` can be used to select the corresponding *locale resources*, which are files containing locale-specific configurations. These files are grouped per locale and can usually be found under the `resources` directory. These resources are used to configure an instance of `java.util.ResourceBundle` that can be used to manage locale-specific resources.

To build a proper use case for localization, we will modify the previous JavaFX application: instead of singer names, the list will contain a list of animal names with labels that can be translated into various languages. We'll also add a list with the available languages, and when a language is selected from this list, a `Locale` static variable will be set with the corresponding locale and the window will be reinitialized so that all labels can be translated to the new language. Let's start by creating the resource files.

Resource files have the `.properties` extension and contain, as the name says, a list of properties and values. Each line respects the following pattern: `property_name=property_value`, and if it doesn't it is not considered an internationalization resource file. Each property name must be unique in the file; if there is a duplicate, it will be ignored and IntelliJ IDEA will complain by underlining the property with red.

For every language that needs to be supported, we need to create one resource file that contains the same property names as the other files but different property values, as the values will represent the translation of that value in each language. All files must have names that contain a common suffix and end with the language name and the country, separated by underscores, because these are the two elements needed to create a `Locale` instance. For our JavaFX application we have four files, depicted in Figure 10-10.

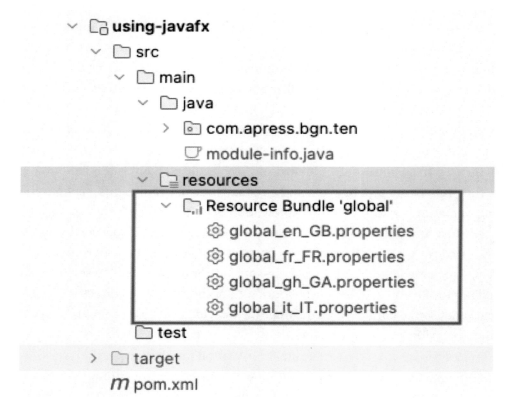

Figure 10-10. *Resource bundle with three resource files*

The suffix is `global`, and this will be our resource bundle name as well. This is made quite obvious by IntelliJ IDEA, which figures out what our resource files are used for and depicts them in an obvious way. The contents of the files are depicted in Table 10-1.

Table 10-1. *Contents of Resource Files*

Property Name	Property Value in global_en_GB	Property Value in global_fr_FR	Property Value in global_it_IT	Property Value in global_gh_GA
English	English	Anglais	Inglese	Beurla
French	French	Français	Francese	Fhraing
Italian	Italian	Italien	Italiano	Eadailteach
Gaelic	Gaelic	Gaélique	Gaelico	Gàidhlig
Cat	Cat	Chat	Gatto	Cat
Dog	Dog	Chien	Cane	Cù
Parrot	Parrot	Chien	Pappagallo	Pioraid
Mouse	Mouse	Souris	Topo	Luch
Cow	Cow	Perroquet	Mucca	Bò
Pig	Pig	Porc	Maiale	Muc
WindowTitle	Java FX Demo Window!	Java FX Démo Fenêtre!	Java FX Dimostratione Finestra!	Java FX Demo Uinneag!
Byebye	Bye bye!	Bye bye!	Ciao!	Tìoraidh!
ChoosePet	Choose Pet:	Choisir un animal de compagnie:	Scegli un animale domestico:	Tagh peata:
ChooseLanguage	Choose Language:	Choisissez la langue:	Scegli la lingua:	Tagh cànan:

IntelliJ IDEA can help you to edit resource bundle files easily and make sure you are not missing any keys from any of them by providing a special view for them. When you open a resource file in IntelliJ IDEA, in the bottom left corner you should see two tabs: Text and Resource Bundle. Clicking the **Text** tab allows you to edit a properties file as a normal text file. Clicking the **Resource Bundle** tab opens a special view that has on the left all the property names in the resource files and on the right views from all resource files containing values for property names selected. In Figure 10-11 you can see this view and the values for property ChooseLanguage.

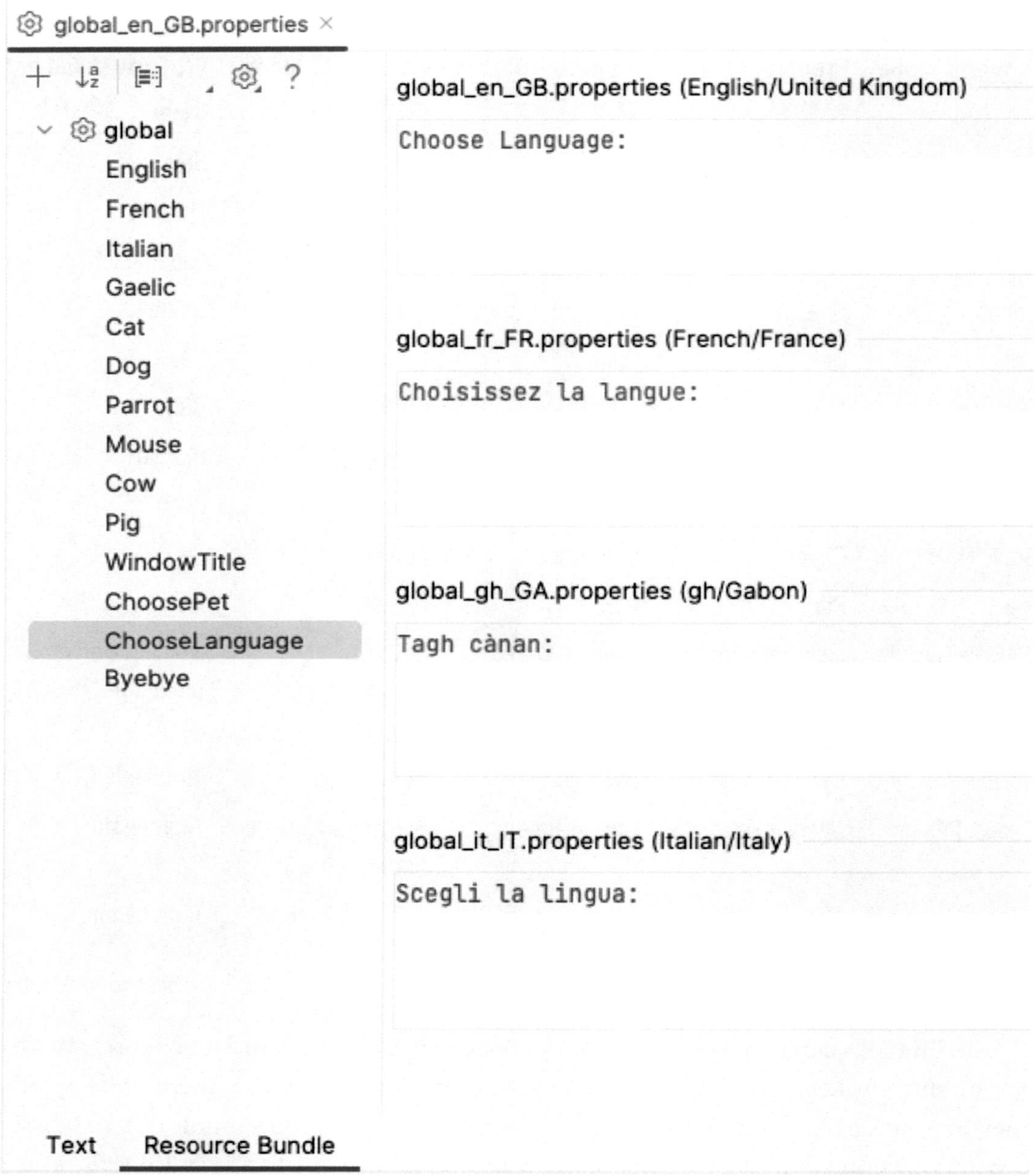

Figure 10-11. *IntelliJ IDEA Resource Bundle editor*

Property names can contain special characters underscore (_) and dot (.) to separate parts of them. In this book example the property names are simple, because we have so few of them. In bigger applications, property names usually contain a prefix that is relevant to their purpose; for example, if the property value is a title, the name will be prefixed with `title`. The property names in our files could be changed to those listed in Listing 10-22.

Listing 10-22. Recommended Internationalization Property Names

```
English --> label.lang.english
French --> label.lang.french
Italian --> label.lang.italian
Gaelic --> label.lang.gaelic
Cat --> label.pet.cat
Dog --> label.pet.dog
Parrot --> label.pet.parrot
Mouse --> label.pet.mouse
Cow --> label.pet.cow
Pig --> label.pet.pig
WindowTitle --> title.window
Byebye --> label.button.byebye
ChoosePet --> label.choose.pet
ChooseLanguage --> label.choose.language
```

Now that we have covered how the resource files should be written, let's see how they can be used. To create a `ResourceBundle` instance, we first need a locale. Applications have a default locale that can be obtained by calling `Locale.getDefault()`, and a `ResourceBundle` instance can be obtained by using a bundle name and a Locale instance, as depicted in the code snippet here:

```
Locale locale = Locale.getDefault();
ResourceBundle labels = ResourceBundle.getBundle("global", locale);
```

When a valid `ResourceBundle` is obtained, it can be used to replace all hard-coded `String` instances with calls to return text values from the resource file matching the selected locale. So every time we need to set a label for a node, instead of using the actual text, we use a call to `resourceBundle.getString("[property_name]")` to get the localized text.

673

When a JavaFX window is reloaded, all its nodes are re-created. To be able to influence how they are re-created, we need to add a couple of static properties to keep the selected locale set. For the application built so far, after internationalizing it, the code looks like the code in Listing 10-23.

Listing 10-23. JavaFX Internationalized Application

```java
package com.apress.bgn.ten;

import javafx.application.*;
import javafx.geometry.*;
import javafx.scene.*;
import javafx.stage.*;

import java.io.File;
import java.net.URL;
import java.net.URLClassLoader;
import java.util.Locale;
import java.util.ResourceBundle;

public class InternationalizationDemo extends Application {

    private static final String BUNDLE_LOCATION = "chapter10/using-javafx/
    src/main/resources";

    private static ResourceBundle resourceBundle = null;
    private static Locale locale = Locale.of("en", "GB");
    private static int selectedLang = 0;

    void main() {
        launch();
    }

    @Override
    public void start(Stage primaryStage) throws Exception {
        loadLocale(locale);
        primaryStage.setTitle(resourceBundle.getString("WindowTitle"));

        String[] data = {resourceBundle.getString("Cat"),
                resourceBundle.getString("Dog"),
```

```
        resourceBundle.getString("Parrot"),
        resourceBundle.getString("Mouse"),
        resourceBundle.getString("Cow"),
        resourceBundle.getString("Pig")};

var borderPane = new BorderPane();

//Top
final ComboBox<String> comboBox = new ComboBox<>();
comboBox.getItems().addAll(data);

final ComboBox<String> langList = new ComboBox<>();
String[] languages = {
        resourceBundle.getString("English"),
        resourceBundle.getString("French"),
        resourceBundle.getString("Italian"),
        resourceBundle.getString("Gaelic")};

langList.getItems().addAll(languages);
langList.getSelectionModel().select(selectedLang);

var gridPane = new GridPane();
gridPane.setHgap(10);
gridPane.setVgap(10);

var labelLang = new Label(resourceBundle.
                getString("ChooseLanguage"));
gridPane.add(labelLang, 0, 0);
gridPane.add(langList, 1, 0);

var labelPet = new Label(resourceBundle.getString("ChoosePet"));
gridPane.add(labelPet, 0, 1);
gridPane.add(comboBox, 1, 1);

borderPane.setTop(gridPane);

//Center
final TextArea textArea = new TextArea();
textArea.setEditable(false);
borderPane.setCenter(textArea);
```

```
comboBox.valueProperty().addListener((_, _, newValue)
        -> textArea.appendText(newValue + "\n"));

langList.valueProperty().addListener((_, _, _)
        -> {
    int idx = langList.getSelectionModel().getSelectedIndex();
    selectedLang = idx;
    locale = switch (idx) {
        case 1 -> Locale.of("fr", "FR");
        case 2 -> Locale.of("it", "IT");
        case 3 -> Locale.of("gh", "GA"); // Scottish Gaelic
        default -> Locale.of("en", "GB");
    };

    primaryStage.close();
    Platform.runLater(() -> {
        try {
            new InternationalizationDemo().start(new Stage());
        } catch (Exception e) {
            System.err.println("Could not reload application!");
        }
    });
});

var box = new HBox();
box.setPadding(new Insets(10, 12, 10, 12));
box.setSpacing(10);
box.setAlignment(Pos.BASELINE_RIGHT);
box.setStyle("-fx-background-color: #85929e;");
Button exitButton = new Button();
exitButton.setText(resourceBundle.getString("Byebye"));
exitButton.setOnAction(event -> Platform.exit());
box.getChildren().add(exitButton);
borderPane.setBottom(box);

//Bottom
var root = new StackPane();
root.getChildren().add(borderPane);
```

```
        primaryStage.setScene(new Scene(root, 500, 500));
        primaryStage.show();
    }

    private void loadLocale(Locale locale) throws Exception {
        var file = new File(BUNDLE_LOCATION);
        URL[] url = {file.toURI().toURL()};
        var loader = new URLClassLoader(url);

        resourceBundle = ResourceBundle.getBundle("global", locale, loader);
    }
}
```

You might be wondering why we used another way of loading the resource bundle and why the full relative path to the bundle location was used. If we want the application to be runnable from the IntelliJ interface, we have to provide a path relative to the execution context of the application. When the application is built and packed up in a runnable Java archive, the resource files are part of it and in the classpath. When running the application by executing the `main()` method in a Java IDE, the classpath is relative to the actual location of the project.

The code snippet in Listing 10-24 restarts the scene by closing the `Stage`, then instantiates a `JavaFxDemo` object and calls `start(..)`. This means the whole hierarchical node structure is re-created and the only state that is kept is the one that was defined in static objects. This is needed for the locale setting, because the `start(..)` method execution now starts with a call to `loadLocale(locale)`, which selects the locale of the application and loads the `ResourceBundle` so that all nodes can be labeled with text returned by it.

Listing 10-24. JavaFX Code Snippet to Restart the Scene

```
primaryStage.close();
Platform.runLater(() -> {
    try {
        new JavaFxDemo().start(new Stage());
    } catch (Exception e) {
        System.err.println("Could not reload application!");
    }
});
```

The result of the very simple application that we have built and modified thus far is depicted in Figure 10-12.

Figure 10-12. *JavaFX internationalized application*

If you ever need to build interfaces that are more complex and require internationalization, you will need to configure more than translations. You might need to have files with different number and date formats, or multiple resource bundles.

Internationalization is quite a big topic, and a quite important one, as an application is rarely built nowadays to be used in a single region. For a Java beginner, just knowing what the supporting classes are and how they can be used is a very good starting point.

Building a Web Application

A web application is an application that runs on a server and can be accessed using a browser. Until recently, most Java applications had to be hosted on web servers like Apache Tomcat or Eclipse GlassFish or enterprise servers like JBoss (currently known as WildFly) or Apache TomEE so that they could be accessed. You would write the web application with the classes and HTML or Jakarta Server Pages (JSP) files, pack it in a WAR (Web Archive) file or an EAR (Enterprise Archive) file, deploy it to a server, and start the server. The server would provide the context of the application and map requests to classes that would provide the answers to be served as responses. Assuming the application would be deployed on a Tomcat server, in Figure 10-13 you can see an abstract schema of the deployed application functionality.

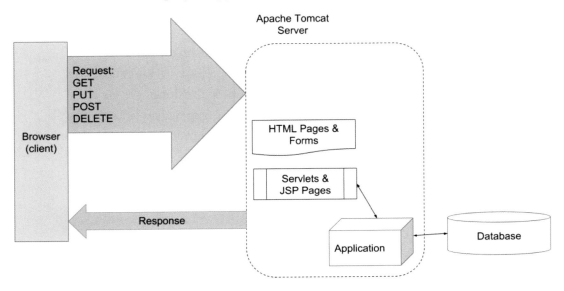

Figure 10-13. *Web application deployed on an Apache Tomcat server*

Requests to a web application can also come from clients other than browsers (e.g., mobile applications), but because this section covers web applications, we'll assume all requests to our application come from a browser.

Before we build a web application, let's briefly explain a very important thing: the Internet. The Internet is an information system made up of a lot of computers linked together. Some computers host application servers that provide access to applications, some computers access these applications, and some do both. The communication between these computers is done over a network through a list of protocols: HTTP, FTP, SMTP, POP, and so on. The most popular protocol is HTTP (Hypertext Transfer Protocol), which is an asymmetric request-response client-server protocol, meaning that the client makes a request to the server and then the server sends a response. Subsequent requests have no knowledge of one another and they do not share any state, thus they are *stateless*.

HTTP requests can be of different types, categorized by the action they require the application on the server to perform, but there are four types that are most commonly used by developers (the ones listed under "Request" in the arrow in Figure 10-13). We won't go into depth regarding request components, as they are not really related to Java, but we'll cover enough details to understand how a web application works. The following list presents the four request types (also called *request methods*) and the types of responses the server sends back for each of them:

- **GET**: Whenever a user enters a URL in the browser, such as `https://my-site.com/index.html`, the browser transforms the address into a Request message and sends it to the web server. What the browser does can be easily viewed by opening the debugger view in **Firefox**, clicking the **Network** tab, and trying to access `https://www.google.com/`. In Figure 10-14 you can see Firefox debugger view showing the URL being requested and the contents of the Request message.

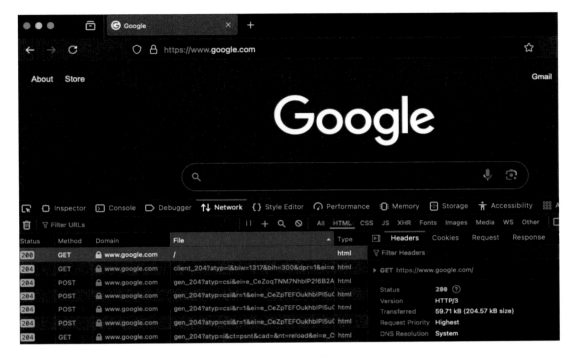

Figure 10-14. *Network debugger view in Firefox*

In the right part of the image, you can see the URL being
requested, the type of request (which is GET in this case), and the
Remote address of the server where the request was sent to. GET
requests are used to retrieve something from the server, in this
example, a web page. If the web page can be found, the response
is sent with the page to be displayed by the browser and other
attributes, such as a status code to communicate that all went fine.
There is a long list of HTTP status codes, but the most important
one is the 200 code, which means all went fine. In Figure 10-14,
you can see that to display the page a lot of additional requests
are done, after the initial request is replied to, and all subsequent
requests are successful, because the status returned by the server
is put in the first column in the table, and it's always 200 or 204.

- **PUT**: This type of request is used to send data to the server to be used to update existing data. In enterprise applications, a PUT request is interpreted as a request to update an existing object. The request contains the updated version of the object and the means to identify it. A successful PUT request generates a response with a status code of 204.

- **POST**: This type of request is used to send data to the server, but the server is instructed to save data for storage as well. The difference from a PUT request is that the data in a POST request does not exist on the server yet. In enterprise applications a POST request is used either to send credentials so that the user can be authenticated or to send data that will be used to create a new object. When a POST request is used to send credentials, the response status code is 200 when the user is authenticated and 401 (Unauthorized) when the user credentials are not good. When a POST request is used to send data to be saved, the 201 status code is returned if the object was created.

- **DELETE**: This type of request is used to instruct the server to delete data. The response code is 200 when all went okay, and if it did not, an error code related to the cause is sent.

There are a few other HTTP methods that are used in more complex applications. If you want to know more about request methods, status codes, and HTTP basics overall, I confidently recommend you to look at this tutorial[7]. Now let's get back to writing Java web applications.

As previously mentioned, until a while ago, we needed a server to host a web application. This is no longer the case as of a few years ago. As databases were replaced for testing purposes and applications with minimum functionality with embedded databases, the same happened to web servers as well. If you want to quickly write a simple web application, you now have the option of using an embedded server such as the Simple Web Server introduced in Java 18, Eclipse Jetty, or Apache Tomcat Embedded. Supporting complex pages with an embedded server is pretty difficult, but embedded servers are usually used for microservices that only need simple REST APIs. The following sections will scratch the surface on building Java web applications.

---

[7] https://dev.to/devlawrence/understanding-http-basics-for-beginners-3f28

Simple Application Server

Java 18 introduced the Simple Web Server, a minimal HTTP static file server, via JEP 408[8]. It can be used as a command-line tool to start a minimal web server that serves static files only; servlets and JSP pages are not supported. It serves only static files over HTTP/1.1; dynamic content and other HTTP versions are not supported. The purpose of its introduction is to make the JDK more approachable for beginner developers.

The way the Simple Web Server works can be summarized as follows:

- It serves a single directory hierarchy, and it serves only static files over HTTP/1.1

- If the requested resource is a file, its content is served.

- If the directory contains an index file, the content of the index file is served. If not, the contents of the directory are listed.

- It supports only the HEAD and GET request methods; any other requests receive either a 501 - Not Implemented or a 405 - Not Allowed response.

This section will show you how to use the jwebserver command-line tool first, and then how create and customize a server instance from your Java code.

The **jwebserver** Command-Line Tool

After you have set up your Java development system as instructed in **Chapter 2**, you should have all the JDK binaries in the system path. So if you open a terminal and run jwebserver –help, you will see all the options available for starting a simple web server, just like shown in Listing 10-25.

Listing 10-25. jwebserver --help Output

```
> jwebserver --help
Usage: jwebserver [-b bind address] [-p port] [-d directory]
                  [-o none|info|verbose] [-h to show options]
                  [-version to show version information]
```

---

[8]https://openjdk.org/jeps/408

```
Options:
-b, --bind-address     - Address to bind to. Default: 127.0.0.1 (loopback).
                         For all interfaces use "-b 0.0.0.0" or "-b ::".
-d, --directory        - Directory to serve. Default: current directory.
-o, --output           - Output format. none|info|verbose. Default: info.
-p, --port             - Port to listen on. Default:mkdocs serve --dev-
                         addr=0.0.0.0:8002 8000.
-h, -?, --help         - Prints this help message and exits.
-version, --version    - Prints version information and exits.
To stop the server, press Ctrl + C.
```

If you just run jwebserver in the terminal, a web server will start on the default port 8000, and it will serve the contents of the directory in which the server was started. So if you run jwebserver in a terminal in java-23-for-absolute-beginners/chapter10/using-simplewebserver and then open http://127.0.0.1:8000/ in the browser, you should see the typical Maven project structure, as shown in Figure 10-15.

Directory listing for /

- target/
- pom.xml
- src/

Figure 10-15. *Java Simple Web Server CLI showing the current directory*

If port 8000 is not occupied by another process, the server starts successfully. If you navigate the directory structure, you will see all the GET requests being logged in the console. In Listing 10-26, you can see a sample output.

Listing 10-26. jwebserver Output

```
127.0.0.1 - - [27/Jul/2024:23:09:08 +0100] "GET / HTTP/1.1" 200 -
127.0.0.1 - - [27/Jul/2024:23:09:10 +0100] "GET /target/ HTTP/1.1" 200 -
127.0.0.1 - - [27/Jul/2024:23:09:11 +0100] "GET /target/generated-sources/
                                            HTTP/1.1" 200 -
127.0.0.1 - - [27/Jul/2024:23:09:12 +0100] "GET /target/generated-sources/
                                            annotations/ HTTP/1.1" 200 -
127.0.0.1 - - [27/Jul/2024:23:09:13 +0100] "GET /livereload/149020878/
                                            149023281 HTTP/1.1" 404 -
127.0.0.1 - - [27/Jul/2024:23:09:14 +0100] "GET /target/classes/
                                            HTTP/1.1" 200 -
127.0.0.1 - - [27/Jul/2024:23:09:17 +0100] "GET /livereload/149020878/
                                            149023281 HTTP/1.1" 404 -
127.0.0.1 - - [27/Jul/2024:23:09:17 +0100] "GET /src/ HTTP/1.1" 200 -
127.0.0.1 - - [27/Jul/2024:23:09:18 +0100] "GET /src/main/ HTTP/1.1" 200 -
127.0.0.1 - - [27/Jul/2024:23:09:19 +0100] "GET /src/main/java/
                                            HTTP/1.1" 200 -
```

The purpose of this utility is not to provide the functionalities of a production-grade server—that requires a lot more complexity.

If you want to change the directory being served, you can configure the server using jwebserver -d {path/to/dir}. For example, starting the server using the using-simplewebserver/src/main/resources directory shows the index.html file when http://127.0.0.1:8000/ is accessed in the browser, as shown in Figure 10-16.

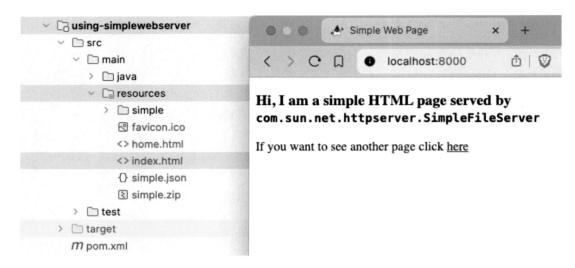

Figure 10-16. *Index page shown by Java Simple Web Server CLI*

Feel free to experiment with the other configurations. To stop the server, just press **Ctrl+C** while in the terminal window.

Beside the CLI, Java 18 introduced a new set of API points for server creation and customization, all grouped under module `jdk.httpserver`. How to configure and start a server from a Java application will be shown in the next section.

Using `SimpleFileServer`

All components that make up the new set of API points for server creation and customization are grouped under the `com.sun.net.httpserver` package. The new class `SimpleFileServer` offers the key components of the server via three static methods:

- `createFileServer(InetSocketAddress addr, Path rootDirectory, OutputLevel outputLevel)`: Creates a file server bound to a given address, from a given path, and logs request details according to the specified logging level.

- `createFileHandler(Path rootDirectory)`: Creates a file handler that serves files from a given directory path (and its subdirectories). A file handler is an instance of `HttpHandler` and is invoked to process HTTP exchanges. A file handler is used as an argument for the `HttpServer#create(..)` method to configure the server to be started.

- createOutputFilter(OutputStream out, OutputLevel
  outputLevel): Creates a post-processing Filter that prints log
  messages about exchanges.

By invoking the createFileServer(..) method, a simple in-memory web server
is created. The type of the returned instance is HttpServerImpl, which extends the
HttpServer abstract class. This class implements a simple HTTP server. An HttpServer
is bound to an IP address and port number and listens for incoming TCP connections
from clients on this address. The code in Listing 10-27 depicts the creation of an in-
memory server that serves the contents of the using-simplewebserver/src/main/
resources directory.

Listing 10-27. Configuring a Simple Web Server Using SimpleFileServer.
createFileServer(..)

```
package com.apress.bgn.ten;

import com.sun.net.httpserver.SimpleFileServer;

import java.io.File;
import java.io.IOException;
import java.net.InetAddress;
import java.net.InetSocketAddress;
import java.nio.file.Path;

import static java.lang.System.in;
import static java.lang.System.out;

public class MostSimpleServer {
    public static final InetSocketAddress SERVER_ADDR =
            new InetSocketAddress(InetAddress.getLoopbackAddress(), 8080);
    private static final String SERVER_DATA = "using-simplewebserver/";

    void main() throws IOException {
        var serverDataLocation = new File(SERVER_DATA);
        var server = SimpleFileServer.createFileServer(SERVER_ADDR,
                Path.of(serverDataLocation.getAbsolutePath()),
                SimpleFileServer.OutputLevel.VERBOSE);
```

```
        server.start();
        out.println("Press any key to exit!");
        in.read();
        server.stop(2);
    }
}
```

To keep the server running, a System.in.read() invocation is added to wait for a user input before stopping it. The contents of the using-simplewebserver directory are listed when http://127.0.0.1:8080/ is accessed in the browser. Thus, using Java code, we have configured and created a simple web server that could have been created using the CLI by running jwebserver -p 8080 -d using-simplewebserver.

To configure the file handler separately, we need to use HttpServer.create(..) to create the server, as shown in Listing 10-28.

Listing 10-28. Configure the file handler separately

```
package com.apress.bgn.ten;

import com.sun.net.httpserver.HttpServer;
import static com.apress.bgn.ten.MostSimpleServer.SERVER_ADDR;
// other import statements omitted

/**
 └── resources
 ├── favicon.ico
 ├── home.html
 ├── index.html
 ├── simple.json
 └── simple.zip
 */
public class ContextServer {
    public static final String SERVER_DATA = "using-simplewebserver/src/
                                              main/resources";

    void main() throws IOException {
        var serverDataLocation = new File(SERVER_DATA);
```

```
        var handler = SimpleFileServer.createFileHandler(Path.
                    of(serverDataLocation.getAbsolutePath()));
        var server = HttpServer.create(SERVER_ADDR, 10, "/simple",
                    handler);

        server.start();
        out.println("Press any key to exit!");
        in.read();
        server.stop(2);
    }
}
```

Notice that the HttpServer.create() method provides more configurations, like the context under which the files are served, in this case simple/, and the maximum number of TCP connections to queue internally, in this case 10.

Handlers can also be created using the utility method HttpHandlers. of(statusCode, headers, body). The extra configuration is useful because it provides the opportunity to serve other type of files, like JSON files for example. The code in Listing 10-29 defines a handler for serving JSON files, but also uses HttpHandlers. handleOrElse(predicate, mainHandler, fallbackHandler) to enforce that only GET requests are allowed.

Listing 10-29. Configuring a Simple Web Server to Serve JSON Files

```
package com.apress.bgn.ten;
// import statements omitted

public class JsonServingServer {

    public static Predicate<Request> IS_GET = r -> r.getRequestMethod().
                                              equals("GET");

    void main() throws IOException {
        var serverDataLocation = new File(SERVER_DATA);

        var jsonHandler = HttpHandlers.of(200,
                Headers.of("Content-Type", "application/json"),
                Files.readString(Path.of(serverDataLocation.
                getAbsolutePath() + File.separator + "simple.json")));
```

```
        var methodNotAllowedHandler = HttpHandlers.of(405,
                Headers.of("Allow", "GET"), "");

        var handler = HttpHandlers.handleOrElse(IS_GET, jsonHandler,
                    methodNotAllowedHandler);
        var server = HttpServer.create(SERVER_ADDR, 10, "/simple/",
                    handler);

    server.start();
    out.println("Press any key to exit!");
    in.read();
    server.stop(2);
    }
}
```

If you want to test this server, the easiest way is to use the IntelliJ IDEA HTTPie[9] web client. In the using-simplewebserver/src/test/resources directory, there are a few HTTPie request files containing requests for each of the servers configured in this section. Listing 10-30 shows the contents of the json-serving-server-tests.http file.

Listing 10-30. json-serving-server-tests.http Contents

```
### GET request to simple server created by JsonServingServer
GET http://localhost:8080/simple/simple.json
# expect 200 + contents of 'simple.json'
###

### PATCH request to example server
PATCH http://localhost:8080/simple/simple.json
# expect 405 Method Not Allowed
###
```

These requests are submitted in IntelliJ IDEA in a similar way JUnit tests are run. Just click the green triangles in the gutter or right-click the file contents and, from the menu that appears, select the option that is prefixed with a green triangle. Figure 10-17 shows the menu item that runs the PATCH request.

---

[9] https://httpie.io

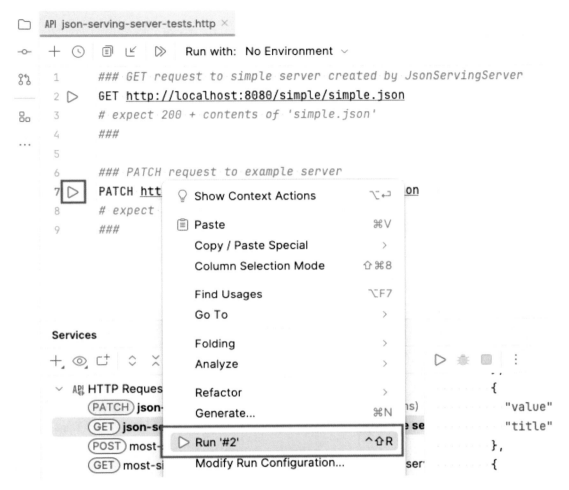

Figure 10-17. *IntelliJ IDEA HTTPie web client menu*

Now let's add a filter to log the requests better. This means we'll make use of both `SimpleFileServer.createFileHandler(..)` and `SimpleFileServer.createOutputFilter()`. To create the server, we need the `HttpServer.create(..)` version that takes a filter as an argument too. The code is depicted in Listing 10-31.

Listing 10-31. Adding a filter to log requests

```
package com.apress.bgn.ten;

// import statements omitted

public class FilterServer {
```

```
void main() throws IOException {
    var serverDataLocation = new File(SERVER_DATA);

    var handler = SimpleFileServer.createFileHandler(Path.
                    of(serverDataLocation.getAbsolutePath()));
    var outputFilter = SimpleFileServer.createOutputFilter(System.out,
                    SimpleFileServer.OutputLevel.VERBOSE);
    var headerAppenderFilter = Filter.adaptRequest("Add Timestamp
                    header",
            request -> request.with("Timestamp", List.of(LocalDateTime.
            now().toString()))));

    var server = HttpServer.create(SERVER_ADDR, 10, "/simple/",
                    handler, headerAppenderFilter, outputFilter);

    server.start();
    out.println("Press any key to exit!");
    in.read();
    server.stop(2);
  }
}
```

Filters can also be used to modify requests. In the example in Listing 10-31, the headerAppenderFilter is used to add a header named Timestamp to the request. Because the outputFilter declares the log level to be VERBOSE and is added last, when opening http://127.0.0.1:8080/simple/ in the console, you can see all the details of the request, including the Timestamp. Listing 10-32 shows a snippet of this output.

Listing 10-32. Detailed Request Log Snippet for the http://127.0.0.1:8080/ simple/ Request

```
127.0.0.1 - - [28/Jul/2024:13:03:33 +0100] "GET /simple/ HTTP/1.1" 200 -
Resource requested: ../chapter10/using-simplewebserver/src/main/resources
> Accept-encoding: gzip, deflate, br, zstd
...
> Sec-ch-ua-platform: "macOS"
```

```
> Timestamp: 2024-07-28T13:03:33.048932
...
< Content-type: text/html
< Content-length: 308
```

Warning   Notice that in the examples in this section the path to the directory to be served is relative to the `chapter10` directory. For your IntelliJ IDEA launchers to work, you might need to customize the Working directory to the absolute path to this directory, like shown in Figure 10-18.

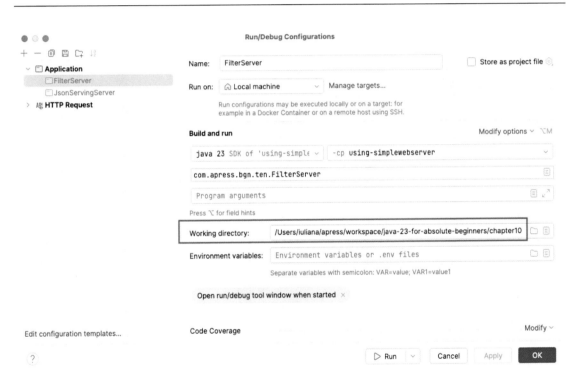

Figure 10-18. *IntelliJ IDEA's customized launcher for* `FilterServer`

The Java Simple Web Server is pretty much the equivalent of Apache HTTPD: it is not cumbersome to configure and use, it does not require a JDK external container to host your web application, and despite its limitations it is a quick and easy way for a beginner to get up and running with writing web applications in Java.

Java Web Application with an Embedded Server

For this section, an embedded Apache Tomcat server is used to display a few simple web pages, using Java servlets *(patience young padawan, they will be explained shortly)*. Tomcat version 11 is used, which means Java modules are supported. The advantage of using an embedded Tomcat server is that you can run a web application by executing a main method. The code, depicted in Listing 10-33, declares a single, very simple servlet that serves as the main page of the application.

Listing 10-33. Simple Java Application with an Embedded Server

```java
package com.apress.bgn.ten;

import jakarta.servlet.http.HttpServlet;
import jakarta.servlet.http.HttpServletRequest;
import jakarta.servlet.http.HttpServletResponse;
import org.apache.catalina.Context;
import org.apache.catalina.LifecycleException;
import org.apache.catalina.startup.Tomcat;
// other import statements omitted

public class WebDemo {

    private static final Logger LOGGER = Logger.getLogger(WebDemo.class.
    getName());

    public static final Integer PORT = Optional.ofNullable(System.
    getenv("PORT")).map(Integer::parseInt).orElse(8080);
    public static final String TMP_DIR = Optional.ofNullable(System.
    getenv("TMP_DIR")).orElse("/tmp/tomcat-tmp");
    public static final String STATIC_DIR = Optional.ofNullable(System.
    getenv("STATIC_DIR")).orElse("/tmp/tomcat-static");

    void main() throws IOException, LifecycleException {
        var tomcat = new Tomcat();
        tomcat.setBaseDir(TMP_DIR);
        tomcat.setPort(PORT);
        tomcat.getConnector();

        tomcat.setAddDefaultWebXmlToWebapp(false);
```

```
var contextPath = ""; // root context
boolean createDirs =  new File(STATIC_DIR).mkdirs();
if(createDirs) {
    LOGGER.info("Tomcat static directory created successfully.");
} else {
    LOGGER.severe("Tomcat static directory could not be created.");
}
var docBase = new File(STATIC_DIR).getCanonicalPath();
var context = tomcat.addWebapp(contextPath, docBase);

addIndexServlet(tomcat, contextPath, context); // omitted
// needed for proper servlets disposal
Runtime.getRuntime().addShutdownHook(new Thread(() -> {
    try {
        tomcat.getServer().stop();
    } catch (LifecycleException e) {
        LOGGER.warning("Unable to stop Tomcat server");
    }
}));

tomcat.start();
tomcat.getServer().await();
    }
}
```

Writing an application with an embedded Tomcat server is quite easy when you don't need complex web pages, making use of templating libraries for HTML generation, like JSP, for example. The code snippet in Listing 10-33 only requires the tomcat-embed-core library as a dependency, and the simple steps to create the server are explained here:

1. Create an org.apache.catalina.startup.Tomcat instance and select the port to expose it. In this case it is 8080, the default value of the PORT variable, unless declared using a system environment variable with the same name.

2. Set a base directory for the Tomcat instance, where the running server will save its various generated files, such as logs. In this case, the directory is configured to be /tmp/tomcat-tmp unless declared using a system environment variable with the name TMPDIR. The user running the application should have writing rights over that location.

3. Set a directory where static files for Tomcat are located. In this case, the directory is configured to be /tmp/tomcat-static unless declared using a system environment variable with the name STATICDIR. The user running the application should have writing rights over that location.

4. Disable default configurations for Tomcat by calling tomcat.setA ddDefaultWebXmlToWebapp(false). In this case this prevents the org.apache.jasper.servlet.JspServlet from being registered. This servlet enables using JSP files in the web app, but when configured it automatically takes over and assumes any request must resolve to a JSP page, so the Java servlets are ignored. Since we want to keep the application simple and use Java servlets, we disable it.

5. Make sure the server shuts down gracefully when the application is closed, by adding a shutdown hook.

6. Write a simple servlet to display the main page of the application to test that the server was started correctly and works as intended. This is done by the addIndexServlet(..) method that was omitted from Listing 10-33 to make sure the focus would be on the Tomcat instance. The method is shown in Listing 10-34.

Listing 10-34. A Simple Method That Creates a Very Simple Servlet and Registers It with a Tomcat Instance

```
private static void addIndexServlet(Tomcat tomcat, String contextPath,
Context context) {
    var indexServlet = new HttpServlet() {
        @Override
        protected void doGet(HttpServletRequest req, HttpServletResponse resp)
```

```
        throws IOException {
    var writer = resp.getWriter();
    writer.print("""
            <!DOCTYPE html>
            <html lang="en">
                <!-- body omitted -->
            </html>
            """);
    }
};
var servletName = "IndexServlet";
var urlPattern = "/";
tomcat.addServlet(contextPath, servletName, indexServlet);
context.addServletMappingDecoded(urlPattern, servletName);
}
```

The servlet instance must be associated with a name and a URL pattern, and when the user tries to open the serverURL/contextPath/urlPattern page, the doGet(..) method is called that returns the response constructed in its body.

A Java web application deployed on a server (even an embedded one) needs a context path. The context path value is a part of the URL to access the application. A URL is made up of four parts:

- protocol: The application-level protocol used by the client and server to communicate, such as http, https, ftp, and so on.

- hostname: The DNS domain name (e.g., www.google.com) or IP address (e.g., 192.168.0.255) or any alias recognized in a network. For example, when an application is accessed from the same computer the server is installed on, either 127.0.0.1, localhost, or 0.0.0.0 can be used.

- path and filename: The name and location of the resource, under the server document base directory. Users usually request to view specific pages hosted on servers, which is why URLs look like this: https://docs.oracle.com/index.html. For security reasons, a common practice is to hide the paths and filenames by using internal mappings (called *URL redirection*).

So where does the `contextPath` value mentioned previously come in? When we have an embedded server declared as in Listing 10-34, any files that are hosted by it can be accessed by using `http://localhost:8080/`. But on a dedicated server, more than one application can be running at the same time, and there must be a way to separate them, right? This is where the `contextPath` value comes in handy. By setting the `contextPath` value to `/demo` instead of the empty string, the `WebDemo` application and the resources it provides to the users can be accessed at `http://localhost:8080/demo/`.

Anyway, back to Java web applications. Java web applications are dynamic: the pages are generated from Java code using servlets and JSP pages. Because of that, Java web applications run not on a server but inside a web container on the server. (This is why Tomcat and Jetty are sometimes called *servlet containers*.) The web container provides a Java runtime environment for Java web applications. Apache Tomcat is such a container running in the JVM, which supports execution of servlets and JSP pages. A **servlet** is a Java class that is a subclass of `jakarta.servlet.http.HttpServlet`. Instances of this type answer HTTP Requests within a web container.

Caution   Apache Tomcat 11.x is an open source software implementation of a subset of the Jakarta EE (formally Java EE) technologies. Tomcat is based on Servlet 5.0, JSP 3.0, EL 4.0, WS 2.0, and JASIC 2.0. Up to Tomcat 9.x, a **servlet** is a Java class that is a subclass of `javax.servlet.http.HttpServlet`. The migration from `javax.*` packages to `jakarta.*` was needed in Tomcat 10.x to separate Oracle official Java products from the open source ones, built using Eclipse build servers[10].

A **JSP page** is a file with `.jsp` extension that contains HTML and Java code. A JSP page gets compiled into a servlet by the web container the first time the page is accessed. In essence, the servlet is the core element of a Java web application. The server must also know that the servlet exists and how to identify it, which is where the call to `tomcat.addServlet(contextPath, servletName, servlet)` comes in. It basically says to add the servlet with name `servletName` to the application context with the `contextPath` value and then to associate a URL pattern to the servlet, the `context.addServletMapping(urlPattern, servletName)` is called.

---

[10] `https://blogs.oracle.com/javamagazine/post/transition-from-java-ee-to-jakarta-ee`

When a Java web application is running, all its servlets and JSP are running into its context, but they have to be added into the context in the code and mapped to a URL pattern. The request URL which matches that URL pattern will be handled by the configured servlet. In Listing 10-34 the servlet was created on the spot by instantiating the HttpServlet abstract class and resulted in an anonymous servlet instance. Listing 10-35 depicts a concrete class named SampleServlet that extends the HttpServlet class. The advantage of doing this is that the URL pattern and the servlet name can become properties of this class, simplifying the syntax of adding them to the application context.

Listing 10-35. The SampleServlet Class

```
package com.apress.bgn.ten;

import jakarta.servlet.http.HttpServlet;
import jakarta.servlet.http.HttpServletRequest;
import jakarta.servlet.http.HttpServletResponse;

import java.io.IOException;
import java.util.logging.Logger;

public class SampleServlet  extends HttpServlet {
    private static final Logger LOGGER = Logger.getLogger(SampleServlet.
                                  class.getName());

    private final String servletName = "sampleServlet";
    private final String urlPattern = "/sample";

    @Override
    protected void doGet(HttpServletRequest req, HttpServletResponse resp)
            throws IOException {
        PrintWriter writer = resp.getWriter();
        try {
            writer.println(WebResourceUtils.readResource("index.html"));
        } catch (Exception e) {
            LOGGER.warning("Could not read static file : " +
            e.getMessage());
        }
    }
}
```

```
    @Override
    public String getServletName() {
        return servletName;
    }

    public String getUrlPattern() {
        return urlPattern;
    }
}
```

The urlPattern property was added to this class for practical reasons, to keep everything related to this servlet in one place. The same goes for servletName. If the intention were to instantiate this class multiple times to create multiple servlets, these two properties should be declared as configurable. Adding this servlet to the application is pretty easy. An object of this type needs to be created and then the tomcat. addServlet(..) and context.addServletMappingDecoded(..) methods must be called, as depicted in Listing 10-36.

Listing 10-36. Adding the SampleServlet Class to the Web Application

```
SampleServlet sampleServlet = new SampleServlet();
tomcat.addServlet(contextPath, sampleServlet.getServletName(),
sampleServlet);
context.addServletMappingDecoded(sampleServlet.getUrlPattern(),
sampleServlet.getServletName());
```

Inside the doGet(..) method the contents of the index.html file are read (using WebResourceUtils, which is part of the project for this chapter but not relevant to this chapter) and are written in the response object using the response PrintWriter.

As you can see, the doGet(..) method receives as arguments two objects: the HttpServletRequest instance is read, and all contents of the request sent from the client can be accessed using appropriate methods, and the HttpServletResponse instance, which is used to add information to the response. In Listing 10-36, we are just writing HTML code read from another file. An extra method that can be called is response. setStatus(HttpServletResponse.SC_OK), which sets the response status.

Aside from the doGet(..) method, there are do*(..) methods matching each HTTP method that declare the same type of parameters.

Starting with the Java Servlet 3.0 specification, servlets can be written using the @ WebServlet annotation, which removes the necessity to be explicitly added to the web application and mapped in the context as shown in Listing 10-36, because they are picked automatically when Tomcat starts. Also, there is no need to instantiate the servlet class either.

The SampleServlet class after Servlet 3.0 is shown in Listing 10-37.

Listing 10-37. Annotated SampleServlet Class

```java
package com.apress.bgn.ten;

import jakarta.servlet.annotation.WebServlet;
import jakarta.servlet.http.*;
// other import statements omitted

@WebServlet(
        name = "sampleServlet",
        urlPatterns = {"/sample"}
)
public class SampleServlet  extends HttpServlet {
    private static final Logger LOGGER = Logger.getLogger(SampleServlet.
                                    class.getName());

    @Override
    protected void doGet(HttpServletRequest req, HttpServletResponse resp)
            throws IOException {
        PrintWriter writer = resp.getWriter();
        try {
            writer.println(WebResourceUtils.readResource("index.html"));
        } catch (Exception e) {
            LOGGER.warning("Could not read static file : " +
            e.getMessage());
        }
    }
}
```

So this is how we handle servlets, but how do we handle JSP pages using an embedded server? It's not impossible, but it is not easy either. That is why, for this task, usually people rely on smarter frameworks such as Spring Boot.[11]

Java Web Application on a Standalone Server

Java web applications that are designed to be deployed on an application server are either packaged as a Web Archive (war) file or Enterprise Archive (ear) file. These are special types of Java Archive (jar) files that are used to group together other Jars, JSPs, Java classes, static pages, and other resources that are part of a web application. There is a maven plugin named `maven-war-plugin` that packs an artifact as a war file. EAR is a file format used by Jakarta EE to package one or more modules into a single deployment onto an application server; it basically links a group of jars and wars together into a single application.

In this section we'll build a very simple web application, packaged as a war file and containing Java Server Pages, and deploy it to a stand-alone instance of an Apache Tomcat server.

To install Apache Tomcat server locally, go to the official site[12] and download Apache Tomcat version 11 and follow the instructions for your operating system. Since Apache Tomcat is provided as an archive (zip or gz), the installation process should be as simple as unpacking it somewhere on your computer. In this section an IntelliJ IDEA Tomcat launcher is used to run the web application, so the interaction with the server will be minimal.

A Java web application has a different structure than a typical Java application. It contains the typical `main` and `test` directories, but it also contains a `webapp` directory that contains the web resources. The project structure is depicted in Figure 10-19.

---

[11] https://spring.io/projects/spring-boot
[12] https://tomcat.apache.org/download-11.cgi

Figure 10-19. *Web application structure change*

Notice the web.xml file located under the WEB-INF directory. This file defines the structure of the web application. Before Servlet 3.0 this file was the only way to map servlets onto url patterns and configure them to be part of the application. After Servlet 3.0 and the introduction of annotations, this file is mostly empty.

When the web application is built, the bytecode of the application is saved under WEB-INF/classes. If the application uses third-party libraries, they are all saved into WEB-INF/lib.

Now, back to Jakarta Pages.

There are two ways of writing JSP pages. The simplest one, which is rarely used these days because it couples HTML code with Java code, is to use **JSP scriptlets**. JSP scriptlets are pieces of Java code embedded in HTML code using directive tags. There are three types of directive tags:

- <%@ page ... %> is used to provide instructions to the container. Instructions declared using this directive belong to the current page and can be used anywhere in the page. Such a directive can be used to import Java types or define page properties. Example:

```
<%@ page import="java.util.Date" %>
<%@ page language="java" contentType="text/html; charset=US-ASCII"
pageEncoding="US-ASCII" %>
```

- `<%@ include ... %>` is used to include a file during the translation phase. Thus, the current JSP file where this directive is used is a composition of its content and the content of the file that is declared using this directive: `<%@ include file = "footer.jsp" >`

- `<%@ taglib ... %>` is used to declare a tag library with elements that will be used in the JSP page. This declarative is important because it is used to import a library with custom tags and elements that will be used to write the JSP page. These tags provide dynamic functionality without the need for scriptlets.

The `index.jsp` page shown in Figure 10-19 is quite simple, as its content in Listing 10-38 demonstrates.

Listing 10-38. The Very Simple `index.jsp` Page Contents

```
<%@ page import="java.util.Date" %>
<%@ page language="java" contentType="text/html; charset=US-ASCII"
pageEncoding="US-ASCII" %>
<!DOCTYPE html PUBLIC "-//W3C//DTD HTML 4.01 Transitional//EN" "http://www.
w3.org/TR/html4/loose.dtd">
<html>
        <head><title>Web Application Demo JSP Page</title></head>
        <body style="background-color:black">
                <h1 style="color:#ffd200"> Today is <%= new Date() %></h1>
        </body>
</html>
```

The `index.jsp` page does nothing else but print today's date, and it does so by calling `new Date()`. As you can see, we are using Java code in what looks like an HTML page. Because those directives are included and the extension is `.jsp`, the container knows this file must be compiled into a servlet. The default page a web application opens with when its root domain is accessed (if nothing was mapped to the default URL pattern, /) is a file named `index.html`, `index.htm`, or `index.jsp` in this case.

After adding the index.jsp file in the WEB-INF directory and thus making sure the container can find it, all that is left to do is to configure an Apache Tomcat launcher in IntelliJ IDEA and configure it to deploy the war file that results when this application is built before starting Tomcat.

To configure an Apache Tomcat launcher, IntelliJ IDEA needs to have the Tomcat and TomEE plugin enabled. If you install IntelliJ IDEA without customizing it, this plugin is installed by default. If you managed somehow to uninstall it, just open the IntelliJ IDE **Settings** window, select **Plugins**, look for it in the **Marketplace** tab, and check its box, as depicted in Figure 10-20 (but with the **Installed** tab selected, because I already have the plugin installed).

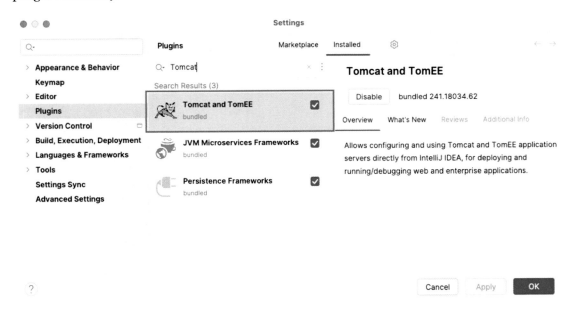

Figure 10-20. *Enabling Tomcat and TomEE plugin in IntelliJ IDEA*

Once the plugin is installed, click the **Launch** section and click the three dots (labeled 1 in Figure 10-21), click **Edit** (2) in the dialog window that pops up, and then click the **Edit configuration templates** link (3) in the lower left corner. In the Run/ Debug Configuration Templates dialog window that opens, select **Tomcat Server ➤ Local** (4) from the list on the left, and then click the **Configure** button (5). In the Application Servers dialog window, set the **Tomcat Home** field to the location where you unzipped the Apache Tomcat server on your system, as depicted in Figure 10-21.

Figure 10-21. *Configuring Apache Tomcat instance to be used in web launchers in IntelliJ IDEA*

After configuring the instance of Tomcat to use with the web launchers, we need to create a launcher. Start again by clicking the three dots in the **Launch** section, then click **Edit…**, but this time, in the Run/Debug Configurations dialog window that pops up, select the + (plus) button (labeled 1 in Figure 10-22) in the upper left corner. Then from the list, select **Tomcat Server ➤ Local** (2). On the right side, a form with the launcher details appears, as shown in Figure 10-22.

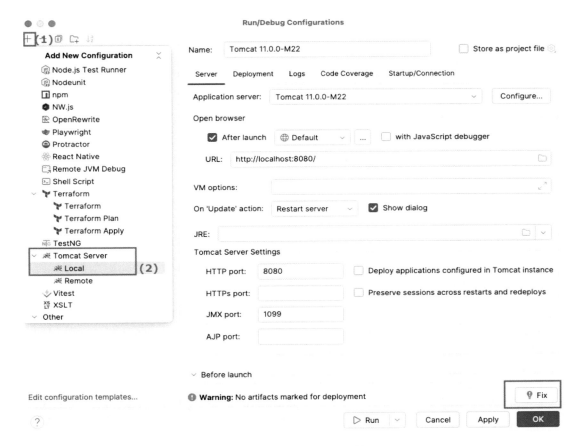

Figure 10-22. *Configuring a web launcher in IntelliJ IDEA*

Set a more relevant name for the launcher, such as web-app. Then click the **Fix** button or the **Deployment** tab and click the + button to select an artifact, as shown in Figure 10-23. IntelliJ IDEA will identify all web applications in the project and provide a list to choose from. Select web-app:war, as depicted in Figure 10-23.

Figure 10-23. *Creating Apache Tomcat launcher in IntelliJ IDEA—selecting the web application to deploy*

In the **Deployment** tab there is also a text field named Application Context. IntelliJ IDEA generates a default context name based on the application name. Change it to **demo**.

After configuring the launcher, start the server and open the http://localhost:8080/demo page in your browser. You should see a simple message like this on the page:

```
Today is Sun Jul 28 23:56:18 BST 2024
```

The depicted date will be the one on your system when you run the application yourself.

Since *tag libraries* (a.k.a. *taglibs*) have been mentioned, let's talk a little about them as well. The most basic tag library is named **JSTL**, which stands for **JSP Standard Tag Library**. Other, more evolved tag libraries are provided by JSF (Jakarta Server Faces), Thymeleaf, or Spring. Tags defined in this library can be used to write JSP pages that change behavior depending on request attributes. JSTL tags can be used to iterate, test and format values and to configure internationalization. Based on the JSTL functions provided, the tags are grouped into five categories, and they can be used in a JSP page only after specifying the appropriate directive. Following are the five directives listed together with the overall topic the tags are covering:

- `<%@ taglib uri="http://java.sun.com/jsp/jstl/core" prefix="c" %>`: JSTL Core tags provide support for displaying values, iteration, conditional logic, catch exception, url, forward or redirect responses.

- `<%@ taglib uri="http://java.sun.com/jsp/jstl/fmt" prefix="fmt" %>`: JSTL Formatting tags are provided for formatting of numbers, dates, and i18n support through locales and resource bundles.

- `<%@ taglib uri="http://java.sun.com/jsp/jstl/sql" prefix="sql" %>`: JSTL SQL tags provide support for interaction with relational databases—but you should never use SQL in a web page because it is very easily hackable (look up **SQL injection** on a search engine to see why).

- `<%@ taglib uri="http://java.sun.com/jsp/jstl/xml" prefix="x" %>`: JSTL XML tags provide support for handling XML documents, parsing, transformations, and XPath expressions evaluation.

- `<%@ taglib uri="http://java.sun.com/jsp/jstl/functions" prefix="fn" %>`: JSTL Function tags provide a number of functions that can be used to perform common operations such as text manipulations.

Now that you know the basic tag categories, which ones do you think we will need to use to redesign our `index.jsp` page? If you're thinking **FMT** and **Core**, you are right. Also, JSP pages that use taglibs are almost always backed up by a servlet that sets the proper attributes on the request that will be used within the JSP page. So let's modify the `index.jsp` page as depicted in Listing 10-39.

Listing 10-39. Using FMT and Core Taglibs to Rewrite `index.jsp`

```
<%@ page language="java" contentType="text/html;charset=US-ASCII"
pageEncoding="US-ASCII"%>
<%@ taglib uri="http://java.sun.com/jsp/jstl/fmt" prefix="fmt" %>
<%@ taglib uri="http://java.sun.com/jsp/jstl/core" prefix="c" %>
<!DOCTYPE html PUBLIC "-//W3C//DTD HTML 4.01 Transitional//EN" "http://www.
w3.org/TR/html4/loose.dtd">
<html>
    <head>
        <title>Web Application Demo JSP Page</title>
    </head>
    <body style="background-color:black">
        <fmt:formatDate value="${requestScope.today}" pattern="dd/MM/yyyy"
        var="todayFormatted"/>
        <p style="color:#ffd200"> Today is <c:out
        value="${todayFormatted}" /> </p>
    </body>
</html>
```

And while we are at it, let's rename `index.jsp` to `date.jsp` to make it obvious what it is used for, and write a servlet class named `DateServlet` to add to the request the `today` attribute, which will be formatted by the `<fmt:formatDate>` tag and the result saved into the `todayFormatted` variable, later printed out by the `<c:out>` tag. The `DateServlet` is depicted in Listing 10-40.

Listing 10-40. DateServlet Class That Provides the `today` Attribute for `date.jsp`

```
package com.apress.bgn.ten;

import jakarta.servlet.RequestDispatcher;
import jakarta.servlet.ServletException;
import jakarta.servlet.annotation.WebServlet;
import jakarta.servlet.http.HttpServlet;
import jakarta.servlet.http.HttpServletRequest;
import jakarta.servlet.http.HttpServletResponse;
```

```java
import java.io.IOException;
import java.util.Date;
import java.util.logging.Logger;

import static java.lang.System.out;

@WebServlet(
        name = "dateServlet",
        urlPatterns = {"/date"}
)
public class DateServlet extends HttpServlet {

    @Override
    protected void doGet(HttpServletRequest request, HttpServletResponse
    response)
            throws IOException, ServletException {
        out.println(" ->>> Getting date ");
        request.setAttribute("today", new Date());
        RequestDispatcher rd = getServletContext().getRequestDispatcher
                                ("/date.jsp");
        rd.forward(request, response);
    }
}
```

Now we just restart the application and the first page will display Today is 06/07/2021, and you will see the date on your system when the code is run.

If you think writing Java web applications is cumbersome, you are quite right. Pure Java is quite tedious for such a task. Professional Java web applications are usually written by using frameworks (e.g., JSF, Vaadin, Thymeleaf, Mustache, etc.) that make the job of creating pages and linking them to the back end easy. Even more, nowadays the tendency is to create web interfaces in JavaScript, using powerful JavaScript frameworks like Angular and React, and to use advanced CSS4; many UI designs can now be done 100% in CSS3 or CSS4 and communicate to a Java back-end application hosted on an enterprise server using web service calls, usually REST. Anyway, look up these options if you are curious; the subject is vast, but frameworks such as Spring make it quite easy to set up your environment and start developing. Just don't fall into the trap of using a framework without understanding its fundamentals.

Summary

This chapter has covered important development tools and techniques, the classes in JDK that provide support for them, and important Java libraries that you will most likely end up working with that could make your development job practical and pleasant. The JDK has never shined when it comes to GUI support, but JavaFX is quite an evolution from AWT and Swing and just might have a future. A complete list of topics from this chapter is provided here:

- How to write an interactive console application
- How to write an interactive application with a Swing interface
- The basics of JavaFX architecture
- How to write an interactive application with a JavaFX interface
- How to internationalize your application
- How to serve static files using the Java Simple Web Server
- How to write a web application using an embedded server
- What a servlet is
- What a JSP scriptlet is
- How to use taglibs to write JSP pages
- How to deploy a Java web application to Apache Tomcat

712

CHAPTER 11

Working with Files

One of the most important functions of software is to organize and store information"? with the goal of using it and sharing it. The traditional (and fading) way of organizing and storing information is to write it on paper and store the paper in organized file cabinets from which it can be retrieved when needed. Software applications do something similar: information is written in files, files are organized in directories, and in most situations data is stored in more complex structures named databases. Java provides classes to read information from files and databases and classes to write files and write information to databases. Databases have been mentioned in previous chapters, and **Chapter 9** introduced a simple example using an Apache Derby in-memory database to show you how heavy dependencies like databases can be mocked to allow unit testing. This chapter is not about using databases, because writing Java applications to use databases is an advanced topic and would require that you install extra software. Instead, the chapter focuses on reading and writing files and the many ways in which this can be done.

Java IO and NIO APIs

Before starting to show you how to read or write files, we need to show you how to access them from the code, how to check if they exist, check their size and list their properties, and so on. The core packages for file handling in Java are named `java.io`[1] and `java.nio`[2]. The package names give a pretty good hint about the components they contain:

---

[1] https://docs.oracle.com/en/java/javase/23/docs/api/java.base/java/io/package-summary.html

[2] https://docs.oracle.com/en/java/javase/23/docs/api/java.base/java/nio/package-summary.html

713

© Iuliana Cosmina 2024
I. Cosmina, *Java 23 for Absolute Beginners*, https://doi.org/10.1007/979-8-8688-1041-1_11

- `java.io` is basically an acronym for Java input/output. This package groups together components designed to facilitate input and output operations for accessing the file system through data streams and serialization.

- `java.nio` is basically an acronym for Java nonblocking input/output. This package was introduced in version 1.4 and is a collection of Java programming language APIs that offer features for intensive I/O operations. A package named `java.nio.file` that was added in JDK 7 contains a collection of utility classes providing comprehensive support for file I/O and for accessing the file system.

The main difference between Java IO and Java NIO is that Java IO is stream oriented, whereas Java NIO is buffer oriented. What this means is that with the old Java IO API, files are read one or more bytes at a time from a stream. Bytes are not cached anywhere and stream traversal is unidirectional. Once the stream is exhausted, there is no way to traverse it again. If you need to walk the stream in both directions, data must be stored in a buffer first.

With the Java NIO API, the data is read directly into a buffer, which means bytes are cached in a web browser and the browser supports bidirectional operations. This gives more flexibility during processing, but extra checks are required to make sure the buffer contains all the data needed for processing.

The second main difference is that Java IO operations are blocking. Once a method to read or write a file is called, the thread is blocked until there is no more data to read or the data was fully written.

Java NIO operations are nonblocking. A thread can request data from a resource (e.g., a file) via an open channel and only get what is currently available, or nothing at all if no data is currently available. Rather than waiting until some data is there, the thread can go ahead and do something else, and later check if the data buffer was populated.

The third difference is not so much a difference but something that Java NIO has extra: **selectors**. These components allow a thread to monitor multiple input channels and select for processing only the ones that have available data. By comparison, the classic Java IO API cannot have selectors because a thread blocks until a file operation is done.

Depending on the problem you are trying to solve, you can use one API or the other, but it all starts with a **file handler**.

File Handlers

The most important class when working with files in Java is `java.io.File`, which is an abstract representation of a file and directory pathname. Instances of this class are named **file handlers** because they allow developers to handle files and directories in the Java code using references of this type, instead of complete path names. A `File` instance can be created by using different arguments.

The simplest way to create a `File` instance is to use the constructor that receives as an argument a `String` value containing the absolute file pathname. In the code sample in Listing 11-1, the `printFileStats(..)` method is used to print file details.

Listing 11-1. Printing File Details

```java
package com.apress.bgn.eleven;

import org.slf4j.Logger;
import org.slf4j.LoggerFactory;

import java.io.File;

public class Main {
    private static final Logger LOGGER = LoggerFactory.getLogger(Main.class);

    void main() {
        // replace [workspace] with your workspace path
        var file = new File("[workspace]/java-23-for-absolute-beginners/
        README.adoc");
        printFileStats(file);
    }

    private static void printFileStats(File f) {
        if (f.exists()) {
            LOGGER.info("File Details:");
            LOGGER.info("\tName : {}", f.getName());
            LOGGER.info("\tParent :{}", f.getParent());
            LOGGER.info("\tType : {}", f.isFile() ? "file" : "directory or
                                    symlink");
            LOGGER.info("\tLocation :{}", f.getAbsolutePath());
```

```
            double kilobytes = f.length() / (double)1024;
            LOGGER.info("\tSize : {} ", kilobytes);

            LOGGER.info("\tIs Hidden : {}", f.isHidden());
            LOGGER.info("\tIs Readable? : {}", f.canRead());
            LOGGER.info("\tIs Writable? : {}", f.canWrite());
        } else {
            err.println("File does not exist!");
        }
    }
}
```

The file handler instance in Listing 11-1 is created by providing the absolute file pathname on my computer. If you want to run the code on your computer, you must provide a pathname to a file on your computer (replace [workspace] with it in the example). If you are using Windows, keep in mind that the pathname contains the \ (backslash) character that is a special character in Java and must be escaped by doubling it, \\ (see **Chapter 5** for more details).

The printFileStats(..) method makes use of a lot of methods that can be called on a file handler. The full list of methods that you can call is long, and you can see them all in the official API documentation.[3] The methods are explained in the following subsections.

isFile

The isFile() method returns true if the pathname points to a file and returns false if the pathname points to a directory or a *symlink* (a special type of file that exists only for the purpose of linking to another file, which can be quite useful when you want to shorten the pathname to a file and incredibly useful on Windows where the pathname length limit is 256 characters). In Listing 11-1 the method returns true and the logger prints

```
INFO  c.a.b.e.Main - Type : file
```

If you want to see if the method works for a directory, just delete the file name from the pathname:

```
var file = new File("/[workspace]/java-17-for-absolute-beginners/");
```

---

[3] https://docs.oracle.com/en/java/javase/23/docs/api/java.base/java/io/File.html

The log prints

```
INFO  c.a.b.e.Main - Type : directory or symlink
```

getAbsolutePath

The getAbsolutePath() method returns the absolute pathname to a file or a directory. When creating a file handler, the absolute pathname is not always needed, but if you need to use it later in the code or make sure the relative path was resolved correctly, this method is just what you need. The following piece of code creates a file handler to a file in the resources directory, by using the path relative to the root project directory (in our case the java-17-for-absolute-beginners directory):

```
var d = new File("chapter11/read-write-file/src/main/resources/input/");
```

The getAbsolutePath() method returns the full pathname, which is printed by the log statement as

```
INFO  c.a.b.e.Main - Location :/[workspace]/java-17-for-absolute-beginners/
chapter11/read-write-file/src/main/resources/input
```

The Java File class is quite powerful; it can be used to point to a shared file on another computer. There is a special constructor for that which receives an argument of type java.net.URI, where URI stands for **Uniform Resource Identifier**. To test this constructor, select a text file on your computer and open it in a web browser so that you can get its URI from the browser address bar. The code in Listing 11-2 depicts the File class being instantiated using a local URI.

Listing 11-2. Printing File Details using an URI

```
package com.apress.bgn.eleven;

import java.net.URI;
import java.net.URISyntaxException;
// other imports & wrapper code omitted

 try {
    var localUri = new URI("file:///[workspace]/java-17-for-absolute-
                  beginners/README.adoc");
    var localFile =  new File (localUri);
```

```
    printFileStats(localFile);
} catch (URISyntaxException use) {
    LOGGER.error("Malformed URI, no file there", use);
}
```

The URI might be incorrect, as in having an incorrect prefix or containing a wrong path, so the URI constructor is declared to throw a `java.net.URISyntaxException`. This is a checked exception, so the code you write must handle it. In the case of a URI being used to create a file handler, the `getAbsolutePath()` method returns the absolute pathname of the file on the computer and drive where the file is located.

Caution   The `file:///` protocol is used in macOS (and other operating systems) to specify a file path in a URL format. This allows applications and web browsers to access files directly from the file system. It will work on Windows as well, as long as you replace `[workspace]` with a real path.

Info   Since both Listing 11-1 and 11-2 call `printFileStats(..)` on the same file, the console output is identical. Feel free to try running the code yourself.

---

getParent, getName, length, isHidden, canRead, and canWrite

Since there is not much to say about each of these method, I grouped them together in this section. Here's the brief summary:

- `getParent()` returns the absolute path to the directory containing the file, because hierarchically, a file cannot have another file as a parent.

- `getName()` returns the file name. The file name contains the extension as the suffix after `"."` is called, which is used to indicate they type of file and what it is intended to be used for.

- length() returns the length of the file in bytes. This method does not work for directories, as directories can contain files restricted to the user executing the program and exceptions might be thrown. So if you ever need the size of a directory, you have to write the code yourself.

- isHidden() returns true if the file is not visible to the current user, and returns false otherwise. On a macOS/Linux system, files with names starting with "." are hidden, so if we want to see that method returning true we have to create a handler to one of the system configuration files, such as .gitconfig. So calling the printFileStats(..) method on a file handler created using a pathname to a hidden file results in output similar to the output in Listing 11-3.

Listing 11-3. Printing File Details for a Hidden File

```
INFO  c.a.b.e.Main - File Details:
INFO  c.a.b.e.Main - Type : file
INFO  c.a.b.e.Main - Location :/Users/[userDir]/.gitconfig
INFO  c.a.b.e.Main - Parent :/Users/[userDir]
INFO  c.a.b.e.Main - Name : .gitconfig
INFO  c.a.b.e.Main - Size : 3.865234375
INFO  c.a.b.e.Main - Is Hidden : true
INFO  c.a.b.e.Main - Is Readable? : true
INFO  c.a.b.e.Main - Is Writable? : true
```

- canRead() and canWrite() are obvious, as files can be secured from normal users. Both methods return true when the user has the specific right on the file and return false otherwise.

Handling Directories: list() and listFiles()

File handlers can be created for pathnames pointing to directories, which means there are available methods to call that are specific only to directories. The most common thing to do with a directory is to list its contents. The list() method returns a String array containing the names of the files (and directories) under this directory. Using lambda expressions makes printing the items in a directory pretty practical:

```
var d = new File("/[workspace]/java-17-for-absolute-beginners");
Arrays.stream(Objects.requireNonNull(d.list())).forEach(ff -> LOGGER.
info("\t File Name : {}", ff));
```

Files names are not really useful in most cases; having a File array with file handlers to each of them would be better. That is why listFiles() method was added in version 1.2:

```
Arrays.stream(Objects.requireNonNull(d.listFiles())).forEach(ff -> LOGGER.
info("\t File : {}", ff.getAbsolutePath()));
```

This method has more than one form, because it can be used to filter the files and return file handlers only for files or directories matching a certain requirement when called with an instance of FileFilter. The code sample in Listing 11-4 filters the entries under the directories and keeps only the directories with names that start with chapter.

Listing 11-4. Filtering Content of a Directory Using a FileFilter Instance

```
package com.apress.bgn.eleven.io;

import java.io.File;
import java.io.FileFilter;
// other imports and wrapper code omitted

var d = new File("/[workspace]/java-17-for-absolute-beginners");
        Arrays.stream(d.listFiles(new FileFilter() {
          @Override
          public boolean accept(File childFile) {
            return childFile.isDirectory() && childFile.getName().
            startsWith("chapter");
          }
        })).forEach(ff -> LOGGER.info("Chapter Source : {}",
        ff.getName()));
```

Listing 11-4 is written in expanded form to make it obvious that you should provide a concrete implementation for the accept(..) method. By using lambda expressions as follows, the previous code can be simplified and even made less prone to exceptions being thrown:

```
Arrays.stream(
    Objects.requireNonNull(d.listFiles(
        childFile -> childFile.isDirectory() && childFile.getName().
        startsWith("chapter")))
    ).forEach(ff -> LOGGER.info("Chapter Source : {}", ff.getName())
);
```

In Listing 11-4 we implemented the accept(..) method to filter by file type and name, but the filter can involve anything. When the filter you need strictly involves the file name, you can use the other version of the method, which receives a FilenameFilter instance as argument:

```
Arrays.stream(Objects.requireNonNull(d.listFiles(new FilenameFilter() {
        @Override
        public boolean accept(File dir, String name) {
            return name.startsWith("chapter");
        }
}))).forEach(ff -> LOGGER.info("\t Chapter directory : {}",
ff.getAbsolutePath()));
```

createNewFile(), exists(), createTempFile(..), and deleteOnExit()

Aside from listing properties of file, a file handler can also be used to create a file. To create a file, the createNewFile() method must be called after creating a file handler with a specific pathname, as shown in Listing 11-5.

Listing 11-5. Creating a File

```
package com.apress.bgn.eleven.io;

import java.io.IOException;
// other imports and wrapper code omitted

var created = new File(
        "chapter11/read-write-file/src/main/resources/output/created.txt");
if (!created.exists()) {
    try {
```

721

```
        var result = created.createNewFile();
        LOGGER.info("File was created ? {}", result);
    } catch (IOException e) {
        LOGGER.error("Could not create file.", e);
    }
}
```

The exists() method returns true when the file hander is associated with a concrete file or directory, and returns false otherwise. It can be used to test if the file we are trying to create already exists. If the file exists, the method has no effect. If the user does not have proper rights to create the file at the specified pathname, a SecurityException will be thrown.

In certain cases, we might need to create a file that needs to be used only during the execution of the program. This means we either have to create the file and delete it explicitly or create a temporary file. Temporary files are created by calling createTempFile(prefix, suffix) and they are created in the temporary directory defined for the operating system. The prefix argument is of type String and its value will be the prefix of the name of the created file. The suffix argument is of type String as well, and it can be used to specify an extension for the file. The rest of the file name is generated by the operating system. The code to create a temporary file is depicted in Listing 11-6.

Listing 11-6. Creating a Temporary File

```
package com.apress.bgn.eleven.io;

import java.io.IOException;
// other imports and wrapper code omitted

try {
    File temp = File.createTempFile("java_bgn_", ".tmp");
    LOGGER.info("File created at: {}", temp.getAbsolutePath());
    temp.deleteOnExit();
} catch (IOException e) {
        LOGGER.error("Could not create temporary file.", e);
}
```

Files in the temporary directory of an operating system are periodically deleted by the operating system, but if you want to make sure a temporary file will be deleted, you can explicitly call deleteOnExit() on the file handler for the temporary file. In the code sample in Listing 11-6, the absolute path to the file is printed to show the exact location where the temporary file was created, and on a macOS system the full pathname looks very similar to this:

```
/var/folders/gg/nm_cb2lx72q1lz7xwwdh7tnc0000gn/T/java_
bgn_14652264510049064218.tmp
```

You can stop the execution of the Main class by running it in debug mode and putting a break point on the logging statement to check where temporary files are saved on your system, like shown in Figure 11-1.

Figure 11-1. *IntelliJ IDEA debugger showing absolute path of temporary file*

renameTo

A file can also be renamed using a Java file handler. The rename(f) method is called with a file handler argument pointing to the location and desired name that the file should have. The method returns true if the renaming succeeded and returns false otherwise. The code for doing this is depicted in Listing 11-7.

Listing 11-7. Renaming a File

```
package com.apress.bgn.eleven.io;

import java.io.IOException;
// other imports and wrapper code omitted

file = new File(
        "chapter11/read-write-file/src/main/resources/output/created.txt");
var renamed = new File(
        "chapter11/read-write-file/src/main/resources/output/renamed.txt");
boolean result = file.renameTo(renamed);
        LOGGER.info("Renaming succeeded? : {} ", result);
```

Most methods in the class File throw IOException, because manipulating a file can fail for various reasons, including a hardware problem or an operating system problem. This type of exception is a checked exception, and developers using file handlers are forced to catch and treat this type of exception.

Methods that require special rights for accessing a file throw SecurityException. This type extends RuntimeException so exceptions are not checked. They become obvious when the application is running.

You now know all the basics of working with file handlers.

Path Handlers

The java.nio.file.Path interface was introduced in Java 7 together with utility classes java.nio.file.Files and java.nio.file.Paths to provide new and more practical ways to work with files. A Path instance may be used to locate a file in a file system, and thus represents a system-dependent file path. Path instances are more practical than File instances because they can provide methods to access components of a path, combine paths, and compare paths.

Path instances cannot be directly created, because an interface cannot be instantiated, but the interface provides static utility methods to create them, and so does the class Paths. Use whichever you want depending on your situation.

The simplest way to create a Path instance is to start with a file handler and call Paths.get(fileURI), as shown in Listing 11-8.

Listing 11-8. Creating a Path Instance

```
package com.apress.bgn.eleven.io;

// other imports omitted
import java.io.File;
import java.nio.file.Path;
import java.nio.file.Paths;

public class PathDemo {

    private static final Logger LOGGER = LoggerFactory.
    getLogger(PathDemo.class);

    void main() {
        File file = new File(
                "/[workspace]/java-23-for-absolute-beginners/README.adoc");
        Path path = Path.of(file.toURI());
        LOGGER.info(path.toString());
    }
}
```

Starting with Java 11, `Paths.get(file.toURI())` can be replaced with `Path.of(file.toURI())`. The other way to create a `Path` instance is to use the other form of the `Paths.get(..)` that receives as arguments multiple pieces of the path:

```
Path composedPath = Paths.get("/[workspace]",
    "java-23-for-absolute-beginners",
    "README.adoc");
LOGGER.info(composedPath.toString());
```

Both paths created previously point to the same location, thus if compared with each other using the `compareTo(..)` method (because `Path` extends interface `Comparable<Path>`), the result returned will be 0 (zero), which means the paths are equal:

```
LOGGER.info("Is the same path? : {} ", path.compareTo(composedPath) = =0 ?
"yes" : "no");
// prints : INFO com.apress.bgn.ch11.PathDemo - Is the same path? : yes
```

725

In the code sample in Listing 11-9, a few Path methods are called on the path instance.

Listing 11-9. Inspecting Path Details

```
package com.apress.bgn.eleven.io;
// import section omitted

public class PathDemo {
    private static final Logger LOGGER = LoggerFactory.
    getLogger(PathDemo.class);

    public static void main(String... args) {
        var path = Paths.get("/[workspace]",
                    "java-23-for-absolute-beginners",
                    "README.adoc");
        printPathDetails(path);
    }

    private static void printPathDetails(Path path) {
      LOGGER.info("Path Details:");
      LOGGER.info("\tFileName : {}", path.getFileName());
      LOGGER.info("\tParent :{}", path.getParent());
      LOGGER.info("\tLocation :{}", path.toAbsolutePath());
      LOGGER.info("\tIs Absolute? : {}", path.isAbsolute());
      LOGGER.info("\tRoot :{}", path.getRoot());
      LOGGER.info("\tFileSystem : {}", path.getFileSystem());
      LOGGER.info("\tIsFileReadOnly : {}", path.getFileSystem().
                                    isReadOnly());
    }
}
```

The following list explains each method and its outcome:

- toAbsolutePath() returns a Path instance representing the
  absolute path of this path. When called on the Path instance created
  previously, as it is already absolute, the method will just return the
  path object the method is called on. Also, calling path.isAbsolute()
  will return true.

- getParent() returns the parent Path instance. Calling this method on the Path instance will print:

  ```
  INFO com.apress.bgn.ch11.PathDemo - Parent :/[workspace]/java-23-
  for-absolute-beginners/README.adoc
  ```

- getRoot() returns the root component of this path as a Path instance. On a Linux or macOS system it prints "/", and on Windows it prints something like "C:\".

- getFileName() returns the name of the file or directory denoted by this path as a Path instance; basically, the path is split by the system path separator, and the most far away from the root element is returned.

- getFileSystem() returns the file system that created this object. For macOS, it is an instance of type sun.nio.fs.MacOSXFileSystem.

Another useful Path method is resolve(..). This method takes a String instance that is a representation of a path and resolves it against the Path instance it is called on. This means that path separators are added according to the operating system the program runs on and a Path instance will be returned. This is depicted in Listing 11-10.

Listing 11-10. Inspecting Path Details (again)

```
var chapterPath = Paths.get("/Users/iuliana/apress/workspace",
            "java-23-for-absolute-beginners/chapter11");
Path filePath = chapterPath.resolve(
        "read-write-file/src/main/resources/input/data.txt") ;
LOGGER.info("Resolved Path :{}", filePath.toAbsolutePath());
```

The Listing 11-10 code sample will print the following:

```
INFO  c.a.b.e.PathDemo - Resolved Path :/[workspace]/java-23-for-absolute-
beginners/chapter11/read-write-file/src/main/resources/input/data.txt
```

Using Path instances, writing code that manages files or retrieves their properties becomes easier to write in combination with Files utility methods. The code sample in Listing 11-11 makes use of a few of these methods to print properties of a file, in the same way we did previously using a file handler.

Listing 11-11. Printing Even More Path Details

```
package com.apress.bgn.eleven.io;
// import section omitted

public class PathDemo {
  private static final Logger log = LoggerFactory.
  getLogger(PathDemo.class);

  public static void main(String... args) {
    var outputPath = FileSystems.getDefault()
            .getPath("/[workspace]/java-23-for-absolute-beginners/" +
                "chapter11/read-write-file/src/main/resources/output/
                sample");
    try {
      Path dirPath = Files.createDirectory(outputPath);
      printPathStats(dirPath);
    } catch (FileAlreadyExistsException faee) {
      LOGGER.error("Directory already exists.", faee);
    } catch (IOException e) {
      LOGGER.error("Could not create directory.", e);
    }
  }

  private static void printPathStats(Path path) {
    if (Files.exists(path)) {
      LOGGER.info("Path Details:");
      LOGGER.info("\tType: {}", Files.isDirectory(path) ? "yes" : "no");
      LOGGER.info("\tType: {}", Files.isRegularFile(path) ? "yes" : "no");
      LOGGER.info("\tType: {}", Files.isSymbolicLink(path) ? "yes" : "no");
      LOGGER.info("\tLocation :{}", path.toAbsolutePath());
      LOGGER.info("\tParent :{}", path.getParent());
      LOGGER.info("\tName : {}", path.getFileName());

      try {
        double kilobytes = Files.size(path) / (double)1024;
        LOGGER.info("\tSize : {} ", kilobytes);
        LOGGER.info("\tIs Hidden: {}", Files.isHidden(path) ? "yes" : "no");
```

```
    } catch (IOException e) {
      LOGGER.error("Could not access file.", e);
    }
    LOGGER.info("\tIs Readable: {}", Files.isReadable(path) ? "yes"
    : "no");
    LOGGER.info("\tIs Writable: {}", Files.isWritable(path) ? "yes"
    : "no");

    }
  }
}
```

As you can see, the Files class provides the same functionality as the File class. The Files class consists exclusively of static methods that operate on files, directories, or other types of files. It was introduced in Java 7 and its advantage is the clearer syntax. The power and practicality of using java.nio classes is more obvious when managing files, creating them, renaming them, deleting them, and reading and writing them. The code sample in Listing 11-12 shows a file being created, renamed, and deleted using Java NIO classes.

Listing 11-12. Copying and Moving Files

```
package com.apress.bgn.eleven.io;
// import section omitted
import java.nio.FileAlreadyExistsException;

public class PathDemo {
  private static final Logger LOGGER = LoggerFactory.
  getLogger(PathDemo.class);

  public static void main(String... args) {
    Path filePath = chapterPath.resolve(
            "read-write-file/src/main/resources/input/data.txt");
    Path copyFilePath = Paths.get(outputPath.toAbsolutePath().toString(),
                        "data.adoc");
    try {
      Files.copy(filePath, copyFilePath);
      LOGGER.info("Exists? : {}", Files.exists(copyFilePath)? "yes": "no");
```

```
      LOGGER.info("File copied to: {}", copyFilePath.toAbsolutePath());
    } catch (FileAlreadyExistsException faee) {
      LOGGER.error("File already exists.", faee);
    } catch (IOException e) {
      LOGGER.error("Could not copy file.", e);
    }
    Path movedFilePath = Paths.get(outputPath.toAbsolutePath().toString(),
                      "copy-data.adoc");
    try {
      Files.move(copyFilePath, movedFilePath);
      LOGGER.info("File moved to: {}", movedFilePath.toAbsolutePath());
      Files.deleteIfExists(copyFilePath);
    } catch (FileAlreadyExistsException faee) {
      LOGGER.error("File already exists.", faee);
    }  catch (IOException e) {
      LOGGER.error("Could not move file.", e);
    }
  }
}
```

Information   Although compact `catch` exception statements were introduced in **Chapter 5**, in code samples where the different types of exceptions have distinct causes and should be handled differently, the expanded form will be used.

Notice the `FileAlreadyExistsException`, an exception type added in Java 7 that extends `IOException` and is used to provide more data about the situation that determined the failure of a file operation. It is thrown by methods `createDirectory(..)`, `createFile(..)`, and `move(..)`.

The `delete(..)` method that is not used in Listing 11-12 throws a `java.nio.file.NoSuchFileException` if the file to be deleted does not exist. To avoid an exception being thrown, `deleteIfEFileAlreadyExistsExceptionxists(..)` is used in Listing 11-12.

The list of methods in `Files` is even longer, but since the size of this chapter is limited, you can go ahead and check it out yourself in the official Javadoc API.

Reading Files

Every file is a succession of bits on a hard drive. A File handler does not provide methods to read the content of a file, but a group of other classes can be used to do so, all of which are created using a file handler instance. Java provides many ways to read files, the choice of which depends on what actually needs to be done with the contents of a file. This section will cover the four most common ways.

Using Scanner to Read Files

The Scanner class was used previously to read input from the command line. System.in can be replaced with a File and Scanner methods can be used to read file contents, as depicted in Listing 11-13.

Listing 11-13. Using Scanner to Read a File

```
package com.apress.bgn.eleven.io;
import java.util.Scanner;
// other import statements omitted

public class ScannerDemo {
    private static final Logger LOGGER = LoggerFactory.
    getLogger(ScannerDemo.class);

    void main() {
        try {
            final String inDir = "chapter11/read-write-file/src/main/
                            resources/input/";
            var scanner = new Scanner(new File("chapter11/read-write-file/
                        src/main/resources/input/data.txt"));
            var content = "";
            while (scanner.hasNextLine()) {
                content += scanner.nextLine() + "\n";
            }
            scanner.close();
            LOGGER.info("Read with Scanner --> {}", content);
```

```
        } catch (IOException e) {
            LOGGER.error("Something went wrong! ", e);
        }
    }
}
```

Instead of a file, a `java.nio.file.Path` instance can be used as well:

```
scanner = new Scanner(Paths.get(new File("chapter11/read-write-file/src/
main/resources/input/data.txt").toURI()), StandardCharsets.UTF_8.name());
```

Files can be written using different sets of characters, referred to in Java by `java.nio.charset.Charset` instances. To ensure they are read correctly, it is a good practice to read them using the same charset. The `Scanner` constructor receives a charset name as an argument. The `StandardCharsets.UTF_8.name()` method is called to extract the name of the UTF-8 charset.

Using Files Utility Methods to Read Files

The first code sample in Listing 11-14 shows the simplest way to read a file.

Listing 11-14. The Simplest Way to Read a File

```
package com.apress.bgn.eleven.io;

import java.nio.file.Files;
import java.nio.file.Paths;
// other import statements omitted

public class FilesReadDemo {
    private static final Logger LOGGER = LoggerFactory.
    getLogger(FilesReadDemo.class);

    void main() {
        final String inDir = "chapter11/read-write-file/src/main/resources/
                            input/";
        var file = new File(inDir + "data.txt");
```

```
    try {
        var content = new String(Files.readAllBytes(Paths.get(file.
                      toURI()))));
        LOGGER.info("Read with Files.readAllBytes --> {}", content);
    } catch (IOException e) {
        LOGGER.info("Something went wrong! ", e);
    }
  }
}
```

This approach works well when the file size can be approximated (the file size can be estimated and is relatively small) and storing it in a `String` object would not be a problem.

The advantage of using `Files.readAllBytes(..)` is that no loop is needed, and we do not have to construct the `String` value line by line, because this method just reads all the bytes in the files that can be given as an argument to the `String` constructor. The disadvantage is that no `Charset` is used, so the text value might not be the one we expect. There is a way to overcome this, by calling `Files.readAllLines(..)` that returns the file content as a list of `String` values, and has two forms one of them declaring a `Charset` as a parameter. This version of reading a file is depicted in Listing 11-15.

Listing 11-15. A Simple Way to Read a File Specifying a `Charset`

```
try {
    List<String> lyricList = Files.readAllLines(Paths.get(file.toURI()),
                             StandardCharsets.UTF_8);
    lyricList.forEach(System.out::println);
} catch (IOException e) {
    LOGGER.info("Something went wrong! ", e);
}
```

But what if we do not need a `List<String>`, but the one `String` instance? Java 11 introduced a method for that: `readString(..)`. The code sample using it is shown in Listing 11-16.

Listing 11-16. The Simplest Way to Read a File into a Single `String` Specifying a `Charset`

```
try {
var content = Files.readString(Paths.get(file.toURI()),
            StandardCharsets.UTF_8);
    LOGGER.info("Read with Files.readString --> {}", content);
} catch (IOException e) {
    LOGGER.info("Something went wrong! ", e);
}
```

Using Readers to Read Files

Before the `Files` class and its fancy methods were introduced, there were other ways to read files. The fancy methods are also not designed for reading big files, or for reading only parts of a file. Let's take a trip to the past and slowly analyze how things have evolved.

Before Java 6, to read a file line by line, you would have to write a contraption such as the one in Listing 11-17.

Listing 11-17. Reading a File Line by Line, Before Java 6

```
package com.apress.bgn.eleven.io;

import java.io.BufferedReader;
import java.io.FileReader;
// other imports omitted

public class ReadersDemo {
  private static final Logger LOGGER = LoggerFactory.
getLogger(ReadersDemo.class);

  void main() {
    BufferedReader reader = null;
    final String inDir = "chapter11/read-write-file/src/main/resources/
                      input/";
```

```
try {
  reader = new BufferedReader(new FileReader(new File(inDir +
          "data.txt"), StandardCharsets.UTF_8));
  StringBuilder sb = new StringBuilder();
  String line;
  while ((line = reader.readLine()) != null) {
    sb.append(line).append("\n");
  }
  LOGGER.info("Read with BufferedReader --> {}", sb.toString());
} catch (Exception e) {
  LOGGER.error("File could not be read! ", e);
} finally {
  if (reader != null) {
    try {
      reader.close();
    } catch (IOException ioe) {
      LOGGER.error("Something went wrong! ", ioe);
    }
  }
}
}
```

Whoa, what is that, right? After Java 6, the syntax was simplified a little, but the biggest changes came in Java 7. Before Java 7, if you wanted to read a file line by line, you had to write code as follows:

1. Create a `File` handler.

2. Wrap the file handler into a `FileReader`. This type of instance could do the job of reading, but only in chunks of `char[]`, which is not very useful when you need the actual text.

3. Wrap the `FileReader` instance into an instance of `BufferedReader` that provides this functionality by reading the characters in an internal buffer. This involved calling `reader.readLine()` until there is nothing more to read because the end of the file was reached, at which point this method returned `null`.

4.   At the end of the reading, call `reader.close()` explicitly; otherwise, a lock might be kept on the file, and it might become unreadable until a restart.

Java 7 introduced a lot of changes to reduce the boilerplate needed to work with files. One of those changes was that all classes used to access file contents and that could keep a lock on the file were enriched by being declared to implement the `java.io.Closeable` interface, which marks resources of these types as *closable* and a `close()` method is invoked to release resources transparently by the JVM before execution ends. Also, Java 7 introduced the `try-with-resources` statement. By making use of all these features, the pre–Java 6 code in Listing 11-17 can be written as depicted in Listing 11-18.

Listing 11-18. Reading a File Line by Line, Starting with Java 7

```
try (BufferedReader br = new BufferedReader(new FileReader(new File(inDir
+ "data.txt")))){
    StringBuilder sb = new StringBuilder();
    String line;
    while ((line = br.readLine()) != null) {
        sb.append(line).append("\n");
    }
    LOGGER.info("Read with BufferedReader --> {}", sb.toString() );
} catch (Exception e) {
    LOGGER.info("Something went wrong! ", e);
}
```

The code can be further simplified, as the `FileReader` can take the absolute path to a file as `String` as a parameter. But the code cannot be made to take encoding into consideration. This became possible in Java 8, when a constructor was introduced for the `FileReader` class that accepts a `Charset` argument. In Java 7, we still have nested constructor calls in the previous example, and it is quite ugly. Here is where Java 8 comes to the rescue, by introducing the `Files.newBufferedReader(Path)` and the `Files.newBufferedReader(Path, Charset)` method.

So, the code in Listing 11-18 can be written as shown in Listing 11-19.

Listing 11-19. Reading a File Line by Line, Taking Encoding into Consideration
Starting with Java 8

```
File file = new File(inDir + "data.txt");
try (BufferedReader br = Files.newBufferedReader(file.toPath(),
StandardCharsets.UTF_8)){
    StringBuilder sb = new StringBuilder();
    String line;
    while ((line = br.readLine()) != null) {
        sb.append(line).append("\n");
    }
    LOGGER.info("Read with BufferedReader --> {}", sb.toString());
} catch (Exception e) {
    LOGGER.info("Something went wrong! ", e);
}
```

If we know that the size of the file is manageable and we are interested in not only logging the contents but also saving the individual lines for further processing, the easiest way to do this is by using `Files.readAllLines(..)` method combined with lambda expressions. Streams can be added in the mix, so the lines can be filtered or processed on the spot as shown here:

```
List<String> dataList = Files.readAllLines(Paths.get(file.toURI()),
StandardCharsets.UTF_8)
  .stream()
  .filter(line -> line!= null && !line.isBlank())
  .map(String::toUpperCase)
  .collect(Collectors.toList());
```

Or we can write it another way, using the `Files.lines(..)` method, also introduced in Java 8, and get all contents as a stream directly:

```
dataList = Files.lines(Paths.get(file.toURI()), StandardCharsets.UTF_8)
  .filter(line -> line!= null && !line.isBlank() )
  .map(String::toUpperCase)
  .toList();
```

Anyway, back to file readers. The BufferedReader class is a member of a class group that extend the abstract Reader class. This is an abstract class used for reading character streams and is part of the java.io package. A simplified hierarchy showing the most-used implementations is depicted in Figure 11-2.

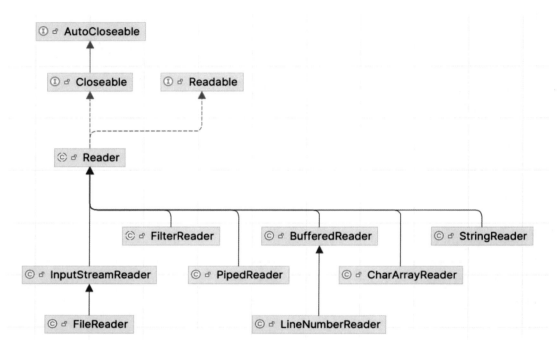

Figure 11-2. *Reader class hierarchy (as shown in IntelliJ IDEA)*

Character streams can have different sources, files being the most common. They provide sequential access to data stored in the file. The BufferedReader class does not provide support for character encoding, but a BufferedReader instance is based on another Reader instance. And as you have noticed in the previous examples, a FileReader instance was used as argument when instantiating a BufferedReader, and FileReader was modified in Java 8 to support character encoding. Before Java 8, to read from a file and take character encoding into consideration, an InputStreamReader instance was used, as depicted in Listing 11-20.

Listing 11-20. Reading a File Line by Line, Taking Encoding into Consideration
Before Java 8

```
try (BufferedReader br = new BufferedReader(new InputStreamReader(new
FileInputStream(file), StandardCharsets.UTF_8))){
    StringBuilder sb = new StringBuilder();
    String line;
    while ((line = br.readLine()) != null) {
        sb.append(line).append("\n");
    }
    LOGGER.info("Read with BufferedReader(InputStreamReader(FileInput
    Stream(..))) --> {}", sb.toString() );
} catch (Exception e) {
    LOGGER.info("Something went wrong! ", e);
}
```

In Java 11, the Reader class was enriched with the nullReader() method, which
returns a Reader instance that does nothing. This was requested by developers for testing
purposes and is nothing else but a pseudo-Reader implementation.

Using InputStream to Read Files

Classes in the Reader family are advanced classes for reading data as text, but
technically speaking files are just a sequence of bytes, so these classes are themselves
wrappers around classes in a family of classes used for reading byte streams. This
becomes quite obvious when trying to use the proper character encoding, and when
reading text (as shown at the end of the previous section) using the BufferedReader,
as the InputStreamReader instance given as an argument is based on a java.
io.FileInputStream instance, a type that is a subclass of java.io.InputStream.

The root class of this hierarchy is java.io.InputStream. A simplified hierarchy,
showing the most commonly used implementations is depicted in Figure 11-3.

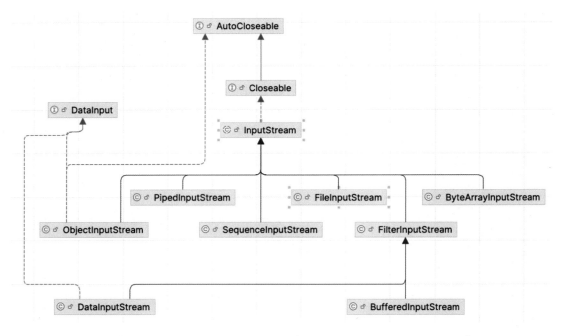

Figure 11-3. *InputStream class hierarchy (as shown in IntelliJ IDEA)*

The class BufferedInputStream is the equivalent of BufferedReader for reading streams of bytes. The System.in that we previously used to read user data from the console is of this type, and the Scanner instance converts the bytes from its buffer into user-understandable data. When the data we are interested in is not text that was stored using Unicode conventions, but raw numeric data (binary files such as images, media files, PDFs, etc.), classes for using streams of bytes are more suitable. Just for the purpose of showing you how it's done, we'll read the contents of the data.txt file using FileInputStream, as depicted in Listing 11-21.

Listing 11-21. Reading a File Using FileInputStream

```
package com.apress.bgn.eleven.io;

import java.io.FileInputStream;
// other imports omitted

public class FileInputStreamReadingDemo {
    private static final Logger LOGGER = LoggerFactory.getLogger(FileInput
    StreamReadingDemo.class);
```

```
public static void main(String... args) {
    final String inDir = "chapter11/read-write-file/src/main/resources/
                        input/";
    File file = new File(inDir + "data.txt");
    try (FileInputStream fis = new FileInputStream(file)) {
        byte[] buffer = new byte[1024];
        StringBuilder sb = new StringBuilder();
        while (fis.read(buffer) != -1) {
            sb.append(new String(buffer));
            buffer = new byte[1024];
        }
        LOGGER.info("Read with FileInputStream --> {}", sb.toString() );
    } catch (IOException e) {
        LOGGER.error("Something went wrong! ", e);
    }
}
}
```

If you run the code in Listing 11-21, you will notice that the expected output is printed in the console, but you might also notice something odd: after the text is printed, a set of strange characters is printed too. On a macOS system they look as depicted in Figure 11-4.

```
···   41 ▷   public class FileInputStreamReadingDemo {  new *
      42          private static final Logger LOGGER = LoggerFactory.getLogger(FileInputStreamRea
      43
      44 ▷       public static void main(String... args) {  new *
      45              final String inDir = "chapter11/read-write-file/src/main/resources/input/";
      46              File file = new File( pathname: inDir + "data.txt");
      47              try (FileInputStream fis = new FileInputStream(file)) {
      48                  byte[] buffer = new byte[1024];
                         StringBuilder sb = new StringBuilder();
```

Run   FileInputStreamReadingDemo ×

```
Whatcha gonna do about it?
Whatcha gonna do about it?
Whatcha gonna do about it?
Don't give up, give up
Don't give up, give up, give up
Don't give up, give up
Don't give up, give up, give up▨▨▨▨▨▨▨▨▨▨▨▨▨▨▨▨▨▨▨▨▨▨▨▨▨▨▨▨▨▨▨▨▨▨▨▨▨▨▨▨▨▨▨▨▨▨▨▨
```

Figure 11-4. Text read with FileInputStream

741

Do you have any idea what those characters might be?

It's okay if you have no idea; I did not either, the first time I had to use `FileInputStream` to read a file. Those characters appear there because the file size is not a multiple of 1024, so the `FileInputReader` ends up filling the rest of the last buffer with zeros. A fix for this involves computing the size of the file in bytes and making sure we adapt the `byte[]` buffer size accordingly. You can try doing that as an exercise if you are in the mood for some coding. And now that we've explored how to read files in a lot of ways, we can continue by examining how to write files, since you already know how to create them.

In Java 11, the `InputStream` was also enriched with a method that returns an `InputStream` that does nothing: the `nullInputStream()` method is designed for testing purposes and is nothing but a pseudo-`InputStream` implementation.

All classes presented so far are the ones you will encounter most while working with files in Java. If you need more specialized file handling tools, feel free to read the official documentation or use custom implementations provided by third-party libraries such as Apache Commons IO[4], which is frequently used in the Java world.

Writing Files

Writing files in Java is quite similar to reading them, only different classes have to be used, because streams are unidirectional. A stream that is used for reading data cannot be used for writing data as well. For almost any class or method of reading files there is one for writing files. Without further ado, let's start.

Writing Files Using Files Utility Methods

Smaller files can be easily written starting with Java 7, using the `Files.write(Path, byte[], OpenOption... options)` method. It takes two arguments: a `Path` representing the location of a file and an array of bytes representing the data to be written. This method is a practical one-liner when the data required to be written is small enough. The last argument is actually a *varargs* (introduced in **Chapter 3**) and represents none, one, or more operations the file is opened for. The method can be used without specifying any argument of that type, as shown in Listing 11-22.

---

[4] `https://commons.apache.org/proper/commons-io`

Listing 11-22. Writing a String to a File, Starting with Java 7

```
package com.apress.bgn.eleven.io;

import java.io.File;
import java.io.IOException;
import java.nio.file.Files;
import java.nio.file.Path;
// other import statements omitted

public class FilesWritingDemo {
    private static final Logger LOGGER = LoggerFactory.
    getLogger(FilesWritingDemo.class);

    void maim() {
        var file = new File("chapter11/read-write-file/src/main/resources/
                    output/data.txt");

        byte[] data = "Some of us, we're hardly ever here".getBytes();
        try {
            Path dataPath = Files.write(file.toPath(), data);
            LOGGER.info("String written to {}", dataPath.toAbsolutePath());
        } catch (IOException e) {
            LOGGER.debug("Could not write data to file", e);
        }
    }
}
```

If the file already exists, the contents will be simply overwritten. This means that since no argument was specified to configure what we want to do with the file, the default behavior was to open the file for writing and truncate its size to zero and start writing from there, thus overwriting it. The list of available options is modeled by the values in the java.nio.file.StandardOpenOption enum. The value corresponding to the default behavior is TRUNCATE_EXISTING. So this line in the example in Listing 11-22:

```
Path dataPath = Files.write(file.toPath(), data);
```

is equivalent to

```
import java.nio.file.StandardOpenOption
//...
Path dataPath = Files.write(file.toPath(), data, StandardOpenOption.
               TRUNCATE_EXISTING);
```

If the desired behavior is to modify a file if it exists and append the new data at its end, the option to use as an argument for the Files.write(..) method is APPEND:

```
Path dataPath = Files.write(file.toPath(), data, StandardOpenOption.APPEND);
```

Also notice how the string needs to be converted to an array of bytes before being written. In Java 11, this is no longer necessary, because finally some JDK developer thought that most people would probably write a simple String to a file and realized that forcing them to explicitly call getBytes() is pretty silly. As a result the Files. writeString(..) method family was introduced, and one of them also supports specifying an encoding. An example of this method being used to write a string into a file can be seen in Listing 11-23.

Listing 11-23. Writing a String to a File, Starting with Java 11

```
package com.apress.bgn.eleven.io;

import java.nio.charset.StandardCharsets;
import static java.nio.file.StandardOpenOption.APPEND;
// import statements omitted

var file = new File("chapter11/read-write-file/src/main/resources/output/
data.txt");
 try {
    Path dataPath = Files.writeString(file.toPath(),
            "\nThe rest of us, we're born to disappear",
            StandardCharsets.UTF_8,
            APPEND);
    log.info("String written to {}", dataPath.toAbsolutePath());
} catch (IOException e) {
    e.printStackTrace();
}
```

Another version of Files.write(..) takes an argument of type Iterable<? extends CharSequence>, which means that a list of String values can be written using it, as shown in Listing 11-24.

Listing 11-24. Writing a List<String> to a File Using Files.write(..)

```java
var file = new File("chapter11/read-write-file/src/main/resources/output/
        data.txt");

List<String> dataList = List.of(
        "How do I stop myself from",
        "Being just a number?");
try {
    Path dataPath = Files.write(file.toPath(), dataList,
            StandardCharsets.UTF_8,
            APPEND);
    log.info("String written to {}", dataPath.toAbsolutePath());
} catch (IOException e) {
    e.printStackTrace();
}
```

Next we are going to look into writing files using classes in the Writer hierarchy.

Using Writer to Write Files

Similar to the Reader hierarchy for reading files, there is an abstract class named Writer, but before we get to that, I'll introduce the BufferedWriter, the correspondent of BufferedReader for writing files, because this is one of the most used in practice. This class too has an internal buffer, and when write methods are called, the arguments are stored into the buffer, and when the buffer is full, its contents are written to the file. The buffer can be emptied earlier by calling the flush() method. It is definitely recommended to call this method explicitly before calling close() to make sure all output was written to the file. The code snippet in Listing 11-25 depicts how a list of String instances is written to a file.

Listing 11-25. Writing a List<String> to a File Using BufferedWriter

```
package com.apress.bgn.eleven.io;

import java.io.BufferedWriter;
import java.io.FileWriter;
// other import statements omitted

public class BufferedWritingDemo {
  private static final Logger LOGGER = LoggerFactory.
getLogger(BufferedWritingDemo.class);

  void main() {
    var file = new File("chapter11/read-write-file/src/main/resources/
              output/data.txt");
    var dataList = List.of ("How will I hold my head" ,
          "To keep from going under");

    BufferedWriter writer = null;
    try {
      writer = new BufferedWriter(new FileWriter(file));
      for (String entry : dataList) {
        writer.write(entry);
        writer.newLine();
      }
      LOGGER.info("String written using BufferedWriter before Java 7");
    } catch (IOException e) {
      LOGGER.info("Something went wrong! ", e);
    } finally {
      if(writer!= null) {
        try {
          writer.flush();
          writer.close();
        } catch (IOException e) {
          LOGGER.info("Something went wrong! ", e);
        }
```

```
        }
      }
    }
}
```

Yet another code contraption is needed, because writing files is a sensitive operation that can fail for many reasons. The code in Listing 11-25 is what you had to write before Java 7, when try-with-resources reduced the boilerplate and allowed that code to be reduced as shown in Listing 11-26.

Listing 11-26. Writing a List<String> to a File Using BufferedWriter and try-with-resources

```
try (final BufferedWriter wr = new BufferedWriter(new FileWriter(file))){
    dataList.forEach(entry -> {
        try {
            wr.write(entry);
            wr.newLine();
        } catch (IOException e) {
            LOGGER.info("Something went wrong! ", e);
        }
    });
    wr.flush();
    LOGGER.info("String written using BufferedWriter after Java 7");
} catch (IOException e) {
    LOGGER.info("Something went wrong! ", e);
}
```

Notice that there is no need to call wr.close(), because in Java 7 the java.io.Closeable interface was modified to extend java.lang.AutoCloseable, which declares a version of the close() method that is called automatically when exiting a try-with-resources block. Still, the code looks pretty stuffy, right? Especially since a BufferedWriter needs to be declared and needs to be wrapped around a FileWriter instance. This was simplified in Java 8 with the addition of the Files utility class, which contains a method named newBufferedWriter(Path path) that returns a

BufferedWriter instance, so that the developer no longer has to write that code explicitly. So the initialization expression in the try-with-resources in Listing 11-26 can be replaced with

```
final BufferedWriter wr = Files.newBufferedWriter(file.toPath());
```

Also, there is a version of this method taking a charset argument:

```
final BufferedWriter wr = Files.newBufferedWriter(file.
toPath(),StandardCharsets.UTF_8);
```

Before this method was introduced, writing text to a file with a specified charset required a java.io.OutputWriter instance:

```
final OutputStreamWriter wr = new OutputStreamWriter(new
FileOutputStream(file), StandardCharsets.UTF_8);
```

There is also a version of this method that takes an argument of type OpenOption that allows you to specify how the file should be opened:

```
final BufferedWriter wr = Files.newBufferedWriter(file.
toPath(),StandardCharsets.UTF_8, StandardOpenOption.APPEND);
```

This is very useful, since a BufferedWriter created explicitly (without specifying a file option) overrides an existing file, unless the FileWriter that is wrapped around is configured to append data to an existing file, like depicted here:

```
final BufferedWriter wr = new BufferedWriter(new FileWriter(file, true))
```

The second parameter is a boolean value representing if the file should be opened for appending text (true) or not (false).

Now that the basics of using BufferedWriter have been covered, it's time to meet the most useful members of the Writer family, depicted in Figure 11-5.

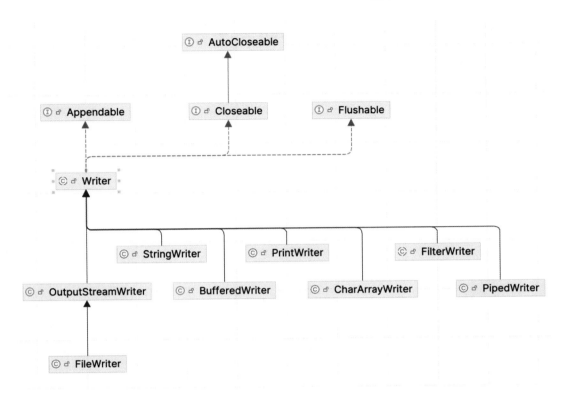

Figure 11-5. *The* `Writer` *class hierarchy*

The `Writer` class is abstract, so it cannot be used directly; the appending API comes from the `java.io.Appendable` interface that `Writer` implements. The other `Writer` classes are used for different purposes. As we've already seen, the `OutputStreamWriter` is used to write text using a special character encoding.

The `PrintWriter` is used to write formatted representations of objects to a text-output stream (we've already used it to write HTML code, in **Chapter 10**).

The `StringWriter` is used to collect output into its internal buffer and write it to a `String` instance.

In Java 11, the `Writer` class was enriched with the `nullWriter()` method, which returns a `Writer` instance that does nothing. This was requested by developers for testing purposes.

Using OutputStream to Write Files

Classes in the Writer family are advanced classes for writing data as text using character streams, but essentially, before data is written it is turned into bytes. This obviously means that files can be written by using streams of bytes as well. This probably became obvious when trying to use the proper character encoding when writing text using the OutputStreamWriter, as the OutputStreamWriter instance given as an argument is based on a FileOutputStream instance, a type that is used to write byte streams to a file.

The root class of this hierarchy is java.io.OutputStream, and the most common members of the hierarchy are depicted in Figure 11-6.

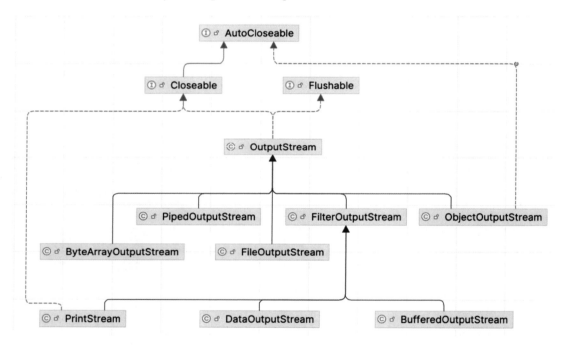

Figure 11-6. *The OutputStream class hierarchy*

Listing 11-27 shows how to use FileOutputStream to write a list of String entries.

Listing 11-27. Writing a List<String> to a File Using FileOutputStream

```
package com.apress.bgn.eleven.io;

import java.io.FileNotFoundException;
import java.io.FileOutputStream;
// other import statements omitted
```

```java
public class OutputStreamWritingDemo {
    private static final Logger log = LoggerFactory.getLogger(OutputStream
                                    WritingDemo.class);

    public static void main(String... args) {
        var file = new File("chapter11/read-write-file/src/main/resources/
                output/data.txt");

        var dataList = List.of("Down to the wire" ,
                "I wanted water but" ,
                "I'll walk through the fire" ,
                "If this is what it takes");

        try (FileOutputStream output = new FileOutputStream(file)){
            dataList.forEach(entry -> {
                try {
                    output.write(entry.getBytes());
                    output.write("\n".getBytes());
                } catch (IOException e) {
                    log.info("Something went wrong! ", e);
                }
            });
            output.flush();
        } catch (FileNotFoundException e) {
            log.info("Something went wrong! ", e);
        } catch (IOException e) {
            e.printStackTrace();
        }
    }
}
```

The OutputStream family class is used for writing streams of bytes that represent raw data, unreadable by users directly, such as the ones contained in binary files like images, media, PDFs, and so on. For example, the code in Listing 11-28 makes a copy of an image using FileInputStream to read it and FileOutputStream to write it.

Listing 11-28. Making a Copy of an Image File Using `FileOutputStream`

```
package com.apress.bgn.eleven.io;

import java.io.*;
// other import statements missing

public class DuplicateImageDemo {
    private static final Logger LOGGER = LoggerFactory.
    getLogger(DuplicateImageDemo.class);
    void main() {
        final String inDir = "chapter11/read-write-file/src/main/resources/
                             input/";
        final String outDir = "chapter11/read-write-file/src/main/
                              resources/output/";

        File src = new File(inDir + "the-beach.jpg");
        File dest = new File(outDir + "copy-the-beach.jpg");
        try(FileInputStream fis = new FileInputStream(src);
            FileOutputStream fos = new FileOutputStream(dest)) {
            int content;
            while ((content = fis.read()) != -1) {
                fos.write(content);
            }
        } catch (Exception e) {
            LOGGER.debug("Image could not be copied! ", e);
        }
    }
}
```

However, writing code like this is no longer necessary, thanks to the introduction of the `Files.copy(src.toPath(), dest.toPath())` method in Java 7.

In Java 11, the `OutputStream` was enriched with the `nullOutputStream()` method, which returns an `OutputStream` instance that does nothing. This was requested by developers for testing purposes.

Using Java NIO to Manage Files

The java.nio package was introduced at the beginning of the chapter in conjunction with the java.io package. Most classes and methods we have used up to this section of this book were part of the java.io package and blocked the main thread while the data was read/written. The utility classes java.nio.file.Paths and java.nio.file.Files introduced in the previous section contain methods that make use of classes in the java.nio package as well as in the java.io package. It is time to show you how to manipulate files using java.nio classes as well.

Manipulating a file using java.nio requires an instance of java.nio.channels.FileChannel. This a special class that describes a channel for reading, writing, mapping, and manipulating a file. A FileChannel instance is connected to a file and holds a position within a file that can be queried and modified.

To read data from a file using a FileChannel instance, the following are needed:

- A file handler instance
- A FileInputStream instance the channel is based on
- A FileChannel instance
- A java.nio.Buffer instance

Being nonblocking, a thread can ask a channel to read data from a buffer and then do other things until the data is available. Java NIO's buffers allow moving back and forth in the buffer as needed. The data is read into a buffer and cached there until it is processed. There are buffer implementations for all primitive types in the java.nio package and, depending on the purpose of the data, you can use any of them. Listing 11-29 shows how to read data from a file into a ByteBuffer. Since the ByteBuffer can be instantiated with an initial size, by configuring the ByteBuffer capacity in bytes to be the same as the file size, the file can be read in one go.

Listing 11-29. Reading a File Using FileChannel Using a ByteBuffer

```
package com.apress.bgn.eleven.nio;

import java.nio.ByteBuffer;
import java.nio.channels.FileChannel;
// other import statements omitted
```

```java
public class ChannelDemo {
    private static final Logger LOGGER = LoggerFactory.
    getLogger(ChannelDemo.class);

    void main() {
        var sb = new StringBuilder();
        final String inDir = "chapter11/read-write-file/src/main/resources/
                             input/";
        try (FileInputStream is = new FileInputStream(new File(inDir +
                                   "data.txt"));
            FileChannel inChannel = is.getChannel()) {
            long fileSize = inChannel.size();
            ByteBuffer buffer = ByteBuffer.allocate((int) fileSize);
            inChannel.read(buffer);
            buffer.flip();
            while (buffer.hasRemaining()) {
                sb.append((char) buffer.get());
            }
        } catch (IOException e) {
            LOGGER.debug("File could not be read! ", e);
        }
        LOGGER.info("Read with FileChannel [1]--> {}", sb);
    }
}
```

The method getChannel() returns the unique FileChannel object associated with this file input stream. The most important statement in Listing 11-29 is the buffer.flip() call. Calling this method *flips the buffer*, meaning that a buffer is switched from writing mode to reading mode. Initially this means that the channel is the able to write data in the buffer because it is in writing mode, but after the buffer is full, the buffer is switched to reading mode, so the main thread can read its contents.

After reading the contents of a buffer, if there is a need to do it again, the buffer.rewind() method sets the position to zero.

If the file is big, the ByteBuffer can be reinitialized multiple times, but in this case the buffer must be cleared before new data is written by the channel, and this can be done by calling buffer.close(). Also, using a FileInputStream to obtain a channel is not the correct way to do it, since it limits it to reading from the file. But a channel can both read and write from a file, so the recommended way is to use a `java.io.RandomAccessFile` instance as a file handler, as depicted in Listing 11-30.

Listing 11-30. Reading a File Using `FileChannel` Using a Smaller `ByteBuffer`

```
import java.io.RandomAccessFile;
import java.nio.ByteBuffer;
import java.nio.channels.FileChannel;
// ...
var sb = new StringBuilder();
try (var file = new RandomAccessFile(inDir + "data.txt", "r");
     var inChannel = file.getChannel()) {

    var buffer = ByteBuffer.allocate(48);
    while(inChannel.read(buffer) > 0) {
        buffer.flip();
        for (int i = 0; i < buffer.limit(); i++) {
            sb.append((char) buffer.get());
        }
        buffer.clear();
    }
} catch (IOException e) {
    LOGGER.debug("File could not be read! ", e);
}
LOGGER.info("Read with FileChannel [3] --> {}", sb);
```

The `RandomAccessFile` class constructor has a second argument named `mode` that specifies the access mode in which the file is to be opened. Or in more human language: the mode describes what your code intends to do with the file. The `mode` parameter can be set any of the following values:

- `r`: The file is open for reading only. Attempts to write to this file will cause an `IOException` to be thrown.

- `rw`: The file is open for reading and writing.

- rws: The file is open for reading and writing and also requires that every update to the file's content or metadata be written synchronously to the underlying storage device.

- rwd: The file is open for reading and writing and also requires that every update to the file's content be written synchronously to the underlying storage device.

If the mode parameter it is set to anything else, an IllegalArgumentException is thrown.

Making a copy of a file is simple as well; it's just about moving the data from a channel to another using a buffer, as shown in Listing 11-31.

Listing 11-31. Duplicating an Image Using FileChannel and a ByteBuffer

```
package com.apress.bgn.eleven.nio;

import java.io.RandomAccessFile;
import java.nio.ByteBuffer;
import java.nio.channels.FileChannel;
// other import statements omitted

public class DuplicateImageDemo {
    private static final Logger LOGGER = LoggerFactory.getLogger(Duplicate
                                    ImageDemo.class);

    void main() {
        LOGGER.info("-- Image duplicated using FileChannel -- ");
        final String inDir = "chapter11/read-write-file/src/main/resources/
                        input/";
        final String outDir = "chapter11/read-write-file/src/main/
                        resources/output/";
        try (FileChannel source = new RandomAccessFile(inDir + "the-beach.
                            jpg", "r").getChannel();
            FileChannel dest = new RandomAccessFile(outDir + "copy-the-
                            beach.jpg", "rw").getChannel()) {
            ByteBuffer buffer = ByteBuffer.allocateDirect(48);
            while (source.read(buffer) != -1) {
```

```
                buffer.flip();
                while (buffer.hasRemaining()) {
                    dest.write(buffer);
                }
                buffer.clear();
            }
        } catch (Exception e) {
            LOGGER.debug("Image could not be copied! ", e);
        }
    }
}
```

Another way to do it is to use dedicated ReadableByteChannel and WritableByteChannel, as shown in Listing 11-32.

Listing 11-32. Duplicating an Image Using ReadableByteChannel and a ByteBuffer

```
import java.nio.channels.ReadableByteChannel;
import java.nio.channels.WritableByteChannel;
// ...
try(ReadableByteChannel source = new FileInputStream(inDir + "the-beach.
                                  jpg").getChannel();
    WritableByteChannel dest = new FileOutputStream(outDir + "2nd-copy-the-
                                  beach.jpg").getChannel()) {
    ByteBuffer buffer = ByteBuffer.allocateDirect(48);
    while (source.read(buffer) != -1) {
        buffer.flip();
        while (buffer.hasRemaining()) {
            dest.write(buffer);
        }
        buffer.clear();
    }
} catch (Exception e) {
    LOGGER.error("Image could not be copied! ", e);
}
```

Because of their nonblocking nature, Java channels are suitable for applications that handle data provided by multiple sources, such as applications that manage connections with multiple sources over a network. Figure 11-7 depicts the most important members of the Channel hierarchy.

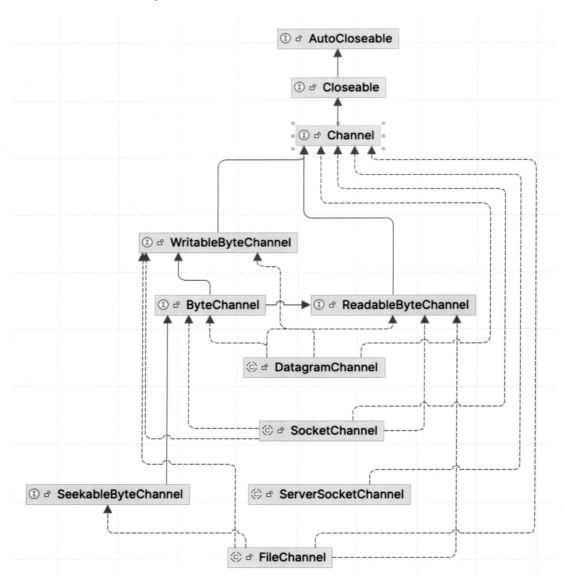

Figure 11-7. *The Channel class/interface hierarchy*

The DatagramChannel can read and write data over the network via UDP. The SocketChannel can read and write data over the network via TCP, and the ServerSocketChannel allows you to listen for incoming TCP connections, like a web server does. For each incoming connection, a SocketChannel is created.

The Java NIO components (interfaces and classes) were introduced to complement existing Java IO functionality. Java IO reads or writes one byte or character at a time. Buffering makes use of Java heap memory, which can become problematic when files of considerable sizes are used. When Java NIO was released, there was a statement from Oracle that NIO was more efficient and had better performance than pure Java I/O, but it all depends on the application you are trying to build. Java NIO introduces the possibility to handle raw bytes in bulk, the possibility of asynchronous operations, and off-heap buffering. Buffers are created outside the central memory of the JVM, in portions of memory not handled by the garbage collector. This allows for larger buffers to be created, so bigger files can be read without the danger of an OutOfMemoryException being thrown because the JVM is out of memory.

If you ever find yourself needing to handle a lot of data, make sure to read the JDK NIO documentation very well, because this section has just scratched the surface.

Serialization and Deserialization

Serialization is the name given to the operation of converting the state of an object to a byte sequence. In this format it can be sent over a network or written to a file and reverted into a copy of that object. The operation to convert the byte sequence back to an object is named *deserialization*. Java serialization has been a controversial topic, with Java Platform Chief Architect Mark Reinhold describing it as a horrible mistake made in 1997. Apparently, most Java vulnerabilities are somehow related to the way serialization is done in Java, and there is a project named Project Amber[5] that is dedicated to removing Java serialization completely and allowing developers to choose the serialization in a format of their choice.

---

[5] https://openjdk.org/projects/amber

Byte Serialization

The java.io.Serializable interface has no methods or fields and serves only to mark classes as being serializable. When an object is serialized, the information that identifies the object type is serialized as well. Most Java classes are serializable. Any subclass of a serializable class is by default considered serializable.

If any new fields are nonserializable, then an exception of type NotSerializableException will be thrown. Classes written by developers that contain nonserializable fields must implement the Serializable interface and provide a concrete implementation for the methods shown in Listing 11-33.

Listing 11-33. Methods That Need to Be Implemented to Make a Custom Class Serializable

```
private void writeObject(java.io.ObjectOutputStream out)
    throws IOException;
private void readObject(java.io.ObjectInputStream in)
    throws IOException, ClassNotFoundException;
private void readObjectNoData()
    throws ObjectStreamException;
```

These are not methods that are part of a specific Java interface, so implementing them in this context just means writing a body for them in the class you want to make serializable. The reason they are grouped in Listing 11-33 is to depict the signatures of these methods.

The writeObject(..) method is used for writing the state of the object, so that the readObject(..) method can restore it. The readObjectNoData() method is used to initialize the state of the object when the deserialization operation failed for some reason, so this method provides a default state despite the issues (e.g., incomplete stream, client application does not recognize the deserialized class, etc.). This method is not really mandatory, if you are an optimist.

Also, when making a class serializable, a static field of type long must be added as a unique identifier for the class to make sure both the application that sends the object as a byte stream and the client application receiving it have the same loaded classes. If the application that receives the byte stream has a class with a different identifier, a java.io.InvalidClassException will be thrown. When this happens, it means that the application was not updated, or you might even suspect some foul play from a hacker.

The field has to be named `serialVersionUID`, and if the developer does not explicitly add one, the serialization runtime will. The code snippet in Listing 11-34 depicts a class named `Singer` that contains serialization and deserialization methods shown in the Listing 11-33 code snippet.

Listing 11-34. Serializable Singer Class

```java
package com.apress.bgn.eleven;

import java.io.*;
import java.time.LocalDate;
import java.util.Objects;

public class Singer  implements Serializable {
    private static final long serialVersionUID = 42L;

    private String name;

    private Double rating;

    private LocalDate birthDate;

    public Singer() {
        /* required for deserialization */
    }

    public Singer(String name, Double rating, LocalDate birthDate) {
        this.name = name;
        this.rating = rating;
        this.birthDate = birthDate;
    }

    private void writeObject(ObjectOutputStream out) throws IOException {
        out.defaultWriteObject();
    }

    private void readObject(ObjectInputStream in) throws IOException,
    ClassNotFoundException {
        in.defaultReadObject();
    }
```

761

```
    private void readObjectNoData() throws ObjectStreamException {
        this.name = "undefined";
        this.rating = 0.0;
        this.birthDate = LocalDate.now();
    }
    // setter, getters, toString, equals and hashCode omitted
}
```

Now that we have the class, let's instantiate it, serialize it, save it to a file, and then deserialize the contents of the file into another object that we will compare with the initial object. All these operations are depicted in Listing 11-35.

Listing 11-35. Serializing and Deserializing a Singer Class

```
package com.apress.bgn.eleven;

import org.slf4j.Logger;
import org.slf4j.LoggerFactory;

import java.io.*;
import java.time.LocalDate;
import java.time.Month;

public class BinarySerializationDemo {
    private static final Logger log = LoggerFactory.getLogger(BinarySeriali
                                      zationDemo.class);

    public static void main(String... args) throws ClassNotFoundException {
        LocalDate johnBd = LocalDate.of(1977, Month.OCTOBER, 16);
        Singer john = new Singer("John Mayer", 5.0, johnBd);
        File file = new File("chapter11/serialization/src/test/resources/
                    output/john.txt");
        try (var out = new ObjectOutputStream(new FileOutputStream(file))){
            file.createNewFile();
            out.writeObject(john);
        } catch (IOException e) {
            log.info("Something went wrong! ", e);
        }
```

```
    try(var in = new ObjectInputStream(new FileInputStream(file))){
        Singer copyOfJohn = (Singer) in.readObject();
        log.info("Are objects equal? {}", copyOfJohn.equals(john));
        log.info("--> {}", copyOfJohn);
    } catch (IOException e) {
        log.info("Something went wrong! ", e);
    }
  }
}
```

When the code in Listing 11-35 is run, everything works as expected, and `writeObject(..)` and `readObject(..)` are called by the `ObjectOutputStream` and `ObjectInputStream`, respectively, via reflection. If you want to test that they are actually called, you can add logging, or you can place breakpoints inside them and run the program in debug mode. If you open the `john.txt` file, you won't be able to understand much. The text written in there does not make much sense, because it is binary, raw data. If you open the file, you might see something like what is depicted in Figure 11-8.

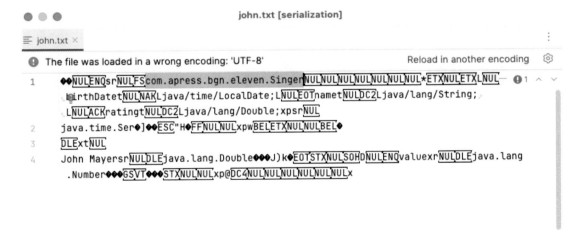

Figure 11-8. *Serialized Singer instance*

XML Serialization

Java serialization does not have to result in cryptic files, however. Objects can be serialized to readable formats. One of the most-used serialization formats is XML, and the JDK provides classes to convert objects to XML and from XML back to the initial object.

763

Java Architecture for XML Binding (JAXB) used to provide a fast and convenient way to bind XML schemas and Java representations, making it easy for Java developers to incorporate XML data and processing functions in Java applications. The operation to serialize an object to XML is named **marshalling**. The operation to deserialize an object from XML is named **unmarshalling**.

JAXB was removed from the JDK starting with version 11, and its successor JAXB2 did not gain the expected traction. This was not a surprise, because for years the Jackson collection of libraries has been the default go-to for XML, JSON, and (more recently) YAML serialization and deserialization for most projects. Jackson has been known for quite a while in the Java ecosystem as the ultimate *Java JSON library*, but it also has modules that support serialization to quite a few other formats, among them XML, CSV, YAML, and TAML. Just check the project page (`https://github.com/FasterXML/jackson`); chances are that if there is a new catchy serialization format emerging, there might already be a module for that.

There are a few things to keep in mind when serializing to XML using Jackson:

- There is a different set of annotations to use, the most important of which are listed here:

    - `@JacksonXmlRootElement(localName = "...")` is a top-level annotation that is placed at the class level to tell Jackson that the class name will become an XML element at serialization time; if a different name is needed for the XML element, it can be specified via the `localName` attribute.

    - `@JacksonXmlProperty(localName = "...")` is a method- or field-level annotation that is used to tell Jackson that the field or method name will become an XML element at serialization time; if a different name is needed for the XML element, it can be specified via the `localName` attribute.

    - `@JacksonXmlProperty(localName = "...", isAttribute = true)` with the `isAttribute = true` parameter is used when the property is configured to become an XML attribute.

- To serialize and deserialize with Jackson, an instance of `com.fasterxml.jackson.dataformat.xml.XmlMapper` is used.

- The XmlMapper instance has to be configured to support special types such as the new Java 8 Date API types, and this is done by registering and configuring the com.fasterxml.jackson.datatype.jsr310. JavaTimeModule.

- When using Java modules, you have to make sure they are configured correctly. Exceptions will not always be easy to read, and solving them might require a combination of Apache Maven and module configuration to solve.

This being said, let's start with the module configuration, shown in Listing 11-36.

Listing 11-36. Module Configuration for XML Serialization with Jackson

```
module chapter.eleven.serialization {
    requires org.slf4j;
    requires com.fasterxml.jackson.databind;
    requires com.fasterxml.jackson.dataformat.xml;
    requires com.fasterxml.jackson.datatype.jsr310;

    opens com.apress.bgn.eleven.xml to com.fasterxml.jackson.databind;
}
```

The first two requires com.fasterxml.jackson.* directives are needed so that Jackson annotations and XmlMapper can be used. The jsr310 is required for serialization of Java 8 Date API types.

The last statement, opens com.apress.bgn.eleven.xml to com.fasterxml. jackson.databind, is necessary so that Jackson can access the classes in package com. apress.bgn.eleven.xml, because that is where the version of the Singer class written using the Jackson annotation is located. The class is depicted in Listing 11-37.

Listing 11-37. A Singer Class with Jackson XML Annotations

```
package com.apress.bgn.eleven.xml;
// other imports omitted
import com.fasterxml.jackson.dataformat.xml.annotation.JacksonXmlProperty;
import
com.fasterxml.jackson.dataformat.xml.annotation.JacksonXmlRootElement;
```

```java
@JacksonXmlRootElement(localName = "singer")
public class Singer implements Serializable {
    private static final long serialVersionUID = 42L;

    private String name;

    private Double rating;

    private LocalDate birthDate;

    public Singer() {
        /* required for deserialization */
    }

    public Singer(String name, Double rating, LocalDate birthDate) {
        this.name = name;
        this.rating = rating;
        this.birthDate = birthDate;
    }

    @JacksonXmlProperty(localName = "name", isAttribute = true)
    public String getName() {
        return name;
    }

    @JacksonXmlProperty(localName = "rating", isAttribute = true)
    public Double getRating() {
        return rating;
    }

    @JacksonXmlProperty(localName = "birthdate")
    public LocalDate getBirthDate() {
        return birthDate;
    }
    // other code omitted
}
```

Notice the location where the annotations were placed. Based on the placement
of the annotations and their configurations in Listing 11-37 when the john object is
serialized, the john.xml file is expected to contain the snippet depicted in Listing 11-38.

Listing 11-38. The john Singer Instance in XML Format

```
<singer name="John Mayer" rating="5.0">
  <birthdate>1977-10-16</birthdate>
</singer>
```

It's more readable than the binary version, right? Listing 11-39 depicts the code that saves the Singer instance to the john.xml file, and then it loads it back into a copy to compare it with the original instance.

Listing 11-39. Serializing and Deserializing a Singer Class with Jackson's XmlMapper

```
package com.apress.bgn.eleven.xml;

import com.fasterxml.jackson.databind.SerializationFeature;
import com.fasterxml.jackson.dataformat.xml.XmlMapper;
import com.fasterxml.jackson.datatype.jsr310.JavaTimeModule;
// other import statements omitted

public class XMLSerializationDemo {
    private static final Logger LOGGER = LoggerFactory.getLogger(
                                        XMLSerializationDemo.class);

    void main(){
        var johnBd = LocalDate.of(1977, Month.OCTOBER, 16);
        var john = new Singer("John Mayer", 5.0, johnBd);

        var xmlMapper = new XmlMapper();
        xmlMapper.registerModule(new JavaTimeModule());
        xmlMapper.enable(SerializationFeature.INDENT_OUTPUT);
        xmlMapper.configure(SerializationFeature.WRITE_DATES_AS_
        TIMESTAMPS, false);

    var path = Path.of("chapter11/serialization/src/test/resources/
            output/john.xml");
    try {
        var xml = xmlMapper.writeValueAsString(john);
        Files.writeString(path, xml, StandardCharsets.UTF_8);
```

```
    } catch (Exception e) {
        LOGGER.info("Serialization to XML failed! ", e);
    }

    try {
        var copyOfJohn = xmlMapper.readValue(path.toFile(),
                         Singer.class);
        LOGGER.info("Are objects equal? {}", copyOfJohn.equals(john));
        LOGGER.info("--> {}", copyOfJohn);
    } catch (IOException e) {
        LOGGER.info("Deserialization of XML failed! ", e);
    }
  }
}
```

The XmlMapper instance can be used to serialize any class in the project that contains Jackson annotations. The example in Listing 11-39 is also configured to support default serialization of Java 8 Date API types and keep types readable, by not converting them to numeric time stamps using the following two lines:

```
xmlMapper.registerModule(new JavaTimeModule());
xmlMapper.configure(SerializationFeature.WRITE_DATES_AS_TIMESTAMPS, false);
```

Since the chosen format is XML, it would look pretty ugly if all of it was written in a single line, so indented formatting is supported using this statement:

```
xmlMapper.enable(SerializationFeature.INDENT_OUTPUT)
```

Information   The annotations are not necessary; as long as an XmlMapper instance is used and the class to be serialized is a plain old Java object (POJO), an XML file is generated, with all fields becoming XML elements under a root element named as the class. The annotations are useful for customizing the generated XML, naming elements, converting some fields into attributes, and specifying which converters to use for complex types. If you are curious about the default XML file generated for a Singer instance, comment the annotations in the Singer class and run the XMLSerializationDemo example from Listing 11-39.

XML serialization has been dominating the development field for many years, being used in most web services and remote communication. However, XML files tend to become crowded, redundant, and painful to read as they become bigger, so a new format stole the show: JSON.

JSON Serialization

JSON (JavaScript Object Notation) is a lightweight data-interchange format. It is readable for humans and is easy for machines to parse and generate. JSON is the favorite format for data being used in JavaScript applications, for REST-based applications and as the internal format for quite a few NoSQL databases. Therefore, it is only appropriate to show you how to serialize/deserialize Java objects using this format as well. The advantage of serializing Java objects to JSON is that there is more than one library providing classes to do so, which means at least one of them is stable with Java 9+ versions.

JSON format is in essence a collection of key-pair values. The values can be arrays, or collection of key/pairs themselves. The most preferred library for JSON serialization is the Jackson library as well, because it can convert Java objects to JSON objects and back again without requiring much code to be written. The best part for this chapter is that the same module configuration can be used for JSON too. All we need to do is change the annotations used and change the type of mapper used to do the serialization/deserialization. Jackson supports a multitude of annotations for JSON serialization, but for the simple example in this book, we don't really need any. A Jackson `com.fasterxml.jackson.databind.json.JsonMapper` instance is smart enough to auto-detect the publicly accessible properties (public fields, or private fields with public getters) of a class and use them when serializing/deserializing instances of this class.

The `@JsonAutoDetect` annotation from the package `com.fasterxml.jackson.annotation` can be used to annotate a class. It can be configured to tell the mapper which class members should be serialized. There are a few options, grouped in the `Visibility` enum declared within the annotation body:

- ANY: All kinds of access modifiers (`public`, `protected`, `private`) are auto-detected.
- NON_PRIVATE: All modifiers except `private` are auto-detected.
- PROTECTED_AND_PUBLIC: Only `protected` and `public` modifiers are auto-detected.
- PUBLIC_ONLY: Only `public` modifiers are auto-detected.

- NONE: Disable auto-detection for fields or methods. In this case configuration has to be done explicitly using @JsonProperty annotations on fields.

- DEFAULT: Default rules apply, depending on the context (sometimes inherited from a parent).

This single annotation placed on the Singer class combined with the proper mapper and the JavaTimeModule ensures that an instance of the Singer class can be serialized to JSON correctly; and also deserialized from JSON. Listing 11-40 shows the simple configuration of the Singer class (even if redundant).

Listing 11-40. Annotating a Singer Class with Jackson @JsonAutoDetect Just to Show How It's Done

```java
package com.apress.bgn.eleven.json;
// some import statements omitted
import com.fasterxml.jackson.annotation.JsonAutoDetect;

@JsonAutoDetect(getterVisibility = JsonAutoDetect.Visibility.PUBLIC_ONLY)
public class Singer  implements Serializable {
  private static final long serialVersionUID = 42L;
  private String name;
  private Double rating;
  private LocalDate birthDate;

  public String getName() { // auto-detected
    return name;
  }

  public Double getRating() { // auto-detected
    return rating;
  }

  public LocalDate getBirthDate() { // auto-detected
    return birthDate;
  }
  // other code omitted
}
```

For serializing a Singer instance, an instance of JsonMapper is needed. This class was introduced in Jackson version 2.10. Up to that version the com.fasterxml.jackson.databind.ObjectMapper was used for the same purpose. ObjectMapper is intended to become the root class for all mappers in future versions. The XmlMapper used in the previous section extends ObjectMapper too. The JsonMapper is a JSON format–specific ObjectMapper implementation and is intended to replace the generic implementation. Listing 11-41 depicts an example how it can be used to serialize/deserialize a Singer instance.

Listing 11-41. Serializing and Deserializing a Singer Class with Jackson's JsonMapper

```
package com.apress.bgn.eleven.json;

import com.apress.bgn.eleven.xml.Singer;
import com.fasterxml.jackson.databind.SerializationFeature;
import com.fasterxml.jackson.databind.json.JsonMapper;
import com.fasterxml.jackson.datatype.jsr310.JavaTimeModule;
// other import statements omitted

public class JSONSerializationDemo {
    private static final Logger LOGGER = LoggerFactory.getLogger(JSON
                                        SerializationDemo.class);

    void main(){
        var johnBd = LocalDate.of(1977, Month.OCTOBER, 16);
        var john = new Singer("John Mayer", 5.0, johnBd);

        JsonMapper jsonMapper = new JsonMapper();
        jsonMapper.registerModule(new JavaTimeModule());
        jsonMapper.enable(SerializationFeature.INDENT_OUTPUT);
        jsonMapper.configure(SerializationFeature.WRITE_DATES_AS_
        TIMESTAMPS, false);

        var path = Path.of("chapter11/serialization/src/test/resources/
                    output/john.json");
        try {
            var xml = jsonMapper.writeValueAsString(john);
            Files.writeString(path, xml,
                    StandardCharsets.UTF_8);
```

```
        } catch (Exception e) {
            LOGGER.info("Serialization to JSON failed! ", e);
        }

        try {
            var copyOfJohn = jsonMapper.readValue(path.toFile(),
                            Singer.class);
            LOGGER.info("Are objects equal? {}", copyOfJohn.equals(john));
            LOGGER.info("--> {}", copyOfJohn);
        } catch (IOException e) {
            LOGGER.info("Deserialization of JSON failed! ", e);
        }
    }
}
```

As you can see, except the type of mapper used, not much in this code sample has changed when making the switch from XML. Jackson is pretty great, right?

The field birthDate in class Singer is of type java.time.LocalDate. Registering the JavaTimeModule allows control over how this type of field is serialized/deserialized at the mapper level. The other way to do it is to declare a custom serializer class and a custom deserializer class for this type of data and configure them to be used by annotating the birthDate with the @JsonSerialize and @JsonDeserialize annotations. Listing 11-42 shows the custom serializer and deserializer classes configured on the birthDate field.

Listing 11-42. Configuring Custom Serialization and Deserialization for java.time.LocalDate Fields

```
package com.apress.bgn.eleven.json2;
import com.fasterxml.jackson.databind.annotation.JsonDeserialize;
import com.fasterxml.jackson.databind.annotation.JsonSerialize;
// other import statements omitted

@JsonAutoDetect(getterVisibility = JsonAutoDetect.Visibility.PUBLIC_ONLY)
public class Singer  implements Serializable {
    private static final long serialVersionUID = 42L;

    private String name;

    private Double rating;
```

```
@JsonSerialize(converter = LocalDateTimeToStringConverter.class)
@JsonDeserialize(converter = StringToLocalDatetimeConverter.class)
private LocalDate birthDate;
// other code omitted
}
```

Listing 11-43 shows the implementation of the custom serializer and deserializer classes.

Listing 11-43. Implementing Custom Serialization and Deserialization Classes

```
package com.apress.bgn.eleven.json2;

import com.fasterxml.jackson.databind.util.StdConverter;
import java.time.LocalDateTime;
import java.time.format.DateTimeFormatter;
import java.time.format.FormatStyle;

public class LocalDateTimeToStringConverter extends
StdConverter<LocalDateTime, String> {
  static final DateTimeFormatter DATE_FORMATTER = DateTimeFormatter.
  ofLocalizedDateTime(FormatStyle.LONG);

  @Override
  public String convert(LocalDateTime value) {
    return value.format(DATE_FORMATTER);
  }
}

public class StringToLocalDatetimeConverter extends StdConverter<String,
LocalDateTime> {

  @Override
  public LocalDateTime convert(String value) {
    return LocalDateTime.parse(value, LocalDateTimeToStringConverter.DATE_
    FORMATTER);
  }
}
```

773

For the scope of this book, this is all that can be said about JSON serialization with Jackson. Feel free to read more yourself if this subject looks appealing to you.

Important   There is also a Jackson library for serializing Java instances to YAML, which is *the new kid in town* when it comes to configuration files. The library is named `jackson-dataformat-yaml`.

The Media API

Besides text data, Java can be used to manipulate binary files such as images. The Java Media API contains a set of image encoder/decoder (codec) classes for several popular image storage formats: BMP, GIF (decoder only), FlashPix (decoder only), JPEG, PNG, PNM3, TIFF, and WBMP.

In Java 9, the Java media API was transformed as well, with functionality added to encapsulate many images with different resolutions into a multiresolution image. The core of the Java Media API is the `java.awt.Image` abstract class that is the super class of all classes used to represent graphical images. The most important image-representing classes and the relationships between them are depicted in Figure 11-9.

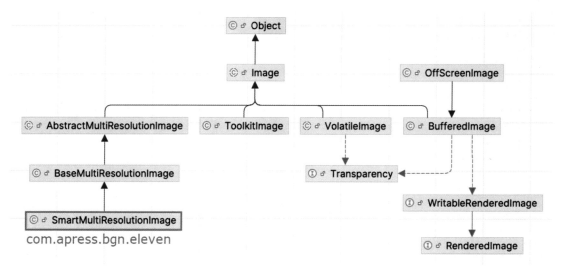

Figure 11-9. *Image classes hierarchy (as shown by IntelliJ IDEA)*

The `SmartMultiResolutionImage` class is used later in this section.

Although the `java.awt.Image` class is the root class in this hierarchy, the class used the most is `java.awt.BufferedImage`, which is an implementation with an accessible buffer of image data. It provides a lot of methods that can be used to create an image, to set its size and its contents, to extract its contents and analyze them, and so much more. In this section we will use this class to read and write images.

An image file is a complex file. Aside from the picture itself, it contains a lot of additional information, the most important of which nowadays is the location where that image was created. If you have ever wondered how a social network proposes a check-in location for an image you are posting, this is where the information is found. This might not seem that important, but posting a picture of your cat, taken in your house, exposes your location to the whole world. I'm not sure what you think about it, but to me this is terrifying. I used to post on my person blog pictures of my cat sitting comfortably on the computer where I was writing this book, which meant that I basically exposed my location and that of a quite expensive laptop to the whole world. Sure, most people do not care about my cat, nor the laptop, but somebody looking to make an easy buck might. So after a friendly and knowledgeable reader sent me a private email telling me about something called Exchangeable Image File Format (EXIF) data and how he knows where I live because of the latest cat picture I posted on my blog, I looked into it. A photo's EXIF data contains a ton of information about your camera and where the picture was taken (GPS coordinates). Most smartphones embed EXIF data into pictures taken with their camera.

In Figure 11-10 you can see the EXIF information depicted by the macOS Preview application.

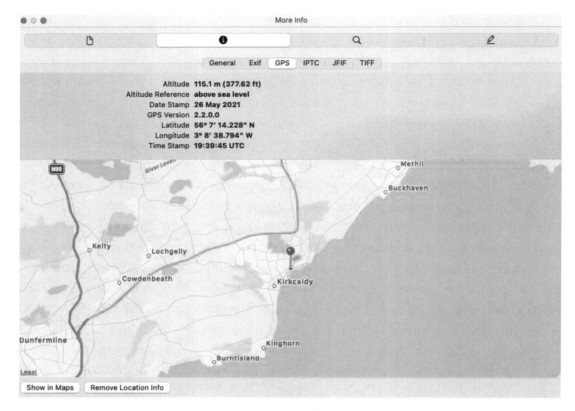

Figure 11-10. *EXIF information on a JPG image*

Notice that the EXIF info contains the exact location, latitude and longitude included, where the picture was taken. There are utilities to remove EXIF data, but when you post a lot of pictures on your blog (like I do) or social media sites, it takes too much time to clean them one by one. This is where Java comes in, and in Listing 11-44 I share with you a snippet of code I use to clean my pictures of EXIF data.

Listing 11-44. Code Snippet to Strip EXIF Data from Images

```
package com.apress.bgn.eleven;
// some import statement omitted
import org.apache.commons.imaging.formats.jpeg.exif.ExifRewriter;
import java.awt.image.BufferedImage;

public class MediaDemo {
```

```
    private static final Logger LOGGER = LoggerFactory.
    getLogger(MediaDemo.class);

    void main() {
        File src = new File("chapter11/media-handling/src/main/resources/
                    input/the-beach.jpg");
        try {
            LOGGER.info(" --- Removing EXIF info ---");
            File destNoExif = new File("chapter11/media-handling/src/main/
                            resources/output/the-beach-no-exif.jpg");
            removeExifMetadata(src, destNoExif);
        } catch (Exception e) {
            LOGGER.error("Something bad happened.", e);
        }
    }

    public void removeExifMetadata(final File jpegImageFile, final File dst)
    throws IndexOutOfBoundsException, IOException {
        try (FileOutputStream fos = new FileOutputStream(dst);
             OutputStream os = new BufferedOutputStream(fos)) {
            new ExifRewriter().removeExifMetadata(jpegImageFile, os);
        }
    }
}
```

Removing EXIF data is pretty easy, since `javax.imageio.ImageIO` does not persist in the image file EXIF information, or any other information, that is not linked to the actual image.

Note   The utility library that provides classes that do the stripping of the EXIF information with better performance than the Java AWT classes is named Apache Commons Imaging[6]. This project is the continuation of Apache Sanselan, which was used in the first edition of this book.

---

[6] https://commons.apache.org/proper/commons-imaging

The removeExifMetadata(..) method is given as an argument the source of the image and a File handler managing the location where the new image should be saved. To test that the resulting image has no EXIF data, just open it in an image viewer. Any option that shows EXIF should either be disabled or display nothing. In the Preview image viewer from macOS, the option is grayed out.

If your project requires avoiding third-party solutions at all costs, JDK comes with its own way of removing EXIF data. The javax.imageio.ImageIO class provides a method to write a BufferedImage instance that leaves the EXIF data out. So the removeExifMetadata(..) method can be simply written as:

```java
private static void removeExifMetadata(final File src, final File dest)
throws Exception {
    BufferedImage originalImage = ImageIO.read(src);
    ImageIO.write(originalImage, "jpg", dest);
}
```

Now that we have that out of the way, let's resize the original image. To resize an image, we need to create a BufferedImage instance from the original image to get the image dimensions. After that, we modify the dimensions and use them as arguments to create a new BufferedImage that will be populated with data by a java.awt.Graphics2D instance, a special type of class that is used to render 2-D shapes, text, and images. The code is depicted in Listing 11-45 (the method is called to create an image 25% smaller, an image 50% smaller, and one 75% smaller).

Listing 11-45. Code Snippet to Resize an Image

```java
package com.apress.bgn.eleven;

import org.apache.commons.imaging.formats.jpeg.exif.ExifRewriter;
import org.slf4j.Logger;
import org.slf4j.LoggerFactory;

import javax.imageio.ImageIO;
import java.awt.*;
import java.awt.image.BufferedImage;
import java.awt.image.MultiResolutionImage;
import java.io.*;
```

```java
public class MediaDemo {
    private static final Logger LOGGER = LoggerFactory.
    getLogger(MediaDemo.class);
    void main() {
        var src = new File("chapter11/media-handling/src/main/resources/
                input/the-beach.jpg");

        try {
            BufferedImage originalImage = ImageIO.read(src);
            LOGGER.debug(" --- Original image sizes {} x {} ---",
            originalImage.getWidth(), originalImage.getHeight() );

            LOGGER.info(" --- Creating 25% image ---");
            File dest25 = new File("chapter11/media-handling/src/main/
                    resources/output/the-beach_25.jpg");
            resize(dest25, src, 0.25f);
            BufferedImage dest25Image = ImageIO.read(dest25);
            LOGGER.debug(" --- 25% image sizes {} x {} ---", dest25Image.
            getWidth(), dest25Image.getHeight() );

            LOGGER.info(" --- Creating 50% image ---");
            File dest50 = new File("chapter11/media-handling/src/main/
                    resources/output/the-beach_50.jpg");
            resize(dest50, src, 0.5f);
            BufferedImage dest50Image = ImageIO.read(dest50);
            LOGGER.debug(" --- 50% image sizes {} x {} ---", dest50Image.
            getWidth(), dest50Image.getHeight() );

            LOGGER.info(" --- Creating 75% image ---");
            File dest75 = new File("chapter11/media-handling/src/main/
                    resources/output/the-beach_75.jpg");
            resize(dest75, src, 0.75f);

        } catch (Exception e) {
            LOGGER.error("Something bad happened.", e);
        }
    }
}
```

```
private static void resize(final File dest, final File src, final float
percent) throws IOException {
  BufferedImage originalImage = ImageIO.read(src);

  int scaledWidth = (int) (originalImage.getWidth() * percent);
  int scaledHeight = (int) (originalImage.getHeight() * percent);

  Image resultingImage = originalImage.getScaledInstance(scaledWidth,
                    scaledHeight, Image.SCALE_SMOOTH);
  BufferedImage outputImage = new BufferedImage(scaledWidth,
                    scaledHeight, BufferedImage.TYPE_INT_RGB);
  outputImage.getGraphics().drawImage(resultingImage, 0, 0, null);
  ImageIO.write(outputImage, "jpg", dest);
  }
}
```

To make things easier, the ImageIO class utility methods come in handy for reading images from files, or for writing them to a specific location. If you want to test to see that the resizing works, you can just look in the resources directory. The output files have already been named accordingly, but just to make sure, you can double-check in a file viewer.

This version of the resize(..) method is not that precise; the Image.SCALE_SMOOTH might not help that much if you require a lot of clarity. If more clarity is required, the best way to resize the image is by using a java.awt.Graphics2D instance, like shown in Listing 11-46.

Listing 11-46. Graphics2D Version of the resize(..) Method

```
private static void resize(final File dest, final File src, final float
percent) throws IOException {
    BufferedImage originalImage = ImageIO.read(src);
    int scaledWidth = (int) (originalImage.getWidth() * percent);
    int scaledHeight = (int) (originalImage.getHeight() * percent);

    BufferedImage outputImage = new BufferedImage(scaledWidth,
                    scaledHeight, originalImage.getType());
```

```
Graphics2D g2d = outputImage.createGraphics();
g2d.setRenderingHint(RenderingHints.KEY_INTERPOLATION, RenderingHints.
VALUE_INTERPOLATION_BILINEAR);
g2d.drawImage(originalImage, 0, 0, scaledWidth, scaledHeight, null);
g2d.dispose();
outputImage.flush();

ImageIO.write(outputImage, "jpg", dest);
}
```

If you run the MediaDemo example using both methods, you might not even notice a difference between the generated images, because details like that might not be obvious to the naked eye.

Tip   The method to resize images shown in Listing 11-45 is the one that is possible using JDK classes. For more efficient resizing, there are quite a few libraries out there like Imgscalr[7] and Thumbnailator[8].

You should see something similar to what is depicted in Figure 11-11.

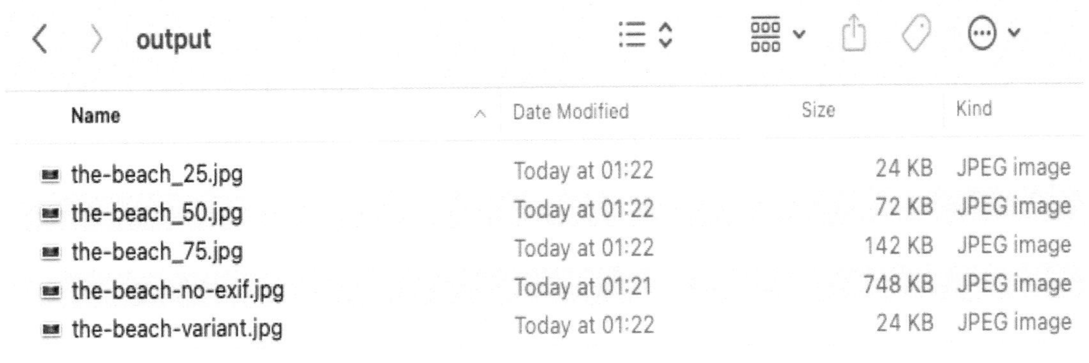

Name	Date Modified	Size	Kind
the-beach_25.jpg	Today at 01:22	24 KB	JPEG image
the-beach_50.jpg	Today at 01:22	72 KB	JPEG image
the-beach_75.jpg	Today at 01:22	142 KB	JPEG image
the-beach-no-exif.jpg	Today at 01:21	748 KB	JPEG image
the-beach-variant.jpg	Today at 01:22	24 KB	JPEG image

Figure 11-11. *Images resized using Java*

The resulting images are not as high in quality as the original image, because compressing the pixels does not result in high quality, but they do fit the sizes we intended.

---

[7] https://github.com/rkalla/imgscalr
[8] https://github.com/coobird/thumbnailator

Now that we have all these versions of the same image, we can use them to create a multiresolution image using class BaseMultiResolutionImage, introduced in Java 9. An instance of this class is created from a set of images, all copies of a single image but with different resolutions. This is why earlier we created more than one resized copy of the image. A BaseMultiResolutionImage can be used to retrieve images based on specific screen resolutions, and it is suitable for applications designed to be accessed from multiple devices. Let's look at the code first, shown in Listing 11-47, and then examine the results.

Listing 11-47. Code Snippet to Create a Multiresolution Image

```java
package com.apress.bgn.eleven;

import org.apache.commons.imaging.formats.jpeg.exif.ExifRewriter;

import java.awt.image.BufferedImage;
import java.awt.image.MultiResolutionImage;
// other import statements omitted

public class MediaDemo {
    private static final Logger LOGGER = LoggerFactory.
    getLogger(MediaDemo.class);
    void main() {
        var src = new File("chapter11/media-handling/src/main/resources/
                input/the-beach.jpg");

        try {
            // omitted code for generating scaled images
            Image[] imgList = new Image[]{
                    ImageIO.read(src), // 2000 x 972
                    ImageIO.read(dest25), // 500 x 243
                    ImageIO.read(dest50), // 1000 x 486
                    ImageIO.read(dest75) // 1500 x 729
            };

            LOGGER.info(" --- Creating multi-resolution image ---");
            File destVariant = new File("chapter11/media-handling/src/main/
                            resources/output/the-beach-variant.jpg");
            createMultiResImage(destVariant, imgList);
```

```
        BufferedImage variantImg = ImageIO.read(destVariant);
        LOGGER.info("variant width x height :  {} x {}", variantImg.
        getWidth(), variantImg.getHeight());
        BufferedImage dest25Img = ImageIO.read(dest25);
        LOGGER.info("dest25Img width x height :  {} x {}", dest25Img.
        getWidth(), dest25Img.getHeight());
        LOGGER.info("Are identical? {}", variantImg.equals(dest25Img));
    } catch (Exception e) {
        LOGGER.error("Something bad happened.", e);
    }
}

private static void createMultiResImage(final File dest, final Image[]
imgList) throws IOException {
    MultiResolutionImage mrImage = new BaseMultiResolutionImage
                                       (0,imgList);

    var variants = mrImage.getResolutionVariants();
    variants.forEach(i -> LOGGER.info(i.toString()));

    Image img = mrImage.getResolutionVariant(500, 200);
    LOGGER.info("Most fit to the requested size<{},{}>: <{},{}>", 500,
    200, img.getWidth(null), img.getHeight(null));
    if (img instanceof BufferedImage) {
        ImageIO.write((BufferedImage) img, "jpg", dest);
    }
}
}
```

The BaseMultiResolutionImage instance is created from an array of Image instances. This class is an implementation of the MultiResolutionImage interface, designed to be an optional additional API supported by some implementations of Image to allow them to provide alternate images for various rendering resolutions.

To make really obvious in Listing 11-47 which image will be selected, the resolution of each image is put in a comment next to it. When getResolutionVariant(..) is called, the arguments are compared to the corresponding image properties, and even if both are less then equal to one of the images, that image is returned. In Listing 11-48, the code of the BaseMultiResolutionImage.getResolutionVariant(..) is depicted.

Listing 11-48. Code for Getting an Image Variant, Based on Size

```
@Override
public Image getResolutionVariant(double destImageWidth,
                                  double destImageHeight) {

    checkSize(destImageWidth, destImageHeight);

    for (Image rvImage : resolutionVariants) {
        if (destImageWidth <= rvImage.getWidth(null)
                && destImageHeight <= rvImage.getHeight(null)) {
            return rvImage;
        }
    }
    return resolutionVariants[resolutionVariants.length - 1];
}
```

The code looks suited for its purpose. If you call mrImage.
getResolutionVariant(500, 200), you get the dest25 image with resolution 500 × 243.
If you call mrImage.getResolutionVariant(500, 300), you get the dest50 image with
resolution 1000 × 486, because the destImageHeight argument is 300, which is greater
than 243, so the next image in the list with width and height values greater than the
arguments is returned.

But—and this is important to keep in mind—this works only if the images in the
array are sorted in the order of their sizes. If the imgList were to be modified to

```
Image[] imgList = new Image[]{
    ImageIO.read(src),  // 2000 x 972
    ImageIO.read(dest25), // 500 x 243
    ImageIO.read(dest50), // 1000 x 486
    ImageIO.read(dest75) // 1500 x 729
};
```

then both calls return the original image, because that is the first one in the list, and
width is greater than 500 and height is greater than both 200 and 300.

So if the algorithm is not efficient and depends on the order of the images in the array
used to create the multiresolution image, what can be done? It's simple: we can create our
own MultiResolutionImage implementation that extends BaseMultiResolutionImage
and overrides the getResolutionVariant() method. Since we know that all images are

resized copies of the same image, this means that width and height are proportional, so we can write an algorithm that will always return the variant of the image that is most suitable to the desired resolution and will ignore the order of the images in the array. The implementation might look quite similar to the one in Listing 11-49.

Listing 11-49. Better Code for Getting an Image Variant, Based on Size

```
package com.apress.bgn.eleven;
// other import statements omitted
import java.awt.image.BaseMultiResolutionImage;

public class SmartMultiResolutionImage extends BaseMultiResolutionImage {

    public SmartMultiResolutionImage(int baseImageIndex, Image...
    resolutionVariants) {
        super(baseImageIndex, resolutionVariants);
    }

    @Override
    public Image getResolutionVariant(double destImageWidth,
                                      double destImageHeight) {

        checkSize(destImageWidth, destImageHeight);
        Map<Double, Image> result = new HashMap<>();

        for (Image rvImage : getResolutionVariants()) {
            double widthDelta = Math.abs(destImageWidth - rvImage.
                               getWidth(null));
            double heightDelta = Math.abs(destImageHeight - rvImage.
                               getHeight(null));
            double delta = widthDelta + heightDelta;
            result.put(delta, rvImage);
        }
        java.util.List<Double> deltaList = new ArrayList<>(result.
                                   keySet());

        deltaList.sort(Double::compare);

        return result.get(deltaList.get(0));
    }
```

```
private static void checkSize(double width, double height) {
    if (width <= 0 || height <= 0) {
        throw new IllegalArgumentException(String.format(
                "Width (%s) or height (%s) cannot be <= 0", width,
                height));
    }

    if (!Double.isFinite(width) || !Double.isFinite(height)) {
        throw new IllegalArgumentException(String.format(
                "Width (%s) or height (%s) is not finite", width,
                height));
    }
  }
}
```

The checkSize(..) method must be duplicated, as it is private and used inside getResolutionVariant(..), so it cannot be called inside a superclass, but that is a minor inconvenience to having an implementation that has proper behavior. With the previous implementation, we no longer need a sorted array, thus these invocations

```
getResolutionVariant(500, 200), getResolutionVariant(500, 300);
// and
getResolutionVariant(400, 300), and getResolutionVariant(600, 300);
```

all return image dest25.

To use the new class, in Listing 11-47 this line:

```
MultiResolutionImage mrImage = new BaseMultiResolutionImage(0,imgList);
```

must be replaced with

```
MultiResolutionImage mrImage = new SmartMultiResolutionImage(0, imgList);
```

You can reposition the images in the imgList array too, if you want to test it properly. Then running the MediaDemo class produces the output depicted in Listing 11-50.

Listing 11-50. Output Produced by Running the `MediaDemo`

```
[main] INFO com.apress.bgn.eleven.MediaDemo --  --- Creating multi-
resolution image ---
[main] INFO com.apress.bgn.eleven.MediaDemo -- BufferedImage@17211155: type
= 5 ColorModel: #pixelBits = 24 numComponents = 3 color space = java.awt.
color.ICC_ColorSpace@b3d7190 transparency = 1 has alpha = false isAlphaPre
= false ByteInterleavedRaster: width = 2000 height = 972 #numDataElements 3
dataOff[0] = 2
[main] INFO com.apress.bgn.eleven.MediaDemo -- BufferedImage@69379752: type
= 5 ColorModel: #pixelBits = 24 numComponents = 3 color space = java.awt.
color.ICC_ColorSpace@b3d7190 transparency = 1 has alpha = false isAlphaPre
= false ByteInterleavedRaster: width = 500 height = 243 #numDataElements 3
dataOff[0] = 2
[main] INFO com.apress.bgn.eleven.MediaDemo -- BufferedImage@27fe3806: type
= 5 ColorModel: #pixelBits = 24 numComponents = 3 color space = java.awt.
color.ICC_ColorSpace@b3d7190 transparency = 1 has alpha = false isAlphaPre
= false ByteInterleavedRaster: width = 1000 height = 486 #numDataElements 3
dataOff[0] = 2
[main] INFO com.apress.bgn.eleven.MediaDemo -- BufferedImage@5f71c76a: type
= 5 ColorModel: #pixelBits = 24 numComponents = 3 color space = java.awt.
color.ICC_ColorSpace@b3d7190 transparency = 1 has alpha = false isAlphaPre
= false ByteInterleavedRaster: width = 1500 height = 729 #numDataElements 3
dataOff[0] = 2
[main] INFO com.apress.bgn.eleven.MediaDemo -- Most fit to the requested
size<500,200>: <500,243>
[main] INFO com.apress.bgn.eleven.MediaDemo -- Are identical? false
```

Wait, what? Why are the images not identical? They do have the same resolution, but as objects they are not identical, because drawing pixels is not really that precise. But if you really want to make sure, you could use code like the following to print the width and height of the two images, open them with an image viewer, and with the naked eye you would see they look identical:

```
log.info("variant width x height : {} x {}", variantImg.getWidth(),
variantImg.getHeight());
log.info("dest25Img width x height : {} x {}", dest25Img.getWidth(),
dest25Img.getHeight());
```

The output of the previous code makes it obvious that the two images have the same dimensions, just as expected:

```
[main] INFO MediaDemo - variant width x height :   500 x 243
[main] INFO MediaDemo - dest25Img width x height :   500 x 243
```

As you've noticed, most of the image classes are part of the old java.awt, which is rarely used nowadays and is known to be quite slow. So if you want to build an application and image processing is required, you might want to look for alternatives. One such alternative is to use JavaFX, which is presented in the following section.

Using JavaFX Image Classes

Besides the Java Media API, which is centered on components of the java.awt package, another way to display and edit images is provided by JavaFX. The core class for the javafx.scene.image package is named Image and can be used to handle images in a few common formats: PNG, JPEG, BMP, GIF, and others. JavaFX applications display images using an instance of javafx.scene.image.ImageView, and the part that I like most about this class is that the images can also be displayed scaled, without modifying the original image.

To create a javafx.scene.image.Image instance, all we need is either a FileInputStream instance to read the image from the user-provided location or a URL location given as String. The code snippet in Listing 11-51 creates a JavaFX application that displays an image with its original width and height, which can be accessed using methods in class javafx.scene.image.Image.

Listing 11-51. Using JavaFX to Display Images

```
package com.apress.bgn.eleven;
// import statements omitted

public class JavaFxMediaDemo extends Application {
    final static int option = 3;
```

```
public static void main(String... args) {
    Application.launch(args);
}

@Override
public void start(Stage primaryStage) throws Exception {
    primaryStage.setTitle("JavaFX Image Demo");
    File src = new File("chapter11/media-handling/src/main/resources/
                cover.png");
    Image image = new Image(new FileInputStream(src));
    ImageView imageView = new ImageView(image);
    imageView.setFitHeight(image.getHeight());
    imageView.setFitWidth(image.getWidth());
    imageView.setPreserveRatio(true);
    //Creating a Group object
    StackPane root = new StackPane();
    root.getChildren().add(imageView);
    primaryStage.setScene(new Scene(root,
            image.getWidth()+10,
            image.getHeight()+10));
    primaryStage.show();
    }
}
```

The Image instance cannot be added to the Scene of the JavaFX instance directly, as it does not extend the Node abstract class that is required to be implemented by all JavaFX elements that make a JavaFxApplication. That is why this instance must be wrapped in a javafx.scene.image.ImageView instance, which is a class extending Node and that is specialized for rendering images loaded with the Image class. The ImageView class resizes the displayed image, with or without preserving the original aspect ratio, by calling the setPreserveRatio(..) method with the appropriate argument: true to keep the original aspect ratio, false otherwise.

Caution   Check out **Chapter 10** to learn how to install JavaFX for your system so that the examples in this chapter can be run correctly.

As you can see in Listing 11-51, we use the values retuned by `image.getWidth()` and `image.getHeight()` to set the size of the `ImageView` object and the size of the `Scene` instance. But let's get creative and display the scaled image, still preserving the aspect ratio and also using a better-quality filtering algorithm when scaling the image by using the `smooth(..)` method, as shown here:

```
//...
ImageView imageView = new ImageView(image);
imageView.setFitWidth(100);
imageView.setPreserveRatio(true);
imageView.setSmooth(true);
//...
```

Another thing that the `ImageView` class can do is support a `Rectangle2D` view port that can be used to rotate the image:

```
//...
ImageView imageView = new ImageView(image);
Rectangle2D viewportRect = new Rectangle2D(2, 2, 600, 600);
imageView.setViewport(viewportRect);
imageView.setRotate(90);
//...
```

Being an implementation of `Node`, `ImageView` supports clicking events, and it is quite easy to write some code to resize an image as a response to a single mouse click on it. Just take a look at code in Listing 11-52.

Listing 11-52. Using JavaFX to Resize Images on Click Events

```
//...
ImageView imageView = new ImageView(image);
imageView.setFitHeight(image.getHeight());
imageView.setFitWidth(image.getWidth());
imageView.setPreserveRatio(true);
root.getChildren().add(imageView);
imageView.setPickOnBounds(true);
imageView.setOnMouseClicked(mouseEvent -> {
```

```
if(imageView.getFitWidth() > 100) {
imageView.setFitWidth(100);
    imageView.setPreserveRatio(true);
    imageView.setSmooth(true);
} else {
        imageView.setFitHeight(image.getHeight());
imageView.setFitWidth(image.getWidth());
imageView.setPreserveRatio(true);
}
});
//...
```

In the code snippet in Listing 11-52, by calling the setOnMouseClicked(..) method, we attached an EventHandler<? super MouseEvent> instance to the mouse-clicking event on the imageView. EventHandler<T extends Event> is a functional interface containing a single method named handle, and its concrete implementation is the body of the lambda expression in Listing 11-52.

If you are interested in learning more about media processing Oracle provides some really good tutorials[9]. Also, as practice, you can try writing your own code, based on the code in the book, to add a mouse event that rotates the image. This is all the space we can dedicate to playing with images in Java. I hope you found this section useful and that you might get the chance to test your Java Media API skills in the future, at least for cleaning EXIF data from your images.

Writing and Reading from Databases

Note   Establishing a connection and executing a simple query was covered in **Chapter 7** with the purpose of introducing the do-while loop. Details about databases and JDBC were not the focus of that chapter, however, so the subject will be covered lightly in this section.

---

[9] https://docs.oracle.com/javafx/2/image_ops/jfxpub-image_ops.htm

A *database* is a storage of data. The data is organized in such a way that it can easily be read back, searched through, updated, and deleted, all without losing relationships between various pieces of data.

The most-used databases are relational databases that present information in **tables** with rows and columns. A table is a collection of rows with the same structure. Each row in a table is uniquely identified via a **primary key**. Rows in a table can be associated with rows in other tables. These associations are called **relationships**. A database management system (**DBMS**) handles the way data is stored, maintained, and retrieved. Databases containing data organized in related tables are called **relational**, and thus management systems for them are called relational database management systems (**RDBMSs**).

RDBMSs do their job by using Structured Query Language (**SQL**), which is a programming language for storing and processing information in a relational database.

The Java Database Connectivity (JDBC) API is the industry standard for database-independent connectivity between the Java programming language and a wide range of SQL databases and other tabular data sources, such as spreadsheets or flat files. There are generally three main parts of JDBC. The first is the **JDBC API**, which comprises various methods and interfaces, grouped under the java.sql package for easy communication with the database.

The second main part of JDBC is the **JDBC Driver manager** represented by the java.sql.DriverManager class encapsulate the service for managing a set of **JDBC drivers**. Which drivers are loaded and available to an application depends on the libraries on the classpath. For example, the chapter11/database-sample project classpath contains the libraries for the MySQL and PostgreSQL drivers, so invoking the DriverManager.drivers() method introduced in Java 9 returns a stream containing the following drivers:

```
class com.mysql.cj.jdbc.Driver
class org.postgresql.Driver
```

JDBC drivers are implementation-specific components provided by database vendors (Oracle, Microsoft SQL Server, MySQL, PostgreSQL, etc.) that let Java applications talk to their own databases. To be recognized by DriverManager, they have to implement the java.sql.Driver interface.

The JDBC architecture can be summarized as shown in Figure 11-12.

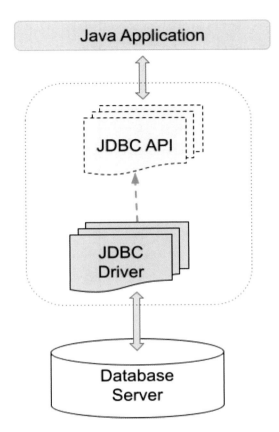

Figure 11-12. *The JDBC architecture*

For stand-alone Java applications that communicate directly with the database, the architecture is referred to as **two-tier**. For applications that get deployed on an application server (like Apache Tomcat, introduced in **Chapter 10**), the server usually provides the JDBC implementation and becomes a layer itself, so the architecture is referred to as **three-tier**. The JDBC API thus becomes the middle tier.

The JDBC driver is known as a pure Java driver direct for the database. This means JDBC is a database driver implementation which makes use of a middle tier (such as an application server) between the calling program and the database.

One of the core components of JDBC is the **connection** to the database. This is modeled by classes implementing java.sql.Connection. Database connections are created by factory objects that are instances of classes implementing the javax.sql. DataSource interface.

The third important part of JDBC is the **JDBC Test Suite** that provides validation of your code compatibility with the JDBC driver used.

So how does it work? How can Java objects be saved to a database, and how can data be turned back into a Java object? In theory, in the simplest of cases, a class is mapped to a table; its fields are mapped to columns in the table columns. You would also need to write code to support various querying and interpretation of the results and much more. This is because JDBC is the low-level API used by multiple frameworks at the end to talk to a database. Without using a higher level API, you have to do all the grunt work yourself (writing SQL queries, mapping results to objects, etc.). There are certain types of applications (financial, usually) that require this approach, because optimizations at SQL level are better than optimizations on the level above it. For the rest of the applications, there are frameworks such as JDO[10], JPA[11], Hibernate[12], and a few others. These frameworks, however, are too advanced for this book, so let's go over how to do some basic things using JDBC to give you an overall idea.

The `database-sample` project for this book contains sources for communicating with a MySQL database and executing some Data Definition Language (DDL) statements and some Data Manipulation Language (DML) SQL commands.

DDL is a subset of SQL commands that define the structure or schema of the database. It deals with creating, modifying, and deleting database structures such as tables, indexes, views, and users.

DML is a subset of SQL commands that deal with managing and manipulating data within the database. It includes common SQL statements such as `SELECT`, `INSERT`, `UPDATE`, and `DELETE`, which allow users to retrieve, add, modify, and delete data from database tables.

Thus, we write DML statements to manipulate data, and we write DDL statements to define the structures that hold the data. The JDBC `java.sql.Statement` interface contains method skeletons that various drivers implement to support both DML and DDL statements.

Following the examples in this section requires you to have a local MySQL database instance or a container set up. The sources available on GitHub provide the means to start up the container, and instructions to install Docker on your computer are available on the official site[13]. Listing 11-53 shows some typical JDBC code to create a connection to the `mysql` database using the `root` user, which has administrative powers, and create a new database named `musicdb` and a user named `sample`.

---

[10] `https://www.jcp.org/en/jsr/detail?id=243`
[11] `https://www.oracle.com/java/technologies/persistence-jsp.html`
[12] `https://hibernate.org`
[13] `https://docs.docker.com/engine/install`

Listing 11-53. Using JDBC to Create a User and Database

```
// snippet from class com.apress.bgn.eleven.DDLMySQLDemo
import java.sql.DriverManager;
import java.sql.SQLException;

// some code omitted
private static final Logger LOGGER = LoggerFactory.
getLogger(DDLMySQLDemo.class);
//...
try (var con = DriverManager.getConnection(
        "jdbc:mysql://localhost:3306/mysql",
        "root", "mypass")) {
    var stmt = con.createStatement();
    stmt.execute("create database musicdb");
    stmt.execute("CREATE USER 'sample'@'%' IDENTIFIED BY 'sample'");
    stmt.execute("GRANT ALL PRIVILEGES ON *.* TO 'sample'@'%'");
    stmt.execute("flush privileges");

    var rs = stmt.executeQuery("SELECT * FROM user");
    var foundUser = false;
    while (rs.next() && !foundUser) {
        foundUser = rs.getString("User") .equals("sample");
    }
    if (foundUser) {
        LOGGER.info("User 'sample' created.");
    }
} catch (SQLException e) {
    LOGGER.error("Well, this is unexpected...", e);
}
```

The code sample in Listing 11-53 executes all the necessary statements to create a database named musicdb, create a user named sample that uses password sample to connect to the database, and give this user administrative rights on the musicdb database.

The con.createStatement() method returns a Statement instance that is used to execute the SQL DDL statements. When using a MySQL driver, the type of the returned instance is com.mysql.cj.jdbc.StatementImpl, which is a MySQL implementation of the Statement interface and is used to execute MySQL statements.

The execute(..) method executes the given SQL statement and returns `true` if the first result is a `ResultSet` object; it returns `false` if it is an update count or there are no results. This method also throws an `SQLException` if anything goes wrong while communicating with the database. This method is suitable for executing SQL DDL statements because they do not return data and SQL DML UPDATE/DELETE statements.

An alternative to this method is executeUpdate(..) that returns the number of affected rows for insert, update, and delete statements and 0 (zero) for SQL DDL statements. So the code in Listing 11-53 can be rewritten as shown in Listing 11-54.

Listing 11-54. Using JDBC to Create a User and Database (Alternative)

```
// snippet from class com.apress.bgn.eleven.DDLMySQLDemoV2
import java.sql.DriverManager;
import java.sql.SQLException;

// some code omitted
private static final Logger LOGGER = LoggerFactory.
getLogger(DDLMySQLDemo.class);
//...
try (var con = DriverManager.getConnection(
        "jdbc:mysql://localhost:3306/mysql",
        "root", "mypass")) {
    var stmt = con.createStatement();
    var stmtIntResult = stmt.executeUpdate("create database musicdb");
    if (stmtIntResult == 0) {
        LOGGER.info("'musicdb' database created.");
    }

    stmt.executeUpdate("CREATE USER 'sample'@'%' IDENTIFIED BY 'sample'");
    stmt.executeUpdate("GRANT ALL PRIVILEGES ON *.* TO 'sample'@'%'");
    stmt.executeUpdate("flush privileges");

    var rs = stmt.executeQuery("SELECT * FROM user");
    var foundUser = false;
    while (rs.next() && !foundUser) {
        foundUser = rs.getString("User") .equals("sample");
    }
```

```
    if (foundUser) {
        LOGGER.info("User 'sample' created.");
    }
} catch (SQLException e) {
    LOGGER.error("Well, this is unexpected...", e);
}
```

The executeQuery(..) method executes the given SQL statement and returns a single ResultSet object. This method allows us to check that the user was created, by inspecting the contents of the MySQL user table.

Besides the methods listed here, the Statement interface provides a few other utility methods. None of them, however, help with converting a ResultSet into a Singer instance, so mapping SQL table rows to Java objects is not possible with JDBC. JDBC is simplistic and efficient, and it is secure and platform-independent; the one thing it is not known for is being friendly to developers.

Summary

This chapter has covered most of the details you need to know to be able to work with various types of files, how to serialize Java objects and save them to a file, and how to then recover them through deserialization. When writing Java applications, you will most likely need to save data to files or read data from files, and this chapter provides quite a wide list of components to do so. This is a short summary of what you learned how to do in this chapter:

- Use File and Path instances

- Use utility methods in java.nio.file.Files and java.nio.file.Paths

- Serialize/deserialize Java objects to/from binary, XML, and JSON

- Resize and modify images using the Java Media API

- Use images in JavaFX applications

- Execute SQL DDL and DML statements using JDBC

CHAPTER 12

The Publish/Subscribe Framework

All the programming concepts explained so far in the book involved data that needed to be processed. Regardless of the form in which data is provided, the Java programs we've written so far took that data, modified it, and printed out the results, whether to console, files, or another software component. You could say that all these components were communicating with each other, and passing processed data from one to another. For example, take Figure 12-1, which abstractly describes the interaction between Java components in a program.

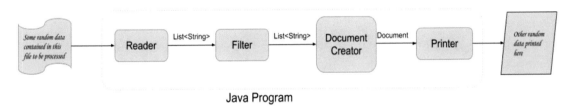

Java Program

Figure 12-1. *Interactions between Java components within a program*

Each of the arrows is labeled with the type of information being passed from one component to another. In this image, you can identify a starting point where information enters the program by being read by the Reader, and an end point where the information is printed to some output component by the Printer. You could say that the Reader provides the data, the Filter and the DocumentCreator are some internal processors, and processing the data and the Printer is the consumer of the data.

What was described so far is something resembling a **point-to-point (P2P) messaging model**, which describes a concept of one message being sent to one consumer. The P2P model is specific to a Java API named *Java Message Service (JMS)* that supports the formal communication known as messaging between computers in

799

© Iuliana Cosmina 2024
I. Cosmina, *Java 23 for Absolute Beginners*, https://doi.org/10.1007/979-8-8688-1041-1_12

a network. The example depicted in Figure 12-1 shows that communication between components of a Java program works similarly. The design of a solution to implement a process as described by Figure 12-1 could be created by considering all components linked into a messaging style communication model.

There is more than one communication model—producer/consumer, publish/subscribe, and sender/receiver—each with its own specifics, but this chapter is focused on **publish/subscribe** because this is the model that reactive programming is based on.

Note   If you are interested in knowing more about other communication models, search the Web for Enterprise Integration Patterns.

Reactive Programming and the Reactive Manifesto

Reactive programming is a declarative programming style that involves using data streams and propagation of change. It revolves around asynchronous and event-driven programming principles, and implies building solutions to manage streams of data and asynchronous operations efficiently. Reactive Streams is an initiative to provide a standard for asynchronous stream processing with nonblocking back pressure. Reactive streams are extremely useful for solving problems that require complex coordination across thread boundaries. The operators allow you to gather your data on to the desired threads and ensure thread-safe operations without requiring, in most cases, excessive use of synchronized and volatile constructs.

It was assumed in the Java world that the introduction of virtual threads in Java 21 would kill the interest in building reactive solutions, but reactive programming is a programming paradigm, while virtual threads are a technical implementation. Thus, I am retaining this reactive programming chapter in this edition too.

Java took a step toward reactive programming after introducing the Stream API in version 8, but reactive streams were not available until version 9. You've already learned how to use streams in **Chapter 8**, so now all you have to do is understand how to use reactive streams to do some reactive programming.

Using reactive streams is not a new idea. The Reactive Manifesto was first made public in 2014[1] and proposed that software be developed in such a way that **systems are "Responsive, Resilient, Elastic and Message Driven"**—in short, they should be **reactive**.

Each of the four terms use in the Reactive Manifesto is briefly explained here:

- **Responsive**: Systems should provide fast and consistent response times.

- **Resilient**: Systems should remain responsive in case of failure and be able to recover.

- **Elastic**: Systems should remain responsive under various workloads.

- **Message Driven**: Systems should communicate using asynchronous messages, avoid blocking, and apply back pressure when necessary.

Systems designed this way are supposed to be more flexible, loosely coupled, and scalable, but at the same time they should be easier to develop, amenable to change, and more tolerant of failure. To be able to achieve all that, the systems need a common API for communication. As previously mentioned, Reactive Streams is an initiative to provide such a standard API for asynchronous, nonblocking stream processing that also supports back pressure. I'll explain what **back pressure** means in a moment. Let's start with the basics of reactive stream processing.

Any type of stream processing involves a producer of data, a consumer of data, and components in the middle between them that process the data. Obviously, the direction of the data flow is from the producer to the consumer. The abstract schema of a system described thus far is depicted in Figure 12-2.

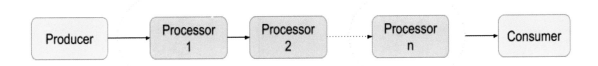

Figure 12-2. *Producer/consumer system*

---

[1] https://www.reactivemanifesto.org

The system might end up in a pickle when the producer is faster than the consumer, so the extra data that cannot be processed must be dealt with. There is more than one way of doing that:

- The extra data is discarded (this is done in network hardware).

- The producer is blocked so the consumer has time to catch up.

- The data is buffered. However, buffers are limited, and if we have a fast producer and a slow consumer, there is a danger of the buffer overflowing.

- **Back pressure** is applied, which involves giving the consumer the power to regulate the producer and control how much data is produced. Back pressure can be viewed as a message being sent from the consumer to the producer to let the producer know that the consumer has to slow its data production rate. With this in mind, we can complete the design in the previous image, which will result in Figure 12-3.

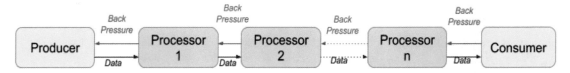

Figure 12-3. *Reactive producer/consumer system*

If the producer, processors, and consumer are not synchronized, solving the problem of too much data by blocking until each one is ready to process it is not an option, as it would transform the system into a synchronous one. Discarding it is not an option either, and buffering is unpredictable, so all we're left with for a reactive system is applying **nonblocking back pressure**.

Tip   If the software example is too puzzling for you, imagine the following scenario: You have a friend named Jim. You also have a bucket of differently colored balls. Jim tells you to give him all the red balls. You have two ways of doing this:

- You pick all the red balls, put them in another bucket, and hand the bucket to Jim. This is the typical request - complete response model. It is an asynchronous model. If selecting the red balls takes too long, Jim just goes and does other things while you do the sorting, and when you are done, you notify him that his bucket of red balls is ready. It is asynchronous because Jim is not blocked by you sorting the balls and is able to go do other things and then get the balls when they are ready.

- You get the red balls one by one from your bucket and throw them at Jim. This is your data flow, or a ball flow in this case. If you are faster at finding the balls and throwing them than Jim is at catching them, you have a blockage. So Jim tells you to slow down. This is him regulating the flow of balls, which is the real-world equivalent of back pressure.

Writing applications that can be aggregated in reactive systems was not possible in Java before version 9, so developers had to make do with external libraries. A reactive application must be designed according to the principle of reactive programming and use reactive streams for handling the data. The standard API for reactive programming was first described by the **reactive-streams** library, which could be used with Java 8 as well. In Java 9, the standard API was added to the JDK and the next version of the reactive-streams library included a set of classes declared nested into the org.reactivestreams.FlowAdapters class that represents bridges between the analogous components in the two APIs (the Reactive Streams API and the Reactive Streams Flow API).

In Figure 12-4 you can see the interfaces from org.reactivestreams that are meant to be implemented by components with the roles defined previously.

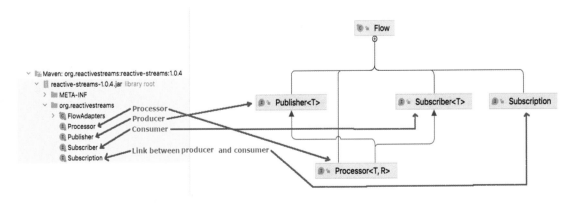

Figure 12-4. *Reactive Streams interfaces (as shown in IntelliJ IDEA)*

The Reactive Streams API is made of four basic interfaces:

- `Publisher<T>` exposes one method named `void subscribe(Subscriber<? super T>)`, which is called to add a `Subscriber<T>` instance and produces elements of type T, which will be consumed by the `Subscriber<T>`. The purpose of a `Publisher<T>` implementation is to publish values according to the demand received from its subscribers.

- `Subscriber<T>` consumes elements from the `Publisher<T>` and exposes four methods that must be implemented to define concrete behavior of the instance depending on the event type received by the `Publisher<T>` instance:

  - `void onSubscribe(Subscription)` is the first method called on a subscriber and is the method that links the `Publisher<T>` to the `Subscriber<T>` instance using the `Subscription` argument; if this method throws an exception, the following behavior is not guaranteed.

  - `void onNext(T)` is the method invoked with a `Subscription`'s next item to receive the data; if it throws an exception, the `Subscription` might be cancelled.

  - `void onError(Throwable)` is the method invoked upon an unrecoverable error encountered by a `Publisher<T>` or `Subscription<T>`.

  - `void onComplete()` is the method called when there is no more data to consume, thus no additional `Subscriber<T>` method invocations will occur.

- `Processor<T,R>` extends both `Publisher<T>` and `Subscriber<R>`, because it needs to consume data and produce it to send it further upstream.

- `Subscription` links the `Publisher<T>` and the `Subscriber<T>` and can be used to apply back pressure by calling the `request(long)` to set the number of items to be produced and sent to the consumer. It also allows the cancellation of a flow, by calling the `cancel()` method to tell a `Subscriber<T>` to stop receiving messages.

In the JDK, all the previously listed interfaces are defined in the `java.util.`
`concurrent.Flow` class. The name of this class is obvious in nature, as the previous
interfaces are used to create flow-controlled components that can be linked together to
create a reactive application. Figure 12-5 shows the correspondence between the JDK
Reactive Streams API and the Reactive Streams library API.

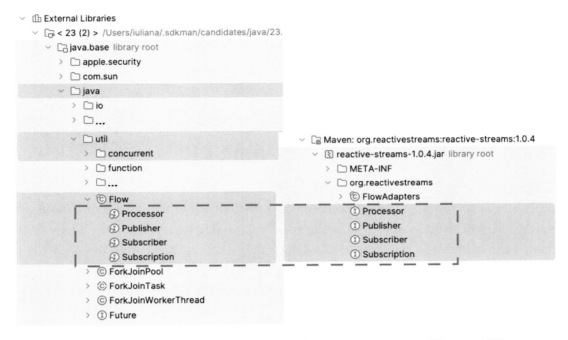

Figure 12-5. *JDK Reactive Streams API and Reactive Streams library API*
correspondence

Aside from these four interfaces, there is a single JDK implementation, the `java.`
`util.concurrent.SubmissionPublisher<T>` class implementing `Publisher<T>`, which
is a convenient base for subclasses that generate items and use the methods in this class
to publish them.

The `Flow` interfaces are quite basic and can be used when writing reactive
applications, but this requires a lot of work. Currently, there are multiple
implementations, by various teams, that provide a more practical way to develop
reactive applications. Using implementations of these interfaces, you can write reactive
applications without needing to write the logic for synchronization of threads processing
the data.

The following list contains the most well-known Reactive Streams API implementations (and there are more, because in a big data world, reactive data processing is no longer a luxury, but a necessity):

- Project Reactor[2], embraced by Spring for its Web Reactive Framework

- Akka Streams[3]

- MongoDB Reactive Streams Java Driver[4]

- Ratpack[5]

- ReactiveX[6]

Using the JDK Reactive Streams API

The JDK-provided interfaces for reactive programming are quite basic, so implementation is quite cumbersome, but nevertheless we'll make an attempt in this section. We will build an application that generates an infinite number of integer values, filters these values, and selects the values that are less than 127. For the values that are even and between 98 and 122, the application will subtract 32 (basically converting lowercase letters to uppercase letters) and then convert them to a character and print them.

The most basic solution, without reactive streams, is depicted in Listing 12-1.

Listing 12-1. Generating an Infinite Number of Integers < 127

```
package com.apress.bgn.twelve.dummy;
// some input statements omitted

import java.security.SecureRandom;
```

---

[2] https://projectreactor.io
[3] https://doc.akka.io/docs/akka/current/stream/stream-flows-and-basics.html
[4] https://mongodb.github.io/mongo-java-driver-reactivestreams/
[5] https://ratpack.io
[6] https://reactivex.io/

```
public class BasicIntTransformer {
    private static final Logger LOGGER = LoggerFactory.
    getLogger(BasicIntTransformer.class);
    private static final SecureRandom random = new SecureRandom();

    void main() {
        int rndNo = random.nextInt(130);
        if (rndNo < 127) {
            LOGGER.info("Initial value: {} ", rndNo);
            if(rndNo % 2 == 0 && rndNo >=98 && rndNo <=122) {
                rndNo -=32;
            }
            char res = (char) rndNo;
            LOGGER.info("Result: {}", res);
        } else {
            LOGGER.debug("Number {} discarded.", rndNo);
        }
    }
}
// sample output
//[main] INFO com.apress.bgn.twelve.dummy.BasicIntTransformer -- Initial
value: 95
//[main] INFO com.apress.bgn.twelve.dummy.BasicIntTransformer -- Result: _
//[main] INFO com.apress.bgn.twelve.dummy.BasicIntTransformer -- Initial
value: 33
//[main] INFO com.apress.bgn.twelve.dummy.BasicIntTransformer -- Result: !
// ..
```

Each line of code in Listing 12-1 has a purpose, a desired outcome. This approach is called *imperative programming*, because it sequentially executes a series of statements to produce a desired output. However, this is not what we are aiming for. In this section, we will implement a reactive solution using implementations of the JDK reactive interfaces, so we'll need the following:

- A publisher component that makes use of an infinite stream to generate random integer values. The class should implement the Flow.Publisher<Integer> interface.

- A processor that selects only integer values that can be converted to visible characters, which in our solution will be all characters with codes between [0,127]. The class should implement the `Flow.Processor<Integer, Integer>`.

- A processor that modifies elements received that are even and between 98 and 122 by subtracting 32. This class should also implement the `Flow.Processor<Integer, Integer>`.

- A processor that transforms integer elements into the equivalent characters. This is a special type of processor that maps one value to another of another type and should implement `Flow.Processor<Integer, Character>`.

- A subscriber that prints the received elements from the last processor in the chain. This class will implement the `Flow.Subscriber<Character>` interface.

Let's start by declaring the `Publisher<T>` that will wrap around an infinite stream to produce values to be consumed. We will implement the `Flow.Publisher<Integer>` interface by providing a full concrete implementation to submit the elements asynchronously. To buffer them in case of need, a lot of code would need to be added. Fortunately, the class `SubmissionPublisher<T>` does that already, so internally, in our class we'll make use of a `SubmissionPublisher<Integer>` object. The code for the publisher is depicted in Listing 12-2.

Listing 12-2. Publisher Generating an Infinite Number of Integers

```
package com.apress.bgn.twelve.jdkstreams;

import java.util.concurrent.Flow;
import java.util.concurrent.SubmissionPublisher;
import java.util.random.RandomGenerator;
import java.util.stream.IntStream;

public class IntPublisher implements Flow.Publisher<Integer> {
    static RandomGenerator randomGenerator = RandomGenerator.of
                                              ("SecureRandom");
    protected final IntStream intStream;
```

```java
public IntPublisher(long limit) {
    intStream = limit == 0 ? IntStream.generate(() -> randomGenerator.
    nextInt(150)) :
            IntStream.generate(() -> randomGenerator.nextInt(150)).
            limit(30);
}

private final SubmissionPublisher<Integer> submissionPublisher = new
SubmissionPublisher<>();

@Override
public void subscribe(Flow.Subscriber<? super Integer> subscriber) {
    submissionPublisher.subscribe(subscriber);
}

public void start() {
    intStream.forEach(element -> {
        submissionPublisher.submit(element);
        sleep();
    });
}

private void sleep() {
    try {
        Thread.sleep(1000);
    } catch (InterruptedException _) {
        }
    }
}
```

Tip Notice how the constructor of the IntPublisher class takes a single argument. If the value provided as argument at instantiation time is 0 (zero), an infinite stream is created. If the argument value is different from 0, a finite stream is created. This is useful if you want to run the example and not forcefully stop the execution.

As expected, we've provided an implementation for the subscribe() method. In this case we simply have to forward the subscriber to the internal submissionPublisher. This is necessary because we've created our publisher by wrapping it around submissionPublisher; otherwise, our flow won't work as expected. Also, we've added a start() method that takes elements from the infinite IntStream and submits them using the internal submissionPublisher.

The IntStream makes use of a RandomGenerator instance to generate integer values in the [0,150] interval. This interval is chosen so that we can see how values greater than 127 are discarded by the first Flow.Processor<T,R> instance connected to the publisher. To be able to slow down the element submission, we've added a call to Thread.sleep(1000) that basically guarantees one element per second will be forwarded up the chain.

The name of the first processor will be FilterCharProcessor and will make use of an internal SubmissionPublisher<Integer> instance to send the elements it processes onward to the next processor.

Exceptions thrown will be also forwarded using the SubmissionPublisher<Integer>. The processor acts as a publisher, but as a subscriber as well, so the implementation on the onNext(..) method will have to include a call to subscription.request(..) to apply back pressure. From the figures presented earlier in the chapter, you could see that the processor is basically a component that allows data flow in both directions, and it does that by implementing both Publisher<T> and Subscriber<T>.

The processor must subscribe to the publisher, and when the publisher subscribe(..) method is called, it will cause the onSubscribe(Flow.Subscription subscription) method to be invoked. The subscription must be stored locally, so that it can be used to apply back pressure. But when accepting a subscription, we must make sure that the field was not already initialized, because, according to the Reactive Streams specification, there can only be one subscriber for a publisher, otherwise the results are unpredictable. If and when a new subscription arrives, it must be cancelled, and this is done by calling cancel(). The full code for the processor is depicted in Listing 12-3.

Listing 12-3. Flow.Processor<T,R> Implementation FilterCharProcessor<Integer,Integer> That Filters Integers > 127

```
package com.apress.bgn.twelve.jdkstreams;

import java.util.concurrent.Flow;
import java.util.concurrent.SubmissionPublisher;
// some input statements omitted
```

```java
public class FilterCharProcessor extends Flow.Processor<Integer, Integer> {
  private static final Logger LOGGER = LoggerFactory.getLogger
                                       (FilterCharProcessor.class);

  private final SubmissionPublisher<Integer> submissionPublisher = new
  SubmissionPublisher<>();
  private Flow.Subscription subscription;
  @Override
  public void subscribe(Flow.Subscriber<? super Integer> subscriber) {
    submissionPublisher.subscribe(subscriber);
  }
  @Override
  public void onSubscribe(Flow.Subscription subscription) {
    if (this.subscription == null) {
      this.subscription = subscription;
      // apply back pressure - request one element
      this.subscription.request(1);
    } else {
      subscription.cancel();
    }
  }
  @Override
  public void onNext(Integer element) {
    if (element >=0 && element < 127){
      submit(element);
    } else {
      log.debug("Element {} discarded.", element);
    }
    subscription.request(1);
  }
  @Override
  public void onError(Throwable throwable) {
    submissionPublisher.closeExceptionally(throwable);
  }
```

```
  @Override
  public void onComplete() {
    submissionPublisher.close();
  }
  protected void submit(Integer element){
    submissionPublisher.submit(element);
  }
}
```

This processor is very specific, and a processing flow usually requires more than one processor. In this scenario we need a few, and since the rest of the implementation is mostly boilerplate code (except the onNext(..) method) that allows for processors to be linked together in the flow we are designing, it would be more practical to wrap up this code in an AbstractProcessor that all processors needed for this solution can extend.

Because the last processor in the flow needs to convert the received Integer value to a Character, we need to keep the returned type of this implementation generic. The code is depicted in Listing 12-4.

Listing 12-4. AbstractProcessor<Integer,T> Implementation

```
package com.apress.bgn.twelve.jdkstreams;

import java.util.concurrent.Flow;
import java.util.concurrent.SubmissionPublisher;

public abstract class AbstractProcessor <T> implements Flow.
Processor<Integer, T> {
    protected final SubmissionPublisher<T> submissionPublisher = new
    SubmissionPublisher<>();
    protected Flow.Subscription subscription;

    @Override
    public void subscribe(Flow.Subscriber<? super T> subscriber) {
        submissionPublisher.subscribe(subscriber);
    }

    @Override
    public void onSubscribe(Flow.Subscription subscription) {
        if (this.subscription == null) {
```

```java
            this.subscription = subscription;
            // apply back pressure - ask one or more than one
            this.subscription.request(1);
        } else {
            //avoid more than one Publisher sending elements to this
            Subscriber
            // do not accept other subscriptions
            subscription.cancel();
        }
    }

    @Override
    public void onError(Throwable throwable) {
        submissionPublisher.closeExceptionally(throwable);
    }

    @Override
    public void onComplete() {
        submissionPublisher.close();
    }

    protected void submit(T element) {
        submissionPublisher.submit(element);
    }
}
```

This simplifies the implementation of the FilterCharProcessor<Integer, Integer> and the other processors as well. The FilterCharProcessor<Integer, Integer> simplified implementation is depicted in Listing 12-5.

Listing 12-5. FilterCharProcessor Extending AbstractProcessor<Integer>

```java
package com.apress.bgn.twelve.jdkstreams;

import org.slf4j.Logger;
import org.slf4j.LoggerFactory;

public class FilterCharProcessor extends AbstractProcessor<Integer> {
```

```java
    private static final Logger LOGGER = LoggerFactory.
    getLogger(FilterCharProcessor.class);

    @Override
    public void onNext(Integer element) {
        if (element >= 0 && element < 127) {
            submit(element);
        } else {
            LOGGER.debug("Element {} discarded.", element);
        }
        subscription.request(1);
    }
}
```

We have a publisher and a processor, so now what? We connect them, of course. The dots (..) in Listing 12-6 replace all the processors and the subscribers being connected to each other, which we have yet to build in this section.

Listing 12-6. Executing a Reactive Flow

```java
package com.apress.bgn.twelve.jdkstreams;

public class ReactiveDemo {
    void main() {
        var publisher = new IntPublisher(0);
        var filterCharProcessor = new FilterCharProcessor();
        // some code omitted

        publisher.subscribe(filterCharProcessor);

        // some code omitted
        publisher.start();
    }
}
```

The next processor implementation is the one that transforms smaller letters into big letters by subtracting 32. It can be easily implemented by extending AbstractProcessor<Integer, T> as well, and the implementation is depicted in Listing 12-7.

Listing 12-7. The `TransformerProcessor` Implementation

```
package com.apress.bgn.twelve.jdkstreams;

public class TransformerProcessor extends AbstractProcessor<Integer>{
    @Override
    public void onNext(Integer element) {
        if(element % 2 == 0 && element >=98 && element <=122) {
            element -=32;
        }
        submit(element);
        subscription.request(1);
    }
}
```

To plug in this processor in the flow, we just need to instantiate it and call the `filterCharProcessor.subscribe(..)` and provide this instance as an argument. Listing 12-8 shows the next step in creating our reactive flow.

Listing 12-8. A `TransformerProcessor` Instance Being Added to a Reactive Flow

```
package com.apress.bgn.twelve.jdkstreams;

public class ReactiveDemo {
  void main() {
    var publisher = new IntPublisher(0);
    var filterCharProcessor = new FilterCharProcessor();
    var transformerProcessor = new TransformerProcessor();
    // some code omitted

    publisher.subscribe(filterCharProcessor);
    filterCharProcessor.subscribe(transformerProcessor);
    // some code omitted

    publisher.start();
  }
}
```

The next processor to implement is the final processor that we need for this solution and is the one that converts an Integer value to a String value. To keep the implementation as declarative as possible, the processor will be provided in the mapping function as an argument. The code is shown in Listing 12-9.

Listing 12-9. The MappingProcessor Implementation

```java
package com.apress.bgn.twelve.jdkstreams;

import java.util.function.Function;

public class MappingProcessor extends AbstractProcessor<Character> {
    private final Function<Integer, Character> function;

    public MappingProcessor(Function<Integer, Character> function) {
        this.function = function;
    }
    @Override
    public void onNext(Integer element) {
        submit(function.apply(element));
        subscription.request(1);
    }
}
```

In Listing 12-10, you can see a MappingProcessor instance being added to the reactive flow.

Listing 12-10. A MappingProcessor Instance Being Added to a Reactive Flow

```java
package com.apress.bgn.twelve.jdkstreams;

public class ReactiveDemo {
  void main() {
    var publisher = new IntPublisher(0);
    var filterCharProcessor = new FilterCharProcessor();
    var transformerProcessor = new TransformerProcessor();
    var mappingProcessor = new MappingProcessor(element -> (char) element.
                           intValue());
```

```
// some code omitted

publisher.subscribe(filterCharProcessor);
filterCharProcessor.subscribe(transformerProcessor);
transformerProcessor.subscribe(mappingProcessor);
// some code omitted

publisher.start();
  }
}
```

The last component of this flow is the subscriber. The subscriber is the most important component in a flow—until a subscriber is added to the flow and a Subscription instance is created, nothing actually happens. Our subscriber implements the Flow.Subscriber<Character> and most of it is identical to the code we've isolated in the AbstractProcessor<T>, which might look a little bit redundant, but makes things very easy as well. Listing 12-11 depicts the Subscriber implementation.

Listing 12-11. Subscriber<Character> Implementation

```
package com.apress.bgn.twelve.jdkstreams;
// some import statements omitted

import java.util.concurrent.Flow;

public class CharPrinter  implements Flow.Subscriber<Character> {
    private static final Logger LOGGER = LoggerFactory.getLogger
                                        (CharPrinter.class);

    private Flow.Subscription subscription;

    @Override
    public void onSubscribe(Flow.Subscription subscription) {
        if (this.subscription == null) {
            this.subscription = subscription;
            this.subscription.request(1);
        } else {
            subscription.cancel();
        }
    }
}
```

```
    @Override
    public void onNext(Character element) {
        LOGGER.info("Result: {}", element);
        //apply back-pressure again
        subscription.request(1);
    }

    @Override
    public void onError(Throwable throwable) {
        LOGGER.error("Something went wrong.", throwable);
    }

    @Override
    public void onComplete() {
        LOGGER.info("Printing complete.");
    }
}
```

Using this subscriber class, the flow can now be completed like shown in Listing 12-12.

Listing 12-12. Reactive Pipeline Complete Implementation

```
package com.apress.bgn.twelve.jdkstreams;

public class ReactiveDemo {
    void main() {
        var publisher = new IntPublisher(0);
        var filterCharProcessor = new FilterCharProcessor();
        var transformerProcessor = new TransformerProcessor();
        var mappingProcessor = new MappingProcessor(element -> (char)
                            element.intValue());
        var charPrinter = new CharPrinter();

        publisher.subscribe(filterCharProcessor);
        filterCharProcessor.subscribe(transformerProcessor);
        transformerProcessor.subscribe(mappingProcessor);
```

```
        mappingProcessor.subscribe(charPrinter);
        publisher.start();
    }
}
```

It would be nice if the subscribe(..) method would return the caller instance, so that we could chain the subscribe(..) calls, but we'll work with what is provided for us. When the code in Listing 12-12 is run, a log similar to the one depicted in Listing 12-13 is printed in the console.

Listing 12-13. Console Output of a Reactive Flow Being Executed

```
...
INFO  c.a.b.t.j.CharPrinter - Result: `
INFO  c.a.b.t.j.CharPrinter - Result: I
DEBUG c.a.b.t.j.FilterCharProcessor - Element 128 discarded.
INFO  c.a.b.t.j.CharPrinter - Result: Z
INFO  c.a.b.t.j.CharPrinter - Result: \
INFO  c.a.b.t.j.CharPrinter - Result: %
DEBUG c.a.b.t.j.FilterCharProcessor - Element 147 discarded.
INFO  c.a.b.t.j.CharPrinter - Result: _
DEBUG c.a.b.t.j.FilterCharProcessor - Element 137 discarded.
...
```

The earlier example presented in Listing 12-2 uses an infinite IntStream to generate elements to be published, processed, and consumed. This leads to the execution program running forever, so you will have to stop it manually. Another consequence of this is that the onComplete() method will never be called. If we want to use it, we must make sure the number of items being published is finite by initializing the IntPublisher with a value different from 0.

Another thing to mention is that back-pressure handling is done more in a conceptual way. The Reactive Streams Flow API doesn't provide any mechanism to signal about back pressure or to deal with it. So the subscription.request(1) just makes sure that when onNext(..) is called, the element-producing rate is reduced to one. Various strategies can be devised to deal with back pressure based on the fine-tuning of the subscriber, but it is challenging to show something like this in a basic example that does not involve two microservices reactively interacting with each other.

Support for reactive streams is quite thin in the JDK, even in version 23, released on September 17, 2024. It was expected that more useful classes would be added in future versions. However, apparently Oracle is focused on other aspects, like virtual threads, structured concurrency and Class-File API, reorganizing the module structure, and deciding how to better monetize usage of the JDK. That is why the last section of this chapter covers a short example of reactive programming done with the Project Reactor library.

Reactive Streams Technology Compatibility Kit

When building applications that use reactive streams, a lot of things can go wrong. To make sure things go as expected, the **Reactive Streams Technology Compatibility Kit** project, also known as **TCK**[7], is an invaluable library to write tests. This library contains classes that can be used to test reactive implementations against the Reactive Streams specifications. TCK is intended to verify the interfaces contained in the JDK's `java.util.concurrent.Flow` class. For some reason the team that created the library decided to use TestNG as a testing library.

TCK contains the following four classes that have to be implemented to provide their `Flow.Publisher<T>`, `Flow.Subscriber<T>`, and `Flow.Processor<T,R>` implementations for the test harness to validate:

- `org.reactivestreams.tck.PublisherVerification<T>` is used to test `Publisher<T>` implementations.

- `org.reactivestreams.tck.SubscriberWhiteboxVerification<T>` is used for white-box testing `Subscriber<T>` implementations and `Subscription` instances.

- `org.reactivestreams.tck.SubscriberBlackboxVerification<T>` is used for black-box testing `Subscriber<T>` implementations and `Subscription` instances

- `org.reactivestreams.tck.IdentityProcessorVerification<T>` is used to test `Processor<T,R>` implementations.

---

[7] `https://github.com/reactive-streams/reactive-streams-jvm/tree/master/tck`

To make the purpose of each test obvious, the library test methods' names follow this pattern: TYPE_spec####_DESC, where TYPE is one of required, optional, stochastic, or untested, which refers to the importance of the rule being tested. The hash signs in spec#### represent the rule number, with the first one being 1 for Publisher<T> instances and 2 for Subscriber<T> instances. The DESC is a short explanation of the test purpose.

Let's see how we could test the IntPublisher instance that we defined previously. The PublisherVerification<T> class requires implementation of two test methods: one to test a working Publisher<T> (the createPublisher(..) method) instance that emits a number of elements, and one to test a "failed" Publisher<T> (the createFailedPublisher(..) method) instance, which was unable to initialize a connection it needs to emit elements.

The instance tested by the createPublisher(..) is created by passing an argument with a value different from 0, so the IntPublisher instance emits a limited set of elements so the test execution is finite as well.

The PublisherVerification<Integer> implementation is depicted in Listing 12-14.

Listing 12-14. TestNG Test Class for Testing an IntPublisher Instance

```
package com.apress.bgn.twelve.jdkstreams;

import org.reactivestreams.FlowAdapters;
import org.reactivestreams.Publisher;
import org.reactivestreams.tck.PublisherVerification;
import org.reactivestreams.tck.TestEnvironment;
import java.util.concurrent.Flow;
// other import statements omitted

public class IntPublisherTest  extends PublisherVerification<Integer> {
    private static final Logger log = LoggerFactory.
    getLogger(IntPublisherTest.class);

    public IntPublisherTest() {
        super(new TestEnvironment(300));
    }

    @Override
    public Publisher<Integer> createPublisher(final long elements) {
```

```
        return FlowAdapters.toPublisher(new IntPublisher(30) {
            @Override
            public void subscribe(Flow.Subscriber<? super Integer>
            subscriber) {
                intStream.forEach(subscriber::onNext);
                subscriber.onComplete();
            }
        });
    }

    @Override
    public Publisher<Integer> createFailedPublisher() {
        return FlowAdapters.toPublisher(new IntPublisher(0) {
            @Override
            public void subscribe(Flow.Subscriber<? super Integer>
            subscriber) {
                subscriber.onError(new RuntimeException("There be
                dragons!"));
            }
        });
    }
}
```

Another thing that should be mentioned about the previous test class is that since the implementation is designed to work with the Reactive Streams API, it cannot be used to test the JDK-based IntPublisher. However, the Reactive Streams API was enriched in version 1.0.3 with a set of classes used as bridges between the Reactive Streams API and the JDK Reactive Streams API. Thus, IntPublisher must be provided as an argument to the FlowAdapters.toPublisher(..) method that converts it to an equivalent org. reactivestreams.Publisher that the IntPublisherTest can test.

A Publisher<T> implementation might not pass all the tests, because of design decisions that are specific to the application you are building. In our case the IntPublisher implementation is quite simplistic, and when running the createPublisher(..) method of all the executed tests, few of them pass and most are ignored, as depicted in Figure 12-6.

Figure 12-6. *TestNG reactive publisher execution results*

The reason tests do not pass or are ignored is that our implementation does not implement behaviors targeted by those specific tests (e.g., `maySupportMultiSubscribe`, `maySignalLessThanRequestedAndTerminateSubscription`, and `mustSignalOnMethodsSequentially`).

We can test the processor and subscriber we defined in the previous section by extending the previously mentioned testing classes as well. However, I'll leave that as an exercise for you, because there is one more interesting thing I would like to cover in this chapter.

Using Project Reactor

As mentioned previously, the JDK support for reactive programming is quite scarce. Publishers, processors, and subscribers should function asynchronously, and all that behavior must be implemented by the developer, which can be a bit of a pain. The only thing that the JDK is suitable for at the moment is providing a common interface between all the other already existing implementations. There are a lot of them, providing many more useful classes for more specialized reactive components and utility methods to create and connect them easier. The one I personally fancy the most as a Spring aficionado is **Project Reactor**, the same one favored by the Spring development team.

Project Reactor is one of the first libraries for reactive programming, and its classes provide a nonblocking stable foundation with efficient demand management for building reactive applications. It works with Java 8, but does provide adapter classes for JDK 9+ reactive streams classes.

Project Reactor is suitable for microservices applications and provides a lot more classes designed to make programming reactive applications more practical than the JDK does. Project Reactor provides two main publisher implementations: `reactor.core.publisher.Mono<T>`, which is a reactive stream publisher limited to publishing zero or one element, and `reactor.core.publisher.Flux<T>`, which is a reactive stream publisher with basic flow operators.

The advantages of using Project Reactor is that we have a lot more classes and methods to work with, there are static factories that can be used to create publishers, and operations can be chained way more easily. The Project Reactor team did not like the name processor, though, so the intermediary components are named **operators**.

If you look in the official documentation, you will most likely encounter the schema in Figure 12-7[8].

---

[8] `http://projectreactor.io/docs/core/release/api/reactor/core/publisher/Flux.html`

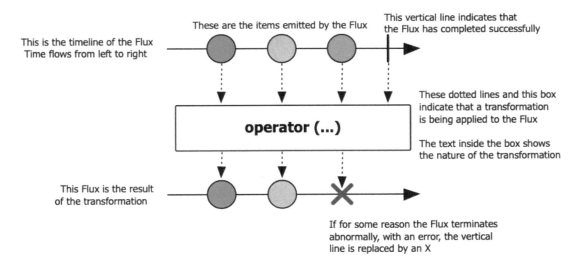

Figure 12-7. *Project Reactor Flux publisher implementation*

This is an abstract schema of how the Flux<T> publisher works. The Flux<T> emits elements, can throw exceptions, and completes when there are no more elements to publish—the same behavior explained previously, but the Project Reactor team found a prettier way to draw it. The drawing for the Mono implementation is quite similar[9].

But let's put that aside and look at a few code samples. Creating Flux<T> instances is very easy using the multiple utility methods in this class. Before starting to publish elements, let's design a general subscriber that does nothing else than print values, because we will need it to make sure our Flux<T> publishers actually work. To write a subscriber using the Project Reactor API, you have multiple options. First, you can implement the org.reactivestreams.Subscriber<T> directly, as shown in Listing 12-15.

Listing 12-15. org.reactivestreams.Subscriber<T> Implementation

```
package com.apress.bgn.twelve.reactor;

import org.reactivestreams.Subscriber;
import org.reactivestreams.Subscription;
// other import statements omitted
```

---

[9] http://projectreactor.io/docs/core/release/api/reactor/core/publisher/Mono.html

```java
public class GenericSubscriber<T> implements Subscriber<T> {
  private static final Logger LOGGER = LoggerFactory.getLogger
                                        (GenericSubscriber.class);

  private Subscription subscription;
  @Override
  public void onSubscribe(Subscription subscription) {
    if (this.subscription == null) {
      this.subscription = subscription;
      this.subscription.request(1);
    } else {
      subscription.cancel();
    }
  }
  @Override
  public void onNext(T element) {
    LOGGER.info("consumed {} ", element);
    subscription.request(1);
  }
  @Override
  public void onError(Throwable t) {
    LOGGER.error("Unexpected issue!", t);
  }
  @Override
  public void onComplete() {
    LOGGER.info("All done!");
  }
}
```

To avoid implementing that many methods with boilerplate code, there is also
the option of implementing reactor.core.CoreSubscriber<T>, the reactor base
interface for subscribers, or even better, by extending the reactor.core.publisher.
BaseSubscriber<T> class, which provides basic subscriber functionality. The behavior of
typical subscriber methods can be modified by overriding methods with the same name,
but prefixed with hook. In Listing 12-16, you can see how easy it is to write a subscriber
using Project Reactor.

Listing 12-16. `reactor.core.publisher.BaseSubscriber<T>` Extension

```
package com.apress.bgn.twelve.reactor;

import reactor.core.publisher.BaseSubscriber;
// other import statements omitted

public class GenericSubscriber <T> extends BaseSubscriber<T> {
    private static final Logger LOGGER = LoggerFactory.getLogger
                                        (GenericSubscriber.class);

    @Override
    protected void hookOnNext(T value) {
        LOGGER.info("consumed {} ", value);
        super.hookOnNext(value);
    }

    @Override
    protected void hookOnComplete() {
        LOGGER.info("call done.");
        super.hookOnComplete();
    }
}
```

Ta, da! Now we have a subscriber class, so let's create a reactive publisher that serves integers from an infinite integer stream, to use an instance of this class. The implementation is shown in Listing 12-17.

Listing 12-17. Creating a Reactive Publisher Using Project Reactor's `Flux<T>`

```
package com.apress.bgn.twelve.reactor;

import reactor.core.publisher.Flux;

import java.util.random.RandomGenerator;
import java.util.stream.Stream;

public class ReactorDemo {
    static RandomGenerator randomGenerator = RandomGenerator.of
                                        ("SecureRandom");
```

```
    void main() {
        Flux<Integer> intFlux = Flux.fromStream(
                Stream.generate(() -> randomGenerator.nextInt(150))
        );
        intFlux.subscribe(new GenericSubscriber<>());
    }
}
// sample output
/*
INFO  c.a.b.t.r.GenericSubscriber - consumed 14
INFO  c.a.b.t.r.GenericSubscriber - consumed 35
INFO  c.a.b.t.r.GenericSubscriber - consumed 115
 */
```

If you run the preceding code, you will see that all the generated integer values are printed by the subscriber. A Flux<T> can be created from a multitude of sources, including arrays and other publishers. For special situations, to avoid returning a null value, an empty Flux<T> can be created by calling the empty() method:

```
String[] names = {"Joy", "John", "Anemona", "Takeshi"};
Flux.fromArray(names).subscribe(new GenericSubscriber<>());

Flux<Integer> intFlux = Flux.empty();
intFlux.subscribe(new GenericSubscriber<>());
```

The most awesome method in my opinion is named just(..) and it is provided for both Flux and Mono. It takes one or more values and returns a publisher, a Flux<T> or a Mono<T>, depending on the type being called on:

```
Flux<String> dummyStr = Flux.just("one", "two", "three");
Flux<Integer> dummyInt = Flux.just(1,2,3);

Mono<Integer> one = Mono.just(1);
Mono<String> empty = Mono.empty();
```

Another method that you might find useful is concat(..), which allows you to concatenate two Flux<T> instances:

```
String[] names = {"Joy", "John", "Anemona", "Takeshi"};
Flux<String> namesFlux = Flux.fromArray(names);

String[] names2 = {"Hanna", "Eugen", "Anthony", "David"};
Flux<String> names2Flux = Flux.fromArray(names2);
Flux<String> combined = Flux.concat(namesFlux, names2Flux);
combined.subscribe(new GenericSubscriber<>());
```

Another thing that you might like: remember how the IntPublisher class had to be slowed down using a Thread.sleep(1000) call? With Flux<T> you do not need to do that, because there are two utility methods that when combined lead to the same behavior:

```
Flux<Integer> infiniteFlux = Flux.fromStream(
        Stream.generate(() -> randomGenerator.nextInt(150))
    );

Flux<Long> delay = Flux.interval(Duration.ofSeconds(1));
Flux<Integer> delayedInfiniteFlux = infiniteFlux.zipWith(delay, (s,l) -> s);
delayedInfiniteFlux.subscribe(new GenericSubscriber<>());
```

The interval(..) method creates a publisher that emits long values starting with 0 and incrementing at specified time intervals on the global timer; it receives an argument of type Duration, and in the previous example seconds were used. The zipWith(..) method zips the Flux<T> instance received as a parameter. The zip operation is a specific stream operation that translates as both publishers emitting one element and combining these elements using a java.util.function.BiFunction<T, U, R>. In our case, the function just discards the second elements and returns the elements of the calling stream slowed down by the number of seconds generated by the second stream.

The good part about the components provided by Project Reactor is that they return mostly the same type of objects they are being called on, and this means they can be easily chained. A reactive piece of code equivalent to the previously implemented JDK-based implementation can be written with the Project Reactor API as shown in Listing 12-18.

Listing 12-18. Writing a Reactive Pipeline Using Project Reactor

```
Flux<Integer> infiniteFlux = Flux.fromStream(
        Stream.generate(() -> random.nextInt(150))
    );

Flux<Long> delay = Flux.interval(Duration.ofSeconds(1));
Flux<Integer> delayedInfiniteFlux = infiniteFlux.zipWith(delay, (s, l) -> s);

delayedInfiniteFlux
    .filter(element -> (element >= 0 && element < 127))
    .map(item -> {
        if (item % 2 == 0 && item >= 98 && item <= 122) {
            item -= 32;
        }
        return item;
    })
.map(element -> (char) element.intValue())
.subscribe(new GenericSubscriber<>());
```

Most functions that you remember from the Stream API have been implemented for a reactive usage in Project Reactor, so if the previous code seems familiar, this is the reason why.

Regarding the Project Reactor API, if you are ever in need of a reactive library, you could consider this one first. The official documentation[10] is great and full of examples. Oracle apparently has postponed for now its plans to provide a rich API for programming reactive applications.

Summary

Reactive programming is not an easy topic, but reactive applications are the most suitable for modeling event-driven, asynchronous, responsive, and resilient systems. This chapter did not need to get into really advanced topics to show the true power of a reactive solution. Being a book for absolute beginners in Java, this is not a suitable

---

[10] https://projectreactor.io/docs/core/milestone/reference/aboutDoc.html

subject for it. However, if you want to learn more about building reactive applications, the book *Pro Spring MVC with WebFlux*[11] (second edition) published by Apress in January 2021 has a few great chapters about building reactive applications with Spring and Project Reactor.

Important   What you must keep in mind is that reactive implementations are useless with implementations that are not reactive, so to build a truly reactive application, all layers must be reactive.

There is no use in designing and using reactive components with nonreactive components, because you might actually introduce failure points and slow things down. For example, if you are using an Oracle database, there is no point in defining a repository class that returns elements using reactive streams, because an Oracle database does not support reactive access. You would just be adding a reactive layer that adds extra implementation, because there are no real benefits in this case. But if your database of choice is MongoDB, you can use reactive programming confidently, because MongoDB databases support reactive access. Also, if you are building a web application with a ReactJS or Angular interface, you can design your controller classes to provide data reactively to be displayed by the interface.

The contents of this chapter can be summarized as follows:

- Reactive programming was explained.

- The behavior of reactive streams was explained.

- The JDK reactive streams support was covered.

- How to use the Reactive Streams Technology Compatibility Kit to test your reactive solution was addressed.

- A brief introduction to Project Reactor components for building reactive applications was provided.

---

[11] https://link.springer.com/book/10.1007/978-1-4842-5666-4

CHAPTER 13

Garbage Collection

When executing Java code, objects are created, used, and discarded repeatedly from memory. The process through which unused Java objects are discarded is called **memory management** but is most commonly known as **garbage collection (GC)**. Garbage collection was mentioned in **Chapter 5**, as it was necessary for explaining the difference between primitive and reference types, but in this chapter we will go deep *under the hood* of the JVM to resolve yet another mystery of a running Java application.

When the Java Garbage Collector does its job properly, the memory is cleaned up before new objects are created, and it does not fill up, so you could say that the memory allocated to a program is *recycled*. Programs of low complexity, like the ones we've been writing so far, do not require that much memory to function, but depending on their design (remember recursivity introduced in Chapter 4?), they could end up using more memory than available. In Java, the garbage collector runs automatically. In more low-level languages like C/ C++, there is no automatic memory management, and the developer is responsible for writing the code to allocate memory as needed and deallocate it when it is no longer necessary. Although it seems practical to have automatic memory management, the garbage collector can be a problem if managed incorrectly. This chapter provides enough information about the garbage collector to ensure that you know how to use it wisely and that when problems arise, at least you will have a good place to start fixing them.

Although some ways to tune the garbage collector will be introduced, keep in mind that garbage collector tuning should not be necessary. A program should be written in such a way that it creates only the objects that are needed to perform its function and references are managed correctly; estimations of memory capacity for the server to run the application should be done before the application is put into production, and the maximum amount of memory needed by it should be known and configured before that. If the memory allocated to a Java program is not enough, there is usually something rotten in the implementation.

833

© Iuliana Cosmina 2024
I. Cosmina, *Java 23 for Absolute Beginners*, https://doi.org/10.1007/979-8-8688-1041-1_13

Garbage Collection Basics

Java automatic garbage collection is one of the major features of the Java programming language. The JVM is a virtual machine used to execute Java programs, as mentioned at the beginning of this book. A Java program uses resources of the system that the JVM is running on top of, so it must have a way to release those resources safely. This job is done by the garbage collector.

The performance of a garbage collector is evaluated considering the following three factors:

- **Throughput**: The rate at which processes complete application work. Ideally the JVM should be spending more time running an application and less time performing garbage collection.

- **Memory footprint**: The amount of memory required by the garbage collector.

- **Pause time**: The length of time the application is stopped during a garbage collection.

To understand what the place of the garbage collector is among all JDK components, we must take a look at the JVM architecture[1].

Oracle HotSpot JVM Architecture

Over the years, some big companies have produced their own variations of the JVM (e.g., IBM), and now that Java is moving into the module age, with a rapid delivery style and a more expensive licensing model, more and more companies have decided to build their own version of the JVM (e.g., Azul, Amazon Corretto, GraalVM, and Eclipse OpenJ9)[2].

Under the new licensing model, Java Support is paid as of January 2019, for all LTS versions after the two-year grace period, so companies will eventually have to pay for the JDK running their Java-based software. The official Oracle JDK can be used on personal computers by developers who are learning to code or building small projects. However, running the resulting software on a server, accessing enterprise features such as full-fledged JMC, and turning that software profitable requires a paid subscription.

---

[1] https://www.oracle.com/java/technologies/whitepaper.html#:~:text=The%20Java%20HotSpot%20Virtual%20Machine,garbage%20collector%2C%20and%20adaptive%20optimizer
[2] https://en.wikipedia.org/wiki/List_of_Java_virtual_machines

Currently, the Oracle's HotSpot is still the most common JVM implementation being used by many applications. When it comes to garbage collection, this JVM provides a mature set of garbage collection options. An abstract representation of its architecture is depicted in Figure 13-1.

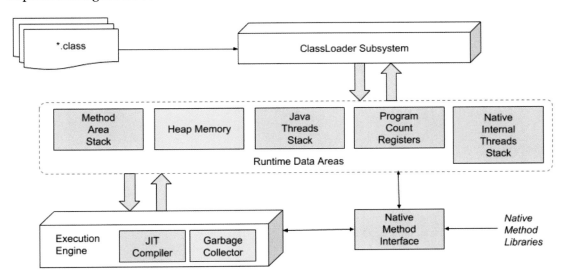

Figure 13-1. *Oracle HotSpot JVM architecture (abstract representation)*

The **heap** memory area is managed by the garbage collector and is split into multiple zones. Objects are moved between these zones until being discarded. The zones depicted in Figure 13-2 are for old-styles garbage collectors and the new style of garbage collector, which will probably follow the model of the current default garbage collector used by the JDK, the G1GC, that was introduced in JDK 8.

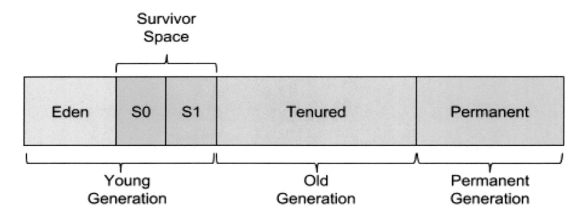

Older GCs: serial, parallel, CMS

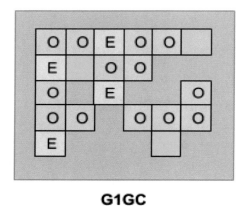

G1GC

Figure 13-2. *The heap structure*

The **G1GC** is a next-generation garbage collector, designed for machines with a lot of resources, which is why its approach to the partitioning of the heap is different. It is the default GC since Java 9. Its heap is partitioned into a set of equal-sized heap regions, each a contiguous range of virtual memory. Certain region sets are assigned the same roles (eden, survivor, old) as in the older collectors, but there is not a fixed size for them. This provides greater flexibility in memory usage. You can read more about the different types of garbage collectors in the next section, but for now the focus will remain on the heap memory and its zones, which are named **generations**.

When an application is running, objects created by it are stored in the **young generation area**. When an object is created, it starts its life in a subdivision of this generation named the **eden space**. When the eden space is filled, this triggers a **minor garbage collection (minor GC) run** that cleans up this area of unreferenced objects, and moves referenced objects to the **first survivor space (S0)**. The next time the eden space is filled, another minor GC run is triggered, which again deletes unreferenced objects, and referenced objects are moved to the **next survivor space (S1)**.

The objects in S0 have been there for a minor GC run, so their age is incremented. They are moved to S1 as well, so S0 and the eden can be cleaned up.

At the next minor GC run, the operation is performed again, but this time referenced objects are saved into the empty S0. The older objects from S1 have their age incremented and moved to S0 as well, so the S1 and eden can be cleaned up.

After the objects in survivor space reach a certain age (value-specific to each type garbage collector), they are moved to *the old generation space* during minor GC runs.

The previously described steps are depicted in Figure 13-3, and the objects o1 and o2 are aged until they are moved to the old generation area.

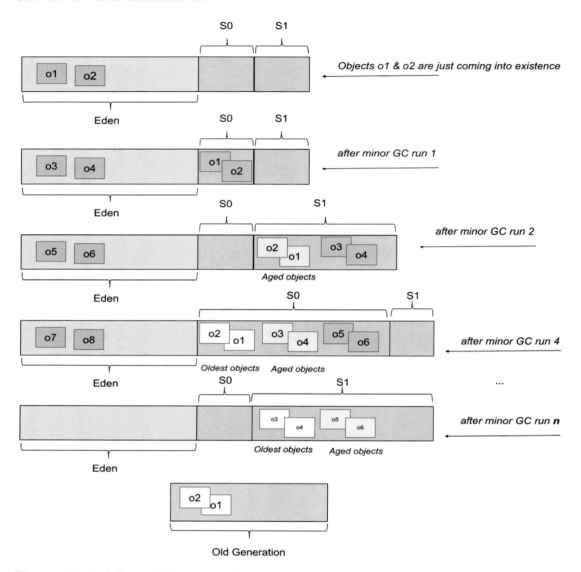

Figure 13-3. *Minor GC runs on the young generation space*

Minor GC collections will happen until the old generation space is filled. That is when a **major garbage collection (major GC) run** is triggered, which will delete unreferenced objects and will compact the memory, moving objects around so that the empty memory left is one big compact space.

The minor garbage collection event is a "stop the world" event. This process basically takes over the run of the application and pauses its execution, so it can free the memory. As the young generation space is quite small (as you will see this in the next section), the application pause is usually negligible. If no memory can be reclaimed from the young generation area after a minor GC run takes place, a major GC run is triggered.

The **permanent generation** area is reserved for JVM metadata such as classes and methods. This area is cleaned too from time to time to remove classes that are no longer used in the application. The cleanup of this area is triggered when there are no more objects in the heap.

The garbage collection process just described is specific to generational garbage collectors, such as the G1GC. Before JDK 8, garbage collection was done using an older garbage collector that used an algorithm called **Concurrent Mark Sweep**. This type of garbage collector ran in parallel with the application and marked used and unused zones of memory. Then it would delete unreferenced objects and would compact the memory into a contiguous zone, by moving objects around. This process was quite inefficient and time-consuming. As more and more objects were created, the garbage collection took more and more time to be performed, but as most objects are quite short-lived, this was not really a problem. So the CMS garbage collector was okay for a while.

The G1GC has a similar approach, but after the marking phase is finished, G1 focuses on regions that are mostly empty to recover as much unused memory as possible. That is why this garbage collector is also named **Garbage First**. G1 also uses a pause prediction model to decide how many memory regions can be processed based on the pause time set for the application. Objects from the processed region are copied to a single region of the heap, thus realizing a memory compaction at the same time. Also, G1GC does not have a fixed size for the eden and survivor spaces; it decides their size after every minor GC run.

How Many Garbage Collectors Are There?

The Oracle HotSpot JVM provides the following types of garbage collectors:

- **The serial collector**: All garbage collection events are conducted serially in one thread. Memory compaction happens after each garbage collection.

- **The parallel collector**: Multiple threads are used for minor garbage collection. A single thread is used for a major garbage collection and old generation compaction.

- **Garbage First (G1)**: Introduced in Oracle JDK 7, update 4, it was designed to permanently replace the CMS GC and is suitable for applications that can operate concurrently with the CMS collector, that need memory compaction, that need more predictable GC pause durations, and that do not require a much larger heap. The G1 collector is a server-style garbage collector, targeted for multiprocessor machines with large memories, but considering that most laptops now have at least eight cores and 16GB RAM, it is quite suitable for them as well. G1 has both concurrent (runs along with application threads; e.g., refinement, marking, cleanup) and parallel (multithreaded; e.g., stop-the-world events) phases. Full garbage collections are still single threaded, but if tuned properly your applications should avoid full garbage collections.

- **Z Garbage Collector (ZGC)**: This is a scalable low-latency garbage collector introduced in Java 11. ZGC performs all expensive work concurrently, without stopping the execution of application threads for more than 10ms, which makes it suitable for applications that require low latency and/or use a huge heap (multiple terabytes)

- **Shenandoah Garbage Collector**: Shenandoah is the low-pause-time garbage collector, introduced in Java 12, that reduces GC pause times by performing more garbage collection work concurrently with the running Java program. Shenandoah does the bulk of GC work concurrently, including the concurrent compaction, which means its pause times are no longer directly proportional to the size of the heap.

- **Epsilon no-op collector**: Introduced in Java 11, this type of collector is actually a dummy GC that does not recycle or clean up the memory. When the heap is full, the JVM just shuts down. This type of collector can be used for performance tests, memory allocation analysis, VM interface testing, and extremely short-lived jobs and applications that are super-limited when it comes to memory usage. Evidently, developers must estimate the application memory footprint as exactly as possible.

We've listed the garbage collector types, but how do we know which is the one used by our local JVM? There is more than one way. The simplest way is to add `-verbose:gc` as a VM option when running a simple class with a `main()` method.

Using Java 23, without any other configuration, the following output is shown:

```
[0.011s][info][gc] Using G1
```

Note   The simplest way to run a Java class with VM options is to create an IntelliJ IDEA launcher and introduce the VM options in the appropriate text field. The other way is to run a simple class from the command line and add the arguments to the command. The following example reuses the `Practice01.java` file introduced in **Chapter 2**:

```
java --enable-preview -Xlog:gc* Practice01.java
```

Caution   Using a launcher avoids complications that might be caused by the shell used to execute commands. For example, Zsh (or Z shell) requires the * (asterisk) to be escaped; otherwise, it will not execute the command and will complain that `zsh: no matches found: -Xlog:gc*`.

As you've read, the G1 garbage collector is used by default. To show even more details of this garbage collector, `-Xlog:gc*` can be added to the VM arguments when running a Java class, as shown in Listing 13-1.

Listing 13-1. Showing G1GC Details Using `-verbose:gc` `-Xlog:gc*` VM Options When Running ShowGCDemo

```
[0.015s][info][gc,init] CardTable entry size: 512     # (1)
[0.014s][info][gc      ] Using G1
[0.017s][info][gc,init] Version: 23+37-2369 (release)
[0.017s][info][gc,init] CPUs: 16 total, 16 available
[0.017s][info][gc,init] Memory: 32768M
[0.017s][info][gc,init] Large Page Support: Disabled
[0.017s][info][gc,init] NUMA Support: Disabled
```

```
[0.017s][info][gc,init] Compressed Oops: Enabled (Zero based)
```
[0.017s][info][gc,init] Heap Region Size: 4M # (2)
```
[0.017s][info][gc,init] Heap Min Capacity: 8M
[0.017s][info][gc,init] Heap Initial Capacity: 512M
```
[0.017s][info][gc,init] Heap Max Capacity: 8G # (3)
```
[0.017s][info][gc,init] Pre-touch: Disabled
[0.017s][info][gc,init] Parallel Workers: 13
[0.017s][info][gc,init] Concurrent Workers: 3
[0.017s][info][gc,init] Concurrent Refinement Workers: 13
[0.017s][info][gc,init] Periodic GC: Disabled
[0.030s][info][gc,metaspace] CDS archive(s) mapped at: [0x000000012b000000-
0x000000012bd94000-0x000000012bd94000), size 14237696, SharedBaseAddress:
0x000000012b000000, ArchiveRelocationMode: 1.
[0.030s][info][gc,metaspace] Compressed class space mapped at: 0x000000012
c000000-0x000000016c000000, reserved size: 1073741824
[0.030s][info][gc,metaspace] Narrow klass base: 0x000000012b000000, Narrow
klass shift: 0, Narrow klass range: 0x100000000
... Hey ma' look the GC! ...
[0.209s][info][gc,heap,exit] Heap
```
[0.209s][info][gc,heap,exit] garbage-first heap   total reserved
8388608K, committed 528384K, used 5236K [0x0000000600000000,
0x0000000800000000) # (4)
```
[0.209s][info][gc,heap,exit]   region size 4096K, 1 young (4096K), 0
survivors (OK)
[0.209s][info][gc,heap,exit]  Metaspace       used 996K, committed 1152K,
reserved 1114112K
[0.209s][info][gc,heap,exit]   class space     used 85K, committed 192K,
reserved 1048576K
```

In the Java HotSpot VM, the GC uses a data structure called a *card table*. The card table speeds up finding references that are no longer used. The old generation is split into 512-byte chunks called **cards**, as shown in the log line labeled with **(1)** in Listing 13-1. JDK 18 introduced configurable card table card sizes. The available card sizes are 128, 256, 512 (default), and 1024 (the last is 64 bits only). To customize the card size, add VM option -XX:GCCardSizeInBytes=<card-size> when running the ShowGCDemo class, and the first console log message should reflect the desired card size.

We can see in Listing 13-1 that the memory region size is 4M **(2)**, the heap maximum size is 8G **(3)**, size and occupation for each generation **(4)**.

In **Chapter 5**, the java -XX:+PrintFlagsFinal -version command was introduced to show all JVM flags. Filtering the results returned by the "GC" and "NewSize" shows all the GC-specific flags and their values. There are quite a few of them, and they are shown in Listing 13-2.

Listing 13-2. Showing G1GC Flags Using java -XX:+PrintFlagsFinal -version | grep 'GC\|NewSize'

```
> java -XX:+PrintFlagsFinal -version | grep 'GC\|NewSize'
    uintx AdaptiveSizeMajorGCDecayTimeScale  = 10      {product} {default}
     uint ConcGCThreads                      = 3       {product} {ergonomic}
     bool DisableExplicitGC                  = false {product} {default}
     uint GCCardSizeInBytes                  = 512     {product} {default} # (1)
     uint GCDrainStackTargetSize             = 64      {product} {default}
     uint GCHeapFreeLimit                    = 2       {product} {default}
    uintx GCPauseIntervalMillis              = 201     {product} {default}
     uint GCTimeLimit                        = 98      {product} {default}
     uint GCTimeRatio                        = 12      {product} {default}
    uintx MaxGCPauseMillis                   = 200     {product} {default}
   size_t MaxNewSize                         = 5150605312  {product} {ergonomic}
   size_t NewSize                            = 1363144   {product}
{default}  # (2)
     uint ParallelGCThreads                  = 13        {product} {default}
     bool PrintGC                            = false     {product} {default}
     bool PrintGCDetails                     = false     {product} {default}
     bool UseG1GC                            = true      {product}
                                                         {ergonomic} # (3)
     bool UseGCOverheadLimit                 = true      {product} {default}
     bool UseMaximumCompactionOnSystemGC = true      {product} {default}
     bool UseParallelGC                      = false     {product} {default}
     bool UseSerialGC                        = false     {product} {default}
     bool UseShenandoahGC                    = false     {product} {default}
     bool UseZGC                             = false     {product} {default}
 # some logs omitted
```

843

The UseG1GC is set to true by default, which means when the JVM is used to execute a Java application, the G1 garbage collector is used. The "NewSize" filter picks up flags with values relevant for the young generation size. And the default card size is shown too.

All these flags (and a few not depicted here) can be used separately as VM options preceded by -XX:+ when running an application to customize the GC behavior or show extra details in the logs.

The last entries in the log show the options to use to enable a specific GC. For example, if we run the ShowGCDemo class and add the -XX:+UseSerialGC -verbose:gc -Xlog:gc* VM options, the console log produced will look differently, as shown in Listing 13-3 (notice the lack of parallel, concurrent workers and the different heap structure).

Listing 13-3. Showing Serial GC Details

```
[0.016s][info][gc,init] CardTable entry size: 512
[0.017s][info][gc       ] Using Serial
[0.019s][info][gc,init] Version: 23+37-2369 (release)
[0.019s][info][gc,init] CPUs: 16 total, 16 available
[0.019s][info][gc,init] Memory: 32768M
[0.019s][info][gc,init] Large Page Support: Disabled
[0.019s][info][gc,init] NUMA Support: Disabled
[0.019s][info][gc,init] Compressed Oops: Enabled (Zero based)
[0.019s][info][gc,init] Heap Min Capacity: 8M
[0.019s][info][gc,init] Heap Initial Capacity: 512M
[0.019s][info][gc,init] Heap Max Capacity: 8G
[0.019s][info][gc,init] Pre-touch: Disabled
[0.034s][info][gc,metaspace] CDS archive(s) mapped at: [0x0000000127000000-
0x0000000127d94000-0x0000000127d94000), size 14237696, SharedBaseAddress:
0x0000000127000000, ArchiveRelocationMode: 1.
[0.034s][info][gc,metaspace] Compressed class space mapped at:
0x0000000128000000-0x0000000168000000, reserved size: 1073741824
[0.034s][info][gc,metaspace] Narrow klass base: 0x0000000127000000, Narrow
klass shift: 0, Narrow klass range: 0x100000000
... Hey ma' look the GC! ...
[0.229s][info][gc,heap,exit] Heap
```

[0.229s][info][gc,heap,exit]   def new generation   total 157248K, used 16773K [0x0000000600000000, 0x000000060aaa0000, 0x00000006aaaa0000)

[0.229s][info][gc,heap,exit]   eden space 139776K,   12% used [0x0000000600000000, 0x0000000601061590, 0x0000000608880000)

[0.229s][info][gc,heap,exit]   from space 17472K,   0% used [0x0000000608880000, 0x0000000608880000, 0x0000000609990000)

[0.229s][info][gc,heap,exit]   to   space 17472K,   0% used [0x0000000609990000, 0x0000000609990000, 0x000000060aaa0000)

[0.229s][info][gc,heap,exit]   tenured generation   total 349568K, used 1140K [0x00000006aaaa0000, 0x00000006c0000000, 0x0000000800000000)

[0.229s][info][gc,heap,exit]   the space 349568K,   0% used [0x00000006aaaa0000, 0x00000006aabbd0b0, 0x00000006c0000000)

[0.229s][info][gc,heap,exit]   Metaspace   used 1008K, committed 1152K, reserved 1114112K

[0.229s][info][gc,heap,exit]   class space   used 86K, committed 192K, reserved 1048576K

Use -XX:+UseParallelGC to use the parallel GC. In this case adding the -verbose:gc -Xlog:gc*VM options as well produces the output in Listing 13-4 (notice the parallel workers and the different heap structure.)

Listing 13-4. Showing Parallel GC Details

[0.013s][info][gc,init] CardTable entry size: 512

[0.013s][info][gc   ] Using Parallel

[0.015s][info][gc,init] Version: 23+37-2369 (release)

[0.015s][info][gc,init] CPUs: 16 total, 16 available

[0.015s][info][gc,init] Memory: 32768M

[0.015s][info][gc,init] Large Page Support: Disabled

[0.015s][info][gc,init] NUMA Support: Disabled

[0.015s][info][gc,init] Compressed Oops: Enabled (Zero based)

[0.015s][info][gc,init] Alignments: Space 512K, Generation 512K, Heap 2M

[0.015s][info][gc,init] Heap Min Capacity: 8M

[0.015s][info][gc,init] Heap Initial Capacity: 512M

[0.015s][info][gc,init] Heap Max Capacity: 8G

[0.015s][info][gc,init] Pre-touch: Disabled

[0.015s][info][gc,init] Parallel Workers: 13

[0.028s][info][gc,metaspace] CDS archive(s) mapped at: [0x0000000131000000-0x0000000131d94000-0x0000000131d94000), size 14237696, SharedBaseAddress: 0x0000000131000000, ArchiveRelocationMode: 1.

[0.028s][info][gc,metaspace] Compressed class space mapped at: 0x0000000132000000-0x0000000172000000, reserved size: 1073741824

[0.028s][info][gc,metaspace] Narrow klass base: 0x0000000131000000, Narrow klass shift: 0, Narrow klass range: 0x100000000

... Hey ma' look the GC! ...

[0.189s][info][gc,heap,exit] Heap

[0.189s][info][gc,heap,exit]   PSYoungGen   total 153088K, used 15790K [0x0000000755580000, 0x0000000760000000, 0x0000000800000000)

[0.189s][info][gc,heap,exit]   eden space 131584K, 12% used [0x0000000755580000,0x00000007564eb980,0x000000075d600000)

[0.189s][info][gc,heap,exit]   from space 21504K, 0% used [0x000000075eb00000,0x000000075eb00000,0x0000000760000000)

[0.189s][info][gc,heap,exit]   to space 21504K, 0% used [0x000000075d600000,0x000000075d600000,0x000000075eb00000)

[0.189s][info][gc,heap,exit] ParOldGen   total 349696K, used 1140K [0x0000000600000000, 0x0000000615580000, 0x0000000755580000)

[0.189s][info][gc,heap,exit]   object space 349696K, 0% used [0x0000000600000000,0x000000060011d0b0,0x0000000615580000)

[0.189s][info][gc,heap,exit] Metaspace   used 997K, committed 1152K, reserved 1114112K

[0.189s][info][gc,heap,exit]   class space   used 85K, committed 192K, reserved 1048576K

Although it is enabled by default, you would use -XX:+UseG1GC to enable the default garbage collector (already covered).

As previously introduced, Shenandoah is the low-pause-time garbage collector that reduces GC pause times by performing more garbage collection work concurrently with the running Java program. The -XX:+UseShenandoahGC option enables the use of Shenandoah GC.

> **Caution**   Although the flag for Shenandoah exists, Oracle has chosen not to build Shenandoah, instead directing all focus to G1's successor, ZGC. However, Shenandoah is available in various OpenJDK builds listed on the Shenandoah official documentation[3].

The -XX:+UseZGC VM option enables the ZGC. In this case adding the -verbose:gc -Xlog:gc* VM options as well produces the output in Listing 13-5 (notice the GC and Runtime workers and the different heap structure).

Listing 13-5. Showing ZGC Details

```
[0.015s][info][gc,init] Initializing The Z Garbage Collector  [0.015s]
[info][gc,init] Version: 23+37-2369 (release)
[0.015s][info][gc,init] NUMA Support: Disabled
[0.015s][info][gc,init] CPUs: 16 total, 16 available
[0.016s][info][gc,init] Memory: 32768M
[0.016s][info][gc,init] Large Page Support: Disabled
[0.016s][info][gc,init] Address Space Type: Contiguous/Unrestricted/
Complete
[0.016s][info][gc,init] Address Space Size: 131072M
[0.017s][info][gc,init] Min Capacity: 8M
[0.017s][info][gc,init] Initial Capacity: 512M
[0.017s][info][gc,init] Max Capacity: 8192M
[0.017s][info][gc,init] Soft Max Capacity: 7372M
[0.017s][info][gc,init] Medium Page Size: 32M
# .. additional log entries omitted ..
[0.020s][info][gc,init] GC Workers Max: 4 (dynamic)
[0.020s][info][gc,init] Runtime Workers: 10
[0.021s][info][gc    ] Using The Z Garbage Collector [0.076s][info]
[gc,metaspace] CDS archive(s) mapped at: [0x000000071f000000-0x
000000071fd94000-0x000000071fd94000), size 14237696, SharedBaseAddress:
0x000000071f000000, ArchiveRelocationMode: 1.
```

---

[3] https://wiki.openjdk.java.net/display/shenandoah/Main#Main-JDKSupport

```
[0.076s][info][gc,metaspace] Compressed class space mapped at:
0x0000000720000000-0x0000000760000000, reserved size: 1073741824
[0.076s][info][gc,metaspace] Narrow klass base: 0x000000071f000000, Narrow
klass shift: 0, Narrow klass range: 0x100000000
... Hey ma' look the GC! ...
[0.259s][info][gc,exit      ] Stopping ZGC
[0.259s][info][gc,stats     ] === Garbage Collection Statistics ============
========================================================
# .. statistics data omitted for brevity ..
[0.260s][info][gc,heap,exit] Heap
[0.260s][info][gc,heap,exit]  ZHeap            used 8M, capacity 512M, max
capacity 8192M
[0.260s][info][gc,heap,exit]  Metaspace        used 1013K, committed 1216K,
reserved 1114112K
[0.260s][info][gc,heap,exit]   class space     used 86K, committed 192K,
reserved 1048576K
```

Use the -XX:+UseEpsilonGC VM option to use the no-op garbage collector. Since this GC is experimental, the -XX:+UnlockExperimentalVMOptions VM option is also required to unlock experimental features. Adding the -verbose:gc -Xlog:gc* VM options as well produces the output in Listing 13-6 (notice the lack of any workers, and the TLAB options).

Listing 13-6. Showing Epsilon GC Details

[0.013s][info][gc] Using Epsilon
```
[0.013s][info][gc,init] Version: 23+37-2369 (release)
[0.013s][info][gc,init] CPUs: 16 total, 16 available
[0.013s][info][gc,init] Memory: 32768M
[0.013s][info][gc,init] Large Page Support: Disabled
[0.013s][info][gc,init] NUMA Support: Disabled
[0.013s][info][gc,init] Compressed Oops: Enabled (Zero based)
[0.013s][info][gc,init] Heap Min Capacity: 6656K
[0.013s][info][gc,init] Heap Initial Capacity: 512M
[0.013s][info][gc,init] Heap Max Capacity: 8G
[0.013s][info][gc,init] Pre-touch: Disabled
```

[0.013s][warning][gc,init] Consider setting -Xms equal to -Xmx to avoid resizing hiccups

[0.013s][warning][gc,init] Consider enabling -XX:+AlwaysPreTouch to avoid memory commit hiccups

[0.013s][info   ][gc,init] TLAB Size Max: 4M

[0.013s][info   ][gc,init] TLAB Size Elasticity: 1.10x

[0.013s][info   ][gc,init] TLAB Size Decay Time: 1000ms

[0.024s][info   ][gc,metaspace] CDS archive(s) mapped at: [0x0000000126000000-0x0000000126d94000-0x0000000126d94000), size 14237696, SharedBaseAddress: 0x0000000126000000, ArchiveRelocationMode: 1.

[0.024s][info   ][gc,metaspace] Compressed class space mapped at: 0x0000000127000000-0x0000000167000000, reserved size: 1073741824

[0.024s][info   ][gc,metaspace] Narrow klass base: 0x0000000126000000, Narrow klass shift: 0, Narrow klass range: 0x100000000

... Hey ma' look the GC! ...

[0.186s][info   ][gc,heap,exit] Heap

[0.186s][info   ][gc,heap,exit] Epsilon Heap

[0.186s][info   ][gc,heap,exit] Allocation space:

[0.186s][info   ][gc,heap,exit] space 524288K,   0% used [0x0000000600000000, 0x000000060031fe10, 0x0000000620000000)

[0.186s][info   ][gc,heap,exit] Metaspace   used 990K, committed 1152K, reserved 1114112K

[0.186s][info   ][gc,heap,exit]   class space   used 84K, committed 192K, reserved 1048576K

[0.186s][info   ][gc   ] Heap: 8192M reserved, 512M (6.25%) committed, 3199K (0.04%) used

[0.186s][info   ][gc,metaspace] Metaspace: 1088M reserved, 1152K (0.10%) committed, 994K (0.09%) used

The data printed for these GCs has common elements, such as the initial size of heap, which will always be 512M at the start of the application and has a maximum size of 8GB **on my computer**. The eden and the young generation differ between them as well, the G1GC using just 4096K for the young generation, whereas the ParallelGC requires 153088K (a lot more).

The most interesting here is the Epsilon garbage collector because, as expected, it does not have a heap split into generation areas, as this type of garbage collector does not perform garbage collection at all. **TLAB** is an acronym for **Thread Local Allocation Buffer**, which is a memory area where objects are stored. Only bigger objects are stored outside of TLABs. The TLABs are dynamically resized during the execution for each thread individually. So, if a thread allocates very much memory, the new TLABs that it gets from the heap will increase in size. The minimum size of a TLAB can be controlled using the VM -XX:MinTLABSize option.

For the small empty class that we ran with the previous VM options, this output is not really relevant. However, you can play with these options when running the code presented in the next sections, because that is when the statistics printed here have some relevance.

Also, there is a VM option named -XX:+PrintCommandLineFlags that can be used when a class is run to depict configurations of the garbage collector, as the number of threads it makes use of, heap size, and so on. These options are shown in Listing 13-7.

Listing 13-7. G1GC VM Options

```
-XX:ConcGCThreads=3
-XX:G1ConcRefinementThreads=13
-XX:InitialHeapSize=536870912
-XX:MarkStackSize=4194304
-XX:MaxHeapSize=8589934592
-XX:MinHeapSize=6815736
-XX:+PrintCommandLineFlags
-XX:ReservedCodeCacheSize=251658240
-XX:+SegmentedCodeCache
-XX:+UseCompressedOops
-XX:+UseG1GC
```

Most of these VM options have obvious names that allow developers to infer what they are used for; for those that do not have obvious names, the official documentation from Oracle provides the answers. If you ever need to dissect the Oracle memory management, there are quite a few good official Oracle articles about this topic[4].

---

[4] For example, https://www.oracle.com/java/technologies/javase/javase-core-technologies-apis.html

Working with Garbage Collection from the Code

For most applications, garbage collection is not something a developer must really consider. The JVM starts a GC thread from time to time, which does its job usually without hindering the execution of the application. For developers who want to have more than Java basic skills, understanding how the Java garbage collection works and how it can be tuned is a must. The first thing a developer must accept about Java garbage collection is that it cannot be controlled at runtime. As you will see in the next section, there is a way to suggest to the JVM that some memory cleaning is necessary, but there is no guarantee that a memory cleaning will actually be performed. The only thing that can be done from the code is to configure some code to be run when an object is discarded.

Using the `finalize()` Method

As introduced back in **Chapter 4**, every Java class is automatically a subclass of the JDK `java.lang.Object` class. This class is at the root of the JDK hierarchy and is the root of all classes in an application. It provides quite a few useful methods that can be extended or overwritten to implement behavior specific to the subclass. The `equals()`, `hashCode()`, and `toString()` methods have already been covered in previous chapters. The `finalize()` method was deprecated in Java 9, but it has not yet been removed from the JDK in the interest of backward compatibility.

Caution   The finalization mechanism is somewhat problematic. Finalization can lead to performance issues, deadlocks, and hangs. Errors in finalizers can lead to resource leaks, and there is no way to cancel finalization if it is no longer necessary.

Since you might end up working with Java projects using earlier versions of the JDK, it is good to know that the `finalize()` method exists, in case you might ever need it, or just to know where to look for weird bugs.

This method is called by the garbage collector when there are no longer any references to that object in the code. Before we move forward, take a look at the code in Listing 13-8.

Listing 13-8. Class Generating Infinite Number of Singer Instances

```java
package com.apress.bgn.thirteen;

import com.apress.bgn.thirteen.util.NameGenerator;
import org.slf4j.Logger;
import org.slf4j.LoggerFactory;

import java.time.LocalDate;

import static com.apress.bgn.thirteen.util.NameGenerator.RND;

public class InfiniteSingerGenerator {
    private static final Logger LOGGER = LoggerFactory.getLogger(Infinite
                                    SingerGenerator.class);
    private static final NameGenerator nameGenerator = new NameGenerator();
    void main() {
        while (true) {
            genSinger();
        }
    }

    private static void genSinger() {
        Singer s = new Singer(nameGenerator.genName(), RND.nextDouble(),
                    LocalDate.now());
        LOGGER.info("JVM created: {}", s.getName());
    }
}
```

The action performed by the code in Listing 13-8 should be obvious even without knowing how the NameGenerator or the Singer class look. The main method calls the genSinger() method in an infinite loop. This means that infinite Singer instances are created. So what happens? Will the code run? For how long? If you can answer these questions in your mind, *my work here is complete; you can stop reading the book now!*

Recall that **Chapter 5** included some figures representing the memory contents for a small program. Similarly, Figure 13-4 represents how the Java heap and stack memory might look during the execution of the program in Listing 13-8.

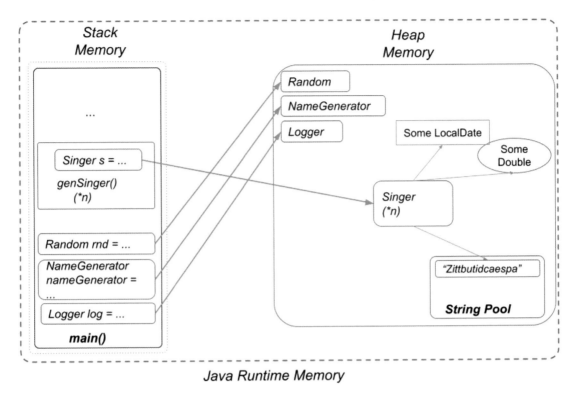

Figure 13-4. *Java stack and heap memory during execution of the*
`InfiniteSingerGenerator` *class*

Only one `genSinger()` call is represented and only one `Singer` instance, for obvious reasons. As you can see, when the `main(..)` method is called, references to the static instances are created; that will be relevant to the program until the end of its execution. Then, `genSinger()` methods are called. Each of these methods has its own stack where it saves references to the objects created within the context of that method, in this case the `Singer` instance. This reference is used just to print the name of the `Singer` instance that was created in the body of this method. Then the method exists, without returning the reference. This means that the instance that was created is no longer necessary, as it was created to be used only in the context of this method.

When the execution of the `genSinger()` method ends, the reference to the `Singer` is discarded from the stack. The `Singer` instance still exists, in the heap memory, but can no longer be accessed from the program, thus it is no longer necessary to it. It now just keeps a memory block occupied with its own contents, its references to other instances, in this case, a `String`, a `Double`, and a `LocalDate`.

Considering that the genString() is called an infinite number of times (represented by (*n) in Figure 13-4), more Singer instances will be created. They will keep the memory occupied, and the program will be unable at some point to create others, because there will be no more memory available.

This is where the garbage collector comes into the picture. The Singer instances that are no longer being referenced from the program, and thus unreachable, are considered garbage (now you know where the name comes from) because they are no longer necessary, and the memory can be safely cleaned up. The GC is a cleanup thread that runs in parallel with the main execution thread and from time to time starts deleting the unreferenced objects in the heap memory. And because the finalize() method is still available for use, we will overwrite it for the Singer type to print a log message, so we can see in our console directly when the garbage collector is destroying an instance, because before that we will call the finalize() method. The code snippet in Listing 13-9 depicts our Singer instance.

Listing 13-9. The Singer Class with the Overridden finalize() Method

```
package com.apress.bgn.thirteen;

import org.slf4j.Logger;
import org.slf4j.LoggerFactory;

import java.time.LocalDate;
import java.util.Objects;

public class Singer {
    private static final Logger LOGGER = LoggerFactory.getLogger
                                        (Singer.class);
    private static final long serialVersionUID = 42L;
    private final long birthtime;

    private String name;

    private Double rating;

    private LocalDate birthDate;

    public Singer(String name, Double rating, LocalDate birthDate) {
        this.name = name;
        this.rating = rating;
```

```
        this.birthDate = birthDate;
        this.birthtime = System.nanoTime();
    }

    // some code omitted

    @Override
    protected void finalize() throws Throwable {
        try {
            long deathtime = System.nanoTime();
            long lifespan = (deathtime - birthtime) / 1_000_000_000;
            LOGGER.info("GC Destroyed: {} after {} seconds", name,
            lifespan);
        } finally {
            super.finalize();
        }
    }
}
```

The field `birthtime` was added just to be able to calculate the time that passes between when the constructor for an instance is called and the time the garbage collector calls the `finalize()` method. As the time is counted in nanoseconds, we are dividing the difference by pow(10, 9) to get the time in seconds.

The code sample used in this section gives the garbage collector a lot of work to do, as every `Singer` instance being created is being used very little before being discarded. If you run the code, you will see a lot of log messages in the console: first a lot of messages about objects being created, and then, if you wait a few seconds, messages about objects being discarded. All output is directed to a file, because the IntelliJ IDEA console is based on a buffer that resets from time to time to prevent the editor from crashing. You will have to stop the program manually, because the `while (true)` never ends, because its condition will never evaluate to `false`. After you stop the program, you will notice a log file at the following location: `/chapter13/out/gc.log`. If you don't, modify the IntelliJ IDEA launcher for this class and add the following VM option:

`-Dlogback.configurationFile=chapter13/src/main/resources/logback.xml`

Then, run it again.

The gc.log contents should look a lot like the snippet depicted in Listing 13-10.

Listing 13-10. The gc.log File Showing the finalize() Method in Class Singer Being Called

```
INFO  c.a.b.t.InfiniteSingerGenerator - JVM created: Kygsmwslzpfsrso
INFO  c.a.b.t.InfiniteSingerGenerator - JVM created: Uuiyihrmq gohll
INFO  c.a.b.t.InfiniteSingerGenerator - JVM created: Elpeyhru eizdpc
INFO  c.a.b.t.InfiniteSingerGenerator - JVM created: Jlblklupwdkyvkw
INFO  c.a.b.t.Singer - GC Destroyed: Agzdgjwvrzeerzw after 0 seconds
INFO  c.a.b.t.InfiniteSingerGenerator - JVM created: Fzgcnjrqqykvjab
INFO  c.a.b.t.Singer - GC Destroyed: Jyyfhkzagazyiny after 0 seconds
INFO  c.a.b.t.InfiniteSingerGenerator - JVM created: Lydeqzjbgcamrfz
INFO  c.a.b.t.InfiniteSingerGenerator - JVM created: Mgogeuokjbrgwaa
INFO  c.a.b.t.Singer - GC Destroyed: Bzwwqkdeykcpefs after 0 seconds
INFO  c.a.b.t.InfiniteSingerGenerator - JVM created: Ieczaazifjehhkv
INFO  c.a.b.t.Singer - GC Destroyed: Zlzoaufqzymepko after 0 seconds
INFO  c.a.b.t.InfiniteSingerGenerator - JVM created: Q bmeugibk eezo
INFO  c.a.b.t.Singer - GC Destroyed: Lqzdgeqqguitbgg after 1 seconds
INFO  c.a.b.t.Singer - GC Destroyed: Ddpzqlbiryelzvr after 1 seconds
INFO  c.a.b.t.Singer - GC Destroyed: Ozkzfubi  vpmj  after 1 seconds
INFO  c.a.b.t.InfiniteSingerGenerator - JVM created: Uegz isigjcrlfj
...
```

When you have the file, you can open it and start analyzing its contents, but because IntelliJ IDEA might not open such a big file, try to open it with a specialized text editor like Notepad++ or Sublime. Or if you use a Unix/Linux operating system, just open your console and use the grep command like this:

```
grep -a 'seconds' gc.log
```

This will display all log entries printed when the finalize() method is called. Then you can select the name of an instance and do something like this:

```
> grep -a 'Fmsnwrtbuldmnjs' gc.log
INFO  c.a.b.t.InfiniteSingerGenerator - JVM created: Fmsnwrtbuldmnjs
INFO  c.a.b.t.Singer - GC Destroyed: Fmsnwrtbuldmnjs after 1 seconds
```

As you can see, the time it takes for a `Singer` instance to be deleted from the heap varies, and this is because the GC is called randomly; the developer has no control over it. There is a way to explicitly request garbage collection to be done...well, two ways. You can call `System.gc()` or `Runtime.getRuntime().gc()`. Note that `System.gc()` calls `Runtime.getRuntime().gc()` anyway.

This doesn't mean that the GC will immediately start cleaning up the memory, though. It is more like a suggestion to the JVM that it should make an effort to recycle unused objects and reclaim unused memory, because it is needed.

Now, back to the `finalize()` method. It was mentioned that it was marked as deprecated in Java 9. This method is meant to be overridden by classes that handle resources that are stored outside the heap. The obvious example here is the I/O handling classes, used to read resources as files or URLs and databases. The `finalize()` method would be called by the JVM when an object can no longer be accessed by any living thread of the running application. This is to make sure that those resources were released and available for other external and unrelated programs to use.

Info   In older versions of Apache Tomcat (a Java-based web server), on Windows there was a bug related to the release of resources. When the server would crash or would be stopped forcefully, it couldn't be started again because some of its log file handlers were not released properly, and the new server instance could not get access to them to start writing the new log entries.*(This is an observation from my personal experience when working with Apache Tomcat on Windows, from a long, long time ago.)*

With the introduction of the `java.lang.AutoCloseable` interface in JDK 7, the `finalize()` method became less and less used. A few problems with this method have been mentioned previously, but the following list gives more context:

- The JVM cannot guarantee which thread will call this method for any given object, so any thread that has access to it can call it, and we might end up with resources being released while the object is still necessary. The method is public, and thus it can be called explicitly in the code, even if it is supposed to be called only by the GC thread.

- If the custom implementation of `finalize()` is not correct, it could throw exceptions or not release resources properly.

- The finalize() method should be called only once, by the JVM, but this cannot be guaranteed.

- finalize() calls are not automatically chained, so a custom implementation of a finalize() method must always explicitly call the finalize() method of the superclass.

- As previously mentioned, once a finalize() is called, there is no way to stop the method from executing or undo its effect, so you are basically left with a reference to an object that no longer exists.

- As you have probably figured out by now, there is a lot of freedom given to the developer when it comes to implementing this method, and this means there is a lot of room for errors to happen.

This list summarizes why the finalization mechanism in Java is flawed and was deprecated in JDK 9 to discourage its use. Improper finalize() implementations could lead to any of the following:

- Memory leaks (memory contents are not discarded)

- Deadlocks (resource is blocked by two processes)

- Hangs (process is in a waiting state it cannot go out of)

To help with memory management, the java.lang.ref.Cleaner class was introduced in Java 9. Before getting into that, I must show you how to check out the status of your memory programmatically.

Heap Memory Statistics

The Runtime class is quite useful when trying to interact with the internals of the JVM while a program is running. As previously mentioned in this chapter, its gc() method can be called to suggest to the JVM that the memory should be cleaned, and a few chapters ago we used methods in this class to start processes from the Java code. There are three methods in this class that are useful to see the status of the memory assigned to a Java program:

- runtime.maxMemory() returns the maximum amount of memory the JVM will attempt to use for its heap, in case of need. The value returned by this method varies from machine to machine and is set implicitly to a quarter of the total existing RAM memory on the machine, unless it is set explicitly by using the JVM option -Xmx followed by the amount of memory; for example, -Xmx8G will allow the JVM to use a maximum of 8GB of memory.

- runtime.totalMemory() returns the total amount of memory of the JVM. The value returned by this method also varies from machine to machine, and it is implementation-dependent unless explicitly set by using the JVM option -Xms followed by the amount of memory; for example, -Xms1G will tell the JVM that the initial size of its heap memory should be 1GB of memory.

- runtime.freeMemory() returns an approximation of the amount of free memory for the Java Virtual Machine. Using the runtime. totalMemory() and runtime.freeMemory() methods, we can write some code to check how much of our memory is occupied at various times during the execution of the program. For this a class named MemAudit is created that will use the current logger to print memory values. The implementation of this class is shown in Listing 13-11.

Listing 13-11. The MemAudit Class Showing Memory Statistics During the Execution of a Java Application

```
package com.apress.bgn.thirteen.util;

import org.slf4j.Logger;

public class MemAudit {
    private static final long MEGABYTE = 1024L * 1024L;
    private static final Runtime runtime = Runtime.getRuntime();

    public static void printBusyMemory(Logger log) {
        long memory = runtime.totalMemory() - runtime.freeMemory();
        log.info("Occupied memory: {} MB", (memory / MEGABYTE));
    }
}
```

```
public static void printTotalMemory(Logger log) {
    log.info("Total Program memory: {} MB", (runtime.totalMemory()/
    MEGABYTE));
    log.info("Max Program memory: {} MB", (runtime.maxMemory()/
    MEGABYTE));
}
}
```

The methods of this class will be called during the execution of our program, as shown in Listing 13-12.

Listing 13-12. The MemAuditDemo Class Using the Class in Listing 13-11 to Print Memory Statistics in the Console

```
package com.apress.bgn.thirteen;

// some imports omitted
import static com.apress.bgn.thirteen.util.MemAudit.*;

public class MemAuditDemo {
    private static final Logger LOGGER = LoggerFactory.
    getLogger(MemAuditDemo.class);
    private static NameGenerator nameGenerator = new NameGenerator();

    public static void main(String... args) {
        printTotalMemory(LOGGER);
        int count = 0;
        while (true) {
            genSinger();
            count++;
            if (count % 1000 == 0) {
                printBusyMemory(LOGGER);
            }
        }
    }
}
```

```
    private static void genSinger() {
        Singer s = new Singer(nameGenerator.genName(), RND.nextDouble(),
                    LocalDate.now());
        LOGGER.info("JVM created: {}", s.getName());
    }
}
```

After we delete the old log file, we should run this class and leave it running for a while. Since it will be impossible again to see the output, this command

```
grep -a 'memory' gc.log
```

is useful to extract all lines containing the word "memory," and the result should look quite similar to one in Listing 13-13.

Listing 13-13. Memory Statistics Printed by Methods in the MemAudit Class During Java Application Execution

```
$  grep -a 'memory' gc.log
INFO  c.a.b.t.MemAuditDemo - Total Program memory: 260 MB # <1>
INFO  c.a.b.t.MemAuditDemo - Max Program memory: 4096 MB  # <2>
INFO  c.a.b.t.MemAuditDemo - Occupied memory: 21 MB       # <3>
INFO  c.a.b.t.MemAuditDemo - Occupied memory: 7 MB        # <4>
INFO  c.a.b.t.MemAuditDemo - Occupied memory: 12 MB
...
INFO  c.a.b.t.MemAuditDemo - Occupied memory: 98 MB
INFO  c.a.b.t.MemAuditDemo - Occupied memory: 104 MB
...
```

The max memory is 4096MB, which means my machine has a total of 16GB of RAM, and the occupied memory is tiny, not even close to the initial 260MB the JVM is given to use. If we want to see real memory being occupied, we can modify the genSinger() method to return the created references and add them to a list. Since the Singer instances are referenced in the main class, the memory is no longer emptied. The modifications mentioned previously are shown in Listing 13-14.

Listing 13-14. Saving the Singer Instances to a List to Avoid Them Being
Collected by the GC and the Memory Cleared

```java
package com.apress.bgn.thirteen;

// some import statements omitted
import static com.apress.bgn.thirteen.util.MemAudit.*;

public class MemoryConsumptionDemo {
    private static final Logger LOGGER = LoggerFactory.
    getLogger(MemoryConsumptionDemo.class);
    private static NameGenerator nameGenerator = new NameGenerator();

    public static void main(String... args) {
        printTotalMemory(LOGGER);
        List<Singer> singers = new ArrayList<>();
        IntStream.range(0, 1_000_000).forEach(i -> {
          singers.add(genSinger());
          if (i % 1000 == 0) {
            printBusyMemory(LOGGER);
          }
      });
    }
    private static Singer genSinger() {
        Singer s = new Singer(nameGenerator.genName(), RND.nextDouble(),
                LocalDate.now());
        LOGGER.info("JVM created: {}", s.getName());
        return s;
    }
}
}
```

After running the program in Listing 13-14, we can actually see the memory being
used gradually increasing. A look in the log filtered magically by grep will show us that
the program keeps the memory occupied until its end, since the references now are
saved into the List<Singer> instance, as shown in Listing 13-15.

Listing 13-15. Memory Statistics Printed by Methods in the `MemAudit` Class During a Java Application Execution, Where Instance Is Saved to a `List<Singer>`

```
$ grep -a 'memory' gc.log
INFO  c.a.b.t.MemoryConsumptionDemo - Total Program memory: 260 MB
INFO  c.a.b.t.MemoryConsumptionDemo - Max Program memory: 4096 MB
INFO  c.a.b.t.MemoryConsumptionDemo - Occupied memory: 14 MB
INFO  c.a.b.t.MemoryConsumptionDemo - Occupied memory: 17 MB
INFO  c.a.b.t.MemoryConsumptionDemo - Occupied memory: 19 MB
INFO  c.a.b.t.MemoryConsumptionDemo - Occupied memory: 22 MB
...
INFO  c.a.b.t.MemoryConsumptionDemo - Occupied memory: 99 MB
INFO  c.a.b.t.MemoryConsumptionDemo - Occupied memory: 101 MB
INFO  c.a.b.t.MemoryConsumptionDemo - Occupied memory: 104 MB
...
INFO  c.a.b.t.MemoryConsumptionDemo - Occupied memory: 474 MB
INFO  c.a.b.t.MemoryConsumptionDemo - Occupied memory: 477 MB
```

And as we print the occupied memory every 1000 steps, we can draw the conclusion that 1000 `Singer` instances occupy approximately 2MB. The preceding code no longer uses an infinite loop to generate instances; if it did, at some point the program would abruptly crash, throwing the following exception:

```
Exception in thread "main" java.lang.OutOfMemoryError: Java heap space
    at chapter.thirteen/com.apress.bgn.thirteen.MemoryConsumptionDemo
        .genSinger(MemoryConsumptionDemo.java:64)
    at chapter.thirteen/com.apress.bgn.thirteen.MemoryConsumptionDemo
        .main(MemoryConsumptionDemo.java:55)
```

Remember the value returned by the `runtime.maxMemory()` method? On my machine, it was 4096MB. If I look in the console, right before the exception just depicted, here is what I see:

```
INFO c.a.b.c.MemoryConsumptionDemo - Occupied memory: 4094 MB
INFO c.a.b.c.MemoryConsumptionDemo - Occupied memory: 4094 MB
INFO c.a.b.c.MemoryConsumptionDemo - Occupied memory: 4095 MB
INFO c.a.b.c.MemoryConsumptionDemo - Occupied memory: 4095 MB
INFO c.a.b.c.MemoryConsumptionDemo - Occupied memory: 4095 MB
```

So the JVM was struggling to create another `Singer` instance, but there was no more memory left. The last value printed before the exception was 4095MB, which is 1MB less than 4096MB, the maximum amount of memory that the JVM was allowed to use. So the poor JVM crashed because there was no more heap memory available. If a program ever ends like that, the problem is always in the design of the solution. The values for total and maximum memory for the JVM can influence the behavior of the GC as well. The `-Xms` and `-Xmx` options introduced previously are quite important, as they decide the initial and the maximum size of the heap memory. Configured properly, they can increase performance, but when unsuitable values are used, they have an adverse effect. For example, never set an initial size for the heap too small. If there is not enough space to fit all objects created by the application, the JVM has to allocate more memory, basically rebuilding the heap repeatedly during the execution of the program. So if this happens a few times during the application run, the overall time consumption will be affected. The maximum size for the heap is crucial: allocating too little will cause the application to crash; allocating too much might hinder another program from running. Deciding these values is usually done through repeated experiments, and starting with JDK 11, the new Epsilon garbage collector is quite handy for this purpose.

If you want to learn more about GC tunning, usually the best documentation is the official one[5].

Now that you know what to expect from the GC, let's see other methods of customizing its behavior so that problems are avoided.

Using Cleaner

It is not clear when the `finalize()` method is to be taken out of the JDK, but if you want to avoid using it, there are a few options. You can develop some classes to implement `java.lang.AutoCloseable`, provide an implementation for the `close()` method, and then make sure that you use your objects in a `try-with-resources` statement.

If you want to avoid implementing the `AutoCloseable` interface, you can use a `java.lang.ref.Cleaner` object. You can instantiate this class and register objects to it together with an action to perform when each object is being discarded by the garbage collector. Using a `Cleaner` instance, the code in Listing 13-9 can be written as depicted in code Listing 13-16:

---

[5] `https://docs.oracle.com/en/java/javase/17/gctuning`

Listing 13-16. Using a Cleaner Instance

```
package com.apress.bgn.thirteen.cleaner;

// some import statements omitted
import java.lang.ref.Cleaner;

public class CleanerDemo {
    private static final Logger LOGGER = LoggerFactory.getLogger
                                        (CleanerDemo.class);
    public static final Cleaner cleaner = Cleaner.create();
    private static NameGenerator nameGenerator = new NameGenerator();

    public static void main(String... args) {
        printTotalMemory(LOGGER);
        int count = 0;
        for (int i = 0; i < 100_000; ++i) {
            genActor();
            count++;
            if (count % 1000 == 0) {
                printBusyMemory(LOGGER);
                System.gc();
            }
        }

        //filling memory with arrays of String to force GC to clean up
        Actor objects
        IntStream.range(0, 10_000).forEach(_ -> {
          var s = new String[10_000];
          try {Thread.sleep(1);} catch (InterruptedException _) {}
        });

    }

    private static Cleaner.Cleanable genActor() {
        Actor a = new Actor(nameGenerator.genName(), LocalDate.now());
        LOGGER.info("JVM created: {}", a.getName());
```

```
        Cleaner.Cleanable handle = cleaner.register(a, new ActorRunnable(a.
                                getName(), LOGGER));
        return handle;
    }

    static class ActorRunnable implements Runnable {
        private final String actorName;
        private final Logger log;

        public ActorRunnable(String actorName, Logger log) {
            this.actorName = actorName;
            this.log = log;
        }

        @Override
        public void run() {
            log.info("GC Destroyed: {} ", actorName);
        }
    }
}
```

Because I wanted to make it easier for you to browse the code, as all these sources are part of the same project, Listing 13-16 uses a class modeling an Actor instead of a Singer, but no worries, the implementation is quite similar.

The Cleaner instance has a method named register(..) that is called to register the action to be performed when the object is cleaned. The action to be performed is specified as a Runnable instance, and I decided to create a class by implementing it, ActorRunnable in this example, so that we could save the name of the object to be destroyed into a field without actually keeping a reference to the object to be destroyed; otherwise, the Cleaner.Cleanable handle would not be used by the GC during the execution of the program, as the object would appear as if it still had references to it.

The cleaner.register(..) method returns an instance of type Cleaner.Cleanable that can be used to explicitly perform the action, by calling the clean() method. This is the method called by the JVM when the object is deleted from memory, when no longer used. If you run the code in Listing 13-16, the printed log would look pretty similar to the one in Listing 13-17.

Listing 13-17. Log Printed by an Execution Using a `Cleaner` Instance to Free Up Memory

```
INFO  c.a.b.t.c.CleanerDemo - Total Program memory: 516 MB
INFO  c.a.b.t.c.CleanerDemo - Max Program memory: 8192 MB
INFO  c.a.b.t.c.CleanerDemo - JVM created: Nuyktryvtkewiwd
INFO  c.a.b.t.c.CleanerDemo - JVM created: Brqivlsbvmteihz
INFO  c.a.b.t.c.CleanerDemo - JVM created: Qzvopg ophjcyho
...
INFO  c.a.b.t.c.CleanerDemo - Occupied memory: 14 MB
INFO  c.a.b.t.c.CleanerDemo - JVM created: Jrliwbjadztvwdm
INFO  c.a.b.t.c.CleanerDemo - JVM created: Evdteelpzinfcfh
INFO  c.a.b.t.c.CleanerDemo - JVM created: Hozfatszogfvzfz
...
INFO  c.a.b.t.c.CleanerDemo - GC Destroyed: Giqojswtuqzs s
INFO  c.a.b.t.c.CleanerDemo - GC Destroyed: Lzdjorokvyzwdu
INFO  c.a.b.t.c.CleanerDemo - JVM created: Igmzjiypo ttkzw
INFO  c.a.b.t.c.CleanerDemo - JVM created: Ljmksqzhzzhuzwl
INFO  c.a.b.t.c.CleanerDemo - Occupied memory: 8 MB
...
```

So the same result as using `finalize()` was obtained, but without implementing a deprecated method.

Tip   As a good practice to take from here, if you are writing your application using Java 9+, avoid using `finalize()`, because this method is clearly on the path toward being removed. Use `Cleaner` instead and you might have less of a hassle when upgrading the Java version your application is using.

Preventing GC from Deleting an Object

In the two previous sections, we focused on objects that were eligible for garbage collection. In an application, there are objects that should not be discarded while the program runs because they are necessary(for example, translation applications that need to keep a huge dictionary in memory). The most obvious references in our classes that were discarded only at the end of the execution were the static fields, and they are final, so they cannot be reinitialized:

```java
private static final Logger log = LoggerFactory.
getLogger(CleanerDemo.class);
public static final Cleaner cleaner = Cleaner.create();
private static NameGenerator nameGenerator = new NameGenerator();
```

The problem with these static values, however, is that they occupy the memory. What if your application uses a big Map<K,V> that contains a dictionary that is not even necessary right when the application starts? To solve this, you can use the Singleton design pattern. The Singleton pattern is a specific design of a class that ensures the class will be instantiated only *once* during the execution of the program. This is done by hiding the constructor (declare it private) and declaring a static reference of the class type and a static method to return it. There is more than one way to write a class according to the Singleton pattern, but the most common way is depicted in Listing 13-18.

Listing 13-18. SingletonDictionary Class

```java
package com.apress.bgn.thirteen.util;
// some import statements omitted

public class SingletonDictionary {
    public static final Cleaner cleaner = Cleaner.create();
    private static final Logger LOGGER = LoggerFactory.getLogger
                                    (SingletonDictionary.class);

    private static final SingletonDictionary instance = new
    SingletonDictionary();
    private Map<String, String> dictionary = new HashMap<>();

    private SingletonDictionary() {
        // init dictionary
        LOGGER.info("Starting to create dictionary: {}", System.
        currentTimeMillis());
        final NameGenerator keyGen = new NameGenerator(20);
        final NameGenerator valGen = new NameGenerator(200);
```

```
    IntStream.range(0, 100_000).forEach(_ -> dictionary.put(keyGen.
    genName(), valGen.genName()));
    LOGGER.info("Done creating dictionary: {}", System.
    currentTimeMillis());
}

public synchronized static SingletonDictionary getInstance(){
    return instance;
}
}
```

The code in Listing 13-18 simulates a dictionary with 100,000 entries, all generated by a modified version of the NameGenerator class. Log messages are printed in its constructor, to be really obvious when the instance is created. There are four things you must remember about the Singleton pattern:

- The constructor must be private, as it should not be called outside the class.

- The class must contain a static reference to an object of its type that can be initialized in place by calling the private constructor.

- A method to retrieve this instance must be defined, so it must be static.

- The method to retrieve the static instance also has to be synchronized, so that no two threads can call it at the same time and gain access to the instance, because the core idea of the Singleton pattern is to allow the class to be instantiated only once during the duration of the execution of the program and ensure that no concurrent access is allowed, as it might lead to unexpected behavior. There are multiple ways to initialize and work with a Singleton, so feel free to do your own research if you are interested in the details.

In a Singleton class, a static reference to an instance is created and this static reference prevents the garbage collector from cleaning up this instance during the execution of the program. This is because a static reference is a class variable, and classes are the last to be deleted by the GC, toward the end of the program execution. To test this, we'll write a main class that declares a Cleaner instance and registers a Cleanable for the SingletonDictionary instance. The main method will create a lot of String arrays to fill up the memory to try to convince the GC to delete the SingletonDictionary instance, and we'll even set its own reference to it to null, as depicted in Listing 13-19.

Listing 13-19. SingletonDictionaryDemo Class

```
package com.apress.bgn.thirteen;
// import statements omitted

public class SingletonDictionaryDemo {
    public static final Cleaner cleaner = Cleaner.create();
    private static final Logger LOGGER = LoggerFactory.getLogger(Singleton
                                         DictionaryDemo.class);

    void main() {
      LOGGER.info("Testing SingletonDictionary...");
      //filling memory with arrays of String to force GC
      IntStream.range(0, 10_000).forEach(_ -> {
        var s = new String[10_000];
        try {Thread.sleep(1);} catch (InterruptedException _) {}
      });
      SingletonDictionary singletonDictionary = SingletonDictionary.
                                                getInstance();

      cleaner.register(singletonDictionary, ()-> LOGGER.info("Cleaned up
      the dictionary!"));
      // we delete the reference
      singletonDictionary = null;

      //filling memory with arrays of String to force GC
      IntStream.range(0, 10_000).forEach(_ -> {
        var s = new String[10_000];
        try {Thread.sleep(1);} catch (InterruptedException _) {}
      });
      LOGGER.info("DONE.");
    }
}
```

If we run the code in Listing 13-19 and expect to see the "Cleaned up the dictionary!" message in the console, we're expecting in vain. That static reference in the `SingletonDictionary` will not allow the GC to touch that object until the program ends. The static reference that we have in class `SingletonDictionary` is also called a strong reference, because it prevents the object from being discarded from memory.

Using Weak References

If there are strong references, we should be able to use weak references as well, for objects that we actually want cleaned, right? Right.

In Java, three classes can be used to hold a reference to an object that will not protect that object from garbage collection. This is useful for objects that are too big and thus inefficient to keep in memory. With this kind of object, it is worth the cost of time consumed to be reinitialized, because keeping them in memory would slow down the overall performance of the application.

The three classes are as follows:

- `java.lang.ref.SoftReference<T>`: Objects referred by these types of references are cleared at the discretion of the garbage collector in response to memory demand. Soft references are most often used to implement memory-sensitive caches.

- `java.lang.ref.WeakReference<T>`: Objects referred by these types of references do not prevent their referents from being made finalizable, finalized, and then reclaimed. Weak references are most often used to implement canonicalizing mappings. **Canonicalizing** mapping refers to containers where weak references can be kept in and can be accessed by other objects, but their link to the container does not prevent them from being collected.

- `java.lang.ref.PhantomReference<T>`: Objects referred by these types of references are enqueued after the collector determines that their referents may otherwise be reclaimed. Phantom references are most often used to schedule postmortem cleanup actions.

Our SingletonDictionary contains a Map<K,V> that is actually the big object stored in memory. This map can be wrapped in a WeakReference, since weak references are most often used to implement canonicalizing mappings. We can write some logic that when the dictionary instance is accessed, if it is not there, it should be reinitialized. Because we need to access the map, the implementation will change a little, aside from wrapping the Map<K,V> into a WeakReference. The new class, named WeakDictionary, is depicted in Listing 13-20.

Listing 13-20. WeakDictionary Class

```
package com.apress.bgn.thirteen.util;
// other import statements omitted
import java.lang.ref.WeakReference;

public class WeakDictionary {
    private static final Logger LOGGER = LoggerFactory.
    getLogger(WeakDictionary.class);
    private static WeakDictionary instance = new WeakDictionary();
    private static Cleaner cleaner;
    private WeakReference<Map<Integer, String>> dictionary;

    private WeakDictionary() {
        cleaner = Cleaner.create();
        dictionary = new WeakReference<>(initDictionary());
    }

    public synchronized String getExplanationFor(Integer key) {
        Map<Integer, String> dict = dictionary.get();
        if (dict == null) {
            dict = initDictionary();
            dictionary = new WeakReference<>(dict);
            return dict.get(key);
        } else {
            return dict.get(key);
        }
    }
}
```

```java
    public WeakReference<Map<Integer, String>> getDictionary() {
        return dictionary;
    }

    public synchronized static WeakDictionary getInstance() {
        return instance;
    }

    private Map<Integer, String> initDictionary() {
        final Map<Integer, String> dict = new HashMap<>();
        LOGGER.info("Starting to create dictionary: {}", System.
        currentTimeMillis());
        final NameGenerator valGen = new NameGenerator(200);
        IntStream.range(0, 100_000).forEach(i -> dict.put(i, valGen.
        genName()));
        LOGGER.info("Done creating dictionary: {}", System.
        currentTimeMillis());
        cleaner.register(dict, ()-> LOGGER.info("Cleaned up the
        dictionary!"));
        return dict;
    }
}
```

The getExplanationFor(..) method is used to access the map and get the value corresponding to a key. Before doing that, however, we have to check if the Map<K,V> is still there. This is done by calling the get() method on the dictionary reference that is of type WeakReference<Map<Integer, String>>. If the GC did not collect the map, the key is extracted and returned; otherwise, the Map<K,V> is reinitialized and the weak reference is re-created.

The Cleaner instance is used here as well, and registers a Cleanable for the Map<K,V> so that we can see the map being collected. So how do we test this? In a similar way that we tested SingletonDictionary; the WeakDictionaryDemo class is not that different. The code is depicted in Listing 13-21.

Listing 13-21. WeakDictionaryDemo Class

```
package com.apress.bgn.thirteen;
// import statements omitted

public class WeakDictionaryDemo {
  private static final Logger LOGGER = LoggerFactory.
  getLogger(WeakDictionaryDemo.class);
  //try using the following VM options: -verbose:gc -Xlog:gc*

  void main() {
    LOGGER.info("Testing WeakDictionaryDemo...");
    //filling memory with arrays of String to force GC
    IntStream.range(0, 10_000).forEach(_ -> {
      var s = new String[10_000];
      try {Thread.sleep(1);} catch (InterruptedException _) {}
    });

    WeakDictionary weakDictionary = WeakDictionary.getInstance();

    //filling memory with arrays of String to force GC
    IntStream.range(0, 10_000).forEach(_ -> {
      var s = new String[10_000];
      try {
        Thread.sleep(1);
      } catch (InterruptedException _) {}
    });
    LOGGER.info("Getting val for 3 =  {}", weakDictionary.
    getExplanationFor(3));
    LOGGER.info("DONE.");
  }
}
```

After retrieving the `WeakDictionary` reference, a lot of `String` arrays are created to force the GC to delete the map from memory. After that, we try to access the problematic map. Will it work? Listing 13-22 shows a few output snippets proving that indeed the GC collects the map when the memory fills up.

Listing 13-22. WeakDictionaryDemo Class Output Snippet

```
INFO  c.a.b.t.WeakDictionaryDemo - Testing WeakDictionaryDemo...
INFO  c.a.b.t.u.WeakDictionary - Starting to create dictionary: 1724873056151
INFO  c.a.b.t.u.WeakDictionary - Done creating dictionary: 1724873074643
INFO  c.a.b.t.u.WeakDictionary - Cleaned up the dictionary!
INFO  c.a.b.t.u.WeakDictionary - Starting to create dictionary:
1724873071268
INFO  c.a.b.t.WeakDictionaryDemo - Getting val for 3 =  Skzfekoct pt
vfnhpvgshvdthynyrgzgftwteywantrioacckfdzvhuwybhgkv wyfvigysrazqgkisw
oalosooupmfzfkqrkqzyjqisdhffidcvbmmbghyvubzzzhcuaskjcewwbcosgpukpgtgv
ekunupnourzm dscafvoiqfdfrjbabhzkdysnlcnpjoziualz
INFO  c.a.b.t.WeakDictionaryDemo - DONE.
```

The log in Listing 13-22 not only proves that deleting the map from memory works, but also shows us the map being discarded by GC and then reinitialized when needed. This demonstrates the power of soft references.

The garbage collection process is nondeterministic, because it cannot be controlled much from the code. A Java program cannot tell it to start, pause, or stop, but by using the appropriate VM options, we can control the resources it has. By using the proper code implementation, we can tell the GC what to collect and not to collect, and most times this is sufficient. If you want more details about garbage collection, there are quite a few articles[6] available publicly on the Internet.

Garbage Collection Exceptions and Causes

It was mentioned before that if objects cannot be discarded from the memory, an exception of type OutOfMemoryError will be thrown. OutOfMemoryError does not actually extend java.lang.Exception, so calling it an "exception" is inaccurate. The exception class hierarchy was mentioned in **Chapter 4**. That hierarchy includes a class named java.lang.Error that implements java.lang.Throwable, and it was mentioned that these types of objects are thrown by a program when there is a critical issue that the program cannot recover from. The full hierarchy of the java.lang.OutOfMemoryError class is depicted here:

---

[6] For example, https://www.oracle.com/technetwork/tutorials/tutorials-1876574.html

```
java.lang.Object
    java.lang.Throwable
        java.lang.Error
            java.lang.VirtualMachineError
                java.lang.OutOfMemoryError
```

OutOfMemoryError is actually one of those ugly things you do not want thrown when your program is running, because this means your program is actually no longer running. The reason why it is not running is that it has no memory left to store new objects being created.

This error is thrown by the JVM when anything goes wrong when it is doing memory management. Although the most common cause is that the heap memory is depleted, there are other causes. When heap memory allocated to the JVM is depleted, the error has the following message:

Exception in thread "main" java.lang.OutOfMemoryError: Java heap space

But there is another message that you might see:

Exception in thread "main" java.lang.OutOfMemoryError: GC Overhead Limit Exceeded

This message is still related to the heap size. The error is thrown with this message when the data for the program barely fits the size of the heap, so the heap is almost full, which allows the GC to run, but because it cannot redeem any memory, the GC keeps running, and it is actually hindering the normal execution of the application. This message is added to the error when the GC spends 98% of execution time and the application spends the other 2%.

These two are the most common error messages you will see when the GC cannot do its job properly for whatever reason. A complete list can be found at: https://docs.oracle.com/javase/8/docs/technotes/guides/troubleshoot/memleaks002.html, but since most GC issues relate to the heap size, G1GC mostly throws errors with the Java heap space messages.

Summary

This is the final chapter of the book (two appendixes follow). When it comes to the Java ecosystem, there are a lot of books and tutorials available on the Internet. This book only scratched the surface to give you a good starting point as a Java developer, and the whole team that worked on it hopes it satisfied your needs and raised your curiosity to find out more. As this chapter clearly demonstrated, there is no perfect solution to make sure memory is always managed right regardless of the application scope. If you get into trouble, experimentation is always a step of determining the right garbage collector for your JVM.

This chapter has covered the following topics:

- What garbage collection is, and the steps involved

- How the heap memory is structured

- The many types of garbage collectors available in the Oracle HotSpot JVM and how to switch between them

- How to list all GC flags and use them as VM options

- How to view GC configurations and statistics using VM options

- How to view the garbage collection in action using `finalize()` and `Cleaner`

- How to stop the garbage collector from collecting important objects

- How to create objects that are easily collected by using soft references

APPENDIX A

Java Modules

Java 23 was released on September 17, 2024. The Java world has changed a lot since I, the author, was first introduced to the Java language. Nowadays, Java is still free, but the Oracle JDK isn't. Developers can use the Oracle JDK to learn, but applications that are deployed in production require a license.

The workaround is to use an OpenJDK like the Eclipse Temurin[1] build, but this does not come with Oracle support. JDK 23 is not a major release—it will not benefit from long-term support—but this book is still valuable because it covers the best features in the current Long-Term Support (LST) version, Java 21, and introduces you to what to expect from Java 25, the next LTS version.

If you are curious about the Oracle terms of use, you can find them on the official Oracle page[2].

The Oracle license restrictions have led to an expansion of the Java market to provide more options. Companies like Zulu and IBM have developed their own JDKs, and Amazon has its own no-cost, multiplatform, production-ready distribution of the Open Java Development Kit (OpenJDK) named Corretto. All these companies provide support for JDKs that Oracle doesn't. Probably more companies will emerge to provide cheaper support and open source JDKs. Now that access to an important resource has been restricted, humanity will do what it does best—creatively adapt to get access to the resource or develop similar resources. Either way, diversity will be blooming in the following years for the Java open source community, and I can barely wait to see what is coming.

---

[1] Download it from `https://adoptium.net`

[2] `https://www.oracle.com/downloads/licenses/javase-license1.html`

The purpose of this appendix is to gracefully end the book by covering more advanced details regarding Java modules that were not suitable for a Java beginner developer earlier in the book. It contains an extended version of the modules section in **Chapter 3**, covering configuration of Java modules in a complex project, including good, bad, and recommended practices for working with modules. The code snippets presented in this appendix are already part of the project associated with the book. Enjoy!

Modules

Starting with Java 9, a new concept was introduced: modules. In the Java world, the concept of modules existed in different forms, either by grouping sources in bundles using OSGI, or Maven/Gradle modules. Java modules represent a more powerful mechanism to organize and aggregate packages. The implementation of this new concept took more than ten years. The discussion about modules started in 2005, and the hope was for them to be implemented for Java 7. Under the name **Project Jigsaw**, an exploratory phase eventually started in 2008. Java developers hoped a modular JDK would be available with Java 8, but that did not happen.

Modules finally arrived in Java 9 after three years of work (and almost seven years of analysis). Supporting modules delayed the official release date of Java 9 to September 2017[3].

A Java module is a way to group packages and configure more granulated access to package contents. A Java module is a uniquely named, reusable group of packages and resources (e.g., XML files and other types of non-Java files) described by a file named `module-info.java`, located at the root of the source directory. This file contains the following information:

- The module's name

- The module's dependencies (that is, other modules this module depends on)

---

[3] `https://openjdk.org/projects/jigsaw/`

- The packages the module explicitly makes available to other modules (all other packages in the module are implicitly unavailable to other modules)

- The services the module offers

- The services the module consumes

- To what other modules it allows reflection

- Native code

- Resources

- Configuration data

In theory, module naming resembles package naming and follows the reversed-domain-name convention. In practice, just make sure the module name does not contain any numbers and that it reveals clearly what its purpose is. The `module-info.java` file is compiled into a module descriptor, which is a file named `module-info.class` that is packed together with classes into a plain old jar file. The file is located at the root of the Java source directory, outside any package. For the `chapter03` project introduced in **Chapter 3**, the `module-info.java` file is located in the `src/main/java` directory, at the same level with the `com` directory; the root of the `com.apress.bgn.three` package is shown again in Figure A-1.

```
) cd ~/apress/workspace/java-23-for-absolute-beginners/chapter03
) tree
.
├── pom.xml
└── src
    └── main
        ├── java
        │       ├── com
        │       │   └── apress
        │       │       └── bgn
        │       │           └── three
        │       │               ├── Main.java
        │       │               ├── SimpleReader.java
        │       │               ├── helloworld
        │       │               │   └── HelloWorld.java
        │       │               ├── other
        │       │               │   ├── AnotherPropRequester.java
        │       │               │   └── SubClassedProvider.java
        │       │               ├── package-info.java
        │       │               └── same
        │       │                   ├── PropProvider.java
        │       │                   └── PropRequester.java
        │       └── module-info.java
```

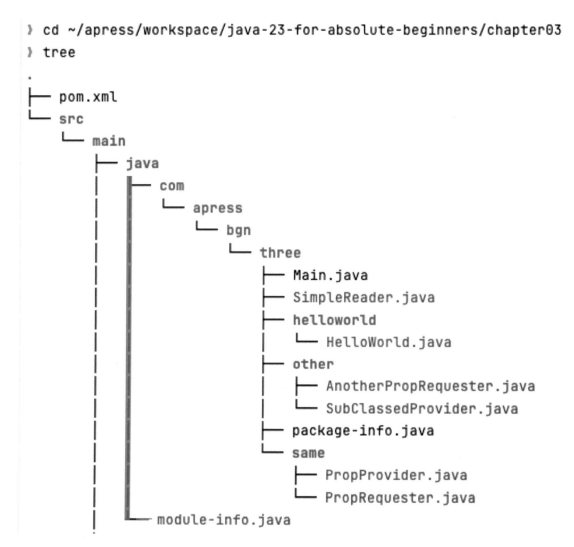

Figure A-1. *Location of the* module-info.java *file*

As with any file with the *.java extension, the module-info.java file is compiled
into a *.class file. As the module declaration is not a part of Java type declaration,
module is not a Java keyword, so it can still be used when writing code for Java types (as
a variable name, for example). For package the situation is different, as every Java type
declaration must start with a package declaration. Just take a look at the SimpleReader
class declared in Listing A-1.

Listing A-1. SimpleReader Class

```
package com.apress.bgn.three;

public class SimpleReader {
  private String source;
  // code omitted
}
```

You can see the package declaration, but where is the module? Well, the module is an abstract concept, described by the module-info.java file. So, starting with Java 9, if you are configuring Java modules in your application, Figure A-2 (also repeated from **Chapter 3**) evolves into Figure A-2.

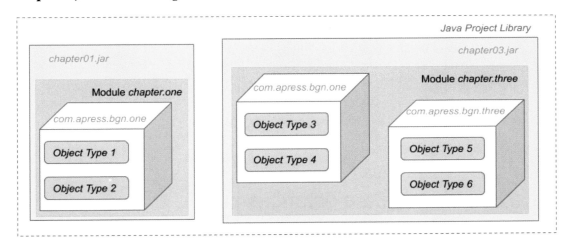

Figure A-2. *Java modules represented visually*

A Java module is a way to logically group Java packages that belong together.

The introduction of modules allows for the JDK to be divided into modules too. The java --list-modules command lists all modules in your local JDK installation. Listing A-2 depicts the output of this command executed on my personal computer, where currently JDK 23 is installed.

Listing A-2. JDK 23 Modules

```
$ java --list-modules
java.base@23
java.compiler@23
java.datatransfer@23
java.desktop@23
# output omitted
```

Each module name is followed by a version string, @23 in Listing A-2, which means that the module belongs to Java version 23.

There are multiple benefits of introducing modules that more experienced developers have been waiting for years to take advantage of. But configuring modules for bigger and more complex projects is no walk in the park, and most software companies prefer to avoid configuring modules altogether. The contents of the `module-info.java` file can be as simple as the name of the module and two brackets containing the body, as shown in Listing A-3.

Listing A-3. A Simple `module-info.java` Configuration

```
module chapter.three {}
```

Advanced Module Configurations

A Java module declaration body contains one or more **directives** that are constructed using the keywords in Table A-1. These directives represent access configurations and dependency requirements for the packages and classes contained in the modules.

Table A-1. *Java Module Directives*

Directive	Purpose
requires	Specifies that the module depends on another module.
exports	One of the module's packages whose `public` types (and their `nested` `public` and `protected` types) should be accessible to code in all other modules.
exports ... to	Qualified version of the `exports` directive that enables specifying in a comma-separated list precisely which module's or modules' code can access the exported package.
open	Used at module-level declaration (`open module mm {}`) and allows reflective access to all module's packages.
opens	Used inside the body of a module's declaration to selectively configure access through reflection only to certain packages.
opens ... to	Qualified version of the `opens` directive that enables specifying in a comma-separated list precisely which module's or modules' code can access its packages reflectively.
uses	Specifies a service used by this module, making the module a **service consumer**. A service in this case represents the full name of an interface/ abstract class that another module provides an implementation for.
provides ... with	Specifies that a module provides a service with a specific implementation, making the module a **service provider**.
transitive	Used together with `requires` to specify a dependency on another module and to ensure that other modules reading your module also read that dependency—known as *implied readability*.

As you've in this book, *modules can depend on one another*. The project for this book consists of 13 modules, and most on them depend on module `chapter.zero`. This module contains the basic components used to build more complex components in the other modules. For example, classes inside module `chapter.three` need access to packages and classes in module `chapter.zero`. Declaring a module dependency is done by using the `requires` directive, as depicted in Listing A-4.

Listing A-4. Another Simple `module-info.java` Configuration

```
module chapter.three {
  requires chapter.zero;
}
```

The preceding dependency is an **explicit** one. But there are also **implicit** dependencies. For example, any module declared by a developer implicitly requires the JDK `java.base` module. This module contains the foundational APIs of the Java SE Platform, and no Java application could be written without it. This implicit directive ensures access to a minimal set of Java types, so basic Java code can be written. Listing A-4 is equivalent to Listing A-5.

Listing A-5. A Simple `module-info.java` Configuration with an Explicit Directive of `requires java.base`

```
module chapter.three {
  requires java.base;

  requires chapter.zero;
}
```

Important   Declaring a module as required means that the module is required when the code is compiled (frequently referred to as *compile time*) and when the code is executed (frequently referred to as *runtime*). If a module is required only at runtime, the `requires static` keywords are used to declare the dependency.

Now `chapter.three` depends on module `chapter.zero`. But does this mean `chapter.three` can access all `public` types(and their nested `public` and `protected` types) in all the packages in module `chapter.zero`? If you are thinking that this is not enough, you are right. Just because a module depends on another, it does not mean it has access to the packages and classes it actually needs to. The required module must be configured to expose its *insides*. How can this be done? In our case, we need to make sure module `chapter.zero` gives access to the required packages. We can do so by customizing the `module-info.java` file for this module by adding the `exports` directive, followed by the necessary package names. Listing A-6 depicts the `module-info.java` file for the `chapter.zero` module that exposes its single package.

Listing A-6. The `module-info.java` Configuration File for the `chapter.zero` Module

```
module chapter.zero {
  exports com.apress.bgn.zero;
}
```

Tip   Think about it like this: You are in your room cutting out Christmas decorations, and you need a template for your decorations. Your roommate has all the templates. But just because you need them doesn't mean they will magically appear. You need to go and talk to your roommate. Needing your roommate's assistance can be viewed as the *requires room-mate* directive. After talking to your roommate, your roommate will probably say: *Sure, come in, they are on the desk! Take as many as you need.* This can be considered the *exports all-templates-on-desk* directive. The desk is probably a good analogy for a package.

Using the configuration in listing A-6, we have just given access to the `com.apress.bgn.zero` package to any module configured with a `requires module.zero;` directive. What if we do not want that? (Considering the previous tip, your roommate just left the door to their room open, so anybody can enter and get those templates!)

What if we want to limit the access to module contents only to the `chapter.three` module? (So, your roommate has to give their templates only to you.) This can be done by adding the `to` keyword followed by the module name to clarify that only this module is allowed to access the components. This is the qualified version of the `exports` directive mentioned in **Table A-1**.

Listing A-7 depicts the `module-info.java` file for the `chapter.zero` module that exposes its single package only to the `chapter.three` module.

Listing A-7. Advanced `module-info.java` Configuration File for the `chapter.zero` Module

```
module chapter.zero {
    exports com.apress.bgn.zero to chapter.three;
}
```

More than one module can be specified to have access, by listing the desired modules separated by commas, as depicted in Listing A-8.

Listing A-8. Advanced `module-info.java` Configuration File for the `chapter.zero` Module with Multiple Modules

```
module chapter.zero {
    exports com.apress.bgn.zero to chapter.two, chapter.three;
}
```

The order of the modules in an `exports` directive is not important. The order of packages being exported by `exports` directives is not important either, and if there is more of them, you can place them on multiple lines. Just make sure to end the declaration with a ; (semicolon).

Caution   Multiple packages cannot be exported using a single `exports` directive because that would lead to conflicts in the different packages exported from different modules, which defies the purpose of modularizing the code. So a construction like the following, using a wildcard to export multiple packages, is not supported:

```
module chapter.zero {
    exports com.apress.bgn.* to chapter.two, chapter.three;
}
```

This is all good and well, and we can go even one step further. What if module `chapter.three` requires access to a class defined in a module that is a dependency of `chapter.zero`? In technical language, this is called a **transitive** dependency, because it is more practical to use a dependency that is already there instead of declaring it again. Modules support this as well and the keyword to declare such a dependency is (as you probably suspected): `transitive`.

For this scenario, we'll make our module `chapter.zero` depend on the external module of Log4j (Apache Log4j 2). Log4j is a simple library for logging of application behavior, but we also want any module depending on `chapter.zero` to be able to use classes in the `org.apache.logging.log4j` module. In this case, the contents of the `module-info.java` for module `chapter.zero` become as shown in Listing A-9.

Listing A-9. `module-info.java` Configuration File for the `chapter.zero` Requiring a Dependency Being Shared with Its Dependents

```
module chapter.zero {
  requires transitive org.apache.logging.log4j;

  exports com.apress.bgn.zero to chapter.three;
}
```

By using `requires transitive`, we have given read access to module `org.apache.logging.log4j` to our `chapter.three` module. This means that types in `chapter.three` can be declared by making use of types defined in packages exported by module `org.apache.logging.log4j`. To test this, class `com.apress.bgn.three.transitive.LoggingSample` has been introduced in project `chapter03`. This class uses a Log4j 2 logger to print a simple log message.

And this is where simple, basic things end. There are a few more module directives to cover, and this is what this appendix is for.

As mentioned a few times throughout the book (and in Table A-1), Java has a feature named **reflection**. Reflection can be used to inspect a package and access information of all its contents, including private members. As you can imagine, this is not always such a good thing, especially in a production application that requires higher levels of security. Plus, such a feature makes it useless to have so many types of accessors, right? Up to Java 9, this is how things were, and using reflection led to problems included in the **JAR Hell** category. By introducing modules, reflection can be restricted as well. That is, reflection is no longer possible unless the module is configured to allow it. There are three forms of the same directive that can be used to configure access using reflection:

- open is used at the module-declaration level and allows reflective access to all packages in the module. A configuration to allow reflective access to all packages in module `chapter.zero` is depicted in Listing A-10.

889

Listing A-10. `module-info.java` Configuration File for the `chapter.zero` Allowing Reflective Access to All Its Packages

```
open module chapter.zero {
  requires transitive org.apache.logging.log4j;
  exports com.apress.bgn.ch0 to chapter.three;
}
```

- opens is used inside the module declaration to selectively configure access through reflection only to certain packages. A configuration to allow reflective access only to package `com.apress.bgn.three.helloworld` is depicted in Listing A-11.

Listing A-11. `module-info.java` Configuration File for the `chapter.three` Allowing Reflective Access Only to Package `com.apress.bgn.three.helloworld`

```
module chapter.three {
  requires chapter.zero;
  opens com.apress.bgn.three.helloworld;
}
```

- opens ... to is used inside the module declaration to selectively configure access through reflection only to certain packages and to a specific module. It's a little difficult to give an example here, but let's imagine this project uses Spring Boot. Spring is a very popular framework written in Java, and Spring Boot is used to build production-ready Spring applications[4]. Spring Boot uses reflection to instantiate objects of types defined in our `chapter.three` module. A configuration to allow reflective access only to package `com.apress.bgn.three.helloworld` and only to a specific Spring module named `spring.core` is depicted in Listing A-12.

---

[4] `https://spring.io/projects/spring-boot`

Listing A-12. `module-info.java` Configuration File for the `chapter.three` Allowing Reflective Access Only to Package `com.apress.bgn.three.helloworld` to a Module Named `spring.core`

```
module chapter.three {
  requires chapter.zero;
  requires spring.boot;
  requires spring.web;
  requires spring.context;
  requires spring.boot.autoconfigure;
  opens com.apress.bgn.three.helloworld to spring.core;
}
```

Besides opening a package or a module for reflection, the preceding directives also provide access to the package's (respectively all packages in the module) public types (and their nested public and protected types) at runtime only.

If you are curious about how reflection is used, take a look at class `com.apress.bgn.three.ReflectionDemo` from project `chapter03`. This class inspects the structure of the Base class and uses this knowledge to try to modify the value of a private field of a Base instance. The code is depicted in Listing A-13.

Listing A-13. The `ReflectionDemo` Class

```
package com.apress.bgn.three;

import com.apress.bgn.zero.Base;
import org.apache.logging.log4j.Logger;
import org.apache.logging.log4j.LogManager;

import java.lang.reflect.Field;

public class ReflectionDemo {

  private static final Logger LOGGER = LogManager.getLogger();

  void main(){
    //testing access to Base class from module chapter.zero
    Base base = new Base();
    LOGGER.info("Base object was created? > {} ", (base != null));
```

```
//testing reflection
try {
  Field field = base.getClass().getDeclaredField("secret"); // <1>
  field.setAccessible(true); // make the private field accessible
  field.set(base, 1); // set the value of the private field
  base.printSecret(); // call public method to display value of
  private field
} catch (NoSuchFieldException nsf) {
  LOGGER.error("Field 'secret' cannot be accessed!" );
} catch (IllegalAccessException e) {
  LOGGER.error("Field 'secret' cannot be set!" );
}
}
}
```

Initially the attempt fails, and this exception is shown in the console:

Exception in thread "main" java.lang.reflect.InaccessibleObjectException:
Unable to make field private int com.apress.bgn.zero.Base.secret
accessible: module chapter.zero does not "opens com.apress.bgn.zero" to
module chapter.three
    at java.base/java.lang.reflect.AccessibleObject.checkCanSetAccessible(A
    ccessibleObject.java:354)
    at java.base/java.lang.reflect.AccessibleObject.checkCanSetAccessible(A
    ccessibleObject.java:297)
    at java.base/java.lang.reflect.Field.checkCanSetAccessible(Field.
    java:178)
    at java.base/java.lang.reflect.Field.setAccessible(Field.java:172)
    at chapter.three/com.apress.bgn.three.ReflectionDemo.
    main(ReflectionDemo.java:52)

Edit the module-info.java in project chapter00 and remove the comment
from line 9:

opens com.apress.bgn.zero to chapter.three;

This enables reflection access to package `com.apress.bgn.zero` where the `Base` class is located. If you run the `ReflectionDemo` class again, the exception is gone and instead the value is set correctly, as shown by the execution of the `base.printSecret()` method. Expect to see the following message in the console:

```
[main] INFO  com.apress.bgn.three.ReflectionDemo - Base object was
created? >  true
```

There are two directives left to cover that were too difficult to explain in **Chapter 3**, since they make more sense after you understand Java a little more: `uses` and `provides`. Module declarations that contain directives `provides` or `provides...` with are named service providers because these modules provide a service implementation.

Java has a class named `java.util.ServiceLoader` that can be used to modularize an application and load implementations of a service. What is a service in this case? It is a Java type that defines only a contract, and that service providers need to provide a concrete implementation for.

Tip   Essentially, a service is modeled using an interface, and a service implementation is modeled by a class implementing the interface. An interface is analogous to the earliest specification version for a car before being built: it covers what it should do, but not how. When the car is actually being built, that is the implementation part, when *the how* is decided. And cars do the same things but in different ways depending on their type of engine, for example. An electric car will have a different implementation (under the hood) for the braking function (during braking, electric cars also recharge their battery) than a diesel-based car. You can refresh your understanding of interfaces in **Chapter 4**.

Assuming the service needed to be implemented is named `NakedService`, a module that contains a class that provides an implementation for it is declared as shown in Listing A-14.

Listing A-14. Module Providing an Implementation for the `NakedService`

```
// yes, import statements are supported in module configuration file
import com.apress.bgn.one.service.Provider;
import com.apress.bgn.zero.service.NakedService;
```

```
module chapter.one {
    requires chapter.zero;

    // needed for Appendix A.
    exports com.apress.bgn.one.service;
    provides NakedService with Provider;
}
```

By using the provides declarative like that, this module just became a **service provider**. The module retrieves the service using the java.util.ServiceLoader<S> class and uses it, and thus it is called a **service consumer**. The ServiceLoader class is generic, and the S type provided as a parameter is the type of service (the interface type) the ServiceLoader tries to find and load from the project classpath.

To declare the fact that a service consumer uses an implementation of that service, its module-info.java must contain the directive configuration shown in Listing A-15.

Listing A-15. Module Using an Implementation of the NakedService

```
import com.apress.bgn.zero.service.NakedService;

module chapter.three {
    requires chapter.zero;
    uses NakedService;
}
```

You might be wondering at this point what is the difference from normally accessing module contents. If you noticed, there is no requires chapter.one directive in the module configuration file depicted previously. Why? Because when using services, it is only necessary to have the module that provides the service type as a dependency *in the classpath, at runtime* (this is done in this project by using Maven configurations in the pom.xml file). This way module chapter.three does not really care who provides the implementation. As long as it is there, it is retrieved by the java.util.ServiceLoader. Why is this important? Because it decouples an application and removes explicit dependencies on concrete implementation (the module-info.java for module chapter.three does not need to explicitly declare a dependency on module chapter.one).

This is the Java simple way to support *Inversion of Control*.

Important   It was mentioned in **Chapter 1** that this book will introduce you to the core components of programming, which are data structures, algorithms, design patterns, and the most-used coding principles. They will be explained as they come up in the book, so there is no predefined order or sequence that you should expect.

To explain **Inversion of Control**, **Dependency Injection** must be explained. The action performed by any program (not only Java) is the result of interaction between its interdependent components, usually named objects.

Dependency injection is a concept that describes how dependent objects are connected at runtime by an external party. Look at Figure A-3. It describes two types of relationships between objects, and how those objects "meet" each other.

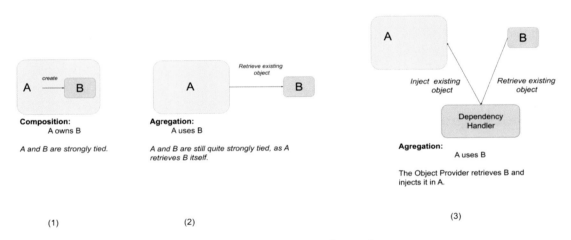

Figure A-3. *Object relationships and how they "meet"*

Because object A needs an object of type B to perform its functions, *A depends on B*. Object A can directly create object B, which is case (1), composition. Or object A can retrieve a reference to an existing object itself, which is case (2), aggregation, but this ties them up together.

Dependency injection allows severing that tie by using an external party to provide an object of type B to the object of type A, as shown in case (3), which is still aggregation, but with no direct ties and one twist.

NaN

Inversion of Control is a design principle in which generic reusable components are used to control the execution of problem-specific code, as in retrieving dependencies. Thus, the `java.util.ServiceLoader` is a **dependency handler** used to perform dependency injection, and it was designed following the inversion of control principle. It is also known as the Hollywood Principle: *Don't call us, we'll call you.*

This is where the *under the hood* section ends. I hope it has given you enough understanding of Java code and the reasons behind it that you will enjoy reading this appendix and experimenting with code confidently.

Before I digressed into explaining inversion of control and dependency injection, we configured our service provider, module `chapter.one`, and our service consumer, module `chapter.three`. Looking at Listings A-14 and A-15, you might have noticed that both require `chapter.zero`. This is because both provider and consumer must know what the API of the service is. The provider needs access so that it can implement it. The consumer needs access so that it can "consume" it, which in this case is to call its methods. The interface modeling the API is declared in the `chapter.zero` module and is depicted in Listing A-16.

Listing A-16. The `NakedService` Interface

```
// in module 'chapter.zero'
package com.apress.bgn.zero.service;

public interface NakedService {

    String theSecret();
}
```

The service implementation, provided by the `Provider` class in `chapter.one` module, is depicted in Listing A-17.

Listing A-17. The `NakedService` Implementation

```
// in module 'chapter.one'
package com.apress.bgn.one.service;

import com.apress.bgn.zero.service.NakedService;

public class Provider implements NakedService {
  @Override
```

```
  public String theSecret() {
    return "I am the implementation of NakedService provided by module
    'chapter.one'.";
  }
}
```

The ServiceConsumerDemo class using the service in the chapter.three module is depicted in Listing A-18.

Listing A-18. The NakedService Demo Class

```
package com.apress.bgn.three;

import com.apress.bgn.zero.service.NakedService;
import org.apache.logging.log4j.LogManager;
import org.apache.logging.log4j.Logger;

import java.util.ServiceLoader;

public class ServiceConsumerDemo {
    //testing to classes in transitive module slf4j.org
    private static final Logger LOGGER = LogManager.getLogger();

    void main(){
        ServiceLoader<NakedService> loader = ServiceLoader.
        load(NakedService.class);
        loader.findFirst().ifPresent( service -> LOGGER.info("Service
        found: {}, with secret '{}'",service.getClass(), service.
        theSecret()));
    }
}
```

When the module configuration is correct, running the class in Listing A-18 results in the following message printed in the console:

```
[main] INFO  com.apress.bgn.three.ServiceConsumerDemo - Service found:
class com.apress.bgn.one.service.Provider, with secret 'I am the
implementation of NakedService provided by module 'chapter.one'.'
```

Figure A-4 shows all the module configuration files side by side, together with the Maven configuration for the service consumer module (`chapter.three`).

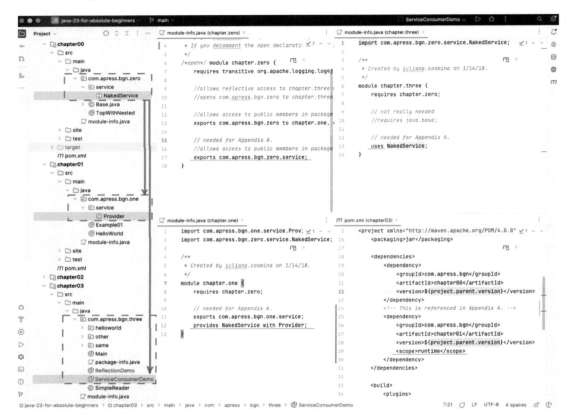

Figure A-4. *Service API, producer, and consumer module configurations*

After the modules system was introduced in Java 9, it has been practically ignored by the industry, so there haven't been a lot of improvements on the modules system. It has even been ignored by Oracle, with the exception of a change (JEP 396[5] in JDK 16) to strongly encapsulate all internal elements of the JDK by default, except for critical internal APIs such as `sun.misc.Unsafe`.

Java 23 intends to change that through **JEP 476: Module Import Declarations**[6]. Here's a quick summary of what this JEP introduces: when you write a complex class that references a lot of components, the import section might get a little too long. Some

---

[5] https://openjdk.org/jeps/396
[6] https://openjdk.org/jeps/476

companies do not like collapsing imports because classes with identical names do exist in different packages, and collapsed (wildcard) imports might cause issues. The size of the imports section has been the bane of existence for quite a few developers. Oracle finally decided to do something about it, because JEP 476 proposes the introduction of module imports. Essentially, instead of importing a list of classes and interfaces, in your class declaration you could just import the module exporting the package they are in, and you are done. Take a look at the class in Listing A-19; it has more import lines than code lines.

Listing A-19. Example Class with Multiple Imports

```java
import java.util.Map;
import java.util.function.Function;
import java.util.stream.Collectors;
import java.util.stream.Stream;

public class ModuleImportDemo {
    void main(){
        String[] singers = new String[] { "john mayer", "danny o'donoghue",
        "nina simone" };
        Map<String, String> m =
                Stream.of(singers)
                        .collect(Collectors.toMap(s -> s.toUpperCase().
                        substring(0,1),
                                Function.identity())));
    System.out.println(m);
    }
}
```

With the JEP 476 feature, the code in Listing A-19 can be rewritten as shown in Listing A-20.

Listing A-20. Example Class with a Module Import

```java
import module java.base;

public class ModuleImportDemo {
    void main(){
```

```
        String[] singers = new String[] { "john mayer", "danny o'donoghue",
        "nina simone" };
        Map<String, String> m =
                Stream.of(singers)
                        .collect(Collectors.toMap(s -> s.toUpperCase().
                        substring(0,1),
                                Function.identity()));
    System.out.println(m);
    }
}
```

The import module statement imports all public top-level types in the packages exported by the module being imported. Related to this feature, JEP 477 is the third preview of **Implicitly Declared Classes and Instance Main Methods**[7] feature that proposes for the java.base module to be implicitly imported if a main class is not explicitly defined. This means that we can write a Java file—let's name it ModuleImportDemoV2.java–containing just the main() method shown in Listing A-20, and run it with java --enable-preview --source 23 ModuleImportDemoV2.java and it will work, because all packages exported by the java.base module are imported implicitly, including the java.util package that includes the collection classes used in the example.

The good part about the module import feature is that you can use it even if your project does not configure modules.

Java modules adoption has been slow, but maybe this is because until Java 21, migrating to newer versions of Java has been slow too. Projects like Spring, Log4J, Logback, and many others used in the project for this book are leading the way by providing module builds, but it will probably be a while until declaring modules become a routine step in Java project configuration.

All we are missing is the introduction of import aliases. This would allow us to easily import classes with identical names from different packages, without the need for one of them to be used in the code with their entire qualified name. This is an improvement that would make me so happy.

---

[7] https://openjdk.org/jeps/477

APPENDIX B

IntelliJ IDEA Modules

If you've inspected the structure of the `java-23-for-absolute-beginners` project in IntelliJ IDEA, you might have noticed a **Modules** tab. If not, feel free to do so from the **File ➤ Project Structure** menu, as shown in Figure B-1.

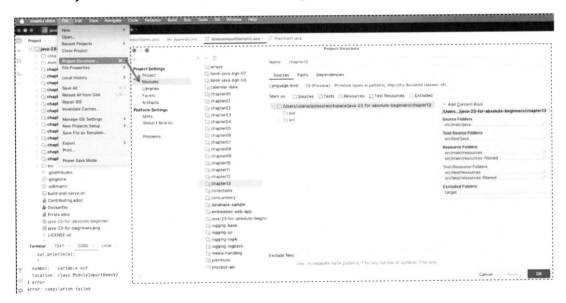

Figure B-1. *IntelliJ IDEA Modules tab*

You might think that the Modules tab is related to the Java modules, but that is not the case. This section explains the existence of this tab.

Let's consider a banking web application. It probably is quite complex, right? A lot of code has to be written to handle user requests, process banking transactions, saving and retrieving data. Can you imagine how this code is organized? Most applications have three basic layers: presentation, services, and data access. Figure B-2 depicts this common structure.

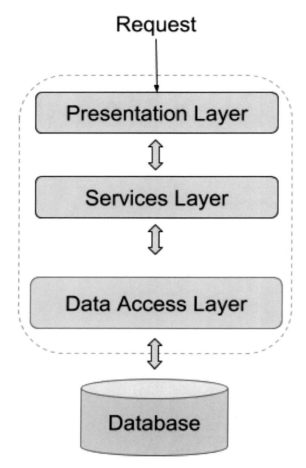

Figure B-2. *The three most common layers of a Java application*

In the simplest applications, each layer is represented by a subproject or module that contains all the code used to perform a group of related operations. For example, all code in the presentation layer implements functionalities for interaction with the user, processing user requests and transforming them into calls for layers under it. Before there were Java modules, Java projects were themselves organized as multimodule projects. That is why the Modules tab exits in IntelliJ IDEA.

As you've probably noticed in Figure B-1, the `java-23-for-absolute-beginners` project is multimodular as well. The module names shown in the IntelliJ IDEA Modules tab are not the Java module names, configured in the `module-info.java` files, but the names of the Maven modules, configured in `pom.xml` files.

Index

A

Abstract class, 161, 163, 176, 182
Abstraction, 161, 164, 461
Abstract method, 162, 184, 186, 200, 621
Abstract Window Toolkit (AWT), 11, 13, 643, 666
  applets, 645
  GUI components, 643
  heavyweight components, 643
  Java desktop applications, 645
  JavaFX, 666, 712
  native OS equivalent components, 643
  OS native GUI, 644
  swing, 644
accept() method, 491
accept(..) method, 491, 720, 721
Access modifiers, 84
  Bass class, 84, 85
  fields and methods, 87
  member-level accessors scope, 87
  nested class, 88
  package-private, 85
  PropProvider, 88
  PropRequester, 90
  subclass, 90, 91
  superclass, 90
  World column, 91, 92
Accessors, 88–92, 149, 187
Actor class, 160, 168, 177
addIndexServlet(..) method, 696

add(..) method, 231, 232
add(T t) method, 472
Advanced module configurations, Java modules
  dependency injection, 895
  example class
    module imports, 899
    multiple imports, 899
  import module statement, 900
  inversion of control, 896
  Java module directives, 885
  JEP 476: Module Import Declarations, 898
  JEP 477, 900
  java.util.ServiceLoader, 893, 894, 896
  module-info.java configuration, 886
    chapter.zero module, 886–889
    chapter.zero module with multiple modules, 888
    explicit directive, java.base, 886
  NakedService, 893, 894
    Demo Class, 897
    Implementation, 896
    Interface, 896
  projects, 900
  provides declarative, 894
  reflection, 889–891
  ReflectionDemo class, 891, 893
  service API, producer and consumer module configurations, 898
  transitive dependency, 888

B

Printed in the United States
by Baker & Taylor Publisher Services